# MUST WE BE SILENT?

## Issues Dividing Our Church

By

**Samuel Koranteng-Pipim**

Berean Books
Ann Arbor Michigan

**Berean Books** *seek to restore among Bible-believing Christians the spirit of the early Bereans (Acts 17:11), by subjecting contemporary views to the Bible as advocated and exhibited by the foremost Seventh-day Adventist theologian, Ellen G. White. In addressing today's critical issues, each book adopts a serious tone, provocative style, and a reassuring outlook. These books are for all who seek the lordship of Jesus Christ in their lives, the sole authority of His inspired Word as their infallible guide, the proclamation of His everlasting gospel as their life vocation, and the revival of primitive godliness as the most urgent need in their churches.*



Published by Berean Books, P. O. Box 2799, Ann Arbor, Michigan 48106
**www.bereanbooks.org**
FAX: 734-669-0050
E-mail: 105323.612@compuserve.com



Unless otherwise stated, all Bible quotations are taken from the King James family of translations, *King James Version, New King James Version, and Revised Standard Version.*

For your own copy of *Must We Be Silent?* or for additional copies, contact your ABC or mail your prepaid order (US $19.95, plus US$3.00 shipping and handling) to:
**Berean Books, P. O. Box 2799, Ann Arbor, Michigan 48106, USA.**

For quantity discounts to churches or groups, contact author at the above address or FAX: 734-669-0050; E-mail: 105323.612@compuserve.com

---

Koranteng-Pipim, Samuel
Must We Be Silent? Issues Dividing Our Church / Samuel Koranteng-Pipim

1. Apologetics. 2. Contemporary Issues 3. Doctrines 4. Seventh-day Adventists 5. Theology
I. Title
BX6154.4 K67 2001
ISBN 1-890014-03-6

---

Cover Design & Layout by Remnant Publications and PQ Design


*Printed in the United States of America*

# Dedication

To
The Faithful Believers in Congo and Rwanda
*Your Uncompromising Loyalty to Christ Inspired the Writing of this Book*

&

My Family, Becky, Ellen, & Sam
*Your Patience and Understanding Made this Book Possible*

# Contents

## III. Amazing Grace and Our Mazing Race (The Ideology of Racism)



## IV. The Babble Over the Bible (The Ideology of Higher Criticism)



## Part V. The Vocal Few and the Local Pew (The Ideology of Congregationalism)



## Epilogue

# Acknowledgments

*Thanks to Good Friends Whose Contributions to this Effort Are Known to the Lord*

# 1

# AUTHOR'S INTRODUCTION

*"If I profess with the loudest voice and clearest exposition every position of the truth of God except precisely that little point which the world and the devil are at that moment attacking, I am not confessing Christ, however boldly I may be professing Christ. Where the battle rages, there the loyalty of the soldier is proved; and to be steady on all the battle field besides, is mere flight and disgrace if he flinches at that point."*

**—Martin Luther**

This volume is not a bedtime story, although some Bible students will stay up late reading it. Neither is it a devotional book, though it will lead some to serious heart-searching. It is certainly not an inspirational volume, although it will fire up some saints to rejoice and encourage them to hold on. *Must We Be Silent?* is an apologetic book, to use the technical term, a work designed to defend sound biblical teaching by counteracting the false. For this reason, I expect the book to receive harsh treatment from certain quarters of the church. Let me explain why.

Homosexuality, women's ordination, racism and racially separate conferences, liberal higher criticism, and congregationalism are among the hottest potato items on today's theological menu. They are so hot that anyone attempting to touch them is bound to be burned.

Already, in certain quarters of our own Seventh-day Adventist church, individuals who forthrightly express their views on these subjects are considered "divisive," "controversial," "intolerant," "fundamentalist," "immature," or even "third world." These uncomplimentary labels have exerted powerful psychological pressure on some church leaders and scholars to either endorse the unbiblical practices or, at a minimum, remain silent.

But should Bible-believing Christians be intimidated by these labels? Should they remain silent or neutral when established biblical doctrines are being undermined? Should they uncritically embrace secular ideologies that masquerade in the church as sound theologies? Ellen G. White responds:

> "If God abhors one sin above another, of which His people are guilty, it is doing nothing in case of an emergency. Indifference and neutrality in a religious crisis is regarded of God as a grievous crime and equal to the very worst type of hostility against God" (*Testimonies,* vol. 3, p. 281).

**What the Book Is About.** The book you are holding deals with forbidden subjects. Because it tackles the most contentious and politicized issues to have plagued our church in recent times, permit me to explain at the outset what the book is about.

First, *Must We Be Silent?* is an honest attempt by an inquiring Bible student to offer some clarity and direction to some controversial issues in the church.

Second, *Must We Be Silent?* is an evaluation of ideas circulating in certain quarters of our church in North America. But the ideas have also spread to other parts of the world. These views have been put in print and are all in the public arena, where they continue to have influence.

Third, *Must We Be Silent?* is *not* about personalities, but about biblical truth. Those unfamiliar with scholarly discussions may question the legitimacy of my citing and reviewing published works put out by thought leaders of the church. However, references to these published materials should be seen as objective or scholarly citations. It is a well-established fact that whenever people publicize their views in print they automatically invite others to subject their works to careful scrutiny. Taking issue with published works does not involve questioning the sincerity of their authors as well-meaning thought leaders of the church.

Also, the candid evaluation of certain positions does not mean an expression of personal dislike for those whose works are being reviewed. Furthermore, challenging those authors on specific issues does not mean that whatever they have written in other areas is necessarily suspect or invalid.

Fourth, *Must We Be Silent?* is not an autopsy report on the body of Christ. It is a pathology report on the church. It is not an autopsy because the church of Christ cannot die. Jesus Himself has assured us that "the gates of hell" shall not prevail against it (Matt 16:18). To paraphrase Ellen White, the church may be imperfect, even enfeebled. But it is still the only object upon which Christ bestows His supreme regard (see *Acts of the Apostles,* p. 12). Therefore, let no one read this book and conclude that it evidences the final inscription on the tombstone of a dead church.

Although this work is not a postmortem, it is a much needed pathology report on our church today. For, like many other Christian denominations, ours also has been infected by some malignant ideological tumors. By undertaking this critical examination, we may correctly understand the true nature of the church's condition and the kind of surgery it needs. The process may be painful. But the pathological exam and surgery are necessary for the survival and well-being of the church.

**Anticipated Reactions.** I am aware that it is risky these days for anyone to question the biblical legitimacy of the ideologies that are invading our church. Scholars and leaders who courageously stand up against them are often vilified, if not persecuted. The issues have torn apart friendships and churches. In places where the ideologies have become entrenched, opposing views have not always been welcome, even if those views are still embraced by an overwhelming majority of the church through official action. And sometimes it is very difficult for loyal Adventists to be hired or retained, despite the fact that they may be the most qualified. The policy is usually unwritten, but those familiar with several situations can testify to the intolerant attitude toward those who uphold the longstanding biblical position on the ideological issues. It is partly in response to this kind of intimidation that I have reproduced Ellen G. White's defiant statement on the front cover of *Must We Be Silent?*

Since the book deals with explosive issues, allow me to address candidly the kinds of reactions I anticipate from certain quarters of the church.

While many will greatly benefit from this book, *Must We Be Silent?* will undoubtedly upset some readers. This is understandable. It always hurts whenever error is pointed out. It hurts even more when those errors are cherished and promoted by respected church leaders and scholars, some of whom I esteem as close friends. But I want to believe that most of the scholars whose views I am challenging genuinely desire to know and to do God's will. Such thought leaders would gladly accept biblical correction and willingly renounce their published errors. Wrote Ellen White: "Those who sincerely desire truth will not be reluctant to lay open their positions for investigation and criticism, and will not be annoyed if their opinions and ideas are crossed" (*Review and Herald*, July 26, 1892).

But, as I mentioned earlier, I have no illusions whatsoever regarding reactions the book will generate from certain quarters of the church. Human nature being what it is, some people are bound to denounce the book merely because it has touched their ideological sacred cows and called into question some of their innovative interpretations of Scripture.

We may, however, ask the critics: Must we have sacred cows in the church? Are certain positions sacrosanct simply because they are articulated or promoted by some influential thought leaders and administrators? Should there be views that are off-limits to biblical investigation? I don't think so. For, no one—including the author of this book—is infallible. Thus, the Bible urges us always to "prove all things [and] hold fast to that which is good" (1 Thess 5:21).

On my part, I will welcome those who make a painstaking effort to refute the arguments in *Must We Be Silent?* I will also appreciate the labors of those who offer compelling scriptural correctives to the positions I have advanced in this volume. But I will ignore all negative criticisms that fail to demonstrate objectively that the views presented in this book are biblically incorrect or out of harmony with the long-standing Seventh-day Adventist beliefs and practices.

There are also some who will subtly try to shift the focus away from the issues raised in *Must We Be Silent?* They will misconstrue the candid evaluation of aberrant views as evidence of theological fault finding. Let me say to such that though I have tried to write carefully and compassionately, I plead guilty with explanation for the serious tone and provocative style with which I fault the theological arguments for homosexuality, women's ordination, racism and racially separate conferences, liberal higher criticism, and congregationalism. In the words of A. E. Housman, "I have spent most of my time finding faults because finding faults, if they are real and not imaginary is the most useful sort of criticism" (*Selected Prose* [Cambridge: Cambridge University Press, 1961], xii).

Finally, a few will attempt to gain sympathy for their questionable views by putting on the disguise of injured innocence. Set in their ways and putting their ideological commitments above Scripture, they will conceal their wounded pride by projecting themselves as courageous defenders of acceptance and compassion (in the case of homosexuality), of equality, fairness, and justice (with reference to women's ordination), of cultural sensitivity and ethnic diversity (as regards issues on racism and racially separate conferences), of open-mindedness and academic freedom (in the matter of liberalism's higher criticism), and of diversity in unity, freedom of conscience, and the Holy Spirit's leading (in the case of congregationalism). They will thus consider it a moral imperative to silence the message and messenger of *Must We Be Silent?*

Ellen G. White spoke poignantly to this kind of situation when she wrote: "While some under correction will acknowledge that they have been an injury to the cause, there are others who will charge with having an unkind spirit the one who has manifested true friendship by pointing out their wrongs, and will either be impudent or disrespectful to the reprover or will put on the disguise of injured innocence. This martyr-like appearance is a specious hypocrisy and is calculated to deceive those who are easily blinded, who are always ready to sympathize with the wrongdoer. . . . When the servants of God are called upon to do the disagreeable duty of correcting the erring, let not those upon whom the Lord has not laid this burden stand between the offender and God. If you cannot see matters in the light in which they have been presented, hold your peace; let the arrows of the Almighty fall just where He has directed they shall fall. . . . But we may still rejoice in the fact that it is not yet too late for wrongs to be righted" (*Christ Triumphant,* p. 125).

**My Ernest Prayer.** *Must We Be Silent?* has been published for one, and only one, purpose: To caution us against our proneness to hastily embrace secular ideologies which from time to time come knocking at our church doors. The example of the Bereans in "receiving the word" and "searching the Scriptures" to see "whether those things were so" (Acts 17:11) suggests that whenever articulate scholars, influential leaders, and vocal interest groups urge innovative ideas or practices on the church, members who are committed to biblical fidelity should always ask, "Are those things so?"

The volume in your hand brings together and updates articles I have previously published in journals, magazines, booklets, and books. But the messages contained in these articles have not lost their relevance or timeliness. By assembling them into this one volume, I am making available to a larger number of readers works that may not otherwise have been readily accessible.

As an Adventist, you long for Jesus to return. You desire the peace and harmony of heaven. My earnest prayer is that as you read *Must We Be Silent?* you will heed the counsel of the apostle Paul to "prove all things; [and] hold fast that which is good" (1 Thess 5:21).

Samuel Koranteng-Pipim, Ph.D.
Ann Arbor, Michigan
January 2001

*Why are Christians changing their attitudes on the question of homosexuality? What are the three major views on the subject? Are the arguments being used to justify homosexuality biblically valid? Can homosexuals change?*

Section I

# BORN A GAY AND BORN AGAIN?

## The Ideology of Homosexuality

# 2

# A BRIEF BACKGROUND

*"Some issues are so controversial that confronting them is too painful. Rather than discussing them in an emotionally charged atmosphere, we prefer not to discuss them at all. Other issues are so important that confronting them is necessary even when this is unavoidably painful. We prefer to find an approach to them at almost any cost, including the risk of pain. The issue of homosexuality is, at present and generally speaking, in the first category in the churches and in the second category in society."*

**—Pim Pronk**

Just when I was completing this manuscript for publication, I received an e-mail from Joe (pseudonym), a homosexual who claims to be a Seventh-day Adventist (SDA). In a subsequent e-mail, he indicated that his gay partner was not an Adventist but was considering baptism. The purpose of his writing to me was to inquire about the availability of gay friendly Christian groups in the Ann Arbor area where I currently live and about whether or not the Ann Arbor SDA church (or some other SDA church in the area) will offer a gay friendly environment for him and his homosexual male partner. The relevant section of his e-mail reads:

> My partner and I will be graduate students at the University of Michigan in January (if all goes as planned!). We are looking for a gay-friendly church to attend, or possibly a gay Christian Bible study group on campus. Do you have contact names for g[ay]-l[esbian and] b[isexual] Christian groups in the area? If the SDA churches in Ann Arbor are not gay-friendly, do you have a list of non-SDA accepting congregations? Also, is there an active

> Kinship chapter in Ann Arbor? [Kinship is a pro-homosexual group operating within the SDA church] We are looking forward to finding a new church home.

Joe is not alone in his request. Today "Adventist" homosexuals are coming out of the closet and clamoring for acceptance. And in response some of our churches are embracing homosexuals who still cling to that lifestyle. A Winter 1999 issue of *Scanner,* a newsletter published by the Glendale City SDA Church in California, includes an interview with Donald, a "gay Adventist" who is apparently very active in the church. He is quoted as saying that "going by conservative estimations, there are at least 5,000 gay Adventists in Southern California."[1] The November 18, 2000 church bulletin of that church even carries an announcement of a homosexual couple "who are celebrating their 14-year anniversary."

The presence of Adventist homosexuals is not limited to California. There even exists a national organization known as *Kinship,* which functions, to use its own words, as "a support group for gay and lesbian Seventh-day Adventists." Its aim is to convert Adventists to its belief that "God can bless a committed homosexual relationship." They want the church to accept homosexuality as a natural gift from God. The influence of this ideology can be seen and felt on some of our North American SDA college campuses where some students and faculty openly discuss their homosexual or lesbian relationships in the students' newspapers.[2]

There are also other gay and lesbian "ministries" or support groups, which are operating in the church. While claiming to distance themselves from the pro-gay theology of *Kinship,* these so-called outreach ministries nonetheless teach that homosexuality is not a sin, but a morally neutral condition that cannot always be "cured."[3]

Some readers may even be surprised to learn that pro-gay views of *Kinship* were actively promoted in booth #1109 at the 2000 Toronto General Conference (GC) session. The booth was listed as "Someone to Talk To" in the General Conference Exhibition book given to all delegates to the session. The "Someone to Talk To" organization claims to be for "Adventist Families and Friends of Gays and Lesbians." Its organizers placed a two page advertisement in the GC Exhibition book in which they mentioned that the North American Division Family Ministries Department has recognized their organization.[4]

In an attempt to convince the church to embrace homosexuality as morally acceptable, the above organization passed out hundreds of brochures to the Toronto GC session delegates and visitors. One of their materials explains why:

> I hope the church will no longer take an ostrich-in-the-sand approach, but face the reality that its gay brothers and sisters are everywhere in the Church: from congregational laity to college faculty, church pastors and General Conference workers. We are hurting and isolated, and as much in need of denominational acceptance and the forgiving grace of Christ as anyone else. Please don't continue to ignore us.[5]

The above facts confirm that Joe's e-mail to me cannot be dismissed as an isolated request. Whether we recognize it or not, homosexuals "are everywhere in the Church" and are calling for "denominational acceptance." The crucial question therefore is, How should we respond to their calls? Does the church have an official position on the issue?

A satisfactory answer requires a clear understanding of the Bible's teaching on the nature and morality of homosexuality. This understanding should help us address the question of how to relate or minister to homosexuals. Just in case a reader of this book is wondering about how I responded to Joe's e-mail, here it is:

> Hello Joe:
>
> This is in response to your inquiry about "gay friendly" Christian groups in the Ann Arbor area, and whether or not the Ann Arbor SDA church (or some other SDA church) will offer a "gay friendly" environment for you and your male partner should you decide to relocate to Ann Arbor in January.
>
> To the best of my knowledge the SDA churches in the area uphold Fundamental Belief #22 as well as the Official SDA Statement on Homosexuality. The former reads in part: "Marriage was divinely established in Eden and affirmed by Jesus to be a lifelong union between a man and a woman in loving companionship." The Official Statement

reiterates: "Sexual intimacy belongs only within the marital relationship of a man and a woman."

But while as a church we are "opposed to homosexual practices and relationships," the SDA church recognizes that "every human being is valuable in the sight of God, and we seek to minister to all men and women in the spirit of Jesus. We also believe that by God's grace and through the encouragement of the community of faith, an individual may live in harmony with the principles of God's Word." Consequently, we "endeavor to follow the instruction and example of Jesus. He affirmed the dignity of all human beings and reached out compassionately to persons and families suffering the consequences of sin. He offered caring ministry and words of solace to struggling people, while differentiating His love for sinners from His clear teaching about sinful practices" (Official SDA Statement on Homosexuality, 1999).

Consistent with our SDA Fundamental Belief #22 and the Official Statement, you can understand why the Ann Arbor SDA church cannot support an openly gay lifestyle or the activities of Kinship. However, the church is open to all homosexuals who recognize that homosexuality is sin, who are willing to turn away from that lifestyle, and who, by the grace of God, seek to order their lives in accordance with His Word. I am in full agreement with the church's position.

Joe, I recognize that you may or may not agree with the church's position. But I want to assure you that while my own personal and ethical convictions do not allow me to refer you to any gay group that condones a homosexual lifestyle, I would still be more than willing to assist you in any way possible—such as help in moving, ride from the airport, having you in our home for meals, spiritual counseling or Bible study, etc. as desired."[6]

Joe graciously responded to my reply. But quite often, those who challenge attempts to reconcile homosexuality with the Christian lifestyle incur the wrath of pro-gay advocates. These Christians are misrepresented as being uninformed, judgmental or uncompassionate legalists. At times, they are caricatured as some right-wing homophobic fundamentalists. It is partly to avoid being so labeled that many Adventist thought leaders have chosen to be silent (or at most ambiguous) on the subject of homosexuality.

**Must We Be Silent?** There are at least three reasons why the church must not be silent on crucial issues raised by the gay theology. First, it is a betrayal of Christ and His gospel when, for reasons of political expediency, we choose to remain silent or neutral on established biblical teachings that are being undermined.[7] Moreover, since the advocates of homosexuality are freely disseminating their opinions in the church, it is not out of place for Bible-believing Adventists also to express their views on the subject.

Furthermore, the issue of homosexuality is creating some confusion and hurt in the church. On the one hand, those who consider themselves as homosexuals in orientation are hurt because they often feel misunderstood, rejected, and even discriminated against. On the other hand, those who believe that homosexuality is a violation of the teachings and norms of biblical Christianity are also hurt because they feel that the church has betrayed their trust by accommodating itself to the objectionable practice of homosexuality, thereby encouraging and exposing its members to gross sexual deviations. A truly caring church cannot refuse to respond to an issue that is creating so much confusion and hurt.[8]

**What the Issue Is Not.** The issue to be addressed is *not* whether homosexuals have legitimate civil rights to practice their lifestyle. Like every other human being, the homosexual is of equal value in God's sight and has the same rights and freedom of choice as all others.

**What the Issue Is.** The specific issue to be addressed is whether or not homosexuality is compatible with the Christian lifestyle. In other words, are the pro-gay arguments biblically defensible?

While addressing this crucial question, I will attempt to: (1) explain why Adventist attitudes are changing on the issue of homosexuality; (2) summarize the three major options on the church's dealing with homosexuality; (3) briefly respond to some of the main arguments being put forth by those attempting to reconcile their "born a gay" experience with the Bible's "born again" theology, and (4) point out how we must deal redemptively with homosexuals seeking help to overcome their sin.

**Working Definitions.** In this article, the term "homosexual" or "gay" will be applied to any person (male or female) who, for whatever reasons (genetic, hormonal, environmental, situational, etc.), either engages in a same-gender sexual activity or has a sexual attraction, preference, desire, fantasy, or lust for, members of the same sex. "Lesbianism" refers to a female homosexual. While a "bisexual" is one who engages in or has an erotic attraction to members of both sexes, a "heterosexual" is a person who practices or has an erotic attraction to members of the opposite sex. Gay or homosexual theology refers to the attempt to make homosexuality compatible with biblical Christianity.

Observe carefully that homosexuality, contrary to the claims by some, is *not* simply a same gender attraction (SGA). After all, there is often a same gender attraction between a father and a son, a mother and a daughter, a little brother and his older brothers, a little sister and her big sisters, etc. Individuals experiencing such same-gender attractions cannot be correctly termed homosexuals. A same-gender attraction can be rightly termed homosexuality if, and only if, the attraction is *sexual* or *erotic.* In the same way, an attraction between a child and an adult is not necessarily pedophilia unless that attraction is sexual or erotic.

From our definition above, homosexuality (regardless of its cause or whether considered constitutional or situational [9]) is a same gender *sexual* practice and/or an erotic attraction, preference, desire, or lust for members of the same sex. Outward expressions of homosexuality include sexual contact, erotic noncontact behavior (exhibitionism, telephone sex), and the use of pornography. Indirect expressions of homosexuality include such conscious acts of the imagination as lusting and sexual fantasies.

**The Forbidden Issue.** In order to decide whether or not the Seventh-day Adventist church should embrace the born-a-gay gospel, we must address this crucial question: Is the homosexual *orientation/tendency* (i.e. sexual attraction, preference, desire, or lust), regardless of its cause (genetic, hormonal, environmental, etc.), a morally neutral mark of a person's identity which cannot be changed?

The above question is loaded with major theological and ethical concerns that have to do with our interpretation and understanding of the Bible's teaching.[10] This first section of *Must We Be Silent* will address these issues.

**Endnotes**

[1]Reni Dupertuis, "To Every Nation, Kindred, Tongue and People (Including Sexual Orientation?)," An Interview with Donald J. Freeman, *Scanner*, Winter 1999, 9-11.

[2]The next chapter of this book will document some of these.

[3]I can think of organizations like *GLOW* (God's Love Our Witness) and *God's Rainbow* (an Adventist Gay/Lesbian Ministry at San Francisco Central SDA Church which claims official recognition by the Central California Conference). Apparently believing that homosexuality is a mark of a person's identity (like being born with a particular color of skin, hair, eyes) these "ministries" and support groups teach that being a homosexual is not sin, but (lustful and inappropriate) homosexual activity is sin and therefore, must be avoided. In subsequent pages I will argue that, despite their best intentions, those who hold to this view fail to realize that their position on homosexuality is neither consistent nor biblical.

[4]In his comments on "the inappropriate presentations made in booth1109 at the 2000 Toronto GC session" Howard 'duke' Holtz, a member of the Adventist Gay/Lesbian Ministry at San Francisco Central SDA Church, and "originator" of God's Rainbow, gives some background on how the pro-gay organization managed to get a booth at the GC session. He indicates that the booth was obtained by Carrol Grady, one who appears "to drift towards the Kinship philosophy. . . . Carrol then went and knowingly allowed *Kinship* members to work the booth for her. This resulted in *Kinship* having access to a booth to promote their non-Adventist beliefs at the GC session. When Carrol asked me to send her some of our *God's Rainbow* brochures to hand out, I also expressed my feelings that her actions were not in-line with the goals and standards of our ministry. I have no idea how Carrol could obtain a booth without adhering to SDA principles, and I believe that this is an issue which should be investigated and corrected because incidents like this set back the sincere SDA efforts of such ministries as ours and GLOW's." See Howard Holtz's Internet comments, "End-Time Issues: Homosexuality and the SDA Church," October 30, 2000; *http://www.sdanet.org/archive/2000/Oct32000/0323.html.* While distancing itself from *Kinship,* both Holtz's own *God's Rainbow* and the GLOW organization he highly recommends maintain that homosexuality is morally neutral. In fact GLOW holds that homosexuality is not sin, and that homosexuals cannot be "cured" of their homosexuality.

[5]Mark Edwards (pseudonym), "My World," 2, document distributed in booth #1109 at the 2000 Toronto GC session. The booth was listed in the GC Exhibition book as "Someone to Talk To," an organization claiming to be for "Adventist Families and Friends of Gays and Lesbians."

[6]The official Seventh-day Adventist statement on homosexuality was voted during the Annual Council of the General Conference Executive Committee on Sunday, October 3, 1999, in Silver Spring, Maryland. It reads in its entirety:

"The Seventh-day Adventist Church recognizes that every human being is valuable in the sight of God, and we seek to minister to all men and women in the spirit of Jesus. We also believe that by God's grace and through the encouragement of the community of faith, an individual may live in harmony with the principles of God's Word.

"Seventh-day Adventists believe that sexual intimacy belongs only within the marital relationship of a man and a woman. This was the design established by God at creation. The

Scriptures declare: 'For this reason a man will leave his father and mother and be united to his wife, and they will become one flesh' (Gen. 2:24, NIV). Throughout Scripture this heterosexual pattern is affirmed. The Bible makes no accommodation for homosexual activity or relationships. Sexual acts outside the circle of a heterosexual marriage are forbidden (Lev. 20:7-21; Rom. 1:24-27; 1 Cor. 6:9-11). Jesus Christ reaffirmed the divine creation intent: 'Haven't you read,' he replied, 'that at the beginning the Creator made them male and female,' and said, 'For this reason a man will leave his father and mother and be united to his wife, and the two will become one flesh? So they are no longer two, but one' (Matt. 19:4-6, NIV). For these reasons Adventists are opposed to homosexual practices and relationships.

"Seventh-day Adventists endeavor to follow the instruction and example of Jesus. He affirmed the dignity of all human beings and reached out compassionately to persons and families suffering the consequences of sin. He offered caring ministry and words of solace to struggling people, while differentiating His love for sinners from His clear teaching about sinful practices" (The official Seventh-day Adventist statement on homosexuality was voted during the Annual Council of the General Conference Executive Committee on Sunday, October 3, 1999, in Silver Spring, Maryland).

[7]I am aware that, in today's climate of theological pluralism, it is almost suicidal for anyone to speak out against homosexuality and other disputed theological or ethical issues. Already, in certain quarters of the church, those who forthrightly express their views on such issues as racism or tribalism, women's ordination, contemporary higher criticism, homosexuality, and worship styles are considered "divisive," "controversial" and "extreme fundamentalists". For my views on some of the issues, see my "Saved by Grace and Living by Race: The Religion Called Racism," *Journal of the Adventist Theological Society* 5/2 (Autumn 1994): 37-78; *Searching the Scriptures: Women's Ordination and the Call to Biblical Fidelity* (Berrien Springs, MI: Adventists Affirm, 1995); *Receiving the Word: How New Approaches to the Bible Impact Our Biblical Faith and Lifestyle* (Berrien Springs, MI: Berean Books, 1996).

[8]Cf. Richard J. Foster, *The Challenge of the Disciplined Life: Christian Reflections on Money, Sex and Power* (San Francisco: Harper and Row, 1985), 107.

[9]It should also be noted that in the literature on homosexuality, a distinction is often made between "constitutional" and "situational" homosexuals. "Constitutional" or "true" homosexuals (also referred to as "inverts" or "ontological" homosexuals) are those who are believed to have been born gay, and therefore, are considered to be the genuine homosexuals. Because their *condition/orientation* is said to be a permanent part of their constitutional make up (and not a transitory phase of life nor an accommodation to situational pressure), it is maintained that those who are "ontological" homosexuals should not be held morally responsible for their condition. In and of itself, homosexual *orientation* is believed to be morally neutral, like the normal condition of heterosexuality. On the other hand, "situational" homosexuals (also referred to as "perverts") are not considered as true homosexuals but as heterosexuals who are forced by circumstances (e. g., restrictions on their sexual expression, such as is the case in prison, military camps, boarding schools, monasteries, and other single sex environments) to resort to homosexual practices to gratify their sexual needs. Because situational homosexuality is believed to be a transitory phase in their lives (i. e. they are forced to engage in homosexual practices merely to accommodate situational pressure), their homosexuality is regarded as a perversion of true

sexuality; those who engage in these practices are culpable for their actions. See D. S. Bailey, *Homosexuality and the Western Christian Tradition* (London/New York: Longmans, Green, 1955), xi; H. K. Jones, *A Christian Understanding of the Homosexual* (New York: Association Press, 1966), 20-23.

[10]At issue is the authority of Scripture and the relevance of the biblical text for every generation. "If one discounts the authority of Scripture and its relevance, it matters little what the Bible says about homosexuality or any other subject. If, on the one hand, one holds Scripture in high regard and accepts it as the inspired Word of God, it must be allowed to judge the conduct of every individual. Principles of moral conduct should not change with time or place, contrary to the doctrines of situation ethics common in our day" (Donald J. Wold, *Out of Order: Homosexuality in the Bible and the Ancient Near East* [Grand Rapids, MI: Baker Books, 1998], 9).

# 3

# WHY ATTITUDES ARE CHANGING

All manner of sin can be forgiven, provided we admit our wrongdoing, repent, and turn away from it. But there can be no forgiveness when sinners are in denial—when they insist that their lustful desires and practices are not sinful, when they reinterpret Scripture to justify their sins, and when they defiantly maintain that they will not turn from their sinful ways.

Such is the case today with a sin called homosexuality.

Almost two dozen years ago, a former dean of the Theological Seminary at Andrews University perceptively noted: "The gay crisis has come to church. Some homosexuals are coming to church not only for forgiveness and mercy but to say to the church, as they have to the world, 'Homosexuality is not sinful; it is natural to me. God made me this way. He accepts me and my homosexuality as good. Therefore the time has come for the church to accept me as I am and join me in saying that gayness is good.'"[11]

The above statement aptly captures the essence of the born-a-gay gospel and its varied "ministries" or support groups. Though advocates of this gospel employ the term ministry to describe their "outreach" to gay and lesbians, such ministries for the most part do not teach homosexuals to repent of their particular sin. Instead, they suggest that the church itself must be "educated" to own up to its alleged "immoral" past, when it failed to understand or recognize homosexuality as a morally legitimate lifestyle. Regrettably, an increasing number of Christians are uncritically embracing this new gospel!

Even in our own Seventh-day Adventist church the attitudes of some are changing on the issue of homosexuality. We may find evidence for this change in Adventist discussions on the Internet, in written declarations by some scholars, in discussions at annual professional meetings of the church's Bible teachers, in some carefully written, yet troubling, articles that have been published in our church publications, and in the mumblings, if not deafening silence, from our pulpits.[2]

The question before us is: Why are some within our ranks embracing the born a gay gospel as a morally legitimate part of the Christian lifestyle?

**What Is New About the Born A Gay Gospel?**

The practice of homosexuality is not a new phenomenon of sexual behavior that has suddenly burst upon our modern culture; the practice has been present in almost every human society. Not unexpectedly, the Bible also deals with the subject in such texts as Gen. 19 (cf. Jude 7; 2 Pet. 2:6-10); Lev. 18:22; 20:13; Rom 1:24-27; 1 Cor. 6:9-11; 1 Tim. 1:8-11).

If there is anything new about the practice of homosexuality, the newness lies in the fact that unlike the past centuries of Christian history, many churches in our day are accepting homosexuality as a morally legitimate lifestyle. Advocates of gay theology have employed two major methods to silence or challenge the Bible's negative valuation of homosexuality.

First, they argue that the Bible texts which have been understood historically as condemning homosexuality are either obscure or refer to the *abuse* of homosexuality. By this they mean certain kinds of homosexual practices, notably gang rape, idolatry, promiscuity, and prostitution, but not genuine homosexual orientation as we know it today.

Second, they put forward some Bible characters as examples of allegedly healthy and loving homosexual relationships. For example, the friendship love (*philia*) between biblical characters like Ruth and Naomi (Ruth 1-4) and David and Jonathan (1 Sam 18-20) they interpret to mean sexual love (*eros*). Consequently, they present these Bible characters as Christian models of lesbian and gay relationships. Advocates often argue that Ruth and Naomi exchanged their lesbian marriage vows when Ruth said to Naomi: "Wherever you go, I will go with you, wherever you stay I will stay with you; your people will be my people, and your God will be my

God. . . . *Till death do us part"* (Ruth 1:16-17, my translation).

Regarding David and Jonathan, advocates of gay theology string together the following interesting argument to suggest that they were two "male lovers": The Bible itself says Jonathan "loved" David (1 Sam18:3); David declared publicly that Jonathan's love was "wonderful"—passing even "the love of women" (2 Sam 1:23); Jonathan allegedly "stripped" in David's presence (1 Sam 18:4), the two "kissed" each other (1 Sam 20:41), subsequently "wept together" and (David) "exceeded" (1 Sam 20:41)—terms advocates take to mean a sexual encounter! (Readers may wish to read the Scriptural account of the relationship between David and Jonathan to ascertain for themselves what the Bible actually says.)

Other proponents of gay theology also consider Joseph and Potiphar (Gen 39), Nebuchadnezzar and Daniel (Dan 2, 4), as well as Jesus and John ("the disciple whom Jesus loved"—John 13:23; 19:26; 20:2) as genuine models of loving and committed homosexual relationships. Some even consider the virgin Mary a lesbian, describing her as "one courageous woman who did not need a man to have a child."

Even though we may easily dismiss the above examples of allegedly healthy gay and lesbian relationships in the Bible as frivolous inventions, not all the arguments of pro-gay theology can be so rebuffed so handily. Some of the arguments are quite sophisticated, often invoking scientific, philosophical, or logical arguments to show that (i) people are born homosexual (i.e., homosexuality is genetic or inborn); (ii) the sexual orientation of people born gay should be viewed as a natural or normal trait of their identity, like the color of the skin, eyes, or hair, or as a God given gift; (iii) a person's so-called God-given homosexual orientation is morally neutral and unchangeable; and (iv) the Bible is silent, or does not condemn, homosexuality as such, but only its abuse.

Sincere, Bible-believing Christians are often caught off-guard by the subtle and plausible-sounding arguments in favor of homosexuality today. In an effort to clear away the smokescreen which often clouds this issue, subsequent chapters of this section of *Must We Be Silent* will list some of the arguments in circulation. Following each is a response which I hope will make clear the fundamental issue at stake for the Christian. I believe that the reader will find in Scripture a clear and consistent guide to God's will in this highly charged matter.

This chapter will identify some major reasons why Christian attitudes are changing on the question of homosexuality.

**Reasons for the Changing Attitudes**

The favorable disposition of some towards the practice of homosexuality may be attributed to a number of factors. The following are some of the major reasons:

**1. Campaign by Pro-Homosexual Groups.** The successful campaigns by various homosexual lobbying and civil rights organizations to end not only discrimination against homosexuals generally, but also to decriminalize homosexual practices between consenting adults, and to liberalize public opinion, attitudes, laws, and policies on homosexuality have contributed to the favorable attitude of some on homosexuality.

For example, in 1973 the American Bar Association called for the repeal of laws which in the past had placed homosexuality in the category of *crime*. That same year, the American Psychiatric Association removed homosexuality from its official list of mental *illness*, and the American Psychological Association also decided that homosexuality was no longer an *abnormal* behavior. With such influential actions to remove homosexuality from the categories of crime, illness, and abnormal behavior, it did not take long before Christian churches began to hear calls from pro-gay advocates, urging the church to remove homosexuality from the category of *sin*.

In the effort to remove homosexuality from the category of sin, advocates of gay theology have often presented testimonies of homosexuals and latest research findings (scientific and biblical) in such a manner as to silence or challenge the Bible's negative valuation of homosexuality. They portray those who do not embrace the revisionist interpretations of Scripture as being hopelessly uninformed or judgmental. Worse still, those opposed to the homosexual agenda are portrayed as cherishing the mean spirit of some right wing fundamentalists, the kind of spirit that encourages gay bashing and gay hate-crimes.[3]

Gay activists also employ specific strategies to turn the public against the church, and the church against itself. In an insightful exposé of how they silence conservative churches' opposition to the gay lifestyle, one researcher quotes the following from a 1987 *Guide Magazine,* a publication for gays:

> When conservative churches condemn gays . . . we can use talk to muddy the moral waters. This means publicizing support for gays by more moderate churches. . . . We can undermine the

> moral authority of homophobic churches by portraying them as antiquated backwaters, badly out of step with the times and with the latest findings of psychology. Against the mighty pull of institutional Religion one must set the mightier draw of Science and Public Opinion. Such an unholy alliance has worked well against churches before, on such topics as divorce and abortion . . . that alliance can work again here.[4]

By removing homosexuality from the category of sin, and by employing strategies such as outlined above, pro-gay advocates have been successful in splitting major churches over gay clergy and gay marriage. The ultimate goal is not simply toleration, but total approval of the homosexual lifestyle.

**2. Departure from Biblical Revelation to Empirical Research:** The changing attitude toward homosexuality may also be attributed to the skepticism in certain quarters of the church about the trustworthiness and reliability of the Bible. Under the influence of contemporary higher-criticism, the Bible's sole authority is being replaced by other sources: reason, tradition, and experience. If the Bible is not authoritative in matters dealing with science, history, psychology, etc., why should it be relied upon on questions dealing with homosexuality?[5]

Thus, those who seek to neutralize the biblical witness against homosexuality often do so on the basis of alleged research findings (scientific, statistical, etc.), or on the basis of testimonies by homosexuals of their happy, healthy, and fulfilling relationships, instead of on Scripture.

For example, on the basis of a highly questionable study showing that homosexuals in the San Francisco Bay area who are involved in reciprocal, permanent, and sexually exclusive relationships tended to be the happiest, healthiest, and most well-adjusted people of the entire group being analyzed, an Adventist ethicist concluded: "Christians therefore have every reason to encourage homosexuals who are honestly convinced that they should neither attempt to function heterosexually nor remain celibate to form Closed-Coupled homosexual unions."[6]

Notice that the reason given for endorsing closed couple homosexual unions is not Biblical revelation, but rather an empirical finding regarding the experience of homosexuals. This new way of knowing truth (what scholars refer to as epistemology) is also illustrated in the testimony of one lesbian, who describes herself as an "Adventist-connected" theologian, Bible instructor/academy teacher-turned minister.

She speaks about her naiveté in blindly following the teaching of the Seventh-day Adventist church that "told me that my own nature was sinful, so looking to myself would be my downfall. . . . It did not tell me to look at the rest of the natural world and discover that same-gender nesting occurs in many species." She explains, however, that following "an unusual calling" or "Martin Luther experience" (the "ecstasy and torment" of her lesbian encounter), she came to value the importance of "inner knowing"—listening to "the voice of God within me."[7]

The above examples illustrate the increasing departure from Biblical revelation towards empirical experience as an authority base on religious issues. Not only does this trend raise questions for Bible believing Christians regarding the starting point for discussions on homosexuality—Should it be *observation, introspection,* or biblical *revelation*?—but it also explains why some will jettison biblical teaching for "latest research findings."

**3. Impact of Behaviorist Philosophy on Recent Research Findings.** Another factor that is shaping the homosexual debate is the impact of behavioristic philosophy. This philosophy, which has adherents among biologists, zoologists, physicists, and other social scientists, simply states that individuals have practically no choice in their moral actions, and therefore, may not be held morally accountable for their actions. Human behavior, it is said, is largely, if not exclusively, predetermined by one's environment and one's genetic code.[8]

Given the impact of the behavioristic philosophy, it is not coincidental that researchers are discovering that some are "born gay," that is to say they hold their homosexual orientation or identity from birth.[9] Although the findings of genetic research are at the present time inconclusive, and although the studies often cited have been compellingly challenged,[10] already some Adventist writers are making the following deductions from the new light of scientific research: (a) homosexuals are born gay, (b) homosexuality is a normal or natural condition, (c) what is natural cannot be immoral, and (d) "blaming the homosexual for his or her sexual orientation is both wrong-spirited and wrong."[11]

Observe that while perceptive critics, including some homosexuals, have questioned the value of these "born a gay" discoveries, and while others have exposed the intellectual and psychological inconsistency in this "outmoded version of natural law,"[12] for some Adventist advocates of homosexual theology, these research findings validate their new understanding of "the truth about homosexuality." They argue that "whatever may cause a homosexual orientation, it is not something a person *chooses*."[13]

Another writer approvingly explains the born a gay argument using the words of an Adventist homosexual (notice her emphases):

> As God is in His heaven I did not *choose* this orientation, this lifestyle. Why would I *choose* a lifestyle that's kept me from following my choice of profession? Why would I *choose* a lifestyle that's kept me from marrying any of several girls who offered me a "normal" lifestyle with a home and family? Why would I *choose* to live in a world that thinks I am disgusting, repulsive, and totally unacceptable? Why would I *choose* a lifestyle that can lead to loss of employment, friends, family, and love? If I would *choose* this, then I truly need to be put away! . . . What I am saying is that I did not *choose* this lifestyle. God allowed it, though He did not give it to me. I cannot change, because I have tried.[14]

The belief that homosexual orientation, like the color of the skin, eye, or hair, is inborn—i.e., the homosexual was born gay, and has no choice over his/her homosexual condition—is one of the main reasons for the changing attitudes within Adventism on the question of homosexuality. Some go so far as to say that if God has allowed some people to be born gay, why should we not accept the person's sexual orientation?

More, probably, see homosexuality as an unfortunate birth defect, like a harelip, crossed eyes, or Down syndrome, to be corrected if possible. My contention, however, is that if we accept homosexual orientation as something inherited or acquired rather than *chosen*, it is *inevitable* that we will soon be called to see it as natural, then normal, then acceptable, and finally laudable. (Consider, for example, how those with AIDS are now valorized for their courage.)

**4. New Sexual Paradigms.** The acceptance of homosexuality as a morally legitimate sexual expression in certain quarters of the Adventist church should also be seen as a reflection of the growing challenge to traditional Adventist views on human sexuality. In what is emerging in the church as a "new sexual paradigm," permissible sex is no longer limited to sex within the biblically prescribed monogamous, heterosexual, marriage relationship. Instead, it is one which is engaged in by consenting individuals, according to their own self-imposed boundaries. Accordingly, premarital sex, masturbation (also known as solo sex, self sex, or partnerless sex), and homosexuality are all viewed as morally justifiable.

For example, one Adventist university chaplain and teacher who argues for pre-marital sex and masturbation writes that "sexual exploration and experimentation before marriage" is acceptable as long as a person does not put his or her unmarried partner "in the position of feeling guilty or sinful."[15]

Another Adventist, a professor of psychology, defines sexual sin as "*behaving* in a way that *harms* yourself or others." Among the "radical reforms of the Adventist sexual paradigm" that he recommends to the church is this: "The pleasures of occasional guilt-free orgasm ought to be available to all post-pubescent parishioners." The "guilt-free" sex includes sex with "myself" (masturbation), with "a person of the same gender" (homosexuality), and with "someone ['not-yet- married'] of the opposite gender" (premarital sex).[16]

**5. Climate of "Enlightened" Ethical Sensitivity.** Our generation is painfully aware of the existence in our world of injustice and bigotry—slavery, racism, sexism, anti-Semitism, homophobia[17] (fear, hysteria, disgust and/or hatred of the homosexual), etc. Because ignorance and religious bigotry have often played a part in these oppressive acts, it has become potentially harmful to quote the Bible when questioning anyone's sexual conduct—however objectionable it may be. Thus, the condemnation of any of today's new sexual paradigms is perceived as a judgmental act that may hurt the ethical feelings of sexual minorities—individuals with alternate sexual preferences or orientations.

In the desire to appear more informed and compassionate, those who have adopted this posture of enlightened ethical sensitivity are treating biblical prohibitions of certain sexual deviations as culturally-conditioned or offensive relics of a pre-scientific (or puritanical) morality.[18] Additionally, biblical virtues such as love, compassion, and acceptance are emphasized in such a way as to counter any efforts not to accept the new sexual paradigms. Bible-believing Christians who speak against homosexuality are accused of being *judgmental* (as in the case of Christ's disciples, who condemned a congenitally blind person as a sinner [John 9]) and un-Christlike (Didn't Jesus say, "Judge not, lest ye be judged?" And didn't He also say to the woman caught in adultery, "Neither do I condemn thee?").

To digress for a moment, it would seem that Jesus' statement, "Neither do I condemn thee: go, and sin no more" (John 8:11), has been abused by all classes of Christians in their attitude to homosexuality. On one hand, strong advocates of pro-gay theology would read the statement as: "*Neither do I condemn thee: go, and sin . . .*" On the other hand, some strong opponents of gay theology would adopt the attitude: ". . . *I condemn thee: go!*" A true Adventist position does not condemn the sinner ("neither do I condemn thee"); it does condemn the sin ("Go, and sin no more").

In any case, given today's climate of enlightened ethical sensitivity, anyone who does not accept homosexuality as morally justifiable is looked upon as being legalistic, insensitive, hypocritical, bigoted, or homophobic—characteristics that are incompatible with acceptable Christian behavior. This strategy exerts a powerful psychological pressure on Christians to either endorse the homosexual lifestyle or, at a minimum, remain silent on the issue.

**6. The AIDS Crisis.** During the early phases of the AIDS epidemic, when it was discovered that AIDS is largely a sexually transmitted disease, the disease came to be perceived as a judgment from God against all forms of sexual perversion—of which homosexuality was the chief. Since many Adventists viewed homosexuality as *the* unpardonable sin of sexual immorality—the one sin that sealed the doom of Sodom and Gomorrah, and which would signal the end of time, AIDS became associated with homosexuality and the disease came to be seen as a gay disease.[19]

But as heterosexuals and non-promiscuous individuals started coming down with AIDS, Christians were forced not only to rethink their judgmental stance towards victims of AIDS, but also to reconsider their negative valuation of homosexuality. The reasoning was: If both homosexuals and heterosexuals fall to AIDS, perhaps homosexuality is not as sinful as it was traditionally pictured.

Also, when compassion for victims of the AIDS disease soon turned into compassion for homosexuals, it was not long before compassion for the struggling homosexual turned into an acceptance of the sin of homosexuality. This seems to be the unspoken message in an article in *Adventist View*, titled "I'm Homosexual, I'm Adventist, and I Have AIDS."[20]

**7. Kinship's Pro-Gay Theology.** Another major reason for Adventism's changing attitude toward homosexuality is the influence of the work by the pro-homosexual organization known as Kinship. Billing itself as "a support group for gay and lesbian Seventh-day Adventists," Kinship has been quite successful in converting some Adventists to its belief that "God can bless a committed homosexual relationship." As a result, an increasing number of homosexuals are coming out of the closet and demanding that their homosexuality be accepted as either natural, or a "gift from God."[21]

This may explain why in the 1993 Adventist Women's Institute's book referred to earlier, an "Adventist-connected" theologian, Bible instructor/academy teacher-turned-minister, writes that her lesbianism is "an unusual calling" from the Lord and why her lesbian partner also felt that the lesbian relationship was "God's gift for her conversion."[22]

A year earlier the November 4, 1992 issue of the Andrews University student newspaper *(Student Movement)* created a sensation on campus when it published a letter from an Andrews University homosexual couple pleading for acceptance.[23] In the center page article of that issue, some anonymous staff members and students discussed their homosexual and lesbian relationships. Among them was "Ann," a 28-year old lesbian who was seeking the transfer of her church membership to the Pioneer Memorial Church at Andrews University. Speaking about her committed homosexual relationship in which God plays an important role, Ann summed up the basic belief of Kinship: "I am a lesbian because God knows that that's the best thing for me. My homosexuality has actually brought me a lot closer to God than if I was a heterosexual."[24]

It is this kind of view that was actively promoted at the 2000 Toronto GC session by "Someone To Talk To," an organization claiming to be for "Adventist Families and Friends of Gays and Lesbians" and which has apparently been recognized by the North American Division Family Ministries Department. Even some Adventist Gay/Lesbian "ministries" (such as the one at the San Francisco Central SDA Church) and "outreach" groups like God's Rainbow and GLOW, while distancing themselves from Kinship, nonetheless argue that homosexuality is not sin, but rather morally neutral.

As a result of the campaigns by these organizations, groups, and individuals, many Adventists are no longer very sure of the nature and morality of homosexuality.

**8. 1980 Declaration by Some Scholars.** Within the Seventh-day Adventist church, the most significant event that signaled the changing attitudes towards homosexuality occurred when, in August 1980, the church commissioned six well-known representatives to attend a camp meeting (or "*kamp* meeting") organized by the pro-homosexual group Kinship.[25]

Although the church representatives consisted of six influential Bible scholars and pastors, to the surprise of many, the biblical and theological scholars at the Kinship camp meeting concluded that the teaching of Scripture on the subject of homosexuality is not sufficiently clear to settle the question of the morality of homosexual acts or relationships in our world.[26]

The three scholars, all of whom were then teaching at the church's leading theological seminary at Andrews University, declared: "A simplistic English reading of the few scriptural references to homosexual acts would not suffice to determine the Lord's will for homosexual persons today."[27]

Given the ensuing civil war between liberals and conservatives over the legitimacy of contemporary higher criticism in biblical interpretation, the declaration by the church's authorized scholars at the Kinship camp meeting has been understood by some as another indication of the flourishing of liberal methodology in the church.[28]

In any case, declarations such as the one above, and the official opposition to such a position by the church in the volume *Seventh-day Adventists Believe . . .* (1988)[29] and in the GC's Biblical Research Institute's book *Homosexuality in History and Scriptures* (1988),[30] have made the issue of homosexuality a hot potato item within Adventist scholarship.

**9. Troubling Views in Church Publications.** Despite the clamor for the church's acceptance of homosexuality, and despite the fact that the church's Bible scholars have been quietly debating the issue, very few Adventists were aware of the campaign for homosexuality in the Seventh-day Adventist church. But in recent times the homosexual issue has come out of its ideological and academic closets into the mainstream Adventist view. This has taken the form of carefully written yet troubling articles in such church publications as *Ministry*, *Adventist Review*, *Insight*, *Women of Spirit*, *Adventist View*, and the *Collegiate Quarterly*. These articles, sometimes by anonymous authors, have called for new "awareness and understanding on the subject of homosexuality." A careful reading of some of these works reveals a subtle shift from the church's categorical rejection of homosexuality to its qualified acceptance.[31]

As I will show in the next chapter, there are three contending positions on homosexuality that are competing in Christian churches today: (a) the *non-acceptance* view, which maintains that homosexuality is not compatible with biblical Christianity; this is the long-standing SDA position (b) the *qualified acceptance* view, which argues that homosexuality can be compatible with Christianity; this is the new view being promoted in the articles being put out in church publications; (c) the *full acceptance* view, which asserts that homosexuality is fully compatible with the Christian faith; this is the position held by pro-gay organizations like Kinship.

The vexing questions raised by the troubling articles appearing in our church publications can best be illustrated by calling attention to the December 5, 1992, issue of *Insight*, a publication for Seventh-day Adventist teenagers. This particular issue of *Insight* is devoted entirely to the subject of homosexuality. While the then editor of the magazine maintains that "there is no scriptural support for practicing homosexuality," he nevertheless endorses the pro-gay theology when he asserts that: "There's a difference between *being* a homosexual and *practicing* homosexuality"; "Nobody *chooses* to be homosexual"; "Changing one's homosexual orientation is difficult and rare"; "Homosexuals can be genuine, model Christians"; and "Being a homosexual is not a sin."[32]

Perceptive readers will recognize that the above position was rejected by the 1990 and 1995 *Church Manuals* when the church officially condemned "homosexual practices and lesbian practices" as examples of "the obvious perversions of God's original plan," *and made these practices a basis for church discipline.*[33] It is significant that the 1990 and 1995 *Church Manuals* made the practice of homosexuality a basis for church discipline. For, since the 1985 GC session, pro-gay advocates have subtly sought to modify the language in the *Church Manual* towards a qualified acceptance view of homosexuality (see the note below for an insightful account of how this happened).[34]

**10. Obliteration of Gender Role Distinctions.** One overlooked reason for Adventism's changing attitude towards homosexuality is the impact of feminist theology on sexual role distinctions. This fact is evident in the liberal (radical feminist) and conservative (egalitarian or equalitarian) reasoning for ordaining women as elders or pastors. Though employing different sets of arguments, both liberal and conservative proponents of women's ordination are united in their denial of male headship and gender role differentiation *at creation.* They reject the biblical teaching of sexual role distinctions before the fall of Adam and Eve because of their belief that such a teaching suggests the absence of "full equality" and the existence of superiority/inferiority among the first pair.[35]

We should not miss the connection between the above arguments and those used to promote homosexuality. Just as feminists seek "full equality" by getting rid of *gender* or *sex roles* in marriage and the church, gay theology also seeks to bring about "full equality" between homosexuals and heterosexuals by obliterating *sexual identity.* Thus, when radical proponents impose their gender-inclusive reconstructions upon the Bible and suggest that Adam was "an androgynous being" (i.e. bisexual),[36] it is only a few steps from seeing homosexuality as a creation ordinance.

Similarly, when conservative proponents of women's ordination claim that at creation Adam and Eve were "fully equal," enjoying "total egalitarianism in marriage," and when they argue that prior to the fall there was no role differentiation between male and female, whether they are aware of it or not, they also are building a theological nest for advocates of homosexual theology to lay and hatch their gay eggs.[37]

To speak of "full equality" without seriously coming to terms with the nature and extent of this equality and without stating unambiguously that to act as "equal and joint partners" does not mean to act identically, allows advocates of gay theology to build upon the shaky foundation constructed by liberal and conservative advocates of women's ordination. At a time of increasing homosexual demands for marital rights, the failure by proponents of women's ordination to say unambiguously that men are not equal with women personally or even physically *as candidates to be spouses of men* has opened a welcome door for those who seek to nullify the biblical case for divinely instituted role differences and a monogamous heterosexual relationship. This fact has not been lost by proponents of gay theology within Adventism.[38]

For example, speaking at the annual meeting of Seventh-day Adventist college and university Bible teachers in San Francisco, California, in 1992, the "liaison" from the pro-homosexual group Kinship, correctly remarked that the push for women's ordination, when successful, will eventually open the door for the church to embrace homosexuality, since both causes are waging a similar battle of "discrimination" and share the same basic approach to biblical interpretation.

One Adventist homosexual, a member of the "Adventist Gay/Lesbian" Ministry at San Francisco Central SDA Church, makes an insightful observation regarding the similarities of the pro-gay and pro-women's ordination arguments. He expresses his amusement that proponents of women's ordination "use a set of arguments to validate women being ordained, almost exactly the same as us gays used to approve of 'monogamous gay relationships.' Junia and Phoebe rank right in there with David and Jonathan, and Ruth and Naomi. In this [Internet Web site] thread, I have even seen the Bible translated by first setting aside references to gender because of some women being just as capable of certain tasks as a man is. Well, let me tell you something honey, except for childbirth I have been just as capable as any woman in all of the tasks normally performed by the woman—so I guess I can also set aside all the biblical statements I don't like? To my knowledge, 'Ordination Credentials' are a man-made set of requirements to fill a biblical role, but they are in no way capable of changing the gender to which the role applies."[39]

Despite the objections by some Adventist proponents of women's ordination, the experience of other Christian denominations confirms the above observations that openness towards homosexuality inescapably follows once we jettison the Bible's teaching on sexual role differentiation for an "egalitarian" model.

This is why some delegates at the 2000 Toronto GC session objected to the insertion of a theologically fuzzy feminist language in the "divorce and remarriage" document presented to them at the session. The reason is simple: Whether proponents were aware of it or not, by taking away role distinctions at creation, the divorce and remarriage document which was presented to delegates at the Toronto GC session set a theological foundation not just for women's ordination but also for homosexuality.[40]

**Summary.** The above ten reasons—(1) campaign by pro-homosexual groups, (2) departure from biblical revelation to empirical research, (3) the impact of the behavioristic philosophy on recent research findings, (4) new sexual paradigms, (5) the climate of "enlightened" ethical sensitivity, (6) the AIDS crisis, (7) the impact of Kinship's pro-gay theology, (8) the 1980 declaration by some scholars, (9) troubling views in church publications, and (10) the obliteration of gender role distinctions—may help explain why attitudes are changing within the Adventist church on the issue of homosexuality.

As a result of these reasons (and perhaps others), there is uncertainty in the minds of many church members over the nature and morality of homosexuality. Some pro-gay advocates within our ranks are slowly moving the church towards a full—or qualified-acceptance view of homosexuality. Before evaluating the arguments being used to domesticate homosexuality in the Adventist church, it may first be necessary to summarize the three major positions pleading for audience in the Christian church. The next chapter will take up this issue.

---

**Endnotes**

[1]Raoul Dederen, "Homosexuality: A Biblical Perspective," *Ministry,* September 1988, 14.

[2]At my last count, no less than 150 published works (articles and letters) on the subject of homosexuality have appeared in Adventist publications during the past 20 years (1978-2000). For a detailed discussion of published Adventist views on the subject from the early '50s to the mid '80s, see Michael Pearson, *Millennial Dreams and Moral Dilemmas: Seventh-day Adventism and Contemporary Ethics* (Cambridge; New York: Cambridge University Press, 1990), 240-265.

[3]Mel White's *Stranger At the Gate: To Be Gay and Christian in America* (New York: Simon and Schuster, 1994) also captures this spirit of vindictiveness. A former evangelical, he is now openly homosexual and has served as dean of Dallas's Cathedral of Hope, an affiliate of the gay Universal Fellowship of Metropolitan Community Churches. He dismisses those who do not embrace his attempt to reconcile homosexuality with the biblical faith as being ignorant of "the new biblical, pastoral, psychological and scientific data about homosexuality." In his view, such individuals evidence the spirit of the so-called religious right, a spirit perceived as intolerance and which ultimately leads to the suffering of God's homosexual children. White presents an agenda to "keep the religious right from doing more wrong": "Start your own version of a local 'to prevent a gay/lesbian' holocaust museum. Demonstrate the similarity between Hitler's Third Reich and the current tactics of the religious right." He advocates censorship: "Organize your new coalitions to call radio and television stations quoting the offenders, suggesting they be taken off the air. Follow up with public or even legal pressure when the inflammatory rhetoric continues. Write letters to the editors against the columnists of the religious right" (Mel White, *Stranger At the Gate,* 320, 321). For a biblical response to White's revisionist interpretation of the biblical data, see Donald J. Wold, *Out of Order: Homosexuality in the Bible and the Ancient Near East* (Grand Rapids: Baker, 1998).

[4]See Lynn Vincent, "How Homosexuals Fight," *World,* April 10, 1999, 19.

[5]In *Receiving the Word,* I have attempted to show how higher critical assumptions and conclusions are shaping discussions on homosexuality, the use of alcohol, creation, etc. See chapter 5 of the book, 101-194.

[6]David R. Larson, "Sexuality and Christian Ethics," *Spectrum* 15 (May 1984):16." For a detailed challenge to the dubious research of Kinsey, see, for example, Judith Reisman and Edward W. Eichel, *Kinsey, Sex, and Fraud: The Indoctrination of a People*

(Lafayette, La.: Lochinvar-Huntington House, 1990).

[7]Lin Ennis,"Seeker of Truth, Finder of Reality," in *In Our Own Words: Women Tell of Their Lives and Faith*, ed. Iris M. Yob and Patti Hansen Tompkins (Santa Ana, CA: Adventist Women's Institute, 1993), 237, 238, 230-235. She explains: "I was so naive about God, so blind to the real needs of human beings, so willing to be led as a sheep, mindlessly following, not thinking for myself, except just enough to afford me the illusion of independence of thought. Far more than I cared to admit, I did what the church said, what the *Church Manual* said, what the ministers and evangelists I had worked with said" (Ibid., 234). But after she discovered the truth about God by looking at herself (apparently, the "inner knowing" of listening to God "within me" [234]) and "the rest of the natural world," and rightly understood "the Bible," "I realized that to continue to be active in the Adventist Church in the way I had always been before would not work for me" (Ibid., 237).

[8]*Time* magazine (August 1, 1977):54-63 alerted the world to the growing impact of another version of this behavioristic philosophy when it devoted its cover article—"Why You Do What You Do"—to *sociobiology*, a new theory which maintains that social behavior has a biological basis. One leading sociobiologist at Harvard University is quoted in the *Time* article as making this prediction: "Sooner or later, political science, law, economics, psychology, psychiatry and anthropology will all be branches of sociobiology." In partial fulfillment of this kind of prediction by the prophets of sociobiology, "discoveries" are being made in recent times by researchers that what in the past were considered as habitual sins are actually of biological origin. Thus, it is said that some individuals are "born to smoke," "born alcoholics," and even "born murderers," and are therefore not to be held accountable for their moral actions. According to a *Time* magazine cover story, even infidelity may be due to our genes. (See Robert Wright, "Our Cheating Hearts," August 15, 1994, 44-52.)

[9]The studies often cited as evidence that homosexuality is inborn include: (1) the 1991 study of neuroscientist Dr. Simon LeVay on the brain structures of 41 cadavers; (2) the 1991 research by Northwestern University psychologist Michael Bailey (a gay rights advocate) and Boston University School of Medicine psychiatrist Richard Pillard (who is openly homosexual) on homosexual twins; and (3) the 1993 study by Dr. Dean Hamer of the National Cancer Institute on the genetic markers on 40 non-identical gay brothers. But as I will later show, these oft quoted research findings have been shown to be misleading and exaggerated (at best inconclusive). For a succinct review and evaluation of the findings of the above cited researchers and supporting references, see Thomas E. Schmidt, *Straight and Narrow: Compassion and Clarity in the Homosexuality Debate* (Downers Grove, IL: InterVarsity Press, 1995), 137-142; Joe Dallas, *A Strong Delusion: Confronting the "Gay Christian" Movement* (Eugene, OR: Harvest House Publishers, 1996), 107-131.

[10]See for example, Neil and Briar Whitehead, *My Genes Made Me Do It! A Scientific Look at Sexual Orientation* (Lafayetter, Louisiana, Huntington House Publishers, 1999), who offer a compelling refutation of the arguments often cited in support of the claim that people are born gay.

[11]According to the then editor of *Insight*, a homosexual orientation (or inclination, inversion, desires, or outlook) is "a way of *being* and *feeling*—whether or not those feelings are ever translated into sexual acts." It is a mark of one's identity, "a natural part" of a person—just as possessing green eyes. He quotes approvingly one homosexual as saying: "Oh,

I could cover them up for a while, wear blue or brown contacts, but that wouldn't change the reality. My eyes *are* green, and my sexual orientation *is* gay." Thus, for this Adventist scholar, "blaming the homosexual for his or her sexual orientation is both wrong-spirited and wrong." "Being a homosexual is not a sin," he asserts. See Christopher Blake, "Redeeming Our Sad Gay Situation," *Insight*, December 5, 1992, 6, 7, 11.

[12]Perceptive critics, including some homosexuals, reject this born a gay discovery because they fear that other research findings showing some unacceptable conditions (like alcoholism, schizophrenia, cerebral palsy, etc.) as genetically related will soon make homosexuals look like they are abnormal or less than human (cf. *World* 6 [September 14, 1991]:11). J. B. Nelson exposes the intellectual and psychological inconsistency in this "outmoded version of natural law" which seeks to make a fine distinction between homosexual orientation and behavior. Responding to the view that "while homosexuality as an *orientation* is contrary to God's created intention, the homosexual *person* ought not to be adversely judged or rejected by the church," Nelson counters that while some may deem such a position a more tolerant and compassionate view than outright condemnation, "it places gay men and lesbians in at least two impossible binds." He writes: "One, of course, is the individual's recognition that her or his own sexual orientation is as natural and as fundamental to identity as is the color of the skin. It is both naive and cruel to tell a lesbian or gay man, 'Your sexual orientation is still unnatural and a perversion, but this is no judgment upon you as a person.' The individual knows otherwise. The other bind concerns churchly pressure toward celibacy. When the church presumes to be non-judgmental toward orientation but then draws the line against genital expression, it is difficult to understand how the sense of guilt—even in the celibate—will be significantly alleviated." See J. B. Nelson, "Religious and Moral Issues in Working with Homosexual Clients," in *Homosexuality and Psycho-therapy, a Practitioner's Handbook of Affirmative Models. Journal of Homosexuality* 7, Nos. 2-3, ed. J. C. Gonsiorek (New York: Haworth press, 1982): 168-69.

[13]Kate McLaughlin (pseudonym), "Are Homosexuals God's Children?" *Adventist Review*, April 3, 1997, 26 (emphasis hers); cf. idem, "A Homosexual in My Congregation?" *Ministry*, November 1996, 10-11, 29.

[14]Suzanne Ryan, "When Love Wasn't Enough," *Insight*, December 5, 1992, 3 (emphasis hers). Christopher Blake agrees: "nobody chooses to be homosexual. . . . Whether a person is born with the orientation or it develops as a result of his or her upbringing, or it's a complex combination of both (which is most likely), it is *not* a matter of choice. A child chooses neither how she is born nor how he is raised. We shouldn't hold a person responsible for her or his sexual *orientation* any more than we hold a person responsible for skin color (nature) or how a preschooler is dressed (nurture)" (Blake, "Redeeming Our Sad Gay Situation, 6-7; emphasis his).

[15]Steven G. Daily, *Adventism for a New Generation* (Portland/Clackamas, OR: Better Living Publishers, 1993), 298. According to Daily, the Seventh-day Adventist church's negative valuation of pre-marital sex and masturbation arises from "our Victorian heritage, which has been well preserved through the work of Ellen White. Most Adventists are not aware of what bizarre and extreme views of sexuality were commonly held by our nineteenth century ancestors. Books like *Messages to Young People* have served to perpetuate such baggage throughout much of the twentieth century as well" (ibid., 296-297).

[16]John Berecz, "About Orgasms and Other Things," *Student Movement* [Andrews University Newspaper], February 26, 1997, 9, 11, emphasis mine. A few weeks later

Berecz published another article in the *Student Movement* in which he offered "suggested boundaries to Christian solo sex [masturbation]." See his "An Essay on a Sensitive Subject," *Student Movement*, April 2, 1997, 5.

[17]"Homophobia" is an irrational fear of homosexuality which leads to hostility towards homosexuals and others who seek to give help to them.

[18]Thus, morally neutral expressions are now being employed for once forbidden sins: fornication is now premarital or nonmarital sex; adultery is referred to as an extramarital or co-marital affair; permissiveness is euphemisized as sexual variation; the promiscuous is multifriended; and homosexuality and sodomy are now alternate lifestyles (See, for example, John Leo, "Cleansing the Mother Tongue," *Time*, December 27, 1982, 78). In this politically-correct age, sin is no longer perceived as a sin but rather as sickness, and habitual sin is now regarded as an addictive or compulsive behavior. Thus, not too long ago, a newspaper had an article about a 34-bed clinic that had just opened in Southern California to treat "Christian sex addicts." See, Nicole Brodeur, "Center Aids Christian Sex Addicts," *Orange County Register*, February 13, 1989, 1.

[19]This prevalent understanding is reflected in a 1977 *Sabbath School Lessons*: "Jesus said that one of the signs of His near return would be a condition of morality similar to that among the antediluvians and Sodomites. Not only have the same deviant sexual patterns become prominent in our times, being pursued with open boldness, but some professed ministers now defend such practices, organize churches for persons of this lifestyle, and ordain some to the ministry. Such sinful brazenness indicates again the eroding morality of our times and the approaching end of the age" (*Sabbath School Lessons*, October 1977, 48 [British edition, 330]; cf. Ellen G. White, *Mind, Character, and Personality*, vol. 1, 232).

[20]See the story of Jim Miller (as told to Celeste Ryan), "I'm Homosexual, I'm Adventist, and I have AIDS: The Jim Miller Story," *Adventist View* (Winter 1993), 9, 15. Cf. Bruce Moyer's interview with Ron (pseudonym), "A Cry from the Valley of Death," *Ministry* (November 1996):23-25, 29; Christopher Blake, "Redeeming Our Sad Gay Situation," *Insight*, December 5, 1992, 5; Beth Schaefer, "Homosexual Warfare," *View* (Special 1999 issue):18-21 (*View* is a quarterly publication by the Young Adult Ministries of the North American Division of SDA; this special 1999 issue has the theme, "Is There Room for Me in Your Church?").

[21]According to Elvin Benton, "in early January 1977, a handful who had responded to a newspaper ad placed by a gay Adventist met in Palm Desert, California. It was the beginning of Kinship, and by April there were 75 members, a temporary chairman and four committees: membership, educational, social, and spiritual. . . . The organization was incorporated in March 1981 as Seventh-day Adventist Kinship International, Incorporated. Its mailing list in 10 countries now approaches 500 and includes a broad spectrum of occupations. The ratio of professional people is disproportionately high. A significant number are denominational employees, most of whom, understandably, use pseudonyms in their relationship to Kinship. Almost all are or have been Seventh-day Adventist church members. Several are friends of Adventists and would become church members except for what they perceive to be the church's negative attitude toward their homosexuality" (Elvin Benton, "Adventists Face Homosexuality," *Spectrum* 12/3 [April 1982]: 33). Because the pro-gay stance of Kinship is at variance with the position of the Seventh-day Adventist Church, the SDA church has dissociated itself from Kinship. For a discussion of the

relationship between Kinship and the SDA Church, see Michael Pearson, *Millennial Dreams and Moral Dilemmas: Seventh-day Adventism and Contemporary Ethics* (Cambridge; New York: Cambridge University Press, 1990), 256-265.

[22]Lin Ennis, "Seeker of Truth, Finder of Reality," in *In Our Own Words,*227-239, 232.

[23]The entire issue of the November 4, 1992, *Student Movement* was devoted to homosexuality. The letter from the homosexual couple is found on page 15 of that issue.

[24]Yoonah Kim, "The Love that Dares Not Speak Its Name," *Student Movement,* November 4, 1992, 9

[25]The idea of having a special camp meeting (or *kamp* meeting) for homosexual Adventists was born at an early 1980 Kinship board meeting. According to Benton, the August 1980 camp meeting "was a major event in the long story of Adventist homosexuals" (Benton, "Adventists Face Homosexuality," 32, 33).

[26]The six scholars and pastors consisted of three biblical and theological scholars (James J. C. Cox, Lawrence Geraty and Fritz Guy), two representing pastoral concerns (James Londis and Josephine Benton) and one, an outspoken opponent of Kinship, who had run a recovery ministry for homosexuals for many years, disagreed with the majority conclusion (Colin Cook). For a summary of the meeting, see Elvin Benton, "Adventists Face Homosexuality," *Spectrum* 12/3 (April 1982):32-38.

[27]Elvin Benton, "Adventists Face Homosexuality," *Spectrum* 12/3 (1982):35. At the time of the 1980 Kinship camp meeting, James J. C. Cox was professor of New Testament at the Andrews University Theological Seminary; he has since served as president of Avondale College in Australia. Old Testament scholar Lawrence T. Geraty was professor of archeology and history of antiquity at the Seminary at Andrews University; he has since served as president of Atlantic Union College and currently serves as president of La Sierra University. Fritz Guy was professor of systematic theology at the Seminary; he currently teaches theology and philosophy at La Sierra University, Riverside, California.

[28]See my *Receiving the Word*, chapters 4 and 5 (part 1), 75-113.

[29]*Seventh-day Adventists Believe . . . A Biblical Exposition of 27 Fundamental Doctrines* (Washington, DC: Ministerial Association of the General Conference of Seventh-day Adventists, 1988), 303. Produced by some 194 SDA thought leaders around the world, this "carefully researched" volume is to be received "as representative of . . . [what] Seventh-day Adventists around the globe cherish and proclaim," and as furnishing "reliable information on the beliefs of our [SDA] church" (ibid., vii, iv, v).

[30]The articulation of the official church position on homosexuality was taken up by the Biblical Research Institute of the General Conference. See Ronald Springett, *Homosexuality in History and the Scriptures* (Washington, DC: Biblical Research Institute, 1988).

[31]See, for example, Kate McLaughlin (pseudonym), "A Homosexual in My Congregation?" *Ministry,* November 1996, 10-11, 29; idem, "Are Homosexuals God's Children?" *Adventist Review,* April 3, 1997, 26-29; *Insight,* December 5, 1992, 1-16; Phillip Whidden, "Gays, Gabriel, and Dynamo Truth," in the *Collegiate Quarterly* (January-March 2000), 97; Jim Miller (as told to Celeste Ryan), "I'm Homosexual, I'm Adventist, and I have AIDS: The Jim Miller Story," *Adventist View,* Winter 1993, 9, 15; Beth Schaefer, "Homosexual Warfare," *View,* Special 1999 issue, 18-21; Tessa Willow (pseudonym), "Still Our Son," *Women of Spirit,* May-June 2000; Katie Tonn-Oliver, "Virginia Cason: More

Than A Daughter," *Women of Spirit,* Winter 1996; Kate McLaughlin, "When Your Child Doesn't Choose Your Lifestyle," *Women of Spirit,* Spring 1995. Occasionally, the published works take the form of well-crafted "interviews" with Adventist homosexuals. See, for example, Bruce Moyer's interview with Ron (pseudonym), "A Cry from the Valley of Death," *Ministry,* November 1996, 23-25, 29; Reni Dupertuis's interview with Donald J. Freeman, "To Every Nation, Tongue and People (Including Sexual Orientation)," *Scanner* [a publication of the Glendale City, California,SDA Church], Winter 1999, 9-11. These eye-opening interviews may reveal as much about the views of the interviewees as that of the interviewers.

[32]Christopher Blake, "Redeeming Our Sad Gay Situation: A Christian Response to the Question of Homosexuality," *Insight,* December 5, 1992, 4-16. Similar views are presented in articles carried in the July-August 1999 issue of *Adventist Today.* The cover title of that issue of *Adventist Today* is "Adventism and Homosexuality Today: What's in the Closet?" The troubling articles include Kate McLaughlin's (pseudonym) "Mom, Dad, I'm Gay," 10-11; Norman Brown's (pseudonym) "Reluctant Homosexual, Forgiving Marriage," 13-15; [Anonymous SDA Pastor's] "Adventist Pastor, Husband, Homosexual," 16; Jim Miller's "The Bible on Homosexuality," 17-19. Though it not an official publication of the church, many of it's writers hold membership in the Seventh-day Adventist church.

[33]*Seventh-day Adventist Church Manual* (1995), 154, 169; emphasis mine. The wording in the current (1995) *Church Manual* is based on the revisions made at the 1990 GC session in Indianapolis (see, 1990 *Church Manual,* 147, 160, 173). It may be argued that both the 1990 and 1995 *Church Manuals* do not explicitly condemn "homosexuality and lesbianism" (which would have implied an adherence to the *non-acceptance* position), but merely condemn "homosexual practices and lesbian practices" (which implies a tacit endorsement of the *qualified-acceptance* position). Christopher Blake makes this argument (see his "Redeeming Our Sad Gay Situation," 11). However, by making the practice of homosexuality a basis for church discipline, the delegates at the 1990 and 1995 GC sessions made it clear that they still adhered to a "non-acceptance" position on homosexuality.

[34]Ronald Lawson, the "liaison" between the SDA Kinship organization and the SDA Church, maintains that the attempted subtle shift in the position of the SDA Church is attributed to the role of an SDA Kinship "kampmeeting graduate" who was on the committee drafting changes in the *Church Manual.* The original drafted document had explicitly condemned "homosexuality and lesbianism." The "kampmeeting graduate," Lawson explains, "feeling that the presence of large numbers of conservative Third World delegates would make it impossible to liberalize the statement once it reached the floor [1985 General Conference Session], he got together with friends, including several other veterans of kampmeetings, to try to modify the draft in advance. As they read the situation, it was impossible at that stage to avert the change totally. Consequently, they focused their efforts on changing language which would have condemned 'homosexuality and lesbianism', a sweeping rejection of their very being, to a somewhat more limited condemnation of 'homosexual and lesbian practices.' They were successful in this. Nevertheless, the new statement, which replaced much vaguer language, for the first time labeled this 'practice' as unacceptable and a basis for discipline." See Ronald Lawson, "The Caring Church?: The Seventh-day Adventist Church and Its Homosexual Members," a paper prepared for the meeting of the Society for the Scientific Study of Religion (Washington, DC, November

1992), 7; the same paper was presented at the meeting of the Andrews Society for Religious Study at San Francisco, November 1992. Some perceptive Adventists have argued that the attempt made at the 1995 GC session to modify the relevant sections on homosexuality was yet another attempt by advocates of pro-gay theology to chip away the church's non-acceptance position.

[35]In the Seventh-day Adventist Church the two influential books endorsing women's ordination are: Patricia A. Habada and Rebecca Frost Brillhart, eds., *The Welcome Table: Setting A Place for Ordained Women* (Langley Park, MD: TEAMPress, 1995); and Nancy Vyhmeister, ed., *Women in Ministry: Biblical and Historical Perspectives* (Berrien Springs, MI: Andrews University Press, 1998). While the former often employs the arguments of liberal feminism, the latter adopts the egalitarian arguments of Evangelical feminism. Whereas my response to the former volume is found in *Receiving the Word*, 119-129, my detailed critique of the latter will appear in the next section of *Must We Be Silent?*

[36]Jeane Haerich, "Genesis Revisited," in *The Welcome Table*, 101, 100. The obliteration of gender differentiation in Genesis 2 is only a few steps away from positing homosexuality or bisexuality in the first created pair. And since human beings were created in God's image, if Adam was "an androgynous being" does it not mean that God also is androgynous? One wonders what is really behind the gender-inclusive reconstructions of the Bible: "*Son* of God" becomes "*Child* of God"; "*Son* of Man" becomes "*Human* one"; "our heavenly *Father*" becomes "our heavenly *Parent*". Is this also the reason an Adventist author promotes the Holy Spirit as the female member of the Godhead and repeatedly refers to the Creator as "He/She"? See Steve Daily, *Adventism for a New Generation* (Portland/Clackamas, Ore.: Better Living Publishers, 1993), 88, 105, 113.

[37]This basic argument underlies *Women in Ministry*, the pro-ordination book by some faculty of Andrews University. The clearest articulation of this view in the book is Richard M. Davidson's article "Headship, Submission, and Equality in Scripture," 259-295. Denying that God made man the head of the home at creation, the article argues that God's original plan for the home was "total equality in marriage" (267), or "total egalitarianism in the marriage relationship" (269), or "headship among equals" (270), expressions understood to mean the absence of role differentiation before the Fall (264, 267, 269). For him the biblical teaching of male headship and female submission implies "functional superiority/inferiority" (260). Though he believes that "headship" was instituted *after the Fall*, it is his view that God's original plan of "total egalitarianism in the marriage relationship" is still the same in the post-fall situation "as it was for Adam and Eve in the beginning" (269). In other words, today, as at the beginning, there should be no "ontological or functional" role distinctions. Rather, Christians should aspire for the "ideal" of "full equality" in their homes (284). Cf. Peter M. Van Bemmelen, "Equality, Headship, and Submission in the Writings of Ellen G. White," in *Women in Ministry*, 297-311.

[38]For a response to the "full equality" argument, see my unpublished article "Ideology or Theology: An Analysis and Evaluation of *Women in Ministry*" (1999).

[39]Howard 'duke' Holtz, "Re: Women's Ordination," October 29, 2000. *http://www.sdanet.org/archive/2000/Oct32000/0313.html.* As I will show in the next section of this book, indeed, the so-called biblical arguments for women's ordination are as flimsy as those being used to support homosexuality.

[40]I raised that point on the GC session floor in Toronto, but I'm not sure how many people fully understood the theological implications of my point. To them, homosexuality

and women's ordination issues where unrelated to the divorce and remarriage discussion on the floor. In fact one associate editor of the *Adventist Review* expressed "surprise" at my comment. He apparently believed the comment by one delegate that those of us questioning the theological fuzziness of the divorce and remarriage proposal were appealing to those with "a scare mentality." See Roy Adams, "Fireworks in the Dome," *Adventist Review*, July 5, 2000, 2-3.

# 4

# WHAT MUST THE CHURCH DO?

The Christian church is, today, being called upon to decide what homosexuals should do when they become Christians. Should homosexuals change their orientation, control their orientation, or celebrate their orientation?

The answer to this question has given birth to three contending positions in Christian churches: (a) the *non-acceptance* view, which maintains that homosexuality is not compatible with biblical Christianity (b) the *qualified-acceptance* view, which argues that homosexuality can be compatible with Christianity, and (c) the *full-acceptance* view, which asserts that homosexuality is fully compatible with the Christian faith.

Seventh-day Adventists historically have adopted the *non-acceptance* view. But as pro-homosexual groups (like Kinship) continue their campaign for the *full-acceptance* view some segments within contemporary Adventism are moving towards the *qualified-acceptance* view. Since all three views are represented in contemporary Seventh-day Adventism, and since each is based on a set of theological and ethical assumptions, I will briefly summarize the respective views. In the next two chapters, I will raise some critical questions for those seeking to move the church towards qualified-acceptance and full-acceptance of homosexuality.

### Non-Acceptance View

Historically embraced by the Christian church, this position maintains that homosexuality is incompatible with biblical Christianity.[1] Despite the efforts by some thought leaders within our ranks, the non-acceptance view remains the official position of the Seventh-day Adventist church. The following are some of its basic tenets:

**(a) Nature of Homosexuality:** This view holds that homosexuality is a post-fall distortion of human sexuality. Whether constitutional (i.e., believed to be born gay) or situational (i.e., forced by single sex environments, e.g., prisons, military camps, monasteries), homosexuality is no different from other depraved sexual deviations (such as bisexuality, bestiality, adultery, fornication etc.). The popular statement, "If God had intended homosexuality to be a legitimate expression of human sexuality, He would have created Adam and Steve, not Adam and Eve," aptly summarizes the non-acceptance position.

**(b) Morality of Homosexuality:** According to the non-acceptance position, homosexuality is both sinful (like pride, adultery, and murder) and evil (like sickness and death). Like all other morally corrupt tendencies, homosexual orientation or disposition does not excuse the sin of homosexuality. All people are tempted to act upon their besetting sexual desires, cravings or tendencies (homosexual and heterosexual). The temptation is not sin, but yielding to it is morally wrong.

**(c) Way Out of Homosexuality:** Believing that there is no sin that is outside the scope of the sanctifying work of the Holy Spirit, the non-acceptance position maintains that the Creator of human sexuality can fix every sexual problem. Homosexuality and homosexual lifestyle can, therefore, be overcome by God's transforming power (in the conversion/new birth experience) and by God's enabling or sustaining grace (in the gradual work of sanctification). God is able to deliver a homosexual from his/her sin and keep such a person from falling. Therefore, the non-acceptance view denies the claim that homosexuality is incurable.

**(d) Response to Homosexuality:** The church should accord all homosexuals their full rights as human beings created in the image of God, show compassion, kindness, and Christian love to all those struggling with sexual sins, and point them to Jesus Christ as the Answer to all their needs. Homosexuals should be urged to repent and accept God's forgiveness.

Homosexuals who acknowledge the sinfulness of homosexuality, who accept Christ's offer of forgiveness, who cut themselves loose from homosexual relationships, and who, by faith, commit themselves to a life of sexual purity should be accepted into church fellowship. But those who do not acknowledge homosexuality as sin and/or those who are engaged in homosexual relationships or practices should not be accepted into church membership.[2]

The *non-acceptance* view, therefore, *rejects* the view that "once a homosexual, always a homosexual."

### Qualified-Acceptance View

Currently gaining currency in certain quarters of the Adventist church, this accommodating view argues that homosexuality *can be* compatible with Christianity.[3] The following are some of its essential teachings:

**(a) Nature of Homosexuality:** Unlike the non-acceptance position which holds that homosexuality is post-fall distortion, the qualified-acceptance maintains that homosexuality is a post-fall *aberration* of human sexuality. Homosexual condition/orientation (constitutional homosexuality or inversion), according to this view, is a non ideal condition of human sexuality (just as poor eye-sight, asthma or allergies). "God didn't create homosexuality, as He didn't create loneliness or disabilities."[4] Homosexuality is not God's ideal plan for people, and therefore must be removed *wherever possible.*

**(b) Morality of Homosexuality:** The qualified-acceptance position argues that the homosexual condition is not sin but a condition of sinfulness. What advocates mean is that homosexual condition or orientation is one evidence of the brokenness and fallenness of our present world. The condition may be classified with disease (such as alcoholism, or allergies), with handicap (such as congenital blindness), and eccentricity (such as left-handedness). It may even be evil (like sickness or death), but not necessarily sinful (like pride, blasphemy, or murder).

Because homosexuals presumably did not choose to be born gay, "we shouldn't hold a person responsible for her or his sexual *orientation* any more than we hold a person responsible for skin color (nature)."[5] Being a homosexual is not sin,[6] but lustful and inappropriate homosexual activity is sin and therefore, must be avoided.[7]

**(c) Way Out of Homosexuality:** In very rare situations, God may deliver some homosexuals from their condition/orientation. Generally, however, since genuine homosexuals did not choose their orientation, and since in most cases there is no possibility of change in orientation, homosexuals must aim at controlling (i.e. putting in subjection) their homosexual drives. One Adventist scholar writes:

> We must teach them to live with their condition. In a sense it is like being born left-handed. . . . However, it does not give license to practice homosexual acts, which violate Christian moral standards. In this situation we must consider the homosexual on the same basis as the heterosexual. . . . The homosexual may not be able to do anything about his attraction for his own sex, but by God's grace he can control his impulses. He may not have had any real choice regarding his condition, but he has choice about his actions.[8]

Cure or deliverance may not always be possible for those with homosexual orientations. But through prayer, counseling, human therapy, and other methods of behavior modification (skills of self-discipline or self-control), homosexuals can cope with their sexual predicament.

**(d) Response to Homosexuality:** While accepting their condition as a "thorn in the flesh," and while controlling their desires, homosexuals should accept God's unconditional love and acceptance. On the other hand, the church should treat people with homosexual orientation as one would treat heterosexuals—i. e., as real human beings, of equal value in God's sight and having the same rights as all others. It should show understanding, compassion, and love to them "neither condemning them for an orientation over which they have no control, nor encouraging them to accept something less than God's best for their lives,"[9] as homosexuals are led to accept Jesus as their Savior.

Homosexuals who renounce homosexual practices and make a commitment to remain celibates must be accepted as members in good and regular standing in Church. They can hold church offices and can be ordained as ministers. "If an alcoholic who never drinks alcohol can hold any church office, a homosexual who never practices homosexuality can hold any church office."[10]

The *qualified acceptance* view, therefore, assumes that "once a homosexual (almost) always a homosexual."

**Full-Acceptance View**

Historically rejected by the church, this revisionist view of morality asserts that homosexuality is *fully compatible* with Christianity.[11] In the Adventist church, this view is actively promoted by Kinship, an organization that claims to be "a support group for gay and lesbian Seventh-day Adventists." The following are some of its primary precepts:

**(a) Nature of Homosexuality:** The full-acceptance position sees homosexuality as part of the *pre-fall natural order.* In its view, genuine (constitutional) homosexuality is not a distortion of human sexuality (as held by the non-acceptance view), nor an aberration (as argued by the qualified-acceptance position.) Instead, homosexuality is an immutable sexual orientation given or created by God as a gift to some people—just as is heterosexuality. It is an eccentricity (a characteristic of a minority) or a mark of one's individual identity (just like possessing a particular color of the skin, eye, or hair).

**(b) Morality of Homosexuality:** Homosexuality is morally neutral; it is neither evil nor sinful. An article in the *Newsletter* of SDA Kinship states this position well:

> Homosexuality and heterosexuality are two aspects of sexuality, neither being the counterfeit of the other, both being right or wrong depending upon the context of their expression. . . . Both the homosexual and the heterosexual are capable of lusting or loving, worshiping the creature or the Creator, and of seeking salvation by works or accepting it as a gift of God.[12]

Homosexuality may be eccentric, but it definitely is not sinful (like murder, or pride) or evil (like congenital blindness or the sickness of alcoholism).[13] The *abuse* of homosexuality (e. g., promiscuity, rape, or prostitution) is wrong, but not its legitimate expression (as in loving, consensual, monogamous, homosexual relationships).

**(c) Way Out of Homosexuality**: According to the full-acceptance view, to insist that homosexuals should change their orientation is equivalent to asking an Ethiopian to change his skin, or asking a person five feet tall to become six feet. Homosexuals do not have to be transformed into heterosexuals, nor should they just control themselves until they become heterosexualized. Because of the long years during which they have been victimized as "sexual minorities," homosexuals must claim the assurance of God's acceptance and leading in their homosexual lifestyle.

**(d) Response to Homosexuality:** Homosexuals should not be condemned, despised, or singled out as the embodiment of sexual perversion. They, like all others, deserve love, dignity, and respect. Effort must be expended to present the living Christ to the homosexual who is not yet a Christian (i. e. the person who was born a gay but has not yet been born again). But whether converted or unconverted, all homosexuals should celebrate God's "gift" (homosexual orientation), and *practice* homosexuality within a permanent relationship of love and fidelity or within the biblical guidelines for sexual morality.

Homosexuals who accept Jesus Christ as their Lord and Savior must be considered as full and regular members of the church, and if they choose, they must be encouraged to date other homosexuals—as long as the relationship is kept pure. In other words, homosexuals should be affirmed in their same sex relationships, be allowed to "marry" or to form "closed-couple homosexual unions,"[14] and whenever necessary, be permitted to adopt children. The rules of marriage should apply in homosexual marriages just as in heterosexual marriage. Converted homosexuals who have a calling or the requisite spiritual gifts should be ordained as pastors.

The full-acceptance view, therefore, maintains that "once a homosexual, always a homosexual."

**Summary.** All three views—non-acceptance, qualified acceptance, and full-acceptance positions—are competing for converts within the Seventh-day Adventist church. The hot potato issue is whether to regard homosexuality as: (a) a morally-sinful practice to be renounced, (b) a morally-neutral condition to be controlled, or (c) a morally acceptable gift to be celebrated.

Each of the three views raises crucial theological, ethical, and hermeneutical issues. Of the three views, only the non-acceptance and full-acceptance positions are consistent. Of these two, only the non-acceptance view is biblical. The qualified acceptance view is neither consistent nor biblical. In other words, it is my contention that whereas the non-acceptance position is consistent *and* biblical, and while the full-acceptance view is consistent but not biblical, the qualified-acceptance position is neither consistent nor biblical.

Yet, it appears that the qualified-acceptance view is that which is being widely promoted in church publications. Before the Adventist church renounces its traditional non-acceptance position in favor of the qualified acceptance position, or even the full-acceptance view, the church should demand biblically consistent answers from advocates of these versions of pro-gay theology.

The next two chapters will concern itself with these issues, evaluating some of the common arguments often put forth in defense of these views of homosexuality. I wish to make it clear, however, that on this hot potato item, just as on any other controversial subject, "it is better to debate a question without settling it than to settle a question without debating it."[15]

---

**Endnotes**

[1]Representatives include Westmont College New Testament scholar Thomas E. Schmidt, *Straight and Narrow? Compassion and Clarity in the Homosexual Debate* (Downers Grove, IL: InterVarsity, 1995), Louisville Seminary New Testament professor Marion Soards, *Scripture and Homosexuality: Biblical Authority and the Church* (Westminster, PA: John Knox, 1995), Gordon-Conwell Seminary church historian Richard Lovelace, *The Church and Homosexuality* (Old Tappan, NJ: Flemming H. Revell, 1978), and Don Williams (Biblical scholar at Claremont Men's College), *The Bond That Breaks: Will Homosexuality Split the Church* (Los Angeles, CA: BIM Publications, 1978). In their theological discussions, Schmidt, Soards, Lovelace and Williams pay greater attention to church history and Biblical theology than to contemporary scientific findings on homosexuality.

[2]Ronald M. Springett concludes his study on homosexuality: "The church must accept the individual of homosexual orientation who needs help and support and [who] struggles against same-sex tendencies. But those who insist on and promote the active homosexual lifestyle as normal, natural, or even superior to heterosexual relations by that very act disregard and undermine the sole authority upon which the church's very existence and mission is based, namely, the Scriptures" (Ronald M. Springett, *Homosexuality in History and the Scriptures* [Washington, D.C.: Biblical Research Institute, 1988], 164).

[3]Helmut Thielicke, *The Ethics of Sex*, trans. John Doberstein (New York: Harper &

Row, 1964), and Lewis Smedes, *Sex for Christians* (Grand Rapids, MI: Eerdmans, 1976) adopt this view. While the latter is a more popular version than the former, they both seek to deal pastorally with the tragedy of "an ethically upright, mature homosexual who is struggling with his condition" (Thielicke, 271). They seem to accept, as equal partners, both the Bible and the testimonies of homosexuals and research by social scientists in their theological discussion of the issue.

[4]Blake, "Redeeming Our Sad Gay Situation," *Insight*, December 5, 1992, 11.

[5]Christopher Blake, "Redeeming Our Sad Gay Situation: A Christian Response to the Question of Homosexuality," *Insight* (December 5, 1992):7.

[6]"I don't deny the *evil* of the thing, for evil it certainly is, but I do deny the *sinfulness* of it. The homosexual condition is to be classified with disease, weakness, death, as an evil; not with gluttony, blasphemy, murder, as a sin. Both sin and evil are the work of Satan, were brought into the world at the Fall, and will one day be destroyed by Christ, but they are not identical. Sin, which we must avoid and need never commit, is represented in our situation by homosexual lust and the activity to which it leads. Evil is different. We pray to be delivered from it, but may nevertheless find ourselves left in it, and then have to aim at using and transforming it. In our situation that means a homosexual nature. I'm sure that in this sense it is morally neutral . . ." (Alex Davidson, *The Returns of Love: Letters of a Christian Homosexual* [London: Intervarsity Press, 1970], 80).

[7]Christopher Blake, "Redeeming Our Sad Gay Situation," 11, equates homosexual *orientation* with temptation, and states: "We cannot condone homosexual activity. Homosexual sexual activity is sinful—it is apart from God's will. Yet a difference exists between the person who fights against homosexual tendencies and the one who experiments with or revels in them. It's a sin to cave in to temptation. It's not a sin to be tempted."

[8]Sakae Kubo, *Theology and Ethics of Sex* (Washington, DC: Review and Herald, 1980), 83.

[9]Kate McLaughlin, "Are Homosexuals God's Children?" *Adventist Review*, April 3, 1997, 29.

[10]Christopher Blake, "Redeeming Our Sad Gay Situation," *Insight* (December 5, 1992):16. Blake, who wrote this long before reading my response in the next chapter, insists that the difference between our positions is primarily semantic and that his use of terms is in line with the *Church Manual*. I would say that an alcoholic who never drinks alcohol is no longer an alcoholic, and a person who does not practice homosexuality is no longer a homosexual. That individual may have been born gay, but once converted (i.e., once *reborn* as a Christian), he cannot claim to be a homosexual. He may be tempted to go back to his former ways of homosexuality (it is not a sin to be tempted). But unless he acts upon the temptation, it is incorrect to refer to the former homosexual by the label homosexual.

[11]Representing this position are Norman Pittenger, *Time for Consent: A Christian's Approach to Homosexuality* (London: SCM Press, 1970); Letha Scanzoni and Virginia Ramey Mollenkott, *Is the Homosexual My Neighbor?—Another Christian View* (New York: Harper & Row, 1978), a work that draws heavily on findings of social scientists. The same position is advocated by SDA Kinship International, Inc., "a support group for gay and lesbian Seventh-day Adventists"—and a group which maintains that "God can bless a committed homosexual relationship."

[12]See J. Stuart, "Counterfeits," *SDA Kinship Newsletter* (May 1980):4 (cited by Pearson, *Millennial Dreams and Moral Dilemmas*, 257).

[13]In 1973, *Trends*, a publication of the United Presbyterian Church, devoted a full issue to the topic: "Homosexuality: Neither Sin or Sickness" (see *Trends* 5 [July-August 1973]).

[14]For example, Scanzoni and Mollenkot, *Is the Homosexual My Neighbor?*, 111, 71, 72, argue for "the possibility of a permanent, committed relationship of love between homosexuals analogous to heterosexual marriage." Adventist ethicist David R. Larson, "Sexuality and Christian Ethics," *Spectrum* 15 (May 1984):16, also writes: "Christians therefore have every reason to encourage homosexuals who are honestly convinced that they should neither attempt to function heterosexually nor remain celibate to form Closed-Coupled homosexual unions."

[15]The above statement is attributed to Joseph Joubert (1754-1824); see David L. Bender, "Why Consider Opposing Viewpoints?" in Bruno Leone, ed., *Racism: Opposing Viewpoints*, rev. ed. (St. Paul, MN: Greenhaven Press, 1986), 9.

# 5

# COMMON MYTHS ABOUT HOMOSEXUALITY

In order to silence or challenge the Bible's negative valuation of homosexuality, advocates of pro-gay theology often put forward several arguments. Although the arguments often invoked in defense of the qualified- and full-acceptance views on homosexuality tend to be scientific, philosophical, or logical, they also have theological or ethical implications. Their basic thrust is to show that: people are born homosexual—i.e., conclusive evidence exists to prove that homosexuality is genetic or inborn; and since homosexuals are born gay, their sexual orientation is a natural or normal trait of their identity (like the color of the skin or hair), and the orientation is allowed or given by God; a person's homosexual orientation is morally neutral and unchangeable.

In this chapter, I will state and respond to the myths often advanced in support of homosexuality. The next chapter will address specific arguments that are often presented to cast doubt on the Bible's teaching.

**1. "To learn the truth about homosexuality, talk to real homosexuals."**

For many advocates of gay theology, it is not sufficient to trust the Bible writers as the dependable source of truth on this matter. They argue that in order to learn the truth about homosexuality, we must update our knowledge by actually listening to homosexuals themselves. This seems to be the point in some recent Adventist publications.

For example, one Adventist mother wrote that after she had spent "years of reading, observing, and eventually talking to people," her homosexual son finally confirmed to her that indeed, "homosexuality is a condition, not a behavior. Whatever may cause a homosexual orientation, it is not something a person chooses." Her son "told us that from his earliest memories he knew he was 'different.'" She also reported learning that God may change a persons's sexual orientation only "on rare occasions," and that one can be a homosexual and be "deeply spiritual."[1]

A non-Adventist scholar has explained why we supposedly need to go to homosexuals themselves to learn the truth about homosexuality. In his article entitled, "A Newly Revealed Christian Experience," a self-avowed gay Christian on the Presbyterian task force studying homosexuality, explains that gay Christians are "the best source" for the Church to understand homosexuality.[2] Similarly, a United Church of Christ minister states this new approach to knowing (epistemology):

> Rather than looking to the psychologists and the psychiatrists and the sociologists, and even to the theologians, to find out about gay people, there is a need to listen to gay people within our churches and within the society, to begin to understand what we perceive to be the problems, and then together to work on those problems.[3]

A Princeton Theological Seminary professor of Old Testament Language and Literature, an ordained elder in the Presbyterian Church (USA), best articulated why we supposedly need to go to homosexuals themselves to learn the truth about homosexuality. He wrote:

> I used to believe that homosexual acts are always wrong. Listening to gay and lesbian students and friends, however, I have had to rethink my position and reread the scriptures. . . . I have no choice but to take the testimonies of gays and lesbians seriously. I do so with some comfort, however, for the scriptures themselves give me the warrant to trust that human beings can know truths apart from divine revelation.[4]

**Response to Argument #1.** We must offer a sympathetic ear to the pains and genuine struggles of homosexuals. But Bible-believing Adventists need to ask whether the testimonies and claims of homosexuals are an adequate basis to learn the truth about homosexuality. Are homosexuals, by virtue of their experience, more qualified than the Bible writers to speak on homosexuality? The inspired writers of the Bible served as dependable spokespersons for the Creator of human sexuality. Is the attempt to justify homosexuality on the grounds of personal experience or empirical studies, rather than biblical revelation, a legitimate starting point for any investigation regarding sexual morality? Are the testimonies and claims of homosexuals necessarily true?

We are dealing with the fundamental question of how to know truth, a study philosophers call *epistemology*. I will restate my response: Does one really have to be a homosexual in order to fully understand the truth about homosexuality? Must we experience a particular kind of sinful tendency in order to understand that sinful reality? Assuming even that homosexual orientation is part of a person's constitutional make up (just as a person's color or gender is), can true knowledge about that condition be accurately obtained by only persons with that kind of sexual identity? If so, does this mean, for example, that one has to be black, African, and a woman in order to fully understand and accurately address the pains of people in that category? By analogy, could Jesus, a single Jewish male, have understood the experience of, say, Maria, a single parent Hispanic woman?

Could it be that in a desire to appear more "informed" and perhaps more "compassionate," some Christians are giving the impression that they are ethically and religiously more knowledgeable and "sensitive" than the inspired Bible writers who condemned the practice of homosexuality? How can pro-homosexual advocates be wiser than the One who has given His written Word and His moral laws as the basis of true human joy and self-fulfillment? How can they be more compassionate than the One who has given His life for all humanity? Is it, perhaps, that they do not view the Bible and its God as did the Bible writers—the pioneers of biblical Christianity?

### 2. "People Are Born Homosexual."

When advocates of pro-gay theology assert that people are born gay, they actually go beyond the generally accepted view that genetics and environmental factors *influence* a person's behavior. They suggest that homosexuality is largely *caused by* a person's genes.[5]

This belief, which is itself based on the deterministic philosophy of behaviorism, is designed to suggest that what is inborn is (a) natural or normal,

(b) unchangeable, (c) allowed or created by God—as with a congenital defect or one's eye color, and that it is (d) morally legitimate.

The logic and implications of this view are as follows: If a person is homosexual because of inbred homosexual condition, there is no hope or possibility for change. And because the homosexual cannot change, all aspects of society must change, including education, religion, and law. Not only must homosexuality be accepted as socially legal for homosexuals, it must also be promoted as a normal lifestyle option and, if necessary, the church must be pressured to abandon its alleged immoral discrimination against homosexuals seeking church membership.

**Response to Argument #2.** Even if one could prove that homosexuality is of genetic or hormonal origin, would this make homosexuality morally legitimate? I am aware that scientists, such as the authors of *My Genes Made Me Do It!*, have compellingly challenged the claim that homosexuality is biologically fated.[6] But even if true, does being born alcoholic, pedophiliac, or gay make alcoholism, pedophilia, or homosexuality normal? Moreover, does the fact that something is normal make it morally right?

Is behaviorism or biological determinism compatible with biblical anthropology, which teaches that human beings are created in the image of God and endowed with freedom of choice? Can we correlate this naturalistic philosophy with the biblical doctrine that we are accountable to God for our conduct (doctrine of judgment)? Does not this "I did not choose, I cannot change" philosophy raise serious questions about Christ's power to help us "overcome all hereditary and cultivated tendencies to sin"?[7]

Does not this behavioristic philosophy lead to a "once a sinner, always a sinner" doctrine? In other words, would it be biblically correct to maintain that even after conversion, an alcoholic/drug addict or a habitual/compulsive liar or sexual pervert will always remain an alcoholic/drug addict or habitual/compulsive liar or a sexual pervert? Is not this born a gay philosophy in conflict with the born again promise of the living Christ?

To clarify the issue further, we will look at other aspects of this born a gay theory. For example: (1) Do studies show that homosexuality is inborn? (2) Is homosexual orientation natural or normal? (3) Is homosexual orientation God given? (4) Is homosexual orientation morally neutral? (5) Is homosexual orientation unchangeable? (6) Does God want homosexuals to give up who they are? (7) Is it true that "once a homosexual, (almost) always a homosexual"?

### 3. "Studies Show that Homosexuality is Inborn"

Like every other sinful practice, one's genes, environment, and many other factors may greatly influence a person's predisposition to a particular sin. But pro-gay advocates go further, claiming that scientific studies offer conclusive proof that people are born gay.

**Response to Argument #3.** Although some future studies may one day bear this out, the research findings often cited as evidence of the born a gay condition are, at best, inconclusive; they are questionable at worst.[8] Two of these deserve mention because of the prominence often given them in Adventist publications.

***(a) Neurobiologist Simon LeVay's 1991 Study on the Brains of 41 Cadavers.*** The cadavers consisted of nineteen allegedly homosexual men, sixteen allegedly heterosexual men, and six allegedly heterosexual women. LeVay reported that a cluster of neurons in a distinct section of the brain (called the interstitial nuclei of the anterior hypothalamus, or the INAH3) were generally smaller in the homosexual men as compared to the heterosexual men. As a result, he hypothesized that the size of these neurons may cause a person to be either heterosexual or homosexual.[9] This study is often cited as proof that people are born gay.

As others have shown, LeVay's study is exaggerated, misleading, and fraught with major weaknesses. (1) In order for his theory to be valid, studies would have to show that the difference in size of that section of the brain occurred 100% of the time. But LeVay's own study showed 17% of his total study group contradicted his theory. Three of the nineteen allegedly homosexual men actually had larger neurons than their heterosexual counterparts, and three of the heterosexual men had smaller neurons than did the homosexual men. (2) There is no proof that the section of the brain he measured actually has anything to do with sexual preference. (3) The study did not show whether the size of the neurons caused the sexual preference or whether the sexual preference caused the size. (4) The scientific community has not by any means unanimously accepted LeVay's finding. (5) LeVay's own objectivity in the research is in question, since he admitted in a September 9, 1991, *Newsweek* magazine that after the death of his homosexual lover, he was determined to find a genetic cause for homosexuality, or he would abandon science altogether.

***(b) J. Michael Bailey and Richard Pillard's 1991 Study of Twins.*** Bailey and Pillard investigated how widespread homosexuality is among identical twins (whose genetic makeup are the same) and fraternal twins (whose genetic ties are less close). Among other things, they discovered that 52% of the identical twins studied were both homosexual. Bailey and Pillard hypothesized that the higher incidence of homosexuality among the identical twins implies that homosexuality is genetic in origin.

Bailey and Pillard's theory is also misleading and exaggerated. For their theory to be a fact, the following should hold: (1) There should never be a case when one identical twin is heterosexual and the other homosexual, since both identical twins share 100% of the same genes. If sexual orientation is genetic, then both identical twins will in 100% of cases always be either homosexual or heterosexual. Bailey and Pillard's findings of only 52% challenges their own hypothesis. On the contrary, their research confirms that non-genetic factors play a significant role in shaping sexual preference. (2) The twins should be raised in different homes to eliminate the possible effect of environmental factors in their sexual preferences. But all twins studied by Bailey and Pillard were raised in the same homes. (3) A later study on twins by other scholars yielded different results. (4) Bailey and Pillard, like LeVay, may not have approached their study objectively, given their personal feelings about homosexuality. Because Bailey is a gay rights advocate and Pillard is openly homosexual, their objectivity in the research may be questioned. (5) There are also questions about whether the sample was representative, since Bailey and Pillard requested subjects by solicitation through homosexual organizations and publications.

Other studies have been done. However, to date, we know of no study that supports the claim by pro-gay advocates that conclusive evidence exists showing people are born gay or that homosexuality is inborn or of genetic origin. We are not suggesting that genetics does not influence one's homosexual predisposition. Our contention is simply that the studies usually cited for the claim that people are born gay are not as conclusive as proponents would have us believe. It seems that the studies are put forth to intimate that homosexuality is not a sin to be repented of but a mark of one's identity to be celebrated.

**4. "Homosexuality is not a sin, but a condition of sinfulness."**

This variation of the born gay argument is perhaps the most popular in Christian circles. Unlike the previous argument which sees homosexuality as normal or natural, proponents of the current argument suggest that homosexuality is an abnormal or unnatural condition, or even an illness brought about by a number of factors beyond the control of the individual. The causes include biological/genetic defect, gender confusion (a female mind in a male body and vice versa), or prenatal hormonal irregularities (e.g., endocrine-mimicking chemicals or chemical toxicity in the brains of homosexuals during the formative period of their embryos or fetuses). Based on these alleged causes, some pro-gay advocates maintain that homosexuals have no choice in the matter of their sexual predisposition towards persons of the same gender.

The homosexual condition or orientation, it is argued, is an evidence of the brokenness and fallenness of our present world. The condition may be classified with disease (such as alcoholism, or allergies), with handicap (such as congenital blindness), and eccentricity (such as left-handedness). It may even be evil (like sickness or death), but not necessarily sinful (like pride, blasphemy, or murder). Because homosexuals did not choose to be born gay, "we shouldn't hold a person responsible for her or his sexual *orientation* any more than we hold a person responsible for skin color (nature)."[10] Being a homosexual is not sin,[11] but lustful and inappropriate homosexual activity is sin and therefore, must be avoided.[12] Since it is believed that homosexuals did not chose to be gay, but were born that way, God deserves the credit (or blame) for who or what they are. And since homosexuality is presumably not a sin, but a sinful condition, homosexuals need compassion and acceptance from the church.

One ex-homosexual explains why he "accepted" his homosexuality:

> I was not responsible for who and what I was. I was God's creation, and if He had not wanted me to be gay (homosexual), then He wouldn't have made me this way. If being gay was a choice, I would never have made that choice, for with it came the consequences of hurting those I loved, the break up of my home, the loss of my children, alienation from my family and friends and church, the scorn and ridicule of the general public. It was all God's fault. As far as choices were concerned, I had made all the right choices. I had chosen a Christian education for myself. I had chosen to be a student missionary for two years in the Far East. I had chosen to study theology and pre-med preparatory to becoming a medical missionary some day. I had chosen to

> marry a Christian girl, and to have little Christian children. But eventually, no longer able to deny to myself who and what I really was inside, I had 'accepted' being homosexual, and, in extreme frustration, turned my back on family, friends, God, and everything I had worked for, and entered into the gay life 'rightfully' giving God all the credit (or blame).[13]

**Response to Argument #4:** While not denying the possibility that homosexuality *may* be caused by many combinations of variables, including biological/genetic or hormonal irregularities, there are serious problems with the argument that homosexuals are somewhat sick or abnormal, or that homosexuality is not a sin, but a condition of sinfulness.

First, perceptive critics, including advocates of the Gay Right Movement, are moving away from the theories of genetic-defect and hormonal irregularities for fear that other research findings showing some unacceptable conditions (like alcoholism, schizophrenia, cerebral palsy, etc.) as genetically or biologically related will soon make homosexuals look like they are abnormal, sick, or less than human. Such a perception, in their opinion, will be a reversal of the gains they made when the Gay Right Movement successfully lobbied to have the American Psychological Association and the American Psychiatric Association remove homosexuality from the categories of abnormal behavior and mental illness

For example, one scholar exposes the intellectual and psychological inconsistency in this "outmoded version of natural law" which seeks to make a fine distinction between homosexual orientation and behavior. Responding to the view that "while homosexuality as an orientation is contrary to God's created intention, the homosexual person ought not to be adversely judged or rejected by the church," this researcher counters that while some may deem such a position a more tolerant and compassionate view than outright condemnation, "it places gay men and lesbians in at least two impossible binds." He continues:

> One, of course, is the individual's recognition that her or his own sexual orientation is as natural and as fundamental to identity as is the color of the skin. It is both naive and cruel to tell a lesbian or gay man, 'Your sexual orientation is still unnatural and a perversion, but this is no judgment upon you as a person.' The individual knows otherwise. The other bind concerns

> churchly pressure toward celibacy. When the church presumes to be non-judgmental toward orientation but then draws the line against genital expression, it is difficult to understand how the sense of guilt—even in the celibate—will be significantly alleviated.[14]

The point is that many homosexuals don't want to be perceived as abnormal or sick. They see themselves as normal people with full control over their choices. They don't consider themselves driven by some defective genes to do things contrary to their choice. When they describe themselves as born gays, they don't understand their condition to be the result of genetic defect or gender-confusion, or hormonal/chemical accident. Instead, they argue that their homosexuality is an alternative expression of human sexuality, created by God Himself, and therefore not a sin. This is why they prefer to see their homosexual orientation as normal, natural, morally neutral, and a gift from God.

Second, assuming even that homosexuality is of biological/genetic origin, does it make it right. For example, is stealing right just because a person was born a kleptomaniac? Is alcoholism right, just because a person was born alcoholic (i.e. born with a strong genetic predisposition towards alcoholism)? Undoubtedly, the kleptomaniac/alcoholic is sick and needs help. But stealing/drunkenness, regardless of its cause, is never right. Thus, a person who is born gay (either because of genetic defect, hormonal problem, gender confusion, etc.) is at best abnormal or sick. That person may be suffering from a compulsive immoral tendency. But would the cause of that compulsive or uncontrollable homosexual lust or behavior make the tendency or behavior morally right?

> Adulterers, or pedophiles, or pornographers, will gain little sympathy from the claim that their genes made them do it. Why should the homosexual be considered in a different genetic light? No, however fascinating or apparently comforting it may be to explore how the patterns of genetic structure and social surroundings combine to create for each of us a moral context, we must nevertheless also recognize our responsibility to act obediently within that context. As moral agents we say yes or no to each potential sexual encounter.[15]

Third, even if a biological/genetic link is found, would that prove that God created homosexuality? Jesus dismissed the suggestion that God is responsible for genetic deficiencies with which people are born. When asked why a man was born blind, Christ did not say, "Because God made him this way." "Rather, He said that God was to be glorified through healing the man of the effects of his faulty genes (John 9:1-7). So it is with homosexuals who *might* have a genetic predisposition. (Notice I said 'might.' The verdict is still out.) God didn't make them this way. It [homosexuality] is the result of the degeneration of humankind by thousands of years of sin. God doesn't create any of the aberrations sin causes. However he can be glorified in genetically challenged people. Jesus will provide victory over what genetics might influence."[16]

**5. "Homosexual Orientation Is Natural or Normal"**

Based on the assumption that homosexuality is inborn, i.e. of genetic origin, advocates argue that homosexuality should be accepted as a natural or normal human condition.

**Response to Argument #5.** This argument is also flawed. Leaving aside the important issues of the manner in which the scientific research is conducted and the kind of interpretation given to the research findings,[17] even proving that homosexual orientation is inborn (i.e., of genetic origin) will not make homosexuality normal or desirable. Many defects or handicaps today are inborn, but hardly anyone would call them normal for that reason alone. Why should homosexuality be considered natural or normal, just because it may be inborn?

When we say that something is natural, we refer to what happens repeatedly in the world of nature—in which case we do not assign moral judgment to it. For example, spiders kill and eat other spiders, including their mates. "But as a moral category natural refers to something that is in accord with God's intention. Actions are good or bad: for example, people sometimes kill and eat other people. But the fact that cannibalism happens in the world—perhaps in satisfaction of deeply held religious beliefs or peculiar culinary tastes—does not make it *natural* in the sense that it conforms to God's will. In summary: that which is *natural* to human experience or human desire is not necessarily *natural* in God's moral design."[18]

### 6. "Homosexual Orientation Is God-given."

The argument here is that because many homosexuals claim that since their childhood they have *always* had homosexual feelings, their "natural" homosexual tendencies are from God.

**Response to Argument #6.** Scripture nowhere suggests that if a thing seems natural it is inevitably God given. On the contrary, the Bible teaches that many "natural" states and desires are not of God and are contrary to His will.

For example, "The natural man does not receive the things of God" (1 Cor 2:14). Before conversion, we "were by nature the children of wrath" (Eph 2:3). "The carnal mind is enmity against God, for it is not subject to the law of God, nor indeed can be" (Rom 8:7). Scripture teaches that we are a fallen race, born in sin: "Behold, I was brought forth in iniquity" (Ps 51:5; cf. Jer 17:9; Rom 5:12). Sin has marred our physical and spiritual nature (1 Cor 15:1-54; John 3:5-6). We cannot therefore assume that because something is natural or inborn, it must be God ordained.

### 7. "Homosexual Orientation Is Morally Neutral"

From the assumption that people are born gay, proponents argue that homosexuality should be viewed as a neutral expression of human sexuality. Like heterosexuality, homosexuality can be rightly used or abused. The abuse is wrong. But its use within a loving, consensual, and monogamous relationship is morally right.

**Response to Argument #7.** As to the assumption that because homosexuality may be natural or inborn (an unproven assertion) it is morally neutral or legitimate, we may ask: If we would demonstrate conclusively that adultery, incest, pedophilia, violence, lying are inherited, would we be justified in considering them legitimate or neutral? Should the standard for morality be determined by what is inborn?

Contrary to this view, homosexuality is still immoral, whether inborn or acquired. "And immoral behavior cannot be legitimized by a quick baptism in the gene pool."[19]

Morality is not determined by what is inborn. Those wishing to discover God's moral standards must look to the Bible. The Ten Commandments and God's pre-fall order, rather than the latest discoveries of science regarding the post-fall sinful condition, provide the moral guidelines on whether homosexuality is moral and immoral. The leap from *what is* (alleged facts of the homosexual condition) to *what ought to be* (the morality of homosexuality) is too large to make.

If some men and women are born with homosexual or lesbian genes, then the rest of us are born with adulterous and lying genes. Will God excuse adultery and lying because we were supposedly born with those genes? We are counseled: "Never should we lower the standard of righteousness in order to accommodate inherited or cultivated tendencies to wrong-doing" (*Christ's Object Lessons,* 330).

**8. "Changing the Homosexual Orientation Is Difficult and Rare"**

It is claimed that because homosexuality is an inbred condition, the homosexual has no (or very little) hope of ever changing.

**Response to Argument #8**. The oft-repeated claim that "changing one's homosexual orientation is difficult and rare" is not supported by Scripture or Ellen G. White. In fact, the Bible itself says that sinners such as fornicators, adulterers, thieves and *homosexuals* were actually able to overcome their sinful practice through the transforming power of Christ (1 Cor. 6:9-11). Similarly, Ellen G. White states unequivocally that "a genuine conversion changes hereditary and cultivated tendencies to wrong."[20]

But even when we suppose, for the sake of argument, that the homosexual condition is unchangeable—i.e., that no amount of prayer, counseling, and effort of any kind can make a homosexual change his orientation—do these facts make homosexuality less sinful? Definitely not. One former homosexual's statement is worth quoting:

> There is no contingency factor in any scriptural reference to any kind of sin, in either the Old or the New Testament. We never read anything like: "Thou shalt not do thus and so!" ("Unless, of course, you tried hard to change, went for prayer and counseling, and found you just couldn't stop wanting to do thus and so. If that's the case, then thus and so is no longer sin. It's an inborn, immutable gift and you can darn well [feel free to] indulge in it!)"[21]

The truth, however, is that "whether the homosexual is in denial, latent, 'in the closet,' openly gay, 'married,' militant, or even a 'flaming queen'; whether he believes to have been born 'gay' or conditioned to be gay, . . . it does not really matter. If someone is drowning, it matters not whether he *fell* into the water, *fell asleep* in the water, *jumped* into the water, or was *thrown* into the water. The bottom line is that he needs a life guard, a savior."[22] Jesus is that Lifeguard. He is mighty to save every sinner, both heterosexual and homosexual, provided they admit that they are sinners, repent, and turn from their sinful ways.

### 9. "Once A Homosexual, (Almost) Always A Homosexual"

This is where the logic of biological predestination eventually leads: People are born gay; they cannot change their condition; they will always remain gay. If anyone has to change, it must be the institutions of society and the church, not the homosexual. The laws of society and the Bible must change to accommodate the homosexual who, once gay, will always be gay.

**Response to Argument #9.** Perhaps the most important question raised by the issue of homosexuality is whether Christ has power to help people overcome sin in their lives. This is of course an important question if homosexuality is sin. For if homosexuality is just a sickness or addictive/compulsive behavior, then homosexuals need therapy, not repentance; they need medical cure and not moral correction. And if homosexuality is simply a morally neutral part of a person's identity, then "once a homosexual, (almost) always a homosexual."

The latter claim has been made by the editor of a leading Adventist church paper:

> You attempt to make a point that neither the Bible nor human experience can support—that a person's sexual orientation is itself sinful and must and can be overcome by the new birth. As Jesus and our common sense tell us, no amount of praying or piety can turn a person five feet tall into one six feet tall; and a person who is an alcoholic is an alcoholic for life. The only question is whether the alcoholic will *practice* on the basis of her [sic] or her orientation.[23]

The above quotation summarizes the issues raised in this chapter. Not only does it raise questions about the normative source of one's religious authority (Bible? human experience? Jesus? common sense?), but also it raises the question about whether or not (a) we can distinguish between *being* a homosexual and *practicing* homosexuality, whether or not the experience of conversion—the new birth—can help a person to overcome his/her sinful sexual orientation (whether homosexual, bisexual, or heterosexual) and whether (c) a person who is an alcoholic or homosexual can overcome all these sinful tendencies and cease to be an alcoholic and homosexual.

If the Bible's diagnosis of homosexuality as sin can be established scripturally, then the Bible's prescription is the same for homosexuals as it is for all other sinners: a call to conversion and an invitation to participate in the process of biblical sanctification. If this is true, then the Bible's approach cannot be disdained as naive, simplistic, or inadequate, nor belittled as pat answers that are incomplete for people struggling with sexual addiction. It forces us to answer the question of whether the transforming power of God is more effective than the impotent power of psychological therapy.[24]

The testimony of Scripture exposes the lie that "once a homosexual, always a homosexual." Homosexuals can be, and have actually been, changed through the transforming power of Christ (1 Cor 6:9-11). Those who deny this fact not only deny the veracity of Scripture on this issue, but they also unwittingly portray God as impotent, rather than omnipotent. Jesus can save to the uttermost any sinner. This includes the homosexual.

### 10. "There's A Difference Between Being A Homosexual And Practicing Homosexuality"

Discussions on homosexuality often define it in two ways: (a) homosexual *orientation* or *inclination* or *tendency*—an inborn sexual attraction, predisposition, or desire toward a member of one's own sex, and (b) homosexual *behavior* or *practice*—an erotic activity with a member of one's own sex, an activity that may or may not be morally right.[25]

On the basis of this distinction some Adventist writers argue that homosexual *orientation/condition* (also referred to as ontological or constitutional homosexuality or inversion) is a permanent and unchangeable part of the individual's constitutional make up.[26] It is like the color of a person's skin—a non-behavioral trait that is to be viewed as morally neutral and a condition from which no one can change. On the other hand, homosexual *practice/activity* must be judged according to morally acceptable norms. "Being a homosexual is not sin," it is argued, but "homosexual sexual activity is sinful—it is apart from God's will."[27]

**Response to Argument #10:** This argument is meaningless, if not misleading. Is homosexuality something you are, like being black or elderly or handicapped or female, or is it something you do, like adultery or incest or lying? This question goes to the heart of the pro-homosexual statement that "there is a difference between *being* a homosexual and *practicing* homosexuality." In order for the pro-gay argument to be valid, one must assume that homosexuality is not a sin. On the other hand, if homosexuality is a sin, as the Bible teaches, then the distinction between being a homosexual and practicing homosexuality is artificial and invalid.

Let's think a little more carefully: Can a person really be a homosexual without practicing homosexuality? If this is so, can a person be an adulterer without practicing adultery? Can a person be a kleptomaniac without stealing? Can an individual be a liar without practicing lying? Also, if a person repents of his besetting sin, and through the enabling grace of God gains victory over, say, stealing, lying, immorality, etc., would it be theologically appropriate to continue viewing the person as though he were still in bondage to that particular sin, even though he may still be tempted?

Rather than distinguishing between *being* a homosexual and *practicing* homosexuality, perhaps it is more theologically sound to distinguish between the temptation to act upon one's sinful homosexual tendency (which is not wrong) and actually choosing to cherish and act upon that temptation (a wrongful choice).

If allowed to stand unchallenged, the distinction made between being homosexual and practicing homosexuality would raise a number of biblical and theological questions. First, does the Bible make such a distinction between homosexual *orientation*/condition and homosexual *practice*/behavior?—between *inversion* (constitutional homosexuality) and *perversion* (the abuse of homosexuality)? Adventist scholars disagree on this issue.

For example, one New Testament scholar admits that, "Such a distinction [between *inverts* and *perverts*] does not appear in Scripture, nor does the Bible reflect the understanding of homosexuality that we have today." But he seems to negate this categorical statement when, in the very next sentence, he writes: "Nevertheless, Paul must have had reference to the perverted sexual practices common in the degenerate pagan society of his time. Obviously he is referring to perverts, not inverts who do not participate in homosexual practices."[28]

If the Bible makes no such distinction, how is it "obvious" for Paul to be referring to a non-existent distinction? In other words, if Scripture does not make the contemporary distinction between homosexual orientation (inversion) and homosexual practice (perversion), how is it possible that "the New Testament statements directed themselves primarily if not exclusively to perverts, not inverts"?[29] In order not to be accused of forcing the Bible into the mold of today's sociological dichotomy between perversion and inversion, Adventist exegetes would need to establish whether the Bible makes such a distinction or not. The Bible condemns sin in thought and deed. It teaches that we all have sinful natures but offers victory through rebirth.

Second, the distinction between orientation and practice—the former being morally neutral and the latter morally wrong—also raises theological and ethical questions. Does the universal sinfulness of all humanity and the fact that they are born with weakness and tendencies to evil (Ps 51:5; 143:2; cf. 14:3; 1 Kings 8:46; Pro 20:9; Rom 3:23; 7:14-24; 1 John 1:8) allow one to suggest that this sinful tendency or propensity is morally neutral, and therefore, not a sin to be repented of or overcome by the power of Christ (Rom 7:25; 8:1; Eph 2:1-10; John 1:13; 3:5; 2 Cor 5:17)?

Third, if Adventists adopt the social scientists' distinction between homosexual *orientation* and homosexual *practice*, would not such a dichotomy be a biblically questionable rending of actions and attitudes? In other words, how can the *practice* of homosexuality be wrong, and yet, the inclination toward or the longing for that action be neutral (cf. Matt. 5:27, 28; 1 John 3:15)?

Is it Scriptural to argue that a homosexual *orientation* is morally neutral (and hence, not a sin) but the *action* itself is that which is sinful? If there exists an *orientation* toward a wrong act, does not a person need as much help to overcome that inclination as the individual who has succumbed to that wrong desire—whether it be lying, stealing, adultery or killing, etc.? The Bible teaches that all sinful acts, including deceit, adultery, murder, etc., proceed from the sinful human heart (Prov 12:20; Matt 5:27, 28; 1 John 3:15; Mark 7:21-27).

Instead of referring to homosexuality as a morally neutral orientation, is it not more biblical to say that a homosexual orientation is nothing more than an almost helpless sinful tendency or propensity (such as kleptomania, nymphomania, inveterate adultery), a condition that makes temptation to sin almost irresistible? And if homosexual orientation, like kleptomania and nymphomania, is a sinful human condition, does not this diagnosis suggest that the cure for this problem has to be Divine?

Could it be that the failure to recognize homosexuality as sin is one reason why it cannot be overcome? If homosexual orientation excuses the sin of homosexual desires, does it not imply that other sinful orientations (such as compulsive lying, compulsive adultery, compulsive racism, compulsive stealing, compulsive disobedience to authority, etc.) should all be excused as irreversible sinful conditions? Wherein then, lies the power of God's transforming grace?

### 11. "Being A Homosexual Is Not A Sin"

Another variation of the previous pro-gay argument is the belief that being a homosexual is not a sin. In the view of proponents, the *condition* of homosexuality is not a sin. Therefore, in the words of one Adventist scholar, "homosexuals can be genuine, model Christians."[30] They do not consider it an oxymoron to speak about a gay Christian or a gay Adventist. For in their view, individuals can be a non-practicing homosexual when they choose to be "celibate homosexuals."[31]

**Response to Argument #11.** The above statement is based on the questionable argument that a person can be a homosexual without practicing homosexuality. It also wrongly assumes that homosexuality is a morally neutral condition or mark of a person's identity (like being black, white, Italian, woman, etc.). For the statement ("being a homosexual is not a sin") to be valid, we have to show from the Scriptures that homosexuality itself is not a sin. As we shall later see, this cannot be established from Scripture.

A person is no more a non-practicing homosexual as a non-practicing adulterer or a non-practicing polygamist. Once individuals cease to practice adultery or polygamy, they can no longer be referred to as adulterers or polygamists. They are *ex*-adulterers and *ex*-polygamists. Therefore homosexuals who do not practice (or cherish or lust after) homosexuality are *ex*-homosexuals.

The apostle Paul did not refer to the converted believers in Corinth as non-practicing fornicators, idolaters, adulterers, or homosexuals. That they were *ex*-fornicators, *ex*-idolaters, *ex*-adulterers and *ex*-homosexuals is indicated by his statement, "such *were* some of you" [past tense] (1 Cor 6:9-11).

**12. "God Does Not Want Homosexuals to Give Up 'Who They Are'"**

Based on the assumption that people are born gay, and on the basis of texts like Psalm 139:13 ("For you created my inmost parts") and Psalm 100:3 ("It is he that hath made us and not we ourselves"), pro-gay advocates maintain that peoples' homosexual *orientation/condition* is part of their identity, defining who they are as sexual human beings. Consequently, it is argued: "Since God made me the way I am, and since I have had my orientation from my earliest memories, why shouldn't I express my God-given sexuality? Why would God ask me to change something which He Himself has given me?"[32]

**Response to Argument #12.** The fact is that God wants every one of us, including homosexuals, to give up something we have had all our lives—*our selves,* our sinful selves. The Bible condemns all forms of self-love or self-indulgence as expressions of idolatry and presents *self-denial* as the hall-mark of Christian discipleship (Luke 14:26-27; cf. Rev 12:11). The only way really to find one's self is by losing it (Mark 8:34-37). We cannot change ourselves but Christ can change us if we truly want to be changed from our besetting sexual tendencies.

---

**Endnotes**

[1]Kate McLaughlin, "Are Homosexuals God's Children?" *Adventist Review,* April 3, 1997, 26-29. Cf. Suzanne Ryan, "When Love Wasn't Enough," *Insight,* December 5, 1992, 2-3; Christopher Blake, "Redeeming Our Sad Gay Situation," *Insight,* December 5, 1992, 4-5, 6.

[2]Chris Glaser, "A Newly Revealed Christian Experience," *Church and Society* 67 (May-June 1977):5.

[3]William Muehl and William Johnson, "Issues Raised by Homosexuality," *Raising the Issues* (materials distributed as Packet 1, Task Force to Study Homosexuality, United Presbyterian Church), 4, cited in Robert K. Johnston, *Evangelicals at an Impasse* (Atlanta, GA: John Knox Press, 1984), 116-117.

[4]Choon-Leong Seouw, "A Heterotexual Perspective," in *Homosexuality and Christian Community,* ed. Choon-Leong Seouw (Louisville, KY: Westminster John Knox Press, 1996), 25.

[5]This argument has to do with the causes of homosexuality and the possibility of change. If the root cause of the homosexual orientation is strictly genetic, then the chances of change are very slim. If, on the other hand, homosexual orientation has to do with one's

environment or choice, then changing one's environment or exercising the power of choice can effect a change in a homosexual's condition.

[6]Neil and Briar Whitehead, *My Genes Made Me Do It! A Scientific Look at Sexual Orientation* (Lafayette, Louisiana, Huntington House Publishers, 1999).

[7]Ellen G. White, *The Desire of Ages*, 671; cf. *The Ministry of Healing*, 175-176.

[8]For a more detailed discussion, with supporting references, see Neil and Briar Whitehead, *My Genes Made Me Do It*, 125-169; William Byne, "The Biological Evidence Challenged," *Scientific American* 270/5 (1994):50-55; Thomas E. Schmidt, *Straight and Narrow: Compassion and Clarity in the Homosexuality Debate* (Downers Grove, IL: InterVarsity Press, 1995), 137-142; Joe Dallas, *A Strong Delusion: Confronting the "Gay Christian" Movement* (Eugene, OR: Harvest House Publishers, 1996), 107-131. What follows is a brief summary from these works.

[9]Simon LeVay's findings were published as "A Difference in Hypothalamic Structure Between Heterosexual and Homosexual Men," *Science*, August 30, 1991, 1034-1037.

[10]Christopher Blake, "Redeeming Our Sad Gay Situation: A Christian Response to the Question of Homosexuality," *Insight*, December 5, 1992, 7.

[11]"I don't deny the *evil* of the thing, for evil it certainly is, but I do deny the *sinfulness* of it. The homosexual condition is to be classified with disease, weakness, death, as an evil; not with gluttony, blasphemy, murder, as a sin. Both sin and evil are the work of Satan, were brought into the world at the Fall, and will one day be destroyed by Christ, but they are not identical. Sin, which we must avoid and need never commit, is represented in our situation by homosexual lust and the activity to which it leads. Evil is different. We pray to be delivered from it, but may nevertheless find ourselves left in it, and then have to aim at using and transforming it. In our situation that means a homosexual nature. I'm sure that in this sense it is morally neutral . . ." (Alex Davidson, *The Returns of Love: Letters of a Christian Homosexual* [London: Intervarsity Press, 1970], 80).

[12]Christopher Blake, "Redeeming Our Sad Gay Situation," 11, equates homosexual *orientation* with temptation, and states: "We cannot condone homosexual activity. Homosexual sexual activity is sinful—it is apart from God's will. Yet a difference exists between the person who fights against homosexual tendencies and the one who experiments with or revels in them. It's a sin to cave in to temptation. It's not a sin to be tempted."

[13]Victor J. Adamson, *"That Kind Can Never Change!" Can They . . .?: One Man's Struggle with His Homosexuality* (Lafayette, Louisiana: Huntington House Publishers, 2000), 18-19. Adamson no longer holds this view. In chapters 7 and 8 of *Must We Be Silent?* he explains why.

[14]J. B. Nelson, "Religious and Moral Issues in Working with Homosexual Clients," in *Homosexuality and Psycho-therapy, a Practitioner's Handbook of Affirmative Models. Journal of Homosexuality* 7, Nos. 2-3, ed. J. C. Gonsiorek (New York: Haworth Press, 1982): 168-69. Cf. *World* 6 (September 14, 1991):11.

[15]Thomas E. Schmidt, "Homosexuality: Establishing a Christian Backdrop for Pastoral Care," *Ministry*, November 1996, 14.

[16]Garry Gibbs, *Homosexuality: Return to Sodom* (Roseville, CA: Amazing Facts, 1996), 16-17.

[17]For more on this, see Joe Dallas, "Born Gay?" *Christianity Today*, June 22, 1992, 20-23.

[18]Thomas E. Schmidt, *Straight and Narrow?* 133.

[19]Joe Dallas, *A Strong Delusion: Confronting the "Gay Christian Movement"* (Eugene, OR: Harvest House Publishers, 1996), 117.

[20]Ellen G. White, *Seventh-day Adventist Bible Commentary*, ed., Francis D. Nichol, rev. ed. (Washington, DC: Review and Herald, 1980), vol. 6, 1101.

[21]Dallas, *A Strong Delusion*, 121.

[22]Victor J. Adamson, *"That Kind Can Never Change!" Can They . . .?: One Man's Struggle with His Homosexuality* (Lafayette, Louisiana: Huntington House Publishers, 2000), ix.

[23]Official letter, dated May 28, 1993, from New Testament scholar William G. Johnsson, editor, *Adventist Review*, to Samuel Koranteng-Pipim. In this letter, Johnsson was responding to an article I had submitted for publication. The above quotation presents the first of three reasons given why my article—titled then as "'Born A Gay' Or 'Born Again'?"—was "not acceptable" for publication in the *Adventist Review*. The editor suggested that the article should be re-worked "to bring it in line with the general thinking of the Seventh-day Adventist Church in this matter [of homosexuality]" if it should be considered for publication. The "general thinking" that the editor endorses seems to be the *qualified-acceptance position*. In addition to the above reason, the editor also suggested that the article should (1) deal with the pro-gay reconstructions of the Biblical texts that challenge homosexual lifestyle and (2) be "shaped within the framework of a greater compassion." I am indebted to Dr. Johnsson for the suggestion. This section of *Must We Be Silent?* is a partial response to his invitation.

[24]See Andrews University psychology professor John Berecz's, "How I Treat Gay and Lesbian Persons," *Student Movement*, November 11, 1992, 7, where he asserts that seeking help in the complex area of homosexuality from "untrained nonprofessionals," such as a local pastor, "is a bit like asking your mailman to remove your gall bladder. If you're seeking sexual reorientation therapy, a competent professional trained in sex therapy is your best hope."

[25]Writes Anglican theologian D. S. Bailey: "It is important to understand that the genuine homosexual condition, or *inversion*, as it is often termed, is something for which the subject can in no way be held responsible; in itself, it is morally neutral. Like the normal condition of heterosexuality, however, it may find expression in specific sexual acts; and such acts are subject to moral judgement no less than those which may take place between man and woman. It must be made quite clear that the genuine invert is not necessarily given to homosexual practices, and may exercise as careful a control over his or her physical impulses as the heterosexual." D. S. Bailey, *Homosexuality and the Western Christian Tradition* [London/New York: Longmans, Green, 1955], xi).

[26]As I pointed out earlier, in the literature on homosexuality, a distinction is often made between constitutional and situational homosexuals. Constitutional or true homosexuals (also referred to as inverts or ontological homosexuals) are those who are believed to have been born gay, and therefore, are considered to be the genuine homosexuals. Because their *condition/orientation* is said to be a permanent part of their constitutional make up (and not a transitory phase of life nor an accommodation to situational pressure), it is maintained that those who are ontological homosexuals should not be held morally responsible for their condition. In and of itself, homosexual *orientation* is morally neutral, like the normal condition of heterosexuality. On the other hand, situational homosexuals (also referred to

as perverts) are not true homosexuals but are heterosexuals who are forced by circumstances (e. g., restrictions on their sexual expression, such as is the case in prison, military camps, boarding schools, monasteries, and other single sex environments) to resort to homosexual practices to gratify their sexual needs. Because situational homosexuality is believed to be a transitory phase in their lives (i. e. they are forced to engage in homosexual practices merely to accommodate situational pressure), their homosexuality is regarded as a perversion of true sexuality; those who engage in these practices are culpable for their actions. See D. S. Bailey, *Homosexuality and the Western Christian Tradition* (London/New York: Longmans, Green, 1955), xi; H. K. Jones, *A Christian Understanding of the Homosexual* (New York: Association Press, 1966), 20-23.

[27]Blake, "Redeeming Our Sad Gay Situation," 11. To be fair, I should make it very clear that though Blake argues that "being a homosexual is not sin," he does believe that homosexual *practice* is sin. He is not preaching that "It's okay to be gay." Instead he is calling for an end to persecution of those who face homosexual temptation so they can be brought to Christ rather than driven from Him. He is right to argue that name calling, ostracism, and violence against homosexuals are not Christian.

[28]Sakae Kubo, *Theology and Ethics of Sex* (Washington, DC: Review and Herald, 1980), 75. It appears that in the Old Testament, the assumption is that everyone will marry, if possible. Not only is there no allowance for an inverted homosexual, but there is no suggestion that some might choose not to marry but to remain single. Not until the New Testament do we find Jesus calling disciples to be willing to forsake their families and follow Him and Paul urging disciples to forego marriage if possible and devote themselves to God's work.

[29]Writes Kubo: "Thus in treating the New Testament evidence we must keep two things in mind. Scripture does not reflect the understanding of homosexuality that we have today. The contemporary practices indicate that the New Testament statements directed themselves primarily if not exclusively to perverts, not inverts" (Sakae Kubo, *Theology and Ethics of Sex*, 76).

[30]Blake, Redeeming Our Sad Gay Situation," 10, 11.

[31]See Reni Dupertuis's interview with a 51 year old businessman who describes himself as a "gay Adventist." (Reni Dupertuis, "To Every Nation, Kindred, Tongue and People," *Scanner* [a newsletter published by the Glendale City, California, SDA Church], Winter 1999, 9). The article claims that there are "at least 5,000 gay Adventists in Southern California" (ibid.).

[32] The Andrews University student newspaper carried an article by David Rodgers (pseudonym), a denominationally employed Andrews University campus outreach coordinator for the gay group, Kinship. Rodgers states that his homosexuality "certainly wasn't a choice. . . . God made me this way and it's not something I should change. Or can change" (Yoonah Kim, "The Love that Dares Not Speak Its Name," *Student Movement*, November 4, 1992, 9). The same article refers to Ann, a 28-year old lesbian who seeks to transfer her church membership to the Pioneer Memorial Church at Andrews University. Ann speaks about her committed homosexual relationship in which God plays an important role: "I am a lesbian because God knows that that's the best thing for me. My homosexuality has actually brought me a lot closer to God than if I was a heterosexual" (ibid).

# 6

# IS THE BIBLE REALLY SILENT?

On the basis of Scripture, Seventh-day Adventists historically have rejected homosexuality as morally unacceptable. Today, however, some are reinterpreting the Bible to allow for the practice. Proponents claim that scriptural references to homosexual acts are culturally-conditioned, and thus do not suffice to determine God's will for homosexuals today.

Because of space limitations I can only summarize and respond to some of the major scriptural arguments justifying pro-gay theology. Those who seek more information may want to consult the in-depth analysis and evaluation provided in some other excellent works.[1] We will take up numbering of the arguments where the list in the previous chapter left off.

### 13. "Scriptural references to homosexual acts do not suffice to determine God's will for homosexuals today. They are 'culturally conditioned'"

Probably the major reason why Christian churches accept homosexuality as an acceptable lifestyle is the sophisticated scriptural arguments many employ to justify the practice.

Proponents either maintain that the Bible is "silent" on the issue or that scriptural passages which condemn homosexuality (Gen 19 [cf. Jude 7; 2 Pet 2:6-10]; Lev 18:22; 20:13; Rom 1:24-27; 1 Cor 6:9-11; 1 Tim 1:8-11), if "rightly" understood, are either ambiguous, irrelevant to contemporary homosexual practice, or refer to pederasty or cultic prostitution.[2]

In short, advocates of gay theology argue that because Bible passages on homosexuality only deal with specific historical situations, they are "culturally conditioned" and no longer relevant for Christian sexual ethics today.

**Response to Argument #13.** Undergirding these new reformulations of biblical teaching on homosexuality is liberalism's unscriptural view of biblical inspiration, interpretation, and authority. One writer has correctly noted: "There are only two ways one can neutralize the biblical witness against homosexual behavior: by gross misinterpretation or by moving away from a high view of Scripture."[3] Indeed, many of the homosexuals' biblical arguments are "strained, speculative and implausible, the product of wishful thinking and special pleading."[4]

Jesus refuted the culturally conditioned argument when He stated unequivocally that God's will for our moral life is the original ideal He instituted in the Garden of Eden. He asked the Pharisees, "Have ye not read, that he which made them at the beginning made them male and female, And said, For this cause shall a man leave father and mother, and shall cleave to his wife: and they twain shall be one flesh?" (Mt 19: 4-5; cf. Mk 10:6-8).

With the expression "at the beginning" or "from the beginning" (Mt 19:8; Mk 10:6), Christ teaches that *all cultures* must bow before the unchangeable standard He instituted at creation. That standard is that only "male and female" can legitimately "cleave" and become "one flesh." Indeed, if Christ intended a homosexual relationship He would have created "Adam and Steve, not Adam and Eve."

**14. "Jesus said nothing about homosexuality in any of the Gospels"**

The argument is that, as followers of Christ, Christians should base their beliefs on the teachings of Christ. If Jesus Christ, the founder of biblical Christianity, was silent on the issue of homosexuality, why should we go beyond our Master by condemning the practice?

**Response to Argument #14:** The lack of record in the Gospels of a statement from Christ on homosexuality does not mean that He never addressed it during His earthly ministry. According to John, if the Gospel writers had attempted to record all the works of Christ, the world could not contain all the books (John 21:25).

Morever, the recorded teachings of Christ in the Gospels are not the Christian's only source of authority. "All Scripture"—from Genesis to Revelation—constitutes the normative authority (2 Tim 3:16-17). The fact that one section of the Bible says nothing explicitly on a subject does not mean the other sections are silent.

Furthermore, it is incorrect to say that Jesus is silent on homosexuality. As we pointed out earlier, Christ's statement in Matthew 19:3-8 and Mark 10:2-9 ("Have ye not read, that he which made them at the beginning made them male and female, And said, For this cause shall a man leave father and mother, and shall cleave to his wife: and they twain shall be one flesh?") reveals that God's intention at Creation regarding human sexuality—namely, a monogamous, heterosexual relationship—is the only context for the expression of human sexuality.[5]

### 15. "The Bible writers did not know about homosexuality as we know it today"

Some argue that the kind of homosexuality the Bible writers condemned was that which was connected with rape, prostitution, or idolatry. They claim that even if the Bible writers did condemn homosexuality as we know it today (i.e., the so-called loving, committed, and faithful homosexual relationships), this is not the first time Bible writers have been wrong. They were wrong on many things, including the practice of slavery, polygamy, and the subjugation of women. These practices were later allegedly corrected by the Spirit's leading. If the Bible writers were wrong on these issues, they argue, why can't they be wrong on homosexuality? And if under the Spirit's leading the church came to embrace slave emancipation, monogamy, and women's equal rights, why should not the church, led by the same Spirit, accept homosexuality?

**Response to Argument #15:** First, if we believe that the Bible is God's inspired Word and not simply the personal opinions of ancient writers, and if we believe that the Bible is the all-sufficient guide in doctrine and practice for all people living at all times (2 Tim 3:16-17; cf. 2 Pet 1:20-21), then "it is unthinkable that God—who is no respecter of persons—would be so careless as to offer no guidance in His revealed Word to the thousands of homosexuals He knew would exist throughout time, if indeed their relationships were legitimate in His sight."[6]

Second, it is without foundation to argue that the Bible writers

(Moses and Paul) were ignorant of today's more "enlightened" scientific and theological view of homosexuality. These men were erudite in their intellectual training and discerning in their calling as God's prophets. They never made the fine distinctions cited by today's pro-homosexual advocates because there is no validity to recent distinctions between the homosexual act and the condition, the latter being something about which homosexuals allegedly have no choice. The Bible writers condemned homosexuality of itself. They also offered God's miraculous transformation as the cure for this sin (1 Cor 6:9-11).

Third, the suggestion that the Bible writers were wrong on a number of issues arises from contemporary higher criticism (the so-called historical-critical method). In an earlier work I have challenged this discredited method of liberal interpretation as incompatible with the tenets of biblical Christianity.[7]

Moreover, the claim that the Bible writers accommodated or tolerated (some say encouraged) slavery, polygamy, and the subjugation of women, practices later allegedly corrected by the Spirit's leading, is a scholarly *myth* that has been challenged by responsible Bible scholars.[8] The Bible writers never once *commended* the practice of slavery, polygamy, and the subjugation of women. But they did repeatedly condemn the practice of homosexuality (see, for example, Lev 18:22; 20:13; Rom 1:26ff. 1 Cor 6; 1 Tim 1:8ff).

### 16. "The Bible does not speak directly to the issue of behavior by consenting adults of homosexual orientation"

This argument, though similar to the previous one, deals with the matter of choice, i.e., consent and orientation. The suggestion here is that because of one's homosexual orientation (believed to be caused by one's genes or other biological and environmental factors) one has no choice and, therefore, should not be held morally responsible for acting it out.

**Response to Argument #16.** It is a mistake to think that the Bible does not speak directly to the matter of consensual (or choice) sex between persons of the same gender. The Scriptures make it plain that homosexual conduct, like other sexual deviations, is a *deliberate* action against God's expressed Law. The fact that the Bible warns against it, and imposes punishment upon those who engage in the practice (Lev 18:22, 29; 20:13), shows that a homosexual is culpable. The sanctions for same-gender sex would be meaningless if homosexuality was not a matter of choice.

Moreover, the Bible does not support the use of the term *orientation* as a shelter to escape the consequences of a deliberate choice. In the context of today's discussion of homosexuality, the word orientation is used to denote a person's sexual bent, proclivity, tendency, inclination, attraction, frame of mind, or desires believed to have been caused by genetic, biological, or environmental causes. The Hebrew word that comes closest in meaning to the modern nuances of *orientation* is the term *yētser.*

This word is frequently used for "that which is formed in the mind, e.g., plans and purposes (Gen 6:5; 8:21); Deut 31:21) or even the state of mind (Isa 26:31)."[9] For example, in reference to the orientation of the humanity in the days of Noah, the King James Version (KJV) of the Bible translates the word as the "imaginations "of the heart (Genesis 6:5 and 8:21). The KJV marginal reference correctly explains that the word *yētser.* describes "the whole imagination, with the *purposes and desires of the heart*" (emphasis mine).

The sin condition (*yētser.*) is the foundation for homosexual conduct (as it is for all sin). The individual is morally responsible for this inclination, which can be directed toward either good or evil, toward the Spirit or the flesh (Rom 8). Thus, whereas pro-gay advocates use the term orientation as a justification to escape moral responsibility of a homosexual's conduct, Scripture always attaches intentionality or choice to a person's conduct. Rightly understood, homosexual orientation refers to one's mind-set, not an inherited trait over which a person has no choice:

> In the Bible, the cause for all violations against the divine standard is ultimately traceable to the mind-set of the individual: is it subordinated to the will of God? Thus not some but *all* of the passages relating to same-gender sexual intercourse are categorically against it. There are no seams in the biblical view. No concession is made to semantic labels. A bottle of poison labeled with anything but the customary skull and bones is *more* dangerous to society, not less so. . . . No reference to causes, apart from the one located in the mind-set of the individual, can be found in the biblical text.[10]

### 17. "Sodom was destroyed because of pride, inhospitality, and/or gang rape, not because of homosexuality"

When the men of Sodom demanded of Lot, "Where are the men who came to you tonight? Bring them out to us so that we can have sex with them" (Gen 19:5), pro-gay advocates argue that the men of Sodom were only violating the ancient rules of hospitality. Some assert that the Hebrew word *yadah,* which is translated "have sex with" (or "know" in KJV) appears 943 times in the Old Testament, and carries sexual meaning only about ten times. They thus argue that the men of Sodom had no sexual intentions towards Lot's visitors; they only wanted to get acquainted with them or interrogate them, fearing that they were foreign spies being harbored by Lot, himself a foreigner. Furthermore, even if they had sexual intentions, the condemnation of their action would be the condemnation of homosexual gang rape, not of a consensual homosexuality as such.

**Response to Argument #17:** Indeed, Sodom was destroyed because of pride and inhospitality (cf. Ezek 16:49-50; Jer 23:14; Lk 17:28-29). But it is a false distinction to separate inhospitality from sexual sin. What the men of Sodom sought to do was another form of inhospitality. Also, inhospitality and pride were not the only reasons for Sodom's destruction. The city was punished also because of its abominations (Ezek 16:50), a veiled reference to its sexual deviations. The Bible describes various things as abomination, a word of strong disapproval, meaning literally something detestable and hated by God. But since the word is used in the so-called inhospitality passages of Ezekiel 16 to describe sexual sin (v. 22, 58), and since the word refers to same-sex acts in Leviticus 18:22 and 20:13, the abominations of Sodom are not exclusive of sexual deviations.

Two New Testament passages make this point explicitly. The apostle Peter indicates that, among other things, Sodom and Gomorrah were destroyed because of their "filthy conversation," "unlawful deeds," and their "walk after the *lust of the flesh"* (2 Pet 2:6-10), a reference that includes adultery, fornication, and other sexual perversions (cf. Gal 5:19-21). Jude specifically linked the destruction of these wicked cities to their sexual deviations: "Even as Sodom and Gomorrah and the cities about them in like manner, giving themselves over to *fornication, and going after strange flesh* are set forth for an example, suffering the vengeance of eternal fire" (Jude 7, emphasis supplied). The "fornication and going after strange flesh" are obvious references to sexual perversions (so NIV, RSV, NRSV, Phillips, TEV).

Pro-gay advocates incorrectly assert that the Hebrew word *yadah* as used in Genesis 19 means "to get acquainted with," not "to have sex with." They base this on the fact that, out of some 943 occurrences in the Old Testament, *yadah* clearly refers to sexual intercourse in only twelve instances. The problem with this argument is that mere word counting is no criterion of meaning; the usage of a word in its specific context is the decisive consideration. Thus, Lot's reply to the men of Sodom shows that he understood their demand in sexual terms: "No, my friends. Don't do this *wicked thing*" (Gen 19:7). In fact, in the very next verse the word *yadah* is translated "slept with." Lot, acting out of sheer desperation and hopelessness proposed: "Look, I have two daughters who have never *slept with* (*yadah*) a man. Let me bring them out to you, and you can do what you like with them" (v. 8). Lot definitely had no reason to think that the men of Sodom merely wanted to question or get acquainted with his daughters. One Bible commentary puts it neatly: "It would be grotesquely inconsequent that Lot should reply to a demand for credentials by an offer of daughters."[11] The fact that Lot refers to his daughters' virgin status also indicates he understood the *sexual* content of the request. Clearly, then, *yadah* in this passage refers to sexual intercourse.

This much can be said: The men of Sodom were not interested in Lot's desperate offer of his virgin daughters. They were proposing a homosexual rape. But for such rape to have involved "all the men of the city, both young and old" (Gen 19:4), homosexual activity must have been commonly practiced—one reason why Jude records that their "fornication, and going after strange flesh are set forth [in Scripture] for an example [and warning unto us]" (Jude 7). As we will see, other Bible passages condemn all homosexual activity, not just homosexual rape.

### 18. "The Leviticus 18:22 and 20:13 passages, condemning homosexual activity as sinful, do not condemn homosexuality as we know it today"

In these passages, God forbids a man to "lie with" another man "as with a woman." Doing so is an "abomination." Advocates of gay theology, however, argue that the practices condemned as "abomination" (Heb. *to'evah*) in these passages of Leviticus have to do with the kind of homosexuality associated with pagan religious practices. In the view of pro-gay writers, God was not prohibiting the kind of homosexuality practiced today by Christians but only the kind connected with idolatry.

Some also argue that, even if the passages condemn homosexuality in general, these passages in Leviticus are part of the ceremonial holiness code that has no permanent binding obligation on Christians. They reason that the prohibition of sexual intercourse with a woman during her menstrual flow (Lev 18:19) shows that the prohibition against homosexual intercourse, which closely follows it in the text (18:22) was ceremonial in nature. It was a temporary obligation upon the Jews, not a universal law.

**Response to Argument #18:** First, if these passages condemn homosexuality only because of its association with idolatry, then it would logically follow that other practices mentioned in these passages—incest, adultery, polygamy, bestiality, and child sacrifice—are also condemned as sinful only because of their association with idolatry. Conversely, if incest, adultery, polygamy, bestiality, etc., are morally objectionable regardless of their connection with pagan practices, then homosexuality is also morally wrong, regardless of the context in which it is practiced.

Second, in context, both Leviticus 18 and 20 deal primarily with morality, not idolatrous worship. When God wants specifically to mention the practices of cultic or idolatrous prostitutes, He does so, as in Deuteronomy 23:17: "No Israelite man or woman is to become a shrine prostitute." The lack of such mention in Leviticus 18:22 and 20:13 indicates that God is dealing with homosexuality per se, not with any alleged specific form of Canaanite religious practice.

As for the contention that Scripture always connects the word "abomination" (Heb. *to'evah*) with idolatry or pagan ceremonies, one biblical example will discredit the claim. Proverbs 6:16-19 describes God as hating such abominations as a proud look, a lying tongue, murder, etc. Are we to believe that pride, lying, and murder are morally acceptable as long as they are not carried out in idolatrous pagan contexts? Certainly not.

Pro-gay advocates also argue that because Leviticus 18 prohibits intercourse during a woman's menstrual flow (v. 19) and proceeds in the same text to prohibit homosexual intercourse (v. 22), the condemnation of homosexuality should be viewed as a temporary ceremonial obligation, not a universal moral injunction. But this argument is also untenable in that the prohibitions appear with others of a clearly moral nature—namely, prohibitions against various types of unlawful sexual relations including incest (18:6-17), polygamy (18:18), adultery (18:20), child sacrifice (18:21), and bestiality (18:23).[12] The fact that child sacrifice violated two provisions in the moral law, namely prohibitions against idolatry and killing (cf. Exo 20:3, 13), and the fact that the list of unlawful behaviors in Leviticus 18 is condemned in the strongest terms (vv. 24ff.) suggests that these moral concerns are universal in nature, and thus, still relevant today.[13]

Also, since the New Testament again denounces these sexual deviations, we may conclude that the moral content of these Leviticus passages is permanently normative, not part of the ceremonial holiness code.[14]

### 19. "In Romans 1:26-27 Paul does not condemn individuals who are homosexuals by nature; rather, he refers to idolatrous heterosexuals who have 'changed their nature' by committing homosexual acts"

According to this argument, the real sin condemned by Paul is two-fold: (I) the changing of what is natural to a person into what is unnatural, and (ii) homosexuality committed by people who worship images, not God.

**Response to Argument #19:** Advocates of pro-gay theology often argue that if a person is homosexual, he or she can never become truly heterosexual. And yet they often quote the Romans 1 passage as an example of truly *heterosexual* people committing a sin by becoming truly *homosexual.* We may therefore ask: If a person who is a heterosexual can change and become a homosexual, why cannot a person who is a homosexual be changed and become a heterosexual? It appears, however, that advocates of the pro-gay view point do not see the inconsistency of their position.

For a number of reasons, it seems inconceivable that Paul could be describing predominantly heterosexual people indulging in homosexual acts. First, he describes the men and women committing these homosexual acts as "burning in lust" for each other. Are we to understand this as heterosexuals who are simply experimenting with an alternate lifestyle?

Also, if verses 26 and 27 condemn only homosexual actions by people to whom they did not come naturally (i.e., heterosexuals who are practicing homosexual acts), but don't apply to individuals to whom those same actions allegedly *do* come naturally (so called true homosexuals), then consistency and intellectual integrity demand that the sinful practices mentioned in verses 29 and 30—fornication, backbiting, deceit, etc.—are permissible as long as the people who commit them are people to whom they come naturally.

Is Paul's use of "natural" purely subjective (what is "natural for me" in my orientation) or is it objective (what is "natural for everyone" regardless of orientation)? The context of Romans 1 suggests that Paul is describing homosexual behavior and other sinful practices as objectively unnatural. They are part of the practices that result when men "exchange the truth about God for a lie and worship and serve the creature rather than the Creator." "He was talking about an objective condition of depravity experienced by people who rejected God's will."[15]

In other words, it is the very nature of the sexual conduct itself that Paul considers unnatural. Homosexuality is unnatural to the man as a male (*arsen*) and to the woman as a female (*gune*), not because of what may or may not be natural to their personality, but because of what is unnatural according to God's design when he created male and female.

Finally, if we are to accept pro-gay arguments that Romans 1 condemns only homosexuality committed by people who worship idols, then consistency and honesty demand that we also argue that the other sins listed in that chapter—fornication, wickedness, covetousness, maliciousness, envy, murder, pride, etc. (vv. 28-32)—are sinful only because they are committed by idol worshipers. I don't believe that even the most strident advocates of homosexuality will embrace this logic. The point is thus obvious: Homosexuality is unnatural, whether it is committed by idolaters or those who worship the true God.[16]

**20. "Paul's *arsenokoitai* and *malakoi* statements in 1 Cor 6:9-10 and 1 Tim 1:9-10, denouncing the 'effeminate and them that defile themselves with mankind' are actually a condemnation of an 'offensive kind of homosexuality,' not the 'offense of homosexuality'"**

In both passages, Paul lists those who engage in homosexual behavior among such lawless people as fornicators, idolaters, adulterers, thieves, drunkards, kidnapers, etc. According to pro-gay advocates, the Greek terms *arsenokoitai* (translated in 1 Cor 6 and 1 Tim 1 as "them that defile themselves with mankind") and *malakoi* (translated "effeminate" or "soft" in 1 Cor 6), which the apostle uses to denounce homosexual activity, refer to homosexual *abuse*, not its right use. Thus, these passages do not condemn today's loving and committed homosexual relationships, but rather offensive kinds of homosexual activity, such as homosexual prostitution.

**Response to Argument #20:** For good reason the terms *arsenokoitai* and *malakoi* have been understood traditionally as a reference to the active and passive partners in a homosexual relationship. The first term (*arsenokoitai*) literally means "male bedders" (reference to a man who "beds" another) and the second term (*malakoi*) refers to "soft" or "effeminate" men, specifically males who play female sexual roles with the "male bedder." There is no hint in these words that Paul was condemning only a certain kind of homosexual abuse, as in prostitution, rape, or pagan ceremonies. He condemns homosexuality in itself as sin.

Further, note that *arsenokoitai* is derived from two words—*arsen* (referring to man as male) and *koite* (a term that appears only twice in the New Testament, and literally means "bed" or "couch." In Romans 13:13, it appears in "Let us walk honestly . . . not in chambering [*koite*])"; and in Hebrews 13:4, "Marriage is honorable . . . and the bed [*koite*] undefiled"). The combination of the two terms *arsen* (male) and *koite* (bed) does not even suggest prostitution, rape or idolatry—only sexual contact between two men. In other words, homosexuality is wrong, regardless of the reason why it is practiced.

Note also that when Paul used the term *arsenokoitai* to condemn the sinful practice of homosexuality, he apparently derived it directly from the Greek translation of two verses in Leviticus 18, which reads in part:

> ". . . *kai meta* ***arsenos*** *ou koimethese* ***koiten*** *gynaikos*" ("and you shall not sleep in bed with a man as with a woman"; Lev 18:22);
> " . . . *kai hos an koimethe meta* ***arsenos koiten*** *gynaikos*" ("and whoever may lie in bed with a man as with a woman"; Lev 20:13).

Therefore, Paul's condemnation of homosexuality in 1 Corinthians 6:9-10 and 1 Timothy 1:9-10 presupposes Leviticus's condemnation of homosexual acts. Is it any wonder that Paul lists homosexuality among lawless deeds that would bar a person from the kingdom of God?[17] Homosexuality in any form is sinful. To attempt to sanitize a sinful practice by describing it as loving and committed and to attempt to silence the Bible's categorical condemnation of the practice is an irresponsible exercise in biblical gamesmanship.

In summary, the Bible is not morally neutral on homosexuality. Paul's statements in Romans 1, 1 Corinthians 6, and 1 Timothy 1,[18] along with the Leviticus 18:22 and 20:13 passages, clearly show that homosexuality in all of its various forms is a sinful practice. Homosexual behavior, like heterosexual fornication, is sin, whether it results from one's orientation or from conscious choice. In other words, the Bible condemns all homosexual lust and behavior, including today's so-called loving and consensual homosexual relationships. *It is not wrong to be tempted either homosexually or heterosexually, but it is wrong to yield to one's sexual temptation.*

### 21. "Homosexuality cannot be cured; therefore the church must welcome gays and lesbians into full membership and embrace their homosexual lifestyle"

Based on the mistaken notion that homosexuality is not a sin, but a trait of one's identity, and based on the apparent failure of prayer, counseling, human therapy, and other methods of behavior modification (skills of self-discipline or self-control), advocates of pro-gay theology argue that cure or deliverance may not always be possible for those with homosexual orientations. Consequently they urge the church to be mature enough to welcome homosexuals into membership and leadership. When proponents employ the terms "outreach" or "ministries" for gays and lesbians, they simply mean an affirmation of homosexuals in their homosexuality.

**Response to Argument #21.** I have argued in this chapter and the preceding one that homosexuality is a sin, no less or worse than other sins condemned in the Bible: "Do you not know that the wicked will not inherit the kingdom of God? Do not be deceived: Neither the sexually immoral nor idolaters nor adulterers nor male prostitutes nor *homosexual offenders* nor thieves nor the greedy nor drunkards nor slanderers nor swindlers will inherit the kingdom of God" (1 Cor 6:9-10).

The good news, however, is that there is a cure for all manner of sin including homosexual sin—provided sinners admit their wrongdoing, repent, and turn away from it. It is significant that the steps to overcome homosexuality are clearly outlined by the apostle Paul in the verse immediately following the above: *"And that is what some of you were. But you were washed, you were sanctified, you were justified in the name of the Lord Jesus Christ and by the Spirit of our God"* (1 Cor 6:11).

The change described in this verse is specific with respect to a list of violations, including homosexual conduct. In other words, the cure for homosexuality is the same as for all other sins. Also, the use of the past tense in verse 11 emphasizes that what the Corinthians were in the past is not what they are in the present, because they have been changed.

According to Paul it is possible for one to be freed from homosexual bondage. The transformation of the homosexual does not come through the sinner's struggle nor from some humanistic methods of behavior modification. Since homosexuality is a problem of the heart, and not simply genetic or environmental, the only way out is through a transformation of the heart. It comes through Christ and His spirit. The process by which this change takes place is defined by three terms: cleansing, sanctification, and justification.

In the Greek, each verb is introduced by the strong adversative conjunction *alla*, a word that is normally translated in English as "but." Thus, the KJV states: "*but* ye are washed, *but* ye are sanctified, *but* ye are justified . . ." The force of the word "but" (Greek, *alla)* is that it expresses a sharp contrast to what has come before. It also has a confirming or emphatic nuance. In other words, there was a radical difference between what the Corinthians were in the past and what they currently were when they were converted.

Given the completeness of the transformation, the apostle would therefore reject any suggestion that a person can be gay and Christian or Adventist at the same time. The two don't mix. You are either gay or a Christian. It is an oxymoron to refer to a person as a "gay Adventist." "In choosing the aorist [past tense] for these three verbs ['washed,' 'sanctified,' and 'justified'], Paul emphasizes that the actions of cleansing, sanctifying, and justifying have been accomplished. They have completed a change in the condition and orientation of those who were practicing homosexuality and the other vices listed in 1 Corinthians 6:9-10."[19]

The Bible also challenges the pro-gay suggestion that the church must welcome unrepentant homosexuals into church membership. When the Old Testament urged that those who engaged in adultery, homosexuality, incest, bestiality, etc. should be "cut off from among their people," and even imposed the death penalty upon these sexual offenders (cf. Lev 18:7-30), it indicates clearly that homosexuals were not to be entertained in the community of faith.

In the New Testament Paul apparently applies this Old Testament principle to disfellowshiping people from the church. Concerning the sexual immorality of incest and other blatant sins, he exhorted the Corinthian church, "not to associate with sexually immoral people. . . . I am writing you that you must not associate with anyone who calls himself a brother but is sexually immoral or greedy, an idolater or a slanderer, a drunkard or swindler. With such a man do not even eat. . . . Expel the wicked man from among you" (vv. 9, 11, 13, NIV).

The Bible's position is clear. Homosexuals who acknowledge the sinfulness of homosexuality, who accept Christ's offer of forgiveness, who cut themselves loose from homosexual relationships, and who, by faith, commit themselves to a life of sexual purity should be accepted into church fellowship. But those who do not acknowledge homosexuality as sin, who reinterpret Scripture to justify their sins, who defiantly maintain that they will not turn from their sinful ways, and/or those who are engaged in homosexual relationships or practices should not be accepted into church membership. Accordingly, the church must not endorse any so-called outreach or ministries for gays and lesbians that teaches that homosexuality is morally neutral or not a sin, which affirms homosexuals in their homosexuality, and which seeks to make homosexuality compatible with the Christian faith.

**Conclusion**

The questions that have been raised in the preceding chapters are some of the major issues confronting Bible-believing Seventh-day Adventists as they respond to the attempts by some within our ranks to reconcile the homosexual lifestyle with biblical Christianity. Unless biblically consistent answers are given to the questions, one cannot but conclude that the qualified-acceptance position on homosexuality, just like the full-acceptance position, cannot be a biblically-defensible option for Seventh-day Adventists.

What then should we say in response to homosexuals who are coming to church "not only for forgiveness and mercy but to say to the church, as they have to the world, 'Homosexuality is not sinful; it is natural to me. God made me this way. He accepts me and my homosexuality as good. Therefore the time has come for the church to accept me as I am and join me in saying that gayness is good'"? Should the born a gay lifestyle be baptized?

In the light of our discussion in the preceding pages, we cannot but borrow the following words to respond to attempts at domesticating homosexuality and lesbianism in the Seventh-day Adventist Church:

> The church cannot condone homosexual activity without betraying its biblical, historical, and spiritual heritage. Its conscious acceptance of the authority and inspiration of Scripture

> would need to undergo such a radical, liberalizing change that the fundamental teachings of the church would be left without foundation.
>
> The consequences of such change with its ramifications for theological, ethical, and moral teaching might be labeled by some as progressive, calculated to enlighten the church and produce a more compassionate laity accommodated to the modern society in which it lives. But in reality such a move would be a giant step toward repaganization of the church. The resulting religion would not be a Bible religion or that of the prophets, the Lord, or the apostles, not Christianity except in name.[20]

In today's climate of enlightened ethical sensitivity, the above words and the theological position adopted in this section of *Must We Be Silent?* may seem judgmental or uncompassionate to some. If so, we must make it absolutely clear that God's grace covers every kind of sin for any believer in Jesus who contritely turns toward God and makes a decisive commitment to turn away from sin. "God can forgive homosexual sin as well as heterosexual sin, sin which is socially acceptable as sin and sin which is not. But the first step in receiving forgiveness is to recognize our wrongdoing as sin."[21]

Seventh-day Adventists believe that the biblical world view presents a loving Father who is interested in all aspects of our being and our lifestyle (3 John 2). His written Word is the surest and most trustworthy guide for every human thought and conduct (2 Tim 3:16-19). It tells of a compassionate and powerful God who is abundantly able and willing to assist us in overcoming our human weaknesses (Heb 4:15-16; Jude 24; Eph 3:20). And the Bible introduces us to a faithful Savior and his dependable promises. Writes Ellen G. White:

> Are you tempted? He will deliver. Are you weak? He will strengthen. Are you ignorant? He will enlighten. Are you wounded? He will heal. . . . 'Come unto Me,' is His invitation. Whatever your anxieties and trials, spread out your case before the Lord. Your spirit will be braced for endurance. The way will be opened for you to disentangle yourself from embarrassment and difficulty. The weaker and more helpless

> you know yourself to be, the stronger will you become in His strength. The heavier your burdens, the more blessed the rest in casting them upon the Burden Bearer (Ellen G. White, *The Desire of Ages,* 329).

We all can receive help if we are willing to believe that whatever God commands we may accomplish in His strength. The apostle Paul, a few verses after his condemnation of sinful practices such as homosexuality, declared that though he was "the chief of sinners," Christ's enabling grace was able to turn his life around (1 Tim. 1:9-16). If Jesus can change "the chief of sinners," certainly, He can change you and me (1 John 1:9). But this is possible if, and only if: (1) we accept that the homosexual lifestyle is morally wrong and resolve to change and if (2) we are willing to accept Christ's abiding offer of pardon and cleansing (Matt 11:28-30; 1 John 1:9; Isa 1:18). The choice is ours.

---

**Endnotes**

[1]See, for example, Donald J. Wold, *Out of Order: Homosexuality in the Bible and the Ancient Near East* (Grand Rapids: Baker, 1998); Thomas E. Schmidt's *Straight and Narrow? Compassion and Clarity in the Homosexual Debate* (Downers Grove, IL: InterVarsity, 1995), and Marion L. Soards' *Scripture and Homosexuality: Biblical Authority and the Church Today* (Louisville, KY: Westminster John Knox, 1995). To date, the most detailed Adventist response to scriptural arguments of pro-gay advocates is the GC Biblical Research Institute's commissioned work by Ronald Springett, *Homosexuality in History and the Scriptures* (Washington, DC: Biblical Research Institute, 1988); cf. Raoul Dederen, "Homosexuality: A Biblical Perspective," *Ministry,* September 1988, 1416. I am indebted to the following works for their excellent readable review and evaluation of the scriptural arguments by pro-gay advocates: Carl Bridges, Jr. "The Bible Does Have Something to Say About Homosexuality," in *Gay Rights Or Wrongs: A Christian's Guide to Homosexual Issues and Ministry,* ed. Michael Mazzalongo (Joplin, MO: College Press, 1995), 147169; Joe Dallas, *A Strong Delusion: Confronting the "Gay Christian" Movement,* 185202; John R. W. Stott, *Homosexual Partnerships?: Why Same-Sex Relationships Are Not A Christian Option* (Downers Grove, IL: InterVarsity, 1985).

[2]These pro-gay arguments are best articulated by former Yale University professor of history John Boswell, *Christianity, Social Tolerance and Homosexuality* (Chicago: University of Chicago Press, 1980), and Anglican theologian Derrick Sherwin Bailey, *Homosexuality and the Western Christian Tradition* (London: Longmans, Green, 1955). John R. W. Stott describes Bailey as "the first Christian theologian to reevaluate the traditional understanding of the biblical prohibitions regarding homosexuality" (Stott, "Homosexual Marriage," *Christianity Today,* November 22, 1985, 22).

[3]Stanton L. Jones, "The Loving Opposition," *Christianity Today,* July 19, 1993, 13.

[4]Richard Lovelace, *The Church and Homosexuality* (Old Tappan, NJ: Flemming H. Revell, 1978), 113.

[5]"While Jesus is not reported to have spoken on homosexuality or homosexual behavior, his one recorded statement [in Matt 19:38 and Mark 10:29] about human sexuality reveals that he understood males and females to be created by God for mutual relations that unite and fulfill both male and female in a (permanent) complementary union. There is no room here for an argument from silence concerning what Jesus 'might have' or 'must have' thought about homosexuality. But from Jesus' own words we see that he understood human sexuality to be God's own creation for the purpose of male and female uniting in a complementary relationship" (Marion L. Soards' *Scripture and Homosexuality: Biblical Authority and the Church Today* [Louisville, KY: Westminster/John Knox, 1995], 28).

[6]Joe Dallas, *Desires in Conflict: Answering the Struggle for Sexual Identity* (Eugene OR: Harvest House Publishers, 1991), 276.

[7]See my *Receiving the Word*, 241249, esp. 279321. Cf. my unpublished article, "A Bug in Adventist Hermeneutic," 1999, a summary version of which is to be published in a future issue of *Ministry* under the title, "Questions in the Quest for a Unifying Hermeneutic."

[8]Readers will benefit from the following works which challenge the above "accommodation" hypotheses: Ronald A. G. du Preez, *Polygamy in the Bible* (Berrien Springs, MI: Adventist Theological Society Publications, 1993); Theodore D. Weld, *The Bible Against Slavery: Or, An Inquiry into the Genius of the Mosaic System, and the Teachings of the Old Testament on the Subject of Human Rights* (Pittsburgh: United Presbyterian Board of Publication, 1864); cf. Dale B. Martin, *Slavery As Salvation: The Metaphor of Slavery in Pauline Christianity* (New Haven: Yale UP, 1990). These works offer biblical evidence showing that God at no time tolerated polygamy and slavery as morally legitimate practices for His people. On the issue of the subjugation of women or "patriarchy," George Knight, *Role Relationships of Men and Women: New Testament Teaching* (Chicago, IL: Moody, 1985), and Guenther Haas, "Patriarchy as An Evil that God Tolerated: Analysis and Implications for the Authority of Scripture," *Journal of the Evangelical Theological Society,* September 1995, 321-326, have challenged the notion that male headship (in the home and church) is an evil practice that God tolerated.

[9]R. Laird Harris, Gleason L. Archer, Jr., and Bruce K. Waltke, *Theological Wordbook of the Old Testament,* vol. 1 (Chicago: Moody Press), 396.

[10]Donald J. Wold, *Out of Order: Homosexuality in the Bible and the Ancient Near East* (Grand Rapids, MI: Baker, 1998), 22-23 (emphasis his).

[11]Derek Kidner, "Additional Note on the Sin of Sodom," in *Genesis: An Introduction and Commentary* (Downers Grove: InterVarsity, 1967), 136-137.

[12]For an insightful discussion of Leviticus 18, see Ronald A. G. du Preez, *Polygamy in the Bible* (Berrien Springs, MI: Adventist Theological Society, 1993), 70-81.

[13]Based on the repeated references to "aliens" in Leviticus 17 and 18, Gerhard F. Hasel concludes that these laws are not ceremonial, ritual, or cultic, "cannot be restricted to Israelites," but "are universal in nature" (see Hasel, "Clean and Unclean Meats in Leviticus 11: Still Relevant?" *Journal of the Adventist Theological Society* 2 [Autumn 1991]: 103-104. Richard M. Davidson concurs. He maintains that the practices outlawed in Lev 18 "are not just destructive for Israel. They are universal abominations." See,

Davidson, "Revelation/Inspiration in the Old Testament: A Critique of Alden Thomposon's 'Incarnational' Model," in *Isses in Revelation and Inspiration*, ed. Frank Holbrook and Leo Van Dolson (Berrien Springs, MI: Adventist Theological Society, 1992), 121. Cf. Walter C. Kaiser, Jr., *Toward Old Testament Ethics* (Grand Rapids, MI: Zondervan, 1983), 117-119, 196, 197.

[14]For an argument supporting the permanently binding nature of these passages, see Michael Ukleja, "Homosexuality and the Old Testament," *Bibliotheca Sacra* 140/3 (JulySeptember 1983): 259-266, especially 264ff. on "The Relevance of the Law."

[15]Carl Bridges, Jr. "The Bible Does Have Something to Say About Homosexuality," in *Gay Rights Or Wrongs: A Christian's Guide to Homosexuals Issues and Ministry*, ed. Michael Mazzalongo (Joplin, MO: College Press, 1995), 160.

[16]A detailed exegetical study of Romans 1:26-27 appears in Schmidt, *Straight and Narrow*, 64-85.

[17]For more on this, see D. F. Wright, "Homosexuals or Prostitutes? The Meaning of *Arsenokoitai* (1 Cor 6:9, 1 Tim 1:10)," *Vigiliae Christianae* 38 (1984):125153, especially 126-129. Cf. Zaas, "1 Corinthians 6:9ff.: Was Homosexuality Condoned in the Corinthian Church?" *Society of Biblical Literature Seminar Papers* 17 (1979): 205-212.

[18]For more on this, see Michael Ukleja, "Homosexuality in the New Testament," *Bibliotheca Sacra* 140/4 (October-December 1983):350-358; David E. Malick, "The Condemnation of Homosexuality in Romans 1:26-27," *Bibliotheca Sacra* 150/3 (JulySeptember 1993): 327-340, and "The Condemnation of Homosexuality in 1 Corinthians 6:9," *Bibliotheca Sacra* 150/4 (October-December 1993): 479-492.

[19]Donald Wold, *Out of Order: Homosexuality in the Bible and the Ancient Near East,* 198.

[20]Ronald Springett, *Homosexuality in History and the Scriptures*, 163-164.

[21]Bridges, Jr., "The Bible Does Have Something to Say About Homosexuality," in *Gay Rights Or Wrongs*, 169. Noel Weeks states it well: "It may seem kind to say that a person is not responsible for his sin. But it has the harsh and cruel consequence that sin is therefore outside the scope of the sanctifying work of the Spirit. The homosexual is doomed to live with the misery of sin. Make no mistake. Sin and misery go together. When we deny the homosexual the gospel we tell him to expect a continuance of his misery. The point is often made that the church should show compassion to the homosexual. So it should. The first item of that compassion is telling him how escape is possible. Why should he seek the church that tells him that nothing can be done for him? He may like such a church to ease the burden of his guilty conscience, but such a church has nothing to offer him" (Noel Weeks, *The Sufficiency of Scripture* [Carlisle, Pa.: Banner of Truth Trust, 1988], 172).

# 7

# TESTIMONY FROM AN EX-GAY [1]

The testimony you are about to read is written by an *ex*-homosexual who has experienced freedom from homosexual bondage. Today, he is serving God as a writer, pastor, radio evangelist, and international speaker. His reassuring testimony underscores the all-sufficient power of Jesus to save *to the uttermost*; to save His people, *whosoever* they may be, from their sins *of whatever nature.* Yes, as is true for any other sinner, God can save even homosexuals from their lifestyle of sin. For, *Homosexuals Are God's Children, Too!*

**Homosexuals are God's Children, Too![2]**

If you had asked me nine years ago why I had *chosen* to be "gay", or homosexual, I would have answered you as I had answered others countless times before, "I did not *choose* to be 'gay'! I *chose* to be a Seventh-day Adventist Christian. I *chose* to be educated in Seventh-day Adventist Christian schools. I *chose* to be a student missionary. I *chose* to earn a degree in Theology and to graduate with honors. I *chose* to marry a Seventh-day Adventist young lady. I *chose* to father Seventh-day Adventist babies. I did *not choose* to be 'gay'! I just finally came to grips with reality and *accepted* that I was 'gay', that I was *born* 'gay'."

For years after my "coming out of the closet" and the devastating breakup of my home that resulted, I dared anyone to tell me my "condition" was a matter of choice. I had made all the right "choices" in my life. While struggling with the nagging yearnings of my heart, I had prayed relentlessly that God would "Create in me a clean heart, and renew a right spirit within me," and help me to love and to be in love with my wife. But, to no avail.

Finally, I had succumbed to those nagging yearnings and had fallen into the gay life of homosexuality, totally convinced that my condition, or behavior, was not something a person chooses. Who would willingly choose to be so radically out of sync with society, and the church, if a Christian?! I had to be either the victim of my own environment, or just born that way.

My parents, friends, and family all thought of me as a gentle person, thoughtful and considerate of others. In their eyes I was intelligent, likeable, courteous, and talented in many areas. Most of all, I was known to be deeply spiritual.

**The Tensions of My "Gay" Lifestyle**

Upon entering the gay life, I upheld that image except that of being deeply spiritual. Reared a Seventh-day Adventist, I just could not reconcile my homosexuality with being a part of the people who love God and *keep* His commandments, for that seemed to be a hypocritical exercise in futility. To me, the Bible was very clear in stating that I would not enter heaven in my condition. For example, ". . . Be not deceived: neither fornicators, . . . nor adulterers, nor effeminate, nor abusers of themselves with mankind, . . . shall inherit the kingdom of God." (1 Cor. 6:9,10)

As I now reflect upon my years in the "gay" lifestyle, I can honestly say that my life became full of disgusting, depraved, and perverted behavior. I, along with every homosexual I knew, was lustful and obsessed with sex. Yet, in the work place, in public, and when among friends and family, I masterfully maintained the image of a decent, gentle, thoughtful, polite, considerate person, both loving and loveable.

For sixteen years I blamed God for everything wrong with my life, especially my homosexuality, because I had prayed that He would take it away, and He hadn't. "So, wasn't it rightfully His fault that I was 'gay'?" I reasoned.

During those self-serving years of "love," promiscuity, and pleasure, self-advancement, self-exaltation, and self-gratification, there was also much loneliness, misery and heartache. However, my parents and family never made me feel unloved, unappreciated, or unaccepted. The Lord, in His mercy and patience, worked through them to reveal to me the true meaning of unconditional love for the sinner, while not condoning the sin. Not only did they manifest this love and acceptance towards me, but also towards my friends and lovers. In their relationship to me was demonstrated the words of Jesus, "Neither do I condemn thee." However, neither in word nor in practice did they dismiss the rest of Jesus' statement: "go, and sin no more." (John 8:11)

**Searching for Answers**

Eventually, I stopped blaming God for my condition and tried to look honestly at myself. "After all," I reasoned, "I can blame God all my life; I am still lost! And what point is there in pretending there are no consequences to my lifestyle, or in pretending that I am saved?" I had been deceiving myself. Simple logic revealed my only hope to be in the Word of God. I had to stop running and hiding, and begin searching out what the Word says.

We are counseled that "All who endeavor to excuse or conceal their sins, and permit them to remain upon the books of heaven, unconfessed and unforgiven, will be overcome by Satan." (GC 620) That was me—totally overcome!

I began to think, "Wouldn't it be tragic to find myself standing some day outside the New Jerusalem;—with 'a good excuse . . .'?" In fact, for several years I had been having a recurring dream in which I experienced the horror of being lost as I gazed into the face of Jesus coming in the clouds of glory.

Jesus had warned of this horror in stating, "Not every one that saith unto me, Lord, Lord, shall enter into the kingdom of heaven; but he that *doeth* the will of my Father which is in heaven. Many will say to me in that day, Lord, Lord, have we not . . . in thy name done many wonderful works? And then will I profess unto them, I never knew you: depart from me, ye that work iniquity." (Matthew 7:21-23; emphasis mine)

Tragically, the lake of fire will contain an innumerable host whom God dearly loves, unconditionally; people He loves so much that He gave His only begotten Son that they need not perish. But they have chosen not eternal life. And God honors their choice, the consequence of which is eternal separation from the Source of eternal life.

I now believe that through my recurring nightmare Jesus was reaching out to me, a homosexual, saying, "My son, give me thine heart." With childlike reasoning and logic, I began to prayerfully study God's Word to find either justification *in* my homosexuality, or salvation *from* it. Try as I might, I could not find justification anywhere in God's word for continuing in my lifestyle of sin.

Instead, I re-discovered the simple truth that "Sin is the transgression of the law" (1 John 3:4), in other words, "disobedience." And God's Word clearly states in John 14:15 & Exodus 20:14, "*If ye love me* . . . Thou shalt not commit adultery," adultery being sexual relations outside of the marriage institution. And God, the Creator of marriage, designed that one man should be united with one woman, becoming *one* flesh, and that they were to be fruitful and to multiply . . . !! Man with man, or woman with woman, cannot fulfill this purpose of God in marriage.

Furthermore, God expressed very clearly His feelings about homosexuality in Leviticus 20:13, (and elsewhere throughout Scripture), "If a man also lie with mankind, as he lieth with a woman, both of them have committed an abomination . . ."

I was again drawn to 1 Corinthians 6:9, 10: "Know ye not that the unrighteous shall not inherit the kingdom of God? *Be not deceived*: neither fornicators, . . . nor adulterers, nor effeminate, nor abusers of themselves with mankind shall inherit the kingdom of God."

And, "The wages of sin [disobedience] is death"(Romans 6:23)

These, and many other texts, clearly revealed to me that I could not be justified *in* my homosexuality. It is the deception of Satan that leads us to believe "Thou shalt not surely die" when we choose to disobey, when we choose to remain in our inherited and cultivated fallen condition of disobedience.

This understanding left me just feeling more helpless. And in retrospect, I know that the purpose of God's law is to do just that, to show us where we have come short of God's ideal, and to awaken within us a realization of *our need of a Savior.* "For all have sinned (disobeyed), and come short of the glory of God" (Romans 3:23) in one way or another.

**Self-Examination**

As a homosexual, I could not picture myself back in harmony with God's plan. Addicted to my sexual inclinations, I was repulsed by the idea of "one man and one woman" as God intended.

Nevertheless, I continued to honestly examine myself to determine who I really was, how and why I was homosexual, and how I could fit in with God's plan for mankind in general and for myself in particular. Was homosexuality really sin? If I was born that way, how could it be sin?

As I considered the question as to whether I was born homosexual, or whether I had chosen to be so, I eventually came to realize that *it really doesn't matter!* Every descendent of Adam was born with tendencies to sin in more respects than one. Many have created even more tendencies on their own by choice, or have been victimized into additional tendencies by their environment. And we all have *cultivated* to some extent these tendencies to evil, whatever they might be.

Again, in short, we *all need a Savior*! And it was for this purpose that God "gave His only begotten Son, that *whosoever* ["gays" included] believeth in him should not perish, but have everlasting life" (John 3:16); that whosoever was broken might be repaired and restored to the image of his Maker in accordance with His original plan.

The homosexual needs to be saved from his/her sin, just as the unfaithful spouse needs to be saved from sin, just as the thief, the murderer, and the liar need to be saved from their sins. Salvation from sin is a work of divine therapy, of reprogramming, of redirection, of re-creation.

As I continued to study and pray, the Lord revealed to me even more answers to my questions. He also disclosed His unconditional love for me His child—even though a homosexual, and His omnipotent power to save me *from* my sins, *whatever* they might be. Paul warned us to turn away from "Christians" who have a form of godliness, but deny the power thereof in 2 Timothy 3:5. Any Christian who does not accept the power of God to transform even the homosexual is sadly underestimating His grace and cannot fully appreciate, nor fully benefit from, the gospel, which I discovered to be stated very simply in Matthew 1:21: ". . . thou shalt call his name JESUS for he shall save his people *from* their sins." (Emphasis mine) He shall save *even me* from *my* sins!! *From* my homosexuality!!

Our loving God is the Author of, and Creator of the plan of salvation. We cannot alter that plan in any way, for it is perfect, just as the law of the Lord is perfect, and just as God Himself is perfect. Our role in the plan of salvation is to *choose* to accept it, or *choose* to reject it. And the only way we can make the correct choice is to recognize our need of a Savior.

Do we really need to be saved? Yes, of course. From what? From sin. From what sin? For some it may be from intemperance: alcohol, tobacco, drugs, and gluttony. For others it may be dishonesty, or bad temper, or having other gods, as the god of this world and its goods. For still others it may be adultery—sex *of any kind* outside of the marriage of God's design and creation.

Some may look at homosexuality as being a greater sin than cheating on a spouse or pre-marital sex, but God does not. Sin is sin, the wages thereof being eternal death. However, three sins *are* stated to be especially offensive to God, (homosexuality not included . . .). They are pride, selfishness, and covetousness (*Testimonies for the Church,* 5:337), for it seems these are the roots of all other sin. These are the sins that festered in the heart of the covering cherub and eventually made a devil out of Lucifer.

### Discovering Victory Through Christ

My continued study revealed that in order for one to overcome homosexuality, or any other besetting sin, he must first develop a hatred for sin and a love for truth and righteousness (doing what is right by God's standard). Jesus promised Satan, "I will put enmity (hatred) between thee and the woman" (Genesis 3:15).

The beautiful thing about this promise is that Jesus says He will develop within us that hatred, if we permit Him to, if we ask Him to. "For it is [He] which worketh in you both to will and to do of his good pleasure." And we can be confident "of this very thing, that he which hath begun a good work in you will perform it until the day of Jesus Christ." (Philippians 2:13; 1:6) Jesus says "Ask, and it shall be given you . . ." (Matthew 7:7).

If we choose to not permit this transformation within ourselves, and receive not the love of the truth, that we might be saved, God Himself shall send us strong delusion, that we should believe a lie, ["sin and live"?] who believe not the truth, but have pleasure in unrighteousness [what is right by our own standard]. See 2 Thessalonians 2:10-12.

Also, if we choose not the miraculous transformation and re-creation work of God in our lives, He will eventually give us "over to a reprobate mind . . ." (Romans 1:28)

I was given the assurance in 1 Corinthians 6:9-11 that I could be cured of my homosexuality. Changed! Re-created! For Paul speaks of this very sin, among others, when he says, "And such *were* some of you (past tense): but ye *are* washed (present tense), but ye *are* sanctified, but ye *are* justified . . ." How? "In the name of the Lord Jesus and by the Spirit of our God."

What a wonderful promise to someone who has permitted the Lord to give him a hatred for his sin and a longing desire for truth and victory!

As I continued my self-evaluation, I began to realize more and more that I had been deceived into thinking I was living a life of freedom, when in actuality I was in terrible bondage. Freedom from God's law is not freedom at all. James 1:5 refers to God's law as "the perfect law of liberty," and I began to see that it was freedom from sin that I desperately needed, not freedom from God's law. Yet, I was totally helpless to set myself free. I truly needed a Savior and salvation *from* my bondage of sin, my addictive sexual perversion.

It was presumptuous of me to continue living as though I had the gift of eternal life while knowingly earning the wages of sin—death. In honestly facing eternal realities, I was convicted that my life had to be changed. Yet, I knew I was powerless to make that change in and of myself.

God, however, is not powerless. He is the omnipotent Re-Creator. So, trusting in His Word, I decided to step out in faith and depend upon the promise of Jesus Christ to save His people from their sins.

Today I understand that, of all Bible-believing Christians, only Seventh-day Adventists have the message of real, lasting hope in the message of salvation from sin. For, any religious denomination, or person, teaching that we can practice breaking any one of God's Ten Commandments and still have eternal life cannot consistently show the homosexual the way to victory over his sin.

And Seventh-day Adventists who believe God is impotent to save the homosexual from his/her sin will .find themselves impotent in explaining to non-Adventists why keeping the Sabbath is important. For Sabbath-keeping is a witness that we serve the Omnipotent Creator God, the all-powerful Re-Creator God who can and will save His people personally *from* their sins—even those especially offensive sins: pride, selfishness, and covetousness. . . .

**Facing Skepticism and Doubt**

Once having come back to the Lord, imagine my distress over hearing of Seventh-day Adventist ministers and laity alike discrediting my experience by saying, "Sure, I believe in victory over sin. But *that* kind can never change! Furthermore, I advise you to keep your children away from him." Or, "I've never known anyone coming out of the "gay" lifestyle who has ever been able to remain straight for more than two years!"

Is this not a lack of faith manifested toward God? Is this not revealing in the "believer" a *form* of godliness, denying the power thereof?"

Frequently I am faced with questions such as:

1) Were feelings and emotions toward men miraculously changed upon conversion? Or,

2) Did the same gender orientation still persist? And,

3) Since conversion, has there been a radical change of attitude, a psychological change in sexual orientation?

These questions are of paramount importance for the sincere seeker for deliverance from besetting sin of whatever nature. And they deserve a definitive explanation.

In my autobiography[3] I tell the painful story of my exodus from the "gay" lifestyle. To be honest, it was the one most traumatic experience of my entire lifetime up to that point. I had to terminate my relationship with one in whom I was deeply in love. My feelings and emotions had not changed toward him at all. But my feelings and emotions toward the Man Jesus Christ had changed tremendously.

Being faced with a choice, based upon God's word of truth, I chose to follow the Man Jesus, regardless of consequences. Like the words of the famous hymn sung through the lips of every Christian, (but too often without comprehension), it was a matter of "Trust and Obey." I began to *trust* my Creator, realizing that "Father truly does know best." And in this ever increasing trust, I began to *obey* Him in spite of my feelings and emotions, knowing that His will for me was for my own present, as well as eternal, happiness and well-being. God's children are instructed that the just shall live by faith, not by feelings and emotions!

In practicing this Biblical principle, I discovered that right feelings and emotions did not come first, but later, as a result of my accepting by faith the will of my Creator. If we wait until we have victory over feelings and emotions before trusting and obeying Christ, then what need have we of a Savior . . . ? And what is the purpose of faith?

Choosing to leave behind the love of my life, to be born again as a helpless, newborn babe, I entered my new world. As an infant begins his life with inherited tendencies to evil, I began my new life in the family of God with all the same tendencies I had cultivated my entire previous life, i.e., homosexuality, drinking, smoking, dancing, love of the world and its entertainment, perverted appetite, ad infinitum.

However, looking to Jesus and God my Father, I *renounced* my homosexuality and all these things of the world, and I *submitted* to His divine upbringing within the family of God.

Am I ever tempted in these areas?

Is Satan still alive and well . . . ?

**All-Sufficient Grace**

To this day, every time someone lights up a cigarette near me, I am attracted to the smell; attracted to that which used to repulse me but for which I purposely created and cultivated a taste and tendency. But I choose not to smoke. And God's grace is all-sufficient.

To this day, the smell of freshly brewed coffee, or the thought of an icy margarita, work to arouse within me an old cultivated tendency to indulgence. But I choose not to drink. And God's grace is all-sufficient.

To this day, when encountered, the music of the world pulls and tugs at me, luring me back, making my happy feet want to dance. So I avoid it and replace it with music that uplifts. When faced with worldly "gospel" music in the church, I am made extremely uncomfortable. But God's grace is all-sufficient.

To this day, I do not trust myself to walk into a "gay" bar or nightclub or to socialize with practicing homosexuals. I do not trust myself to go where God does not lead, where I cannot be assured of His companionship and protection. Instead, I enjoy the companionship of my wife and fill my life with associations that can receive the favor and blessing of God. And His grace is all-sufficient.

However, to say that I am above temptation in any of the areas of sin cultivated by years of indulgence would be to give false hope to others desperately seeking salvation from like besetting sins. It was just such expectation during my youth, that of being delivered from temptation, that caused me to give up on God in the first place and to plunge headlong into a life of sin, misery, and woe.

God has not promised to save His people from their temptations. He has promised to save His people from their sins, from giving in to those temptations. And it is not an admission of failure for one to admit the continued existence of inherited, created, and cultivated tendencies to evil—infirmities. A lack of these tendencies would be to have "holy flesh."

"And he said unto me, My grace is sufficient for thee: for my strength is made perfect in weakness. Most gladly therefore will I rather glory in my infirmities, that the power of Christ may rest upon me." (2 Corinthians 12:9)

To this day, I must choose daily whom I will serve.

To this day, like the apostle Paul, I must "keep under my body, and bring it into subjection: lest that by any means, when I have preached to others, I myself should be a castaway." (1 Corinthians 9:27)

To this day, I realize the importance of protecting my environment. I must starve the old evil tendencies while feeding and nurturing the new nature. Evil must be replaced with good. Perverted feelings and emotions can be starved out and replaced by righteous ones as I trustingly and self-*less*-ly follow the instructions laid out for me in the "Operator's Manual" given by the Creator of sexuality.

Just as when fleeing from God years earlier, turning my back upon everything and everyone I knew, in coming back to God I had to separate myself totally from the gay scene and lifestyle, fleeing, as it were, Sodom and Gomorrah for my very life. In starting a new life, I surrounded myself with everything I *knew* to be right for me, which was not everything I *felt* like having around me . . . ! No Christian should risk depending upon what feels right. Neither could I. "Come now; let us reason together," God says. As children created in the image of God we are to use that marvelous gift of reason and the power of choice. The spiritual mind is to rule over and bring into subjection the lusts of the flesh.

To this day, like any other Christian, I must guard well all the avenues to my soul. God's grace, (His strength and power), as promised, is sufficient for His child the homosexual, enabling him also to bring "into captivity every thought to the obedience of Christ" (2 Corinthians 10:15), and to have complete and total victory over his sin of homosexuality.

Based upon my experience and study of God's word, I have outlined in my book specific sequential steps that a person can take to experience freedom from the bondage of besetting sin, including the sin of homosexuality.[4]

As a result of putting into practice these and other Biblical principles, I have become totally comfortable in my new life as an *ex*-gay heterosexual. The thought of returning to my old life has become foreign and repugnant to me. Submitting myself to divine reconditioning and therapy has truly resulted in a new creation. And I rejoice in the words of Paul that I have experienced in my own personal life, "Therefore if any man be in

Christ, he is a new creature: old things are passed away; behold, all things are become new. (2 Cor.5:17)

Why should we as Christians doubt that this promise can be true for the homosexual as well as for anyone else? Every day I live victoriously in my new heterosexual life I testify to the power of God to save His people from their sins. And I praise Him for the privilege to have this demonstration of His grace played out through my own personal experience.

Our Savior has commissioned me in the same words He spoke to the cleansed demoniac in Mark 5:19, "Go home to thy friends, and tell them how great things the Lord hath done for thee, and hath had compassion on thee." Accordingly, my life of falling from grace to the depths of degradation, and rising to new life through Jesus Christ has now been published to His glory as a "How To" autobiography: "'*That* Kind Can Never Change!' Can They . . . ?"[5]

This story is meant to be of assistance to homosexuals in need; to parents, family and friends in distress; to pastors and counselors in search of answers; and for anyone struggling with besetting sins of whatever nature.

Not through human reasoning, logic, philosophy and counseling was I able to change; but through the Word of God and the power of Jesus Christ to save His people from their sins, according to His promise. By God's grace, this homosexual prodigal child of God has been delivered from his sin and redirected into a productive and fruitful new life as a Seventh-day Adventist minister of the gospel, happily married, with children.

I praise the Lord for the great things He has done for me, and for His compassion towards me, for His mercy and patience, and for His marvelous power to save even me from my life of sin!

"*That* kind can never change! Can they . . . ?," some may question.

Yes, they can! Homosexuals are God's children, too! To them, as to every other child of God in need of a Savior, is the promise given, "Thou shalt call his name JESUS: for he shall save his people from their sins" (Matthew 1:21, emphasis mine).

---

**Endnotes**

[1]A modified version of the current testimony has already been circulated on the Internet. This is, however, the full, unedited version.

[2]Readers who are familiar with what is being published in our church publications will recognize that this title is a direct response to the article by Kate McLaughlin (pseudonym),

"Are Homosexuals God's Children?" *Adventist Review,* April 3, 1997, 26-29. McLaughlin has also publicized her views in other church publications. See, for example, her "A Homosexual in My Congregation?" *Ministry,* November 1996, 10-11, 29; and "When Your Child Doesn't Choose Your Lifestyle," *Women of Spirit,* Spring 1995. Views similar to the above have been articulated in *Insight*, December 5, 1992, pp. 1-16; Phillip Whidden, "Gays, Gabriel, and Dynamo Truth," in the *Collegiate Quarterly* (January-March 2000), 97; Jim Miller (as told to Celeste Ryan), "I'm Homosexual, I'm Adventist, and I have AIDS: The Jim Miller Story," *Adventist View*, Winter 1993, 9, 15; Beth Schaefer, "Homosexual Warfare," *View,* Special 1999 issue, 18-21; Tessa Willow (pseudonym), "Still Our Son," *Women of Spirit,* May-June 2000; Katie Tonn-Oliver, "Virginia Cason: More Than A Daughter," *Women of Spirit,* Winter 1996. Occasionally, the published works take the form of well-crafted interviews with Adventist homosexuals. See, for example, Bruce Moyer's interview with Ron (pseudonym), "A Cry from the Valley of Death," *Ministry*, November 1996, 23-25, 29; Reni Dupertuis's interview with Donald J. Freeman, "To Every Nation, Tongue and People (Including Sexual Orientation)," *Scanner* [a publication of the Glendale City, California, SDA Church], Winter 1999, 9-11.

[3]Victor J. Adamson (pseudonym), *"That Kind Can Never Change!" Can They . . . ?: One Man's Struggle with His Homosexuality* (Lafayette, Louisiana: Huntington House Publishers, 2000). Available through 800-749-4009. Also available through the Adventist Book Center.

[4]Read about this in the next chapter of *Must We Be Silent?* ("You, Too, Can Be Made Whole!").

[5]Victor J. Adamson (pseudonym), *"That Kind Can Never Change!" Can They . . . ?: One Man's Struggle with His Homosexuality* (Lafayette, Louisiana: Huntington House Publishers, 2000). Available through 800-749-4009. Also available through the Adventist Book Center.

# 8

# YOU, TOO, CAN BE MADE WHOLE!

All sin is *generic* to the human species, including the sin of homosexuality, but no sin is *genetic.* Because it is a function of choice, God holds everyone accountable for it. To overcome the tendency to sin, the sinner must be transformed: 'Therefore if any man is in Christ, he is a new creature; the old things passed away behold, new things have come (2 Cor. 5:17)."[1]

But what specific steps can a person take to experience freedom from the bondage of sin, including homosexual sin?

This final chapter of our discussion of the ideology of homosexuality is a continuation of the previous one. Written by an ex-homosexual who is currently a Seventh-day Adventist minister, it offers some practical suggestions to assist pastors and counselors, family and friends, the homosexual himself, and any person struggling with seemingly insurmountable besetting sins of whatever nature.

### "That Kind Can Never Change!"

Considering my having been born into and raised within a Seventh-day Adventist Christian home, please try to imagine the anxiety, the frustration, and the despair I experienced through childhood and youth growing into the realization that I was homosexual. Why! No one I knew was attracted sexually to another of his own gender! And, clearly, from the Word of God, homosexuality was condemned.

Being ashamed of my sexual orientation, I tried desperately to hide my true feelings and emotions, and practiced living a lie. But deep inside, this thing festered until one day it ruptured, and I came "out of the closet" to openly live the homosexual lifestyle. My family was devastated, and my home was broken.

However, before terminating our marriage, my wife and I counseled with a number of Seventh-day Adventist professionals. Sadly, no one was able to help me. The psychiatrists advised my wife, in essence, that "That kind can never change," and that she should then seek counseling for herself. Two very prominent Seventh-day Adventist ministers counseled with my wife alone. Without ever contacting me to offer counseling, they both advised her to divorce me, because "That kind can never change . . . !"

In hopeless despair, I turned my back upon my God, my church, my friends, and my family. For the next sixteen years I blamed God for all the heartache, pain, and suffering that I caused others and that I experienced myself, believing that I could not be changed.

However, in total selfless love and compassion for me, God followed me and would not let me go without giving His all. In my book, *"'That Kind Can Never Change!' Can They . . . ?,"* I share the story of my life, my fall from grace, the feelings and emotions of being trapped in a lifestyle some call "gay," a lifestyle of unfulfilled expectations, guilt, shame, hopelessness, and despair. I also share the story of my conversion, and rehabilitation, and my "Jonah Call" into the ministry I had fled in my youth. Most importantly, however, I share the "how to's" of victory in Jesus for homosexuals, (and other sinners), based upon my own personal experience, study, and application.[2]

The attitude expressed in the title quote, "That Kind Can Never Change!", is held by many Christians today in regard to the homosexual in particular, but this attitude could also extend to those of any socially unacceptable besetting sin or lifestyle. This title is based upon an unfortunate direct pronouncement against and denouncement of me by a local pastor one year after my conversion; a pastor who just could not believe that even God could change someone like the homosexual. The same point was made repeatedly by an elder of my local church two years after my conversion.

Such Seventh-day Adventist Christians need to understand that their faith may be no more than a mere "form of godliness, denying the power thereof."

May the same come to know and understand our God as being mighty to save; even to the uttermost. "Whosoever" includes the homosexual.

While elements within our own church choose to remain silent upon this subject, or to even promote the idea that our church needs to revise its stand on this issue, non-Adventist Christian and secular talk shows alike around the country are promoting the message of my book, bravely taking a public stand and speaking out for victory over homosexuality through Jesus Christ.

I know of 109 ministries in 40 countries working successfully to save the homosexual from his lifestyle of sin. Numerous gays have responded and now bravely give their testimonies of victory in newsletters from these ministries.[3]

Must our church be silent . . . ?!

We are the repositories of God's law! Who better should be able to assist the homosexual sinner overcome his sin than we?!

The following excerpt from my book is entitled "You, Too, Can Be Made Whole." Laying out the sequential steps to victory that worked for me, a homosexual, it is meant to be of assistance to pastors and counselors, family and friends, the homosexual himself, and any person struggling with seemingly insurmountable besetting sins of whatever nature. Jesus' plan of salvation is for the "whosoevers." For He came to save His people from their sins, not in their sins, and to save to the uttermost. Yes! Even you, dear reader . . .

**"You, Too, Can Be Made Whole!"** [4]

"I've never known anyone coming from a homosexual lifestyle that has ever been able to remain straight for more than two years!"

"Sure, I believe in victory over sin. But that kind can never change!"

"You'd better keep your children away from him . . . !"

"I've been a preacher for forty years, and I've never met a perfect person yet!"

If you are a sin sick soul seeking deliverance from bondage in this life, how do remarks such as these affect you? Do they give you hope, or leave you despondent and in despair?

Statements such as these coming from the mouths of some Christians reveal their focus to be upon the ability and works of man, the sinner, the helpless victim, rather than upon the omnipotent ability and works of the Savior. They unwittingly portray God as impotent, rather than omnipotent. He it is who has promised to save you, dear reader, from sin. He it is who has promised to cleanse you, to work within you, to perform that good work He has begun in you until the day of Jesus Christ, to keep you from falling and to present you faultless. He it is that paid the infinite price for your redemption. He has a vested interest in you and will finish what He has started, if you only will stop resisting Him. He is the Alpha and the Omega, the first and the last, the beginning and the end. He is not a quitter!

Without this understanding, what hope does the Christian have to offer any sin sick soul who wants deliverance *in this life* from the bondage of sin? Without this understanding, the best the Christian can portray to the world is a *form* of godliness, denying the *power* thereof. The call for repentance can be heard from every pulpit in the land, but when a homosexual repents, too many Christians reveal their lack of faith in the God of love Who is mighty to save *to the uttermost*, and express doubt in the ability of the victim to be saved by the Savior.

As I by God's grace was leaving behind my homosexual life, a gay friend of mine who himself had been a pastor for several years made the following statement. "Jesse, I'm going to be keeping my eye on you. If you last for two years in the straight world, then I'll believe that just maybe I would be able to do the same."

I pray to God that this dear friend of the past will somehow find this book in his hands, for at the time of publication of this book, it will have been *nine* years of victorious living for me.

Friend, you, too, can be made whole!

May the following suggestions help you find restoration and victory at last, even as they have been so sustaining for me.

**1. Know, and believe:** first of all **that "God is love"** (1 John 4:8). Know and believe that whoever you are, whatever you are, God loves you unconditionally, just as you are. For God the Father so loved you, the homosexual, that He gave His only begotten son, that *whosoever* believeth in Him, (whosoever means even the homosexual), should not perish, but have everlasting life (John 3:16). He loved the world, as it was, and poured out His love upon the world in the gift of His son, demonstrating and revealing that incomprehensible love, while the world was still in rebellion. His love has been manifested toward you, the sinner, the homosexual, in that while you are yet at odds with Him and His will for you; yes, even while you see Him as the enemy, blaming Him for everything wrong in your life; even while in this attitude of enmity towards Him, He poured out His love for you in the gift of His Son.

"For when we were yet without strength, in due time Christ died for the ungodly. [That is you!] But God commendeth his love toward us, in that, while we were yet sinners, Christ died for us. . . . when we were enemies, we were reconciled to God by the death of his Son. . . ." (Romans 5:6, 8, 10).

God the Father paid the redemptive price for you, which just happens to be the infinite cost of His own Son, knowing who and what you are before you were ever born. As with Jeremiah, He can say of you, "Before I formed thee in the belly, I knew thee."

"Not only that, knowing that you would become homosexual, I paid the redemptive price for you, allowed you to be born, loving you anyway and wanting to spend eternity with you. Therefore, I have preserved you in life with a stay of execution provided by My only begotten Son, even though you have been totally out of sync with my plan for you up to this point. But, if you will slow down and look at Me, comprehend how much I love you, and allow Me the opportunity, I can and will save you personally from your lifestyle of sin. I can heal you, recreate you, wash you and make you clean. It is your choice. May I have you for my very own . . . ?"

Dear reader, God is love, and He loves you with an immeasurable love, regardless of whether you love Him back or not. In the end, the lake of fire of Revelation 20:10,13 will be the final resting place for billions of people whom God loves unconditionally. But they have rejected that love, refusing to respond by allowing Him to prepare them with a fitness to dwell in His presence for all eternity. Sin is consumed in His presence. If it is enthroned in the heart, the soul will be consumed with the sin.

**2. Now, step up to the mirror and face yourself.** Do not be afraid to take an honest look at who and what you really are. Eternal Reality is the real issue to consider. If you are truly OK, then it doesn't hurt to examine yourself closely. Truth can bear scrutiny. So scrutinize your condition and your position.

Jesus invites you with great love, compassion, and sincere personal interest in you, *whosoever* you may be: "Come now, and *let us reason together."*

He pleads with you, "Though your sins be as scarlet, don't be afraid to come to me; they shall be as white as snow, I promise; though they be red like crimson, don't refuse me; they shall be as wool, I promise. If you be willing and obedient, you shall eat the good of the land, I promise: But *only* if you refuse and rebel in determined stubbornness and self-deception, shall you be devoured. . . ." (Isaiah 1:18, 19; paraphrased and personalized).

**3. Acknowledge: who and what you really are.** Face up to it; you are a sinner. "For all have sinned and come short of the glory of God" (Rom 3:23). Don't deny it, for you will only be deceiving yourself to your own eternal ruin.

"Only acknowledge thine iniquity, that thou hast transgressed against the Lord thy God . . . Turn, O backsliding children, saith the Lord; for I am married unto you . . . You have perverted your way and forgotten the Lord your God. Return, ye backsliding children. Come back to me, and I will heal your backslidings" (Jer 3:13, 14, 21, 22; paraphrased).

If you will but confess your sin, God is faithful and just to not only forgive you of your sin, but to also cleanse you from *all* unrighteousness; to change you; to recreate you into His image, into His character (1John 1:9).

**4. Realize:** The wages of your sin is no greater nor less than the wages of the sins of others who may have a particular disdain for your particular besetting sin. For the wages of any sin is death. . . . Yes, the Bible does call homosexuality abomination. The Bible seems to call all sin abomination. Notice:

"If a man also lie with mankind, as he lieth with a woman, both of them have committed an abomination" (Lev. 20:13; & 18:22)

Other abominations: idolatry (Deut. 13:14); an impure sacrifice (Deut. 17:1); occultic practices (Deut. 18:10-12); wearing that which pertaineth to the opposite sex (Deut. 22:5); certain remarriages to former spouses (Deut. 24:4); dishonesty (Deut. 25:13-16); perverse behavior (Deut. 3:32); A proud look, a lying tongue, murder, wicked imaginations, mischief, false witness that speaks lies, and he that sows discord among brethren (Pro. 6:16-19); justifying evil and condemning the just (Pro. 17:15); adultery (Eze. 22:11).

It should especially be noticed in this line up of abominations that adultery of *any kind* is included. The heterosexual sinner need not look down his nose with condescension upon the homosexual sinner, for *any* sexual behavior outside the marriage institution as designed and created by God is sin; abomination. In short, we all need a Savior from sin and from abomination of one kind or another.

**5. Understand:** If you are homosexual, *it matters not how you became so.* Being *born* homosexual, *choosing* to be so, or being environmentally *conditioned* to be so is not the issue that should really be of concern. Rather, how do we arouse you, the homosexual, to your need, if there is one; and how do we answer to that *need*, regardless of how and why you happen to be what you are? Do we just accept homosexuality in ourselves or in others as an acceptable alternative lifestyle, or do we see a need for redirection, and a means to accomplish that end? Is the issue of homosexuality a salvation issue or is it a non-issue? Is it an "eternal reality" issue? Did Jesus come to save the homosexual *in* his homosexuality, or *from* his homosexuality? (Matt 1:21).

Perhaps a simple little allegory can illustrate this point:

A person floundering helplessly in the stormy sea is happened upon by a lifeboat. As it draws up alongside the helpless victim, before throwing out the lifeline the life guard calls out to him over the din of the screaming wind and billowing waves the qualifying questions, "How did you get yourself into this predicament anyway? Did you fall off your boat, or did you jump in? Did someone playfully push you into the sea, or did someone maliciously throw you in? Is it my fault that you are drowning in this sea? Is it something I have done . . . ? Are you in this plight against your will, of no fault of your own, or did you *choose* to swim out here of your own volition?

The spitting, sputtering victim weakly calls back, "No! I did not *choose* to be this way!"

Having now qualified the drowning victim, the all important questions being answered, the lifeguard skillfully throws out the lifeline, only to see the victim refuse to grab hold.

"Take hold!" shouts the lifeguard.

"What's the use?" calls back the drowning victim. "I didn't *choose* to be in this quandary!"

And so the allegory ends, in tragedy.

In just such a light, many homosexuals and heterosexuals alike view their own state in life. More grievous than this, so do many people picture Jesus the Lifeguard and His plan of salvation, as qualifying the victim first, as if God cannot, or chooses not, to save to the uttermost . . . !

The *good news,* however, is: Unlike the allegory above, Jesus cares not how you became the homosexual, or sinner, that you may be! Whether you be in denial, latent, "in the closet", openly gay, "married", militant, or even a "flaming queen," the fact still remains: if you are a homosexual, you are a sinner. However, Jesus is mighty to save *you.* He has come as the Lifeguard, asking no questions, except "Will you take my hand?"

"Come unto me", he says, "and I will give you rest."

God's re-creative plan of salvation and redemption is as much for the homosexual, sin sick and desperate for deliverance, as it is for any other element of society, all of whom were born with inherited tendencies to sin of one kind or another that were later cultivated.

Every baby ever born was born with a *self-centered* nature that must be overcome if he is to become fit for the kingdom of heaven and God. Every person on earth living in sin of any kind is only doing that which comes naturally from a heart centered in self-gratification: the murderer, the liar, the thief, the drug addict, the whoremonger, the street walker, the alcoholic, the smoker, the overeater, the cheating spouse, the promiscuous teenager, the idolater seeking to avenge an angry god or working for reward, the Christian likewise obeying God in fear of punishment or hope of reward . . . ; all are allowing "self" to be their rule of faith and practice.

Homosexuality is but one of many fruits, or manifestations, of the innocuous root of "self." Self-gratification is paramount in this sexual orientation. Pride is also very rooted in the heart of the homosexual; as is covetousness, wanting that which God has forbidden us to have. Like the forbidden fruit in the garden of Eden, homosexual behavior is forbidden by the explicit word of God.

Three sins especially offensive to God are pride, selfishness, and covetousness. Why? They are not so easily detected because they are the hidden roots of all other sins. They are the sins of the heart that manifest themselves, perhaps, many years later in outward "fruit". They are the sins that festered in the heart of Lucifer in heaven that worked so successfully to deceive his own self and one third of all the angels of heaven who stood in the very presence of God Almighty. They are the sins that eventually made a devil out of Lucifer and broke the heart of God. Is it any wonder then that these sins are so offensive to Him?

Recognizing your need, dear reader, will be a major accomplishment, a major stepping stone, on your road to restoration.

**6. Accept the fact: It's all about choices.** God created everyone of us with the power of choice. This is the only barrier He cannot and will not cross, the only obstacle He cannot surmount in your behalf. He must have your permission to wash you, to make you clean, to create within you a clean heart, and to renew a right spirit within you; to re-create you. Ask, dear reader, and you shall receive!

Never forget that you are in good Company. Jesus Himself had also to choose to follow His Father's will. The warfare against self is the greatest battle ever fought.

"If any man will come after me, let him deny himself, and take up his cross daily, and follow me" (Luke 9:23). If He asks you to follow Him in daily self-denial, then He also had to daily practice denial of self.

"I can of mine own self do nothing:" He says, ". . . I seek not mine own will, but the will of the Father which hath sent me" (John 5:30).

"O my Father, if it be possible, let this cup pass from me: nevertheless not as I will, but as thou wilt." (Matthew 26:39) "Not as I want," He said, "but as You want." And this in agony of soul, struggling against His own will in Gethsemane.

Jesus' daily victory was based upon His daily choices, sustained by the power afforded Him from God, even as the same is promised to you and me through the working of the Holy Spirit in the life.

**7. Walk with God:** It is vital that you develop and maintain a relationship with God through communion with Him in prayer and Bible study. He is the power Source for your victorious life. As your Creator, He has self-less love for you and the power to recreate you into His own image. Daily devotion time, plugging in, making that connection with Him, is of utmost importance, for in no other way can you really get to know and appreciate Him and tap into His strength.

This was the secret of success for Daniel, of whom there is no recorded sin in the Bible, though we know that "all [including Daniel] have sinned, and come short of the glory of God" (Rom 3:23) Evidently, Daniel was an overcomer, living the victorious life as one who had been made whole. What was his practice in this respect? "Now when Daniel knew that the writing was signed, he went into his house; and his windows being open in his chamber toward Jerusalem, he kneeled upon his knees three times a day, and prayed, and gave thanks before his God, as he did aforetime" (Dan 6:10).

Apparently, Daniel spent as much time and frequency in communing with God, his power Source, feeding himself spiritually, as he spent in feeding himself physically.

Enoch is another example of one who maintained victory through a close connection with his power Source. "And Enoch walked with God: and he was not; for God took him" (Gen 5:24).

You, too, can have what Enoch had. You, too, can have Christ as your constant companion. Enoch walked with God, and when assaulted by the enemy with temptation, he could talk with Him about it. He made God his confidant and counselor, maintaining a close relationship with Him. While trusting in your heavenly Father for the help you may need, He will not leave you. God has a heaven full of blessings that He wants to bestow upon you, if you are earnestly seeking for that help which only He can give. It was in looking by faith to Jesus, in asking Him in prayer, in believing that every word spoken by God would be verified, that Enoch walked with God. He kept close by the side of God, obeying His every word. Christ was his companion, and He longs to be yours.

**8. Protect your environment:** Guard well the avenues to your soul. Do not place yourself in the path of temptation. Be careful what you watch, what you read, what you behold, what you hear. Give Satan no advantage over you. "Whatsoever things are true, . . . honest, . . . just, whatsoever things are pure, . . . lovely, . . . of good report; if there be any virtue, and if there be any praise, think on these things" (Phil 4:8).

And when Satan plants those impure thoughts and desires into your heart, (and he will . . . !), Paul bids you take every thought captive, ". . . bringing into captivity every thought to the obedience of Christ" (2 Cor 10:5). Use your power of choice to "change the subject." God will help you do this, if you choose.

"Submit [yourself] therefore to God. Resist the devil, and he will flee from you." (James 4:7)

**9. Immerse yourself: into the context of Scripture.** Personalize it as in the following example using Isaiah 53:3-7,11,12:

> As I in my homosexuality was despised and rejected by society, even so, and because of me, Jesus was despised and rejected of men; As I sorrowed and grieved over losing my children because

of my bondage to sin, even so Jesus was a man of sorrows, and acquainted with my personal grief: and, not appreciating his empathy and sympathy, I hid as it were my face from him; I turned my back to him and walked away, blaming Him for every consequence of my own bad choices. But, and nonetheless, as a willing substitute for me, he was really the one despised, and I never realized it.

Surely he has borne my griefs, and carried my sorrows: yet I did not appreciate his being stricken, smitten of God, and afflicted for the sake of my falling into the sin of homosexuality.

But he was wounded for my transgressions of the seventh commandment of His law, he was bruised for the sake of my lifestyle of sin: the somewhat peace of mind I experienced by giving up the battle resulted in reproach upon him; and, looking to the cross, realizing the infinite self-less love for me that put him there, beholding his bruised and bleeding body in my place, all this has brought healing to me, reconciliation toward him. For, how could I not respond to that incomprehensible totally self-less love manifested towards me even while I have maintained my rebellion against him?!

All of us, not just the homosexual, but all of us like sheep have gone astray in one way or another; we have turned every one to his own way. We are all naturally self-centered; and the Lord has laid on Jesus the iniquities of every one of us.

He was oppressed as some of us are, and for our sakes; and he was afflicted as some of us are, and for our sakes; yet he opened not his mouth in complaint, but endured willingly anticipating the joy of seeing me respond and return to him in love and appreciation. He is brought as an innocent, obedient, compliant lamb to the slaughter, and as a sheep before her shearers is dumb, so he opened not his mouth in self-defense, or seeking self-preservation.

He shall see the results someday of the travail, the anguish, the heartache, the suffering and misery of his soul, and shall be satisfied, as I finally respond with a heart appreciation that will cause me to live no longer for self-exaltation, self-ambition, and self-gratification. No! But to honor him, to exalt him, to gratify his self-less will for the good of his creation. Through a knowledge and understanding of what he has done for all mankind, including homosexuals, many shall be brought back into a right relationship with their Creator; that means many homosexuals shall also be brought back into a right relationship with their Creator; for he shall bear their iniquities, the wages of which is the second, or eternal, death.

He was numbered with the transgressors, with the likes of you and me, homosexual sinners and heterosexual sinners, yet he did not participate in our sinful behavior. He did, however, bare the sin of every one of us, and made intercession, arbitration, intervention for us the disobedient ones.

Another one:

"Therefore if any man be in Christ. . . . 'Any man' must include me, the homosexual! Then I, too, am a new creature: old things are passed away; behold, all things are become new. And now all things are of God, now according to his will and pleasure, not my own; God, who hath reconciled us to himself by Jesus Christ, and hath given to us the ministry of reconciliation" (2 Corinthians 5:18; paraphrased and personalized).

**10. Act: upon His word. There is power in the word of God.** "And God said, Let there be light: and there was light . . ." (Gen 1:3)

"For he spake, and it was done; he commanded, and it stood fast" (Ps 33:9).

"The just shall live by faith" (Heb 10:38) we are told. Faith in what? Faith in the Word, Jesus Christ.

When Jesus spoke to Mary, saying "Neither do I condemn thee: go, and sin no more" (John 8:11), she was enabled by faith in His word.

"There hath no temptation taken you but such as is common to man: but God is faithful, who will not suffer you to be tempted above that ye are able; but will with the temptation also make a way to escape that ye may be able to bear it" (1 Cor 10:13)

"Now unto him that is able to do exceeding abundantly above all that we ask or think, according to the power that worketh in us" (Eph 3:20).

"I can do all things through Christ which strengtheneth me" (Phil 4:13).

". . . Greater is he that is in you, than he that is in the world" (1 John 4:4).

*All* God's biddings, dear reader, are enablings. So, take these and other promises of the Word and act upon them.

**11. Be grateful:** Accept with gratitude that which God *has* offered you. In the Garden of Eden, God created an helpmeet for Adam: a woman. In His infinite wisdom and love for the well-being of man, He gave him the gift of a woman to be by his side. There was no alternative. So, did God make a mistake? Did He not know what He was doing? Did He somehow not understand the needs of the man He Himself had just created?

I have children. While on one of my recent engagements overseas I went to great lengths to find what I thought would be a very special surprise for them. I searched in each country I visited for what I had in mind. Finally, I found them. Arriving home at the airport, I had them sticking out the top of my backpack.

"What's that?" they both asked excitedly.

"I have a surprise for you," I said.

"What is it?" they jumped up and down in excitement.

I took down my back pack and gave them each a doll. Little Heidi I gave to my little girl, and little Peter I gave to my little boy. I just knew they would both love these little treasures, because they both played house and "mommy and daddy" with little dolls all the time.

"I don't want it!" whispered my little boy.

"Why not?" I asked in surprise. "You are always wanting to play with your sister's little dolls, so I brought you one of your very own!"

"I don't like it" he answered. "I like hers."

"Well, I'm sorry," I said with great disappointment. "Heidi is for your sister."

My special gift purchased at such "great price . . ." and effort was spurned by my little boy. I had to put it away in the attic, hoping that someday he would appreciate it and want it. (I love him still; he is very dear and precious to me.)

Likewise, God went to great lengths to provide for man the wonderful gift of woman. Some of us have turned up our noses at this gift, and, instead, burn in our lust for one another. Does God stop loving us? No! Of course not. Does he give us the gift that he has created for someone else, that he has provided for the woman? No! It is with great disappointment that he sees man covet for himself what was meant by the Creator to be for the woman.

It is not a sin to do without the gift. But it is wrong for us men to covet what He has forbidden, that which was meant for the woman. It is equally wrong for the woman to lust and covet after another woman whom God has created for man.

"In everything give thanks: for this is the will of God in Christ Jesus concerning you" (1 Thessalonians 5:18).

"Rejoice in the Lord alway" (Philippians 4:4).

Be grateful for what God has provided for your best interest. Father truly knows best!

**12. The Secret to overcoming** the sin of homosexuality, or any other besetting sin, is in helping someone else to overcome his sin. This premise is based upon the heavenly principle for happiness: self-*less*-ness. True happiness comes in helping someone else be happy: Jesus first, Others second, Yourself last creates the acronym for JOY.

Joseph, far from home in the land of his captivity, never forgot this principle. "How can I do this great wickedness and sin against God?" he cried as he fled from the temptation of Potiphar's wife. His concern was not "fear of punishment," nor was it "hope of reward." No; for his faithfulness in obedience resulted in disgrace and confinement to the dungeon. Joseph's concern was a total self-*less* interest in the will and pleasure and honor of his God; regardless of consequences. He also loved and honored his master Potiphar, putting his interests above his own.

All the heavenly host is focused upon the happiness and well-being of others - yours, for example . . . ! All creation, except for sinful man, lives for the benefit of the rest of creation.

The apostle John gave us the concise formula for victory as follows:

"And they overcame him [the accuser of our brethren] by the blood of the Lamb, and by the word of their testimony . . ." (Revelation 12:11)

From the day of my deliverance and victory, I have lived to share the story of "the blood of the Lamb", the incomprehensible demonstration of the love of God for the likes of me that would constrain Him to give His only begotten Son that I, even I the homosexual, might have eternal life with Him! What a price! What love He has for me!

"By the word of my testimony" to others, this love and power of God is kept ever fresh in my own heart and mind. By beholding Him, I am daily changed and sustained in victory. In the face of such beautiful love, I can, like Joseph, respond to the tempter, "How can I do this great wickedness and sin against my God?"

Jesus told the cleansed Gadarene demoniac, "Go home to thy friends, and tell them how great things the Lord hath done for thee, and hath had compassion on thee." He has enjoined me to do the same, and through this book I have.

And I pass along to you, dear reader, this same commission. Now, why don't you also "Go home to thy friends, and tell them how great things the Lord hath done for thee, and hath had compassion on thee?"

When you hear someone say about you, or about someone else, "*That* kind can never change . . . !" Do not believe it, nor accept it. For, *you, too, can be made whole!*

**Benediction:**

> "Now the God of peace, that brought again from the dead our Lord Jesus, that great shepherd of the sheep, through the blood of the everlasting covenant, Make *you* perfect in *every* good work to do *his* will, working in *you* that which is well-pleasing in *his* sight, through Jesus Christ; to whom be glory for ever and ever. Amen." (Heb 13:20, 21; emphasis added)

---

**Endnotes**

[1]Donald J. Wold, *Out of Order: Homosexuality in the Bible and the Ancient Near East* (Grand Rapids: Baker, 1998), 212 (emphasis mine).

[2]Victor J. Adamson (psuedonym), *"That Kind Can Never Change!" Can They . . .?: One Man's Struggle with His Homosexuality* (Lafayette, Louisiana: Huntington House Publishers, 2000). The book is available through the Adventist Book Center and also through its publisher, 1-800-749-4009.

[3]Anyone wishing more information or seeking counsel may contact the following

sources: Exodus International North America, P.O. Box 77652, Seattle, WA 98177; Tel. 206-784-7799; Fax 206-784-7872; Internet: *www.exodusnorthamerica.org;* (2) Regeneration, P.O. Box 9830, Baltimore, MD 21284; (3) New Hope, P.O. Box 10246, San Rafael, CA 94912-0246; (4) Love in Action, P.O. Box 753307, Memphis, TN 38175; (5) Outpost, P.O. Box 15263, Minneapolis, MN 55415-0263.

[4]The discussion that follows is a slight modification of chapter 23 of Adamson's (psuedonym), *"That Kind Can Never Change!" Can They . . .?* ( 199-212). It is reproduced with the permission of the author and publisher.

*Is ordaining women as elders or pastors new light for the church? What strategies are being employed in the campaign for women's ordination? Is the practice biblical? Did women serve as pastors in early Adventist history? Did Ellen G. White ever call for women's ordination? Was she herself ordained? Must our churches ordain women as elders?*

Section II

# A GENDER AGENDA
## (The Ideology of Women's Ordination)

# 9

# A Brief Background

*"Numberless words need not be put upon paper to justify what speaks for itself and shines in its clearness. Truth is straight, plain, clear, and stands out boldly in its own defense; but it is not so with error. It is so winding and twisting that it needs a multitude of words to explain it in its crooked form"*

**—Ellen G. White**

"What is your view on women's ordination?" one of my seminary professors asked me several years ago.

"I have no position on the issue. It does not matter to me one way or the other," I responded, trying to hide the fact that up until that time I had not carefully studied the question.

In those days, my apathy was stronger than my conviction on this controversial theological issue. I prized the feeling of being neutral more than paying the price for taking a stand either for or against women's ordination. This explains why I chose the "neither for nor against" position.

But my professor would not let me remain neutral: "Would it matter to you if you discovered from the Bible and the writings of Ellen G. White that the ordination of women is right, fair, just, and essential to rightly representing God to the world, and that excluding women from ordination is a denial of their spiritual gifts and their call to ministry?"

A simple rhetorical question from a teacher. But, needless to say, it led me to become a believer in women's ordination. At that time, I saw the issue as a question of equality, justice, and fundamental fairness. Refusing to ordain women was, in my view, a form of discrimination. And didn't both the Bible and the writings of Ellen G. White teach that injustice was unchristian?

For about five years I enjoyed the fellowship, respect, and admiration of those with whom I was championing the cause of women's ordination. I was not a radical feminist nor an unbelieving liberal. I was a committed Seventh-day Adventist, upholding the tradition of the Protestant Reformers and Adventist pioneers in standing for what I thought was biblical truth. Our cause was right and our motives were noble.

But was the ordination of women as elders or pastors biblical? Do the Bible and Mrs. White's counsels really support it? Though my motives were noble, were they biblical? These questions ultimately led me, almost ten years ago, to change my mind on women's ordination.

I still believe that women have a legitimate place in the soul-winning ministry of the church and that the Seventh-day Adventist church should make provision to encourage a greater participation of women in ministry. I still believe that the church should show stronger support for the training of women at the Seminary and should offer adequate and fair remuneration to women for their labor and, in some cases (such as in team ministries), should authoritatively commission women for roles and duties that do not violate biblical teaching.

I still believe that, among many lines of ministry, women could be encouraged to participate in the study, teaching and preaching of the gospel in personal and public evangelism; to be involved in ministries of prayer, visitation, counseling, writing and singing; to labor as literature evangelists or health evangelists, to raise new churches; to minister to the needy; to serve in positions of responsibility that do not require ordination as elders or pastors; to serve as colleagues in partnership with ordained men at the various levels of the church organization; to teach in our institutions and seminaries; and above all, to minister to their children at home. But while I affirm the legitimacy of women in ministry, I do not believe that the Bible permits women to be ordained *as elders or pastors,* or that the writings of Mrs. White provide support for it.[1]

Even though today I no longer believe in the biblical correctness of women's ordination, I am grateful to my pro-ordination teacher for helping me realize that a true Adventist cannot (and must not) remain neutral on disputed theological issues. The world today may honor indifference to truth as a sign of open-mindedness, tolerance, or even maturity; but the Bible condemns the attitude as betrayal or cowardice.

In a real sense, the study I am about to undertake in this second section of *Must We Be Silent?* will explain why a Bible-believing Seventh-day

Adventist cannot legitimately support women's ordination. If my critique of pro-ordination arguments at times appears vigorous, it is because I'm disputing with my own earlier views.

**Must We Be Silent?** There are several reasons why we must not remain silent on the question of women's ordination. In the first place, ordaining women *as elders* is creating tensions, divisions, and conflicts in local congregations where advocates are imposing the practice upon loyal church members. These members feel that they are being forced to embrace, or acquiesce to, an unbiblical practice.

The issue has also been politicized in areas where women's ordination has been embraced as an issue of equal rights, fairness, or discrimination. Even after two overwhelming General Conference decisions rejecting the practice, some influential churches in the United States are unilaterally ordaining women *as pastors*. In places where the practice has been entrenched, it is very difficult for Adventists who oppose women's ordination to be hired or retained. The policy is usually unwritten, but those familiar with several situations can testify to the intolerant attitude toward, and sometimes the *a priori* exclusion of, those who uphold the long established Adventist position.

Moreover, emotions are very much involved. We all have close friends, relatives, or other persons who influence our lives and who relate to the issue in a certain way. We do not want to hurt them by taking an opposing view. Besides, many God-fearing and capable women are serving admirably as elders. Hence, questioning whether the ordination of women as elders is biblically proper is misconstrued as an affront to their effectiveness or character.

Finally, the widely promoted book, *Women in Ministry,* by 20 pro-ordination scholars at Andrews University, Berrien Springs, Michigan, is being hailed in certain quarters as providing the definitive biblical and historical basis for ordaining women as elders. Inasmuch as this work overthrows what Adventists have historically understood as the universal teaching of the Old Testament, New Testament, and early Seventh-day Adventist belief, we need to carefully investigate the book's findings.[2]

**What the Issues Are Not.** The issue of women's ordination is *not* a question of whether women and men are equal. Women and men are equal; neither is inferior to the other. Also, the issue should not be confused with whether women can serve in the ministry. Women have been called to the soul winning ministry as surely as have men. Finally, the issue in the women's ordination debate is not whether women can be ordained as elders but not as pastors. In the Bible they are essentially the same office, even though today we divide some of the ministerial responsibilities between elders (presbyters) and pastors (overseers).[3]

**What the Issues Are.** There are two major issues in the debate over women's ordination. First, does the equality of male and female do away with gender-role differences? While maintaining equality of being, has the Bible assigned a headship/leadership role to the man and a supportive role to the woman? If so, were these complementary roles established before or *after* the fall? Are these roles applicable only to the home, or are they also valid in the church? Second, does Scripture permit women in ministry to perform the oversight/leadership roles which ordained elders and/or pastors are called upon to exercise. Does the Bible teach that women in ministry may be ordained as elders and pastors?

Before taking up these questions in subsequent chapters, we must briefly explain the meaning and purpose of ordination.

### The Meaning and Purpose of Ordination

The New Testament teaches that the act of ordination, as such, does not confer any special grace or holiness upon the one ordained. Ordination does not bestow some special magical powers of the Holy Spirit; neither does it confer upon the elder or pastor some special character which sets the person apart as a priest.

Before Paul's ordination, he already possessed the gift of the Holy Spirit (Acts 9:17; 13:3). The same can be said of the seven deacons (Acts 6:3-6; cf. 1 Tim 4:14). Though Christ is the true High Priest (Heb 4:15; 7:24-25; 8:1), all believers in Him constitute a "holy priesthood," a "royal priesthood," and are called to be "kings and priests unto God" (1 Pet 2:5, 9; Rev 1:6).

Thus ordination, per se, does not make anyone spiritual, holy or Spirit filled. Why then is ordination necessary?

**The Necessity of Ordination.** The New Testament attaches special importance to ordination. Paul wrote that the reason he left Titus in Crete was that Titus might "set in order the things that are wanting, and ordain elders in *every city*" (Titus 1:5). Again in Asia Minor, Paul and Barnabas "ordained them elders in *every church*" (Acts 14:23). Evidently elders were to be ordained in all the New Testament churches.

Writing to the many churches that were "scattered abroad," the apostle James urged the sick to "call for the *elders* of the church" (James 1:1; 5:14). In his letter to "the strangers [converted Gentiles] scattered throughout Pontus, Galatia, Cappadocia, Asia, and Bithynia," the apostle Peter wrote, "The *elders* which are among you I exhort" (1 Pet 1:1; 5:1).

Apparently ordination of ministers was essential to the existence of the church. Though ministers were to be ordained in every church and city, their ordination was to be done with great caution and discretion. Paul counseled Timothy, himself an ordained minister, to "lay hands suddenly on no man" (1 Tim 5:22).

**The Meaning of Ordination.** We know that ordination, per se, does not make anyone spiritual, holy or Spirit filled. Yet the Bible teaches that it is essential to the well-being of the organized church. The question then is: What is the meaning of ordination?

Several Greek words in the New Testament are translated "ordain" (KJV); they convey such meanings as to "choose," "appoint," or "set apart." Based on these Greek words, we understand ordination to be the act of the church in choosing, appointing, and setting apart through the laying on of hands certain individuals to perform specific functions on behalf of the church.[4]

By ordination, elders and ministers are authoritatively commissioned to declare the gospel of salvation.[5] Through ordination, setting one apart by the laying on of hands, the church authorizes elders or pastors to counteract false teaching and teachers (1 Tim 1:3; 4:1; Titus 1:9, 10) and to safeguard the sound doctrine that has been entrusted to the church's keeping.[6] As official representatives of the church, ordained elders organize churches and ensure the spiritual well-being of the church (cf. Acts 6).

Our Seventh-day Adventists *Minister's Manual* (1997) rightly recognizes that "Seventh-day Adventists do not believe that ordination is sacramental in the sense of conferring some indelible character or special powers or the ability to formulate right doctrine. It adds 'no new grace or virtual qualification'" (p. 85).

> Ordination, an act of commission, acknowledges God's call, sets the individual apart, and appoints that person to serve the church in a special capacity. Ordination endorses the individuals thus

> set apart as authorized representatives of the church. By this act, the church delegates its authority to its ministers to proclaim the gospel publicly, to administer its ordinances, to organize new congregations, and, within the parameters established by God's Word, to give direction to the believers (Matt. 16:19; Heb. 13:17) (see *Minister's Manual*, pages 84-85).

By means of ordination, "the church sets its seal upon the work of God performed through its ministers and their lay associates. In ordination, the church publicly invokes God's blessing upon the persons He has chosen and devoted to this special work of ministry" (ibid., 85).

**Ellen White's Understanding.** Ellen G. White captured the biblical meaning and importance of ordination: "The biblical background of the rite indicates that it was an acknowledged form of designation to an appointed office and a recognition of one's authority in that office" (*The Acts of the Apostles*, 162).

Concerning Paul and Barnabas, Ellen White wrote: "Before being sent forth as missionaries to the heathen world, these apostles were solemnly dedicated to God by fasting and prayer and the laying on of hands. Thus they were authorized by the church, not only to teach the truth, but to perform the rite of baptism and to organize churches, being invested with full ecclesiastical authority" (*The Acts of the Apostles,* 161, emphasis added).

"God foresaw the difficulties that His servants would be called to meet, and, in order that their work should be above challenge, He instructed the church by revelation to set them apart publicly to the work of the ministry. Their ordination was a public recognition of their divine appointment to bear to the Gentiles the glad tidings of the gospel" (ibid., 161, emphasis added).

Ellen White's understanding that ordination, setting one apart by the laying on of hands, is the church's *recognition* and authoritative *commissioning* of individuals to perform certain functions for the church suggests that, within the guidelines set by Scripture, both men and women may be set apart by the laying on of hands to perform certain functions.

> Women who are willing to consecrate some of their time to the service of the Lord should be appointed to visit the sick, look after the young, and minister to the necessities of the poor. *They*

*should be set apart to this work by prayer and laying on of hands.* In some cases they will need to counsel with the church officers or the minister; but if they are devoted women, maintaining a vital connection with God, they will be a power for good in the church" (Ellen G. White, *The Advent Review and Sabbath Herald,* July 9, 1895, p. 434).

Though this statement has often been taken out of context and misused to claim Ellen White's support for ordaining women as elders or pastors of the church,[7] it does illustrate the legitimacy of the church recognizing and commissioning chosen individuals through an act of consecration/dedication ("laying on of hands") to perform designated functions. Within the guidelines of Scripture, the church may do this for both men and women.

**The Key Issue in the Adventist Debate.** Since both male and female, through an act of dedication (the laying on of hands), can be commissioned *to perform certain specific functions,* the debate over women's ordination is not whether women can or cannot be ordained in this sense. The Bible, confirmed by the Spirit of Prophecy, suggests that both men and women may be commissioned to do certain assigned tasks on behalf of the church.

The key issue to be addressed is whether, among the varied ministries of the church, women may legitimately be commissioned through ordination to perform the leadership functions of elders or pastors. These include the authoritative teaching functions of the elder or pastor, organizing churches, baptism of believers and the spiritual oversight of the flock. Addressing this question will require a careful study of the Scriptures to understand what the Bible teaches about role relationships between men and women in both the home and the church.

In short, the issue in the Adventist debate over women's ordination is not about ordination *per se*, but ordination *to what function*. Specifically, can the church commission (ordain) a person (e.g. a woman) to the headship/leadership office of husband or father (in the home) or elder or pastor (in the church)? The issue is not about women in ministry, but rather women in what kind of soul-winning ministry. The issue is not whether women *can perform* the headship responsibilities of husbands or elders/pastors, but rather whether the Bible *permits* them to do so.

**The Forbidden Issue.** Is there validity in the claim by *Women in Ministry's* authors that the Bible and early Adventist history support women's ordination? More specifically, is ordaining women as *elders* biblical? If it is, we must continue the practice and extend it to include ordaining women as pastors. On the other hand, if ordaining women as local elders is not scriptural, we must reconsider previous church council actions in order to come into harmony with the Bible.

I invite you to put emotions and personalities aside and join me as we reason together on the most divisive and politicized issue to have plagued our church in recent times.

---

**Endnotes**

[1]For the biblical basis for my present position, see my *Searching the Scriptures: Women's Ordination and the Call to Biblical Fidelity* (Berrien Springs, Mich.: Adventists Affirm, 1995).

[2]Nancy Vhymeister, ed., *Women in Ministry: Biblical and Historical Perspectives* (Berrien Springs, Mich.: Andrews University Press, 1998). For an eye-opening response to this book, see Mercedes Dyer, ed., *Prove All Things: A Response to Women in Ministry* (Berrien Springs, Mich.: Adventists Affirm, 2000).

[3]For it is clear from the Bible that (1) those who are permitted to perform the oversight/leadership functions of the ministerial office are elders or pastors; and that (2) the New Testament makes no essential distinction between the two offices.The Greek terms for elder/presbyter (*presbuteros*) and overseer/bishop (*episkopos*) are used interchangeably in the New Testament (Acts 20:17, 28; Titus 1:5-7; 1 Pet 5:1-3). The same qualifications are required of both of these offices (1 Tim 3:1-7; Titus 1:5-9). Both perform the same work of shepherding or pastoring (*poimano*) the flock (Acts 20: 17, 28; 1 Pet 5:1-4; 1 Thess 5:12). The New Testament uses the English term "pastor" only once, in Ephesians 4:11. The same Greek word is translated "shepherd" elsewhere in the New Testament. As a shepherd, the pastor has the care and oversight of the flock. For the convenience of using our contemporary terms, in this study we have frequently used "pastor" as a substitute for "bishop" or "overseer." The *elders* are commissioned to stand as *overseers,* functioning as *pastors/shepherds* to the flock. The book of 1 Peter brings all the terms together: pastor (shepherd), elder (presbyter), and bishop (overseer): "For ye were as sheep going astray; but are now returned unto the Shepherd (*poimen,* = pastor) and Bishop (*episkopos,* overseer) of your souls" (1 Pet 2:25). "The elders (*presbuteros*) which are among you I exhort, who am also an elder . . . : Feed (*poimano,* to tend as a shepherd) the flock of God, taking the oversight (*episkopeo*) thereof. . . . And when the chief Shepherd (*archipoimen*) shall appear, ye shall receive a crown of glory that fadeth not away" (1 Pet 5:1-4). Thus we may conclude that since presbyters (elders) and bishops (overseers) are known by the same names, since they are required to possess the same qualifications, and since they do actually discharge the same oversight duties, the two terms refer to the same office of shepherding the flock. The implication should not be missed: If women can be ordained as local elders, it is equally valid

for them to be ordained as pastors. But by the same token, if the practice of ordaining women as local elders is unbiblical, it is also unbiblical to ordain them as pastors.

[4]For example, Jesus "ordained (*poieo*) twelve" (Mark 3:14); Paul himself was "ordained (*tithemi*) a preacher and an apostle" (1 Tim 2:7; cf., 4:14; 5:22); Titus was urged to "ordain (*kathistemi*) elders in every city" (Titus 1:5). Each of these three Greek words carries the sense of "appoint," "place," or "establish." Another word used in the New Testament for the act of ordination is *cheirotoneo*, which can mean "to stretch forth the hand," or "elect" or "appoint." Thus Paul and Barnabas "*ordained* them elders in every church" (Acts 14:23); and when Titus was appointed by the churches to travel with Paul to Jerusalem, we are told that he was "*chosen* of the churches" (2 Cor 8:19). The compound form of the word, *procheirotoneo*, appears in Acts 10:41, where it describes God's prior appointment of the apostles.

[5]In Romans 10:14-15, having stated that faith comes through the hearing of the word proclaimed by the preacher, Paul asked rhetorically, "How shall they preach except they be *sent?*" The church has to *send* or commission someone to proclaim the message authoritatively. Again, writing to Timothy, Paul declared, "The things that thou hast heard of me among many witnesses, the same *commit to* faithful men, who shall be able to teach others also" (2 Tim 2:2). A person possessing ability to teach, who is faithful to Christ, and who meets the qualifications of 1 Timothy 3:1-7 and Titus 1:5-9 may be commissioned authoritatively to perform the duties of elder or pastor. This was the practice in the New Testament church. Apart from the twelve apostles who were chosen and ordained by Christ Himself, all others apparently were ordained by elders of the church. For a person to be an elder or minister, then, the church must express its approval by recognizing and commissioning that individual for the ministerial task. Even Paul had to be ordained by the church after he received his call from Christ (Acts 13:1-3).

[6]In his pastoral epistles, Paul frequently referred to the "sound words" (1 Tim 6:3; 2 Tim 1:13; cf. 2 Tim 2:15), or "the faith" (1 Tim 3:9; 4:1, 6; 5:8; 6:10, 12, 21; 2 Tim 3:8; 4:7; Titus 1:13; 2:2), or "that which has been entrusted" (1 Tim 6:20; 2 Tim 1:12, 14), and "sound teaching/doctrine" (1 Tim 6:20; 2 Tim 4:3; Titus 1:9; 2:1; cf. 1 Tim 4:6, 16; 6:1, 3; 2 Tim 2:2; Titus 2:10).

[7]Evidence that this statement may not be applied to ordination of women as pastors or elders may be found within the passage itself. (1) This is a part-time ministry, not a calling to a lifework. "Women who are willing to consecrate some of their time. . . ." (2) The work is not that of a minister or a church officer. "In some cases they will need to counsel with the church officers or the minister." Evidently this work is not that of an elder or minister. (3) It was a ministry different from what we were already doing. The portion quoted here is followed immediately by, "This is another means of strengthening and building up the church. We need to branch out more in our methods of labor." (4) It appears in an article entitled, "The Duty of the Minister and the People," which called upon ministers to allow and encourage the church members to use their talents for the Lord. The last sentence of the quoted paragraph reflects this thrust: "Place the burdens upon men and women of the church, that they may grow by reason of the exercise, and thus become effective agents in the hand of the Lord for the enlightenment of those who sit in darkness." This is the only statement from Mrs. White addressing laying on of hands for women. The statement and its context clearly indicat that these women were being dedicated to a specific lay ministry.

# 10

# THE FEMINIST CAMPAIGN FOR EQUALITY

The concept of equality has become crucial in the debate over women's ordination. Though many are not aware of it, the most powerful ideology driving the campaign for women's ordination is feminism. This ideology is very seductive because it is rooted in the pervasive thinking of egalitarianism, which holds that full equality between men and women can be achieved by eliminating gender-role distinctions in the home and in the church.

Proponents of women's ordination who have embraced feminism's mindset often cite the apostle Paul's statement in Galatians 3:28—"there is neither Jew nor Greek, there is neither bond nor free, there is neither male nor female: for ye are all one in Christ Jesus"—as the key proof-text to justify their claim that the Bible teaches full equality between men and women.

In this chapter, I will briefly discuss feminism, showing how it's belief in full equality negatively impacts some fundamental teachings of the Bible. I will also examine the concept of equality, arguing that unqualified statements about the equality of men and women are dangerously imprecise, potentially misleading, and a gross distortion of Paul's statement in Galatians 3:28. I will conclude by stating why feminism's cardinal dogma of full equality poses a direct challenge to our biblical faith.

### The Feminist Ideology

The feminist movement or the so-called women's lib movement is a crusade for freedom, equality and justice. Although Bible-believing Christians have good reasons to distance themselves from the feminist ideology, they share the legitimate concerns of the movement in standing up against any form of injustice, unfairness, and discrimination.

At the heart of the feminist movement are issues concerning unsatisfied and hurt women. Women have all too often been treated unfairly and as second-class citizens in the world. They have been hurt in the home as well, where they have to live with inadequate male leadership. Many are experiencing frustrating marriages as they suffer from abusive, neglectful, and domineering husbands. When they attempt to challenge these injustices, many women feel that society is on the side of the men who have abused them.

Though not a feminist nor a believer in women's ordination, one Christian woman has aptly captured the experiences of many hurt women:

> I am a woman. I have experienced the scorn and prideful superiority with which men have, at times, treated me. I have listened to insults against my capabilities, my intelligence, and my body. I have burned with anger as I have wiped the blood from a battered woman's face. I have wept with women who have been forcefully, brutally raped—violated to the very core of their being. I have been sickened at the perverted sexual abuse of little girls. I have boycotted stores which sell pornographic pictures of women. I have challenged men who sarcastically demean women with their 'humor.' And I have walked out of church services where pastors carelessly malign those whom God has called holy. I am often hurt and angered by sexist, yes, SEXIST demeaning attitudes and actions. And I grieve deeply at the distortion of the relationship that God created as harmonious and good. As a woman I feel the battle. I feel the sin. Feminism identifies real problems which demand real answers.[1]

Indeed, feminism identifies these legitimate issues of women's hurt and unfair treatment. But in seeking to address them, feminists resort to inadequate and unbiblical solutions. The following are some of the worrisome aspects of the feminist ideology.

**1. Obliteration of Gender Roles.** Feminists reason that the role differentiation God established at creation to govern the complementary relationship of male and female makes men superior and women inferior. Believing themselves deprived of their true womanly dignity, some seek self-fulfillment, full equality, and human justice by trying to be like men or by attempting to reject all role distinctions in the home and in the church.

In order to be free from the supposed second-class status resulting from gender role differentiation, some radical feminists have fought against the marriage institution and child-rearing, which they believe confine them to certain roles. Others have taken issue with organized religion, notably Islam and Judeo-Christian religions, whose teachings of male leadership or headship they interpret to mean that women are slaves to men through submission and obedience.

**2. Lesbianism.** Believing that sexual intercourse with men enables males to exercise power over women, many feminists propose sexual encounters that are entirely independent from men. For some, lesbianism is one way women can be free from patriarchy or male leadership in order to know and experience their true inner self. One prominent feminist declares:

> Women's liberation and homosexual liberation are both struggling towards a common goal: a society free from defining and categorizing people by virtue of gender and/or sexual preference. 'Lesbianism' is a label used as a psychic weapon to keep women locked into their male-defined 'feminine role.' The essence of that role is that a woman is defined in terms of her relationship to men.[2]

**3. Witchcraft.** Besides lesbianism, many feminists also see nothing wrong with witchcraft and mother goddess religions characteristic of ancient Canaanite fertility worship. Feminists insist that witches are spiritual women, not evil sorcerers. They point to the burning of witches in the Middle Ages and argue that they were burned as witches "because they were women and because they possessed a power to heal that was unacceptable to the male establishment"[3]

One feminist writer explains: "When the patriarchal, prophetic religions (Judaism, Christianity, Islam) met the Middle Eastern Goddess practices, powerful interests came into conflict. Masculine self-control, social authority, and theological construction (a masculine God) were all bound to see Goddess temple worship as extremely threatening. Since the patriarchal religions won the battle, their scriptural and cultural authorities became 'orthodoxy,' and the female-oriented fertility religion became foul deviance."[4]

**3. Redefinition of God**. While feminists within Christianity may not go this far in their war against marriage and Judeo-Christian religion and in their embracement of lesbianism and witchcraft, some make the effort to redefine God along gender-neutral lines. They attempt to get rid of the alleged offensive (i.e., sexist, male-oriented or patriarchal) language in the Bible and replace it with gender-inclusive terms which blur the male-female distinction. Accordingly, "*Son* of God" becomes "*Child* of God;" "*Son* of Man" becomes "*Human* One;" "heavenly *Father*" becomes "heavenly *Parent*;" and the God of Abraham, Isaac, and Jacob is transformed into a mother goddess named Sophia.[5]

One way by which feminism's "goddess religion" is spreading into major Christian denominations is through its systematic attempt to feminize God. For example, in the new service book of the United church of Canada, the largest Protestant denomination in Canada, baptism is no longer required to be in the name of the Father, Son, and Holy Spirit. Instead, one can now do it in the name of the "Creator, Liberator, and Healer" or, alternatively, in the name of "God, Source of Love; in the name of Jesus Christ, Love incarnate and in the name of the Holy Spirit, Love's Power." In its first 100 pages there is only one reference to God as "Father"; instead, church members pray to "Mother and Father God" or more simply "Mother God."[6]

Even in our own church some scholars are promoting the Holy Spirit as the female member of the Godhead, repeatedly referring to the Creator as "He/She."[7]

**4. Gender-Inclusive Language.** It is the same feminist ideology that undergirds much of the push for gender inclusive language, as in various worship services and Bible translation endeavors.[8] While there may be a legitimate place for gender-inclusive language, it is a mistake to attempt to gender neutralize what God sets aside as gender-specific.

An example of this occurred at the 1990 Indianapolis General Conference session when delegates (perhaps unknowingly) voted to revise the *Church Manual* statement on the office and duties of church elders along gender-neutral lines.[9]

Whether or not they realize it, those who teach unisex roles in the home or in the church are driven by the same feminist ideology. The most recent example of this is found in the much-publicized pro-ordination book *Women in Ministry,* where some of our church scholars attempt to prove that there was at least one woman priest in the Old Testament and some women apostles and women ministers in the New.[10]

Mary Kassian's eye-opening book, *The Feminist Gospel: The Movement to Unite Feminism with the Church,*[11] also shows convincingly that besides shaping contemporary discussions of male and female roles in the home and the church, feminist philosophy also finds expression in various denominations through their women's task forces, in colleges and universities through women's studies courses, and in seminaries through women's feminist theologies.

**5. Questioning of the Bible's Inspiration and Authority.** Feminists perceive the Bible as both a *producer* and *product* of female oppression. Maintaining that some parts of the inspired Scriptures are prejudiced against women's rights and aspirations, they suggest that there are degrees of inspiration in the Bible—the less inspired parts being allegedly tainted with male prejudices and errors. Thus they consider any passage of Scripture that does not uphold the principle of full equality—redefined to mean the absence of role differentiation within the complementary partnership of male and female relationship—as sexist and biased, and therefore not inspired.

One scholar has aptly summarized the view of feminist theologians:

> The Bible was written in a patriarchal society by the people, mostly men, whom the system kept on top. It embodies the androcentric, that is, male-centered, presuppositions of that social world, and it legitimizes the patriarchal, that is male-dominant, social structures that held that world together. Its language is overwhelmingly male-oriented, both in its reference to God and

> in reference to people. In short, the Bible is a book written by men in order to tell *their* story for *their* advantage. As such, it confronts both women and justice-inspired men with an enormous problem. It is not at all certain that the Bible can survive this challenge, that it can retain the allegiance of people called to justice and freedom in a postmodern world.[12]

Notice that since feminists hold that the Bible is the product of a patriarchal, male-dominated (androcentric) culture, and that some of its *content* is oppressive to women, they doubt if the Bible "can retain the allegiance of people called to justice in a postmodern world."

**6. Reinterpretation of Scripture.** To declare gender distinctions as obsolete, feminists adopt an attitude which denies the full inspiration of the Bible and which utilizes higher critical methods of its interpretation. Consequently, feminist interpreters not only pick and choose from the Bible, but they are also *suspicious* of the biblical text. Using the two principles of selectivity and skepticism, feminist interpreters insist that as they approach Scripture, "our ideology takes precedence over the ideology of the [biblical] literature."[13]

A classic example of liberal feminism's liberal interpretation of the Bible is found in *The Welcome Table*, a pro-ordination volume written by 14 Seventh-day Adventist thought leaders[14]. In this work, some of the authors argue that Bible passages (like Eph 5:22-33; Col 3:18-19; 1 Pet 3:1-7; 1 Cor 11:3, 11-12; 14:34-35; 1 Tim 2:11-14; 3:2; and Titus 1:6) which Adventists historically understood as having a bearing on male-female role relations in both the home and the church are the product of the Bible writers' faulty logic or mistaken rabbinic interpretations in vogue in their day. Reasoning along feminist and higher-critical lines, some of the writers maintain that the apostle Paul erred in his interpretation of Genesis 1-3 when he grounded his teaching of role distinctions between male and female in Creation and the Fall. They claim that the apostle Paul's statements were merely expressions of uninspired personal opinions—opinions that reflect his culture and hence do not apply to us. To these authors, Paul was "a man of his own time." He occasionally glimpsed the ideal that Jesus established during His time on earth; yet he never fully arrived at "the gospel ideal" of full equality or complete role interchangeability in both the home and the church.[15]

**7. Mutation of Women's Ministries.** Historically, the Seventh-day Adventist church has always encouraged women's active participation in the soul-winning ministry. They do so without being ordained as elders or pastors. This is still the case, especially in the developing countries. In fact at the time of writing this chapter, the Africa Indian-Ocean Division has launched a major outreach undertaking in which its women are to conduct 10,000 evangelistic campaigns.

But in certain places of our church, women's ministries have been hijacked and transposed into feminist ministries to push the agenda of women's ordination. Then, in very subtle ways, proponents accuse those who justifiably oppose women's ordination as being against women's ministry. They try also to give credibility to their feminist agenda, when they equate their mutation of women's ministry with the legitimate one practiced in the developing countries. Thus, feminists take the term "women's ministries," empty it of its true meaning, and then inject it with a feminist meaning. In this way, unsuspecting church members do not readily see the difference.

One knowledgeable writer offers this succinct summary, contrasting today's feminist ministries and the women's ministries of the early Adventist pioneers is in order:

> Today, feminist ministries contrast sharply with the Women's Ministry back then. Whereas the spirituality of the Adventist sisters was the greatest burden of the first movement, it seems to be assumed in the second; whereas soul-winning was the whole purpose of the first, it does not always seem to be foremost in the second; whereas the first movement stressed the worth and influence of a woman on the domestic scene in the home, such a concept seems nigh-repulsive to many in the second movement; whereas power was equated with the Holy Spirit in the first, one almost senses that it is equated with position in the second.
>
> We can applaud Women's Ministries in developing countries where women are very active in soul-winning and sharing their faith. Praise the Lord for their faith and sacrificial work! The churches are growing because women have captured the spirit of the pioneers in their area. Let us be ashamed to tamper with their form of ministry and infect them with feminist strugglings.[16]

**Summary.** Feminism's campaign for full equality lays the foundation for women's ordination.The ideology's fundamental opposition to Scripture's teaching on role distinctions between male and female in the church leads feminists to embrace lesbianism and witchcraft, to redefine and feminize God, to indiscriminately push for gender-inclusive language, to question the Bible's inspiration and authority, to adopt higher criticism to reinterpret the Bible, and to transpose women's ministries into feminist ministries.

### Egalitarian Ideology

In spite of its worrisome aspects, the feminist movement continues to exert enormous influence on Christian churches in the campaign for the obliteration of gender role-distinctions. The reason why this push has been quite successful is that feminism grows out of an even widespread ideology called *egalitarianism.* Radical egalitarianism (or equalitarianism) holds that all human beings are equal, and therefore they ought to be made to be exactly the same in a whole host of spheres.[17] Consequently, God-ordained differences among people must be abolished.

Our contemporary culture has been greatly influenced by the egalitarian thinking that began with the rationalism and egalitarianism that surrounded the French Revolution. Because the French Revolution dethroned the God of the Bible and enthroned Reason as goddess, the differences that God had ordained among people no longer seemed rational to the egalitarian mind.

Egalitarianism rightly protests exploitation resulting from differences among people, such as rich and poor, male and female, black and white, educated and uneducated, etc. But its attempt to rectify the *abuse* of differences goes too far when it proposes to abolish all distinctions and when it suggests that full equality means equality in every sense.

According to radical egalitarianism, it is unfair for anyone to have authority over another, or to have more power, or money, or influence. Taken to its logical conclusion, egalitarianism would argue that those who stand out and excel should somehow be pulled down and made to fit in with the crowd, lest someone feel inferior.

Thus, communism (or Marxism) embraces this radical ideology when it attempts to make the poor equal to the rich. Feminism also drinks from the egalitarian fountain when it seeks to make women equal to men in every respect. And just as feminists seek full equality by getting rid of *gender* or *sex roles* in marriage and the church, gay theology also seeks to bring about equality between homosexuals and heterosexuals by obliterating *sexual identity.*

**Feminist Egalitarianism.** Feminist egalitarianism is seductive because it builds on something close to biblical truth and then proceeds to distort it. Equality of being and worth (ontological equality) is a clear Biblical teaching, affirming that all human beings—male and female—have equal standing before God as created beings, as sinners in need of salvation through Christ, and as people called to the same destiny. The scriptural evidence for this equality is that (1) both "male and female" were created "in the image of God" (Gen 1:27; Matt 19:4; Mark 10:6); (2) both have been redeemed by Jesus Christ, so that "in Christ" there is neither "male nor female" (Gal 3:28); and (3) both are "joint heirs of the grace of life" (1 Pet 3:7 RSV).

Nowhere does the Bible relegate women to second class status or make men superior and women inferior. To say otherwise is to misrepresent biblical teaching and affront the loving character of the God who created Eve to be Adam's "help meet for him," a partner "fitting" or "suitable" to him. Ellen White was unequivocal: "When God created Eve, He designed that she should possess neither inferiority nor superiority to the man, but that in all things she should be his equal" (*Testimonies for the Church,* 3:484).

Thus, biblical Christianity teaches equality of male and female before God. While feminist egalitarianism appeals to this truth, it does not acknowledge the complementary truth about human differences and gender *role-distinctions.* As will become clear in subsequent chapters, Scripture is clear that within male-female equality, just as gender differences between men and women indicate that they were created to complement one another, so also this complementary nature indicates a *functional* distinction between them.

The issue of women's ordination is, therefore, *not* a question of whether women and men are equal. The Bible, confirmed by the Spirit of Prophecy, has already settled that issue. Women and men are equal; neither is inferior to the other. The real issue in the debate is *whether the equality of male and female does away with role-differences.* While maintaining equality of being, has the Bible assigned a headship/leadership role to the man and a supportive role to the woman?

**Obsession with Equality.** Many have uncritically embraced women's ordination because they have bought into egalitarian feminism's campaign for full equality, without seriously understanding the precise nature of the equality between men and women.

One perceptive Evangelical scholar calls America's obsession with equality as "the great levelling instinct" that "is grounded in the radical egalitarianism which has taken residence deep in her [the evangelical church] heart." Expounding upon the words of Alexis de Tocqueville that, "Americans are so enamored of equality that they would rather be equal in slavery than unequal in freedom," he points to the inconsistency of those who have embraced the ideology of egalitarianism. He writes:

> I've often observed that, in the midst of the egalitarian fervor which has taken the Church, seeking to establish 'full equality' between the sexes, we hear no parallel cries for full equality between professors and their students or parents and their children." He continues: "Somehow those mothers who are levellers in marriage have yet to become levellers in parenthood; rather, mothers fighting for the right to say 'no' to their husbands continue to expect their sons and daughters to say 'yes' to them, and to snap to it clearing off the table, mowing the lawn, and taking out the trash. Similarly, professors who deny the authority of husbands over their wives have yet to initiate a reform movement in the academy, stripping themselves of the perquisites of their Ph.D. or full professorship. Seemingly blind to the whole cloth of various forms of authority, they blithely carry on, grading thier students' papers and processing to commencement exercises in full academic regalia."[18]

The above observation confirms that advocates of egalitarianism do not fully understand the true nature of equality. Let me illustrate:

**The True Nature of Equality.** The US Declaration of Independence states: "We hold these truths to be self-evident, that *all men are created equal*." This profound statement on equality is both true and false, depending on what we mean by "equal." Does equality mean equal in all respects? Does the Declaration statement mean, for example, that all people can play basketball like Michael Jordan, preach like C.D.

Brooks, or write like Arthur S. Maxwell? What exactly does it mean for two entities to be equal?

One illustration will clarify the point.[19] Suppose a seven-year old asks his father, "Does a cup of sugar equal a cup of flour?" the father faces a dilemma. If his son's question means, "Is a cup of one granular material (sugar) the same volume as a cup of another granular material (flour)? The answer is yes. If, however, the child is asking, "Can I put a cup of sugar in this recipe for a cup of flour, since they are equal?" the answer is no. A cup of sugar and a cup of flour are equal in some respects, but not in all respects. In other words, the statement, "A cup of sugar and a cup of flour are equal," is valid and true, provided one understands the manner in which the two entities are equal.

In his excellent work, *Speaking of Equality: An Analysis of the Rhetorical Force of 'Equality' in Moral and Legal Discourse,* Peter Westen points out that in order to call two things equal, one must at least have: (1) two distinct entities, (2) a means of measurement, and (3) a common standard.[20] Westen's basic definition of descriptive equality is worth quoting:

> Descriptive equality is the relationship that obtains among two or more distinct things that have been jointly measured by a common standard and found to be indistinguishable, or identical, as measured by that standard. Things that are equal by one standard of comparison are inevitably unequal by other standards, and vice versa. It therefore follows that the things of this world that we are capable of measuring are not *either* equal *or* unequal. They are *both* equal *and* unequal.[21]

Concerning the examples above, we may conclude that if the common standard employed in the cup of sugar/flour illustration is volume, the two cups are equal. On the other hand, if the common standard is substance, then they are not equal. Similarly, if the common standard in the Declaration of Independence is artistic athletic and oratory ability, then all people are *not* created equal. If, however, the standard is certain rights before God, then all people *are* created equal.

In fact, to avoid confusion, the US Declaration clarifies the meaning of the term *equal* by inserting a series of dependent clauses: "that they are endowed by their Creator with certain unalienable Rights, that among these are Life, Liberty, and the pursuit of Happiness." Equality, as used by the writers of the Declaration, simply means all people have certain unalienable, God-given rights.

The point is that, before we declare two items as equal, it is crucial that we clarify the common standard of comparison. Even two distinct one dollar bills are equal by one standard of comparison (worth) and unequal in other standards (e.g. age or color). As Westen notes in his definition above, things in life are not equal *or* unequal, but both equal *and* unequal, depending on the standard of comparison. It is therefore confusing to call two items equal without clearly delineating the standard of comparison.

Therefore, feminist egalitarianism's rhetoric of full equality as it eliminates all gender role distinctions fails to see the wisdom of Aristotle's words, "The worst form of equality is to try to make unequal things equal." This is precisely what proponents of women's ordination have attempted to do in their forced interpretation of Galatians 3:28.

### Galatians 3:28: Feminism's Missing Link

As we noted at the beginning of the chapter, the concept of equality has become crucial in the debate over women's ordination. Within and without our church, proponents of women's ordination who have embraced feminism's egalitarian mindset often cite the apostle Paul's statement in Galatians 3:28—"there is neither Jew nor Greek, there is neither bond nor free, there is neither male nor female: for ye are all one in Christ Jesus"—as the key proof-text to justify their claim that the Bible teaches full equality between men and women.

This passage has become the missing link for those attempting to import feminist egalitarianism into the church. But does Galatians 3:18 really teach full equality or the obliteration of roles between male and female?

**A New Revelation?** Galatians 3:28 has become a lightening rod in the debate over women's ordination because feminist egalitarians trumpet this text as the new light that now allows men and women to have interchangeable roles in the church. They argue that even though the arrival of Christ brought about the *theological* justification for the full equality of Jew/Gentile, free/slave, and male/female, the concomitant *sociological* changes were manifested gradually over a period of time.

In the rhetoric of feminist egalitarianism, the long range plan for the gospel's transformation of society was laid out by the apostle Paul in

Galatians 3:28. In this view, the barrier between Jew and Gentile was the first in line to be broken down; this allegedly occurred in the first century. Later slavery was overthrown in the nineteenth and twentieth centuries. With the eradication of slavery, feminists argue that it is now time for the church to eliminate gender roles in the home and church.

One Adventist scholar articulates the above view in *Women in Ministry*, the volume produced by pro-ordination scholars at Andrews University:

> The revelation of God's character and our understanding of that character is progressive. What is deemed permissible at one time may eventually come to be understood as not in God's ideal for His children. For example, polygamy, though not in God's original design, was permitted in the Old Testament. By New Testament times 'the overseer must be above reproach, the husband of one wife' (1 Tim 3:2). . . .
>
> The same is true of human slavery. Though New Testament writers did not call for its abolition, Paul laid out a long-rage plan for gospel transformation. . . . [citing Gal 3:28]. Here he set down the principle that the gospel, in its own time, transforms all human relationships.
>
> Much of the New Testament period was devoted to breaking down the barriers between Jew and Gentile. In this struggle God's character was enhanced. Other barriers, such as slavery and gender were to tumble later. . . .
>
> To our modern minds the right and fair course would have been to free those slaves. But Christianity proclaimed its message within its social context then and still does. The time for such a bold advance of justice was not yet, for such concepts of equity were not generally recognized. Still, in the just and fair character of God resided the seeds of the destruction of slavery. . . .
>
> When centuries later the time was ripe for this new revelation of Christian fairness and justice, God had prepared a prophet with his message: "Exact and impartial justice is to be shown to the Negro race," Ellen White wrote. "The religion of the Bible recognizes no caste or color. It ignores rank, wealth, worldly honor . . ."

> Gender might also constitute a caste system. . . . It is generally acknowledged that throughout much of human history women were placed in a position subservient to men simply because they were born female. How would a just God regard a gender caste system?[22]

The rhetoric of the above argument may sound good. But very few may realize that inherent in the above statement are two fatally flawed assumptions. First, the assertion assumes that the religion of the Old and New Testaments ever "deemed permissible" or accommodated the non-ideal practices and injustices of polygamy, Jew/Gentile racism, slavery, and women's subjugation—practices later allegedly corrected by the "new revelation of Christian fairness and justice." This claim is a scholarly *myth* that responsible Bible scholars have invalidated.[23]

Second, though not explicitly stated, the above assertion assumes that the failure of the church to ordain women is a discriminatory practice characteristic of "a gender caste system." This belief also grows out of another commonly accepted paradigm (based on select texts from Rabbinic literature) that women were second class, unjustly oppressed people in the Old and New Testament times, and are now (on the basis of Gal 3:28) to be accorded the same roles as men. This assumption is also highly questionable.[24]

In fact the second assumption would be valid if one believes the correctness of the claim that Galatians 3:28 teaches full equality, understood by feminist egalitarians to mean the complete interchangeability of male-female roles in the church, if not the home. This egalitarian ideology, and not the Galatians passage, is the new revelation that is to eradicate the gender caste discrimination in the church. As we shall see in the next paragraphs, Galatians 3:28 does not support egalitarian feminism's claim that men and women have interchangeable roles in the church.

**The Magna Charta of True Biblical Equality?** In the opinion of one New Testament scholar at Fuller Theological Seminary, Galatians 3:28 is "the fundamental Pauline theological basis for the inclusion of women and men as equal and mutual partners in all of the ministries of the church."[25] Similarly, the author of *Good News for Women: A Biblical Picture of Gender Equality* writes: "Of all the texts that support biblical equality, Galatians 3:26-28 is probably the most important."[26]

Even in our church, virtually every major work endorsing women's ordination has appealed to Galatians 3:28 as a text that removes the theological barriers erected against women serving as elders or pastors. For example, one of the principal authors of *Women in Ministry* considers the text as "the Magna Charta of true biblical equality." Explaining why this passage "upholds the equality of men and women in the church," he argues: "This [Gal 3:28 text] is not merely a statement on equal access to salvation (cf. Gal 2:11-15; Eph 2:14-15). Rather it specifically singles out those three relationships in which God's original plan in Eden had been perverted by making one group unequal to another: (1) Jew-Gentile, (2) slave-free, and (3) male-female."[27]

In another pro-ordination volume, *The Welcome Table: Setting A Place for Ordained Women*, an Adventist New Testament scholar explains why the Galatians passage is "the Bill of Christian Rights":

> Humankind is broken. And it will remain broken as long as men hold dominance over women. For their own good, as well as the good of women, men ought to recognize the need for women to find full equality. Humankind will not be whole until we attain full equality—with equal rights, equal privileges, and equal opportunities for all. And that means, given the Bible of Christian Rights [Gal 3:26-28], full racial, socioeconomic, and gender equality.[28]

But does Galatians 3:28 teach full equality? Does this so-called "Magna Charta of true biblical equality" or "the Bill of Christian Rights" really remove role-distinctions between male and female. Is the apostle speaking about *unity* or *equality?* In short, can our scholars legitimately employ Paul's "neither male nor female" statement to argue for women's ordination?[29]

**Unity or Equality?** It is important to note that when the apostle Paul stated that "there is neither male nor female: for ye are all one in Christ," the word "one" (Greek, *eis*), *never means "equal."*[30] Correspondingly, the lexical options for "you are one" do not include "you are equal."[31]

In what is, perhaps, the most definitive discussion on Galatians 3:28, the author of *Equality in Christ* concludes his extensive study in this way: "A study of every parallel use of the phrase 'we/you/they are one' in the 300 years surrounding the New Testament reveals that this expression fails to express the concept of unqualified equality. In fact, 'you are all one' is used of *diverse* objects to denote one element they share in common; it is not used of similar objects to denote that they are the same."[32]

Furthermore, while the expression "you are all one," points to a shared element, it "nevertheless *assumes differences* between the individual entities. The New Testament examples of 'we/you/they are one,' where a plurality of people are called one, are the planter and waterer (1 Cor. 3:8); Father and Son (John 10:30; 17:11, 21, 22 [2x], 23; husband and wife (Matt. 19:6; Mark 10:8); and different believers with different gifts (Rom. 12:5; 1 Cor. 10:17). *In every instance the groups of people in these pairs have different roles*."[33]

In other words, "you are all one in Christ" emphasizes *unity* in Christ, not *full equality.* But even if egalitarians are right when they insist that "you are all one in Christ" means "you are all equal in Christ," it still does not follow that men and women have the same roles, because the New Testament passage does not assume that "equality in the sight of God implies . . . role interchangeability among all Christians."[34]

**Equality in What Sense?** We must ask proponents of women's ordination what standard of comparison they employ in Galatians 3:28 when they argue for the full equality of male and female. In what sense are they equal? Equal value? Equal abilities? Equal roles? Equal gifts? Equal inheritance in Christ?

As one scholar has correctly noted, "Any meaningful statement on the relationship between *equality* and Galatians 3:28 must clearly state a common standard of comparison. Hence unqualified statements such as 'Galatians 3:28 teaches the equality of men and women' are both dangerously imprecise and potentially misleading."[35]

Contrary to claims of feminist egalitarians, Galatians 3:28 does not teach full equality, in the sense of obliteration of gender role distinctions. Instead, the context makes it very clear that men and women are equal only in the sense that they are both "equally justified by faith (v. 24), equally free from the bondage of legalism (v. 25), equally children of God (v. 26), equally clothed with Christ (v. 27), equally possessed by Christ (v. 29), and equally heirs of the promises to Abraham (v. 29). . . . Galatians 3:28 does not abolish gender-based roles established by God and redeemed by Christ."[36]

Thus, while there is a certain notion of equality taught in Galatians 3:28, the context clearly explains the true nature of this equality. Men and women are "equal members" in Christ, but it does not follow that men and women have equal roles. As we have indicated earlier, simply because two entities are equal in one respect does not follow that they are equal in other respects as well. For example, the twelve tribes were equal members of Israel and were equal heirs of the promised inheritance. But each tribe did not have equal (the same) opportunities or perform the same roles:

> While each tribe has equal *honor*, and each is treated the same way when it comes to fighting battles or settling land, not all the tribes have the same roles (e.g., Gen. 49:10, the scepter will not depart from Judah," and Numbers 3, which details the unique role of the tribe of Levi). Surely all the tribes are equal—in one sense—and surely, as a result of this joint heritage they should work together to do good to one another. But the inheritance, which belongs to each tribe as a result of being part of a whole, does not negate the uniqueness of each tribe.[37]

**The Meaning of Galatians 3:28.** Paul's "neither male nor female" expression does not negate the existence and distinction between male and female. Also, contrary to the egalitarian interpretation, the passage does not obliterate gender role distinctions. He is simply affirming that all believers, regardless of their gender, are one in Christ.

Each of the polar opposites (or couplets)—Jews/Greeks, slaves/free, males/females—is designed to convey the idea of totality or universality. The couplets capture three fundamental ways of viewing the totality of human beings during the New Testament times.

The first couplet, "neither Jew nor Greek," captures the totality of humanity from a salvation-historical perspective. Since Scripture describes the gospel/promise as coming first to the Jews, then to the Gentiles, from the *religious* perspective of the Jew, all the world can be divided into two parts, Jew and Gentile.[38] The second couplet, "neither slave nor free," was the primary *legal* distinction for dividing all people. From a Roman perspective, all men were either free or slaves.[39] And the third couplet, "neither male nor female," divides humanity according to their basic sexual identity given them *at creation*. Accordingly, from creation perspective, all humanity can be divided into two groups—male and female.[40]

Thus, according to the apostle Paul, all of God's people, regardless of how we view them—whether from the salvation-historical perspective of the Jew, or from the legal perspective of the Roman, or from the creation perspective of God—share in the same privilege of union with Christ. It is in this sense that male and female are equal.

But this equal privilege does not suggest that men and women have equal (interchangeable) roles in the home or in church. Therefore, the attempt by proponents of women's ordination to appeal to Galatians 3:28 as evidence that the Bible teaches full equality is indefensible, if not dangerously misleading. Full equality can only be sustained by importing into the text the ideology from the warehouse of egalitarian feminism.

**Feminism's Challenge to Adventism.**

We have seen how feminism's ideology of full equality lays the foundation for women's ordination. Drinking deeply at egalitarianism's fountain, feminism's fundamental opposition to Scripture's teaching on role distinctions between male and female in the church ultimately leads proponents to embrace lesbianism and witchcraft, to redefine and feminize God, to indiscriminately push for gender-inclusive language, to question the Bible's inspiration and authority, to adopt higher-criticism to reinterpret the Bible, to transpose women's ministries into feminist ministries, and to advance a questionable interpretation of Galatians 3:28.

Feminism has always posed a threat to the Seventh-day Adventist church. Long ago, Ellen White warned that "those who feel called out to join the movement in favor of woman's rights and the so-called dress reform might as well sever all connection with the third angel's message. The spirit which attends the one cannot be in harmony with the other. The Scriptures are plain upon the relations and rights of men and women" (*Testimonies for the Church,* 1:421).

In the above warning, Mrs. White described the women's rights (the feminist movement of the 19th century) and the third angel's message as incompatible. The specific reason she gave was that there exist differences on the role relationship between men and women. As has been shown in *Prove All Things,* Sister White also warned against feminism because of its links with spiritualism. This relationship still exists between today's feminist movement and modern spiritualism.[41]

Above all, feminism poses a challenge to Adventism because of its selective interpretation of Scripture, setting some portions of Scripture aside as less inspired than others. Warned Ellen White:

> There are some that may think they are fully capable with their finite judgment to take the Word of God, and to state what are the words of inspiration, and what are not the words of inspiration. I want to warn you off that ground, my brethren in the ministry. 'Put off thy shoes from off thy feet, for the place whereon thou standest is holy ground.' There is no finite man that lives, I care not who he is or whatever is his position, that God has authorized to pick and choose in His Word. . . . I would have both my arms taken off at my shoulders before I would ever make the statement or set my judgment upon the Word of God as to what is inspired and what is not inspired (Ellen G. White comments, *Seventh-day Adventist Bible Commentary*, 7:919).

God speaks to all students of the Bible when He says: "This is the one I esteem: *he who is humble and contrite in spirit, and trembles at my word*" (Isa 66:2 NIV). As we approach Scripture, we must not come with the spirit that possesses feminists, that is, the attitude that seeks to correct the alleged male biases of the Bible writers. Rather, we must be willing to learn from the Spirit of Christ, the One who inspired the Scriptures:

"In the presence of such a Teacher [Jesus], of such opportunity for divine education, what worse than folly is it to seek an education apart from Him—to seek to be wise apart from Wisdom; to be true while rejecting Truth; to seek illumination apart from the Light, and existence without the Life; to turn from the Fountain of living waters, and hew out broken cisterns, that can hold no water" (*Education* , 83).

---

**Endnotes**

[1]Mary A. Kassian, *The Feminist Gospel: The Movement to Unite Feminism with the Church* (Wheaton, IL: Good News, 1992), 242. This book is a must read for those who desire to understand what feminism is all about and how it is hypnotizing Christian churches.

[2]The above statement is attributed to prominent feminist Kate Millet, and cited by Mary A. Kassian, *The Feminist Gospel,* 85.

[3]So argues pagan witch Margot Adler; as cited by Mary A. Kassian, *The Feminist Gospel,* 78; cf. 219.

[4]Denise Lardner Carmody, *Women and World Religions* (Nashville, Tenn.: Abingdon, 1979), 32. Cf. Mary A. Kassian, *The Feminist Gospel,* 155.

[5]See Elizabeth Achtemeier, "Why God Is Not Mother: A Response to Feminist God-talk in the Church," *Christianity Today* (August 16, 1993):16-23. For a shocking account of how this feminist "re-imagining" of God is being actively promoted in Christian churches, see James R. Edwards, "Earthquake in the Mainline," *Christianity Today* (November 14, 1994):38-43.

[6]See Elizabeth Achtemeier's review of United Church of Canada's *An Inclusive Language Lectionary* (3 vols.) in *Interpretation* 38 (1984):64-66; cf. David Lyle Jeffrey, "Death of Father Language: Attacking the Heart of Christian Identity," *Journal for Biblical Manhood and Womanhood* 4/4 (Spring 2000), 1, 11-16.

[7]Steve Daily, *Adventism for a New Generation* (Portland/Clackamas, Ore.: Better Living Publishers, 1993), 88, 105, 113.

[8]To date, the most detailed and complete discussion of gender-neutral Bible translations can be found in Vern S. Poythress and Wayne A. Grudem, *The Gender-Neutral Bible Controversy: Muting the Masculinity of God's Words* (Nashville, TN: Broadman and Holman Publishers, 2000).

[9]C. Mervyn Maxwell has provided an insightful history, showing how church leaders' desire to enjoy United States tax law benefits to ministers led to questionable church policy revisions and *Church Manual* alterations allowing women to serve as elders. See his "A Very Surprising (and Interesting) History," in Mercedes H. Dyer, ed., *Prove All Things: A Response to Women in Ministry* (Berrien Springs, Mich.: Adventists Affirm, 2000), 225-230.

[10]Refer to the articles by Jacques B. Doukhan, "Women Priests in Israel: A Case for Their Absence," and Robert M. Johnston, "Shapes of Ministry in the New Testament," in *Women in Ministry,* 29-43, 45-58, respectively. I will offer a brief evaluation of these articles in subsequent chapters of of *Must We Be Silent?* Those interested in reading a more detailed critique of the above works should consult Gerard Damsteegt's contribution in *Prove All Things: A Response to Women in Ministry,* 123-153.

[11]Mary A. Kassian, *The Feminist Gospel: The Movement to Unite Feminism With the Church* (Wheaton, Ill.: Crossway, 1992).

[12]Sandra M. Schneiders, "Does the Bible Have a Postmodern Message?" in Frederic Burnham, ed., *Postmodern Theology: Christian Faith in a Pluralistic World.* (San Francisco: Harper and Row, 1989), 65.

[13]Donna Nolan Fewell, "Feminist Reading of the Hebrew Bible: Affirmation, Resistance and Transformation," *Journal for the Study of the Old Testament* 39 (1987):78. While C. Raymond Holmes has provided a useful analysis and critique of feminist ideology (see *The Tip of an Iceberg,* 87-132), it is of no less importance that the method feminist interpreters bring to Scripture, like that of other liberation theologians, is an aspect of the historical-critical method (ibid., 31-48). For more on this method, see Gerhard F. Hasel, "Biblical Authority and Feminist Interpretation," *Adventists Affirm* (Fall 1989), 12-23.

[14]*The Welcome Table: Setting A Place for Ordained Women,* edited by Patricia A. Habada and Rebecca Frost Brillhart (Langley Park, Md.: TEAMPress, 1995). The

"fourteen prominent SDA historians, theologians, and professionals" who contributed essays to the book are: Bert Haloviak, Kit Watts, Raymond F. Cottrell, Donna Jeane Haerich, David R. Larson, Fritz Guy, Edwin Zackrison, Halcyon Westphal Wilson, Sheryll Prinz-McMillan, Joyce Hanscom Lorntz, V. Norskov Olsen, Ralph Neall, Ginger Hanks Harwood, and Iris M. Yob.

[15]Although the book's introduction and back-cover recommendations state that *The Welcome Table* comprises "carefully thought-through expositions by some of our most competent writers" and "is a definitive collection of essays for our time from respected church leaders," others have observed that, regarding the key hermeneutical issues of women's ordination, this volume is more noteworthy for its breadth than for its depth. For example, Keith A. Burton, an Adventist New Testament scholar, has exposed the historical-critical assumptions underlying some of the essays in *The Welcome Table.* He concludes his insightful critique of this pro-ordination book: "The table around which we are warmly invited to sit is one that already accommodates those who have attacked the relevance of biblical authority; those who wish to pretend that the gnostic image of the primeval and eschatological androgyne is the one toward which Adventists should be moving; those whose interest is in the acquisition of corporate power rather than the evangelization of a dying world; and finally, those who confuse the undiscriminating limitation of the familial and ecclesiastical roles that have been defined by the same Spirit." See Burton, "The Welcome Table: A Critical Evaluation" (unpublished manuscript, 1995), available at the Adventist Heritage Center, James White Library, Andrews University. In my earlier work *Receiving the Word* (119-129), I spotlighted a few of the troubling aspects of *The Welcome Table's* arguments for women's ordination.

[16]Laurel Damsteegt, "Shall Women Minister?" *Adventists Affirm* 9/1 (Spring 1995):14. For a discussion of how "Women's Ministry" was understood in early Seventh-day Adventism, see also Laurel Damsteegt's "S. M. I. Henry: Pioneer in Women's Ministry," *Adventists Affirm* 9/1 (Spring 1995):17-19, 46; cf. Terri Saelee, "Women of the Spirit," *Adventists Affirm* 9/2 (Fall 1995):60-63.

[17]For the thoughts expressed here, I am indebted to the insights of Vern S. Poythress and Wayne A. Grudem, *The Gender-Neutral Bible Controversy: Muting the Masculinity of God's Words* (Nashville, TN: Broadman and Holman Publishers, 2000), 139-142.

[18]Timothy B. Bayly, "Shepherd's Pie: The Idol of Equality," *Journal for Biblical Manhood and Womanhood* 4/4 (Spring 2000), 18, 19.

[19]For the thoughts expressed in the following discussion, I am indebted to the excellent work by Richard Hove, *Equality in Christ? Galatians 3:28 and the Gender Dispute* (Wheaton, Ill.: Crossway Books, 1999), 110-116.

[20]Peter Westen, *Speaking of Equality: An Analysis of the Rhetorical Force of 'Equality' in Moral and Legal Discourse* (Princeton, N.J.: Princeton University Press, 1990).

[21]Ibid., 41 (emphasis his).

[22]Roger L. Dudley, "The Ordination of Women in the Light of the Character of God," in *Women in Ministry,* 408-409.

[23]The argument above is the same kind used to justify homosexuality. The truth, however is that the Bible writers never once "deemed permissible" the non-ideal practices of polygamy, Jew/Gentile racism, slavery, and the subjugation of women. Readers will benefit from the following works which challenge the above "accommodation" hypotheses: Ronald A. G. du Preez, *Polygamy in the Bible* (Berrien Springs, Mich.: Adventist Theological Society

Publications, 1993); Theodore D. Weld, *The Bible Against Slavery: Or, An Inquiry into the Genius of the Mosaic System, and the Teachings of the Old Testament on the Subject of Human Rights* (Pittsburgh: United Presbyterian Board of Publication, 1864). These two works offer compelling biblical evidence showing that God at no time tolerated polygamy and slavery. Regarding the alleged issue of the subjugation of women or "patriarchy," George Knight, *Role Relationships of Men and Women: New Testament Teaching* (Chicago, IL: Moody, 1985), and Guenther Haas, "Patriarchy as An Evil that God Tolerated: Analysis and Implications for the Authority of Scripture," *Journal of the Evangelical Theological Society,* September 1995, 321-326, have challenged the notion that male headship (in the home and church) is an evil practice that God tolerated.

[24]Based on selected texts from Rabbinic literature, some have argued that the Old and New Testament era were periods of gender inequality and injustice. However, Richard Hove, *Equality in Christ?: Galatians 3:38 and the Gender Dispute,* 104 note 35, has cited other Rabbinic works to counter the anti-women statements in the oft-quoted statements from that time. One of the best summaries of the role of women in biblical history is provided by Dwight Pratt. Contrary to modern revisionist interpretations which claim that women in Bible times were reduced to little more than goods and chattel, he shows that the position of women among God's people in both the Old and New Testaments contrasted markedly with their status in the surrounding heathen nations. Whatever distorted view currently exists regarding women's place in society and ministry is a departure from the religion of the Bible. See Dwight M. Pratt, "Woman," *The International Standard Bible Encyclopaedia*, ed. James Orr, 4 vols. (Grand Rapids, Mich.: Eerdmans, reprint 1986) 4:3100-3104.

[25]David M. Scholer, "Galatians 3:28 and the Ministry of Women in the Church," in *Theology, News and Notes* (Pasadena, Calif.: Fuller Theological Seminary, June 1998), 20 (italics his).

[26]Rebecca Merrill Groothius, *Good News for Women: A Biblical Picture of Gender Equality* (Grand Rapids, MI: Baker, 1997), 25.

[27]Richard M. Davidson, "Headship, Submission, and Equality in Scripture," in Nancy Vyhmeister, ed., *Women in Ministry: Biblical and Historical Perspectives* (Berrien Springs, MI: Andrews University Press, 1998), 281.

[28]Helen Ward Thompson, "Questions and Answers About Women's Ordination and the Seventh-day Adventist Church," in Patricia A. Habada and Rebecca Frost Brillhart, eds., *The Welcome Table: Setting A Place for Ordained Women* (Langley Park, Md.: TEAMPress, 1995), appendix 4, 318. Thompson attributes the above statement to James Cox, when the latter addressed the Sligo Seventh-day Adventist Church in October 1988.

[29]So argues William G. Johnsson, "Galatians 3:28, 29: Its Significance for the Role of Women in the Church," in a paper presented to the Commission on the Role of Women in the Church at Cohutta Springs, Georgia, July 1989. For an insightful analysis of Gal 3:28 and other key New Testament texts bearing on the women's ordination issue, and for crucial methodological issues involved, see Gerhard F. Hasel, "Hermeneutical Issues Relating to the Ordination of Women: Methodological Reflections on Key Passages," an unpublished 56-page document, May 23, 1994, available at the Adventist Heritage Center, James White Library, Andrews University.

[30]See Ann Coble, "The Lexical Horizon of 'One in Christ': The Use of Galatians

3:28 in the Progressive-Historical Debate Over Women's Ordination" (Th.M. thesis, Covenant Theological Seminary, 1995).

[31]E. Stauffer, "*eis*," in Gerhard Kittel, ed., trans. Geoffrey W. Bromiley, *Theological Dictionary of New Testament* (Grand Rapids, MI: Eerdmans, 1964), 2:434. According to Stauffer, *eis* usually means "single," "once-for-all," "unique" or "only," or "unitary," "unanimous," or "one of two or many," or "only one."

[32]Richard Hove, *Equality in Christ: Galatians 3:28 and the Gender Dispute,* 108 (emphasis his). Again, he writes: "In summary, the expression 'you are all one' does not provide specifics regarding the relationship between parts. Rather, the expression simply states that diverse parts share something in common; they are united in some respect, in contrast to their diversity. Lexically the word *one* [Greek, *eis*] can be used many ways, but not to denote equality. In Galatians 3:28 this word is used to express unity in distinction to a plurality: Jews/Greeks, slaves/free, males/females, by virtue of each sharing in one Christ, are one (ibid., 76).

[33]Richard Hove, *Equality in Christ? Galatians 3:28 and the Gender Dispute,* 119.

[34]John Jefferson Davis, "Some Reflections on Galatians 3:28, Sexual Roles, and Biblical Hermeneutics," *Journal of the Evangelical Theological Society* 19 (1976):204.

[35]Richard Hove, *Equality in Christ? Galatians 3:28 and the Gender Dispute,* 116 (emphasis his).

[36]John Piper and Wayne Grudem, "An Overview of Central Concerns: Questions and Answers," in John Piper and Wayne Grudem, eds., *Recovering Biblical Manhood and Womanhood* (Wheaton, Ill.: Crossway, 1991), 71-72.

[37]Richard Hove, *Equality in Christ?* 110 note 46.

[38]Cf. Acts 19:10; 20:21; Rom 1:16; 2:9ff; 3:9; 10:12; 1 Cor 1:24, etc..

[39]"Gaius, the Roman jurist whose *Institutes* are the most complete Roman law book that has come down to us from near the time of Paul, states that the basic distinction in the law of persons is that all men are either free or slaves." See Francis Lyall, *Slaves, Citizens, Sons: Legal Metaphors in the Epistles* (Grand Rapids, Mich.: Zondervan, 1984), 35, cited in Richard Hove, *Equality in Christ,* 65. As explained by Hove, unlike the slavery practiced in the 18th and 19th centuries, New Testament slavery was different in crucial respects: "There were slaves from different races, slaves who volitionally chose to sell themselves into slavery for economic reasons, and slaves from all walks of life, 'from laborers to philosophers, from farmers to physicians'" (Hove, *Equality in Christ,* ibid.; cf. Ceslas Spicq, *Theological Lexicon of the New Testament,* trans. and ed. James D. Ernest [Peabody, Mass.: Hendrickson, 1994], 1:383).

[40]The words chosen by the apostle for "male and female" (*arsen* and *thelu*) are rare terms that are also employed in Romans 1:26-27 in connection with "men [as males] and women [as females] exchanging natural relations for homosexual ones." Jesus also uses these terms in Matthew 19:4 when, citing Genesis 1:27, he taught that in the beginning, God created "male and female" (cf. Mark 10:6).

[41]Laurel Damsteegt, "Spiritualism and Women: Then and Now," in Mercedes H. Dyer, ed., *Prove All Things: A Response to 'Women in Ministry,'* (Berrien Springs, Mich.: Adventists Affirm, 2000), 251-271.

# 11

# NEW LIGHT ON WOMEN'S ORDINATION

Regardless of one's position on women's ordination, this one fact is incontrovertible: Ordaining women as elders or pastors is new light which the worldwide Seventh-day Adventist church is being urged to embrace.[1] Until recently, Adventists have been unanimous in their view that no precedent for the practice of ordaining women can be found in Scripture, nor in the writings of Ellen G. White and the early Seventh-day Adventist church.[2]

By the 1970s, however, this established position began to be reversed in favor of ordaining women as elders and pastors.

This new trend was created by the converging interests of feminism, liberalism, church leaders' desire to enjoy United States tax law benefits to ministers, questionable church policy revisions and *Church Manual* alterations allowing women to serve as elders, calculated attempts by some influential North American churches unilaterally to ordain women as pastors, the relative silence of leadership to this defiance of two General Conference session votes against women's ordination, a well-orchestrated strategy by influential thought leaders and pro-ordination groups to domesticate the practice in the church, and a determined effort by some church scholars to reinterpret the Bible and early Adventist history to justify the practice.

Despite the aggressive campaign, proponents have been unable to convince the world church of the biblical soundness of their arguments to ordain women as elders or pastors. Thus, on the two occasions that the issue has come up at General Conference sessions (Indianapolis, 1990, and Utrecht, 1995), the overwhelming majority of the church has voted "No" to requests to ordain women.

The book, *Women in Ministry: Biblical and Historical Perspectives* (1998), prepared by an Ad Hoc Committee from the Seventh-day Adventist Theological Seminary in Berrien Springs, Michigan, is supposed to offer the much desired justification for the new light of women's ordination.[3]

*Women in Ministry* deserves a careful evaluation because it captures the best biblical and historical arguments that Adventist proponents of women's ordination are capable of presenting. Because it provides readers with the key issues in the current Adventist debate over women's ordination, this chapter and the subsequent ones will focus on this book.

In this chapter I will explain (1) how *Women in Ministry* differs from a previously published pro-ordination volume, *The Welcome Table*, (2) why we must review this Seminary book, (3) how the book came into being, (4) why dissenting scholarly views were not welcome, (5) how the book fits into a well-orchestrated strategy to legislate and legitimize women's ordination in the Seventh-day Adventist church, and (4) the major conclusions of the work. In later chapters, I will offer an evaluation of the book's biblical and historical arguments.

Taking issue with the authors, some of whom I esteem as close friends, does not involve questioning their sincerity as well meaning Adventist scholars. Neither does it mean that whatever they have written in other areas is necessarily suspect or invalid.

### What Is New About *Women in Ministry*?

*Women in Ministry* was published against a backdrop of an ongoing controversy in the church between liberals (Adventist scholars who believe in the use of modified versions of contemporary higher criticism) and conservatives (those who reject the liberal method).[4] The Seminary Ad Hoc Committee on Hermeneutics and Ordination, the group responsible for producing the book, was a gathering of pro-ordination scholars who, though disagreeing on the appropriateness of the higher critical method, are nonetheless united in their view that women should be ordained as elders or pastors.

The first challenge that faced the committee was how to construct a theological justification for women's ordination without tripping the explosive hermeneutical land mine (the use of contemporary higher criticism) that for years a number of scholars at the Seminary have avoided handling and defusing. Another challenge was how to craft a justification for women's ordination that would appeal to a conservative Adventist church which shows no interest in liberal and feminist reinterpretations of Scripture.

After two years of regular meetings and "animated" discussions, "a spirit of camaraderie developed" among these scholars. With this spirit of friendship, "eventually all the chapters [of the book] were written, rewritten, and approved by the committee."[5] Introducing the book at a special Seminary assembly on October 7, 1998, the chair of the Ad Hoc Committee stated that "no chapter was accepted until all members felt they could live with the document." Even though "each chapter was written by a different author and retains the writer's individual style," explains the book's editor, "careful readers will notice slight differences of opinions between chapters. Our agreement was on the big picture."[6]

The "big picture" that kept the pro-ordination committee together was its members' shared belief that the Bible is not against ordaining women *as elders or pastors.* Without doubt, theirs was a daunting task in pursuit of today's unity in diversity—*theological* unity (women's ordination) amidst *hermeneutical* diversity (conflicting approaches to the Bible). But the authors believe that they accomplished their mission: "We believe that the biblical, theological, and historical perspectives elaborated in this book affirm women in pastoral leadership."[7]

It must be noted that the publication of *Women in Ministry* is not the first time that a group of church scholars collaborated to produce a pro-ordination volume. In 1995, fourteen (14) pro-ordination thought leaders produced the 408-page book, *The Welcome Table: Setting a Table for Ordained Women.*[8] This earlier work did not gain much credibility among thoughtful Adventists because its conclusions were based on revisionist interpretation of the Bible and Adventist history.[9]

But unlike the authors of *The Welcome Table,* many of whom seem to put their liberal and feminist commitments above Scripture, the authors of *Women in Ministry* consciously underscore the claim that their approach to the Bible is different. They disavow the feminist and higher critical method of their ideological cousins.[10] Whether the actual practice in the *Women in Ministry* book is consistent with the claim remains to be seen. Still, insofar as the authors claim to uphold the church's generally accepted approach to Scripture on this particular issue, I personally sense a far closer affinity with the authors of the Seminary book than with those of *The Welcome Table.*

The Seminary volume can be viewed as new only in the sense that, for the first time, a group of church scholars attempted to present *conservative* arguments to justify women's ordination. *Women in Ministry* concludes with *The Welcome Table* that there is support in the Bible and the writings of Ellen White to ordain women as elders or pastors. However, the Seminary book presents new arguments and, in some instances articulates more carefully old arguments, to justify women's ordination.

I applaud the authors for making the best case possible for their positions, even though a careful study of their claims will show conclusively that the biblical and historical evidence does not support the ordination of women as elders or pastors.

### Why Review *Women in Ministry?*

Why should one evaluate *Women in Ministry: Biblical and Historical Perspectives* (1998)? After all, its authors describe the book as the product of two years of regular meetings which always began with "prayer, often several prayers—pleading with God for wisdom and understanding, love and firmness, but most of all for God's leading that His will might be done in the meeting and in the book." Why assess a work its writers already believe to be "a contribution to an ongoing dialog"?[11]

Again, why should one take another look at a 438-page volume the editor claims has the support of the ministerial department of the General Conference?[12] And why re-examine a book that a respected scholar and General Conference vice-president has already acclaimed as a "deeply spiritual, highly reasoned, consistently logical approach to the issue of women's ordination"?[13]

First, even a Spirit-guided scholarly contribution deserves careful evaluation. God's inspired Word obliges every Christian to do so: "Quench not the Spirit. Despise not prophesyings. *Prove all things; hold fast that which is good"* (1 Thess 5:19-21).

Second, the twenty authors of the book have invited those who disagree with the volume's findings to engage them in a dialogue: "This volume represents the understanding of the Seminary Ad Hoc Committee on Hermeneutics and Ordination. We do not claim to speak for others, either at the Seminary or in church administration. Some may disagree with our findings. That is their privilege. We welcome their responses and invite them to dialogue."[14]

Third, *Women in Ministry* is the latest attempt by a group of Seventh-day Adventist scholars to find biblical and historical justification for ordaining women *as elders or pastors.* Coming from the Seventh-day Adventist Theological Seminary at Andrews University, the book will undoubtedly influence those members of the worldwide Seventh-day Adventist church who look to the Seminary for sound biblical teaching, training, and guidance.[15] It is this need for safe and discerning theological direction that may have prompted "several" North American Division leaders, shortly after the 1995 Utrecht General Conference session, to approach the Seminary faculty for answers to questions raised by their petition to the world body of Seventh-day Adventists for divisional ordinations.[16]

Fourth, the book provides a critical component in a carefully thought-out, step-by-step strategy to legislate, if not legitimize, the practice of women's ordination in the Seventh-day Adventist church.[17] One such effort is contained in a very significant document that was formally accepted at the October 9, 1997, North American Division year-end meeting. The document is the Division's "President's Commission on Women in Ministry—Report."[18]

Fifth, *Women in Ministry* contains some of the most creative arguments ever marshaled by church scholars to change the minds of a Bible-believing church that has twice overwhelmingly rejected the call to ordain women as pastors.[19] We need to ascertain whether or not the arguments found in the volume will stand the test of biblical and historical scrutiny.

Sixth, the book is being promoted in certain quarters of the Adventist church as the official position of the Seminary and as the product of "sound Biblical and historical scholarship."[20] Even if such statements are dismissed as unfounded, the fact still remains that some Adventists and non-Adventists will consider this work a model of thorough, profound Adventist scholarship on a divisive and controversial issue.[21]

Seven, the book has been sent to church leaders around the world, ostensibly "to provide carefully researched information and foster dialogue."[22] Also proponents of women's ordination distributed *Women in Ministry* to some delegates at the 2000 Toronto GC session. Before church leaders promote and use the book as the basis of informed decision-making in their respective fields, they must ensure that the volume is not fatally defective in biblical and historical scholarship.

Eight, in a recent book, *A Brief History of Seventh-day Adventists*, a work described as an "accurate history of Adventism," the author builds upon the conclusions of both *Women in Ministry* and *The Welcome Table*, and recommends them as volumes that accurately capture the views and practice of the early SDA church on the issue. Before we embrace the revised history found in these recommended works, we must carefully ascertain the factual basis for the claim that "there were female ministers in early Adventism."[23]

These eight reasons offer the justification for the review of *Women in Ministry*. If the book's conclusions are proven to be valid, they should be incorporated into the Seventh-day Adventist church's Bible-based beliefs and lifestyle. And the church should be encouraged immediately to rectify its 150-year-old practice of ministry and ordination.[24] On the other hand, if the evidence and reasoning in the volume are found wanting biblically and historically, then the campaign during the past two or three decades by a few influential scholars and leaders to impose women's ordination on the church should be rejected as a tragic mistake and a misguided endeavor.

Before looking at the new light contained in *Women in Ministry*, it may be helpful to briefly mention how this pro-ordination book from the Seminary came into existence.

**How the Book Came Into Being**

The initial request for the book came from "several union presidents of the North American Division" who, before and during the 1995 Utrecht General Conference session, had urged the North American Division President that there be "no turning back" in their campaign for women's ordination.[25] When their petition was rejected by the world body at Utrecht, certain leaders in the North American Division began calling for "a clarification of the Adventist theology of ordination, *culminating in the ordination of women*," and for steps that would lead to "clear understanding and member education regarding valid Adventist hermeneutical principles [of biblical interpretation]."[26]

Notice that the call for "a clarification of Adventist theology of ordination" was really a quest for a scholarly work that would "culminate in the ordination of women." The meaning of "valid Adventist hermeneutical principles" was later made explicit at the October 1995 Year-end meeting of the North American Division leaders to be an approach to Scripture that would ultimately justify their belief in the biblical correctness of women's ordination.

At that October 1995 Year-end meeting in Battle Creek, just three months after the Utrecht vote, the North American leadership announced that a commission was being appointed to recommend ways to "expand the role of women in ministry," recognize and deploy the gifts God has given to women, and "affirm women in pastoral and other spiritual ministries."[27] In their *Statement of Commitment to Women in Gospel Ministry,* adopted on October 13, 1995, the Union presidents of North America also reaffirmed their belief *"in the biblical rightness of women's ordination"* and pledged their support for a clarification of the church's theology of ordination.[28]

This brief background leads one to conclude that the initial request to the Seminary faculty by "several" of these union presidents for a clarification of the Adventist theology of ordination and for a clear understanding regarding valid Adventist hermeneutical principles was a search for a scholarly work that would justify the ordination of women. Some three months *before* the Seminary appointed its Ad Hoc Committee in January 1996 to study issues related to hermeneutics and ordination, some of the North American Division leaders were already convinced of the "biblical rightness of women's ordination."

Why was there a need for the Seminary to clarify the church's principles for interpreting the Bible when the church already had done so—in the "Methods of Bible Study" document, approved by the church's worldwide leaders in 1986 in Rio de Janeiro, Brazil?[29]And why was there a need to clarify the church's theology of ordination, when the church already had articulated its position in the 1988 volume *Seventh-day Adventists Believe . . . : A Biblical Exposition of 27 Fundamental Doctrines* ( 142-150)[30] and our *Minister's Manual* ( 75-79 [1992 edition]; 83-86 [1997 edition])?[31]

The answer seems obvious. It wasn't because the church had no valid hermeneutical principles for interpreting the Bible, nor a sound theology of ordination. It already had these. Instead, some of the pro-ordination leaders wanted a theological validation of their stance on ordination. This was the only way they could justify earlier church policy revisions and *Church Manual* alterations in response to problems resulting from the North American Division's desire to enjoy United States income tax benefits.[32]

Thus, in the production of the Seminary book *Women in Ministry,* the interests of pro-ordination leaders and that of pro-ordination scholars kissed each other. Or as the book's editor later explained, the North American Division leadership, feeling "let down" at Utrecht, wanted the Seminary to *"do something about it [the Utrecht vote]."*[33]

The conclusion is inescapable. After several years of unsuccessful attempts at *legislating the ideology* of women's ordination, the proponents decided that the time had come to try another strategy: the *proclamation of the theology* of women's ordination. Using one of the leading and most influential church institutions, the Seventh-day Adventist Theological Seminary at Andrews University, some of the North American Division leaders sought to shift their strategy of women's ordination *from ideology to theology.* The Seminary book *Women in Ministry* is the result of this strategy.

**Dissenting Views Not Welcome**

The Seminary volume was an attempt to justify theologically the ideology of women's ordination, not a quest for an open-minded investigation into what the Bible has to say on a divisive and controversial issue in the church. The Seminary committee's "dialogue" did not include Andrews University scholars opposed to women's ordination, some of whom, through their earlier published works, had demonstrated a grasp of the crucial issues in the debate.[34] Though twenty authors collaborated to produce the book, the Seminary Ad Hoc Committee allowed no other viewpoints in the book except those favoring women's ordination.[35]

Although dissenting scholarly views were not represented in the committee, readers are informed that during its two years of regular meetings, "sensitivity to the positions of others, both for and against women's ordination was evident."[36] Lamentably, this is typical of the manner in which the issue has been discussed even in official church publications.[37]

Is it not ironic—and unfortunate—that the views of scholars upholding the long-established Seventh-day Adventist convictions on this question are not always welcome today in church publications and even in the book originating from the Seminary? Whose interest is served when, on *unresolved* theological issues, opposing views are excluded even when those views are still embraced by the overwhelming majority of the church through official action?

Promoters of *Women in Ministry* sometimes offer three major reasons for excluding dissenting scholarly views from the book published and financed by the Seminary. First, they argue that, until the publication of *Women in Ministry,* the church never had the chance of hearing the reasoned views of pro-ordination thought leaders. Some claim that unlike opponents of women's ordination who allegedly defied a 1988 moratorium or ban by the General Conference president on publishing and distributing materials on the issue, proponents loyal to the church chose not to present and publicize their theological defense of women's ordination, in compliance with the supposed moratorium. The alleged ban was apparently lifted in 1995 when "several" North American Division leaders met with some professors from Andrews University Theological Seminary and urged them to "do something about Utrecht."[38]

Second, in the opinion of other proponents, the 1990 General Conference session vote was not a categorical No to women's ordination. Instead of a theological reason against the practice, proponents claim that the GC session simply cited pragmatic reasons—"the widespread lack of support" for it and "the possible risk of disunity, dissension, and diversion from the mission of the Church" that could result had the church gone ahead *at that time* in ordaining women as pastors.[39]

Third, some other proponents of women's ordination claim that the 1995 General Conference session addressed "only the procedural recommendation" of the North American Division, not "the theological appropriateness of women's ordination."[40]

The above justification for *Women in Ministry* is based on a creative reinterpretation of church actions on women's ordination (see the previous three endnotes). Yet, building upon these contestable arguments, advocates and promoters believe that a pro-ordination book from the Seminary would now create the much-needed consensus for women's ordination.

Perhaps the pro-ordination General Conference vice-president who chaired the women's ordination business session at Utrecht and who enthusiastically endorsed the book in *Adventist Review* may have spoken for many of the book's authors when he wrote: "Though unfortunately too late to inform prior [Utrecht] debate, my opinion is that *Women in Ministry* has the *potential to be determinative in future* [General Conference?] *discussion.*"[41]

If indeed the intent of the Seminary book is to provide theological reasons to overturn the worldwide decision at Utrecht, some major questions arise: Is it ever right for the Seventh-day Adventist Theological Seminary to allow its prestige and resources to be hijacked for some ideological agenda rejected by the church? If, for instance, a General Conference session votes against homosexuality, can a group of pro-gay theologians in a church institution use the name and resources of the institution to advance their homosexual agenda?

This question is not about the biblical rightness of women's ordination, homosexuality, or any other issue. My point here is simply about the responsibility of the church's leading theological institution to the community of faith at large. What kind of precedent do we set when the Seminary begins to cave in to ideological pressure or "appeals" from some quarters of church leadership?

Also, the concern here is not about whether theologians may legitimately mass-distribute their published works; they have a right to do so. The issue being raised is simply this: Since the book's editor states in the prologue that the authors of *Women in Ministry* "do not claim to speak for others, either at the Seminary or in church administration," is it appropriate for the Seminary (or Andrews University, or any other church institution) to use its resources, name, and influence to promote some privately held opinions that are contrary to official church actions? Would the Seminary (or Andrews University, or some other church institution) do the same for other scholars holding opposing views on this question, and perhaps on another controversial issue like homosexuality?

The authors of *Women in Ministry* sincerely believe that the church made a great mistake at Utrecht, a mistake that they believe constitutes a hindrance to God's purpose and therefore needs to be ameliorated and/or corrected in order for the church to fulfill God's purpose. Does belief in the rightness of a cause justify the excluding of opposing views from a volume promoted and financed by the church's leading theological Seminary?

*Women in Ministry* would have escaped justifiable criticisms that the Seminary's name and resources are being (mis)used to promote the ideological agenda of women's ordination if it had allowed for opposing views. Since the authors "do not claim to speak for others, either at the seminary or in church administration,"[42] would it not have been better for the pro-ordination scholars of the Seminary to have published and financed their private views independently (as other scholars both for and against ordination had previously done), instead of using the Seminary's prestige and resources to gain credibility for their one-sided view?

The book under review would also have gained much credibility and, as we shall later show, would have avoided some of its theological and historical shortcomings if it had allowed for challenges by opposing views.

### A Well-Orchestrated Strategy

As we noted earlier, the initiative for *Women in Ministry* came from some leaders in the North American Division in response to pressure from a relatively small but influential group which has been pushing for women's ordination during the past thirty or more years.

Initially, advocates convinced *church leaders* at the 1975 Spring Council meeting to approve the biblically-compromising practice of ordaining women as *local elders* in the North American Division if "the greatest discretion and caution" were exercised. Later, they succeeded in persuading *church leaders* at the Fall 1984 Annual Council meeting to reaffirm and expand the 1975 decision, voting to "advise each division that it is free to make provisions as it may deem necessary for the election and ordination of women as local elders."[43]

Thus, even though the 1975 provision departed from the New Testament model of church leadership which assigns to men, not women, the headship roles of elder or pastor, and even though the world church had not formally approved of the provision at a General Conference session, in 1984 ordination of women as *elders* was extended from North America to the world field.

Emboldened by their success in influencing church leaders to allow "women elders," pro-ordination advocates proceeded then to urge the *world church* in General Conference session to ordain women as *pastors,* at least in divisions favorable to it. However, at the General Conference sessions both in 1990 (Indianapolis) and 1995 (Utrecht), the representatives of the world church overwhelmingly rejected the pleas to ordain women into the gospel ministry. The votes were 1173 to 377 (in 1990) and 1481 to 673 (in 1995).

In spite of these decisions, proponents of women's ordination determined upon an all-out campaign, including unilateral ordinations in some influential North American churches and institutions. At the same time that these rebellious ordinations were taking place, advocates were also employing a tactic that had served their cause well in the past—namely, working through church leaders to legislate the unbiblical practice.

Without doubt, the most subtle, and yet most ambitious, effort by pro-ordinationists to overturn the worldwide decision is the proposal contained in the North American Division's document "President's Commission on Women in Ministry—Report." The document was voted during the October 7-10, 1997 year-end meeting of the North American church leaders.[44] If fully implemented, it will allow women to occupy the highest headship positions of church leadership, including local church pastor, conference president, union president, division president, and even General Conference president.

I summarize below the major strategies which the document outlines, offering possible reasons behind some of its provisions. Readers familiar with what is going on will recognize that advocates are already energetically implementing these strategies in church publications, print and video media, schools, local churches, conferences and unions.

1. To make "women pastors" a common fixture in the church, conferences are encouraged "to hire more women in pastoral positions"; they are also requested "to set realistic goals to increase the number of women in pastoral ministry in their field [*sic*] during the next three years [culminating in the year 2000—the year of the Toronto General Conference session]";

2. To enlist young people and their parents and teachers in the pro-ordination campaign, Adventist colleges and universities in North America are encouraged "to recruit young women who sense a call to pastoral ministry to pursue ministerial studies";

3. To get people used to the *concept* of women serving in same roles as men, "the NAD edition of the *Adventist Review* and other general church papers [are to] be asked to publish profiles of women serving in pastoral ministry several times a year";

4. To ensure that church members become accustomed to *seeing* "women pastors," the latter must be given "multiple exposures . . . in congregations throughout the NAD," including the "use of print and video media" and "indirect portrayals of women with men in creative approaches to pastoral ministry";

5. To legislate or make official the ordination of women in the Seventh-day Adventist church without risking another General Conference session defeat, the document encourages the world church "to modify the language" in relevant sections of the current *Church Manual* and North American Division working policy so that wherever the words "ordain" or "ordination" occur they will be replaced by "ordain/commission" or "ordination/commissioning"; this modification makes "commissioning" the functional equivalent of "ordination."

6. To implement modifications suggested in the *Church Manual* and North American Division Working Policy, unions and local conferences

are encouraged "to promptly conduct commissioning services for those women who are eligible";

7. To skillfully quiet opposition to women's ordination/"commissioning" at both the local and higher levels of the church, "the Ministerial Association and/or any appropriate structure" should appoint "an 'ombudsman'—a person with insight in the system and denominational policies who can provide feedback and guidance when women in ministry encounter conflict with employing organizations, as well as provide mediation if necessary";

8. To ensure that pro-ordination views are constantly carried in materials produced by the church, "more of the advocacy for women in ministry [should] be channeled through the union papers and other media of mass distribution"; "preparation and dissemination of educational materials in multiple media designed to raise awareness about women in pastoral ministry and the role of women in the church" should be carried out;

9. To silence or censor views opposing women's ordination, "the Church Resources Consortium [should] monitor and audit all NAD-produced and endorsed materials for compliance with a gender-inclusive model for ministry";

10. To make dissenting church members feel as though *they* are out of harmony with the Bible or the official Seventh-day Adventist position, "the division president [should] issue a clear call to the church for gender-inclusiveness at all levels of the church—boards, committees, pastoral assignments, etc."

11. To ensure the eventual possibility for all conference, union or division pastors to be guided by a "woman pastor," the North American Division is urged to "move with a sense of urgency to include a woman with ministerial background as ministerial secretary or an associate ministerial secretary";

12. To give biblical and historical justification for the women's ordination agenda, there should be "(i) multiple articles in denominational periodicals" and "(ii) a hermeneutics conference by the NAD and/or the GC" to "clarify" the church's understanding of biblical interpretation towards the "goals for gender inclusiveness in church organization."

Actually, most of these strategies had been in operation for many years prior to the voting of the document. Advocates had employed them as they had worked through church leaders in their campaign for ordaining women as *elders*. But now, for the first time, the document puts these strategies clearly into print.

Of the twelve strategies listed above, the last one seems to be the most daunting. This is because an overwhelming majority of Seventh-day Adventists in North America and other parts of the world are theological conservatives—Bible-believers. As such they will strongly oppose the pro-ordination campaign, unless advocates are able to come up with ways to interpret the Bible (hermeneutics) to justify the ordaining of women as elders or pastors. This is one reason why some North American leaders approached the Seminary, urging it to "do something about Utrecht."

The rest is now history. As requested, the Seminary's "Ad Hoc Committee on Hermeneutics and Ordination" has carried out its assignment, producing the book *Women in Ministry.* And consistent with the strategies already outlined in the North American Division's "President's Commission on Women in Ministry—Report," the book has been one-sidedly promoted in church publications and widely distributed around the world. Its producers and promoters believe that they have offered the long awaited reasons for the new light urging women's ordination.

### The New Light in *Women in Ministry*

As we mentioned at the beginning of the chapter, until recently, Adventists have been unanimous in their view that no precedent for the practice of ordaining women can be found in Scripture, nor in the writings of Ellen G. White and the early Seventh-day Adventist church[45]

Thus, in order for anyone to overthrow what has been understood as the universal consensus of the Old Testament, New Testament, and early Seventh-day Adventist belief, and thus succeed in introducing new light in the church, they must come up with compelling reasons for women's ordination.

The *Women in Ministry's* writers believe they have done exactly that: "Our conclusion is that ordination and women can go together, that 'women in pastoral leadership' is not an oxymoron, but a manifestation of God's grace in the church." Or as the prologue states: "We believe that the biblical, theological, and historical perspectives elaborated in this book affirm women in pastoral leadership."[46]

Perceptive readers of *Women in Ministry* will notice slight variations in the views of the authors regarding the above conclusions. A majority of the writers are fully convinced that the New Testament "affirms new roles for women in the church that do not preclude women's ordination to ministry" or that it "never" prohibits women from taking "positions of leadership, including headship positions over men."[47]

But a minority is more modest: "It is time for the Adventist Church to calmly admit that the Scriptures are silent on the matter and that we have no direct word from the Lord either in Scripture or in the writings of Ellen White. This is an opportunity therefore for the exercise of prayerful study and sound judgment. It is our responsibility to seek divine guidance and make a decision as best we can in the light of the Adventist understanding of the church and its mission."[48]

Despite the slight differences among the convinced voices ("there are compelling reasons to ordain women") and the cautious voices ("there are no compelling reasons not to ordain"), the two years of animated discussions, writing, rewriting, careful editing, cross-referencing, and approval by all members of the committee has produced a work in which there seem to be ten basic lines of argument for the ordination of women as elders or pastors. I suggest the following as the essential contours of the biblical and historical arguments advanced by *Women in Ministry*:[49]

(1) Genesis 1-3 teaches that God did not institute headship and submission or male-female role distinctions *at creation.* Adam and Eve enjoyed full equality of "shared leadership" or "shared headship." Male headship and female submission were introduced by God *after the Fall;* even then, this was a non-ideal arrangement designed only for the governance of the home, not the church or covenant community.

(2) New Testament teaching on headship and submission (Eph 5:21-33; Col 3:18-19; 1 Pet 3:1-7) suggests that today Christians should aim at reaching the creation ideal of "total equality," understood to mean the obliteration of any gender-based role differentiation.

(3) A careful study of the Bible reveals that there was actually at least one "woman priest" in the Old Testament. God Himself ordained Eve as a priest alongside Adam when, after the Fall, He dressed both as priests in the garden of Eden using animal skins. Prophetesses Miriam, Deborah, and Huldah exercised headship or leadership roles over men.

(4) The Bible also reveals that there were actually "women apostles and leaders" in the New Testament. Junia (Rom 16:7), for example, was an outstanding "female apostle," and Phoebe (Rom 16:1-2) was a "female minister."

(5) The New Testament teaching of "the priesthood of all believers" suggests that women may be ordained as elders or pastors.

(6) When correctly understood, biblical texts (like 1 Tim 2:11ff., 1 Cor

14:34ff., etc.) which seem to preclude women from headship responsibilities in the home as husbands and fathers and in the church as elders or pastors are temporary restrictions that applied only to specific situations during New Testament times.

(7) Careful study of early Seventh-day Adventist history reveals that women actually served as pastors in those days and were issued ministerial certificates. Ellen G. White apparently endorsed the call of such women to the gospel ministry.

(8) The 1881 General Conference session voted to ordain women. This vote, however, was apparently ignored or killed by the all-male General Conference Committee (comprised of George I. Butler, Stephen Haskell, and Uriah Smith).

(9) A landmark statement in 1895 by Ellen G. White called for ordaining women to the gospel ministry. This statement could have spurred on the male brethren who were reluctant to implement the alleged 1881 General Conference decision.

(10) Ellen G. White was herself ordained and was issued ministerial credentials.

In subsequent chapters I will argue that the above assertions are based on speculative and questionable reinterpretations of Scripture as well as misleading and erroneous claims regarding Adventist history. Yet on the basis of such "biblical, theological, and historical" evidence, *Women in Ministry* seeks to convince readers of the new light of ordaining women *as elders or pastors.*

But there is also a moral-ethical argument. Emphasizing the ethical necessity of ordaining women as elders or pastors, some of the *Women in Ministry* authors argue that "it is morally reprehensible to hold back from women the one thing that formally recognizes their work within the church." "It is imperative" that the church act "with justice, with mercy, and with courage on behalf of its women." The failure of the church to act ethically, or a delay on its part to do so, will compel "the forces of history" (such as the churches in North America which unilaterally engaged in "congregational ordinations") to drag the church along.[50]

Moreover, we are told, unless the new light of women's ordination is implemented, the witness of the church will not only be discredited in countries where it is wrong to discriminate against women, but it will make God "look bad." Thus, the church's rejection of women's ordination will be an affront to the character of God, even as slavery was in the nineteenth century.[51] As we saw in the previous chapter, this new revelation that is to eradicate the gender caste discrimination in the church is built on egalitarian feminism's ideology of full equality, not Galatians 3:28 as alleged by *Women in Ministry.*

If the reader is not yet convinced by *Women in Ministry*'s biblical, theological, historical, and moral or ethical arguments, there is one final argument: We must listen to the voice of the Holy Spirit as He calls upon us today to change our patterns of ministry in response to the pragmatic needs of a growing church. Writes the editor in her summation chapter:

"If circumcision, based on divine [Old Testament] mandate, could be changed [by the apostles, elders, and believers, together with the Holy Spirit, at the Jerusalem Council of Acts 15], how much more could patterns of ministry [ordaining women as elders and pastors], which lack a clear 'Thus says the Lord,' be modified to suit the needs of a growing church?"[52]

Because my later chapters will evaluate the contents of the book, for now I will simply make the following comments in response to the "moral imperative" argument and the appeal to the Holy Spirit's leading to meet the pragmatic needs of a growing church: (1) For believing Christians, there is a "moral imperative" always to trust and obey biblical truth. Whenever they are compelled to believe and practice error, that imperative is not moral—it is coercion. (2) The Holy Spirit cannot lead believers today into new truths or new light that contradict those already established in His inspired Word.

Therefore, *Women in Ministry*'s arguments concerning ethics and the Holy Spirit can only be sustained if the book's biblical, theological, and historical arguments are compelling enough to overthrow the historic understanding of Seventh-day Adventists that ordaining women is an unbiblical practice.

**Conclusion**

"Doing something about Utrecht" is what *Women in Ministry* is all about. It is an attempt by well-meaning scholars to provide a much-desired biblical and historical justification for the ordination of women as elders and pastors. Their motives are noble. But are their conclusions biblical?

While a majority of the worldwide Seventh-day Adventist church has twice voted against women's ordination, a majority of scholars at the Seminary is believed to favor the practice. How should a theological institution of the church conduct itself when the scholarly opinion conflicts with the churchly decision? Should an ideological majority at the Seminary exclude opposing views on theological questions they contend are *unresolved?*

The authors of *Women in Ministry* "do not claim to speak for the others, either at the Seminary or in church administration." Yet the resources, name, and influence of the Seminary at Andrews University have been employed to publish and promote their privately held opinions. Is this appropriate? Should a church institution allow its prestige or resources to be used by *some* church leaders (or even some influential individuals or ideological organizations) to promote controversial views that run contrary to positions taken by the worldwide church?

These questions bring into focus the role we must accord to the opinions of scholars, the voice of the majority, political pressure from some church leaders, and the decisions of church councils, whenever we are called upon to decide on unresolved theological issues.

Ellen G. White reminded us that "God will have a people upon the earth to maintain the Bible, and the Bible only, as the standard of all doctrines and the basis of all reforms. The *opinions of learned men, the deductions of science, the creeds or decisions of ecclesiastical councils,* as numerous and discordant as are the churches which they represent, *the voice of the majority—not one nor all of these* should be regarded as evidence for or against any point of religious faith. Before accepting any doctrine or precept, we should demand a plain 'Thus said the Lord' in its support" (*The Great Controversy,* 595, emphasis mine).

Heeding the above counsel, in subsequent chapters of *Must We Be Silent?* I will attempt to evaluate the biblical and historical evidence marshaled by *Women in Ministry* in support of ordaining women as elders or pastors. As I mentioned earlier, if the book's conclusions are proven to be valid, they should be incorporated into the Seventh-day Adventist church's Bible-based beliefs and lifestyle. And the church should be encouraged immediately to rectify its 150-year-old practice of ministry and ordination.

On the other hand, if the evidence and reasoning in the volume are found wanting biblically and historically, then the campaign during the past two or three decades by a few influential scholars and leaders to impose women's ordination on the worldwide church should be rejected as a tragic mistake and a misguided endeavor. Only as we "prove all things," examining "whether those things are so," can we fully decide whether the determined effort to introduce this new light in the church is inspired by biblical theology or political ideology.

---

**Footnotes**

[1]Christians must always welcome new light from God's Word, as long as the proposed new light does not contradict an established biblical truth. For a careful summary of what Ellen G. White taught about "new light," see P. Gerard Damsteegt, "New Light in the Last Days," *Adventists Affirm* 10/1 (Spring1996): 5-13.

[2]In my *Receiving the Word* ( 123-126), I have challenged revisionist reinterpretations of Adventist beliefs and practice of ministry (see also 138-140, notes 34-44 of my book).

[3]Nancy Vyhmeister, ed., *Women in Ministry: Biblical and Historical Perspectives* (Berrien Springs, Mich.: Andrews University Press, 1998). The generic phrase "women in ministry," employed as a title for the book, can be misleading. For, the authors' goal was not simply the ministry of women in the church (which has never been opposed by the Adventist church), but rather ordaining women as elders and pastors.

[4]See my *Receiving the Word: How New Approaches to the Bible Impact Our Biblical Faith and Lifestyle* (Berrien Springs, Mich.: Berean Books, 1996).

[5]Nancy Vyhmeister, "Prologue," in *Women in Ministry,* 2.

[6]Ibid., 4.

[7]Ibid., 5.

[8]*The Welcome Table: Setting A Place for Ordained Women,* edited by Patricia A. Habada and Rebecca Frost Brillhart (Langley Park, Md.: TEAMPress, 1995). The "fourteen prominent SDA historians, theologians, and professionals" who contributed essays to the book are: Bert Haloviak, Kit Watts, Raymond F. Cottrell, Donna Jeane Haerich, David R. Larson, Fritz Guy, Edwin Zackrison, Halcyon Westphal Wilson, Sheryll Prinz-McMillan, Joyce Hanscom Lorntz, V. Norskov Olsen, Ralph Neall, Ginger Hanks Harwood, and Iris M. Yob.

[9]In the previous chapter, I called attention to the fact that in *The Welcome Table* some of the authors argued that Bible passages (like Eph 5:22-33; Col 3:18-19; 1 Pet 3:1-7; 1 Cor 11:3, 11-12; 14:34-35; 1 Tim 2:11-14; 3:2; and Titus 1:6) which Adventists historically understood as having a bearing on male-female role relations in both the home and the church are the product of the Bible writers' faulty logic or mistaken rabbinic interpretations in vogue in their day. Reasoning along feminist and higher-critical lines, some of the writers maintained that the apostle Paul erred in his interpretation of Genesis 1-3 when he grounded his teaching of role distinctions between male and female in Creation and the Fall. They claimed that the apostle Paul's statements were merely expressions of uninspired personal opinions—opinions that reflect his culture and hence do not apply to us. To these authors, Paul was "a man of his own time." He occasionally glimpsed the ideal that Jesus established during His time on earth; yet he never fully arrived at "the gospel ideal" of "full equality" or complete role interchangeability in both the home and the church. For a brief evaluation of the pro-ordination arguments by some of the authors in *The Welcome Table,* see my *Receiving the Word,* chapter 5, part 2, 126-129.

[10]See Vyhmeister, "Prologue," in *Women in Ministry,* 3, 5, note 1. Observe, however, that contrary to the church's official position in "The Methods of Bible Study" document

(*Adventist Review,* January 22, 1987, pages 18-20), Robert M. Johnston (a *Women in Ministry* author), for example, has recently argued for the use of the historical-critical method. See his "The Case for a Balanced Hermeneutic," *Ministry,* March 1999, 10-12.

[11]Quoted portions are from the prologue and epilogue of the book *Women in Ministry: Biblical and Historical Perspectives,* ed. Nancy Vyhmeister (Berrien Springs, Mich.: Andrews University Press, 1998), 2, 436.

[12]Nancy Vyhmeister, the editor of *Women in Ministry,* is quoted as making this comment during her October 1998 presentation at the meeting of the pro-ordination group Association of Adventist Women held in Loma Linda, California. For an account of her presentation, see Colleen Moore Tinker, "Seminary States Position in *Women in Ministry,*" *Adventist Today,* November-December 1998, 24, 10.

[13]Calvin B. Rock, "Review of *Women in Ministry*," *Adventist Review,* April 15, 1999, 29. Coming from "a general vice president of the General Conference . . . [and a holder of] doctoral degrees in ministry and Christian ethics," the above statement is designed to be taken seriously by readers of *Adventist Review.* Dr. Rock chaired the business session at the 1995 Utrecht General Conference session. In his opinion, the pro-ordination book of the Seminary "offers a sterling challenge to those who see Scripture as forbidding women's ordination. And it provides welcome data for those who support women's ordination but who lack professional materials to bolster their belief and convincing insights for those who have not known quite how or what to decide" (ibid.). Our re-examination of the pro-ordination volume will put the above book review into a better perspective (see my later chapters in the present book).

[14]Vyhmeister, "Prologue" in *Women in Ministry,* 5. Of the 20 scholars whose works are published in *Women in Ministry,* 15 were appointed by the Seminary Dean's Council—a chair of the Ad Hoc Committee and editor of the book (Nancy Vyhmeister) and representatives from each of the six departments of the Seminary (Jo Ann Davidson, Richard Davidson, Walter Douglas, Jacques Doukhan, Roger Dudley, Jon Dybdahl, Denis Fortin, Robert Johnston, George Knight, Jerry Moon, Larry Richards, Russell Staples, Peter van Bemmelen, Randal Wisbey). Of the five remaining writers whose works appear in the book, two were Master of Divinity students (Michael Bernoi, Alicia Worley), and three others are Andrews University scholars, apparently invited because of their pro-ordination stance (Daniel Augsburger, Raoul Dederen, Keith Mattingly). Of the three scholars invited by the committee, the first two are retired (emeritus) Seminary professors and the last is a faculty member in the undergraduate religion department at Andrews University.

[15]One favorable reviewer of the book writes: "It is both appropriate and timely for Seminary professors to lead the church in a study of the theology of women's ordination as it relates to the mission of the Adventist Church. What does the Bible say about this? What is theologically sound? What does our Adventist heritage lead us to do now?" See Beverly Beem, "What If . . . Women in Ministry," *Focus* [Andrews University alumni magazine], Winter 1999, 30. Beem is chair of the Department of English at Walla Walla College. In her opinion, the Seminary book presents such a "powerful argument" for women's ordination that "to say that the ordination of women is contrary to Scripture or to the tradition of the Adventist Church means going against an impressive array of evidence otherwise" (ibid., 31). In later chapters, I will challenge what our pro-ordination reviewer describes as the Seminary authors' "impressive array of evidence" for women's ordination.

[16]According to the editor of the book, "less than one month after the Utrecht vote [rejecting autonomy for Divisions regarding women's ordination], several union presidents of the North American Division met with the faculty of the Seventh-day Adventist Theological Seminary, still asking the same question: May a woman legitimately be ordained to pastoral ministry? If so, on what basis? If not, why not? What are the issues involved—hermeneutics? Bible and theology? custom and culture? history and tradition? pragmatism and missiological needs? And furthermore, how could all these facets of the issue be presented in a logical, coherent manner? Would the Seminary faculty please address these questions and provide answers?" (Vyhmeister, "Prologue," in *Women in Ministry,* 1).

[17]Though historically Seventh-day Adventists did not have women elders and pastors, many women have served the church well in positions of responsibility and outreach, from the local church to the General Conference level. They did so without ordination. However, for about thirty years a small but influential group of people has been working to move the Seventh-day Adventist church a little at a time to legislate the ordination of women as elders and pastors. In the course of their campaign, those pushing for women's ordination have received endorsements from some church leaders who have effected a series of Annual Council policy revisions and *Church Manual* alterations, allowing for a change in the church's longstanding policy regarding the ministry of ordained elders and pastors. For a brief history of how tax-benefit considerations led the church into redefinitions of Adventist practice of ministry, see [C. Mervyn Maxwell,] "A Very Surprising (and Interesting) History," *Adventists Affirm* 12/3 (Fall 1998): 18-22 (included in this volume on 225-230); cf. Laurel Damsteegt, "Pushing the Brethren," ibid., 24-27.

[18]Among the 13 recommendations aimed at "affirming and encouraging women in ministry," the document expresses an "urgent need to study and clarify the church's understanding and application of biblical hermeneutics" and that "this should take the form of: (i) multiple articles in denominational periodicals" and (ii) "a hermeneutics conference by the NAD and/or the GC." See Article XII of the North American Division "President's Commission on Women in Ministry—Report." The entire document, with an analysis, is found in *Adventists Affirm* 12/3 (Fall 1998): 5-17, and is included in this volume Appendix D, 391-404. As I will attempt to show in the next section, the initial request to the Seminary faculty by "several" North American Division union presidents for a clarification of Adventist theology of ordination and for a clear understanding regarding valid Adventist hermeneutical principles was really a search for a scholarly work that would justify the ordination of women. Observe that the generic phrase "women in ministry," employed by the Seminary's Ad Hoc Committee on Hermeneutics and Ordination as a title for their book, is misleading. Like the North American Division President's commission on "Women in Ministry," the Seminary authors' goal was not simply the ministry of women in the church (which has never been opposed by the Adventist church), but rather ordaining women as elders and pastors.

[19]At the 1990 Indianapolis session of the General Conference, by a vote of 1173 to 377, the world field rejected the call to ordain women as pastors. Also, at the 1995 Utrecht session of the General Conference, by a vote of 1481 to 673, the worldwide church refused to grant the North American Division's request to ordain women in its own territory. Despite the "spin" by pro-ordination advocates to the effect that the delegates at the two General Conference sessions didn't quite understand what they were voting for,

the fact remains that at these two world assemblies, the Bible-believing Seventh-day Adventist family, 90% of which lives outside the industrialized countries of North America, Europe, and Australia, made it clear that the arguments for women's ordination are not biblically convincing.

[20]For example, Roger L. Dudley, the author of one of the chapters of the volume, recently stated: "It is important to note that *Women in Ministry* represents the official view of the Seminary and the position of virtually all of its faculty. Whatever the book may accomplish in the church at large, it is the hope of the [Seminary Ad Hoc] committee that it will demonstrate that the Seminary faculty stands for sound Biblical and historical scholarship on this contemporary and controversial issue" (see Roger L. Dudley, "[Letter to the Editor Regarding] *Women in Ministry," Adventist Today,* January-February 1999, 6). Similarly, an article titled "Seminary States Position in *Women in Ministry"* quotes Nancy Vyhmeister, the editor of the Seminary book, as saying: "With the total support of the university and the seminary administration and with the support of about 90% of the seminary faculty [who are believed to favor women's ordination], the book came out." Nancy Vyhmeister made this comment at the annual convention of the Association of Adventist Women held in Loma Linda, California, in October 1998 (see Colleen Moore Tinker, "Seminary States Position in Women in Ministry," *Adventist Today,* November-December, 1998). Apparently, it is the comment by the book's editor that *Women in Ministry* enjoys the "total support of the university and the seminary administration" that has been misunderstood as an official Seminary endorsement of the book. But the chair of the Seminary Ad Hoc Committee and editor of the book has categorically repudiated such a claim (see Vyhmeister, "Prologue," in *Women in Ministry,* 5).

[21]Calvin Rock writes that "the Seventh-day Adventist Church, and the broader Christian community, are indebted to the 20 authors of *Women in Ministry"* for "producing such a thoughtful, thorough treatment of the major aspects of the question 'Should women be ordained as pastors in the Seventh-day Adventist Church?'" In his estimation, the book employs "skillful exegesis of Scripture and careful examination of relevant E. G. White materials," showing why "liberating knowledge of contextual and linguistic backgrounds is absolutely vital in ecclesiastical debate" (Rock, "Review of *Women in Ministry," Adventist Review,* April 15, 1999, 29). Given the one-sided book reviews that have been presented in several Adventist publications, Doug Jones's editorial comment in *Focus* magazine is worth remembering: "The faculty in the Seminary are to be commended for their earnest and critical exploration of women and Christian ministry. . . . I encourage *Focus* readers to read *Women in Ministry* with care as an important step in achieving balance" (see Jones's editorial note to Malcolm Dwyer's letter to the editor, "Seeking Solid Backing," in *Focus,* Spring 1999, 5).

[22]In an accompanying letter on the stationery of the Seventh-day Adventist Theological Seminary, the rationale for the free distribution of the book to church leaders around the world is explained as follows: "Because of your position as a thought leader in the Seventh-day Adventist Church, you have been selected to receive a gift copy of this important study of the place of women in the church's ministry. The book is not intended to incite polemics on ordination, but to provide carefully researched information and foster dialogue. If you have questions or comments, feel free to direct them to the individual authors or to the editor of the book, all of them at Andrews University. May God bless your service in His cause."

[23]In making his claim that there were "female ministers in early Adventism," George R. Knight, *A Brief History of Seventh-day Adventists* (Hagerstown, Md.: Review and Herald, 1999), 104-107, cited *Women in Ministry*, 187-234, and *The Welcome Table*, 27-59. For a helpful corrective to the revisionist interpretation of Adventist history relative to the question of women's ordination, see *Prove All Things*, 231-312.

[24]Until very recently, the Seventh-day Adventist practice has limited ordination of *elders* and *pastors* to males alone. (Biblically speaking there is no distinction between elder and pastor.) However, through a series of Annual Council church policy revisions, a theologically and ethically-inconsistent practice has been instituted in recent times that allows women to be ordained as elders, but not as pastors. We must not miss the implication of this biblically-untenable practice. If women can be ordained as local elders, it is equally valid for them to be ordained as pastors. But by the same token, if the practice of ordaining women as local elders is unbiblical, it is also unbiblical to ordain them as pastors. So the question really facing the church is this: Is ordaining women as *elders* biblical? If it is, we must continue the practice and extend it to include ordaining women as pastors. On the other hand, if ordaining women as local elders is not scriptural, we must *reconsider* previous church council actions in order to come into harmony with the Bible. In an earlier work, *Searching the Scriptures: Women's Ordination and the Call to Biblical Fidelity* (Berrien Springs, Mich.: Adventists Affirm, 1995), I have argued for the latter option—namely for the church to reconsider previous church council actions in order to come into harmony with the Bible. This approach alone preserves the 150-year-old biblical practice of the Adventist church.

[25]See, for example, Alfred C. McClure, "NAD's President Speaks on Women's Ordination: Why Should Ordination be Gender Inclusive?" *Adventist Review* [North American Division edition], February 1995, 14-15; cf. Gary Patterson, "Let Divisions Decide When to Ordain Women," *Spectrum* 24/2 (April 1995), 36-42. For responses to the above view, see the articles by Ethel R. Nelson, "'No Turning Back' on Ordination?" and C. Mervyn Maxwell, "Response to NAD President's Request to Annual Council" in *Adventists Affirm* 9/1 (Spring 1995): 42-46, 30-37, 67; cf. Samuel Koranteng-Pipim, *Searching the Scriptures: Women's Ordination and the Call to Biblical Fidelity* (Berrien Springs, Mich.: Adventists Affirm, 1995), 9-14, 88-90.

[26]After the rejection of the North American Division's petition at Utrecht, the Pacific Union Conference, one of the largest North American union conferences, took an action they considered to be a road map to eventually ordaining women. Among other things, the union executive committee passed a resolution calling upon the General Conference, through the North American Division, to initiate a process that leads to: (A) "a clarification of the Adventist theology of ordination, *culminating in the ordination of women*"; and (B) "action steps that leads to a clear understanding and member education regarding valid Adventist hermeneutical principles." The executive committee of the Pacific Union also released a document affirming the group's commitment to the goal of women's ordination and to working towards the day when it will be realized. See "Pacific Union Executive Committee Maps Course for Women," *Pacific Union Recorder*, October 2, 1995, 3, 11, emphasis mine.

[27]See the introduction to "President's Commission on Women in Ministry—Report" reproduced in *Adventists Affirm* 12/3 (Fall 1998): 13 and in this volume on 399.

[28]"A Statement of Commitment to Women in Gospel Ministry from the North

American Division Union Presidents," October 13, 1995, emphasis mine. Two years after the North American Division President's commission was appointed, its report was formally accepted on October 9, 1997. Among the specific recommendations for "gender inclusiveness in church organization" is an "urgent need to study and clarify the church's understanding and application of biblical hermeneutics. This should take the form of: (i) multiple articles in denominational periodicals; (ii) a hermeneutics conference sponsored by the NAD and/or the GC." See Article XII of the Report of the "President's Commission on Women in Ministry." The entire document is worth reading, if one is to capture the scope of the strategies to achieve a gender-inclusive ministry (see 399-404 in this volume).

[29]At the 1986 Annual Council meeting in Rio de Janeiro, Brazil, church leaders representing all the world fields of the Seventh-day Adventist church approved the report of the General Conference's "Methods of Bible Study Committee" as representative of the church's hermeneutical position. This document was published in the *Adventist Review,* January 22, 1987, pages 18-20, and reproduced as Appendix C in my *Receiving the Word,* 355-362. Generally, loyal Adventists embrace the 1986 "Methods of Bible Study" document as reflecting Adventism's historic principles of interpretation. For a discussion of how Adventist scholars have reacted to the "Methods of Bible Study" document, see my *Receiving the Word,* 75-99. For more on the history of Adventist Bible interpretation, see C. Mervyn Maxwell, "A Brief History of Adventist Hermeneutics," *Journal of the Adventist Theological Society* 4/2 (1993): 209-226; Don F. Neufeld, "Biblical Interpretation in the Advent Movement," in *Symposium on Biblical Hermeneutics,* ed. Gordon Hyde (Washington, D.C.: Biblical Research Institute, 1974), 109-15; George Reid, "Another Look At Adventist Hermeneutics," *Journal of the Adventist Theological Society* 2/1 (1991): 69-76.

[30]*Seventh-day Adventists Believe . . . : A Biblical Exposition of 27 Fundamental Doctrines* (Washington, D.C.: Ministerial Association of the General Conference of Seventh-day Adventists, 1988), esp. 142-150. Produced by some 194 Seventh-day Adventist thought leaders around the world, this "carefully researched" volume is to be received "as representative of . . . [what] Seventh-day Adventists around the globe cherish and proclaim," and as furnishing "reliable information on the beliefs of our [Seventh-day Adventist] church" (ibid., vii, iv, v).

[31]*Seventh-day Adventist Minister's Handbook* (Silver Spring, Md.: Ministerial Association of the General Conference of Seventh-day Adventists, 1997), 83-86. The "Ordination Statement" in the *Minister's Handbook* sets forth Adventists' understanding of the nature, significance, qualifications, and the responsibility of ordination. A note attached to "Statement of Ordination" reads: "This section reproduces the statement on ministerial ordination prepared by the General Conference Ministerial Association and the GC Biblical Research Institute. The statement received broad input from the world field and went through numerous revisions. It purposely omits the gender issue in ministerial ordination, seeking rather to lay down basic principles by which all ministerial ordination issues can be measured" (ibid., 83 [1997 edition]).

[32]For more on the relationship between the issues of income-tax benefits and ordination, see [C. Mervyn Maxwell, editor] "A Very Surprising (and Interesting) History," *Adventists Affirm* 12/3 (Fall 1998): 18-23, appearing on 225-230 of *Prove All Things;* cf. *Receiving the Word,* 125-126; 140, notes 43 and 44.

[33]The editor of the unofficial magazine *Adventist Today* summarizes the circumstances leading to the production of the Seminary book, as narrated by Nancy Vyhmeister, chair of

the Seminary Ad Hoc Committee and editor of the book, at the October 1998 meeting of the pro-ordination group Association of Adventist Women held in Loma Linda, California. On the circumstances leading to the feeling of "let down," Vyhmeister mentioned that in the wake of the Utrecht defeat of the North American Division petition for women's ordination, people from opposite ends of the ordination spectrum blamed or praised the Seminary for sending two representatives with opposing viewpoints. She, however, explained that the two professors who spoke at Utrecht (Raoul Dederen and P. Gerard Damsteegt) did not speak for the Seminary: "Those people were invited by 'someone else,' and they agreed to speak long before the seminary knew anything about it." When, therefore, less than a month after Utrecht "several" North American leaders met with the Seminary faculty and told them, "you let us down [at Utrecht]; you're against women's ordination," reports *Adventist Today*'s editor, "every representative of the seminary who was attending the meeting insisted that they were not against women's ordination. In fact, Nancy said, about 90% of the seminary faculty favor women's ordination." What follows is significant: "*'Then do something about it,'* one union president said. Dr. [Werner] Vyhmeister, dean of the seminary and Nancy's husband, agreed and said that the Dean's Council would decide what to do. The outcome of that decision was a fifteen-person committee which [was] formed to study the subject of hermeneutics and ordination" (see Colleen Moore Tinker, "Seminary States Position in *Women in Ministry,*" *Adventist Today,* November-December, 1998, 24, 10; emphasis mine) "Doing something about Utrecht" is what the Seminary book is all about, rather than being a quest for an open-minded investigation of what the Bible actually teaches on the subject of women in ministry. Some North American leaders wanted the scholars at the Seminary to speak with one voice in favor of women's ordination.

[34]See, for example, Samuele Bacchiocchi, *Women in the Church: A Biblical Study on the Role of Women in the Church* (Berrien Springs, Mich.: Biblical Perspectives, 1987); C. Raymond Holmes, *The Tip of An Iceberg: Biblical Authority, Biblical Interpretation, and the Ordination of Women in Ministry* (Berrien Springs, Mich.: Adventists Affirm and Wakefield, Mich.: Pointer Publications, 1994); Samuel Koranteng-Pipim, *Searching the Scriptures: Women's Ordination and the Call to Biblical Fidelity* (Berrien Springs, Mich.: Adventists Affirm, 1995). At the time they published their works, Samuele Bacchiocchi was a professor of church history and theology in the religion department of Andrews University; C. Raymond Holmes was the director of the Doctor of Ministry Program and professor of Worship and Preaching at the Theological Seminary; and Samuel Koranteng-Pipim was a Ph.D. candidate in systematic theology at the Theological Seminary, having served there as a contract teacher in theology and ethics (see also next note).

[35]Of the 20 authors who collaborated to produce the book, one was the Seminary professor who presented the pro-ordination view at Utrecht (Raoul Dederen); but the other Seminary faculty member who presented the opposing view at Utrecht was excluded (P. Gerard Damsteegt, the principal author of the church's *Seventh-day Adventists Believe*). *Women in Ministry* contains an article by an associate professor in the religion department at Andrews University (Keith Mattingly); but a well-known professor in the same department who had published an opposing view (*Women in the Church*) was left out (Samuele Bacchiocchi). Though not part of the initial committee of 15, other Seminary scholars, including a retired faculty member, were allowed to publish their views in the book (George Knight, Denis Fortin, and Daniel Augsburger); but another equally competent retired faculty member who had earlier challenged women's ordination (in his *The Tip of An Iceberg*)

was not invited to contribute a chapter (C. Raymond Holmes). Two Seminary students' works appear in the book (Michael Bernoi and Alicia Worley); but not a single Seminary student opposing women's ordination was included (at that time Samuel Koranteng-Pipim was a doctoral candidate and had authored the book *Searching the Scriptures*). It is clear that the Seminary Ad Hoc Committee decided that no other viewpoints should be known in the book except those favoring women's ordination. The pro-ordination bias of the committee is also evidenced by the manner in which some cite the works and authors of non-ordination publications (see especially Randal Wisbey, "SDA Women in Ministry, 1970-1998," *Women in Ministry,* 241, 245, 254 note 31).

[36]Vyhmeister, "Prologue," 2.

[37]Space limitations will not permit me to document how, prior to Utrecht, official church publications presented mainly pro-ordination views in their pages. But one of the authors of *Women in Ministry,* despite his pro-ordination bias in chronicling the history of Seventh-day Adventist discussions of the issue, has correctly noted that prior to the 1995 Utrecht General Conference Session, "the *Adventist Review* and *Ministry* published articles dealing with ordination in which the editors took pro-ordination stands" (Randal R. Wisbey, "SDA Women in Ministry: 1970-1998," in *Women in Ministry,* 246). For a recent attempt by editors of a church publication to discredit the works of those attempting to uphold the church's official position, see the editorial comment preceding the article by P. Gerard Damsteegt, "Scripture Faces Current Issues," *Ministry,* April 1999, 23. For a possible explanation of the pro-ordination bias in church publications, see Articles X and XII in the "[North American Division] President's Commission on Women in Ministry—Report," reproduced on 403-404 of the present volume.

[38]In view of these oft-repeated claims by proponents of women's ordination, the following questions deserve a brief response: (1) Was there a ban on publishing and distributing materials on women's ordination between 1988 and 1995? (2) Were advocates of women's ordination relatively silent during the period of the "moratorium" or "ban," while opponents published two books (*The Tip of An Iceberg* [1994] and *Searching the Scriptures* [1995])? These are the facts: In May 1988, while awaiting the July 1989 meeting and recommendation of the "Role of Women Commission," General Conference president Elder Neal C. Wilson appealed to all church members "to abstain from circulating books, pamphlets, letters, and tapes that stir up debate and often generate more confusion [on women's ordination]." Proponents of women's ordination often misinterpret this specific appeal by the General Conference president to mean a permanent moratorium or ban on publishing works on women's ordination. They claim that out of loyalty to the General Conference president they honored his moratorium while those opposed undermined it by publishing and distributing their works. In making these claims, advocates are either unaware of or overlook the facts concerning the General Conference president's appeal and the aggressive campaign mounted by pro-ordination entities. First of all, the president's appeal was not a permanent "ban" or moratorium. Elder Wilson's statement reads: "The 1985 General Conference session action called upon the church to prepare a recommendation by the time of the 1989 Annual Council, so a further meeting of the commission [the Commission on the Role of Women] will be held in July of 1989. Indeed, in such important matters we must at all costs avoid hasty action, and so we will set aside one week to pray together, listen to each other, discuss further papers that will be prepared, and—I hope—come together in a decision dictated by the Holy Spirit. *In the meantime,* I

appeal to all members of the church, whatever their particular convictions on this matter, to avoid further controversy and argument. I request you to abstain from circulating books, pamphlets, letters, and tapes that stir up debate and often generate more confusion. I think it would be much better if we prayed and fasted, and studied the Bible and the writings of Ellen White for ourselves" (Neal C. Wilson, "Role of Women Commission Meets: The General Conference President Reports to the Church," *Adventist Review,* May 12, 1988, 7, emphasis mine). Notice that the president's appeal was not a permanent moratorium or "ban"; it was limited to the period between May 12, 1988 and July 1989 when the Commission was expected to present its theological findings. Even then, the appeal was directed against works that "stir up debate and often generate more confusion." Second, if the moratorium did indeed exist as proponents of women's ordination often claim, (1) then editors of church publications like *Adventist Review* and *Ministry* contravened it when they published several pro-ordination articles during the period between 1988 and 1995; (2) then the pro-ordination authors and some church institutions like Pacific Press, Review and Herald, Andrews University Press, and Loma Linda University Press broke the ban when they published and distributed pro-ordination books like Caleb Rosado's *Broken Walls* (Pacific Press, 1989), and *Women, Church, God: A Socio-Biblical Study* (Loma Linda University Press, 1990), Josephine Benton's *Called by God* (Blackberry Hill Publishers, 1990), V. Norskov Olsen's *Myth and Truth: Church, Priesthood and Ordination* (Loma Linda University Press, 1990), Jennifer Knight's, et al., *The Adventist Woman in the Secular World: Her Ministry and Her Church* (North Ryde, N.S.W., Australia, 1991), Rosa Taylor Banks's, ed., *A Woman's Place* (Review and Herald, 1992), Sakae Kubo's *The God of Relationships* (Review and Herald, 1993), Patricia A. Habada and Rebecca Frost Brillhart's, eds., *The Welcome Table* (TEAMPress, 1995), Lourdes Morales-Gudmundsson's, ed., *Women and the Church: The Feminine Perspective* (Andrews University Press, 1995); (3) then certain authors of the Seminary book violated the alleged "moratorium" by publishing articles in favor of women's ordination; see, for example, Richard M. Davidson's "The Theology of Sexuality in the Beginning: Genesis 1-2" and "The Theology of Sexuality in the Beginning: Genesis 3," *Andrews University Seminary Studies* 26 (1988); Nancy Vyhmeister, "Review of *The Tip of An Iceberg*," *Ministry,* February 1995, 26-28; etc. Space limitations will not allow me to document the fact that during and after the alleged seven-year "moratorium," advocates of women's ordination, including a number of the Seminary authors of *Women in Ministry,* used a number of means to publicize their pro-ordination views. But in spite of their aggressive campaign, proponents failed to convince the world church of the soundness of their theological arguments for women's ordination. A pro-ordination scholar of ethics puts to rest the oft-repeated claim that until the publication of *Women in Ministry* proponents of women's ordination had been relatively silent. He correctly noted that, prior to the more than 2-to-1 defeat of the women's ordination request at Utrecht, "denominational leaders, wit others, had backed ordination with speeches at Annual Council, the speech in Utrecht, and a special strategy committee. The Southeastern California Conference Gender Inclusiveness Commission and others had sent materials to all General Conference delegates. The *Adventist Review* had run special covers, issues, and features promoting women. . . . Some ordination proponents thought that they might win if they got enough materials to the delegates, but found themselves wrong" (Jim Walters, "General Conference Delegates Say NO on Women's Ordination," *Adventist Today,* July-August, 1995, 12-13).

[39]Observe, however, that the above pragmatic reasons—namely, "the widespread lack of support" for it and "the possible risk of disunity, dissension, and diversion from the mission of the Church"—were the secondary reasons stated at the 1990 General Conference session against ordaining women as pastors. Despite the contrary claims of proponents, the primary reason given by those opposing the practice of ordaining women as pastors was that it was unbiblical and out of harmony with the writings of Ellen G. White. Thus, in the opinion of those opposed to women's ordination, to go ahead with a practice that lacked widespread *theological* support could result in "disunity, dissension, and diversion from the mission of the Church." The following are the two recommendations from the "Role of Women Commission" that the 1989 Annual Council brought to the 1990 General Conference session: "1. While the Commission does not have a consensus as to whether or not the Scriptures and the writings of Ellen G. White explicitly advocate or deny the ordination of women to pastoral ministry, it concludes unanimously that these sources affirm a significant, wide ranging, and continuing ministry for women which is being expressed and will be evidenced in the varied and expanding gifts according to the infilling of the Holy Spirit. 2. Further, in view of the widespread lack of support for he ordination of women to the gospel ministry in the world Church and in view of the possible risk of disunity, dissension, and diversion from the mission of the Church, we do not approve ordination of women to the gospel ministry." Notice that whereas the first reason is theological (lack of theological consensus) the second is pragmatic (lack of support and possible risks). By a vote of 1173 to 377, the world church voted against women's ordination. (See *Adventist Review,* July 13, 1990, 15.

[40]One pro-ordination reviewer of the Seminary book sums up the reason for *Women in Ministry* and how the book could be used to justify theologically a possible North American Division "push" of the issue at a future General Conference session: "So why this book? Why now? *Utrecht.* That is the answer given in the prologue to the book. One might think that after the 1995 General Conference session in Utrecht, the discussion would be over and that everyone would go home and quit talking about it. But that has not happened. How could it? The motion voted at Utrecht did not address the theological appropriateness of women's ordination. It addressed only the procedural recommendation of the North American Division that the decision be made by each division. The increasing dissonance between theological understandings and church practice remained unresolved. . . . Now, it is both appropriate and timely for Seminary professors to lead the church in a study of the theology of women's ordination as it relates with the mission of the Adventist church" (Beverly Beem, "What If . . . Women in Ministry," *Focus,* Winter 1999, 30, emphasis hers). In response to the so-called procedural argument, a respected North American church leader has correctly noted: "Though the issue had been presented as a policy matter, whether to allow divisions to decide for themselves about ordination, most delegates knew that they were really voting on the biblical legitimacy of women's ordination. How could the world church make so fundamental a change unless it could find biblical support? How could it allow itself to be divided on something so essential to its unity and function? So as it had done five years earlier, the world church gave an emphatic No" (Jay Gallimore, "The Larger Issues," in *Prove All Things,* 343).

[41]Calvin Rock, "Review of *Women in Ministry,*" *Adventist Review,* April 15, 1999, 29, emphasis mine. Observe also that barely six months into the two years of regular meetings that went into producing the book, at least some of the Seminary Ad Hoc Committee

members were already convinced that the 150-year-old practice of the Seventh-day Adventist church was wrong and needed to be changed. Before all the chapters of the pro-ordination book were written, the tentative thrust of the Seminary volume was to suggest that the "Adventist church structure, however legitimate, has not been, historically, an exact replica of biblical patterns of ministry. While accepting the decision of the Adventist church not to ordain women *at this time* as voted at the 1995 General Conference Session in Utrecht, *the book will attempt to provide data on which to base future decisions."* See, Susan Walters, "Prospectus Revealed for Book on Ordination of Women," *Adventist Today,* March-April, 1997, 24, emphasis mine. Also, following the book's publication, a press release from the public relations office of Andrews University announcing the book-signing concluded: "Whether the book will signal a shift in the worldwide Adventist Church remains to be seen. In Utrecht, conservative factions from Latin America and Africa voted down the women's ordination question. The next General Conference session, to be held in Toronto, Canada, in the year 2000, *could be the site of another theological firestorm if the North American Church pushes the issue."* See, Jack Stenger (Public Information Officer, Andrews University), "Andrews Professors Address Women's Ordination" Press Release, dated October 22, 1998, emphasis mine.

[42]Vyhmeister, "Prologue" in *Women in Ministry,* 5.

[43]Refer to the minutes of the General Conference Spring Meeting (April 1975) and the General Conference Annual Council (October 1984).

[44]The entire document, with helpful commentary, is reproduced as Appendix D in *Prove All Things,* 391-404.

[45]In my *Receiving the Word* ( 123-126), I have challenged revisionist reinterpretations of Adventist beliefs and practice of ministry (see also 138-140, notes 34-44 of my book).

[46]Vyhmeister, *Women in Ministry,* 436, 5.

[47]See the following authors in *Women in Ministry:* Richard M. Davidson, 283, 284; Jo Ann Davidson, 179; cf. Nancy Vyhmeister, 350; Robert M. Johnston, 52-53; Peter van Bemmelen, 306-307; Jacques Doukhan, 39; Daniel Augsburger, 96; Keith Mattingly, 71-72; Randal Wisbey, 251; Denis Fortin, 127-129; Michael Bernoi, 229; Alicia Worley, 370-372; Walter B. T. Douglas, 394; Roger L. Dudley, 414-415.

[48]Russell Staples, in *Women in Ministry,* 251. Jon L. Dybdahl also writes: "Let us be honest. There is no clear specific biblical statement on the issue. No verse gives permission to ordain women, and no passage specifically forbids it" ( 430); cf. Raoul Dederen, 22-23; Jerry Moon, 204; George Knight, 111-112; W. Larry Richards, 327-328.

[49]Source references from *Women in Ministry* for each of the following points will be provided in my evaluation of the book (see chapters 12-16 of *Must We Be Silent?*).

[50]Randal R. Wisbey, "SDA Women in Ministry: 1970-1998," *Women in Ministry,* 251. For my response to the unilateral post-Utrecht ordinations, see my "How the Holy Spirit Leads the Church," *Adventists Affirm* 12/3 (Fall 1998): 28-35.

[51]Roger L. Dudley, "The Ordination of Women in Light of the Character of God," in *Women in Ministry,* 400, 413-414; Walter B. T. Douglas, "The Distance and the Difference: Reflections on Issues of Slavery and Women's Ordination in Adventism," ibid., 379-398; Nancy Vyhmeister, "Epilogue," ibid., 434-435.

[52]Vyhmeister, "Epilogue," in *Women in Ministry,* 436.

# 12

# Women, Equality, and the Apostolic Church

The Apostle Paul commended the Bereans for "receiving the word" and "searching the Scriptures" to see "whether those things were so" (Acts 17:11). Their example suggests that whenever influential scholars and leaders urge new beliefs and practices on the church, members who are committed to biblical fidelity should always ask, "Are those things so?"

The authors of *Women in Ministry,* the pro-ordination book from the Seventh-day Adventist Theological Seminary at Andrews University, have proposed a new understanding of Scripture which would result in the church adopting a new belief and practice. They have submitted their volume as a "resource tool for decision making," correctly recognizing that the ordination of women *as elders or pastors* is a theological issue.[1] As such, it is only through a correct understanding of Scripture—determining "whether those things were so"—that the church can legitimately depart from its 150-year-old practice of ordination.

One supporter of the book adds: "The ultimate purpose of *Women in Ministry* is to provide information for informed decision making, a clear indication that there is a decision to be made. In so doing, the book calls the church to do some serious Bible study. If the basis of our decision is going to be in our interpretation of Scripture, we must do it well."[2]

The question before us is: Did the writers "do their work well"?

The editor of *Women in Ministry* states in the prologue: "We believe that the biblical, theological, and historical perspectives elaborated in this book affirm women in pastoral leadership."[3]

The author of one of the chapters who describes the volume as "the official view of the Seminary and the position of virtually all of its faculty" thinks that this work by twenty Andrews University scholars will "demonstrate that the Seminary faculty stands for sound Biblical and historical scholarship on this contemporary and controversial issue."[4]

Similarly, some influential promoters of *Women in Ministry* are applauding it in Seventh-day Adventist publications as the product of "skillful exegesis of Scripture and careful examination of relevant E. G. White materials,"[5] a volume that presents "a powerful argument" and "an impressive array of evidence" for the ordination of women,[6] and one which "brings together a wealth of material and deserves to be taken seriously."[7]

To evaluate these claims, we must follow Paul's counsel to "prove all things [and] hold fast that which is good" (1 Thess 5:21). Like the Bereans, we must carefully examine *Women in Ministry* to see "whether those things were so."

**Summary of This Analysis**

Contrary to this chorus of claims by authors and reviewers, I am going to argue in this chapter and the four subsequent chapters that there is no evidence in the Bible, in the writings of Ellen G. White, or in the practice of the early Seventh-day Adventist church to support ordaining women as elders or pastors. Despite its authors' noble motives and laudable efforts, I will contend that *Women in Ministry* is constructed upon questionable assumptions and imaginative and speculative interpretations.

The editor alerts readers to this very possibility. She writes in the introduction, "The Seminary Ad Hoc Committee on Hermeneutics and Ordination prayerfully submits this book, not as the final answer to whether or not the Seventh-day Adventist Church should ordain its women in ministry, but rather as a resource tool for decision making. *While recognizing that good decisions are based on hard facts, we are also cognizant of the fact that at times clear evidence may be lacking, thus making necessary the use of sanctified judgment and imagination to resolve questions and issues."*[8]

In evaluating the authors' "use of sanctified judgment and imagination to resolve questions and issues" regarding women's ordination as elders and pastors, my assessment of *Women in Ministry* will show that the book is based on: (1) ambiguity and vagueness, (2) strawman arguments, (3) substantial leaps of logic, (4) arguments from silence, (5) speculative interpretations (6) questionable re-interpretations of the Bible, (7) distorted biblical reasoning, (8) misleading and erroneous claims regarding Adventist history, (9) a seriously flawed concept of "moral imperative," and (10) a fanciful view of the Holy Spirit's leading.[9]

The first four of these will appear in this chapter; the remaining six I will take up in the subsequent chapters of *Must We Be Silent?* At the conclusion of my evaluation, I will mention the implications arising from the book's mistaken conclusions.

### 1. Ambiguity and Vagueness

Several of the chapters in *Women in Ministry* are written in such a way as to be unclear about the issues that divide us. Authors repeatedly avoid a clear statement of what is at issue (the ordination of women *as elders or pastors*) and use a phrase which may be intended to win more support (women in ministry or leadership). To illustrate this fuzziness, I will mention the use of expressions like "full equality," "equal partnership," and "women in leadership and public ministry."

**(a) "Full Equality" and "Equal Partnership."** One of the fundamental arguments underlying *Women in Ministry* is that at creation Adam and Eve were "fully equal," enjoying "total egalitarianism in marriage." According to the book's leading proponent of this view, prior to the Fall there was no role differentiation between male and female. Role distinctions came as the result of the Fall. Because today the relation between husband and wife, even in Christian homes, "does not quite approach total role interchangeableness," Christians should aspire to God's "ultimate ideal" of full equality in their homes. Thus, God's ideal for Christian homes "is still the partnership of equals that is set forth from the beginning."[10]

To speak of full equality as the ideal for today without coming to terms with the nature and extent of this equality leaves the reader to wonder just how far believers in this view are willing to go. Some, no doubt, will take it to mean a partnership of identical roles, and others will probably understand it to mean a partnership with different roles of equal value. Thus the phrase "full and equal" could be hailed by radical feminists who reject the Bible's teaching that because of God's creation arrangement, He calls upon men today to bear the primary headship responsibility as leaders in their homes (e.g., 1 Cor 11:3, 8, 9; Eph 5:23-33; cf. 1 Tim 2:12, 13).

Even more, just as radical feminists seek full equality by getting rid of *gender* or *sex roles* in marriage and in the church, so also does gay theology seek to bring about "equality" between homosexuals and heterosexuals by obliterating *sexual identity.* Radical feminists and pro-gay advocates can also endorse the full equality or "total role interchangeableness" concepts as validations of their claim that there were no gender-based role distinctions at creation.

As far as I know, none of the authors of *Women in Ministry* have endorsed radical feminist and gay theology. Yet this kind of fuzziness or this lack of clarity is a common prelude to liberalism's revisionist theologies. I suggest that we should not speak of "full equality," "equal partnership" or even "shared responsibilities" without stating unambiguously that to act as "equal and joint partners" does not mean to act identically. Individuals in a relationship can be equal and yet have different roles. They can act "jointly" and yet not act identically; they may "share" duties, but not bear the same responsibilities.[11]

This kind of fuzziness on equality mistakenly employs the following statement from Ellen White to support egalitarianism's ideology of full equality:

> Eve was told of the sorrow and pain that must henceforth be her portion. And the Lord said, "Thy desire shall be to thy husband, and he shall rule over thee." *In the creation God had made her the equal of Adam.* Had they remained obedient to God—in harmony with His great law of love—they would ever have been in harmony with each other; but sin had brought discord, and now their union could be maintained and harmony preserved only by submission on the part of the one or the other. *Eve had been the first in transgression; and she had fallen into temptation by separating from her companion, contrary to the divine direction. It was by her solicitation that Adam sinned, and she was now placed in subjection to her husband.* Had the principles joined in the law of God been cherished by the fallen race, this sentence, though growing out of the results of sin, would have proved a blessing to them; but man's abuse of the supremacy thus given him has too often rendered the lot of woman very bitter and made her life a burden" (*Patriarchs and Prophets,* 58-59, emphasis mine).

Those not familiar with the writings of Mrs. White might be misled into believing that the equality of Adam and Eve at creation, and the subjection of Eve to Adam after the Fall implies there was no role distinctions prior to the Fall. But in making this claim, the advocates of women's ordination make three major mistakes.

First, they equate equality with role-interchangeableness, and assume that equality at creation means the absence of gender role distinctions. But the above proof for full equality and equal partnership overlooks the fact that Ellen G. White rejects the egalitarian model of "total role interchangeability." Despite the abuse of God's creation arrangement for role relations in the home, she writes that "heaven's ideal of this sacred [marriage] relation" is one in which the man is the head of the home. This kind of relationship is "what God designed it should be" (*Thoughts from the Mount of Blessing,* 64, 65). And because "the husband is the head of the family, as Christ is the head of the church," she writes, "any course which the wife may pursue to lessen his influence and lead him to come down from that dignified, responsible position is displeasing to God" (*Testimonies for the Church,* 1:307).

Second, advocates fail to mention that in the very next paragraph of the *Patriarchs and Prophets* statement quoted above, Ellen G. White made it clear that prior to the Fall God had already enjoined different roles for Adam and Eve, each with their "assigned spheres." It was because Eve chose to disregard this divine arrangement, that God had to reiterate after the Fall, saying, "Thy desire shall be to thy husband, and he shall rule over thee." Prior to the Fall, Eve's submission was freely and spontaneously expressed. But after the Fall, the Lord had to make explicit the "law" she had, perhaps, been obeying unconsciously.[12]

> Eve had been perfectly happy by her husband's side in her Eden home; but, like restless modern Eves, she was flattered with the hope of entering a higher sphere than that *which God had assigned her.* In attempting to rise above *her original position,* she fell far below it. A similar result will be reached by all who are unwilling to take up cheerfully their life duties in accordance with God's plan. In their efforts to reach positions for which He has not fitted them, many are leaving vacant the place where they might be a blessing. In their desire for a higher sphere, many have sacrificed true womanly dignity and nobility of character,

> and have left undone the very work that Heaven appointed them (*Patriarchs and Prophets,* 59)

Third, advocates of women's ordination fail to call attention to a parallel statement of Ellen White, in which she brings together role distinctions before the Fall, the subjection of Eve after the Fall. Mrs. White taught that male and female were created equal, neither superior or inferior to the other. But because Eve chose to abandon her God-assigned role, God's curse enjoined her to subject herself to her husband. Referring to Eve before the Fall, Mrs. White wrote:

> She was perfectly happy *in her Eden home* by her husband's side; but, like restless modern Eves, she was flattered that there was a higher sphere than that which God had assigned her. But in attempting to climb higher than her original position, she fell far below it. This will most assuredly be the result with the Eves of the present generation if they neglect to cheerfully take up their daily life duties in accordance with God's plan. . . .
>
> A neglect on the part of woman to follow *God's plan in her creation,* an effort to reach for important positions which He has not qualified her to fill, leaves vacant the position that she could fill to acceptance. In getting out of her sphere, she loses true womanly dignity and nobility. When God created Eve, He designed that she should possess neither inferiority nor superiority to the man, but that in all things she should be his equal. The holy pair were to have no interest independent of each other; and yet each had an individuality in thinking and acting. But after Eve's sin, as she was first in the transgression, the Lord told her that Adam should rule over her. She was to be in subjection to her husband, and this was a part of the curse."(*Testimonies,* vol. 4, 483-484).

Contrary to the claims of pro-ordinationist scholars, Sister White never taught the kind of full equality which obliterates role distinctions. Adam and Eve were created equal. But within this partnership of male-female equality, God designed that the man should be the head of the home. The claim in *Women in Ministry* that Adam and Eve enjoyed full equality or "total egalitarianism in marriage" is, therefore, incorrect.

At a time of rampant divorces, sometimes because each party seeks to be the head, we need to be clear on what we mean by "total role interchangeableness" as God's ideal for the home. And at a time of increasing homosexual demands for marital rights, we need to say unambiguously that men were not created equal with women personally or even physically *as candidates to be spouses of men.* Failure to do so will open a welcome door for those who seek to nullify the biblical case for divinely-instituted role differences and a monogamous heterosexual relationship. Proponents of gay theology within Adventism have not lost sight of this fact.[13]

What has been said about the vagueness of expressions like full equality and "joint leadership" also applies to using the expression "mutual submission" as though Ephesians 5:21 ("Submit to one another") means complete reciprocity ("wives submit to husbands and husbands submit to wives *as if there were no role distinctions among you.*")[14]

**(b) "Women in Leadership" and "Women in Public Ministry."** The book frequently refers to women serving in positions of "leadership" and "public ministry." For instance, it is claimed that in Bible times nothing barred women from holding "the highest offices of leadership, including authoritative teaching roles that constituted 'headship' over men," and that "in the late-nineteenth century, women were active in [the Seventh-day Adventist] church leadership and ministry," serving in "both leadership and ministerial positions in the early history of the Seventh-day Adventist denomination."[15]

Another writes: "Throughout both the Old and New Testaments women served not only in home and family administration but also in public and religious spheres. The roles of women in Scripture are varied and vigorous"; "the entire [biblical] canon can be seen to affirm women, whether in the home or in public ministry, or both."[16]

What, exactly, is meant by "leadership" or "public ministry"? These terms are often not clearly defined in *Women in Ministry.* If they mean positions of genuine, significant responsibility in the church, then the implication that women in churches today should likewise be given roles in which they can exercise their spiritual gifts in significant ways is not biblically objectionable. In fact, this is what Seventh-day Adventists historically have believed and practiced.

If, however, "leadership" and "public ministry" mean women served in positions of ultimate responsibility as priests, apostles, and elders or pastors in Bible times and as elders or pastors in early Seventh-day Adventist history, then, as we shall later show, the authors of *Women in Ministry* do not sufficiently substantiate their claim.

My point is this: the basic issue is not "women in ministry" (a non-issue), but "women as ordained ministers-pastors"; not women "in leadership" or "public ministry," but women *as elders or pastors.* Broad, undefined terms can be misleading.

### 2. "Straw Man" Arguments

A straw man is a set of arguments a writer claims his opponent believes so that he can attack them and gain an easy victory. Typically, straw men are presented as unavoidable and unacceptable alternatives to the writers' position. Two examples in *Women in Ministry* grow out of the suggestion that anyone who rejects women's ordination 1) views "women as inferior to men," or 2) wants "all women to be in submission to all men."[17] Let's look at these straw men.

**(a) Male Superiority and Female Inferiority?** When *Women in Ministry* concludes that male headship (and female submission) "is part of God's plan for fallen human beings rather than an original mandate for the sinless world,"[18] it positions itself between liberal feminists (who reject any form of male headship and female submission before and after the Fall) and conservative opponents of women's ordination (who accept headship/submission, before and after the Fall).

Unlike liberal feminists, the authors of *Women in Ministry* believe in a "post-Fall" headship, a loving servant leadership of the husband.[19] (Conservatives opposed to women's ordination also hold to the same kind of loving servant headship, but they argue that headship was instituted by God at creation and reiterated at the Fall.[20]) *Women in Ministry* rejects headship *at creation,* arguing instead for total egalitarianism—an alleged divine ideal of full equality which is void of functional role differentiations between male and female.[21]

But in giving reasons for their rejection of headship before the Fall they resort to "straw man" arguments and misleading reasoning. For example, in the chapter that provides the exegetical and theological framework for the entire book, we read that "there is no hint of ontological or functional superiority-inferiority or headship-submission between male and female."[22] Does a belief in the biblical teaching of headship submission before the Fall necessitate a belief in male superiority and female inferiority at creation? It doesn't, and to my knowledge, this view is not held by any credible Adventist scholar opposed to women's ordination.[23] The opponents I know believe that as human beings Adam and Eve were equal (that is, *ontologically,* neither one was superior or inferior to the other), but they were expected to do different things (that is, there was to be *functional role differentiation*).

The issue in the debate over women's ordination is not whether women were created equal to men (a non-issue), but rather whether God instituted a functional role differentiation between male and female when He created both of them equal. This is the real issue in the headship/submission debate. In my earlier work, *Searching the Scriptures,* I have offered several lines of evidence for headship before the Fall.[24]

Regrettably, the authors did not interact with the biblical evidence. They set up and knocked down strawman arguments about superiority and inferiority. And having shown that Adam and Eve were created equal, neither superior to the other in worth (ontological equality), the writers give the false impression that they have proved that our first parents were created without prescribed role distinctions (functional role differentiations).

If no headship/submission existed at creation, these authors in *Women in Ministry* will need to explain, for example, why Adam (not Eve) is repeatedly held responsible for the entrance of sin and death into the world even though it was Eve who sinned first (Rom 5:12-21; 1 Cor 15:21-22). Note that in Genesis 3, God also approached Adam (not Eve) first after sin, suggesting the reality of male headship before the Fall.[25]

**(b) "All Women Under All Men"?** One writer in the book sees only three options in the discussion of women's relation to men: (1) Scripture instructs "all women to be under the authority of all men" (this is assumed to be the position of conservatives *opposed* to women's ordination); (2) "Women (when married) are [to be] under the headship of their husbands, but in the church men and women stand together in full equality under Christ" (the position of conservatives *for* women's ordination—the posture *Women in Ministry* wants to project); (3) or "the Apostle Paul contradicts himself on this issue in his various New Testament writings and thus should be ignored—or that his counsel is outdated in this modern era" (the liberal or radical feminist position from which the book wants to distance itself).[26]

Writers of *Women in Ministry* must be commended for going to great lengths in distancing themselves from radical feminist and liberal hermeneutics.[27] It is an error, however, to give the impression that view #1 is the position of conservatives opposed to women's ordination. To my knowledge, the conservative Adventist scholars opposed to women's ordination do not argue that "all women must be in submission to all men."[28] Neither do they claim that headship gives "any male preponderance over all females," nor that it gives "males the right to rule over women."[29]

What Adventist opponents of women's ordination hold is that biblical headship/leadership, in contrast to male domination, was instituted by God to govern the relationship of the man and woman, two spiritually-equal human beings, in both the home and the church. In this relation, it is the man who exercises primary responsibility for leading the home and church families in a God glorifying direction (cf. 1 Cor 11:3; Eph 5:21-33), and God holds these men responsible when they abdicate their God-assigned responsibilities as husbands and elders or pastors.

In contrast to the view that "all women must be in submission to all men," Adventist opponents of women's ordination argue that in the home women must be in submission to *their own husbands,* and in the church they must be in submission to *the elders or pastors,* who are appointed by God to positions of headship.

This is why I say the authors created strawman arguments when they attacked the shortcomings of ugly alternatives which are not held by their opponents (i.e, the suggestion that those who reject women's ordination want to "treat women as inferior to men," or view "all women to be in submission to all men"), thus giving the impression that there are no other credible alternatives when in truth there are.

### 3. Substantial Leaps of Logic

Several insightful and otherwise excellent chapters in *Women in Ministry* display substantial leaps of logic. In these instances the conclusions do not follow from the established premises. As examples of leaps of logic, I will discuss the claims about "the priesthood of all believers" and "slavery and women's ordination."

**(a) "Priesthood of All Believers."** A recurring claim in *Women in Ministry* is that the doctrine of "the priesthood of all believers" leads to an egalitarian (i.e., "equalitarian") model of the ordained ministry, in which gender plays no role. The author of the lead chapter writes:

"Males functioned as priests in the days of the biblical patriarchs as well as after God's covenant with Israel at Mount Sinai. With the move from Israel to the Christian church, however, a radical transformation occurred. A new priesthood is unfolded in the New Testament, that of all believers. The Christian church is a fellowship of believer priests. Such an ecclesiology, such an understanding of the nature and mission of the church, no longer poses roadblocks to women serving in any ministry. It in fact demands a partnership of men and women *in all expressions of the ordained ministry.* The recognition of the priesthood of all believers implies a church in which women and men work side by side in various functions and ministries, endowed with gifts distributed by the Holy Spirit according to his sovereign will (1 Cor 12:7-11)."[30]

The claim that women can also function "in all expressions of the ordained ministry" (including the headship roles of elders or pastors) does not follow. The priesthood of all believers is not about particular church functions of men and women. Christians are part of a priesthood because every believer has direct access to God through Christ without any need for other intermediaries (cf. Heb 10:19-22). The New Testament doctrine of the "priesthood of all believers" (1 Pet 2:5, 9-12) also recognizes that the church is a worshiping community (a *priestly* people called to offer spiritual sacrifices of praise and prayer) and also a witnessing community (a *missionary* people called to declare the "praises of him who called you out of darkness into his wonderful light"). Every church member—whether man or woman—has been called to the soul-winning ministry of the church.

It does not follow that every church member may perform an identical function in the church.[31] The Bible itself establishes what the qualities of an elder or pastor should be (1 Tim 3:1-7). Among other things, the elder or pastor must be "the husband of one wife," one who "rules well his own house" (vv. 2, 4, 5; Titus 1:6). This gender-based qualification cannot be legitimately fulfilled by a woman.[32]

Moreover, the apostle Peter makes it clear that the doctrine of "the priesthood of all believers" was not a new innovation "unfolded in the New Testament." Rather, it was based on an Old Testament concept (1 Pet 2:5, 9-12; cf. Ex 19:5-6). In the Old Testament, there was "the priesthood of all believers." God declared, "Ye shall be unto me a kingdom of priests, and an holy nation" (Ex 19:6). Yet, no women served as priests in the Old Testament.

Not even all males served as priests, but only those from the tribe of Levi.[33] And whereas all priests were Levites, not all Levites were priests. Only the family of Aaron and his male descendants were assigned this responsibility (Ex 28:1, 41, 43; Num 3:10, 32; 20:28; 25:10-13).

If there was such a "radical transformation" of the Old Testament concept of "priesthood of all believers" as to demand "a partnership of men and women in all expressions of the ordained ministry," how is it that we cannot find a single unequivocal example of women serving as elders or overseers in the New Testament?

To claim, as many writers in *Women in Ministry* do, that the priesthood of all believers eliminates gender role distinctions requires a substantial leap of logic. It is not validated in the Old Testament or the New Testament. Pro-ordinationists can only sustain their reinterpretation of the concept by imposing on the Bible the feminist concept of "full equality," understood to mean the total obliteration of male-female role differentiation.

**(b) Slavery and Women's Ordination.** Another manifestation of a leap of logic is the claim that because the arguments of those opposed to women's ordination "parallel" those of nineteenth-century slave holders, and because slavery was later shown to be wrong, opposition to women's ordination must also be wrong.[34]

For example, one writer puts in two parallel columns the arguments of those who favored slavery and of those who favor limiting ordination to men. He thus shows that proponents of both positions argue that: (1) their position is based on a high view of Scripture; (2) their view is established on divine creation; (3) Jesus set the precedent (He used a slavery analogy in Luke 17; He ordained only males); (4) the apostles approved Jesus' precedent; (5) there is divine blessing for upholding it; (6) there exists a slippery-slope argument (if you abandon it, it will jeopardize a divine arrangement).[35]

It is puzzling that no committee member caught the fallacy in this kind of argument. Let me illustrate. Are we Adventists to suggest that because our arguments for the Sabbath parallel those used by slave holders (high view of Scripture, divine creation ordinance, the precedent set by Jesus and the apostles, etc.), our doctrine of the Sabbath must necessarily be wrong? Certainly not.

Thus, the fact that pro-slavery theologians argued their case in this manner does not make their case right. And the fact that anti-women's ordination scholars argue for the creation ordinance and the absence of Bible precedents does not make their case wrong. The rightness of a position should be judged on the merits of the issue, in the light of Scripture's witness.[36]

"The headship principle is different from slavery in two major ways: (1) the headship principle was a creation ordinance, while slavery was never instituted by God; and (2) as a pre-Fall creation ordinance, the headship principle is morally right and therefore morally binding on all God's people, irrespective of the place and time in which they live; but slavery, as a post-fall distortion of God's will for humanity, is morally offensive and cannot be justified under biblical Christianity. (The book of Philemon shows this.)"[37]

### 4. Arguments from Silence

These are instances in which the book's authors attempt to deduce some inferences from the silence of Scripture. Most of these deal with the "culture of the times" argument. Let me explain.

There is no record in the Bible of any ordination of women, such as priests in the Old Testament and apostles and elders or pastors in the New Testament. Some *Women in Ministry* authors argue that this lack of biblical precedent should be understood as a cultural accommodation to oppressive structures (race, gender, religion, etc.) in existence during Bible times. Thus, the authors claim, the failure of Jesus to ordain women as apostles and the New Testament church's failure to ordain women as elders and pastors were concessions that had to be made to accommodate the (supposedly) insensitive, male-chauvinistic or anti-women cultural practices of their times so as not to jeopardize their ministries prematurely.

In making this claim, proponents of women's ordination are simply arguing from silence. I will examine how *Women in Ministry* deals with the following examples: "Jesus and the ministry of women," "the apostolic church and women," "women leaders of the NT church," and "Junia as a female apostle." (The claim that Phoebe was a "female minister" will be taken up in a later section.)

**(a) Jesus and the Ministry of Women.** What does *Women in Ministry* have to say in response to the fact that Jesus did not ordain any woman among the twelve apostles? The authors offer two sets of arguments. First, "within the social restraints of his day, Paul and the early church (like Jesus) did not act precipitously."[38] Or as another writer states: "Custom here may have been so entrenched that Jesus simply stopped short of fully implementing a principle that he made explicit and emphatic [i.e., the inclusion of "women, Samaritans and Gentiles"]. . . . However, at this time this may have been an ideal awaiting its time of actualization."[39]

Second, they argue that if opponents to women's ordination insist that Jesus' example of ordaining no women apostles should be followed, by the same logic, Gentiles should also be excluded from the category of apostles since Christ never ordained a Gentile. "While Jesus treated women and Gentiles in a way that was revolutionary for His day," argues one writer, "yet He did not ordain as one of His disciples either a Gentile or a woman. But this pattern was no more normative for the future roles of women in church leadership than for future roles of Gentiles."[40]

These arguments are flawed. First, it would appear that our *Women in Ministry* authors are simply echoing the commonly accepted paradigm that women were second-class, unjustly oppressed people in the Rabbinic writings (and some argue, by implications, the Old Testament). But as other thoughtful scholars have pointed out, "such a position can be argued, citing various chauvinistic Rabbinic sources, but it does not appear that all Rabbinic data fit this paradigm, and it is even more questionable if the O[ld] T[estament], as a whole, can be portrayed as anti-women. More work needs to be done on this."[41]

But even if we assume that the "entrenched custom" of those days were oppressively anti-women, there is still no valid justification to assume that Christ acquiesced to the injustice of women. Thus, with respect to the argument that the "entrenched custom" of those times would not have permitted Christ and the early church to have acted "precipitously," we must point out that such a view, in effect, charges our Lord Jesus Christ with insensitivity or false accommodation to the "injustice" women suffered in His day. How could this be, when Scripture teaches that Jesus never yielded to sin (Heb 4:15)? "Sin" surely includes the sin of gender injustice. The Gospels tell us that Jesus never hesitated to correct his culture when issues of right and wrong were at stake. His treatment of women also contrasted sharply with that of the rabbis of His day. One knowledgeable scholar perceptively writes:

> We can contrast Jesus with the rabbis as seen in the Talmud and Midrash. Jesus does not behave the same way. Women come to him and he helps them directly. He heals them (Mk. 5:25-34).

On occasion he touches them (Mt. 8:14-15). He talks to them individually, regularly in private and sometimes in public (Jn. 11:17-44). On one occasion he even talks to a woman when both of them were unaccompanied (Jn 4:7-24). He teaches women along with the men (Lk 10:38-42). When he teaches, he speaks of women and uses womanly tasks as illustrations. On occasion, he makes use of two parables to illustrate the same point, one drawn from the activities of men, the other from the activities of women (Lk. 15:3-10). He never shows disrespect to women, nor does he ever speak about women in a disparaging way. He relates in a brotherly fashion to women whom he knows. He has some women traveling with him to serve him (Lk. 8:1-3). Finally, he calls women 'daughters of Abraham' (Lk. 13:16), explicitly according them a spiritual status like that accorded to men. One might add that after his resurrection Jesus appears to women first and lets them carry the news to the men (Jn. 20:11-19; Mt. 28:9-10)."[42]

On why Christ never ordained a Gentile, the Bible provides an answer. He chose twelve *Jewish* apostles because in God's divine wisdom, the church began among the Jews, and it was all Jewish at the beginning ("salvation is of the Jews" John 4:22; cf. Rom 3:1, 2; Acts 1:8). Seventh-day Adventists understand that the 70 weeks determined for the Jews (Dan 9:24ff) still had several years to run. There were no Gentile leaders in the church in Christ's day, but there were many qualified, spiritual women. The New Testament actually does report some Gentile apostles (2 Cor 1:19; 1 Thess 1:1; 2 Thess 1:1, Silvanus?), but not one female apostle (we'll look at Junia later). Thus, those who attempt to present a "Gentile" argument to counter the absence of women apostles among Christ's followers apparently fail to understand Christ's prophetic priority of beginning His mission with the house of Israel (cf. Matt 10:5-6).

If Jesus had wanted to demonstrate that women had full access to all leadership roles in the church, He could easily have chosen and ordained six men and their wives as apostles, since the wives of apostles frequently accompanied their husbands (1 Cor 9:5). But He did not. Christ could have chosen and ordained at least one of the women who were actively involved in His ministry, traveling to the places He was teaching, and supporting Him and His disciples with their own money (see Luke 8:1-3). But He did not. He could have ordained His own mother, since she already had heaven's certification as "highly favored" (Luke 1:28, 30). But He did not. He could have chosen and ordained Mary, just as He commissioned her to bear witness to His resurrection (Mark 16:9ff.; John 20:11ff.). But He did not. Christ could have ordained the Samaritan woman as an apostle, since she defied several "cultural" stigmas (a woman five times divorced, living unlawfully with a man, and a Samaritan) to become a powerful and successful evangelist (John 4). But He did not. Instead, after spending all night in prayer (Luke 6:12), Christ appointed twelve men as His apostles (Matt 10:2-4; Mark 3:13-19). Why?

Was it because He did not want to act "precipitously" in light of the "restraints of His day"? Was it because He lacked the courage to stand against gender injustice entrenched in His culture? Or was it because women were not capable or qualified? No. Jesus did not ordain even one woman as an apostle because He understood the headship principle He Himself had instituted at creation, and He submitted to its authority.

**(b) The Apostolic Church and Women.** One author in *Women in Ministry* writes: "While women may not have immediately received full and equal partnership with men in the ministry of the church, evidence of women in leadership roles in the early church is sufficient to demonstrate that they were not barred from positions of influence, leadership and even headship over men."[43]

Here is a paradox. How may women not "immediately" have "received full and equal partnership with men in the ministry" and yet at the same time exercise "leadership and even headship over men"? It can be only one or the other. Either they served as leaders (elders-pastors) or they did not. By inserting the word "immediately" without telling us how much time elapsed before women allegedly received the "equal partnership," is the writer attempting to marry biblical faith with feminist egalitarianism? The New Testament shows that women were actively involved in soul-winning ministry but never served in the headship roles of elder or pastor.

Contrary to the suggestion that women could not "immediately" receive "full and equal partnership with men in the ministry," the New Testament writers note the active role of women in gospel ministry. We read about the significant contributions of Mary, Martha, Joanna, Susanna (Luke 8:2, 3; Acts 1:14), Tabitha (Acts 9:36), Lydia, Phoebe, Lois, Eunice, Priscilla, Tryphena, Tryposa, Persis, Euodia, Syntyche, and Junia (Acts

16:14, 15; 18:26; 21:8, 9; Rom 16:1-4, 6, 7, 12; Phil 4:3). Yet these women were not ordained to the role of apostle, elder or pastor, not because of any "social restraints" against which the early believers chose not to act "precipitously," but because the New Testament church understood that the creation arrangement of headship precluded women from exercising the leadership function of apostle, elder, or pastor in the worshiping community.

**(c) Women Leaders of the New Testament Church?** The above section shows some of the inconsistencies in *Women in Ministry.* On one hand, the authors argue that social restraints precluded women from "equal partnership with men in ministry." Yet they proceed to argue that New Testament evidence suggests that some women actually exercised "positions of influence, leadership and even headship over men." As evidence, an impressive roster of women is listed: Phoebe, Junia, women at Philippi, Euodia and Syntyche, etc.[44]

One of the greatest weaknesses of the book is that while it helpfully provides an inventory of prominent women in the Bible (and in Seventh-day Adventist history), showing that women indeed functioned in spheres of genuine, significant responsibility in soul-winning ministry, *Women in Ministry* proves the exact opposite of what it sets out to demonstrate. Despite the significant ministry of these New Testament women, *not one of them is ever described as apostle, elder or bishop,* whether ordained or non-ordained (we'll look at Junia and Phoebe in chapter 14).

How could the apostle Paul, having established his normative doctrine of headship (God's creational arrangement of functional role distinctions within the partnership of spiritual equals) proceed to violate it in his actual practice? Whenever in doubt, we should supplement our study of the *descriptive* components of the practice in Bible times (which mention women and the significant roles they played) with an analysis of the *prescriptive* teaching of Paul which formed the foundation of what he and the early church practiced. Otherwise, we may give the impression that Paul was merely operating with reference to culture rather than being guided by transcultural norms. But as passages such as Ephesians 5: 21ff., 1 Timothy 2:11ff., and 1 Corinthians 11 show, Paul did in fact establish general parameters (which he already found in the Old Testament creation accounts) for women's roles in the church.[45]

In short, not only Paul's practice, but also the principles underlying the patterns of established churches should be part of the investigation. Paul's norms regarding women's roles in the church are foundational; questionable inferences about what may have been the case are not.

---

**Endnotes**

[1]Nancy Vyhmeister, "Prologue," *Women in Ministry: Biblical and Historical Perspectives,* ed. Nancy Vyhmeister (Berrien Springs, Mich.: Andrews University Press, 1998), 5.

[2]See, Beverly Beem, "What If . . . Women in Ministry?" *Focus* [Andrews University alumni magazine], Winter 1999, 31.

[3]Vyhmeister, "Prologue," *Women in Ministry,* 5. Hereafter, the book *Women in Ministry* will be abbreviated as *WIM.*

[4]Roger L. Dudley, "[Letter to the Editor Regarding] *Women in Ministry,*" *Adventist Today,* January-February 1999, 6.

[5]Calvin Rock, "Review of *Women in Ministry,*" *Adventist Review,* April 15, 1999, 29.

[6]Beverly Beem, see note 2.

[7]Fritz Guy, "Review of *Women in Ministry,*" *Ministry,* January 1999, 29.

[8]Vyhmeister, "Prologue," *WIM,* 5; emphasis mine. Another writes that the silence of the Bible on the ordination of women is an invitation "to careful study, prayer for guidance, and use of sanctified reason" (see Staples, "A Theological Understanding of Ordination," *WIM,* 151). On the proper role of reason in theology, see Frank M. Hasel, "Theology and the Role of Reason," *Journal of the Adventist Theological Society* 4/2 (1993), 172-198.

[9]Space constraints will not allow me to address every flaw I see in *Women in Ministry.* In the following pages I will highlight only a few of the book's biblical, theological, and historical arguments that trouble me.

[10]Richard M. Davidson, "Headship, Submission, and Equality in Scripture," *WIM,* 275. Denying that God made man the head of the home at creation, Davidson argues that God's original plan for the home was "total equality in marriage" (267) or "total egalitarianism in the marriage relationship" (269) or "headship among equals" (270), expressions understood to mean the absence of role differentiation before the Fall (264, 267, 269). Though he believes that "headship" was instituted *after the Fall,* it is his view that God's original plan of "total egalitarianism in the marriage relationship" is still the same in the post-Fall situation "as it was for Adam and Eve in the beginning" (269). In other words, today, as at the beginning, there should be no "ontological or functional" role distinctions. Rather, Christians should aspire for the "ideal" of "full equality" in their homes ( 284; cf. 275). Cf. Peter M. van Bemmelen, "Equality, Headship, and Submission in the Writings of Ellen G. White," *WIM,* 297-311, who also speaks about an "original equality" in which Eve "fully shared in Adam's headship" ( 308, 298).

[11]A friend of mine recently stated, "I know of a pastor who once commented that everyone in the world is willing to love God with all their heart and love their neighbor as themselves—so long as each individual person is allowed to pour into the words 'love,' 'God,' and 'neighbor' whatever definition they want! But God does not allow this. He defines for us what these terms mean. The same is true for 'full equality,' etc." (Jarrod Williamson to Samuel Koranteng-Pipim, correspondence dated June 22, 1999).

[12]The perfect harmony that existed in Eden before the fall may perhaps be likened to the harmony in heaven before the fall of Satan, when "So long as all created beings acknowledged the allegiance of love, there was perfect harmony throughout the universe of God. . . . And while love to God was supreme, love for one another was confiding and unselfish. There was no note of discord to mar the celestial harmonies" (*Patriarchs and Prophets,* 35). Though God's law governed everyone, "When Satan rebelled against the law of Jehovah, the thought that there was a law came to the angels almost as an awakening to something unthought of" (*Thoughts from the Mount of Blessing,* 109). The angels responded freely and spontaneously to God. They seem to have been almost unconscious of a "law" to obey God or to worship Christ. These things were their delight. (See *Patriarchs and Prophets* , 35-37.)

[13]For example, speaking at the annual meeting of North American Seventh-day Adventist college and university Bible teachers in San Francisco, California, in 1992, Ron Lawson, the "liaison" of the pro-homosexual group Kinship, correctly remarked that the push for women's ordination, when successful, will eventually open the door for the church to embrace homosexuality, since both causes are waging a similar battle against "discrimination" and since both share the same basic view of total obliteration of gender-role distinctions. The experience of other Christian denominations which have jettisoned the Bible's teaching on sexual role differentiation for an "egalitarian" model confirms Lawson's observation that an open attitude toward homosexuality inescapably follows once that step is taken. For a discussion of how Seventh-day Adventists' attitudes are changing with respect to the question of homosexuality, see my discussion in chapter 3 of this present volume; Cf. my "Born A Gay and Born Again?: Adventism's Changing Attitude to Homosexuality," *Journal of the Adventist Theological Society* 10/1&2 (Spring-Autumn 1999): 143-156.

[14]For the other side of this issue see Wayne Grudem, "The Myth of 'Mutual Submission,'" *CBMW News,* October 1996, 1, 3, 4; cf. John Piper and Wayne Grudem, eds., *50 Crucial Questions About Manhood and Womanhood* (Wheaton, Ill.: Council on Biblical Manhood and Womanhood, 1992), 13-15; see especially 13 note 4. Cf. C. Mervyn Maxwell, "Let's Be Serious," *Adventists Affirm* 3/2 (Fall 1989), 25, 26.

[15]Richard M. Davidson, "Headship, Submission, and Equality in Scripture," *WIM,* 282; Vyhmeister, "Epilogue," *WIM,* 434; Roger L. Dudley, "The Ordination of Women in Light of the Character of God," *WIM,* 399.

[16]Jo Ann Davidson, "Women in Scripture," *WIM,* 159, 179.

[17]Ibid., 175.

[18]Vyhmeister, "Epilogue," *WIM,* 434; cf. Richard M. Davidson, "Headship, Submission, and Equality in Scripture," *WIM,* 259-295; van Bemmelen, "Equality, Headship, and Submission in the Writings of Ellen G. White," *WIM,* 297-311.

[19]Writes Richard M. Davidson: "The nature of the husband's headship is paralleled to that of Christ, who 'loved the church and gave Himself for it' ([Eph 5] v. 25). The husband's 'headship' is thus a loving servant leadership. It means 'head servant, or taking the lead in serving,' not an authoritarian rule. It consists of the husband's loving his wife as his own body, nourishing and cherishing her, as Christ does the church (vv. 28-29)" (Davidson, "Headship, Submission, and Equality in Scripture," *WIM,* 275). On the basis of Eph 5:33, our author underscores the headship-submission relationship as "love (of the husband for his wife) and respect (of the wife for her husband)"; it is a kind of "mutual submission," though

"this does not quite approach total role interchangeableness in the marriage relation." It "works itself out in different ways involving an ordering of relationships, and exhortations according to gender" (ibid., 275).

[20]This is a summary of my view: "The headship principle was instituted by God at creation, reiterated after the Fall, and upheld as a model of male-female Christian relationships in the home and church. In other words, the male headship role and the female supporting role describe the relationship for which men and women were fitted by nature, unfitted by sin, and refitted by grace. This relationship was formed at creation, deformed by the fall, and re-formed (i.e., transformed for its original purpose) by the gospel" (Samuel Koranteng-Pipim, *Searching the Scriptures,* 49-50).

[21]Richard M. Davidson, "Headship, Submission, and Equality in Scripture," *WIM,* 269, 284; cf. Vyhmeister, "Epilogue," *WIM,* 434; van Bemmelen, "Equality, Headship and Submission in Ellen G. White," *WIM,* 297-311.

[22]Richard M. Davidson, "Headship, Submission, and Equality in Scripture," *WIM,* 260.

[23]Richard M. Davidson summarizes the arguments of those who believe in headship before the Fall as follows: "(a) man is created first and woman last ([Gen] 2:7, 22), *and the first is superior and the last is subordinate or inferior;* (b) woman is formed *for the sake of man*—to be his 'helpmate' or *assistant to cure man's loneliness* (vss. 18-20); (c) woman comes out of man (vss. 21-22), *which implies a derivative and subordinate position;* (d) woman is created from man's rib (vss. 21-22), *which indicates her dependence upon him for life;* and (e) the man names the woman (v. 23), *which indicates his power and authority over her"* (Richard M. Davidson, "Headship, Submission, and Equality in Scripture," *WIM,* 260-261, emphasis added; cf. his "The Theology of Sexuality in the Beginning: Genesis 1-2," *Andrews University Seminary Studies* 26/1 [1988]:14). To my knowledge, no credible Adventist scholar opposing women's ordination uses the above reasons in support of headship before the Fall. It is regrettable that our author goes to great lengths to challenge what is really a non-issue in the Adventist debate over the biblical legitimacy of women's ordination. In fact, in my earlier work, I specifically challenged such reasons as views not held by any Seventh-day Adventist scholar who has written against women's ordination (see my *Searching the Scriptures* (1995), 54 note 3. Our position on the headship principle is *not* the same as these summarized views. I have argued that Genesis 1-2 teaches an ontological equality between the sexes; consequently, no inferiority or superiority exists within the complementary relationship of man and woman (*Searching the Scriptures,* 26-27, 31-32, 45-47; cf. *Receiving the Word,* 120).

[24](1) God expressed His intended arrangement for the family relationship by creating Adam first, then Eve. Therefore, Paul writes, "I do not permit a woman to teach or to have authority over a man; she must be silent. *For Adam was formed first, then Eve"* (1 Tim 2:12, 13 NIV). (2) God gave to Adam the directions for the first pair regarding custody of the garden and the dangers of the forbidden tree (Gen 2:16, 17). This charge to Adam called him to spiritual leadership. (3) God instructed that in marriage it is the man who must act, leaving dependence on father and mother to be united with his wife (Gen 2:24; Matt 19:4, 5), and that in the marriage relationship the woman's role is to complement the man's in his duties (Gen 2:18, 23, 24). In this instruction, God charged the man with the responsibility of lovingly providing for and protecting the woman (cf. Eph 5:25, 28-31; 1 Pet 3:7; 1 Tim 3:4; Titus 1:6). (4) Although Eve first disobeyed, it was only after Adam had joined in the

rebellion that the eyes of *both* of them were opened (Gen 3:4-7). More significantly, after the Fall God first addressed *Adam,* holding him accountable for eating the forbidden fruit: "Where art thou? . . . Hast thou eaten of the tree . . . ?" (Gen 3:9-12; cf. 3:17: *"Because thou hast hearkened unto the voice of thy wife,* and hast eaten of the tree . . ."). It appears inexplicable for God, who in His omniscience already knew what had happened, to act in this way if Adam had not been given headship in the Eden relationship. (5) Despite the fact that the woman initiated the rebellion, it is *Adam,* not Eve, nor even both of them, who is blamed for our Fall (Rom 5:12-21; 1 Cor 15:21, 22), which suggests that as the spiritual head in the partnership of their equal relationship, Adam was the representative of the family. See *Searching the Scriptures,* 46, 47.

[25]For a detailed discussion, see Werner Neuer, *Man and Woman in Christian Perspective,* translated by Gordon J. Wenham (Wheaton, Ill.: Crossway Books, 1991), 59-81; cf. *Women in the Church: Scriptural Principles and Ecclesial Practice,* A Report of the Commission on Theology and Church Relations of the Lutheran Church Missouri Synod (n.p.: 1985), 18-28.

[26]Jo Ann Davidson, "Women in Scripture," *WIM,* 158

[27]See, for example, Jo Ann Davidson, "Women in Scripture," *WIM,* 157-169; cf. Vyhmeister, "Epilogue," *WIM,* 2-4, "Proper Church Behavior in 1 Timothy 2:8-15," *WIM,* 335.

[28]Jo Ann Davidson, "Women in Scripture," *WIM,* 179; cf. 175, 158.

[29]Vyhmeister, "Epilogue," *WIM,* 434; see also her "Proper Church Behavior in 1 Timothy 2:8-15," *WIM,* 350.

[30]Raoul Dederen, "The Priesthood of All Believers," *WIM,* 23, emphasis mine; cf. J. H. Denis Fortin, "Ordination in the Writings of Ellen G. White," *WIM,* 116-118, 128, 129 and Jerry Moon, "Ellen G. White on Women in Ministry," *WIM,* 203.

[31]"This new order, the priesthood of all believers," according to *Seventh-day Adventists Believe . . .*, 143, "means that each church member has a responsibility to minister to others in the name of God, and can communicate directly with Him without any human intermediary. It emphasizes the interdependence of church members, as well as their independence. This priesthood makes no qualitative distinction between clergy and laity, *although it leaves room for a difference in function between these roles"* (emphasis mine).

[32]The phrase "husband of one wife" is a call to *monogamous fidelity*—that is to say, an elder must be "faithful to his one wife." The word *aner* (translated "man" or "husband" in the English translations) means a *male* of the human race. Therefore, the Greek phrase, *mias* [of one] *gynaikos* [woman] *andra* [man] (1 Tim 3:2; Titus 1:6), literally translates as a "man of one woman," or "one-woman man," meaning "a *male* of one woman." When used of the marriage relation it may be translated "husband of one wife" (KJV) or "husband of but one wife" (NIV). Because in this passage the words for "man" and "woman" do not have the definite article, the construction in the Greek emphasizes character or nature. Thus, "one can translate, 'one-wife sort of a husband,' or 'a one-woman sort of a man.' . . . Since character is emphasized by the Greek construction, the bishop should be a man who loves only one woman as his wife." (See Kenneth S. Wuest, *The Pastoral Epistles in the Greek New Testament for the English Reader* [Grand Rapids, Mich.: Eerdmans, 1952], 53.) Also, because the word "one" (*mias*) is positioned at the beginning of the phrase in the Greek, it appears to emphasize this *monogamous* relationship. Thus, the phrase "husband of one wife" is calling for *monogamous fidelity*—that is to say, an elder

must be "faithful to his one wife" (NEB). For an excellent summary of the various interpretations of this text, see Ronald A. G. du Preez, *Polygamy in the Bible with Implications for Seventh-day Adventist Missiology* (D.Min. project dissertation, Andrews University, 1993), 266-277.

[33]Dederen has pointed out that there were a few non-Levites who, on occasion, performed priestly functions: Gideon (Judg 6:24-26); Manoah of Dan (Judg 13:19); Samuel (1 Sam 7:9); David (2 Sam 6:13-17); Elijah (1 Kgs 18:23, 37, 38) (see Dederen, "The Priesthood of All Believers," *WIM,* 11). Acareful study of these specific instances may offer some biblically-consistent explanations. For example, since Samuel was Elkanah's son, he too was a Levite (1 Chron 6:27, 28, 33, 34; cf. *Patriarchs and Prophets,* 569). On David's apparent offer of sacrifices, it appears from 1 Chronicles 15ff. and *Patriarchs and Prophets,* 706, 707, that David did not offer the sacrifices himself but simply paid for and directed them. It is in this sense that he is credited with offering the sacrifices. Regarding Elijah, we have no evidence from Scripture about whether or not he was not a Levite. Without other information, we may have to assume that he was a Levite living in Gilead (1 Kings 17:1). With respect to Gideon, Ellen White makes it clear that though God in this one instance specifically directed him to offer the sacrifice, it was wrong for Gideon to have "concluded he had been appointed to officiate as a priest" (*Patriarchs and Prophets,* 547; cf. 555); the same may apply to Manoah of Dan (Judg 13:19). In any event, even if it can be shown that the above Old Testament characters were all non-Levites and that they actually performed priestly functions, these exceptions only prove the validity of an established rule that only Levites could serve as priests. The phenomenon of "exceptions" to the normal order must always be recognized. But when those exceptions were initiated by humans instead of by God, there were disastrous consequences. See, for example, Korah (Num 16:3-7); Saul (1 Sam 13:8-14); Jeroboam (1 Kings 12:31-13:5; 13:33, 34); Uzzah (2 Chron 26:16-21).

[34]Walter B. T. Douglas, "The Distance and the Difference: Reflections on Issues of Slavery and Women's Ordination in Adventism," *WIM,* 379-398; cf. Vyhmeister, "Epilogue," *WIM,* 434, 435.

[35]Douglas credits Richard M. Davidson for his comparison of pro-slavery and anti-women's ordination arguments, *WIM,* 394, 395; see especially note 44 on 398.

[36]To balance *WIM*'s discussion of "the hermeneutical problem of slavery," see Robert W. Yarbrough, "The Hermeneutics of 1 Timothy 2:9-15," in *Women in the Church: A Fresh Analysis of 1 Timothy 2:9-15,* eds. Andreas J. Köstenberger, Thomas R. Schreiner, and H. Scott Baldwin (Grand Rapids, Mich.: Baker, 1995), 185-190; George W. Knight III, *The Role Relationship of Men and Women: New Testament Teaching* (Chicago, Ill.: Moody Press, 1985), 7-15.

[37]See my *Searching the Scriptures,* 62.

[38]Richard M. Davidson, "Headship, Submission, and Equality in Scripture," *WIM,* 281, 282.

[39]Jo Ann Davidson, "Women in Scripture," *WIM,* 176. Davidson is citing Evelyn and Frank Stagg's response to her questions: "Why did Jesus select twelve male apostles? . . . Why only *Jewish* men?"

[40]Richard M. Davidson, "Headship, Submission, and Equality in Scripture," *WIM,* 294 note 111.

[41]See Richard Hove, *Equality in Christ? Galatians 3:28 and the Gender Dispute*

(Wheaton, Il.: Crossway Books, 1999), 104-105 note 35, where he cites Rabbinic texts that speak quite positively about women.

[42]Stephen Clark, *Man and Woman in Christ: An Examination of the Roles of Men and Women in Light of Scripture and the Social Sciences* (Ann Arbor, Mich.: Servant Books, 1980), 241, 242.

[43]Richard M. Davidson, "Headship, Submission, and Equality in Scripture," *WIM,* 282.

[44]Ibid. Richard Davidson points to the work of Jo Ann Davidson and Robert M. Johnston for support.

[45]For a detailed critique of Richard M. Davidson's chapter in *Women in Ministry,* refer to Samuele Bacchiocchi's "Headship, Submission, and Equality in Scripture," in *Prove All Things,* 65-110.

# 13

# Speculative and Questionable Interpretations

In our discussion of "the feminist campaign for equality" in chapter 10 of this present volume, we saw how pro-ordinations distort Paul's statement in Galatians 3:28 to promote egalitarianism's ideology of "full equality," understood to mean the elimination of all gender role-distinctions in the home as well as in the church. But this is not the only biblical text that they twist.

The previous chapter also showed how advocates of women's ordination attempt to reinterpret the biblical teaching of male headship—a theological concept which means that within the loving relationship of male-female equality and complementarity, God calls upon men to be heads of their homes (as husbands and fathers) and churches (as elders and pastors), and that He holds them accountable if they refuse to shoulder these spiritual leadership responsibilities.

This chapter takes a look at some other innovative interpretations by the authors of *Women in Ministry,* the widely promoted pro-ordination volume by some prominent scholars from Andrews University. Our numbering takes off from the previous chapter's critique of the book.

### 5. Speculative Interpretations

One of the most serious methodological problems in *Women in Ministry* is the frequency of speculations and conjectures. Biblical certainties are downgraded into probabilities and probabilities into possibilities. Then possibilities are upgraded into probabilities and probabilities into certainties. This sounds like hard criticism. But let us look at the effort to construct a religious or cultural background to Paul's statements in 1 Corinthians 11, 14, and 1 Timothy 2:11-15, passages which contain such statements as "the head of the woman is the man," "every woman that prayeth or prophesieth with her head uncovered dishonoreth her head," "neither was the man created for the woman; but the woman for the man," "let your women keep silence in the churches," and "I suffer not a woman to teach, nor to usurp authority over the man. . . . For Adam was first formed, then Eve."

**(a) "Proto-Gnostic" Setting for 1 Corinthians and 1 Timothy?** Instead of accepting Paul's argument from Genesis 2, that Adam was created first and Eve later, as the basis for his teaching that the man occupies a position of headship in the home and in the church, *Women in Ministry* ventures numerous guesses for the real reason behind Paul's statements. These arguments are often propped up with expressions like "perhaps," "seems to," "likely," "apparently," "could be," and "might be."

I find it ironic that one author, who had earlier used some convoluted reasoning of his own to argue for a "female apostle," sees the apostle Paul doing the same here. In this scholar's opinion, "Paul's reasoning at several points in 1 Corinthians 14 is rather convoluted and calls for sophisticated exegesis."[1] Thus, some authors of *Women in Ministry* employ such "sophisticated exegesis" in their discussion of the life setting of 1 Corinthians 11 and 14 and 1 Timothy 2.

For example, in arguing that "any attempt to understand this passage [1 Cor 11 and 14] requires that we first know what was going on in Corinth in the early-to-mid 50s A.D.," one author speculates that Paul was dealing with "incipient gnosticism" or "proto-gnosticism."[2] The editor of the book also sees "incipient gnosticism," together with "the pagan worship of the mother goddess" and Judaism, as the religious background of 1 Timothy 2.[3] Gnosticism, we should note, was a second-century heresy that taught a dualistic (spirit-matter) world view, arguing that matter was bad and spirit good. Consequently, Gnostics held, the Genesis creation account and any teaching that is based on it are flawed, since the Genesis account involves the creation of matter.[4]

On the basis of this alleged "proto-gnostic" background, the authors of *Women in Ministry* claim that Paul was dealing with false teaching introduced by "gnostic Christian" women in Corinth or Ephesus. The problem with this kind of interpretation is that it requires more source material than we have in order to be sure of the cultural surroundings at the time when Paul wrote.

The scholars of *Women in Ministry* see "incipient-" or "proto-gnosticism" as the background of Paul's writings (first century), yet they have to appeal to later sources (second- or third-century writings) to reconstruct the heresy they believe Paul is dealing with. This kind of methodology, called "anachronistic interpretation," is like Sunday keepers' attempts to interpret the meaning of the "Lord's day" in Revelation 1:10 (first-century writing) by the meaning the term assumed in the writings of early church fathers in the second or third centuries. We would make a similar methodological mistake if we were to define the word "gay" in Ellen White's writing by the meaning of the term today. Such methods are open to serious criticism.

In the words of one knowledgeable scholar, "The lack of historical rigor, if I can say this kindly, is nothing less than astonishing. They have clearly not grasped how one should apply the historical method in discerning the nature of false teaching in the Pauline letters."[5]

But even if we suppose that *Women in Ministry* is correct and Paul was opposing an early form of gnosticism, "there is then not the slightest occasion, just because the false teachers who are being opposed are Gnostics, to link them up with the great Gnostic systems of the second century."[6] The appeals to Jewish parallels are also unpersuasive since these sources often postdate the New Testament writings.

**(b) Speculative Interpretations of 1 Tim 2:11-15.** Several of the authors of *Women in Ministry* argue that the traditional interpretation of 1 Timothy 2 has not taken into account what is "now known" to be "the initial situation" that Paul was addressing in Ephesus. Basing their positions partly on the "persuasive" work of a non-Adventist scholar, Sharon Gritz, the authors speculate that Paul's restriction on women's "teaching and having authority over men" (1 Tim 2:11ff) was due to the infiltration of the false teaching of the cult of the Mother Goddess, Artemis, in Ephesus.[7]

But our book's scholars differ on how the questionable claims and assumptions of Gritz's "Mother Goddess" hypothesis help them to understand 1 Timothy 2.[8]

For example, one writer who finds the speculation "persuasive" concludes, "Paul's concern in 1 Tim 2:8-15 is not that women might have authority over men in the church but that *certain assertive women in the church* who had been influenced by false teachers would teach error. For this reason, he charges them to 'be silent.'"[9]

Another writer does not see the issue as a concern about "certain assertive women in church" but rather as "dealing with husband-wife relations" in worship settings. For him, Paul was "correcting a false syncretistic theology in Ephesus . . . [in which] *wives* were apparently domineering over their *husbands* in public church meetings."[10]

The editor of the book speculates in a different direction. Believing the religious background in Ephesus to be "the pagan worship of the mother goddess," Judaism, and "incipient gnosticism," she challenges the husband-wife relation theory.[11] She argues that "the text itself [1 Tim 2] seems to be discussing attitudes [of women] in worship rather than the marriage relationship."[12] In her opinion, "Paul could be saying that he was *currently* not permitting women to teach [and "instigate violence"], because of a number of reasons, or even that he was not permitting women to teach *until such a time as they had learned sufficiently.*"[13]

Believing such conflicting speculations to be the new light that has eluded the Christian church throughout its history, one of the *Women in Ministry* authors asks: "One wonders what might have been the case if the Timothy passage had thus been understood throughout the history of the church"![14]

Fortunately, Seventh-day Adventists and the wider Christian church did not have to wait for this explanation to understand 1 Tim 2. If it is true that Paul wrote his epistle to restrain "certain assertive women in the church" or "wives domineering over their husbands in worship settings" or even some "unlearned" women who at that time were "instigating violence" because "they had not learned sufficiently," why is Paul's prohibition directed to *all women?* Since Paul's prohibition applies to all women, those who believe in these new theories need to show that all (or *any*) Christian women at Ephesus were teaching these kinds of false theologies. Such evidence cannot be found.

What *is* taught in Scripture is that the people who were teaching false doctrine in Ephesus were not women, but men. Paul, for example, talks about Hymenaeus and Alexander (1 Tim 1:20) and Hymenaeus and Philetus (2 Tim 2:17-18), who were all men. Similarly Paul warns the Ephesian elders of men (*andres,* from *aner,* a male) who will arise "speaking perverse things, to draw away disciples after them" (Acts 20:30). These false teachers are men, not women. Until someone shows from Scripture that all the Christian women at Ephesus—or even any of them—were teaching false doctrine, proponents of this new interpretation have no factual basis for it.

It is clear that some of the Ephesian women were being influenced by the false teaching (1 Tim 5:11-15; 2 Tim 3:5-9), but they were not the purveyors. It is also clear from Scripture that women were gossiping at Ephesus (1 Ti 5:13), but gossiping is not the same as teaching false doctrine. We all may know people who gossip but who don't teach false doctrine. Again, it is true that there were pagan religions in Ephesus where *non-Christian* men and women did a number of things not done by Christians (Acts 19:21-41). But to say that they did such things after becoming Christians is speculation without evidence.

How can one say that Paul's prohibition was a temporary restraint on the women of Ephesus until "such a time as they had learned sufficiently"? The apostle Paul did not cite a lack of education, formal training, or teaching skills as the reason why women should not "teach or have authority over men" (1 Tim 2:12 RSV). On the contrary, Paul instructed older women to "teach what is good. Then they can train the younger women" (Titus 2:3, 4 NIV). He also commended the teaching that Eunice and Lois provided for Timothy (2 Tim 1:5; 3:14, 15). Evidently Priscilla was well educated and a capable teacher, since she "expounded to" Apollos, an "eloquent man" who was already "instructed in the way of the Lord" (Acts 18:24-26).

Significantly, Paul's epistle to Timothy—the very epistle which commands that women not be allowed to "teach or to have authority over men," and which restricts the pastoral role of overseer to men—was addressed to the church at Ephesus (1 Tim 1:3), the home church of Priscilla and Aquila. Prior to writing this epistle, Paul had already stayed at the home of Priscilla and Aquila in Corinth for eighteen months (Acts 18:2, 11). The couple later accompanied Paul to Ephesus (Acts 18:18-21). When Paul stayed in Ephesus for another three years, "teaching the whole counsel of God" (Acts 20:27, 31; cf. 1 Cor 16:19), it is likely that Priscilla was among those who received instruction from him.

Yet not even well educated Priscilla, nor godly teachers Eunice and Lois, nor any other accomplished woman, was permitted to "teach or to have authority over men." The reason why women were forbidden to "teach or to have authority over men" was not inadequate education or a lack of ability to teach. Paul instead pointed to the creation order, stating that

"Adam was formed first, then Eve" (1 Tim 2:13).[15] Adam carried the special right and responsibility of leadership which belonged to the "firstborn" in a family (cf. Col 1:15-18).[16]

The editor of *Women in Ministry* offers another idea to prop up the gnostic heresy hypothesis. She argues that Paul's use of the conjunction "for" (*gar*) in 1 Timothy 2:12-13 does not mean that Paul is about to give the reason why women should not "teach and exercise authority over men"; instead, she claims, he uses the term to introduce examples of what happens when women falsely teach men.[17] This explanation is creative, but not convincing.

It is not convincing because in other places in his letter to Timothy, when Paul gives a command, the word "for" (*gar*) that follows almost invariably states the *reason* for the command (see 1 Tim 4:7, 8, 16; 5:4, 11, 15, 18; 2 Tim 1:6, 7; 2:7, 16; 3:5, 6; 4:3, 5, 6, 9-11, 15). In the same way, when he gives the command to women not to "teach or exercise authority over men" (1 Tim 2:11-12), he gives reasons in verses 13-14 why they should not do so ("for [i.e. because] Adam was created first, then Eve"). If the reason for the prohibition was to cite "an example of what happens when false teaching [by women] is propounded and accepted," we should have expected Paul to prohibit all men and all women "to teach and exercise authority over men," for the same bad results follow when men teach falsely.

We therefore conclude: "The suggestion that women were prohibited from teaching because they were mainly responsible for the false teaching finds no substantiation in the text. Even if some women were spreading the heresy (which is uncertain but possible), an explanation is still needed for why Paul proscribes only women from teaching. Since men are specifically named as purveyors of the heresy, would it not make more sense if Paul forbade all false teaching by both men and women? A prohibition against women alone seems to be reasonable only if *all* the women in Ephesus were duped by the false teaching. This latter state of affairs is quite unlikely, and the probable presence of Priscilla in Ephesus (2 Tim. 4:19) also stands against it."[18]

Even if we agree for the sake of argument that Paul was responding to "certain women" or "all women" in Ephesus, such a response to a specific situation does not nullify the universal principle he employs ("Adam was formed first, then Eve") to address that unique situation. If we claim that apostolic letters written to address specific "initial situations" are not applicable to the church today, then the rest of the New Testament would not be applicable to us either, since all the books of the New Testament were addressed to particular communities facing special circumstances.

### 6. Questionable Re-Interpretations of the Bible

By "questionable reinterpretations" I mean interpretations that are unwarranted and contradict Scripture. I will consider how *Women in Ministry* addresses some key questions on the biblical doctrine of male headship and female submission in both the home and the church. In the next chapter I will also examine the claims that there were "women priests" in the Old Testament, "women apostles" and "women ministers" in the New, and that the prophetesses Miriam, Deborah, and Huldah exercised "headship-leadership over men."

**Key Questions on Headship.** Unlike liberal or radical feminists, the authors of *Women in Ministry* accept the biblical teaching of headship in the home. But they insist that this headship was instituted after the Fall and does not apply in the church.[19] Creation headship would strike a fatal blow to the egalitarian concept of ministry. If headship existed before the Fall, with no role interchangeability, the whole enterprise in *Women in Ministry* collapses.

We will focus on three major issues: (a) When did headship begin—at creation or after the Fall? (b) What is the nature of headship—does it call for gender-role distinctions or does it nullify them? (c) What is the extent of headship—is it for the home only or does it also extend to the church? In addressing these questions we will show that the interpretations found in *Women in Ministry* contradict the Bible.

**(a) When Was Headship Instituted: At Creation of After the Fall?** According to the author of chapter 13 of *Women in Ministry,* Genesis 2:24 provides the "ultimate ideal" or the "divine ideal" for husband-wife relations. This Bible text says, "Therefore shall a man leave his father and his mother, and shall cleave unto his wife: and they shall be one flesh." The author repeatedly refers to this passage as revealing "God's original plan for total equality," "full equality with no headship/submission," "equal partnership," and "total role interchangeableness."[20]

In essence, our scholar's study of the creation account of Genesis 2 leads him to deny headship (functional role distinctions) before the Fall. This "equal partnership" or "total role interchangeableness" that was allegedly instituted before the Fall was also to be the ideal after the Fall. He argues that Genesis 2:24 was "clearly written to indicate its applicability to the *post-Fall conditions.* God's ideal for the nature of sexual relationship after the Fall is still the same as it was for Adam and Eve in the beginning—to 'become one flesh.'"[21]

Observe that if we accept this kind of reasoning, we will also have to argue that New Testament passages (like Eph 5:22-33; Col 3:18, 19; 1 Pet 3:7; 1 Cor 11:3, 11, 12) which Adventists have historically understood as God's permanent arrangement for male-female role relations in the home are merely non-ideal accommodations exacted by the Bible writers; Christians who seek to reach the assumed egalitarian ideal may justifiably repudiate the biblical teaching of male headship/leadership and female submission/supporting role. More importantly, however, the author's denial of creation headship, postponing its origin to the "post-Fall conditions," contradicts Paul's explicit use of Genesis 2:24 in Ephesians 5.

Although our scholar correctly recognizes Ephesians 5:21-33 as "the fundamental New Testament passage dealing with husband-wife relations,"[22] he does not take into account the use the inspired apostle himself makes of the verse from Genesis 2. In Ephesians 5, Paul makes it clear that he bases his teaching of headship on the nature of Christ's relation to the church, which he sees revealed as "mystery" in Genesis 2:24 and, thus, in creation itself. From this "mystery" he establishes a pattern of relationship between the husband as head (on the analogy of Christ) and derives the appropriateness of the husband's headship/leadership and the wife's submission/supporting role.

Paul's quotation of Genesis 2:24 in Ephesians 5:31, therefore, indicates that the headship-submission principle in the home ("husbands, love your wives" and "wives, submit to your husbands"), which Christ modeled for us, was established at creation, prior to the Fall. Thus, *Women in Ministry*'s claim that there was no headship before the Fall is directly negated by the apostle Paul's statement in Ephesians 5—"the fundamental New Testament passage dealing with husband-wife relations."[23]

**(b) Nature of Headship: Does It Nullify Gender Roles?** *Women in Ministry* also argues that at creation, there was "total role interchangeableness," so that there were no functional role distinctions before the Fall. This assertion contradicts the Bible's own self-interpretation.

Not only does Paul ground his headship doctrine in Genesis 2, but he also sees male-female role distinctions in the creation account. The inspired apostle's reason given in 1 Timothy 2:13 for not permitting a woman to "teach or have authority over man"—"for Adam was formed first, then Eve"—reflects his understanding of the creation account in Genesis 2:4-25, where we find the narrative of Adam being formed before Eve. The apostle's use of the word "form" (*plasso*, cf. Gen 2:7, 8, 15, 19) instead of "make" (*poieo*, cf. Gen 1:26, 27) also indicates that the reference in 1 Timothy 2 is to Genesis 2, where we find that God "formed man of the dust of the ground" (v. 7). Thus, the apostle Paul understands the order in which Adam and Eve were created as having implications for role differences between male and female (cf. 1 Cor 11:3, 8-11).

"If God indeed fashioned Eve later than Adam, for a purpose for which another male human being was not suited, then it is not difficult to argue that, in principle, there are things for which the woman may be suited for which the man is not, and vice versa. This observation appears to provide some substantiation for the kinds of functional distinctions between men and women in the Creator's purpose that have traditionally been held."[24]

As noted earlier, Ellen G. White rejected the egalitarian model of "total role interchangeability." Despite the abuse of God's creation arrangement for role relations in the home, she wrote that "heaven's ideal of this sacred [marriage] relation" is one in which the man is the constituted head of the home. This kind of relationship is "what God designed it should be."[25] And because "the husband is the head of the family, as Christ is the head of the church, she wrote, "any course which the wife may pursue to lessen his influence and lead him to come down from that dignified, responsible position is displeasing to God" (*Testimonies for the Church,* 1:307).

Thus, not only does Paul see Genesis 2 as an institution of the headship principle, but also his use of the passage in Ephesians 5 ("husbands love your wives, wives submit to your husbands") and 1 Timothy 2 ("I do not permit a woman to teach or have authority over man, for Adam was formed first, then Eve") indicates that headship calls for gender role distinctions. Therefore, the concept of "total egalitarianism" or "total role interchangeableness" as God's original plan for the home directly contradicts the inspired apostle as well as conflicts with Ellen G. White.

**(c) Extent of Headship: Home, Not Church?** *Women in Ministry* also argues that while the headship principle (erroneously believed to have originated at the Fall) is relevant today, the principle is only valid for the *home* situation and not for the *church* family. There are at least three major reasons against this view.

First, the Bible teaches that the church is not just another social institution; it is a worshiping community—a group of people who relate to God through a faith relationship in Christ. Thus the church, in both Old and New Testaments, exists whenever and wherever "two or three have gathered in my [Christ's] name" (Matt 18:20). Rightly understood, the worshiping household is a miniature model of the church. Even before Jesus Christ established the New Testament church (Matt 16:18, 19), the church was already in existence in Old Testament times. Israel, with its priests and ceremonial system of worship, was "the church in the wilderness" (Acts 7:38). But long before the Exodus brought Israel the opportunity to be "a kingdom of priests, and an holy nation" (Ex 19:6), the church existed in the homes, wherever "two or three . . . gathered in my name."[26]

The numerous Bible references to the church as the family of God[27] suggest that the relationship of male and female in the church—"the household of God" (1 Tim 3:15 RSV)—is to be *modeled after the home family,* of which the Eden home was the prototype (Eph 5:22, 23; Col 3:18; 1 Pet 3:1-7; 1 Cor 11:3, 7-9; 14:34, 35; 1 Tim 2:11-3:5). The frequent correspondence between home and church found in Scripture (e.g., Acts 2:46; 5:42; 1 Cor 14:34, 35; cf. Phil 4:22) finds an echo in John Chrysostom's statement that "a household is a little church" and "a church is a large household."[28]

Second, the Bible makes the success of male headship in the home a necessary qualification for one to be elder or overseer in the church. Thus, since only males can legitimately be heads of their homes (as husbands and fathers), according to Scripture, they alone can serve in the headship office of the church (as elders or overseers). For example, the pastoral epistles of Paul to Timothy and Titus, the very books which describe the qualities of an elder-pastor, view the church as the family of God, thus establishing the family structure as the model for church structure: "If a man does not know how to manage his own household, how can he care for God's church?" (1 Tim 3:4, 5 RSV; cf. Titus 1:6). This is why the Bible teaches that the elder or overseer must be "the husband of one wife" (1 Tim 3:2; Titus 1:6).

Third, it is logically and practically inconsistent to propose that God made the husband the spiritual head at home (a smaller family unit) and his wife the spiritual head of the church (a larger family unit). The "total egalitarian" model would create serious conflicts and confusion, yet God is not the author of confusion. Therefore, He is not the author of the idea that women should be the spiritual heads in the church.

The description of the church as "the household of God" (1 Tim 3:15; Eph 2:19) and the patterning of church authority after the headship arrangement in the home reveal the high estimation God places on the home family. Writes Ellen White: "In the home the foundation is laid for the prosperity of the church. The influences that rule in the home life are carried into the church life; therefore, church duties should first begin in the home" (Ellen G. White, *My Life Today,* 284). "Every family in the home life should be a church, a beautiful symbol of the church of God in heaven" (*Child Guidance,* 480).

Not only is authority in the church patterned after the home, but the home government is patterned after the church. Ellen G. White wrote, "The rules and regulations of the home life must be in strict accordance with a 'Thus saith the Lord.' The rules God has given for the government of His church are the rules parents are to follow in the church in the home. It is God's design that there shall be perfect order in the families on earth, preparatory to their union with the family in heaven. Upon the discipline and training received in the home depends the usefulness of men and women in the church and in the world" (*Signs of the Times,* Sept. 25, 1901).

Is it possible that those who wish to drive a wedge between the patterns of authority in the church and in the home do not understand the true nature of male headship and the complementary female supportive role?

One thing is undeniable. The egalitarian interpretations of the Genesis 2 creation account, positing "total role interchangeableness" or "full equality with no headship-submission" as God's divine ideal for the family, contradict the apostle Paul's own interpretation of the Genesis passage. Are those who propose that women should be ordained as elders or pastors better interpreters of Scripture than the inspired apostle?

**Conclusion.** The authors of *Women in Ministry* may be well-intentioned in their desire to offer a biblical justification for women's ordination. But their attempt to reinterpret Scripture's doctrine of headship to allow for feminism's full equality or "total role-interchangeableness" is woefully inadequate, if not totally baseless. The fact that different writers of the Seminary book offer conflicting and biblically questionable opinions on the subject is evidence enough to alert any serious Bible student to the risks of imposing secular ideologies on the Bible.

One scholar who has offered a devastating critique of *Women in Ministry's* view on headship and equality warns of the danger: "The biblical model of different yet complementary roles for men and women in the home and in the church may well be a scandal to liberal and evangelical feminists bent on promoting the egalitarian, partnership paradigm. Nonetheless, Christians committed to the authority and wisdom of the Scriptures cannot ignore or reject a most fundamental biblical principle. Blurring or eliminating the role distinctions God assigned to men and women in the home and in the church is not only contrary to His creational design but also accelerates the breakdown of the family, church structure, and society."[29]

In this respect, the speculative and questionable interpretations in *Women in Ministry* is only the tip of the feminist iceberg.[30] As we pointed out in chapter 10 of *Must We Be Silent?* feminism's efforts at obliterating gender role-distinctions have opened the way for other unbiblical teachings and practices, including lesbianism.

Even a well-known evangelical theologian inclined toward the ordination of women, acknowledges that "it cannot be denied that the women's liberation movement, for all its solid gains, has done much to blur the distinctions between the sexes and that many women who have entered the ministry appear committed to the eradication of these distinctions." This trend, as he observes, "is in no small way responsible for accelerating divorce and the breakdown of the family." He warns that "the fact that some clergywomen today in the mainline Protestant denominations are championing the cause of lesbianism (and a few are even practicing a lesbian life-style) should give the church pause in its rush to promote women's liberation."[31]

"Such things," argues an Adventist scholar, "ought likewise to give us pause in the rush to promote women's ordination, one facet of the women's liberation movement."[32]

---

**Endnotes**

[1]Johnston, "Ministry in the New Testament and Early Church," *Women in Ministry,* 56 note 14.

[2]W. Larry Richards, "How Does A Woman Prophesy and Keep Silence at the Same Time? (1 Corinthians 11 and 14)," *WIM,* 315.

[3]Vyhmeister, "Proper Church Behavior in 1 Timothy 2:8-15," *WIM,* 338-340.

[4]On Gnosticism and its late sources, see Edwin M. Yamauchi, *Pre-Christian Gnosticism: A Survey of the Proposed Evidences,* second edition (Grand Rapids, Mich.: Baker Book House, 1983).

[5]The above criticism was leveled against the hypothesis by Richard and Catherine Kroeger that in 1 Timothy 2:11ff Paul was correcting the "proto-gnostic" heresies in the Ephesian church, See Thomas R. Schreiner, "An Interpretation of 1 Timothy 2:9-15: A Dialogue with Scholarship," in *Women in the Church: A Fresh Analysis of 1 Timothy 2:9-15,* eds. Andreas J. Köstenberger, Thomas R. Schreiner, and H. Scott Baldwin (Grand Rapids, Mich.: Baker, 1995), 109, 110.

[6]Werner G. Kümmel, *Introduction to the New Testament,* 17th ed. (Nashville, Tenn.: Abingdon, 1975), 379.

[7]Jo Ann Davidson, "Women in Scripture," *WIM,* 178; Richard M. Davidson, "Headship, Submission, and Equality in Scripture," *WIM,* 280, 294 note 108; cf. Vyhmeister, "Proper Church Behavior in 1 Timothy 2:8-18," *WIM,* 338-340, 351 note 4. Cf. Sharon Hodgin Gritz, *Paul, Women Teachers, and the Mother Goddess at Ephesus: A Study of 1 Timothy 2:9-15 in Light of the Religious and Cultural Milieu of the First Century* (Lanham, Md.: University Press of America, 1991). On the basis of Gritz's work Jo Ann Davidson lists the "major tenets" of this Mother Goddess worship as the belief that "a female goddess gave birth to the world, that Eve was created before Adam, and that to achieve highest exaltation woman must achieve independence from all males and from child-bearing. Sharon Gritz suggests that such false teaching was endangering the faith of the new Christian converts in Ephesus. And Paul was likely counseling Timothy how to deal with such radical departure from the Christian faith" (Jo Ann Davidson, 178; cf. Richard M. Davidson, 280). In building their work on Gritz, some *Women in Ministry* authors are apparently not aware that Gritz's claims and assumptions "are a thorough misrepresentation of ancient Ephesus and of Artemis Ephesia" (see S. M. Baugh's "A Foreign World: Ephesus in the First Century," in *Women in the Church: A Fresh Analysis of 1 Timothy 2:9-15,* eds. Andreas J. Köstenberger, Thomas R. Schreiner, and H. Scott Baldwin [Grand Rapids, Mich.: Baker, 1995], 50). For more on this, see next note.

[8]"The central weakness of Gritz's work," argues one knowledgeable scholar, "is that she nowhere provides any kind of in-depth argument for the influence of the Artemis cult in 1 Timothy. She records the presence of such a cult in Ephesus and then simply assumes that it functions as the background to the letter [of Paul to Timothy]. To say that sexual impurity (1 Tim. 5:11-14) and greed (1 Tim. 6:3-5) are signs of the Artemis cult is scarcely persuasive! Many religious and nonreligious movements are plagued with these problems. Gritz needs to show that the devotion to myths and genealogies (1 Tim. 1:3-4), the Jewish law (1 Tim. 1:6-11), asceticism (1 Tim. 4:3-4), and knowledge (1 Tim. 6:20-21) indicate that the problem was specifically with the Artemis cult" (Thomas R. Schreiner, "An Interpretation of 1 Timothy 2:9-15: A Dialogue with Scholarship," in *Women in the Church: A Fresh Analysis of 1 Timothy 2:9-15,* eds. Andreas J. Köstenberger, Thomas R. Schreiner, and H. Scott Baldwin [Grand Rapids, Mich.: Baker, 1995], 110).

[9]Jo Ann Davidson, "Women in Scripture," *WIM,* 178, emphasis supplied, citing

Thomas C. Geer, Jr., "Admonitions to Women in 1 Tim 2:8-15," *Essays on Women in Earliest Christianity,* ed. C. D. Osburn (Joplin: College Press, 1993), 1:281-302.

[10]Richard M. Davidson, "Headship, Submission, and Equality in Scripture," *WIM,* 283, 280, emphasis supplied.

[11]According to Vyhmeister, three main religious currents interacted to form the background of 1 Timothy—(1) pagan worship of the mother goddess in Ephesus (Artemis or Diana), (2) Judaism, and (3) "incipient gnosticism." She concludes: "From this mixed environment came the women in the Ephesian congregations. Those from pagan backgrounds would need to learn that the excesses of Artemis worship, along with its ascetic or sensual practices, were inappropriate for Christian women." On the other hand, those from a Jewish background would need encouragement "to study, learn, and serve in the Christian community" (Vyhmeister, "Proper Church Behavior in 1 Timothy 2:8-15," *WIM,* 340).

[12]Ibid., 342, 353 note 50; cf. 352 note 31.

[13]Ibid., 344, emphasis added. Vyhmeister interprets the word translated "authority" (*authentein*) in Paul's statement, "I do not permit women to teach or have authority" to mean "taking independent action, assuming responsibility, o even . . . instigating violence" ( 345). She offers this creative interpretation for 1 Tim 2:11-12: "Paul does not want women to teach at this time, certainly not until they have learned in quietness, submitting to the teaching of the gospel. Neither does he want them to take upon themselves the responsibility for violence or independent action of any kind. They should emulate Eve, who in the next verse is presented as responsible for the fall of the human race" ( 346).

[14]Jo Ann Davidson, "Women in Scripture," *WIM,* 178.

[15]For an alternative to the speculations in *Women in Ministry,* see C. Raymond Holmes's "Does Paul Really Prohibit Women from Speaking in Church?" in *Prove All Things: A Response to Women in Ministry,* 161-174.

[16]Paul's description of Christ in Colossians 1:15-18 RSV as "the first-born of all creation," "the head of the body, the church" suggests His pre-eminent authority. His headship and authority are tied in with His being the "firstborn." Paul's use of "firstborn" language to express the headship and authority of Christ suggests that he attached the same meaning to Adam's being "first formed." If this is the case, it indicates that Paul saw in the priority of Adam's creation the establishment of his right and responsibility as the head of the first home, the first church. This may explain why Adam is presented as the one who brought death into the world, and Christ, the second Adam, as the One who brought life (Rom 5:12-21).

[17]Vyhmeister, "Proper Church Behavior in 1 Timothy 2:8-15," *WIM,* 346, 347.

[18]Thomas R. Schreiner, "An Interpretation of 1 Timothy 2:9-12: A Dialogue with Scholarship," in *Women in the Church: A Fresh Analysis of 1 Timothy 2:9-15,* eds. Andreas J. Köstenberger, Thomas R. Schreiner, and H. Scott Baldwin (Grand Rapids, Mich.: Baker, 1995), 112.

[19]This position is best articulated by a leading conservative among the Seminary scholars. Writes Richard M. Davidson: "The nature of the husband's headship is paralleled to that of Christ, who 'loved the church and gave Himself for it' ([Eph 5] v. 25). The husband's 'headship' is thus a loving servant leadership. It means 'head servant, or taking the lead in serving,' not an authoritarian rule. It consists of the husband's loving his wife as his own body, nourishing and cherishing her, as Christ does the church (vv. 28-29)." On

the basis of Ephesians 5:33, our author underscores the headship-submission relationship as "love (of the husband for his wife) and respect (of the wife for her husband)"; it is a kind of "mutual submission," though "this does not quite approach total role interchangeableness in the marriage relation." It "works itself out in different ways involving an ordering of relationships, and exhortations according to gender" (Richard M. Davidson, "Headship, Submission, and Equality in Scripture," *WIM,* 275). A most penetrating and detailed critique of Davidson's views has been provided by Samuele Bacchiocchi, "Headship, Submission, and Equality in Scripture," in *Prove All Things,* 65-110.

[20]Ibid., 269, 271, 275, 280, 281, 284.

[21]Ibid., 269, emphasis mine. Again he writes: "But just as the equal partnership was described in Gen 2:24 as the divine ideal for *after the Fall* as well as before, so the New Testament counsel calls husbands and wives to a love partnership of mutual submission" (ibid., 280, 281).

[22]Ibid., 274.

[23]Some people try to dismiss the "creation order" principle by claiming that such reasoning would place animals in headship over both men and women, since the animals were created first. Their dispute, clearly, is against the Bible, because Paul cited the creation order as the basis for his counsel (1 Tim 2:13). But the argument also fails to recognize the "firstborn" element in the issue. "When the Hebrews gave a special responsibility to the 'firstborn,' it never entered their minds that this responsibility would be nullified if the father happened to own cattle before he had sons. In other words, when Moses wrote Genesis, he knew that the first readers would not lump animals and humans together as equal candidates for the responsibilities of the 'firstborn.'" See Question #39 of John Piper and Wayne Grudem, "An Overview of Central Concerns: Questions and Answers," in *Recovering Biblical Manhood and Womanhood,* 81.

[24]Harold O. J. Brown, "The New Testament Against Itself: 1 Timothy 2:9-15 and the 'Breakthrough' of Galatians 3:28," in *Women in the Church: A Fresh Analysis of 1 Timothy 2:9-15,* 202. For more on this, see Samuele Bacchiocchi's evaluation of Davidson's chapter in *Prove All Things.*

[25]Ellen G. White writes: "In both the Old and the New Testament the marriage relation is employed to represent the tender and sacred union that exists between Christ and His people, the redeemed ones whom He has purchased at the cost of Calvary. . . . [Quoting Isaiah 54:4, 5; Jeremiah 3:14, and Song of Solomon 2:16; 5:10; 4:7.] In later times Paul the apostle, writing to the Ephesian Christians, declares that *the Lord has constituted the husband the head of the wife,* to be her protector, the house-band, binding the members of the family together, even as Christ is the head of the church and the Saviour of the mystical body. . . . [Quoting Ephesians 5:24-28]. The grace of Christ, and this alone, can make this institution what God designed it should be"an agent for the blessing and uplifting of humanity. And thus the families of earth, in their unity and peace and love, may represent the family of heaven. Now, as in Christ's day, the condition of society presents a sad comment upon *heaven's ideal of this sacred relation.* Yet even for those who have found bitterness and disappointment where they had hoped for companionship and joy, the gospel of Christ offers a solace" (*Thoughts from the Mount of Blessing,* 64, 65, emphasis mine).

[26]"God had a church when Adam and Eve and Abel accepted and hailed with joy the good news that Jesus was their Redeemer. These realized as fully then as we realize now the promise of the presence of God in their midst. Wherever Enoch found one or two who

were willing to hear the message he had for them, Jesus joined with them in their worship of God. In Enoch's day there were some among the wicked inhabitants of earth who believed. The Lord never yet has left His faithful few without His presence nor the world without a witness" (Ellen G. White, *The Upward Look,* 228).

[27]For the various expressions used in the Bible to refer to the church as God's family, see Vern Poythress, "The Church as Family: Why Male Leadership in the Family Requires Male Leadership in the Church," in *Recovering Biblical Manhood and Womanhood: A Response to Evangelical Feminism,* eds. John Piper and Wayne Grudem (Wheaton, Ill.: Crossway, 1991), 233-236.

[28]Chrysostom (A.D. 347-407), *Homily XX on Ephesians,* cited by Stephen B. Clark, *Man and Woman in Christ* (Ann Arbor, Mich.: Servant Books, 1980), 134.

[29]Samuele Bacchiocchi, "Headship, Submission, and Equality in Scripture," in *Prove All Things,* 105.

[30]For more on this, see C. Raymond Holmes, *The Tip of An Iceberg: Biblical Authority, Biblical Interpretation, and the Ordination of Women in Ministry* (Wakefield, Mich.: Adventists Affirm and Pointer Publications, 1994), 87-155.

[31]Donald G. Bloesch, *Is the Bible Sexist?: Beyond Feminism and Patriarchalism* (Westchester, Ill.: Crossway 1982), 56.

[32]Samuele Bacchiocchi, "Headship, Submission, and Equality in Scripture," in *Prove All Things,* 106, commenting on Bloesch's statement above.

# 14

# Women As Priests, Apostles, and Ministers in the Bible?

Until the publication of *Women in Ministry,* Seventh-day Adventist students of the Bible have always recognized the lack of biblical *precedence* for ordaining women. They observed that, despite the significant role of women in ministry, women were not ordained as priests in the Old Testament. Also, though women made major contributions to the ministry of Christ, He did not appoint a single one of them as an apostle; further, when a replacement apostle was sought (Acts 1:15-26), even though women were present and surely met most of the requirements set (vv. 21-22), it was a male who was chosen. In addition, there is no record of any woman's being ordained as an elder or pastor in the New Testament church. Why was this so?[1]

Conflicting answers to these questions fuel the debate over the ordination of women as elders and pastors. Historically, Adventists have explained that women's exclusion from the Old Testament priesthood and from the New Testament roles of apostles and elders/pastors is not based on mere sociological or cultural factors but rather is rooted in God's divine arrangement of gender role-distinctions established at creation.

Proponents of women's ordination, however, offer different explanations for the lack of biblical precedence for ordaining women. On the one hand, while conceding that, indeed, there is no precedence for the practice in the Bible, *liberal* feminist proponents of women's ordination explain this absence by asserting that the Bible itself is time-bound, culturally conditioned, male-centered (androcentric), rabbinic in origin, anti-female in nature, and conditioned by patriarchal mentality or prejudice. Consequently, they argue, the culture of the Old and New Testament times would not have allowed the practice. As we pointed out in chapter 11, this is the view adopted in *The Welcome Table: Setting A Place for Ordained Women* (1995), an Adventist pro-ordination book.

Evangelical or biblical feminists, on the other hand, correctly point out that, since the pagan religions in the Old and New Testament times had women priests, contrary to the claims of liberal feminists, the culture of those times *would have* allowed women priests, apostles, and elders or pastors. *Women in Ministry,* the pro-ordination book from Andrews University Theological Seminary, apparently recognizes this fact. So how does the volume explain the lack of biblical precedence for the practice?

According to the book's authors there *were,* after all, women priests, women apostles, and women elders or pastors in the Bible!

This chapter takes a look at this new light in *Women in Ministry.* Our numbering continues from the previous chapter.

### 7. Distorted Biblical Reasoning

Occasionally, *Women in Ministry* resorts to convoluted and sophisticated explanations to bolster an untenable position. As an example of this, we shall look at the claim that Eve was a "female priest," Junia was a "female apostle" and also that Phoebe was a "female minister."

**(a) Women Priests in the Old Testament?** I was astonished by one suggestion in *Women in Ministry* that women actually served as priests in the Old Testament. The reason given to support the suggestion amazed me even more! The suggestion is that in the Garden of Eden God ordained Eve as a priest alongside Adam. The author of this idea argues:

"Adam and Eve were, indeed, dressed as priests, with one difference, however: instead of the fine linen that characterizes the priestly garment (Ex 28:39), God chose animal skin. This specification not only implies the killing of an animal, the first sacrifice in history, but by the same token, confirms the identification of Adam and Eve as priests, for the skin of the atonement sacrifice was specifically set apart for the officiating priests (Lev 7:8). By bestowing on Adam and Eve the skin of the sin offering, a gift strictly reserved to priests, the Genesis story implicitly recognizes Eve as priest alongside Adam."[2]

Thus our scholar reads Genesis through the lenses of pro-women's ordination and discovers Eve as a "female priest"! In the concluding paragraph of his chapter in *Women in Ministry,* he states: "Thus biblical identification of woman as priest in Eden and the redeemed community ["priesthood of all believers"] complements biblical approval of women's anointing as prophet and judge. In this context, and in reflection upon ordination to pastoral ministry, there is no case for women's exclusion."[3]

If the clothing of Adam and Eve with animal skin meant that they were dressed as priests, does this mean that God congratulated them for sinning?

It is puzzling that this chapter was agreed upon by the Ad Hoc Committee that developed *Women in Ministry.* Perhaps it illustrates where the logic of the "egalitarian" model leads those seeking a biblical justification to ordain women as elders or pastors.[4] Since other scholars in *Prove All Things* have competently challenged the biblical basis for this unbelievable claim,[5] I will concentrate more on the author's cultural arguments.

It seems that our scholar does not accept the biblical explanation that the headship principle instituted at creation is the reason why there is no evidence of female priests in the Old Testament. He has manufactured two reasons—namely God's "reaction to pagan syncretism and sexual perversions" and "the incompatibility of the sacrifice [women performing sacrifices in Israel], normally associated with death and sin, and the physiological nature of the woman traditionally associated in the Bible with life and messianic pregnancy"! In other words, "had it not been for these two factors, ancient Near Eastern cults and more decisively the sacrifices, women might well have been priests in Israel."[6]

It is encouraging that at least one writer, the lead author in *Women in Ministry,* offers a gentle corrective to the speculative "female priest" theory when he observes that "males functioned as priests in the days of the biblical patriarchs as well as after God's covenant with Israel at Mount Sinai."[7] Indeed, the Bible teaches that *only* males served in the headship role of priest in the Old Testament. Prior to Sinai, the head of each household (male) and firstborn sons (males) performed this role.[8] At Sinai, however, this responsibility was assigned "as a gift to Aaron and his sons" (Num 8:19; cf. Num 3:9-13, 32, 45; 25:10-13). Ellen G. White summarized it this way:

> In the earliest times every man [male] was the priest of his own household. In the days of Abraham the priesthood was regarded as the birthright of the eldest son [male]. Now, instead of the first-born of all Israel, the Lord accepted the tribe of Levi for the work of the sanctuary. . . . The priesthood, however, was restricted to the family of Aaron. Aaron and his sons alone [males] were permitted to minister before the Lord" (*Patriarchs and Prophets,* 350).

The absence of female priests in the Old Testament was not due to the culture of those times, since the ancient Near Eastern cultures would have allowed female priests, as was the case in the surrounding Canaanite religions. Also, Israelite women were prohibited from serving as priests not because God did not want them to engage in the kind of immorality that the pagan priestesses engaged in (i.e., God's prohibition was not in "reaction to pagan syncretism and sexual perversions"). Such an argument, besides lacking basis in Scripture, implies that women are more prone to idolatry and sexual immorality than men—a sexist argument which is unproven. Finally, the absence of female priests in the Old Testament was not due to "the physiological nature of the woman traditionally associated in the Bible with life and messianic pregnancy," since it takes both men and women to give birth to human life, and since the anticipated "messianic pregnancy" that resulted in the "virgin birth" of Christ greatly limited the physical involvement of both earthly parents.

The reason for the absence of women priests in the Old Testament can best be explained by God's special divine arrangement at the beginning. The headship principle, instituted by God at creation and reiterated after the Fall, is the only biblically and theologically consistent explanation for why there were no women priests in ancient Israel. The questionable reinterpretations we have been considering contradict this teaching of Scripture.

**(b) The Case of Women Prophets Miriam, Deborah, and Huldah.** Before we look at another astonishing claim in *Women in Ministry*—namely, the assertion that there were women minister's in the New Testament—I will briefly respond to the book's claim that women such as Eve, Sarah, Hagar, Shiphrah and Puah, Jochebed, Miriam, Ruth, Deborah, Hannah, the Shunammite woman, and Huldah occupied headship/leadership positions in the Old Testament. Of these, Miriam the prophetess-musician (Ex

15:20), Deborah, "a prophetess . . . [who] was judging [NIV "leading"] Israel at that time" (Judges 4:4), and Huldah, the prophetess to whom Josiah the king and Hilkiah the high priest looked for spiritual guidance (2 Kings 22), are often cited as exceptional "women leaders exercising headship over men."[9]

On the above assumption, it is claimed that women today should be ordained as elders or pastors. In making this claim, however, *Women in Ministry* seems to confuse the issue of women exercising the leadership authority of elders or pastors with the legitimacy of women filling the messenger role of prophets. It also overlooks the fact that under the Old Testament theocracy, Israel was a nation governed by God and His law. In the Old Testament system, the leaders who were selected—prophets, priests, judges and kings—differed in how they were chosen and in the extent of their respective authority.

Two examples can highlight the separation of the duties of *prophets* and *priests*. In the Old Testament, Amram and Jochebed had three children—Miriam, Aaron, and Moses. All three were prophets. But while their sons both served as priests, Miriam did not. She was a prophetess, but not a priest. Similarly, in the New Testament we read about the prophetess Anna in the temple (Luke 2:36-37). But we never read that she or any other prophetess offered sacrifices. The Bible makes it clear that the priesthood is a male role.

The leadership role of *prophet* (likewise *judge*) was not an elected office. God Himself chose and authoritatively commissioned (ordained) prophets (and judges) as His mouthpiece; they were not elected by the people as leaders to exercise administrative or executive authority. Thus, kings (and judges) and priests were all to be subject to the authority of God, whose prophets delivered His messages.

Similarly, in both the Old and New Testaments, God chose and commissioned (ordained) prophets without regard to gender (e.g., Miriam, Deborah, Huldah). On the other hand, the Bible teaches that elders and pastors are to be chosen and commissioned (ordained) by the church within guidelines stipulated in Scripture. One such criterion for the office of elder or pastor is that the one chosen must be "the husband of one wife" (1 Tim 3:2; Titus 1:6), an expression whose Greek construction emphasizes that the elder or pastor must be the kind of man who loves only one woman as his wife.

Elders and pastors (the Bible makes no distinction in their office) are to be subject to the authority of God's messages coming through His chosen prophets. As leaders of the church, elders and pastors are given administrative and leadership responsibility and authority that prophets are not. Church leaders are responsible to God for their reception of the prophetic message, but they are not under the administrative authority of the prophets.

We may see this difference clearly both in Scripture and in the experience of Ellen G. White. Elijah could give King Ahab God's message, but he did not have executive authority to make the king obey or to countermand Ahab's orders to have Elijah arrested (1 Kings 17:1-3, 18:7-10). Jeremiah proclaimed God's judgments with divine authority, for which he was imprisoned by priest, princes, and king (Jer 20:1, 2; 37:11-38:10). They had authority different from his. Even Deborah's authority as "prophetess [who was] judging Israel" illustrates how God-fearing women are to exercise their unique gifts and leadership in the context of the biblical teaching of headship.[10]

In Seventh-day Adventist history, the closest parallel to the prophetic authority and unique leadership of Deborah is Ellen G. White. Though she never claimed to be a leader of the church, she did exercise her role as a messenger of the Lord. In the early 1870s, Mrs. White had authority to communicate God's plan for Seventh-day Adventist education, but she did not have authority to make the leaders follow it in founding Battle Creek College. Prophetic authority is not the same thing as the administrative responsibility of the chosen leadership. Mrs. White herself refused to be called the leader of the Seventh-day Adventist church, referring to herself as "a messenger with a message": "No one has ever heard me claim the position of leader of the denomination. . . . I am not to appear before the people as holding any other position than that of a messenger with a message" (*Testimonies for the Church,* 8:236-237).

Our conclusion is that Miriam, Huldah and Deborah (like Ellen G. White) were prophets. But their authority as prophets should not be confused with exercising headship authority in the home (as husbands) and in the church (as elder or pastors). We can do so only by resorting to questionable reinterpretations of biblical teaching. *Women in Ministry,* therefore, misleads readers when it compares the headship authority of the elected leadership office in the church (elders or pastors) with the prophetic authority of the non-elected office of prophets and prophetesses.

**(c) Junia, A "Female Apostle"?** Much is made in *Women in Ministry* about Junia being a "female apostle."[11]This claim is based on the apostle Paul's description of Andronicus and Junia as "my kinsmen, and my fellowprisoners, *who are of note among the apostles,* who also were in Christ before me" (Rom 16:7, KJV; emphasis mine).

There are two problems in this text. First, does the name Junia have a feminine ending (proving Junia was a woman), or does it have a masculine ending (proving Junia was a man)? This is a grammatical problem arising from the Greek language. In Romans 16:7, the ending for the name of Junia in the Greek is *-an,* which would be the direct object (accusative) form both for men's names that end in *-as* (like Elias, Zacharias, Silas, Thomas, or Cephas) or women's names that end in *-a* (like Martha, Joanna, or Lydia). Therefore it is impossible to tell from the Greek ending alone whether the person described by the apostle Paul is Juni*as* (male) or Juni*a* (female). This explains the varied opinions among the church fathers. For example, whereas Origen (died A.D. 252) referred to the person as Junias, a man, Chrysostom (died A.D. 407) referred to this person as Junia, a woman. Church historian Epiphanius (died A.D. 403) sees the person as man. Thus, grammatically and historically, both genders are possible.

But let's assume that the person Paul refers to is a woman by the name Junia. Does Romans 16:7 require us to believe that Junia was a female apostle? This is the second problem confronting interpreters. The answer hinges on how one understands the phrase translated "among the apostles" (*en tois apostolois*). In the Greek the phrase is ambiguous. Does it mean that Andronicus and Junia were numbered among the apostles (as the NIV has it, "They are outstanding among the apostles,") or does it mean that their reputation was well known by the apostles (as the KJV puts it, they are "of note among the apostles")?

How do we resolve a problem in which both interpretations are allowed by the Greek? This is where one's hermeneutical principles of interpretation are revealed. The historic Adventist approach is to (1) interpret an obscure passage by a plain passage in Scripture, and (2) look for any applicable precedents in Scripture, noting that one Scripture will never contradict another.

On the basis of this "time-honored" Adventist approach, one should recognize five relevant facts: (1) Paul's doctrine of headship was established on the creation order (1 Tim 2; 1 Cor 11; Eph 5). (2) Jesus Himself ordained only males as apostles, pointing back to the Old Testament patriarchs as foundations of the "church in the wilderness" (Acts 7:38). (3) Every known apostle in the New Testament was a male—Paul and Barnabas (Acts 14:14, 4), Apollos (1 Cor 4:6, 9), Silvanus and Timothy (1 Thess 1:1; 2:6), Titus (2 Cor 8:23, Greek), Epaphroditus (Phil 2:25). (4) While women played significant roles in the early church's soul-winning ministry, none of them is known to have served as apostle, elder, or bishop. (5) The apostle Paul, who worked closely with these active women, taught that the headship function of elder or overseer could be held by only a person who, among other things, was the "husband of one wife" (1 Tim 3:2; Titus 1:6).

The above considerations lead me to the conclusion that the ambiguous phrase "among the apostles" (*en tois apostolois*) should be understood as "of note among the apostles" in the sense that Junia was well known by the apostles, not that she was numbered among them. No New Testament evidence supports the idea that the woman Junia mentioned in Romans 16:7 was an apostle, nor is there any New Testament evidence that the man Andronicus mentioned in the same text was an apostle. The most plausible and biblically-consistent understanding is that both Andronicus and Junia were well known and appreciated by the apostles as Christian converts prior to Paul's own conversion.[12]

Unlike the interpretation in *Women in Ministry,*[13] this interpretation does not violate clear and plain biblical teaching on headship, the example of Jesus Christ in appointing only males as apostles, and the fact that all the known apostles mentioned in the New Testament are males.

My conclusion is that Junia, even if a woman, could not have been an apostle. Any assertion that Junia was a "female apostle" is speculative and arguably false.

**(d) Phoebe: A "Female Minister"?** In Romans 16:1-2, the apostle Paul writes: "I commend unto you Phebe our sister, which is a servant [*diakonos*] of the church which is at Cenchrea: That ye receive her in the Lord, as becometh saints, and that ye assist her in whatsoever business she hath need of you: for she hath been a succourer of many, and of myself also" (KJV).

Based on the above description of Phoebe as a *diakonos* ("servant," KJV, NIV, NASB; or "deaconess," RSV), one of the authors of *Women in Ministry* claims that Phoebe functioned "as Paul's emissary, as did Titus and Timothy" and that her designation as *diakonos* "does not imply the modern 'deaconess' but rather the same position as that of the church leaders designated in 1 Tim 3:8-10."[14] Another author maintains that Phoebe is an example of New Testament "women in church leadership-headship roles."[15]

These writers do not offer any biblical proof for their assertions. They build their cases on the "able" studies provided by another *Women in Ministry* writer who concludes that Phoebe was a "female minister," and that "if there could be one female minister there could as well be many."[16]

However, a careful study of the evidence presented by the book's leading proponent of the "female minister" theory indicates that it involves a convoluted handling of the biblical data and that it contradicts Ellen White's understanding. The following points capture the essential thrust of *Women in Ministry*'s arguments:

(1) The term *diakonos,* used for Phoebe in Romans 16:1, comes from the same root word (*diakonein*) used for the appointive ministry of the seven men in Acts 6.[17]

(2) But this office of *diakonos* assigned to the seven men of Acts 6 is *not* that of deacons as "has often been assumed," even in Ellen G. White's book *The Acts of the Apostles*![18]

(3) Instead, the kind of work for which the seven men of Acts were appointed is the same as "elder," the only appointive ministry originally known in the apostolic church.[19]

(4) Only later did the one appointive ministry of *diakonos* (now redefined by the author to mean "elder" or "minister") divide into two levels of "elder" and "deacon."[20] The alleged later "distinction between deacon and elder/bishop is hardened in the pastoral epistles, especially in 1 Tim 3:1-13."[21]

(5) Phoebe occupied "the same position as the deacons of 1 Timothy 3," which our author claims was originally the same office as that of elder, or possibly that of apostle.[22]

(6) Therefore, the designation of Phoebe as *diakonos* in Romans 16:1 "proves incontrovertibly that the early church had female *diakonia*"—i.e., female ministers. And "if there could be one female minister [Phoebe] there could as well be many."[23]

In responding to this interpretation, we will briefly discuss the meaning of the term *diakonos.* We will note how Ellen G. White understood the function of the seven men of Acts 6 and what bearing it has on the "female minister" theory.

**(e) Meaning of "Diakonos."** In the New Testament the term *diakonos,* like the related terms *diakonia* and *diakoneo,* has both a broad and a narrow meaning. In its broad sense it conveys the idea of a ministry or service carried out on behalf of the church. Thus, services like preparation of a meal (Luke 10:40), serving a meal (Luke 22:27), providing financial and material support (Luke 8:1-3), the employment of any spiritual gift (1 Cor 12:5; 1 Pet 4:10), doing the work of a deacon by taking care of the needy (Acts 6:1-4), and providing spiritual oversight and leadership for the churches by serving as an elder (1 Tim 4:6) or apostle (Acts 1:25) are all termed ministry (*diakonia*). Because in this broad usage anything a person does to advance the work of the church is a ministry, the one who labors in this manner is a minister or servant (*diakonos*) of the Lord.[24]

In its narrow and technical usage, *diakonos* refers to the office of a deacon which among other things can be occupied by only one who is a "husband of one wife" (1 Tim 3:8-13; Phil 1:1). This deacon office, first occupied by the seven men of Acts 6, involved ministering to the poor, needy, and sick. But "although deacons were to care for the temporal affairs of the church, they were also to be actively involved in evangelistic work (Acts 6:8; 8:5-13, 26-40)."[25]

Whether we apply the broad meaning or the narrow one, calling Phoebe a *diakonos* does not prove she was an apostle or a female minister.[26] Indeed, Paul explains why he calls her a deacon—because she is a "succourer [helper] of many" (Rom 16:2). As for the seven deacons, they certainly were not apostles; they were elected specifically to do work the apostles felt unable to do at that time. Until recently, Seventh-day Adventists have upheld the view that Romans 16:1-2 refers to Phoebe's valuable ministry of care and hospitality for church members. To change from this well-established view surely needs better evidence than what *Women in Ministry* provides.[27]

Ellen G. White presents Phoebe not as a "female minister," but rather as an example of how we should "care for the interests of our brethren and sisters." Referring to Romans 16:1, 2, she states, "Phebe entertained the apostle, and she was in a marked manner an entertainer of strangers who needed care. Her example should be followed by the churches of today" (*Testimonies for the Church,* 6:343, 344).

**(f) Ellen White on the Seven Men of Acts 6.** The "female minister" theory proposal in *Women in Ministry* can only be sustained by proving that the seven men of Acts 6 were elders and not deacons. The leading proponent of this theory is wrong when he argues that because the title of chapter 9 ("The Seven Deacons") in Ellen White's *The Acts of the Apostles* may be the work of editors, it therefore does not show that she believed the seven men of Acts 6 were deacons.[28]

During her lifetime, all editorial work on her books was submitted to Ellen G. White for approval before a book was published. We can safely conclude that she approved the chapter heading in *The Acts of the Apostles,* chapter 9. Also, contrary to what *Women in Ministry* says, in that very chapter (91) Mrs. White does indeed refer to the seven men as deacons (not ministers or elders). Furthermore, elsewhere in the book she describes Philip as "one of the seven deacons" (106); she also refers to Stephen as "the foremost of the seven deacons" (*Lift Him Up,* 104). To claim that Acts 6 is describing seven elders and not seven deacons is to interpret the Bible differently from the way Ellen White interprets it. And to assert, as our author does, that Mrs. White describes these men only as officers and not deacons in the text is simply wrong.

**(g) The History of the Appointive Ministry.** Is there a biblical basis on which to speculate that the original appointive ministry in the New Testament church was that of elder, and that this office was later divided into two levels (elders and deacons) so that in the pastoral epistles the distinction between the two was "hardened"?

As *Women in Ministry* notes, the first leaders of the church were the twelve apostles specially chosen by Christ Himself (Matt 10:1-4; Mark 3:13-19; Luke 6:12-16). Like the twelve patriarchs or the leaders of the tribes of Israel, these twelve male apostles constituted the original ministry. We find that to them was entrusted the responsibility of general spiritual leadership of the churches, serving as overseers (*episkope,* "office," a cognate of *episkopos* [bishop or elder], is applied to the apostolate in Acts 1:20) and ministering to believers' needs (*diakonia,* "ministry," is their work in Acts 1:25; cf. the cognate *diakonos,* "deacon," "one who ministers").

But as the gospel work prospered, it was practically impossible for the apostles alone to perform all the functions of spiritual leadership and at the same time minister to members' physical needs. Led by the Holy Spirit, the original ministry of the twelve apostles was expanded to include chosen deacons (*diakonos*) and elders (*presbyteros*) or bishops/overseers (*episkopos*).[29]

Were the offices of elders and deacons really one office originally, later split into those two? *Women in Ministry* offers slim evidence for this, which we will merely comment on here.[30] (1) According to the leading proponent of the "female minister" theory, "The kind of work for which the seven were appointed in Acts 6 is said to be done by the elders in Acts 11:30." But the Bible text does not say this. It records only that the relief money for Judea was delivered to the elders, not that the elders personally conducted the distribution, as the seven did in Acts 6. As the representatives of the believers, the elders would be the appropriate ones to receive the gifts from the distant churches, regardless of who did the actual distribution. (2) The argument that the elders' method of appointment "resembles somewhat" the method for the seven appointed in Acts 6 is a weak basis for claiming that they were the same. Such partial resemblance does not indicate that the offices were identical. (3) Finally, our author argues that because Acts 15 mentions only the offices of apostle and elder in Jerusalem, the office of deacon was not in place by the time of the Jerusalem council. But this is an argument from silence regarding deacons. The kinds of decisions spoken of in Acts 15 may well have been considered the responsibility of the apostles and elders, and not the deacons, to make.

The three points above, together with the denial that Acts 6 instituted the office of deacon, are the bases upon which our *Women in Ministry* scholar constructs his theoretical history of the appointive ministry. But as we have shown, it does not follow from these points that "we must conclude" that the church had only one office of elder at the early stage and that this one office was later split into two (elder and deacon). The New Testament writers and Ellen G. White affirm that the apostles instituted the office of deacon at a very early stage in the history of the Christian church. And each of the deacons mentioned in Acts 6 was a male.

Inasmuch as the New Testament offices of apostles, elders, and deacons were a continuation and extension of the headship and leadership roles instituted at creation (and exercised by male priests in the Old Testament, and male apostles at the time of Christ), the spiritual qualification for these offices included gender specifications ("the husband of one wife," 1 Tim 3:2, 12; Titus 1:6). Though our author claims that this gender specification actually was generic,[31] such a claim overlooks the fact that in two passages in Acts where qualifications are set forth, one for apostle (Acts 1:21) and the other for the deacon office under consideration (Acts 6:3), the text uses the Greek word *aner,* a male, instead of the generic *anthropos,* a person. The term *anthropos* could have been used here without grammatical difficulty if a person of either gender had been intended.

In light of the above facts from Scripture, the speculations about Phoebe in *Women in Ministry* cannot be sustained. Contrary to the authors' claims, Phoebe, being a "sister," could not have occupied "the same position as that of the church leaders designated in 1 Tim 3:8-10." Neither could she have been an example of New Testament "women in church leadership-headship roles."

**(h) Phoebe's Commendation: A Ministerial Credential?** The authors of *Women in Ministry* argue that Paul's commendation of Phoebe (as "a servant of the church") and his request on her behalf ("receive her in the Lord, as becometh saints") imply that Phoebe functioned "as Paul's emissary, as did Titus and Timothy,"[32] or that this commendation is a kind of ministerial credential for Phoebe. Writes the leading proponent of the "female minister" theory:

"Paul requests that she [Phoebe] be given the same kind of reception as his other representatives, the same kind of support and respect that Paul enjoins for Titus and the other *apostoloi* [apostles] (Titus in 2 Cor 8:24; Timothy in 1 Cor 16:10). Such a letter of commendation was the only kind of credential that the early church could offer. If there could be one female minister there could as well be many."[33]

The argument suffers from at least two serious interpretive fallacies. First, it disregards the context, namely Paul's commendations of and personal greetings to several individuals in Romans 16. Second, it is an instance of a procedure known technically as "illegitimate totality transfer," which supposes that the meaning of a word (e.g. *diakonos*) or expression (e.g., Paul's commendation) in a given context is much broader than the context allows. In this way the sense of a word (e.g., *diakonos*) or expression (commendation or request) and its reference (particular individuals, e.g., Phoebe, Titus, Timothy) are linked in an unwarranted fashion, giving the impression that the given word or expression means the same thing in any conceivable context.

Context really is the key for understanding the meaning of a word. While *diakonos* was indeed a church office, the most common meaning of the word was servant. When the apostles call themselves *diakonos,* the translation as minister misses the point—they were specifying that, like Christ, they led by *serving.* They were not identifying themselves as deacons or ministers. Any reference to the *office* of deacon can be determined only from the *context.* The Bible's stated fact of Phoebe's devoted service to the church, making herself the servant of all, does not mean that she held the office of deacon. The context does not suggest that Paul is talking about a church office.

A fair reading of the New Testament shows all church office names were derived from common functions. Serving, then, did not make one a deacon; being elderly did not make one an elder; being sent (*apostolos*) did not make one an apostle like the Twelve; and being an *aggelos* (messenger) did not make one an angel, though the Greek words are the same. The context is crucial to a proper understanding of a word's meaning.

In light of our discussion in the preceding pages, the assertion that Phoebe functioned as "Paul's emissary, as did Titus and Timothy" and that Paul's letter was a "kind of credential" for one of many "female ministers" can be dismissed as a convoluted interpretation. On the contrary, when Paul commended Phoebe as "a servant [*diakonos*] of the church . . . [and] succourer of many, and of myself also" (Rom 16:1-2), he was speaking of her valuable personal ministry to members of the church as well as to himself.

We must conclude that Phoebe was not a female minister. Hence there is no basis for the statement, "if there could be one female minister there could as well be many." From the evidence given us in the New Testament, there weren't *any.*[34]

**Conclusion**

This chapter has examined some of the areas in which Seventh-day Adventists should carefully examine the assertions *Women in Ministry* makes regarding women serving as priests in the Old Testament and as apostles and ministers in the New. The scholars of the pro-ordination volume tried very hard to explain away the lack of biblical precedence for ordaining women as elders or pastors. Their bold effort of attempting to come up with their flashing new light about women priests, women apostles, and women ministers may be innovative. But the assumptions underlying the theories are incorrect, and therefore so are its conclusions about ordaining women as elders and pastors today.

In the next chapter, I will examine how *Women in Ministry* handles certain historical, facts about our early Adventist history.

**Endnotes**

[1]Observe also that, despite the active involvement of women in ministry in the apostolic church, Paul's pastoral epistles to Timothy and Titus (letters specifically written to pastors and laity) contain instruction that only men may aspire to the office of elder or pastor. "I permit no woman to teach or to have authority over men" (1 Tim 2:12 RSV); "a bishop [or elder] must be . . . the husband of one wife" (1 Tim 3:2; Titus 1:6). These passages all use the same Greek word for "man" and "husband." It is not the generic term *anthropos,* from which the English word "anthropology" derives and which refers to human beings, male or female, without regard to gender. Rather, Paul employed the specific word *aner,* a term that means a male person in distinction from a woman (cf. Acts 8:12; 1 Tim 2:12), one capable of being a husband (see Matt 1:16; John 4:16; Rom 7:2; Titus 1:6). Why did Paul prohibit women from exercising the headship/leadership role of elder or pastor?

[2]Jacques B. Doukhan, "Women Priests in Israel: A Case for their Absence," in Nancy Vyhmeister, ed., *Women in Ministry: Biblical and Historical Perspectives* (Berrien Springs, Mich.: Andrews University Press, 1998), 36, 37. The book is cited hereafter as *WIM.*

[3]Ibid., 39.

[4]Apparently, this questionable interpretation of Genesis that is included in *Women in Ministry* is not challenged by members of the Ad Hoc Committee as long as there is "agreement on the big picture" of ordination (borrowing the words of the editor; see Vyhmeister, "Prologue," *WIM,* 4).

[5]P. Gerard Damsteegt has offered a more thorough response to Doukhan's "female priest" concept in *Prove All Things: A Response to Women in Ministry* (Berrien Springs, Mich.: Adventists Affirm, 2000), 123-128). See also Samuele Bacchiocchi's commens in *Prove All Things,* 65-110.

[6]Doukhan, "Women Priests in Israel: A Case for their Absence," *WIM,* 38; cf. 33, 34

[7]Raoul Dederen, "The Priesthood of All Believers," *WIM,* 23. Though Dederen does not believe in "female priests" in the Old Testament, yet as we have shown in an earlier section he goes on to argue mistakenly that a "radical transformation occurred" so that a new "priesthood of all believers" is unfolded in the New Testament which allows women to function "in all expressions of the ordained ministry." Cf. Denis Fortin, "Ordination in the Writings of Ellen G. White," *WIM,* 116; Vyhmeister, "Epilogue," *WIM,* 433.

[8]Thus, prior to Sinai, Noah (Gen 8:20), Abraham (Gen 22:13), Jacob (Gen 35:3) and Job (Job 1:5) performed the headship role of priest of the family. At the time of the Exodus, God claimed all firstborn males as His own (Ex 13:1, 2, 13). Later, because of their faithfulness during the time of the golden-calf apostasy, males from the tribe of Levi took the place of the firstborn males or heads of each family (Num 3:5-13; 8:14-19).

[9]See, for example, Richard M. Davidson, "Headship, Submission, and Equality in Scripture," *WIM,* 272, 273; cf. Vyhmeister, "Epilogue," *WIM,* 434, and Jo Ann Davidson, "Women in Scripture," *WIM,* 161-172.

[10]The unique leadership of Deborah as prophet and judge in Israel is probably the best model of how women can exercise their leadership gifts in the absence of capable men

(Judges 4:4ff.). However, whereas other judges led Israel into victory in battles, God told Deborah that Barak was to do this (vv. 6-7). Apparently she was the only judge in the book of Judges who had no military function. Also, Deborah does not assert leadership for herself, but she gives priority to a man—even though the man was reluctant to go to battle without her (v. 8). Deborah rebuked Barak's failure to exercise his God-appointed leadership; he is told that the glory that day would go to a woman—not Deborah, but Jael (vv. 9, 17-25.). Thomas R. Schreiner therefore concludes that Deborah's "attitude and demeanor were such that she was not asserting her leadership. Instead, she handed over the leadership, contrary to the pattern of all the judges, to a man" (see Schreiner, "The Valuable Ministries of Women in the Context of Male Leadership: A Survey of Old and New Testament Examples and Teaching," in John Piper and Wayne Grudem, eds., *Recovering Biblical Manhood and Womanhood,* 216).

[11]Robert M. Johnston, "Ministry in the New Testament and Early Church," *WIM,* 47; cf. Richard M. Davidson, "Headship, Submission, and Equality in Scripture," *WIM,* 282, 294 note 113; Jo Ann Davidson, "Women in Scripture," *WIM,* 177; Vyhmeister, "Epilogue," *WIM,* 434.

[12]We can only refer to them as apostles in the general usage of the word *apostolos,* meaning a "sent one." In this sense, both Andronicus and Junia could be conceived as missionaries—dedicated individuals engaged in the soul winning ministry of the early church.

[13]Robert M. Johnston lays the foundation for the speculative interpretation that Junia was a "female apostle." While acknowledging that the phrase in Romans 16:7 ("among the apostles") is ambiguous, Johnston believes that it is "more probable" to take it to mean Junia was "numbered among the apostles." He gives the following interesting reasons: "(1) It is the most natural way to take the Greek; (2) Ancient commentaries, when not ambiguous, such as that of Chrysostom, understood it that way . . . ; (3) Paul, who was always anxious to defend his apostleship, would not have spoken of the apostolic opinion in such a way as to seem not to include himself; (4) The first option [i.e., Junia being "well known by the apostles"] is not usually taken when the person in question is thought to be a man named Junias" (Johnston, "Ministry in the New Testament and Early Church," 54, 55 note 11). Readers should understand that the above weak reasons are the sole basis for the belief by the authors of *Women in Ministry* that Junia was a "female apostle."

[14]Jo Ann Davidson, "Women in Scripture," *WIM,* 177.

[15]Richard M. Davidson, "Headship, Submission, and Equality in Scripture," *WIM,* 282; cf. Vyhmeister, "Epilogue," *WIM,* 434.

[16]Robert M. Johnston, "Ministry in the New Testament and Early Church," *WIM,* 51. Jo Ann Davidson points readers to Robert Johnston's work in *Women in Ministry,* where the latter "studies this significant detail" about Phoebe's role as a *diakonos* (Jo Ann Davidson, 185 note 78). Similarly, Richard M. Davidson writes: "Examples of women in church leadership/headship roles have been ably presented in Robert Johnston's and Jo Ann Davidson's chapters (chaps. 3 and 9). Deacons included the woman Phoebe (Rom 16:1) and probably the women referred to in 1 Tim 3:11" (Richard M. Davidson, *WIM,* 282).

[17]Robert M. Johnston argues that the appointive ministry "could be called either *diakonos* (suggested by *diakonein* in Acts 6:2), a word describing function, or *presbyteros,*

a word describing dignity" (Johnston, "Ministry in the New Testament and Early Church," *WIM,* 49).

[18]Johnston is aware that the office of the seven men in Acts 6 is referred to as "deacon" in the chapter heading of Ellen G. White's *The Acts of the Apostles* (chapter 9 of that book is titled "The Seven Deacons," 87-96). But he counters: "It is to be noted, however, that the chapter titles are mostly the work of the editors. The term 'deacon' does not occur in the text itself. Mrs. White simply calls them 'officers' (89)." See Johnston, "Ministry in the New Testament and Early Church," *WIM,* 49, 57 note 19. Note, however, that in *The Acts of the Apostles,* 91, 106, Ellen G. White does refer to the seven as "deacons."

[19]Johnston argues that "at least in the earliest period, what can be said of 'deacon' also applies to 'elder.' Both were ministries which in the beginning were one, and they likely remained one in many places for several decades. Even in the pastoral epistles, Timothy is called *diakonos* (which the RSV translates 'minister') in 1 Tim 4:6, though he had a charismatic gift that was somehow associated with prophetic designation and the laying on of hands (1:18, 4:14)" (Johnston, *WIM,* 51).

[20]Johnston concludes: "To begin with there was only one appointive ministry that could be called either *diakonos* (suggested by *diakonein* in Acts 6:2), a word describing function, or *presbyteros* [elder], a word describing dignity. Only later did this one ministry divide into two levels, and the two terms came to be used to designate the two levels of ministry" (Johnston, "Ministry in the New Testament and Early Church," *WIM,* 49). Explaining the basis of his conclusion, Johnston writes: "The kind of work for which the seven were appointed in Acts 6 is said to be done by the elders in Acts 11:30. Their method of appointment in the churches, reported in 14:23, resembles somewhat that of Acts 6. In Acts 15 we hear of only two offices in Jerusalem, those of apostle and elder. We must conclude that the church at this early stage knew of only one appointive ministry, which Luke designated 'elder'" (ibid., 49).

[21]Ibid., 50.

[22]Ibid., 51. Our author reasons this way: "Paul requests that she [Phoebe] be given the same kind of reception as his other representatives, the same kind of support and respect that Paul enjoins for Titus and the other *apostoloi* [apostles] (Titus in 2 Cor 8:24; Timothy in 1 Cor 16:10). Such a letter of commendation was the only kind of credential that the early church could offer. If there could be one female minister there could as well be many" (Johnston, 51; cf. ibid., 49).

[23]Ibid., 50, 51. Believing that he has "proved" that Phoebe was a "female minister" and speculating that there "could as well be many" female ministers, this scholar transforms his speculations into the following assertion of certainty: "That there were women in the appointive ministry implies something about that ministry that logically should have remained true even after it began to be differentiated into two and then three levels, just as the qualities of a piece of clay remain the same even when it is divided in two. But at some unknown point in history it ceased to be true, and women were squeezed out, at least from certain levels" (Johnston, *WIM,* 52).

[24]Cf. Matt 20:26; 23:11; Mark 9:35; 10:43; John 12:26; Rom 13:4; 15:8; 1 Cor. 3:5; 2 Cor. 3:6; 6:4; 11:23; Gal 2:17; Eph 3:7; 6:21; Col 1:23, 25; 4:7.

[25]*Seventh-day Adventists Believe . . . : A Biblical Exposition of 27 Fundamental Doctrines* (Silver Spring, Md.: Ministerial Association, 1988), 148.

[26]The question confronting Bible students is this: Since in the Greek, the word *diakonos*

can be either male or female in gender, depending on the context, when Paul referred to Phoebe as *diakonos,* was he using this term in the broad and general sense to suggest Phoebe's *activity* of caring for the needy of the church (she was a "succourer of many" [Rom 16:2])? Or was the apostle using the term *diakonos* in the narrow and technical sense to suggest that Phoebe held the male *office* of deacon (1 Tim 3:8-13), the same position held by the seven men of Acts 6?

[27]Because she is described as a "sister" (Rom 16:1), she could not have served in the male office of a "deacon" without contradicting the gender requirement in 1 Tim 3:12 (a deacon must be the "husband of one wife"). Her ministry as "succourer" (KJV) or "helper" (RSV) (i.e., her "great help to many people" [NIV]), however, parallels what we designate today as the position of "deaconess." By describing Phoebe as a *diakonos,* Paul was simply speaking of her valuable ministry to church members as well as to himself. One respected scholar has captured the Adventist understanding: "Though the word for 'servant' [*diakonos*] is the same as is used for [the office of] deacon . . . it is also used to denote the person performing any type of ministry. If Phoebe ministered to the saints, as is evident from [Rom 16] verse 2, then she would be a servant of the church and there is neither need nor warrant to suppose that she occupied or exercised what amounted to an ecclesiastical office comparable to that of the diaconate. The services performed were similar to those devolving upon deacons. Their ministry is one of mercy to the poor, the sick, and the desolate. This is an area in which women likewise exercise their functions and graces. But there is no more warrant to posit an *office* than in the case of the widows who, prior to their becoming the charge of the church, must have borne the features mentioned in 1 Timothy 5:9, 10." See John Murray, *The Epistle to the Romans,* 2 vols., *The New International Commentary on the New Testament* (Grand Rapids, Mich.: Eerdmans, 1965), 2:226. Even if (for the sake of argument) we assume that the term *diakonos* in Romans 16:1 reflects its narrow and technical usage (i.e., to the male office of "deacon") and not its broad and general usage (i.e., the work of "ministry" on behalf of the church), the office of deacon is not the same as that of a "church leader"—either as elder or apostle, as is the case with Titus and Timothy. The authors of *Women in Ministry* who seek to discover an example of "women in church leadership/headship roles" in Romans 16:1 require the use of very powerful egalitarian lenses.

[28]Johnston, "Ministry in the New Testament," *WIM,* 57 note 19.

[29]According to the Bible (1) those who are permitted to perform the oversight-leadership functions of the ministerial office are elders or pastors; and (2) the New Testament makes no essential distinction between the two offices. The Greek terms for elder or presbyter (*presbyteros*) and overseer or bishop (*episkopos*) are used interchangeably in the New Testament (Acts 20:17, 28; Titus 1:5-7; 1 Pet 5:1-3). The same qualifications are required for both (1 Tim 3:1-7; Titus 1:5-9). Both perform the same work of shepherding the flock (Acts 20:17, 28; 1 Pet 5:1-4; 1 Thess 5:12). Thus we may conclude that since presbyters (elders) and bishops (overseers) are known by the same names and are required to possess the same qualifications, and since they do actually discharge the same oversight duties, the two terms refer to the same offce of shepherding the flock. The book of 1 Peter brings all the terms together: pastor (shepherd), elder (presbyter), and bishop (overseer). "For ye were as sheep going astray; but are now returned unto the Shepherd (*poimen,* = pastor) and Bishop (*episkopos,* overseer) of your souls" (1 Pet 2:25). "The elders (*presbyteros*) which are among you I exhort, who am also an elder . . . : Feed (*poimano,* to tend

as a shepherd) the flock of God, taking the oversight (*episkopeo*) thereof. . . . And when the chief Shepherd (*archipoimen*) shall appear, ye shall receive a crown of glory that fadeth not away" (1 Pet 5:1-4). The *elders* are commissioned to stand as *overseers,* functioning as *pastors/shepherds* to the flock.

[30]Johnston, "Ministry in the New Testament," *WIM,* 49.

[31]Johnston, "Ministry in the New Testament and Early Church," *WIM,* 50, 51.

[32]Jo Ann Davidson, "Women in Scripture," *WIM,* 177.

[33]Johnston, "Ministry in the New Testament and Early Church," *WIM,* 51.

[34]*Seventh-day Adventists Believe . . . ,* 150 note 10 correctly observes that because in New Testament times the term *diakonos* had a broad meaning, "it was still employed to describe all who served the church in any capacity. Paul, though an apostle, frequently described himself (see 1 Cor. 3:5; 2 Cor. 3:6; 6:4; 11:23; Eph 3:7; Col. 1:23) and Timothy . . . (see 1 Tim. 4:6), as *diakonoi* (plural of *diakonos*). (*Seventh-day Adventist Bible Commentary,* rev. ed., 7:300). In these instances it has been translated as 'ministers' or 'servants' instead of 'deacons.'" See also P. Gerard Damsteegt's detailed critique of the "female ministry" hypothesis in *Prove All Things,* 129-153.

# 15

# *Misleading and Erroneous Claims Regarding Early Adventist History*

In earlier chapters, we examined some of the biblical and theological arguments of *Women in Ministry,* organized under seven categories. The current chapter and the next will take up the remaining three categories of concern which we mentioned in the introduction section of chapter 12.

The focus in this particular chapter will be on *Women in Ministry*'s handling of historical matters concerning early Seventh-day Adventist history. Once again, we will take up numbering them where the list in the earlier chapter left off.

### 8. Misleading and Erroneous Claims Regarding Seventh-day Adventist History

There are instances in which *Women in Ministry* is "factually challenged." We must remember that the members of the Seminary Ad Hoc Committee had been asked to come up with a basis in the Bible or Ellen G. White's writings on which to support the ordination of women as elders or pastors. There is no such basis in either source; so the committee manufactured one. This may sound like harsh criticism, so let me show you what I mean.

Here are five "facts" that I say the committee "manufactured." See what you think. (a) There were women ministers (preferred term "leaders") in the early Seventh-day Adventist church (at least prior to 1915); (b) our pioneers wrote strongly in support of women ministers; (c) the early Seventh-day Adventist church voted at the 1881 General Conference session to ordain women; (d) Ellen G. White called for women's ordination in an 1895 statement; (e) Ellen G. White herself was ordained.

I will show that, in making the above claims, the authors of *Women in Ministry* make a use of historical sources that is characterized by misunderstanding, a serious inflation of the evidence, and an uncritical reliance on revisionist histories of the early Seventh-day Adventist church offered by feminists and liberal pro-ordinationists.

(a) **Did Early Seventh-day Adventist Women Function as Ministers?** In early Seventh-day Adventist history women played major roles in the publishing and editorial work, home missionary work, the work of Sabbath schools, church finances and administration, frontier missions and evangelism, and medical and educational work. Those women who labored as full-time workers were issued the denomination's ministerial *license* but not the ministerial *credentials* reserved for ordained ministers—indicating that they were not authorized to perform the distinctive functions of ordained ministers.[1]

In *Women in Ministry,* however, some of the authors have left the erroneous impression that because early Adventist women labored faithfully and successfully in the soul-winning ministry, and because they were issued ministerial *licenses,* these women performed the functions of the *ordained* ministry.[2] On this inaccurate basis, they join other revisionist historians in concluding that today the "ordination of women to full gospel ministry is called for by both the historical heritage of the Seventh-day Adventist Church and by the guidance of God through the ministry of Ellen G. White."[3]

One prominent author of *Women in Ministry* has made the same claim in his most recent work, *A Brief History of Seventh-day Adventists,* a book promoted by its publishers as "providing a short but accurate history of Adventism." This church historian states the following under the heading "The Contribution of Female Ministers in Early Adventism":

> Because the bulk of Adventism's ministry has consistently been male, too few have recognized the contribution to the church made by women who have served as ministers and in other

> official positions. . . . What is beyond doubt, however, is that she [Ellen G. White who] was probably the most influential 'minister' ever to serve the Adventist church. Many other women participated during the late nineteenth and early centuries as licensed ministers.[4]

Statements such as the above lend credibility to the spurious claims by women's ordination advocates that "there were many women pastors in early Seventh-day Adventist church."[5]

Contrary to such creative reinterpretations, the Adventist women of the past typically understood that while they had been called to do the work of soul-winning, and while it was biblically legitimate for them to preach, teach, counsel, minister to the needy, do missionary work, serve as Bible workers, etc., the Scriptures prohibited them from exercising the headship responsibility of elder or pastor. These dedicated Adventist women did not view their non-ordination as elders or pastors to be a quenching of their spiritual gifts or as an arbitrary restriction on the countless functions they could perform in gospel ministry. As they labored faithfully within the biblical guidelines of what is appropriate for men and women, the dedicated women of old discovered joy in God's ideal for complementary male-female roles in the church.[6]

In early Adventist records, full-time workers carrying ordained ministers' *credentials* were listed as "Ministers," while the term "Licentiates" was used for unordained workers (men and some women) with ministerial *licenses.* Not until 1942 would the *Yearbook* of the church employ the terms "Ordained Ministers" and "Licensed Ministers" for these two categories of church workers. Both the early and later distinctions between the two groups of workers ensured that unordained laborers in the soul-winning ministry would not be confused with ordained ministers. One author, whom *Women in Ministry* quotes on other matters, noted that by the turn of the century, when about 15% of church employees were women in various roles, "the church classified *none of them* as ministers except Mrs. White"[7] (a reference to her ordained minister credentials; see discussion below).

Indeed, we have yet to see any of these women referred to as ministers in the writings of Mrs. White or the other pioneers. There is, therefore, no valid justification for some contemporary writers to suggest or to create the impression that women listed as "licentiates" or even occasionally as "licensed ministers" performed the functions of ordained ministers or were generally thought of as "woman ministers."[8] Nor does the history of those days support the idea that women today seeking to do full-time work in gospel ministry must be ordained as elders or pastors. The facts from the "historical heritage of the Seventh-day Adventist Church" do not support such a conclusion.[9]

**(b) Did our Adventist Pioneers Endorse Women as Ministers?** Under the heading of "Defense of women in ministry," a chapter in *Women in Ministry* devotes two pages to citations from the *Review and Herald* and other sources which, the author claims, show the pioneers to be "so passionate in defense of 'women preachers.'"[10] By "women preachers," our author seems to want readers to understand "women as pastors." But in fact, most of the articles address a different issue. While none of the pioneers endorses women pastors or elders, they all uphold the right or propriety of women to speak in the church or in other public places.

For example, our *Women in Ministry* author cites a January 7, 1858 *Review and Herald* article by James White, claiming that he "spoke favorably . . . on women's role in the church." It quotes how he dealt with an objection: "Some have excluded females from a share in this work, because it says, 'your young men shall see visions.' . . ." Actually, though, the article is not about "women's role in the church" but about "Unity and Gifts of the Church," specifically addressing the gift of prophecy. It does not mention women as pastors or elders. It has only one paragraph that our author could quote, but he omitted its first sentence, where James White indicates that the role he was referring to was *prophecy.* The paragraph actually begins this way: "Under the influence of the Holy Spirit both sons and daughters will prophesy. Some have excluded females from a share in this work, because it says, 'your young men shall see visions.'" By omitting the first sentence and applying the remainder of the paragraph to a topic James White was not discussing—"women in ministry" and "women preachers"—the author has misled the reader regarding James White's actual concern.

Likewise J. N. Andrews's *Review and Herald* article (January 2, 1879) which the author cites was not addressing whether women could be ministers or could preach. His title, which our author did not give, was "May Women Speak in Meeting?" Andrews's opening sentence shows his real concern: "There are two principal passages cited to prove that women should not take *any part* in speaking in religious meetings" (emphasis mine). Andrews's article did not specifically mention preaching. His purpose was to show that women may freely bear their testimony or take other speaking parts in meeting.

The author next cites a James White article (*Review and Herald,* May 29, 1879) as stating that "Joel's message that 'sons and daughters' would prophesy indicated the participation of women in preaching." In fact, James White never mentioned preaching in the article, and his only comment about Joel's message is that "women receive the same inspiration from God as men." On women's role in the church, he said, "But what does Paul mean by saying, 'Let your women keep silence in the churches'? Certainly he does not mean that women should take no part in those religious services where he would have both men and women take part in prayer and in prophesying, or teaching the word of God to the people." Having women as ministers was not James White's concern.

The author claims that others through the years defended the sisters and their "prominent roles in the work of God." He cites the example of G. C. Tenney, whose article appeared in the *Review and Herald,* May 24, 1892. The author claims Tenney "defended women who labored publicly in the gospel," an undefined expression which leaves the reader to think of women serving as gospel ministers. But in fact, as Uriah Smith's introduction to the article indicates, Tenney was dealing with "the question whether women should take any public part in the worship of God." Where our author says that Tenney "rested his case" by stating that God is no respecter of persons, male or female, Tenney actually was defending women's bearing their testimony, not serving as ministers. The sentence before the one quoted in *Women in Ministry* reads, "But it would be a gross libel on this valiant servant of Christ [Paul] to impute to him the purpose to silence the testimony of the most devoted servants of the cross." Nowhere in his article does Tenney ever mention "preachers" or "preaching," which *Women in Ministry* seems to equate with "pastors" or "pastoring." He speaks only of women participating in the work of the gospel and being able to speak aloud in the meetings of the church.

The chapter quotes Ellen G. White recounting how, prior to her addressing a congregation for more than an hour, S. N. Haskell had been called upon to answer a question from a Campbellite objector who quoted "certain texts prohibiting women from speaking in public." According to Mrs. White, Haskell briefly answered the objection and "very clearly expressed the meaning of the apostle's words" (*Manuscript Releases,* 10:70). Interestingly enough, even here the words "preaching" and "preacher" are not used. As in the other cases, the issue seems to have been just what Mrs. White said it was: the propriety of women "speaking in public."

Only one of the six exhibits found in this section of *Women in Ministry* even mentions women preaching. It is the article by J. A. Mowatt, under the title "Women as Preachers and Lecturers." It was reprinted from an Irish newspaper; evidently it was not written by a Seventh-day Adventist. *Women in Ministry* quotes in full Uriah Smith's introduction to the article. Alert readers will note how Smith qualifies his endorsement of the article. After noting that Mowatt applies the prophecy of Joel to "female preaching," Smith shifts the point: "while it must embrace public speaking *of some kind* [emphasis mine], this we think is but half of its meaning." Smith declines to comment on the work of the non-Adventist female preachers and lecturers whom Mowatt commends so glowingly. His interest, he says, is in the argument that women have the *right* to do such activities.

All of the exhibits, then, contend that women are not required to be silent in public or in the meetings of the church. Only one of them, from a non-Adventist, offers an explicit endorsement of women preachers. Far from being "so passionate in defense of 'women preachers,'" the Adventist sources seem uninterested in that specific aspect of the matter. They are concerned with the right of *all* women to participate in the services of the church, to testify for the Lord, and to have an active part in the work of saving souls.

Given our author's interest in determining the pioneers' views on women as pastors, it is unfortunate that he has overlooked a significant *Signs of the Times* editorial in 1878 which addresses the issue explicitly. J. H. Waggoner, the magazine's resident editor and the author of a treatise on church organization and order, is the presumed author of the unsigned editorial "Women's Place in the Gospel." After defending, as others had done, the right of women to speak in meeting, Waggoner specifically addressed whether Scripture allowed women to serve as pastors or elders. He wrote, "The divine arrangement, even from the beginning, is this, that the man is the head of the woman. Every relation is disregarded or abused in this lawless age. But the Scriptures always maintain this order in the family relation. 'For the husband is the head of the wife, even as Christ is the head of the church.' Eph. 5:23. Man is entitled to certain privileges which are not given to woman; and he is subjected to some duties and burdens from which the woman is exempt. A woman may pray, prophesy, exhort, and comfort the church, but *she cannot occupy the position of a pastor or a ruling elder.* This would be looked upon as usurping authority over the man, which is here [1 Tim 2:12] prohibited" (emphasis mine).

Waggoner's editorial conclusion revealed how this position harmonized with that of the other pioneers we have cited: "Neither do the words of Paul confine the labors of women to the act of prophesying alone. He refers to prayers, and also speaks of certain women who 'labored in the Lord,' an expression which could only refer to the work of the gospel. He also, in remarking on the work of the prophets, speaks of edification, exhortation, and comfort. This 'labor in the Lord,' with prayer, comprises all the duties of public worship. Not all the duties of *business meetings,* which were probably conducted by men, or all the duties of *ruling elders,* and *pastors,* compare 1 Tim. 5:17, with 2:12, but all that pertain to exercises purely religious. We sincerely believe that, according to the Scriptures, women, as a right may, and as duty ought to, engage in these exercises" (*The Signs of the Times,* December 19, 1878, 320, emphasis his). Waggoner's 1878 statement supports the idea that the women licentiates of his time were not serving in the role of pastor or elder.

The views of those opposing ordination of women in the Seventh-day Adventist church today correspond to those of our pioneers. They believe that women may serve the Lord in many ways, both personal and public, even including preaching. It is the headship role of pastor or elder which they believe Scripture restricts to qualified men.

*Women in Ministry*'s attempts to promote ordination of women by misrepresenting the views of our pioneers should concern all fair-minded Seventh-day Adventists.

**(c) Did the 1881 General Conference Session Vote to Ordain Women?** The 1881 General Conference session considered a resolution to permit ordaining women to the gospel ministry (*Review and Herald,* Dec. 20, 1881, 392). The minutes clearly show that instead of approving the resolution (as some today have claimed), the delegates referred it to the General Conference Committee, where it died. Neither Ellen G. White nor the other pioneers brought it up again. The issue did not resurface until recent decades.

Some authors in *Women in Ministry* make the oft-repeated claim that at the 1881 General Conference session, the church voted to ordain its women. Recycling this myth, one of the authors referred to the comments of a current General Conference vice-president who served as chairman of the July 5, 1995, Utrecht business meeting session which considered the ordination question. Our author writes:

> The [SDA] church has often considered the issue of ordaining women, and has, at times, come amazingly close to doing so. . . . The church, at the General Conference session of 1881, had voted that women might, 'with perfect propriety, be set apart for ordination to the work of the Christian ministry.' The action was then referred to the General Conference Committee. After that, as [the current General Conference vice-president] has so eloquently explained, 'Nothing happened.' Nearly 90 years later in 1968, leadership in Finland officially requested that women be ordained to the gospel ministry.[11]

This author apparently didn't know what really happened to the 1881 General Conference session "vote" for women's ordination, but another author suggests that the resolution was "voted" but was either later killed or ignored by a three-member committee consisting of George I. Butler, Stephen Haskell, and Uriah Smith. He cites the 1881 "resolution" (from *Review and Herald,* December 20, 1881, p. 392) thus:

> *Resolved,* That females possessing the necessary qualifications to fill that position, may, with perfect propriety, be set apart by ordination to the work of the Christian ministry.
>
> This was discussed . . . and referred to the General Conference Committee.

Speculating on why "nothing happened," this author suggests: "These brethren [Butler, Haskell, and Smith] seem to have been uncertain at the time whether women could be ordained 'with perfect propriety.' There is no record of further discussion or implementation of the resolution voted. However, . . . [quoting another scholar] 'the fact that this could be at least discussed on the floor of a G. C. Session indicates an open-mindedness on the part of the delegates toward the subject.' It also clearly demonstrates the open-mindedness toward women serving in the gospel ministry during this time period in the Adventist Church's history."[12]

What many readers of *Women in Ministry* may not know is that there is no need to speculate on what happened regarding woman's ordination in 1881. What actually happened is recorded in the *Review and Herald.* The 1881 General Conference session *never* approved the resolution, and therefore the referral to a committee was not for the purpose of implementing the resolution. Here are the facts.

1. In the nineteenth century, items were brought to the General Conference session as "resolutions," in the appropriate debating form: "Resolved that . . ." To untrained modern ears, this sounds like the decision (i.e., the resolution of the matter), when in fact it was only the *starting point* for discussion of the proposal.

2. Once a resolution was presented, it would be debated from the floor, after which it could either be voted on ("Approved" or "Rejected") or handled in some other way appropriate to parliamentary procedure. For example, (a) sometimes a motion was made and passed that the resolution (the issue being discussed) be "tabled," which meant that the members would stop deliberating on it then and take it up at a later time; (b) the delegates could vote to "refer to committee," which meant that they would not take the matter up again until the designated committee had considered it and returned it with a recommendation, after which it could be debated again and a decision reached on it (a process illustrated by another resolution appearing on the same page of minutes); (c) in some cases, referral to committee (then and today) is a polite way of killing a motion—handing it off to another group that is not expected to do anything with it.

These then are the facts regarding the 1881 resolution:

(1) An item was brought to the floor proposing that women be ordained.

(2) After discussion, the resolution was not "approved," as was almost every other resolution on that page, but was "referred to the General Conference Committee," who never sent it back to that session or to any subsequent General Conference session.

(3) In order for an item to be "referred to [any] committee," those present at the session had to vote in favor of referring it to committee. Referral does not happen just because one person calls for it.

(4) The fact that the "resolution" (i.e., the proposal brought to the floor) was "referred to the General Conference Committee" means that the 1881 General Conference delegates *did not accept* the women's ordination proposal.

(5) Therefore, contrary to some widely held assertions, the 1881

General Conference session actually *declined* to approve the proposal to ordain women! For whatever their reasons (we are not told in the minutes of the session), the delegates referred the matter to the General Conference Committee and let it die there. No one brought it to the General Conference delegates again until 1990 (North American Division request at Indianapolis) and 1995 (North American Division request at Utrecht).

(6) The minutes of the meeting, published in the *Review and Herald,* reveal that prior to the matter being "referred to committee," it was discussed by at least eight of the delegates.[13] After that discussion came the decision to refer to committee. Thus, contrary to some pro-ordination scholars (not writers in *Women in Ministry*), the "resolution" *was* entertained on the floor. And having discussed it, the delegates voted that it be "referred to the General Conference Committee."

(7) If the 1881 resolution was referred to the committee to be *implemented,* as *Women in Ministry* alleges, one wonders why at the next General Conference session no one questioned the failure of the committee to implement it. General Conference sessions were held yearly until 1889, after which they were held every two years. One also wonders why Ellen G. White failed to speak out against this alleged injustice against women when a group of three committee men supposedly refused to act upon a General Conference decision. The silence of subsequent General Conference sessions and Ellen G. White is additional evidence showing that in 1881, the church *never approved* the resolution on women's ordination.

Why did the General Conference in 1881 turn away from women's ordination? Was it because the delegates were not bold enough, or open-minded enough, or even prudent enough to act "with perfect propriety" to ordain women who were "serving as gospel ministers"?[14]

For answer, it is best to read the *published* theological position of the leading Seventh-day Adventist pioneers (e.g., through the editorials by resident editors of the *Review* and *Signs*—Uriah Smith, J. H. Waggoner, James White, J. N. Andrews) on their view on the question of women serving in the headship roles of elder or pastor. When we do, we discover that, for them, because of God's "divine arrangement, even from the beginning," women could not serve in the headship roles as husbands in their homes or as elders or pastors in the church. To do so, according to our Adventist pioneers, would be to disregard and abuse God's divine arrangement.[15]

**(d) Did Ellen G. White's 1895 Statement Call for Women's Ordination?** *Women in Ministry* takes a statement by Ellen White out of its context and misuses it to argue for ordaining women as elders or pastors.[16] This is the actual statement:

> Women who are willing to consecrate some of their time to the service of the Lord should be appointed to visit the sick, look after the young, and minister to the necessities of the poor. *They should be set apart to this work by prayer and laying on of hands.* In some cases they will need to counsel with the church officers or the minister; but if they are devoted women, maintaining a vital connection with God, they will be a power for good in the church.[17]

On the basis of this statement, one writer in *Women in Ministry* laments: "If only Ellen White's 1895 landmark statement had come fourteen years sooner [in 1881]!" He apparently believes that this "landmark statement" would have encouraged the General Conference committee brethren who were wondering about the question of "perfect propriety" in implementing the alleged 1881 vote to ordain women "who were serving in the gospel ministry."[18]

But evidence that Ellen G. White's 1895 statement is not applicable to the ordination of women *as pastors or elders* may be found within the passage itself.

(1) This is a part-time ministry, not a calling to a lifework. "Women who are willing to consecrate some of their time. . . ."

(2) The work is not that of a minister or a church officer. "In some cases they will need to counsel with the church officers or the minister." Evidently this work is not that of an elder or pastor.

(3) It was a ministry different from what we were already doing. The portion quoted here is followed immediately by, "This is another means of strengthening and building up the church. We need to branch out more in our methods of labor."

(4) The statement appears in an article entitled, "The Duty of the Minister and the People," which called upon ministers to allow and encourage church members to use their talents for the Lord. The last sentence of the quoted paragraph reflects this thrust: "Place the burdens upon men and women of the church, that they may grow by reason of the exercise, and thus become effective agents in the hand of the Lord for the

enlightenment of those who sit in darkness."

Thus the statement and its context clearly indicate that these women were being dedicated to a specific *lay* ministry, not the ministry of elders or pastors.[19]

This, however, is not the only statement from Mrs. White addressing laying on of hands for women. We could wish that *Women in Ministry* had cited the only known statement in which Mrs. White specifically spoke of ordination for women. Here it is:

> Some matters have been presented to me in regard to the laborers who are seeking to do all in their power to win souls to Jesus Christ. . . . The ministers are paid for their work, and this is well. And if the Lord gives the wife as well as the husband the burden of labor, and if she devotes her time and her strength to visiting from family to family, opening the Scriptures to them, *although the hands of ordination have not been laid upon her,* she is accomplishing a work that is in the line of ministry. Should her labors be counted as nought, and her husband's salary be no more than that of the servant of God whose wife does not give herself to the work, but remains at home to care for her family? (*Manuscript Releases,* 5:323, emphasis mine).[20]

Here, in the opening paragraph of her message, Mrs. White honors the ministry of women and calls for full-time workers to be paid appropriately, but she dismisses the lack of ordination as irrelevant. In this paragraph and elsewhere in her manuscript she highlights the arena in which women could make an especially significant contribution: personal work with women and families. Such work did not require ordination.

When did she write this way about ordination for women? In 1898, three years after *Women in Ministry* says she called for women to be ordained!

**(e) Was Ellen G. White Ordained?** The implication that Mrs. White was ordained involves a serious inflation of the evidence. It rests on the fact that she was issued ministerial *credentials,* the same as those which were given to ordained men.[21] Because Ellen White's ministerial credentials have given rise to some unfortunate misstatements by those seeking her support for women's ordination, I digress briefly to illustrate how this misinformation became institutionalized.

In addition to promoting and distributing *Women in Ministry* and other pro-ordination materials at the 2000 Toronto General Conference session, advocates of women's ordination also handed out a flyer which has its source in the 1995 pro-ordination book *The Welcome Table.* The leaflet is a xeroxed reproduction of two of Ellen White's credentials (dated 1885 and 1887). Immediately below the credentials, the pro-ordination scholar who pulled it together in *The Welcome Table* makes the following comment:

> "Notice her [Ellen G. White's] credentials dated Dec. 6, 1885, where the word *ordained* has been crossed out. However, that is not the case in credentials issued December 27, 1887."[22]

By this comment, readers of the book are left with the erroneous impression that although Ellen White was not ordained in 1885, by 1887 the church's position had evolved to the point of ordaining her. (Some proponents of women's ordination go so far as to suggest that even though the Seventh-day Adventist church has today rejected women's ordination, as allegedly in the [1885] case of Ellen G. White, one day the church will see the light and ordain its women, even as the church allegedly did [in 1887] after "denying" Ellen G. White her rightful ordination in 1885!) But "are those things so?"

The above statement is a half-truth; the other half is "manufactured." The full truth, as we have already noted, is that a number of dedicated women who worked for the church in the late 1800s and early 1900s were issued *licenses* (not ministerial *credentials* that are given to ordained pastors). Ellen White was the only woman ever to be issued ministerial credentials by the Seventh-day Adventist church; she received them from 1871 until her death in 1915. At least *three,* not two, of her ministerial credential certificates from the 1880s are still in the possession of the Ellen G. White Estate. These are dated 1883, 1885, and 1887.

On one of the certificates (dated 1885) the word "ordained" is neatly crossed out, but on the other two it is not. Does this mean that Ellen White was "ordained" in 1883, "unordained" in 1885 and "re-ordained" in 1887? Obviously not. Rather, the crossing out of "ordained" in 1885 highlights the awkwardness of giving credentials to a prophet. No such special category of credentials from the church exists. So the church utilized what it had, giving its highest credentials without an ordination ceremony having been carried out. In actuality, the prophet needed no human credentials. She had functioned for more than twenty-five years (prior to 1871) without any.[23]

Although Ellen G. White was the only woman known to have been issued Seventh-day Adventist ministerial *credentials,* she was never ordained. Mrs. White herself makes this clear.

In 1909, six years before her death, she personally filled out a "Biographical Information Blank" for the General Conference records. In response to the request on Item 26, which asks, "If remarried, give date, and to whom," she wrote an "X," indicating that she had never remarried. Earlier, Item 19 had asked, "If ordained, state when, where, and by whom." Here she also wrote an "X," meaning that she had never been ordained. She was not denying that God had chosen her and commissioned her as His messenger, but she was responding to the obvious intent of the question, indicating that there had never been an ordination ceremony carried out for her.[24]

This clear and unambiguous statement of Ellen White herself should put to rest the unfounded impression left by *Women in Ministry* that the church's issuance of a ministerial credential to Ellen White is an indication that she was ordained.

If any woman was so spiritually gifted as to qualify for ordination *as elder or pastor,* it was Ellen G. White. If any woman was so effective in her ministry as a teacher, preacher, and soul-winner as to qualify for ordination *as elder or pastor,* it was Ellen White. If any Adventist was so justice-inspired, sensitive and caring (and with demonstrable evidence of other fruits of the Spirit) as to qualify for ordination *as elder or pastor,* it was Ellen G. White. If any Adventist was so prolific an author and so gifted a leader as to qualify for ordination *as elder or pastor,* it was Ellen G. White. And if any woman could legitimately claim the title of *Elder or Pastor,* it was Ellen White.

But during her later years, Mrs. White was known mostly as "Sister White" and affectionately as "Mother White." She was never known as "Elder White" or "Pastor Ellen." Every church member knew that "Elder White" was either her husband, James, or her son, W. C. White.

Could it really be that we are ethically and theologically more enlightened than Ellen G. White? Or is it perhaps that we do not view the Bible as she did? Whatever our response is, this much can be said: The claim or implication by some advocates of women's ordination that Ellen White was ordained is clearly wrong.

**Summary.** Throughout our history, Seventh-day Adventist women labored faithfully in the ministry as teachers, preachers, missionaries, Bible workers, etc., and made a vital contribution to the mission of the church, all *without ordination.* Far from providing a case for ordination, the nine women mentioned in the *Women in Ministry* chapter we have been considering illustrate what women may accomplish without it. They are by no means alone. The Bible workers, as an example, offered valuable service in the ministry; they were an important part of the evangelistic team because they often knew more about the people being baptized and joining the church than the minister did; and the minister welcomed their wisdom and judgment. But none of these women was ever ordained. If these women, who were well versed in Scripture, had been asked if they wanted to be ordained as elders or pastors, most would likely have exclaimed, "Oh, no! It isn't biblical!" I say this because it continues to be the attitude of thousands of dedicated Adventist women around the world today.

In light of these facts of Adventist history—such as that Ellen G. White was never ordained, she never called for women to be ordained as elders or pastors, and none of our dedicated Seventh-day Adventist women of the past was ever ordained as elder or pastor—I again ask those who support women's ordination, just as I would ask those who support the attempted change of the Sabbath from Saturday to Sunday:

> Since the testimonies of Scripture indicate that God the Father *did not* do it; the Old Testament is clear that the patriarchs, prophets and kings *never did* do it; the gospels reveal that Jesus, the Desire of Ages, *would not* do it; the epistles and the acts of the apostles declare that the commissioned apostles *could not* do it; Ellen White, with a prophetic vision of the great controversy between Christ and Satan, *dared not* do it, should we who live at the turn of another millennium do it?[25]

What then shall we say in response to these manufactured "facts" in *Women in Ministry*? Simply this: It would have been better to tell the facts as they are, for then *Women in Ministry* would have been what the Ad Hoc Committee wanted it to be, a reliable guide to church members trying to make the right decision regarding the ordination of women as elders or pastors.

Instead of recycling misinformation, half-truths, and errors, we must honestly and accurately state the facts regarding the position and practice of our pioneers on women's ordination. Having done so, we may then be at liberty to: (1) debate the rightness or wrongness of their action or (2) decide either to follow their theological understanding and practice or chart our own course. It is irresponsible, however, to attempt to inject our biases and self-interests into a historical fact or reinterpret it in order to push our ideological agenda.

Even if there was no intent on the part of *Women in Ministry* authors to mislead, neither the church nor her Lord are well served by "scholarly research" which distorts the history it purports to tell.

---

**Endnotes**

[1]See Kit Watts, "Ellen White's Contemporaries: Significant Women in the Early Church," in *A Woman's Place: Seventh-day Adventist Women in Church and Society,* ed. Rosa T. Banks (Hagerstown, Md.: Review and Herald Publishing Assn., 1992), 41-74; Laurel Damsteegt, "S. M. I. Henry: Pioneer in Women's Ministry," *Adventists Affirm* 9/1 (Spring 1995), 17-19, 46. The spirit of the early Adventist women is also reflected in the soul-winning ministries of women in Africa and many other parts of the world. See, for example, J. J. Nortey, "The Bible, Our Surest Guide," *Adventists Affirm* 9/1 (Spring 1995), 47-49, 67; cf. Terri Saelee, "Women of the Spirit," *Adventists Affirm* 9/2 (Fall 1995), 60-63. But contrary to revisionist interpretations of Adventist history, none of these roles required women to be ordained as elders or pastors (see William Fagal, "Ellen White and the Role of Women in the Church," available from the Ellen G. White Estate, and adapted as chapter 10 in Samuele Bacchiocchi's *Women in the Church* (Berrien Springs, Mich.: Biblical Perspectives, 1987). A summary version of Fagal's work is found in his "Did Ellen White Call for Ordaining Women?" *Ministry,* December 1988, 8-11, and "Did Ellen White Support the Ordination of Women?" *Ministry,* February 1989, 6-9, together reproduced as chapter 16 of this book; cf. Samuel Koranteng-Pipim, *Searching the Scriptures,* 70-83, where we discuss "Restless Eves" and "Reckless Adams."

[2]See, for example, Michael Bernoi, "Nineteenth-Century Women in Ministry," *WIM,* 220-229; Randal R. Wisbey, "SDA Women in Ministry, 1970-1998," *WIM,* 235. A more restrained position is found in Jerry Moon's "'A Power that Exceeds that of Men': Ellen G. White on Women in Ministry," *WIM,* 190-204.

[3]Bert Haloviak, "The Adventist Heritage Calls for Ordination of Women," *Spectrum* 16/3 (August 1985), 52.

[4]George R. Knight, *A Brief History of Seventh-day Adventists* (Hagerstown, Md.: Review and Herald, 1999), 104-105.

[5]Kit Watts made this claim in her presentation on June 28, 2000, during the Ministerial Council Meeting preceding the Toronto General Conference session. More examples of

such revisionist interpretation of Seventh-day Adventist history can be found in some pro-ordination works, which leave readers with the wrong impression that the issuance of ministerial licenses to dedicated Adventist women of the past implied that they labored as ordained ministers. See, for example, Josephine Benton, *Called by God: Stories of Seventh-day Adventist Women Ministers* (Smithsburg, Md.: Blackberry Hill Publishers, 1990). Cf. the following chapters in *The Welcome Table:* Bert Haloviak, "A Place at the Table: Women and the Early Years," 27-44; idem, "Ellen G. White Statements Regarding Ministry," 301-308; and Kit Watts, "Moving Away from the Table: A Survey of Historical Factors Affecting Women Leaders," 45-59; cf. "Selected List of 150 Adventist Women in Ministry, 1844-1994," Appendix 6. A careful review of the source references in some of the chapters of *Women in Ministry* shows that their authors followed too closely the trail left by the revisionist interpreters of Adventist history of ordination (see, for example, Michael Bernoi, "Nineteenth-Century Women in Adventist Ministry Against the Backdrop of Their Times," *WIM,* 233 notes 74 and 78; Randal R.Wisbey, "SDA Women in Ministry, 1970-1998," *WIM,* 252 notes 1, 2, 4).

[6]For a helpful corrective to the historical revisionism of some on the issue of ordination, refer to the careful work by William Fagal, "Ellen G. White and Women in Ministry," in *Prove All Things,* 273-286; Larry Kirkpatrick, "Great Flying Leaps: The Use of Ellen G. White's Writings in *Women in Ministry,* in *Prove All Things,* 231-249; cf. Samuel Koranteng-Pipim, *Searching the Scripture,* 70-83, on "Restless Eves" and "Reckless Adams."

[7]John G. Beach, *Notable Women of Spirit: the Historical Role of Women in the Seventh-day Adventist Church* (Nashville, Tenn.: Southern Publishing Association, 1976), 55, emphasis mine.

[8]Of the nine notable "women in Adventist ministry" which Michael Bernoi profiles (*WIM,* 225-229; cf. George R. Knight, *A Brief History of Seventh-day Adventists,* 105-106), only four were licentiates for significant periods of time: Ellen Lane, Sarah A. Lindsey, Hetty Hurd Haskell, and Lulu Wightman, who all gave substantial full-time work to evangelism, whether private or public. The other five women vary from the general picture *Women in Ministry* would like to draw. S. M. I. Henry held a license for about three years while she advocated a "woman ministry" which encouraged women to work for the Lord where they were; female pastors were not a part of her program. Margaret Caro was licensed in 1894 and from 1897 to 1900 (we have not found record yet of her licensing in 1895 and 1896). During this whole time she seems to have continued her dental practice, using the proceeds to help educate young people for the Lord. I found no record of licensing of any kind—not even a missionary license—for Minerva Jane Chapman. But look at her achievements. L. Flora Plummer was licensed in 1893, but in the year before that and the year after she was given a missionary license; I have yet to find another year in which she was a licentiate. This means that during the time she was secretary and, according to *Women in Ministry,* acting president of the Iowa Conference (a claim I could not verify because the references were erroneous), she was not even carrying a ministerial license but was a licensed missionary. This makes the author's claim for her sound inflated: "Of all the women who *labored in the gospel ministry* while Ellen White was still alive, Flora Plummer was perhaps the most notable" (emphasis mine). Finally, Anna Knight was a licensed missionary, not a licensed minister, contrary to what one might assume from her listing among the "women in Adventist ministry." (The above information is drawn from the church's *Yearbooks* and

from the *General Conference Bulletin* Index, which extends only through 1915.) So all of these truly notable women serve as examples of what women may indeed do in the line of ministry. But *Women in Ministry* (and Knight's *A Brief History*) seem to want us to think of them as examples of woman ministers from our history and to consider how we have fallen away from our "roots." The conclusion is inescapable: all nine women cited by Bernoi (and Knight) were certainly part of the Adventist soul-winning ministry; *but none of them was a minister as we use the term today.* See also the next notes.

[9]One example of where *Women in Ministry* fosters a confusion between the duties of ordained ministers and licentiates is found on 225-226, where the author claims that Sarah A. Lindsey's "1872 license permitted her to preach, hold evangelistic meetings, and *lead out in church business and committee sessions*" (emphasis mine). He offers no evidence for the latter point, which may be no more than his assumption. Several pieces of evidence suggest a conclusion different from his. An expression used for licentiates in some conference session minutes at that time indicates a more limited authorization: candidates were "granted license to improve their gift in preaching as the way may open" (see, for example, *Review and Herald* 35/14 [March 22, 1870]: 110). In 1879, in an article our author quotes on another point, James White wrote his understanding that 1 Cor. 14:34, 35 applied to women keeping silence in the *business meetings* of the church (ibid. 53/22 [May 29, 1879]: 172). And, as we will show at the end of the next subsection, J. H. Waggoner mentioned "business meetings" as an area where the scriptural restrictions likely applied. Beyond this one matter, the chapter shows an unwise dependence on feminist secondary sources, which are often unreliable. We cite a few examples from the same two pages of *Women in Ministry.* Ellen Lane was not licensed by the Michigan Conference in 1868, as claimed. The minutes show that the licentiates that year were "Wm. C. Gage, James G. Sterling, and Uriah Smith" (ibid. 31/23 [May 12, 1868]: 357). Though she was indeed licensed in 1878, as the chapter states, she was actually first licensed in 1875 (ibid. 46/8 [August 26, 1875]: 63). Further, she was not the first woman licentiate among Seventh-day Adventists, a distinction which apparently belongs to Sarah A. H. Lindsey. The chapter also mentions Mrs. Lindsey, as we noted above, but it dates her licensing to 1872, though she is known to have been licensed in 1871 (ibid. 38/13 [September 12, 1871]: 102). After citing her licensing, the chapter mentions that in one series of meetings she preached twenty-three times on the second advent, but it fails to note that this series took place in early 1869, three years before the author's date for her licensing (ibid. 33/25 [June 15, 1869]: 200). Thus in fact her example serves to demonstrate that lack of ordination or even licensing need not stand in the way of a woman who wants to serve God. See Michael Bernoi, "Nineteenth-Century Women in Adventist Ministry Against the Backdrop of Their Times," *WIM,* 225, 226.

[10]See Michael Bernoi, "Nineteenth-Century Women in Adventist Ministry Against the Backdrop of Their Times," *WIM,* 211-229. The portions referenced here are from 222-224.

[11]Randal R. Wisbey, "SDA Women in Ministry, 1970-1998," *WIM,* 235. Wisbey is currently the president of Canadian University College. He is quoting Calvin Rock, who served as the chairman of the Utrecht business meeting that considered the North American Division request to ordain its women. Cf. "Thirteenth Business Meeting," *Adventist Review,* July 7, 1995, 23.

[12]Bernoi, "Nineteenth-Century Women in Adventist Ministry Against the Backdrop

of Their Times," *WIM,* 224. The scholar he quotes is Roger W. Coon, former associate director of the Ellen G. White Estate, now retired. Dr. Coon's document says that the resolution was "introduced" and "referred to committee," but it never claims the resolution was voted.

[13]The minutes of the 1881 General Conference session state that the resolution "was discussed by J. O. Corliss, A. C. Bourdeau, E. R. Jones, D. H. Lamson, W. H. Littlejohn, A. S. Hutchins, D. M. Canright, and J. N. Loughborough, and referred to the General Conference Committee" (*Review and Herald,* December 20, 1881).

[14]Cf. Wisbey, *WIM,* 235; Bernoi, *WIM,* 224. A visit to the endnotes of the Seminary scholars reveals their reliance on the pro-ordination authors who also wrote for *The Welcome Table.* There was no reason why these *Women in Ministry* authors should have missed the facts on this matter. The information was readily available in published works by those opposing women's ordination (see, for example, Samuele Bacchiocchi's *Women in the Church* [1987] and my *Searching the Scriptures* [1995] and *Receiving the Word* [1996]). More fundamentally, the primary sources—the minutes themselves—are easily obtained at Andrews University, and their pattern of recording actions is clear and consistent.

[15]For example, see the editorial in the December 19, 1878 *Signs of the Times* which summarized the understanding of the Adventist pioneers on the headship responsibility of the man in both the home and the church. I have already quoted the key points in this chapter, on 291. Cf. Uriah Smith, "Let Your Women Keep Silence in the Churches," *Review and Herald,* June 26, 1866, 28.

[16]Bernoi, "Nineteenth-Century Women in Adventist Ministry," *WIM,* 224, 225; cf. J. H. Denis Fortin, "Ordination in the Writings of Ellen G. White," *WIM,* 127, 128. Cf. Rose Otis, "Ministering to the Whole Church," *Elder's Digest,* Number Nine, 15. *Elder's Digest* is published by the General Conference Ministeral Association. A more nuanced discussion of Ellen White's 1895 statement is provided by Jerry Moon, "'A Power That Exceeds That of Men': Ellen G. White on Women in Ministry," *WIM,* 201, 202.

[17]Ellen G. White, *Review and Herald,* July 9, 1895, 434, emphasis mine.

[18]Bernoi, "Nineteenth-Century Women in Adventist Ministry," *WIM,* 224. Observe that this kind of "historical research" is built on the following questionable assumptions and speculations: (1) "women were serving as gospel workers" [understood as elders or pastors]; (2) the 1881 General Conference session voted to ordain women as pastors; (3) a 3-member male committee failed to implement the alleged 1881 General Conference session vote because they were wondering about the question of "perfect propriety"; (4) it took Ellen G. White 14 long years to speak to the "correctness" of women's ordination.

[19]This fact is acknowledged by Jerry Moon, "'A Power That Exceeds That of Men': Ellen G. White on Women in Ministry," *WIM,* 201. For more on this matter, see William Fagal's reprinted articles in *Prove All Things,* 273-286.

[20]Though no mention of this statement appears in Bernoi's chapter, two other chapters do mention it. One of them gives only a brief summary of the statement and omits the specific reference to ordination (J. H. Denis Fortin, "Ordination in the Writing of Ellen G. White," *WIM,* 127), while the other provides a helpful and much more thorough study of the manuscript in question (Jerry Moon, "'A Power That Exceeds That of Men': Ellen G. White on Women in Ministry," *WIM,* 192-194). The chapter does not quote the reference to ordination as a part of that discussion, but it does quote it later, in the chapter's last sentence.

[21]Michael Bernoi notes, "For a number of years both she [Hetty Hurd Haskell] and Ellen White were listed together in the *Yearbook* as ministers credentialed by the General Conference, Ellen White as ordained and Mrs. Haskell as licensed" (Bernoi, "Nineteenth-Century Women in Adventist Ministry," *WIM,* 227). Given this way without further explanation, such a statement will mislead many into assuming that Mrs. White was ordained.

[22]Bert Haloviak, "Ellen G. White Statements Regarding Ministry," in *The Welcome Table, 308.*

[23]For more on this, see William Fagal's "Ellen G. White and Women in Ministry," in *Prove All Things,* 273-286.

[24]A copy of her Biographical Information Blank may be found in Document File 701 at the Ellen G. White Estate Branch Office, James White Library, Andrews University. Arthur L. White published the information regarding these matters in the introduction to his article, "Ellen G. White the Person," *Spectrum* 4/2 (Spring, 1972), 8.

[25]See my *Searching the Scriptures* (1995), 65.

# 16

# TO ORDAIN OR NOT TO ORDAIN?

It is far too simple to claim, as some do, that our varying positions on women's ordination have arisen merely because of our different cultural backgrounds. They have suggested that those outside democratic cultures are not ready to go along with women's ordination either because their cultures do not have a high view of women, or because their cultures make it difficult for them to understand the Bible correctly or even to discern the Holy Spirit's leading of women who are aspiring to the roles of elder or pastor. The unfortunate implication is that theological knowledge and spiritual insight belong only to some cultures; unless one belongs to those cultures, one cannot legitimately address the issue.

**Not A Cultural Issue.** From the analysis in the preceding chapters, it must be clear that ordination of women as elders or pastors is not a cultural issue to be settled according to a person's prejudice or preference or the sociological structures existing in a particular region of the world, be they "democratic," "patriarchal," "authoritarian," or otherwise. Neither is it an equal rights issue to be resolved through such things as civil laws, lawsuits, or some type of affirmative action to ensure gender parity in the pastoral ministry, or to equalize some supposed power structure. The issue is not a financial matter to be dictated by a desire to enjoy United States tax law benefits to ministers or to be decided on the basis of economic might or threat of economic blackmail. It is not even a political issue to be settled by petition drives, public opinion polls, referenda, surveys, questionable church policy revisions, unilateral ordinations, or some carefully choreographed campaign-style strategies to legitimize women elders or women pastors in our churches, institutions, and publications. The issue is theological. It can only be resolved legitimately on the basis of Scripture.

This is why we must take exception to the recent claim by a prolific church historian, who also contributed to *Women in Ministry,* that the divisive question of women's ordination is a *cultural* issue. Pointing to the 1990 General Conference session when the "majority of the delegates from the United States and Western Europe favored ordination, but the powerful voting blocks representing the denomination's Latin American and African divisions overwhelmingly opposed such a move," this author suggests that the underlying reason for the varied positions on the issue is differences in "cultural norms" or "vastly different cultures and ways of thinking." [1]

Statements such as the above fail to recognize that the issue of women's ordination *is* theological, *not* cultural. They also tend to trivialize discussions on the subject, relegating the issue to one's cultural preference, rather than to one's fidelity to Scripture. Furthermore, such assertions reinforce the false beliefs held by some advocates in the church of the West regarding their fellow brothers and sisters in the rest of the Church. In the view of these ordination proponents, those believers who conscientiously cannot go along with their unbiblical agenda of ordaining women as elders or pastors are theologically, ethically, or hermeneutically "immature." [2] Or in the words of an European church administrator who recently wrote in the *Adventist Review,* those opposed to the ideology of women's ordination belong to the "fundamentalist fringe." [3]

The undertones of cultural and intellectual arrogance in the above comments may, perhaps, be unintended. But the statements betray the prevalent mistaken notion in certain quarters that those who oppose women's ordination are anti-women, deficient in ethical sensitivity, [4] or that they are incapable of serious theological and ethical reflection.

**Position of the Adventist Pioneers.** I am confident that as more and more pro-ordination Adventists move beyond the prevalent superficial knowledge of the issues, they also will be led to conclude with our studious Adventist pioneers that ordaining women as elders or pastors is theological, not cultural, and that gender role-distinctions exist in both the home and the church:

> The divine arrangement, even from the beginning, is this, that the man is the head of the woman. Every relation is disregarded or abused in this lawless age. But the Scriptures always maintain this order in the family relation. 'For the husband is the head of the wife, even as Christ is the head of the church.' Eph. 5:23. Man is entitled to certain privileges which are not given to woman; and he is subjected to some duties and burdens from which the woman is exempt. A woman may pray, prophesy, exhort, and comfort the church, but *she cannot occupy the position of a pastor or a ruling elder.* This would be looked upon as usurping authority over the man, which is here [1 Tim 2:12] prohibited ([J.H. Wagonner, Editor], "Women's Place in the Gospel," *The Signs of the Times,* December 19, 1878, p. 320; emphasis mine).

The overwhelming majority of the worldwide church (not a "fundamentalist fringe") still upholds this long-standing Adventist pioneers' position, as evidenced by the 1990 and 1995 General Conference session votes.

To their credit, many of the authors of *Women in Ministry* have correctly recognized that the issue of women's ordination is theological, not cultural. Hence their effort to provide a biblical justification for the practice. Despite the book's defects in theological and historical scholarship, we must commend the authors for offering the best argument that Adventist pro-ordinationists are capable of presenting to a Bible-believing conservative church, and submitting their findings to others to evaluate."

More than a hundred years ago, Ellen White wrote: "Those who sincerely desire truth will not be reluctant to lay open their positions for investigation and criticism, and will not be annoyed if their opinions and ideas are crossed" (*Review and Herald,* July 26, 1892).

The authors of *Women in Ministry* accept the above counsel by Ellen White. Hence, the book's editor writes: "This volume represents the understanding of the Seminary Ad Hoc Committee on Hermeneutics and Ordination. We do not claim to speak for others, either at the

Seminary or in church administration. Some may disagree with our findings. That is their privilege. We welcome their responses and invite them to dialogue."[5]

Accepting their invitation, I have attempted to review their much-publicized volume, pointing out some of its theological and historical shortcomings. This chapter concludes the evaluation of *Women in Ministry's* new light. After a brief look at the book's "moral imperative" and "Holy Spirit's leading" arguments, I will offer some suggestions on how to move beyond the ideology of women's ordination.

**9. A Seriously Flawed Concept of "Moral Imperative"**

For the Christian, there is a moral imperative always to trust and obey biblical truth. If, however, the Christian is compelled to believe and practice error, that imperative is not moral; it is coercion. In the light of our evaluation of the biblical and historical arguments for women's ordination, we are now better prepared to judge whether there is a "moral imperative" for women's ordination, as claimed in *Women in Ministry.*

As we have shown in our analysis and critique, the two-year investigation by the "Ad Hoc Committee on Hermeneutics and Ordination" produced neither a hermeneutic nor a theology of ordination superior to what the Adventist church historically has upheld. The book's title is misleading, in that the real goal of the book seems not to be "women in ministry" (which the Adventist church has never opposed), but rather the ordaining of women as elders and pastors. The arguments put forth to justify the ideology of women's ordination are biblically and historically deficient; if employed in other areas, they could easily be used to undermine the relevance of many other biblical teachings.

Since the biblical and historical arguments underlying *Women in Ministry* are seriously flawed, the book's moral imperative argument, its concepts of equality, "women's rights," "justice," "fairness," and "character of God," and its appeals to the "Holy Spirit's leading" to meet "the needs of a growing church" cannot be sustained as ethically credible bases for ordaining women *as elders or pastors.*[6]

In fact, what has taken place in the Seventh-day Adventist church over the past two or three decades suggests that the so-called moral imperative argument could easily be used to coerce those who refuse to surrender to this unbiblical ideology of ordaining women. Let me explain.

When church leaders initially agreed that women *could* be ordained as elders, it was with the understanding that there would be liberty of conscience for those who could not accept the practice either because of biblical reasons or because their cultures were thought to prevent them from moving in that direction. In many places, however, this "could be" policy for women's ordination has already developed into an understanding that women *should* be ordained. With the questionable "moral imperative" argument being proposed in *Women in Ministry,* we are coming into a phase that says women *must* be ordained, not only as local elders but also as pastors.

In other words, if the "moral imperative" argument is accepted, the ideological legislation which was originally permissive will become compulsory! Those who are found to be in disagreement with the ordination of women and who believe for biblical reasons that they cannot participate in such ordinations or allow women to be ordained will be looked upon as out of harmony with church policy and possibly considered unfit for employment in areas where the ideology has become entrenched. This serious situation will inevitably take away the right of individual conscience.

Whenever error is legislated as a "moral imperative," such legislation inevitably leads to the persecution of those standing for truth. Already in certain places where the "moral imperative" argument has been embraced it is very difficult for Adventists who oppose women's ordination to be hired or retained. The policy is usually unwritten, but those familiar with several situations can testify to the intolerant attitude toward, and sometimes the *a priori* exclusion of, those who uphold the long-established Adventist position—a position which, by the way, is embraced by an overwhelming majority of the world church, as demonstrated through official General Conference session votes.

The only moral imperative the church should embrace is that which is founded on truth. The Christian's obligation to such an imperative is to trust and obey it, regardless of intimidation and persecution from those who demand compliance with error.

### 10. A Fanciful View of Holy Spirit's Leading

In a final effort to support their "biblical, historical, and ethical" arguments for ordaining women as elders or pastors, *Women in Ministry*'s authors appeal to a mistaken understanding of the Holy Spirit's leading. They urge the Seventh-day Adventist church to listen to the voice of the Holy Spirit as He calls upon us today to change our patterns of ministry in response to the pragmatic needs of a growing church. Writes the editor in her summation chapter: "If circumcision, based on divine [Old Testament] mandate, could be changed [by the apostles, elders, and believers, together with the Holy Spirit, at the Jerusalem Council of Acts 15], how much more could patterns of ministry [ordaining women as elders and pastors], which lack a clear 'Thus says the Lord,' be modified to suit the needs of a growing church?"

By this innovative argument, the *Women in Ministry* authors add their voices to those within our ranks who also are invoking the name of the Spirit to justify their questionable reinterpretations of Scripture. [7] But can we make Scripture mean anything we desire, and then give the Holy Spirit the credit? Christians must always seek the Spirit's guidance to understand Scripture. But should they invoke the Spirit to circumvent the Bible's explicit teaching on male-female roles in both the home and the church or to invent some new theories to justify certain egalitarian ideologies, as *Women in Ministry* seeks to do?

Bible-believing Seventh-day Adventists have always insisted that those who seek to live under the authority of the Spirit must be willing to bow before the teachings of the Word—the Spirit's authoritative textbook. "To the law and to the testimony: if they speak not according to this word, it is because there is no light in them" (Isa 8:20; cf. Gal 1:8, 9). "The Spirit was not given—nor can it ever be bestowed—to supersede the Bible; for the Scriptures explicitly state that the word of God is the standard by which all teaching and experience must be tested" (*The Great Controversy*, vii).

As we have attempted to show in the preceding chapters, besides the misleading and erroneous claims regarding early Seventh-day Adventist beliefs and practice and the seriously flawed concept of moral imperative, *Women in Ministry*'s arguments for ordaining women as elders or pastors are based on questionable re-interpretations of Scripture. Hence, following the kind of Spirit's "leading" proposed by the book will spawn in the church an uncontrollable subjectivism in which interpreters select only the Scriptures pleasing to them and which fit their fanciful interpretations. This is a sure recipe for contradictory doctrinal views in the church (theological pluralism).

Moreover, because the Holy Spirit does not leave us to wander aimlessly without a sure compass, unless our interpretations are in harmony with the Bible, what we may assume to be the Spirit's voice could actually be echoes from the loud noises within our cultures. Thus, the so-called

Holy Spirit's "leading" would be nothing more than promptings from our unrenewed human experiences or feelings. Ellen G. White explained why faith must be established on the Word of God, not on one's subjective experience or feeling:

> Genuine faith is founded on the Scriptures; but Satan uses so many devices to wrest the Scriptures and bring in error, that great care is needed if one would know what they really do teach. It is one of the great delusions of this time to dwell much upon feeling, and to claim honesty while ignoring the plain utterances of the word of God because that word does not coincide with feeling. . . . Feeling may be chaff, but the word of God is the wheat. And "what," says the prophet, "is the chaff to the wheat?" (*Review and Herald,* November 25, 1884).

In short, *Women in Ministry*'s new light of ordaining women as elders or pastors is foreign to the Bible writers and the studious Bible-believing Seventh-day Adventist pioneers, including Ellen G. White. Since this new light contradicts biblical teaching on gender-role differentiation, the authors' attempt to claim the Holy Spirit's "leading" should be dismissed as a fanciful effort to make scholarly ingenuity seem more important than fidelity to the Bible's text and context. The following statement by Mrs. White, referring to the distinctive truths of Seventh-day Adventists, is also appropriate in this regard:

"When the power of God testifies as to what is truth, that truth is to stand forever as the truth. No after suppositions contrary to the light God has given are to be entertained. Men will arise with interpretations of Scripture which are to them truth, but which are not truth. The truth for this time God has given us as a foundation for our faith. One will arise, and still another, with new light, which contradicts the light that God has given under the demonstration of His Holy Spirit. . . . We are not to receive the words of those who come with a message that contradicts the special points of our faith" (*Selected Messages,* 1:161).

**Moving Beyond the Feminist Ideology**

As we noted in an earlier chapter, for more than 100 years the Adventist position on the ordained ministry claimed the support of Scripture as expressed in the teaching and practice of the Adventist pioneers, including

Ellen G. White. By the 1970s, however, this established position began to be reversed in favor of ordaining women as elders and pastors.

This new trend was created by the converging interests of feminism, liberalism, church leaders' desire to enjoy United States tax law benefits to ministers, questionable church policy revisions and *Church Manual* alterations allowing women to serve as elders, calculated attempts by some influential North American churches unilaterally to ordain women as pastors, the silence of leadership to this defiance of two General Conference session votes against women's ordination, the strategy of the North American Division's "President's Commission on Women in Ministry" to obviate the 1995 Utrecht vote, and now, the book *Women in Ministry* by the Seminary Ad Hoc Committee, in response to the request by certain North American Division leaders for the pro-ordination scholars of the Seminary to *"do something about it [Utrecht]."*

**Our Assessment of *Women in Ministry*.** *Women in Ministry* offers the best arguments that Adventist proponents of women's ordination can find to present to a Bible-believing conservative Seventh-day Adventist church. How do we assess the biblical and historical research provided by our pro-ordination authors? Does the book's new light offer a sound theological basis to depart from nearly 150 years of Seventh-day Adventist belief and practice? Can this work be used legitimately at a future time to overturn the General Conference session decisions at Indianapolis (1990) and Utrecht (1995)? [8]

As we noted in chapter 12, a supporter of the book correctly states, "If the basis of our decision is going to be in our interpretation of Scripture, *we must do it well."* [9] The simple question we must ask, therefore, is: Did the twenty authors of *Women in Ministry* do their job well?

The editor of the book believes they did. [10] An author of one of the chapters (a member of the Ad Hoc Committee who seeks to make *Women in Ministry* "the official view of the Seminary and the position of virtually all of its faculty") thinks that this work will "demonstrate that the Seminary faculty stands for sound Biblical and historical scholarship on this contemporary and controversial issue." [11]

We also noted how some influential promoters of the book are applauding it as the product of "skillful exegesis of Scripture and careful examination of relevant E. G. White materials," [12] a volume that presents "a powerful argument" and "an impressive array of evidence" for the ordination of women, [13] and one which "brings together a wealth of material and deserves to be taken seriously." [14]

With all due respect, we disagree with these "opinions of learned men" (*The Great Controversy,* 595). Heeding the Bible's command to "prove all things; [and] hold fast that which is good" (1 Thess 5:19-21), and accepting the invitation from the book's editor for responses by those who may disagree with their findings, we examined the above claims. Our analysis and evaluation in these chapters call into serious question what the authors and promoters are saying.

Contrary to their claims, *Women in Ministry,* like its forerunner *The Welcome Table,* does not present a cogent and defensible way to neutralize the witness of the Bible and the historical precedent of early Seventh-day Adventism. As I have attempted to show in this evaluation, *Women in Ministry* is built largely on: (1) ambiguity and vagueness, (2) straw-man arguments, (3) substantial leaps of logic, (4) arguments from silence, (5) speculative interpretations, (6) questionable re-interpretations of the Bible, (7) distorted biblical reasoning, (8) misleading and erroneous claims regarding Adventist history, (9) a seriously flawed concept of "moral imperative," and (10) a fanciful view of the "Holy Spirit's leading." [15]

The editor of *Women in Ministry* may have had these shortcomings in mind when she stated in her prologue that "at times clear evidence may be lacking, thus making necessary the use of sanctified judgment and imagination to resolve questions and issues" associated with women's ordination as elders and pastors. [16] Given the fact that there is no clear evidence in Scripture for ordaining women, we can now understand why the authors of *Women in Ministry* often resorted to "sanctified judgment and imagination," and why the committee needed two long years of "animated" discussions, writing, rewriting, editing, and cross-referencing to produce their 438-page volume. Ellen G. White's observation is pertinent:

"Numberless words need not be put upon paper to justify what speaks for itself and shines in its clearness. *Truth is straight, plain, clear, and stands out boldly in its own defense; but it is not so with error. It is so winding and twisting that it needs a multitude of words to explain it in its crooked form*" (*Early Writings,* 96, emphasis mine).

Despite the good intentions and best efforts of the authors of *Women in Ministry,* their book falls short of its goal. It does not provide a sound biblical and historical basis for resolving "this contemporary and controversial issue." Perhaps a future work by some other proponents may be able to make a more judicious use of biblical and historical data to provide the much-desired justification for women's ordination. But I doubt it, because the basis for women's ordination as elders or pastors simply doesn't exist, either in the Bible or in the writings of Mrs. White.

Perhaps here is where the Seminary Ad Hoc Committee has provided its greatest service. After two years of hard work and prayer, they have produced a 438-page book that reveals, when carefully examined and tested, that there is no support in either the Bible or the Mrs. White's writings for ordaining women as elders and pastors. Those of us who have for a long time cautioned against this practice gratefully respond, "Thank you, Ad Hoc Committee."

**Some Important Implications.** To the extent that my conclusions about the book are valid, I would say the following:

1. Acting upon any advice that is contrary to Scripture ultimately leads to disobedience of God's Word in general. "The very beginning of the great apostasy was in seeking to supplement the authority of God by that of the church. Rome began by enjoining what God had not forbidden, and she ended by forbidding what He had explicitly enjoined" (*The Great Controversy,* 289, 290).

"True faith consists in doing just what God has enjoined, not manufacturing things He has not enjoined" (*That I May Know Him,* 226).

2. No one can disobey God's Word without experiencing destructive consequences. Because our Lord is merciful and patient, not willing that any should perish, the consequences of our disobedience are often slow in coming. But consequences always follow. Thus, the legislation of any secular ideology instead of the proclamation of sound theology will surely have consequences.

Already the worldwide church is harvesting some of the baneful results of the push to ordain women as elders and pastors. For example, there are tensions and divisions in churches where the ideology of women's ordination is being forced upon loyal members; strained relationships and broken homes where the erroneous doctrine of "total egalitarianism" or "total role interchangeableness" has been accepted; mistrust in and loss of credibility by church scholars and leaders who are perceived as pushing upon the church an alien agenda; disillusionment among dedicated women in ministry, who are made to believe that the church is quenching their desire to be part of the soul-winning work or is discriminating against them; vilification of scholars and leaders who have courageously stood up against women's ordination; erosion of confidence in the Bible and the writings of Mrs. White as dependable sources of answers to today's perplexing questions; and the unwitting laying of a theological foundation for pro-homosexual theology, when we reject God's creation order of gender or sex roles in marriage and in the church.

3. These consequences will continue as long as we do not renounce our errors and embrace God's truth: "The teachings and restrictions of God's Word are not welcome to the proud, sin-loving heart, and those who are unwilling to obey its requirements are ready to doubt its authority" (*Steps to Christ,* 111).

Instead of being faithful to the inspired writings of Moses, David, Isaiah, Matthew, Peter or Paul, those set on their own ways would rather cling to the opinions of their self-appointed experts—be they pastors, professors, parents, or personal acquaintances. In so doing they forget the warning by Ellen G. White: "Satan is constantly endeavoring to attract attention to man in the place of God. He leads the people to look to bishops, to pastors, to professors of theology, as their guides, instead of searching the Scriptures to learn their duty for themselves. Then, by controlling the minds of these leaders, he can influence the multitudes according to his will" (*The Great Controversy,* 595).

4. We can, however, avert these destructive consequences by turning away from our errors. In view of the biblical teaching that only qualified men may legitimately serve in the headship role of elders or pastors, we can take the following specific steps:

(a) *Church Leaders* should call for an immediate moratorium on ordaining women *as elders* and also initiate proceedings to rescind the biblically-compromising 1975 Spring Council and 1984 Annual Council actions that permitted women to be ordained as *elders,* actions that have brought the church to the straits we are in now;

(b) *Church scholars and editors* should renounce ideological proclivities, temptations, or pressures to justify or promote the divisive and unbiblical practice of ordaining women;

(c) *Women ordained as elders* should willingly and courageously give up that office, bringing their practice into line with the Bible (Acts 17:30-31);

(d) *Women laboring in the ministry* should serve in accordance with

God's biblically-prescribed will, resisting ideological attempts to transform "women's ministry" into "feminists' ministry";

(e) *Church members* should respectfully, but courageously, demand a plain "thus saith the Lord" whenever and wherever vocal groups, scholars, leaders, pastors, or even committees urge them to ordain or accept women as elders or as pastors; insisting upon a prayerful, unbiased, and biblically sound investigation of the issue is both a right and a duty of every church member.

Retracing our erroneous steps, as evidence of genuine repentance, may be uncomfortable, humiliating, even costly. But what is more costly than what it cost Jesus to save us? Loyalty to Christ may cost us our pride, but it will surely give us a free conscience.

"God does not require us to give up anything that it is for our best interest to retain. In all that He does, He has the well-being of His children in view. Would that all who have not chosen Christ might realize that he has something vastly better to offer them than they are seeking for themselves. Man is doing the greatest injury and injustice to his own soul when he thinks and acts contrary to the will of God. No real joy can be found in the path forbidden by Him who knows what is best, and who plans for the good of His creatures. The path of transgression is the path of misery and destruction" (*Steps to Christ,* 46).

**Light or Darkness?** Ellen White warned about the danger of holding on to error, after knowing the truth:

> If rational beings really desire the truth, God will give them sufficient light to enable them to decide what is truth. If they have a heart to obey, they will see sufficient evidence to walk in the light. But if they in heart desire to evade the truth, he will not work a miracle to gratify their unbelief. He will never remove every chance or occasion to doubt. If they honestly, sincerely grasp the light, and walk in it, that light will increase until lingering doubts will be dispelled. But if they choose darkness, their questioning and caviling over the truth will increase, their unbelief will be strengthened, and the light which they would not accept will become to them darkness, and how great will be that darkness! It will be as much greater than before the light came, as the light which was rejected was clearer and more

> abundant than the light which first shone upon them. Thus it was with the Jewish nation; thus it will be with the Christian world in every generation. The rejectors of light treasure up to themselves wrath against the day of wrath. There are those who walk amid perpetual doubts. They feed on doubts, enjoy doubts, talk doubts, and question everything that it is for their interest to believe. To those who thus trifle with the plain testimonies of God's word, and who refuse to believe because it is inconvenient and unpopular to do so, the light will finally become darkness; truth will appear to the darkened understanding as error, and error will be accepted as truth. When thus shrouded in error, they will find it perfectly natural and convenient to believe what is false, and will become strong in their faith (*Advent Review and Sabbath Herald,* January 5, 1886).

**The Choice We Face.** In presenting their book to the worldwide Seventh-day Adventist church, the twenty scholars of *Women in Ministry* stated: "We hope and pray that this volume may assist individuals, leaders, and the community of faith at large in deciding how to deal with the issue of ordination and, more specifically, the relationship of ordination to women." [17]

If the "biblical, theological, and historical perspectives" elaborated in *Women in Ministry* are all that these professors can present to the church, then the decision on "how to deal with the issue" of women's ordination *as elders or pastors* is not a difficult one to make. Their well-publicized and widely distributed volume offers compelling evidence against the practice. It is one more proof that the campaign waged during the past two or three decades by a few influential scholars and leaders to impose women's ordination on the church is a tragic mistake.

In light of this fact, we must ask: What should be our individual and collective responses to the teaching of Scripture regarding the ordination of women to the headship office of elder or pastor? Should we go beyond the legitimate role of women in ministry by ordaining them as elders or pastors? [18] Should we risk the displeasure of God by doing what seems right in our own eyes? Or should we seek a scriptural basis for empowering women for ministry and bring an end to the present "divisiveness and disunity," "embarrassment," and "dishonor upon this church that we love"? [19]

**No Turning Back?** A few years ago in the *Adventist Review* (February 1995), the recently retired president of the North American Division president described the church's situation of ordaining women elders but not women pastors as "untenable." He confessed his difficulty at explaining the reason for this to those who inquired. He offered no theological justification for ordaining women elders, stating only that we had "crossed the theological bridge" when we began to do so. Inexplicably, he asserted that there could be "no turning back."[20]

But I join the editor of *Prove All Things* in responding:

> If we have embarked on a practice which violates the teaching of Scripture, why should we be reluctant to turn back? In our evangelism, we call people who have conscientiously kept Sunday all their lives to turn back when they see what the Bible actually teaches about the Sabbath, even if it should cost them their jobs, friends, and family. Are we unwilling to turn back when we find what Scripture actually teaches about the role of women in the church? Such change is not without pain and cost, but should these concerns prevent us from bringing our practice into line with the Bible? We see no end to the division and disunity which rack the church today on this issue, short of coming into harmony with the Word of God. Obedience to the Word is our only strength. Shall we be reluctant to take hold of it?
>
> We believe the church should take a strong, decided stand to obey God, following Him and Him only. We believe the church should stop ordaining women locally and internationally, whether as elders or pastors, and it should not place them in leadership roles which Scripture calls on men to fulfill. Only fully consecrated men who are doing God's will and demonstrating their commitment by their lives should be ordained to the leadership of the Church. It is time to trust God in faith and humility. May God help us to see clearly His will for His children and to walk willingly in it.[21]

**Worthy Examples.** Our Lord Jesus Christ, the church's Head and the true "Shepherd and Bishop of our souls," has set us an example that we should follow (1 Pet 2:21, 25). In the face of the ultimate test of obedience, He could say, "Not my will, but thine, be done," a decision that was immediately rewarded with help from heaven (Luke 22:42, 43).

His own mother, Mary, also leaves us an example of complete submission to the will of God. In becoming the Messiah's mother before she was married, she faced circumstances that would bring her abuse and derision; yet she said, "I am the Lord's servant. May it be to me as you have said" (Luke 1:38 NIV). Later, though she was highly "favored of the Lord" and a faithful disciple of Christ (Luke 1:28, 30; Acts 1:14). In the upper room she submitted to the biblical guidelines for the choice of a male apostle to be added to the eleven (Acts 1:20-26). [22] Mary speaks to all of us—women and men—on this issue of women's ordination, as well as on every other issue, when she says, "Whatsoever he [Christ] saith unto you, do it" (John 2:5).

Finally, the apostle Paul leaves us an example of total surrender of our aims and ambitions to the cross of Christ. If, like him, we all—men and women, church leaders and members, professors and students—also reckon ourselves as "crucified with Christ" and seek to live by the principle, "Not I but Christ" (Gal 2:20), our spirit will be like his. When we are called upon to make decisions of costly discipleship, the kind suggested when we seek to do God's will on the role of women in the soul-winning ministry, the spirit of Paul must always be ours:

Paul "had no ambitions [for himself]—and so had nothing to be jealous about. He had no reputation—and so had nothing to fight about. He had no possessions—and therefore had nothing to worry about. He had no 'rights'—so therefore he could not suffer wrong. He was already broken—so no one could break him. He was 'dead'—so none could kill him. He was less than the least—so who could humble him? He had suffered the loss of all things—so none could defraud him." [23]

May this spirit of faithful, obedient surrender to Christ and His Word inspire us not only to resist attempts at legitimizing and legislating cultural *ideology,* but also to trust and obey the sound *theology* from God's Word.

*1. When we walk with the Lord,*
In the light of His Word,
What a glory He sheds on our way!
While we do His good will,
He abides with us still,

And with all who will trust and obey.

***Chorus:***
Trust and obey,
For there's no other way
To be happy in Jesus,
But to trust and obey.

2. Not a shadow can rise,
Not a cloud in the skies,
But His smile quickly drives it away;
Not a doubt nor a fear,
Not a sigh nor a tear,
Can abide while we trust and obey.

3. Not a burden we bear,
Not a sorrow we share,
But our toil He doth richly repay;
Not a grief nor a loss,
Not a frown nor a cross,
But is blest if we trust and obey.

4. But we never can prove
The delights of His love,
Until all on the altar we lay,
For the favor He shows,
And the joy He bestows,
Are for them who will trust and obey.

5. Then in fellowship sweet
We will sit at His feet,
Or we'll walk by His side in the way;
What He says we will do,
Where He sends we will go,
*Never fear, only trust and obey.*

**Endnotes**

[1]George R. Knight, *A Brief History of Seventh-day Adventists* (Hagerstown, Md.: Review and Herald, 1999), 151, 152, 153; emphasis mine; cf. his "Proving More Than Intended," *Ministry,* March 1996, 26-28. For a response to the latter article, see P. Gerard Damsteegt, "Scripture Faces Current Issues," *Ministry,* April 1999, 23-27.

[2]For example, shortly after the 1995 General Conference session in Utrecht, the Netherlands, an Adventist scholar in ethics wrote the following: "The vote refusing the NAD [North American Division] permission to ordain its women is the real 'tip of the iceberg,' the iceberg being the clash between *scriptural literalism,* a view largely held in the developing world—Africa and much of South America and Inter-America, and a *principle-based approach* to Scripture followed in areas where the church has matured for a century and a half." In contrast to areas where the church has "matured for a century and a half" (i.e., North America, Europe, and possibly Australia), this professor of ethics states that "many African converts, not far removed from bigamous exploitation of women, are naturally drawn to an interpretation of Scripture ['scriptural literalism'] that affirms a millennia-old sentiment toward women." See Jim Walters, "General Conference Delegates Say NO on Women's Ordination," *Adventist Today,* July-August, 1995, 13. Walters is an Adventist ethicist and an editor of *Adventist Today,* an independent publication whose stated purpose is to follow "basic principles of ethics and canons of journalism," striving "for fairness, candor, and good taste." Cf. J. David Newman, "Stuck in the Concrete," *Adventist Today,* July-August, 1995, 13. Newman last served as the editor of *Ministry,* "the international journal of the Seventh-day Adventist Ministerial Association." For a response to this kind of reasoning, see my *Receiving the Word: How New Approaches to the Bible Impact Our Biblical Faith and Lifestyle* (Berrien Springs, Mich.: Berean Books, 1996), 10-11, 91-92. In the light of our evaluation of *Women in Ministry,* a volume that captures the very best case pro-ordinations can offer in defense of their view, can any honest student of the Bible still believe that those opposed to women's ordination are hermeneutically "immature"?

[3]This church leader wrote: "To be honest, at times I am frustrated with my church. Sometimes I feel it is somewhat out of tune with the times and the world I live in. Sometimes I get upset by its frequent failures to deal decisively with important issues. I wish my church could settle the issue of women's ordination (yes, I'm one of those people) and deal with a few other hot potatoes. And I often wonder why the church allows its fundamentalist fringe to set so much of its agenda. And yes, I need a double or triple portion of grace to interact with some people in the church" (Reinder Bruinsma, "Why I Stay," *Adventist Review,* July 1999, 8-12). It appears that for Bruinsma, who is the secretary of one of the European Divisions, "the church" is nothing more than the "church in the west" which is pushing women's ordination; and the "fundamentalist fringe" is the rest of the world church that refuses to go along. Given the fact that the SDA church has twice (at 1990 and 1995 GC sessions) overwhelmingly rejected the call for women's ordination, some will justifiably contend that the real "fundamentalist fringe" in the church comprises those who have embraced the fundamentalism of feminism's egalitarian ideology (see chapter 10 of this book for a discussion of that ideology).

[4]Decrying the "terrible thing" that happened in Utrecht (the vote against women's ordination), one key advocate of women's ordination wrote: "*We who have grown and progressed in our faith development* to understand and value racial and gender equality and

justice are hurt by the lack of understanding, intolerance and animosity that was displayed at Utrecht. . . . The ministry of *sensitive and caring men and women* who voted to support this action [for women's ordination] feel hurt by the abuse that was so forcefully and overwhelmingly hurled at them here in Utrecht." See Penny Miller (chairperson of the Gender Inclusiveness Commission of the Southeastern California Conference), "Women Denied Equal Rights at 56th GC Session in Utrecht," *Dialogue* [Loma Linda University Church Paper] 6/8 (August 1995), 1, emphasis supplied.

[5]Nancy Vyhmeister, "Prologue," *Women in Ministry,* 5.

[6]Randal Wisbey, "SDA Women in Ministry: 1970-1998," *Women in Ministry* (abbreviated as *WIM*), 251; Walter Douglas, "The Distance and the Difference: Reflections on Issues of Slavery and Women's Ordination," *WIM,* 394; Alicia Worley, "Ellen White and Women's Rights," *WIM,* 367-370; Roger Dudley, "The Ordination of Women in Light of the Character of God," *WIM,* 413-415; Nancy Vhymeister, "Epilogue," *WIM,* 436.

[7]In my *In the Spirit of Truth* (Berrien Springs, Mich.: Berean Books, 1997), I have briefly addressed a proposal similar to the one presently offered by the authors of *Women in Ministry.* Readers interested in a detailed treatment of the Holy Spirit's role in Bible interpretation may want to consult my Ph.D. dissertation, "The Role of the Holy Spirit in Biblical Interpretation: A Study in the Writings of James I. Packer" (Andrews University, 1998). This 410-page work explores how the relationship between the Spirit and the inspired Word has been understood by major theological figures and movements since the sixteenth century Reformation and culminating in the works of one of contemporary Evangelicalism's most widely respected theologians.

[8]Earlier in our discussion of the expected use of the book, we pointed to the prologue of the volume, where the authors submit their work to the church "as a resource tool for decision making," a euphemistic expression for the overturning of the previous General Conference session decisions. An admiring reviewer of the book adds, "The ultimate purpose of *Women in Ministry* is to provide information for informed decision making, a clear indication that there is a decision to be made. In so doing, the book calls the church to do some serious Bible study. If the basis of our decision is going to be in our interpretation of Scripture, we must do it well." See Beverly Beem, "What If . . . Women in Ministry?" *Focus,* Winter 1999, 31.

[9]Ibid.

[10]Vyhmeister, "Prologue," *WIM,* 5; idem, "Epilogue," *WIM,* 436. In a letter accompanying *Women in Ministry*'s wide distribution to church leaders around the world, the authors express the belief that they have provided the church with "carefully researched information" that will "foster dialogue."

[11]Roger L. Dudley, "[Letter to the Editor Regarding] *Women in Ministry,*" *Adventist Today,* January-February 1999, 6.

[12]Calvin Rock, "Review of *Women in Ministry,*" *Adventist Review,* April 15, 1999, 29. In his glowing review, Rock offers "special kudos" to the Seminary Ad Hoc Committee for "providing a deeply spiritual, highly reasoned, consistently logical approach to the issue of women's ordination." In his opinion the book provides "incisive arguments" for those who believe in women's ordination, and "a thoughtful, thorough treatment" of the major aspects of the women's ordination question (ibid).

[13]Beverly Beem, "What If . . . Women in Ministry?" *Focus,* Winter 1999, 31.

[14]Fritz Guy, "Review of *Women in Ministry*," *Ministry,* January 1999, 29.

[15]Therefore, Seventh-day Adventists who wish to believe in women's ordination should do so on the basis of better evidence and methods superior to those found in *Women in Ministry.* And the attempt to put the Seminary's imprimatur on a work that is patently biased and arguably defective in biblical and historical scholarship holds the potential of damaging the credibility of the Seminary as a place of sound teaching. Similarly, the attempt to legislate women's ordination as a "moral imperative" could lead to and institutionalize intolerance and persecution of those who uphold the biblical teaching of role relationships in the church. In my opinion, it is a tragic mistake for the Seventh-day Adventist Theological Seminary to have financed the publication of this book, when the same work could have been published independently by the pro-ordination scholars. In this respect, the Seminary has set an unfortunate precedent by opening its door to those who may be seeking ways to commandeer the name and resources of our church's leading theological institution for their own ideological agendas.

[16]Vyhmeister, "Prologue," *WIM,* 5.

[17]Vhymeister, "Prologue," *WIM,* 5.

[18]In an earlier work, I have articulated the legitimate role of women in ministry thus: "Notwithstanding male leadership in the church, (i) the fact that men and women are equal, having a complementary relationship between them, and (ii) the fact that Scripture calls women to labor in ministry suggest that: The Seventh-day Adventist church should make provision that will encourage a greater participation of women in ministry. This may include stronger support for their training at the Seminary, adequate and fair remuneration of women for their labor and, in some cases (such as in team ministries), their being authoritatively commissioned for roles and duties that are not in violation of biblical teaching. Of the many lines of ministry, women could be encouraged to participate in the study, teaching and preaching of the gospel in personal and public evangelism; to be involved in ministries of prayer, visitation, counseling, writing and singing; to labor as literature evangelists, health evangelists, to raise new churches, and to minister to the needy; to serve in positions of responsibility that do not require ordination *as elders or pastors,* serving as colleagues in partnership with ordained men at the various levels of the church organization; to teach in our institutions and seminaries; and above all, to minister to their children at home. But I do not believe that the Bible and Spirit of Prophecy permit women to be ordained elders or pastors" (see my *Searching the Scriptures,* 88, 89).

[19]Alfred C. McClure, "NAD President Speaks on Women's Ordination," *Adventist Review,* February 1995, 14, 15.

[20]Ibid.

[21]Mercedes H. Dyer, ed., *Prove All Things: A Response to Women in Ministry,* 354.

[22]For more on this, see my *Searching the Scriptures,* 56-58.

[23]Leonard Ravenhill, *Why Revival Tarries* (Minneapolis: Bethany Fellowship, 1959), 173, cited in Stephen F. Olford, *Not I, But Christ* (Wheaton, Ill.: Crossway Books, 1995), 55, 56.

# 17

# *My Daughters' Ordinations— A Testimony*

What should "women elders" do after they recognize the practice to be incompatible with biblical teaching? In this chapter, a Seventh-day Adventist pastor shares the account of how her two daughters got ordained as women elders, and what they later decided to do about it. He concludes by discussing why the issue of women's ordination is a question worth fussing about.[1]

**"What Shall I Do"?**

Still eating breakfast at seven a. m., my phone began ringing. I listened to the urgent voice on the other end of the line. "It's our youngest daughter, Gladys, I told my wife.

"Daddy, what shall I do?"

"Do about what?"

"Daddy, the college church is asking me to serve as an elder. What do you think about ordaining women?"

My quick off the cuff answer, "I'm against it."

"Why?" she wanted to know.

"I really haven't thought about it. We're back in the states after serving 21 years overseas where ordaining women was not an option. Now, I'm heavily involved in a church building program and haven't stayed on top of current issues. This is something I need to study."

A feeling of pride began to fill my heart. Happy that the college church recognized my daughter as a spiritual leader, I said, "Gladys, You need to pray and study this out for yourself. Since they asked you to serve, go ahead if that's what God leads you to do. I can't make a decision for you."

After hanging up it hit me. *You've really let your daughter down! She has questions and you gave no Bible reasons "for" or "against."* I remembered—we were overseas when our mission president returned from a trip to the States and announced, "It's been voted for ministerial interns to baptize."

I questioned, "Isn't that kind of like having sex before marriage? Why would a minister want to baptize before being ordained?" It troubled me that the tax authorities and not the Bible would lead to such a decision.

Occupied with the pressures of raising money and building a church, I swept the ordination matter from my mind. My teenage daughter figured church leaders knew what they were doing and accepted ordination. Taking it all very seriously, she bought a black dress to wear in the pulpit.

My older daughter, Gail, working on a masters degree at an Adventist university didn't bother to ask her parents' opinion on women's ordination. She simply wrote home saying she had been ordained as an elder.

We were not delegates, but all of our family, along with a new son-in-law, attended the 1990 General Conference Session at Indianapolis. My ordained daughters looked pleased when the session voted 1173 to 377, "We do not approve ordination of women to the gospel ministry." It was obvious they had been searching Scripture and making decisions on their own. They said "Amen!" when Paul Wangai's mother from Africa stood up and said, "God called women to evangelize, not baptize."

The next day, I watched their distraught expressions when, while many delegates were absent, a vote was taken approving a document making it possible for women ordained as local elders to do just about everything an ordained minister does, including baptizing and marrying.[2]

By 1995 my wife and I were serving in Thailand. We traveled to Utrecht, again joining our family there. I served as a delegate from the Asia Pacific Division. Two seminary professors made presentations. One *against* ordaining women, appealed powerfully to the Bible for authority. The other, *for* women's ordination, was not biblically convincing.

My daughters told me they felt God led when the session voted 1481 to 673 not to let the North American Division go its own way. Their reaction, "What we really need to do now in order to be consistent is to take an action annulling all previous actions permitting the ordination of women as local church elders."

Today my younger daughter is a full-time missionary on an island in the Asia Pacific Division. She looks back on her ordination at a college church and says, "There were no Bible reasons. It was the politically-correct thing. The leaders wanted to be 'cool.'" She did not accept her latest invitation to serve as an elder.

My older daughter and her husband are full-time missionaries in West Africa. Recalling her ordination, she says, "They wanted to make a 'statement.' There was nothing spiritual about my ordination. It was all political."

After moving away from the University she was again asked to serve as an elder, but desiring to be a woman of the Word, she declined. Later she decided to return her ordination certificate to the church that had issued it.

**Why all the Fuss?**

Paul says, ". . . there is neither male nor female; for you are all one in Christ."—*Galatians 3:28*, NKJV. So why all the fuss about ordaining women? It's simple. The Bible provides as much evidence for keeping Sunday as for ordaining women. It's true, not a single text says, "You shall not keep Sunday."

In his *Dies Domini*, Section 12, John Paul II quotes Genesis 2:3: "God blessed the seventh day and made it holy." Eleven lines later in the same document he says: ". . . Sunday is the day of rest because it is the day 'blessed' by God and 'made holy' by him, . . ." Wait a minute! Did God bless both Sabbath and Sunday? We need to pray for the pope.

Not a single Bible verse says, "You shall not ordain women!" Inspired by God, Paul writes clearly: "If a man desires the position of a bishop, he desires a good work A bishop then must be blameless, the husband of one wife, . . . one who rules his own house well having his children in submission . . ."—*1 Timothy 3:1, 2 & 4*, NKJV.

Feminist pressures ask us to revise scripture and say, "If a woman desires the position of a bishop, she desires a good work A bishop then must be blameless, the wife of one husband, . . . one who rules her own house well having her children in submission." Does God really ask both men and women to rule their homes? "Therefore . . . as the church is subject to Christ, so let the wives be to their own husbands in everything.

Husbands, love your wives . . . as Christ also loved the church and gave Himself for it."—*Ephesians 5:24, 25*, NKJV. We need to pray for our church, our leaders and our homes.

The Creator of the universe instituted the Sabbath and the family at the very beginning of earth's history. Jesus chose to make man the head of the family. It's His decision for church leadership to model His plan for families. The breakdown of the family is the world's greatest problem. God calls the last-day church to build strong, loving disciplined families.

Does this mean God has no place for women to serve in His church? Absolutely not! God has given women the most important position on the planet—that of being mothers. But doesn't God want to use women in finishing His work on earth. Yes, Yes, and Yes!

No man in the remnant church has accomplished more for God's work than Ellen White. She wrote: "But God will have a people upon the earth to maintain the Bible, and the Bible only, as the standard of all doctrines and the basis of all reforms. . . . *Before accepting any doctrine or precept, we should demand a plain "Thus saith the Lord' in its* support." (*The Great Controversy*, 595, emphasis supplied).

Let's look at the words omitted by the ellipsis in the preceding statement. "The opinions of learned men, the deductions of science, the creeds or decisions of ecclesiastical councils, as numerous and discordant as are the churches which they represent, the voice of the majority—not one nor all of these should be regarded as evidence for or against any point of religious faith."

In the paragraph preceding our quote, Ellen White tells how Paul looked down to the last days and declared: "The time will come when they will not endure sound doctrine." *(2 Timothy 4:3*, KJV). Then she says, "That time has fully come." (*The Great Controversy*, 595). On the same page she adds, "Satan . . . leads the people to look to Bishops, to pastors, to professors of theology, as their guides, instead of searching the Scriptures to learn their duty for themselves."

### A Cultural Issue?

Isn't all this just a matter of culture? Isn't John Paul II right to suggest that we take Sabbath and find it's fulfillment in Sunday? Wasn't the Roman Church right when they decided to take the popular pagan day of the sun and make it the Christian Sabbath? Isn't it time for Seventh-day Adventists to be sensitive to the culture of our times and give women positions that God reserved for men? Books with feminist ideals have been sold in our college and university bookstores for many years. Can't we get their message?

If culture is the issue, God missed the perfect opportunity. At the time of the Exodus Egyptian culture dictated that it was proper for a woman to become a pharaoh. The Lord could have avoided all the trouble of having Miriam watch over her baby brother in a basket on the Nile and followed the culture of the times by making her the leader of Israel, a position which she later coveted.

God's attitude on culture comes to us in clear language. "According to the doings of the land of Egypt, where you dwelt, you shall not do: and according to the doings of the land of Canaan, where I am bringing you, you shall not do; nor shall you walk in their ordinances." (Leviticus 18:3). It is not the feminist agenda, but the will of Jesus, we must seek. God is getting us ready for the culture of heaven. He wants us to be part of His family. Christ—not a goddess, as "discovered" by some women pastors in other denominations—is the head of His church.

Bible reasons should be enough justification for obeying God, but we can also find some practical reasons for not ordaining or commissioning women:

First, the women's issue affects our own church's unity. If we are honest, we must admit that ordaining women is a divisive issue in the Seventh-day Adventist church, even in North America. Jesus never commanded his followers to ordain women, but He did call upon them to live together in harmony.

**Impact on Outreach**

What is more, the women's issue affects our churches outreach. With a billion Roman Catholics in the world, more Catholic Christians choose to leave Babylon and join the remnant church than any other group. The great majority believe in the biblical teaching of male leadership, and there is no scriptural reason to offend them by ordaining women pastors. Many Protestant groups also believe it is unbiblical. Among them are the Southern Baptists, the largest Protestant denomination in North America. Other large groups in the world who may be offended by women pastors include Buddhists, Muslims, and Hindus.

The impact of this issue on our evangelism was brought home to me forcefully and personally. While serving as a pastor in Bakersfield,

California, I received a call from an attorney. "I'm looking for a church that follows all the Bible," he said.

My response, "You've found the right church."

He questioned, "Does your church ordain women elders?"

Even though my own church had no women elders, I had to admit my daughters had been ordained in Adventist churches. Although I visited him several times, he continued to be offended by a practice not authorized by Scripture, and he turned away from the Adventist church. Jesus has very strong words for those who offend others. "It would be better for him if a millstone were hung around his neck, and he were thrown into the sea, than that he should offend one of these little ones.'"—*Luke 17:2*, NKJV.

Because of our family's 23 years of mission service, we have contact with a lot of overseas leaders and know firsthand that many are offended by what is going on in North America. Whether we call it "ordain" or "commission," it's all the same when we lay hands on the candidate and give them the full authority of the gospel minister. Even the government tax people agree.

To commission women and say, "We uphold the General Conference action not to ordain," is about as true as President Clinton saying, "I did not have an affair with that woman." Commissioning women while ordaining men will not satisfy many. One woman says, "We dream of achieving full recognition as equals in ministry."—*Pacific Union Recorder*, Dec. 7, 1998, p. 10.

We can not afford to be a stumbling block to the rest of the world. Our overseas brothers and sisters expect the best example from North America. We've gone pretty far, but God will forgive us, just as he forgave my daughters for sincerely accepting a non-biblical ordination. And I pray God will forgive me for side stepping the issue when my daughter first asked me about ordination for women.

Elder Charles Bradford was right back in 1989 when he spoke at Annual Council saying, "And if we have made a horrible mistake, there is such a thing as the Spirit's ministry and He will bring us back. Because, as Ellen White says, we are captives of hope. He has us in His hands. We are the remnant people of God."[3]

If the Spirit calls us back—let's go back. Whatever we do, we need to be sure we have a solid Bible basis for our actions and practices. World divisions look to the church in North America for true leadership based on Scripture and we need to give it.

Delegates at the 1990 and 1995 General Conference Sessions, our church's highest authority, made decisions regarding woman as ordained ministers based on Bible principles. We in North America need to demonstrate leadership to the world field. We need to recommend to the next General Conference Session, that based on the Word of God, all previous actions to ordain women as local church elders or commissioned ministers be annulled.

We need to make it clear that ordaining women as elders or pastors is not in harmony with Scripture. There is nothing in the *Seventh-day Adventist Church Manual* about ordaining women as elders. *Seventh-day Adventists Believe . . . A Biblical Exposition of 27 Fundamental Doctrines* presents Scripture showing that men are to be ordained as elders.

### Pray That Jesus Will Guide

We must get on our knees, review the plain instructions in the Word and ask, "Is Jesus truly leading North America to ignore the decision of two General Conference Sessions and promote a book, *Women in Ministry*, which endorses women's ordination?

Jesus calls women and men, pastors, educators, medical workers and administrators to be ready to stand with Him on the sea of glass in Heaven soon. He gives my daughters, my wife and me, all of us, one great task—"The gospel to all the world." The little lady who died in 1915 is right, ". . . God will have a people on earth to maintain the Bible, and the Bible only, as the standard of all doctrines and the basis of all reforms."—*The Great Controversy*, 595.

Why all the fuss? Shall our church follow popular fashions or maintain the Bible as our standard? That's a question worth fussing about.

---

**Endnotes**

[1]With permission from the publisher, this chapter is adapted from Wellesley Muir's "My Daughters' Ordinations" and "Why All the Fuss?" in Mercedes H. Dyer, ed., *Prove All Things: A Response to Women in Ministry* (Berrien Springs, Mich.: Adventists Affirm, 2000), 319-320, and 335-338.

[2]For an insightful account of the circumstances leading to this controversial decision, see C. Mervyn Maxwell, "A Very Surprising (and Interesting) History," in *Prove All Things,* 225-230.

[3]Charles Bradford, cited by Randal Wisbey, in *Women in Ministry*, 243.

*Is there racism in the church? What religious beliefs lie behind this ideology? Why do we have racially separate conferences in North America? Do we still need these black and white church structures? What should we do about racism?*

Section III

# AMAZING GRACE AND OUR MAZING RACE:
## (The Ideology of Racism)

# 18

# A Brief Background

*"Of all the major institutions in our society, the church is still the most segregated. Americans of different races work together, play together, study together, and entertain each other. But seldom do they pray or worship together"*

**—David R. Williams**

Racism still exists in both society and church. But people often deny it, claiming it is a thing of the past. Sometimes we disguise our racism under euphemistic phrases, such as affirming our "ethnic identity or pride," or "being true to one's cultural heritage."

Even when one admits that racism is prevalent, it is not always easy to discuss the subject honestly. In the United States, for example, black people are too angry to speak about racism, and white people are uncomfortable, if not afraid, to address the issue. A *Time* magazine cover story article, "Pride and Prejudice,"captured this fact not too long ago, when it described the two "ugly truths of American life": "A great many black Americans view their white fellow citizens with anger. And a great many white Americans view their black fellow citizens with fear."[1]

Given the unease, it is not surprising that even in the church, whenever the subject of race or racism comes up for discussion, it is dealt with at the most superficial level. We often invoke catchphrases, like "love one another," "celebrate our diversity," "in Christ, there is neither Jew nor Gentile," or "unity in Christ," "racial inclusiveness and harmony," and others. Each Sabbath, we join our children in singing "red and yellow, black and white; they are precious in His sight." But we seldom move beyond these slogans and jingles.

We still cherish our racial attitudes. We still worship in our racially segregated churches. We still hold on to power in our race based church structures. We still practice racial discrimination in our hiring and promotion practices. We still consider ourselves more "enlightened" or "mature" than the rest of the church. And we still pretend that we have no racial problems.

Over three decades ago, one Christian author asked: "Why are there so many Christians who, belonging to the same church, converse with each other only on the most superficial level, smiling and amiable as they meet but never discussing with each other the issues which trouble them most?" He urges Christians to answer this question if they are to discover "why Christian communion is in most churches a pretense, a cordial but uneasy fiction, rather than a strengthening, creative reality."[2]

We should be grateful to the North American Division (NAD) of Seventh-day Adventists for recognizing the need for frank and open discussion on race relations. The 1999 summit on race, themed *Racial Harmony in the New Millennium: Making it Happen,* sought to "concentrate on the important question of how to bring about positive change in race relations, recommend bold initiatives for dismantling racism, and create an on-going mechanism to continually motivate, expand, and monitor the progress of those initiatives."[3]

It is quite remarkable that the North American church has had the moral courage to confront this subject. Whether or not the actual practice of the church will move beyond mere apologies and recommendations remain to be seen. But by opening the discussion at this time, the NAD seems to validate a prediction made by Ellen G. White some one hundred years ago. Speaking to the black and white racial issue that raged in her days, she stated:

"The relation of the two races has been a matter hard to deal with, and I fear that it will ever remain a most perplexing problem."[4] The current attempt to respond to this "most perplexing problem" of racism could also be seen as an affirmation that one day—in our day—the walls of racial prejudice and bigotry "will tumble down of themselves, as did the walls of Jericho, when Christians obey the Word of God, which enjoins on them supreme love to their Maker and impartial love to their neighbors."[5]

**Objective.** In this section I will explain the nature of racism, show why it is a denial of the Christian faith, and suggest what we should do about it. This discussion will show that individuals who maintain a simultaneous allegiance to both Jesus Christ and to their race are practicing a form of syncretistic or polytheistic faith.

**Working Definition.** Race is one great catchword that means different things to different people, and about which much ink and blood have been spilled. Despite this fact, no agreement seems to exist regarding what is a race, how it can be recognized, who constitute the several races, and how the different races are to be ranked in their relative abilities and closeness to some ideal referent (whether an ape, or a Creator). Thus, over the years, in an effort to abstract some defining traits as characteristic of a race, notable individuals—statesmen, scholars, scientists, etc.—have erroneously pointed to certain easily noted human features (such as color of the skin, hair, or eye, the striking appearance of face or body, the unaccustomed mode of speech, language, dress or religion, the shape of skull, an unusual temperament, etc.) as the permanent ineradicable hallmark of a race.[6]

Racism is the attitude, behavior or ideology that is based on the belief that one race is superior to all others. By race, I mean a group of people, distinguished by certain easily noticed physical characteristics, such as the color of skin, hair, or eye, or the striking appearance of face or body, the distinctive mode of speech, language, dress, or religion, or any other external characteristics often associated with an ethnic group.

**A Forbidden Question.** Do we still need race-based churches and Conferences in North America?

---

**Endnotes**

[1]William A. Henry III, "Pride and Prejudice," *Time* (February 28, 1994), 21.

[2]Kyle Haselden, *Mandate for White Christians* (Richmond, VA: John Knox Press, 1966), 24.

[3]On October 27-30, 1999, the NAD brought together a wide representation of lay members, pastors, educators, and leaders to discuss the furthering of race relations in the different areas of church activities. The statement above, outlining the objectives of the "summit on race," is attributed to Rosa Banks, the director of Human Relations for the NAD. See Celeste Ryan, "Adventist Church Hosts Race Relations Summit," *Adventist News Network* [ANN], October 19, 1999.

[4]Ellen G. White, *Testimonies for the Church*, 9 vols. (Boise, ID: Pacific Press, 1948), 9:214; this statement was written on June 5, 1899. See also *The Southern Work* (Oberlin, OH: Laymen's Leadership Conference, 1965), 117-118.

[5]Ellen G. White, *Christian Service* (Hagerstown, MD: Review and Herald, 1983), 217.

[6]For a critique of some of the different definitions of race, see Jacques Barzun's *Race: A Study in Superstition*, revised, with a new preface (New York: Harper & Row, 1965). Barzun argues that the idea of race is a "fiction" (not a fact), a "fatal superstition" that has been put forward from time to time to advance some ideological goal; see also Ashley Montagu, *Race Science and Humanity* (New York: Van Nostrand Co., 1963).

# 19

# CONTEMPORARY RACISM AND THE CHURCH

### Racism in the Church

The world today has become one global city whose highways are interconnected by advanced networks of transportation and communication technology. However, we are yet able to find a sound basis for overcoming hostilities among people of different ethnic and racial backgrounds.

While it is true that many lands are expending much effort to kill racism in its various forms, one can still point to the Rodney King race riots in Los Angeles, the ethnic cleansing in former Yugoslavia, the hundreds of thousands being killed in tribal warfare in Africa, the violence and bloodshed in Asia, the Middle East and Russia, the activities of neo-Nazi hate groups in Europe, the USA and South Africa, as evidences of the fact that racism, "although repeatedly killed, is nevertheless undying."[1]

Racism may be outlawed in the books and laws of the lands, but it remains written in the hearts of people. Unfortunately, the Christian church, the body of people constituted and appointed by Christ to be a counter-voice in our world, is not totally immune to the virus of racism. Forgetting their status as "resident aliens" in this world, and perhaps, out of comfort, fear or blindness, Christians, by and large, have capitulated to the racism of the world.[2] "By and large, the people who have been the racists of the modern world have also been Christians or the heirs of Christian civilization. Among large numbers of Christians, racism has been the other faith or one of the other faiths."[3]

Decades of research offer compelling, but sobering, evidence that more racial prejudice exists in the Christian church than outside of it. For example, several years ago two sociologists concluded their major study on racism in the following words: "Although the Protestant churches stress (1) the dignity and worth of the individual and (2) the brotherhood of man, the racial behavior patterns of most church members have not been substantially affected by these principles."[4]

Recently, an Adventist sociologist and research scientist at the University of Michigan, Ann Arbor, Michigan, also updated *Adventist Review* readers on current studies that have been conducted in the United States on the relationship between racial prejudice and religion. He reported that "there is more racial prejudice in the Christian church than outside it, that church members are more prejudiced than nonmembers, that churchgoers are more biased than those who do not attend, and that regular attenders are more prejudiced than those who attend less often. It's also been shown that persons who hold conservative theological beliefs are more likely to be prejudiced than those who do not.[5]

The above scientific studies have yet to be contradicted. Despite the claims by some that there is "racial progress" in the church, very little is being done. Not too long ago, *Christianity Today* Institute devoted an entire issue to the "The Myth of Racial Progress." Billy Graham remarked in that publication that even though racial and ethnic hostility is *the* number one social problem facing the world and the church, "evangelical Christians have turned a blind eye to racism or have been willing to stand aside while others take the lead in racial reconciliation, saying it was not our responsibility."[6]

**Racism and the Adventist Church.** The Seventh-day Adventist Church is not altogether immune from this infection of racism. Adventist history bears eloquent testimony to the fact that not only has their church been silent and insensitive to racial issues, but also it has often been guilty of ethnic or racial prejudice, discrimination, pride, condescension, paternalism, and scorn to some groups within its membership.[7]

After noting "some marginal progress" during the past three decades in the area of race relations, one prominent North American church leader concedes that "Adventists remain as racially separated as the rest of Christianity and the rest of society. It is still true that 11 o'clock Sabbath morning is the most segregated hour for Adventism in North America. . . . Our church is still riddled with racism and segregation." The church administrator continues:

> Institutional racism is a costly separation, and when African Americans speak frankly to their white counterparts, they receive apathy, indifference, or the attitude that the issue is not really important. Blacks feel angry, hurt, and betrayed by what they see as society's and the Church's failure. White racism in white institutions must be eradicated by white people and not just black people. In fact, white racism is primarily a white problem and responsibility. This includes the Seventh-day Adventist Church. We must get our house in order.[8]

Seventh-day Adventist historian, Richard W. Schwartz, has summarized in his *Light Bearers to the Remnant* how this racial attitude was manifested in the Adventist Church:

> Afro-Americans were not the only group to be treated for years in a paternal, patronizing way. Adventist missionaries going to Africa, Asia, and Latin America in the early years of the twentieth century did not escape the general Western imperialistic attitude practiced by the colonial powers. In general this attitude tended to equate European culture, education, and technology with progress. The more another culture varied from the European or North American model, the more backward it was assumed to be. It was easy to conclude that nationals from non-Western areas could not be trusted in leadership roles until they had absorbed Western ways as well as Adventist doctrines.[9]

One example of how European missionaries viewed Africans is captured in the 1931 Working Policy of the SDA church in South Africa. The caption under "Hints to Our Missionaries" reads:

> It is not customary for Europeans to entertain [African] natives at meals, and the native does not expect it. If you wish to

> give one a meal, let him eat it outside from a plate kept expecially for natives.
>
> Teach your mission students to shake hands only when you, or any white, makes an advance. It is most embarrassing to have a native come up to you in the streets of a city and offer to shake hands. You may not mind, but others will look askance at you and it will bring discredit to your work (see, Constitution, By-laws, Working Policy of the General Conference of Seventh-day Adventists [Southern African Division, 1931], 139).

I am sure that there is an explanation for a statement of this kind. Still, it aptly describes what Schwartz refers to as the paternal and patronizing practice of Adventist missionaries who went to Africa, Asia, and Latin America with the "imperialistic attitude practiced by the colonial powers."

Perceptive Adventists can also point to the cultural snobbery that has been displayed by some in the "church of the West"as they have related to the "rest of the Church" over the question of women's ordination. For example, when at Utrecht the world church rejected as unbiblical the North American Division's request for divisional ordination, some Adventist scholars and leaders in the United States could not accept the fact that Adventists from the Third World were capable of serious theological reflection. They simply looked down upon them as theologically and ethically "immature."[10] Or in the words of an European church administrator who recently wrote in the *Adventist Review,* those opposed to the ideology of women's ordination belong to the "fundamentalist fringe"[11] Though not always acknowledged, and though not always intended, these kinds of statements reflect cultural arrogance, if not racial prejudice.[12]

Explaining why Adventists have "had their share of casualties over racial issues," a church historian argues that "racial prejudice, like other sins, is not totally eradicated in most Christians at conversion. Nor are the racial tensions embodied in a culture easy for the churches existing in that culture to overcome."[13]

The fact that many conferences in the United States have been organized along racial lines is another evidence of the reality of racism in the Seventh-day Adventist church. A recent indication of the challenge of racism in our church is the broad agenda set forth, and the wide representation of people, at the 1999 "Race Summit" held by the North American Division.[14] These facts confirm that, as a church, we still have a long way to go on this issue of racism.

It is rather ironical that the professions (like politics, business, industry, the military, basketball, baseball, football, and entertainment) whose activities are often at cross purposes with the teachings of Christianity are doing more to heal racial divisions in society than are Christians. We may discredit their efforts by arguing that they do so because of the fear of legislative pressures or sanctions from secular authorities, or the violent protests of individuals who can no longer accept the racial status quo. We may even discount secular efforts at curbing racism on the grounds that these are done for some monetary gain. But as Frank Stagg reminded us half a century ago, "To say that these have done it for money removes none of the sting, for it is a humiliation if a pagan for money effects good which a Christian fails to effect for love." [15]

To understand why racism lies embedded in the attitudes of many Christians, we shall briefly offer a historical background to contemporary racism. We shall also attempt to gain an understanding of the nature of racism. These may explain why Christians have been slow in responding to racial problems.

## A History of Western Racism

Wherever there have been different groups of people, ethnocentrism and racism have also existed. Ethnocentrism is the belief in the unique value and rightness of one's own group, and hence the tendency to evaluate other races or groups by criteria that is specific to one's own. Ethnocentrism is not necessarily racism. It turns into racism when an ethnic group believes that it is superior to all others and transposes that belief into serving the vested interest of that particular ethnic or racial group by whatever means necessary.

Thus, ethnocentrism becomes racism when the belief in the superiority of one race over another shapes the attitude or behavior of a group, or when that belief is transposed into an ideology of power. Racial prejudice is the tendency to misjudge an individual primarily on the basis of their identity within an ethnic or racial group. Fascism, for example, is nationalism built on racism.

Racism, the suggestion that some races are *inherently* superior and inferior, is a fairly recent phenomenon, dating back some three-hundred years.[16] We can trace the rise and development of modern race and color prejudices to four major historical events:[17] (1) the discovery of America and the establishment of trade routes to India; (2) the development of the slave trade;[18] (3) the industrial revolution and its contribution to the enormous wealth and prestige of the white people of Europe and America;[19] and (4) Darwin's doctrine of evolution, with the idea of the survival of the fittest, which "was warmly accepted by the people of European stock who saw no reason to doubt that they were the fittest of all."[20]

Significant in this connection is the "social Darwinism" of English philosopher Herbert Spencer. He coined the phrase "survival of the fittest" in reference to the evolution of cultures and Darwin adopted the term to describe the outcome of the process of natural selection.[21] Spencer argued that since some populations are "naturally unfit," they represent a biologically or inherently inferior group of individuals. This teaching has not only provided "the ultimate license for social policies of domination" but also "has lent spurious credence to racism."[22]

This spirit of inherent superiority characterized the attitude of the European nations as they expanded overseas, competing for colonial power and the conversion of "heathen" natives. Since the European conquerors possessed superior economic and military technology over the enslaved people of color, they were able to explain the superiority of their cultural apparatus in terms of a superior human endowment. In other words, the European exploiters "read from right to left—from cultural effect to a natural or congenital cause."[23]

Modern racism in the West, therefore, arose as an ideological justification for the constellations of economic and political power which were expressed in colonialism and slavery. But "gradually the idea of the superior race was heightened and deepened in meaning and value so that it pointed beyond the historical structures of relation, in which it emerged, to human existence itself." The result of this shift was that the alleged superior race "became and now persists as a center of value and an object of devotion," with multitudes of people finding their sense and "power of being" from their membership in and identification with the superior race.[24]

This brief history of racism in the West may explain why some Christians still cherish the view that some groups are *inherently* superior to others. They are simply reflecting the beliefs in their culture, in which the economic and cultural interests of people in the industrialized countries of the West often overlapped with Christianity's. Today, however, such racial prejudice and hatred is almost universal.

**Universality of Racism**

Wherever diverse people meet, and wherever Western civilization has spread, racism exhibits itself in baffling complexity, intensity, and respectability. Some groups treat others as if the latter have no intrinsic value or worth.

Historically, the groups that have been treated as inferior or subhuman, and possessing lives of little personal or societal worth have included people of color, Jews, native Americans, and Gypsies. Other groups, such as women, prisoners, chronically ill, the physically disabled, the mentally retarded, children, the elderly, and unwanted babies, have also frequently been despised, denigrated, and dehumanized.

Recent expressions of racism include: (1) the tribal genocide in Rwanda in which, in just three months, over one million people—some 15,000 of whom were Seventh-day Adventists—were massacred by their neighbors because they were deemed a threat to the superior race; (2) the experiment of ethnic cleansing in Bosnia in which tens of thousands of people were "collected," "concentrated" and "eliminated" by their neighbors because of the belief that some people cannot dwell together with the superior race; (3) the practice, prevalent in some countries, of exploitation, domination and abuse of defenseless children, women, and the physically or economically disadvantaged, because these forms of slavery enhance the quality of life of the superior race; (4) the countless cases of brutality, war, executions, abortions, euthanasia, etc., which are currently being carried out in different places because such acts of violence will make the world safer and better for the superior race.

**A Global Problem.** Though in America the word racism usually denotes conflict between white and black, this is much too narrow a definition. I have seen racism far stronger in Africa, where one tribe in an area or country seeks dominance over another. I have seen it in the Middle East, where the sons of Abraham still fight one another. I have seen it in various countries of Europe in the rise of ultranationalism and neo-Nazism. I have seen it in Canada, where differences in language and culture have fueled hostility among citizens of the same country. I have seen it in the former Soviet Union, where the fallen colossus seems destined to break into ever smaller warring pieces. And I have seen it in Asia, where religious and ethnic differences have ignited flames of violence.

Nor is the phenomenon limited to ethnic or nationalistic concerns. It may be seen in chauvinism of either gender, in the designation of an unborn child by the neutral term "fetus" so that it may be the more easily disposed of, and in the invisibility of people with various handicaps with which we prefer not to deal. No matter what lines we draw to elevate one group and denigrate another, we are dealing with the same issue.

Racism, therefore, has both a broad and a narrow meaning. In its broad sense it conveys the idea of the inhumanity of one group to another. In its narrow usage, it refers to the prejudice and ill-treatment displayed to a group of human beings solely because of such physical characteristics as color of the skin or hair, striking appearance of face or body, or unusual shape of the skull—physical features that are believed to make one group inferior to others.

In this volume, I will use the term racism in the narrow sense. While I will be illustrating with examples from the North American scene, the discussion could be applied to any country or conflict in which one group is treated as inhuman.

### An Ideology of Supremacy

The discussion thus far leads us to conclude that racism is an ideology of supremacy. It is an ideology because it has a set of ideas and beliefs about reality. As an ideology of *supremacy*, it expresses itself in prejudice (prejudged negative *attitude*) and discrimination (unjust *acts* of domination, exploitation, dehumanization, etc.) of one group by another.[25] One scholar explains:

> Racism is an ideology of racial domination that incorporates beliefs in a particular race's cultural and/or inherent biological inferiority. It uses such beliefs to justify and prescribe unequal treatment of that group. In other words, racism is not merely attitudinal, it is structural. It is not merely a vague feeling of racial superiority, it is a system of *domination*, with structures of domination—social, political and economic. To put it another way: racism excludes groups on the basis of race or colour. But it is not only exclusion on the basis of race, but exclusion for the purpose of subjugating or maintaining subjugation.[26]

The common thread in all manifestations of racism—whether it is apartheid, tribalism, white and black racism,[27] anti-Semitism, anti-Arabism, patriotism, male and female chauvinism, etc.—is the idea that one group, distinguished by certain easily noticed features, is inherently superior to all or certain others. Taken to its logical conclusion (as it is in many parts of the world), it holds that since some human beings are not true persons, where necessary (i.e. to enhance the quality of life of the superior persons), the inferior race may be dehumanized, oppressed, even killed.

**Doctrinal Foundation.** While one may trace the roots of racial prejudice to a number of factors,[28] the foundational assumption upon which the different expressions of racism is built is the pseudoscientific doctrine of *biological determinism.* This doctrine holds that natural law or biological or genetically transmitted physical characteristics (such as, the color of the skin, eye, hair, or some physical features) do not simply influence, but define the basic humanness and, hence, the status of a person in society.[29] Such a belief may seem innocuous. But when it becomes the basis of a social policy, such as Hitler sought to employ, the results of this belief can be harmful and devastating.[30]

### An Ideology of Power

Racism is not simply a set of beliefs about the inherent superiority of one race over another. It is also an ideology of power. Despite their claim to superiority, racists have a feeling of being threatened by members of the inferior race. This is especially so in situations where some members of the alleged inferior races display the same level of expectation (intelligence, character, ability, etc.) normally reserved for the superior race.

To overcome their feeling of insecurity, racists seek to retain power (economic, political, military, etc.) exclusively in the hands of the superior. In this way members of the superior race express their self-identity by elaborate acts that systematically deny the essential humanness of people of other races.[31]

It is not only those holding the reins of power who are racists. One scholar's distinction between "imperialistic racism" or "aggressive racism" and "counter-racism" may be helpful here. In imperialistic/aggressive racism, racism is *in power*; it is full-blooded, in that "it can walk on its feet and strike with its feet because its spirit permeates the institutions of power"—political, military, economic, educational, ecclesiastical and other cultural institutions.

"Counter racism" (others will say "reverse racism"), on the other hand is racism that is *out of power.* "It lacks feet to walk on and fists with which to strike. The spirit is present; the hope is compelling; but the will to power cannot find the institutions of power through which it can express itself."[32]

In the context of USA, since power has tended to reside in the hands of Whites, imperialistic racism or institutional racism tends to be white racism. On the other hand since Blacks, Hispanics and Asians, generally speaking, do not possess power, the racism exhibited by these groups tend to bear the characteristics of counter (or reverse) racism. Given the chance and the appropriate conditions of power, Black/Hispanic/Asian racism can become as aggressive and imperialistic as white racism. This is because racism is a function of human nature, not color.

**Manifestation.** As an ideology of power, racism takes two major forms: (1) legal or *de jure* racism, and (2) institutional or *de facto* racism.

In legal or *de jure* racism, discriminatory practices are encoded in the laws of the land (such as was the case in the USA and in apartheid South Africa). In institutional or *de facto* racism, on the other hand, racial practices though not encoded in the laws of the land, are still present (albeit, in subtle and sophisticated form), having been built into the very structure of society.[33]

In the past, believers in racial supremacy were nakedly racist; they were not too squeamish in advocating and putting into practice views overtly racist: racial discrimination, segregation, etc. Today however, with racism outlawed in many countries, it has assumed a sophisticated form, and racists are more covert or subtle in expressing their views and in implementing racial policies. Legal racism may be dead, but institutional racism is still alive.

Of the two forms of racism, institutional racism poses the greatest challenge to the Christian church. Not only is it difficult to detect, but, as explained by Ian Robertson, institutional racism "is difficult to eradicate, since, obviously, it cannot be repealed, and in most cases is not susceptible to remedial legislation."[34]

**Racialization and "Laissez-Faire Racism."** Recent research data indicates that because Christians are not nakedly racists, many are not even aware that they have become "racialized." *Racialization* (a term which is less offensive than racism) is the situation in which a society assigns to a person certain privileges and benefits and certain doors of access solely on the basis of that person's race. Christians who have thus been racialized tend to be blind to racial injustices of society.[35]

Racialization, it must be noted, is an aspect of "laissez-faire racism," which is a "kinder and gentler" version of the ideology of supremacy and power. With reference to the United States context, the phrase "laissez-faire racism" emphasizes that the institutionalized racial inequalities created by the long era of slavery and followed by Jim Crow racial segregation laws (1870's-1890's) has metamorphosized and persists in contemporary society.[36] However, rather than relying on state-enforced inequality as during the Jim Crow era "modern racial inequality relies on the market and informal racial bias to re-create, and in some instances sharply worsen, structured racial inequality. Hence, laissez-faire racism."[37]

One distinctive feature of laissez-faire racism involves its widespread acceptance of negative stereotypes of other races. Racial stereotypes that were once viewed as categorical differences based in biology now appear to be understood as having largely cultural roots.[38] Moreover, biases based on racial stereotypes occur automatically and without conscious awareness even by persons who do not endorse racist beliefs.[39]

Indeed, considerable data suggests that "much discrimination today occurs through behaviors that the perpetrator does not subjectively experience as intentional. Much contemporary discriminatory behavior is unconscious, unthinking, and unintentional."[40]

For example, while most Americans seem to believe in the broad principles of equality and integration, there remains a considerable gap between belief and practice. Thus, in the 1990 General Social Survey (GSS), a highly respected social indicators survey in the United States, the national data on stereotypes reveal that Whites continue to view Blacks and other minorities more negatively than themselves, which presumably would make the latter undesirable as neighbors and employees.[41] These racial attitudes, stereotypes, and discrimination are not the aberrant behavior of a few "bad apples" but a widespread societal problem.[42]

Whether we are aware of it or not, the fact still remains that what lies behind much of our racial attitudes, stereotypes, and discrimination are the beliefs bequeathed to us by old-fashioned naked racism—the ideology of supremacy. Thus, in contrast to legal or *de jure* racism, the first step towards detecting and eradicating institutional or *de facto* racism—whether perceived as racialization or laissez-faire racism—is by being aware of the world view on which racism is established. We shall attempt to do so in the next chapter when we consider racism as a religion.

Unfortunately, many Christian believers fail to appreciate the fact that institutional racism is hard to eradicate. They are often inclined to believe that civil rights laws and similar legislation enacted by secular governments, as well as ecclesiastical statements and policies condemning racism, automatically eliminate expressions of racial prejudice and discrimination within and without the church.

### Conclusion

The Seventh-day Adventist church has from time to time issued some very strong statements against racism. For example, at the 1985 General Conference session in New Orleans, Louisiana, the church released a public statement denouncing racism as "one of the odious evils of our day," "a sin," and "a heresy and in essence a form of idolatry."[43] Yet, racism is still alive in the church. The church in North America is only now, through its "race summit," seeking "bold initiatives for dismantling racism" in the church. Why is this so?

One reason could be because many have failed to fully recognize how deeply embedded racism is in the structures of society and the church. Even when they do, they don't seem to know what to do about it. In this respect, society is doing a much better work than the church in mitigating the effects of institutional racism. But the church is unable to enforce remedial legislations and disciplinary measures to regulate the conduct of its members. In fact, many members and leaders don't even see a need to dismantle the race-based organizations of the church.

Is it any wonder that the church is still the most segregated of all institutions in society? In society the different races study together and work together; but in the church they seldom go to school or worship together. The different races of society entertain each other and play together; but in the church, they hardly ever sing and pray together. The impregnable walls of communism have come down; and yet, the church refuses to the allow its walls of racism to tumble down. Why is this so?

Could it be because we have not realized that *racism is actually a religion* that repudiates all the essential doctrines of Christianity? Perhaps, a correct understanding of the religious nature of racism may help us to see the urgency of doing something about racism. For racism is not simply an ideology of supremacy or an ideology of power. It is a religion.

---

**Endnotes**

[1]Jacques Barzun, *Race: A Study in Superstition* (New York: Harper and Row, 1965), ix.

[2]For a provocative analysis of what has happened to members of the Christian church, and what can be done to recapture their status as "resident aliens," see Stanley Hauerwas and William H. Willimon, *Resident Aliens: Life in the Christian Colony*, 9th printing (Nashville, TN: Abingdon Press, 1992). Speaking on the subject of Christian social concern today, Hauerwas and Willimon argue: "In fact, much of what passes for Christian social concern today, of the left or of the right, is the social concern of a church that seems to have despaired of being the church. Unable through our preaching, baptism, and witness to form a visible community of faith, we content ourselves with ersatz Christian ethical activity—lobbying Congress to support progressive strategies, asking the culture at large to be a little less racist, a little less promiscuous, a little less violent" (ibid., 80). With this kind of worldliness the Churches have become, in the words of Jesus, salt without savor, useful only to be "thrown out and trampled under foot by men" (Matt 5:13). Waldo Beach, "A Theological Analysis of Race Relations," in Paul Ramsey, ed., *Faith and Ethics: The Theology of H. Richard Niebuhr* (New York: Harper and Brothers, 1955), 218, has this worldliness in mind when he writes: "Seeking their life in quantity, they [churches] lose their life in quality and only earn the scorn of men."

[3]George D. Kelsey, *Racism and the Christian Understanding of Man* (New York: Scribner's, 1965), 10.

[4]G. E. Simpson and J. M. Yinger, *Racial and Cultural Minorities, An Analysis of Prejudice and Discrimination* (New York: Harper & Brothers, 1953), 546.

[5]David R. Williams, "The Right Thing to Do," *Adventist Review*, February 20, 1997, 24. Williams referred readers to work by James E. Dittes *Bias and the Pious: The Relationship Between Prejudice and Religion* (Minneapolis, Minn: Augsburg Publishing House, 1973).

[6]Billy Graham, "Racism and the Evangelical Church," *Christianity Today*, October 4, 1993, 27.

[7]For a documentation of how racism has sometimes been manifested in the Seventh-day Adventist Church, see Richard Schwarz, *Light Bearers to the Remnant* (Mountain View, CA: Pacific Press, 1979), 564-578; Calvin B. Rock, "A Better Way," *Spectrum* 2:2 (Spring 1970): 21-30; Louis B. Reynold, *We Have Tomorrow: The Story of American Seventh-day Adventists with an African Heritage* (Washington, DC: Review and Herald, 1984), especially appendix B—"Actions From the Regional Advisory Committee in Miami, April 7-9, 1969," 362-370; W. W. Fordham's autobiography, *Righteous Rebel: The Unforgettable Legacy of a Fearless Advocate for Change* (Washington, DC: Review and Herald, 1990).

[8]Harold L. Lee, *Church Leadership in a Multicultural World: Directions for Cultural Harmony in the Adventist Church* (Lincoln, Nebraska: Center for Creative Ministry, 2000), p. 14.

[9]Schwarz, *Light Bearers to the Remnant,* 571-572.

[10]See Jim Walters, "General Conference Delegates Say NO on Women's Ordination," *Adventist Today,* July-August, 1995, 13; Walters is an Adventist ethicist and an editor of *Adventist Today,* an independent publication whose stated purpose is to follow "basic principles of ethics and canons of journalism," striving "for fairness, candor, and good taste." Cf. J. David Newman, "Stuck in the Concrete," *Adventist Today,* July-August, 1995, 13. Newman last served as the editor of *Ministry,* "the international journal of the Seventh-day Adventist Ministerial Association." For a response to this kind of reasoning, see my *Receiving the Word: How New Approaches to the Bible Impact Our Biblical Faith and Lifestyle* (Berrien Springs, Mich.: Berean Books, 1996), 10-11, 91-92.

[11]This church leader wrote: "To be honest, at times I am frustrated with my church. Sometimes I feel it is somewhat out of tune with the times and the world I live in. Sometimes I get upset by its frequent failures to deal decisively with important issues. I wish my church could settle the issue of women's ordination (yes, I'm one of those people) and deal with a few other hot potatoes. And I often wonder why the church allows its fundamentalist fringe to set so much of its agenda. And yes, I need a double or triple portion of grace to interact with some people in the church" (Reinder Bruinsma, "Why I Stay," *Adventist Review,* July 1999, 8-12). Some readers may justifiably argue that, for Bruinsma, "the church" is nothing more than the "church in the west" which is pushing women's ordination; and the "fundamentalist fringe" is the rest of the world church that refuses to go along. Bruinsma is the secretary of one of the European Divisions.

[12]One can also cite the unilateral ordinations of women in some North American churches, as well as the recent issue of unisex ordination credential in the Southeastern California Conference as further evidences of the undying racial arrogance prevalent in certain quarters of North America.

[13]George R. Knight, *Anticipating the Advent: A Brief History of Seventh-day Adventists* (Boise, Idaho: Pacific Press, 1992), 112. Calvin Rock, has also offered some psychological, sociological, and theological factors that have historically led to white racism in the Adventist Church. Among other factors, Rock points to political expediency (the fear of a loss of prestige, finance, status and even loss of job) should racism be eliminated); an evangelistic strategy that is directed to the upper-lower and lower-middle class—the segment most threatened by racial parity; a certain kind of conservatism and fundamentalism that ignores the ethical dimension of the biblical doctrines; and a tendency to ignore social issues on the pretext that the situation is too hopeless for any meaningful change (Rock, "A Better Way," 22-24).

[14]The Race Summit was held at the Church's headquarters in Silver Spring, Maryland, from October 27-30. "Rather than merely talk about critical racial issues," the organizers of the meeting sought to "concentrate on the important question of how to bring about positive change in race relations, recommend bold initiatives for dismantling racism, and create an ongoing mechanism to continually motivate, expand, and monitor the progress of those initiatives." According to Celeste Ryan, more than 300 administrators and institutional heads were summoned to the summit. The 50 "renowed thought leaders" invited to speak included: Dr. Samuel Betances, futurist, author, motivational speaker, and senior consultant for Chicago-based Souder, Betances, and Associates, Inc.; Dr. Tony Campolo, professor of Sociology at Eastern College in St. Davids, PA, author of 26 books, and producer of "Hashing It Out," a weekly television show on the Odyssey Network; Dr. Edwin Nichols, a Washington, D.C. based psychologist, motivational speaker, and director of

Nichols and Associates, Inc.; Dr. Betty Lentz Siegel, nationally recognized lecturer and president of Kennesaw State University in GA; and Dr. Cain Hope Felder, professor of New Testament in the School of Divinity at Howard University in Washington, D.C. See, Celeste Ryan, "Adventist Church Hosts Race Relations Summit," *Adventist News Network* [ANN], October 19, 1999.

[15]Frank Stagg, *The Book of Acts* (Nashville, TN: Broadman Press, 1955), 124.

[16]With regard to the black/white form of racism, Cornel West, *Prophetic Fragments* (Grand Rapids, MI: Eerdmans, 1988), 100, observes: "The very category of 'race'—denoting primarily skin color—was first employed as a means of classifying human bodies by François Bernier, a French physician, in 1684. The first authoritative racial division of humankind is found in the influential *Natural System* (1735) of the preeminent naturalist Carolus Linnaeus."

[17]T. B. Maston, *The Bible and Race* (Nashville, TN: Broadman Press, 1959), 64.

[18]Slavery was first accepted as an economic way of life, and later justified as a positive good that was sanctioned by Scripture itself as capable of effecting Christian social order based on the observance of mutual duty of slave to master and vice versa. On how Christianity later came to play a part, Albert J. Raboteau, *Slave Religion: The "Invisible Institution" in the Antebellum South* (New York: Oxford University Press, 1978), 96, has remarked: "Right from the very beginning of the Atlantic slave trade, conversion of the slaves to Christianity was viewed by the emerging nations of Western Christendom as a justification for enslavement of Africans. . . . Pangs of guilt over the cruelty inherent in enslaving fellow human beings were assuaged by emphasizing the grace of faith made available to Africans, who otherwise would die as pagans."

[19]Barzun, xix, argues that "since 1850, when industrialization broke traditional bonds and detached man from his native soil without affording him new loyalties, the idea of race has been put forward as a principle of political and emotional union."

[20]Alan Burns, *Colour Prejudice* (London: George Allen and Unwin Ltd., 1948), 23 (cited by T. B. Maston, *The Bible and Race*, 64).

[21]The integration of this idea of Spencer with Darwin's theory of the evolution of species, "produced a seemingly scientific rationalization of the 19th century European and American view of the peoples of the world as two populations, one of which was superior to the other by reason of physical and mental characteristics. . . . This rationalization came to be known as Social Darwinism. . . . [This view] arose during the most active period of industrialization and developing colonialism. The issue was the weeding out of the weak, the ill, the poor, the 'socially unfit.'. . . The 'survival of the fittest' was an appropriate concept for that goal." See E. Tobach, J. Gianutsos, et. al., *The Four Horsemen: Racism, Sexism, Militarism, and Social Darwinism* (New York: Behavioral Publications, 1974), 99, 101.

[22]See Stephen T. Asma, "The New Social Darwinism: Deserving Your Destitution," *The Humanist* 53:5 (September-October, 1993), 12. Asma argues that the social Darwinism (more accurately social Spencerism) of Herbert Spencer, and his American disciples (e.g., John D. Rockefeller and Andrew Carnegie), with its foundation in the "survival of the fittest" ethic, not only fueled Western capitalism but also provided "the ultimate justification for social passivity and acquiescence in the status quo" on matters pertaining to the poor, homeless, unemployed, etc. (ibid., 11).

[23]Kelsey, 22-23; cf. Adolf Hitler, "The Aryan Race Is Superior," in Bruno Leone,

ed., *Racism: Opposing Viewpoints* (St. Paul, MN: Greenhaven Press, 1986), 211-214; Josiah Strong, "The Anglo-Saxon Race Should Colonize the World," in *Racism: Opposing Viewpoints*, 31-34; Albert J. Beveridge, "America Must Colonize," in *Racism: Opposing Viewpoints*, 20-25.

[24]Kelsey, 9.

[25]Manning Nash, "Race and the Ideology of Race," *Current Anthropology* 3 (1962): 285-288; William J. Wilson, *Power, Racism and Privilege* (New York: Free Press, 1973); Donald L. Noel, ed., *The Origins of American Slavery and Racism* (Columbus, OH: Merrill, 1972). An Adventist sociologist thus, defines racism (the ideology of supremacy) in this way: "Racism is both an attitude and an act of superiority that justifies its very existence by giving biological differences, such as skin color, texture of the hair, physical features, language, and cultural differences a negative meaning of inferiority. This negative meaning in turn legitimizes treating the other person as inferior to oneself." See Caleb Rosado, *Broken Walls* (Boise, Idaho: Pacific Press, 1990), 29.

[26]Allan Boesak, "He Made Us All, but . . ." in John W. DeGruchy and Charles Villa-Vicencio, eds., *Apartheid Is a Heresy* (Grand Rapids, MI: Eerdmans, 1983), 3.

[27]While Joseph Arthur comte de Gobineau (1816-1882) argued that "The White Race is Superior" (see Bruno Leone, ed., *Racism: Opposing Viewpoints*, 207-210), and Adolf Hitler, in his *Mein Kampf* (New York: Reynal & Hitchcok, 1939), insisted that "The Aryan Race is Superior" (see *Racism: Opposing Viewpoints*, 211-214), Albert J. Beveridge (1862-1927), a lawyer, US senator and historian, and Josiah Strong (1847-1916), a clergyman, social reformer and author, are two representatives of the views endorsing American or Anglo-Saxon racism (see Bruno Leone, ed., *Racism: Opposing Viewpoints*, 20-25; 31-34. On the other hand, Elijah Muhammad, the founder of the Nation of Islam religion may be cited as one of those advocating the superiority of the Black race (see his "The Black Race is Superior," ibid., 215-219); cf. the article by Leon Jaroff, "Teaching Reverse Racism," *Time,* April 4, 1994, 74-75, which also discusses some extremist views within the Afrocentric movement in which the history of black superiority is taught on the basis of melanism—the "science" of skin-pigmentation.

[28]For a discussion of the six major factors that shape a person's racial outlook—historical, sociocultural, situational, psychodynamic, phenomenological, earned reputation—see for example, Gordon W. Allport's *The Nature of Prejudice*, 4th printing (Reading, MA: Addison-Wesley Publishing Co., 1966), 206-218; cf. Robert Merton, "Discrimination and the American Creed," in Robert M. MacIver, ed., *Discrimination and National Welfare* (New York: Harper, 1949).

[29]In other words, racism's doctrine of biological determinism is "the glue" that defines and separates racial groups according to genes or "blood." Speaking about biological determinism, R. C. Lewontin, "Foreword" in Richard M. Lerner, *Final Solutions: Biology, Prejudice, and Genocide* (Pennsylvania, PA: Pennsylvania State University Press, 1992), vii-ix, states: "It makes the error of equating heritable with unchangeable, a biological mistake of the first magnitude"—a "pseudo-scientific nonsense."

[30]Richard Lerner, *Final Solutions: Biology, Prejudice, and Genocide*, has identified biological determinism as the central dogma of the Nazi ideology or religion, without which Nazism could not have achieved its power and realized its racial program of holocaust. Lerner maintains that biological determinism is the doctrine that underlies the early 20th century embryological work of Ernst Haeckel, F. Lenz, the ideas of the European and

American Social Darwinists of the nineteenth and twentieth centuries, the American and European eugenics movement during the same period, the German racial hygiene movement (Alfred Ploetz, Wilhelm Schallmayer, Karl Binding and Alfred Hoche) of the first half of the twentieth century, and the contemporary 'synthetic' science of sociobiology in biology and in the behavioral and social sciences (J. P. Ruston, E. O. Wilson, R. Dawkins, Daniel Freedman).

[31]Roger Daniels and Harry H. L. Kitano, *American Racism: Exploration of the Nature of Prejudice* (Englewood Cliffs, NJ: Prentice Hall Inc., 1970), 9-28, have argued that a racist society tends to go through four stages, each stage distinguishable by identifiable characteristics. In stage 1, a member of a minority (or despised) group finds himself avoided, stereotyped, and victimized by prejudice (informal rules operate here); in stages 2 and 3, he is deprived through discriminatory laws and insulated through segregation; finally in stage 4 the superior race adopts some extraordinary measures (isolation, exclusion and genocide). Historically this last stage has translated as apartheid, expulsion, exile, lynching, and concentration camps. Of these four stages, Daniels and Kitano maintain that stages two and three (discrimination/deprivation and segregation/insulation stages) "are *the most damaging steps in race relations*," since they provide the necessary condition for stage four (ibid., 20).

[32]Kelsey, *Racism and the Christian Understanding of Man,* 10-11.

[33]Ian Robertson, *Social Problems,* 2nd edition (New York: Random House, 1980), 210-211.

[34]Robertson, *Social Problems,* 211.

[35]See Michael Emerson and Christian Smith, *Divided by Faith: Evangelical Religion and the Problem of Race in America* (Oxford; New York: Oxford University Press, 2000). After conducting nationwide phone surveys of more than 2,000 white Evangelicals in North America, along with 200 face to face interviews, sociologists Emerson and Smith concluded that white Evangelicals cannot foster genuine racial reconciliation because they deny the existence of any ongoing racial problem in America, often blaming the media and oppressed minorities for refusing to forget the racial conflicts of the past. In the opinion of these two authors while many white Evangelicals may not be overtly racists, they are immersed in their "racialized society." For an Evangelical discussion and response to this study, see *Christianity Today,* October 2, 2000, 34-55.

[36]Lawrence Bobo, James R. Kluegel, and Ryan A. Smith, "Laissez-Faire Racism: The Crystallization of a Kinder, Gentler, Antiblack Ideology," in Steven A Tuch and Jack K. Martin, eds., *Racial Attitudes in the 1990s: Continuity and Change* (Westport, CT: Praeger, 1997), 15-42..

[37]Ibid., 16.

[38]Lawrence Bobo, "Group Conflict, Prejudice, and the Paradox of Contemporary Racial Attitudes," in P. A. Katz and D. A. Taylor, ed.s., *Eliminating Racism: Profiles in Controversy* (New York: Plenum, 1988), 85-114.

[39]P.G. Devine, "Stereotypes and Prejudice: Their Automatic and Controlled Components," *Journal of Personality and Social Psychology* 56 (1989):5-18.

[40]David R. Williams and Toni D. Rucker, "Understanding and Addressing Racial Disparities in Health Care," *Health Care Financing Review* 21/4 (Summer 2000):79. Williams and Rucker cite the following works: J. Allen, "A Remedy for Unthinking Discrimination," *Brooklyn Law Review* 61 (Winter 1995):1299-1345; S. L. Johnson,

"Unconscious Racism and the Criminal Law," *Cornell Law Review* 73 (July 1988):1016-1037; C. R. I. Lawrence, "The Id, the Ego, and Equal Protection: Reckoning with Unconscious Racism," *Stanford Law Review* 39 (January 1987):317-338; D. B. Oppenheimer, "Negligent Discrimination," *University of Pennsylvania Law Review* 141 (January 1993):899-972.

[41]See J. A. Davis and T. W. Smith, *General Social Surveys, 1972-1990* (Chicago: National Opinion Research Center, 1990). Two research sociologists summarize the findings thus: "29% of whites viewed most blacks as unintelligent, 44% believed that most blacks are lazy, 56% endorsed the view that most blacks prefer to live off welfare and 51% indicate that most blacks are prone to violence. Similarly, only relatively small percentages of whites were willing to endorse positive stereotypes of blacks. Only 20% of whites believed that most blacks are intelligent, 17% that most blacks are hardworking, 13% that most blacks prefer to be self-supporting, and 15% that most blacks are not prone to violence. Substantial numbers of whites opted for the "neither" category on these questions and about 5% volunteered that they did not know or had no answer to the stereotype question." See, David R. Williams and Ruth Williams-Morris, "Racism and Mental Health: The African American Experience," *Ethnicity and Health* 5/3 (2000):246. To place the stereotypes of Blacks into a comparative context, the survey also noted how Whites view themselves and other major racial or ethnic groups. The national data reveals that Blacks were viewed much more negatively than Whites: "Compared to how whites view most whites, they are five times more likely to view most blacks as unintelligent, nine times more likely to view most blacks as lazy, 15 times more likely to view most blacks as preferring to live off welfare, and three times more likely to be prone to violence. Hispanics and Asians are viewed more negatively than whites but a clear hierarchy of preference is evident. African Americans are viewed more negatively than any other group and Hispanics are viewed at least twice as negatively as Asians. On the other hand, Jews tend to be viewed more positively than whites in general. The persistence of pervasive stereotypes of African Americans suggests that there may be considerable cultural support for racist societal institutions and policies" (ibid., 246-247). Among other things, the above cited article documents and reviews available research data on changes in United States racial attitudes over time, the persistence of negative racial stereotypes, and the ways in which negative beliefs were incorporated into societal policies and institutions.

[42]David R. Williams and Toni D. Rucker, "Understanding and Addressing Racial Disparities in Health Care," *Health Care Financing Review* 21/4 (Summer 2000):75-90.

[43]"GC President Issues Statements on Racism, Peace, Home and Family, and Drugs," *Adventist Review*, June 30, 1985, 2-3. In the code of ethics for the Seventh-day Adventist minister, racism is condemned as a sinful practice (see, *Seventh-day Adventist Church Minister's Manual* [1992], 53). Cf. Victoria VanAllen, "Clergy Conference on Racism Addresses Current Issues" *Visitor* [Columbia Union Paper], June 15, 1993, 6. See also the document, "Christian Declaration on Race Relations," adopted by the Southern New England Conference of Seventh-day Adventists in session on March 1, 1970 (*Spectrum* 2:2 [Spring 1970]:53-55).

# 20

# RACISM AS A RELIGION

Since racism often expresses itself as a conflict among people of different ethnic and racial backgrounds, attempts to understand the nature of racism have typically centered on an analysis of political, economic, and cultural factors. Not much attention has been given to the religious nature of racism.[1]

When we think of religion, what usually comes to mind are the *supernatural* religions, such as the traditional world religions of Buddhism, Judaism, Christianity, Hinduism and Islam. These emphasize the supernatural and otherworldly values (like God, the Devil, angels, heaven, hell, etc.). But there are other kinds of religion which have essentially no place for supernatural realities. These religions, known as *secular* religions, include communism, socialism, fascism, and secular humanism.[2]

Racism may be classed with the latter group of religions. It is one of the most powerful *secular* religions in today's world. Like the other secular religions, racism is competing with Christianity. Let me illustrate by comparing Christianity with the secular religions of communism and racism.[3]

All three religions—Christianity, communism and racism—(1) revere and obey their leaders (Christ, Marx, Hitler, respectively); (2) rely on authoritative writings (Bible, the writings of Marx and Lenin, or Gobineau's *Essay on the Inequality of the Human Races* (1853);[4] (3) condemn the evils in society and seek to provide answers to societal problems (but they differ in their understanding of the nature and causes of the evil); (4) extol lofty ideals of justice, equity and brotherhood as basic to meaningful human existence; (5) require absolute obedience, commitment and self-sacrifice; (6) are zealous in winning converts; (7) require faith and confidence that the ideals of their religion will ultimately triumph.

Apparently, because racism has been so well domesticated among those who profess Christianity, few recognize the religious nature of racism. If, however, racism is seen as another religion in competition with Christianity, then the simultaneous adherence, by some Christians, to the God of the Bible and the idol of race is a form of polytheism, and their religious profession is syncretistic.

Such Christians may claim to live under the authority of the God of the Bible in many respects, but because they serve two different gods, when they are confronted with crucial matters of race it will soon be apparent that the idol of race will determine their attitude, decision, and action.

### Characteristics of the Religion of Racism

Racism is (1) an attempt to find meaning for human existence by looking to one's race as the center of value and the object of devotion; (2) a religious faith in an unverifiable belief in the inherent superiority of a race—a faith for which countless people will gladly work, suffer, kill, and die.

**Characteristics.** As a religion, racism shares all the essential characteristics of every other religion (secular or supernatural). Thus, racism has its own:

(1) *Sacred* realities, which may take the form of a tangible object (such as a Confederate or Nazi flag[5]), or even a person (e.g. Adolf Hitler or Elijah Muhammad);

(2) Sets of *beliefs*, which are creeds and myths that attempt to explain the origin and nature of reality;

(3) *Practices*, which are the active observable sides of religion (and may include acts of discrimination, violence, segregation, etc. and may involve rituals and ceremonies, such as wearing a special kind of clothing or hair style);

(4) *Symbolisms*, which are an attempt to express the essence of the racist faith by evoking a religious emotion in the follower; in Nazi Germany the symbols used included the swastika, the stretched-out hand

and the phrase "*Heil Hitler*";
(5) *Community of worshipers,* which is the social group that shares the beliefs and practices of the racist religion; the racist community may be a church, a tribe (and their practice is tribalism), a gang (whether respectable, like the apartheid government of South Africa, or ignoble, e.g., the Skinheads or Ku Klux Klan), or a nation (in which case the civil religion becomes known as fascism);
(6) *Moral values,* which are the racist community's sense of right and wrong, which it seeks to preserve and transmit to future generations, for the survival of that group (e.g. the view that it is wrong to integrate churches and schools, or marry people of other races, or employ qualified workers of the other races).

**Some Religious Doctrines of Racism**

Racism is not just an ideology of race or power. It is also a religion that has its own sets of beliefs and practices. This fact is rarely recognized. However, in her definition of racism, anthropologist Ruth Benedict has correctly suggested that racism is a religion (1) that is established on a naturalistic world view,[6] and (2) which has the superior race as the focus of its future (or eschatological) hope and its philosophy of history. Identifying the three cardinal dogmas of the racist faith, Benedict writes that racism is:

> the dogma that one ethnic group is condemned by Nature to hereditary inferiority and another group is destined to hereditary superiority. It is the dogma that the hope of civilization depends upon eliminating some races and keeping others pure. It is the dogma that one race has carried progress throughout human history and can alone ensure future progress.[7]

The following remarks will briefly summarize the racist faith and show why it is incompatible with biblical Christianity.

**Epistemology: Religious Starting Point.** Epistemology asks: How does one come to a knowledge of truth? Biblical Christianity teaches that the way to come to a dependable knowledge of truth about reality is "from above"—through the revelation of God in Jesus Christ and His written Word (2 Tim 3:15-17; John 17:3).

The religion of racism, on the other hand, distorts the biblical method by offering two alternative sources of knowledge, both of which are "from below": (1) internal source (self-knowledge), and (2) external source (knowledge of the other race). Both of these are a reflection on the human situation.

Racists hold that in order to really understand what is going on in a given social context, one must belong to the alleged superior race. Thus, a statement like, "You don't understand because you are not black/white/Hispanic," may have racist overtones, in that understanding is predicated on identification with a given race. The subtle implication is that unless one is black/white/Hispanic, one cannot fully appreciate or empathize with people of those races.

In this respect racist epistemology is similar to those reflected in theologies of liberation, feminism, and homosexuality which also assert that one can only know the truth about a particular reality when one is poor or oppressed, a woman, or a gay. One way racism reinforces this idea of self-knowledge is through versions of teaching dubbed ethnic pride/identity.

Alternatively, the external source of religious knowledge for the racist is obtained through a knowledge of the other race. This is illustrated in statements like: "You must know the truth about the black/white man, if ________" or "You've got to understand the black/white/Hispanic person's thinking or ability if ________"). The knowledge being sought usually is in the form of stereotypes (exaggerated beliefs/myths/jokes) about the different races.

There are two major problems with the racist way of knowing. First, it distorts the essential humanness of all races by exaggerating the significance of their outward appearances at the expense of their inner kinship of spirit. This inner relatedness of all races (analogous to what theologians refer to as *congeniality*) is established on the fact that all human beings were created in the image of God, and consequently have been endowed with a capacity to understand, empathize, appreciate, and communicate with all races—irrespective of their racial backgrounds.

Second, since racist epistemology is "from below" and not "from above," racist theology tends to look up to sociology, anthropology, history, and science, rather than to biblical revelation, to provide explanations and answers to racial problems. It should be noted that while the Bible is sometimes consulted by the racists, the Bible plays only a supportive role, bolstering postures that have already been taken; even then, Scriptural passages are used selectively.

For example, those who justify racial segregation on Scriptural grounds often do so on the grounds of an alleged Biblical mandate. They argue that "God himself has separated the races" (a) by geographical barriers (Acts 17:26), (b) by differences in color and other racial characteristics (Gen 10:5, 32; 11:1-9), (c) by His blessings and curse on son of Noah (Gen 9:24-27), and (d) by His notable example of making Israel separate from all other races—forbidding intermarriage of Israelites with others (Gen 24:3-4; 28:1; Deut 7:1-3, 6; Josh 23:12-13; Ezra 9:1-2, 10-12; 1 Kings 8:53; Exod 33:16). But in actual fact, none of these prohibitions are grounded on race.[8]

**Doctrine of Creation.** The Bible's teaching of the biological unity and racial parity of all people is established by its doctrine of creation. When, for example, Paul declared that God "hath made of one blood all nations of men for to dwell on all the face of the earth" (Acts 17:26), his statement emphasizes two important facts: "On one hand, the entire creation is unified in the *One God*. On the other hand, biological unity is affirmed, for all men are of *one blood*."[9]

Commenting on this text, Ellen White wrote: "In the sight of God all are on an equality; and to the Creator every human being owes supreme allegiance."[10] The biblical doctrine of the seventh-day Sabbath is an eternal witness to God as Creator (Exod 20:8-11), and hence, the reason why He alone is worthy of our worship (Rev 14:6, 7). The religion of racism, however, denies this biblical doctrine of creation by (1) challenging the character of God as a perfect Creator; (2) inverting the order *in* creation; and (3) undermining the nature *of* creation.

The Genesis creation account states that at the conclusion of each phase of God's creative activity, God Himself declared His creation as good. Racism's teaching of the genetic or ontological inferiority of some races not only negates this biblical teaching of a perfect creation from the hands of God, but it also affronts the character of God. For if part of God's original creation is inherently defective, it implies that God is no better than the Demiurge of second century Gnosticism, an imperfect creator god who is responsible for introducing error into his creation.

Also, by teaching the supremacy of a race, and hence the domination of one by another, racist theology sets itself against the biblical teaching about the order in creation. This racist teaching implies that some races of human beings belong to the natural order; they are not part of the human family to whom was entrusted the responsibility of having dominion over the created things (Gen 1:26). One theologian has correctly argued that the racist understanding of man involves "an inversion of the very order of creation," and runs "directly counter to the divine purpose of grace upon which the whole creation depends."[11]

Finally, by teaching that his own race is superior to all others, the racist seeks "to think of himself more highly than he ought to think" (Rom 12:3). It is self-glorification or self-religion—the worship of "the creature rather than the Creator" (Rom 1:25).[12]

Thus, racism is the highest form of self-deification. The fact that God's judgment—in the form of guilt, frustration, hostility, etc.—is being visited on the human race is an indication that God will not remain silent when people "exchange the truth of God for a lie" and worship the creature rather than the Creator.

**Doctrine of Human Beings.** The Bible teaches that human beings were created in God's image. Not only do they possess intrinsic value or equal worth before God, but they are also endowed with the power of choice. As the *Seventh-day Adventist Fundamental Belief, #7* puts it, "man and woman were made in the image of God with individuality, the power and freedom to think and to do. . . ."

Because they have the power of choice, human beings are free moral agents, in the sense that "they make their own decisions as to what they will do, choosing as they please in the light of their sense of right and wrong and the inclinations they feel" and as such they are "answerable to God and each other for their voluntary choices."[13]

Racism, however challenges this important biblical doctrine. Its naturalistic teaching of the inherent superiority and inferiority of the races implies a certain kind of biological or genetic determinism.

According to this religion of racism belief, if a person succeeds or fails in a particular field of study (e.g., athletic sport or academics) it is because that person has been "predestined" by his/her genes to succeed or fail. What a person does, or what he/she becomes is biologically predetermined or built into him/her at conception. In other words, a person's personhood or moral worth, or lack of it, is determined by his or her hereditary endowment.

Whenever we make stereotypical comments alleging that Asians/Blacks/Hispanics/Jews/Whites "are by nature ________" or whenever, we try to distance our selves from people of other races because "there's something about them that is repulsive to me," these attitudes and statements are echoes of the naturalistic world view upon which the biological determinism of racism is founded.

Biological determinism is not only pseudoscientific, it is also pessimistic, in that it puts limits on human performance and potential. Moreover, this doctrine of racism is dangerously fatalistic in its suggestion that a particular race cannot transcend the artificial barrier that has been erected upon them by racist theology. If this doctrine of racist theology were true, there would be no human accountability of the actions of people, and there would also be no basis for divine judgment for human conduct, but the latter is a primary teaching of the Bible (Acts 17:31; Rev 14:6, etc.).

**Doctrine of the Fall and Sin.** The Bible teaches that, although human beings were created perfect, as a consequence of Adam's fall "all [including the so-called superior race] have sinned, and come short of the glory of God" (Rom 3:23; 5:12; 1 Cor 15:22). The Seventh-day Adventist Statement of Belief (7) reads:

> When our first parents disobeyed God, they denied their dependence upon Him and fell from their high position. The image of God in them was marred and they became subject to death. Their descendants share this fallen nature and its consequences. They are born with weaknesses and tendencies to evil . . . . [14]

In so far as a fallen human being makes himself or some collective projection of himself the object of love and value, the racist faith denies a fall for the superior race, and therefore denies the biblical doctrine of original sin—universal sin originating from Adam.

Even if racist theology admits that the superior race has also fallen, it has to reinterpret the nature of the fall in order to be true to its racist doctrine of an inferior/superior race. Thus, for example, the doctrine that some human beings are defective in their very being implies that the so-called inferior races have experienced a double-fall—the first being due to the fall of Adam, and the second, a special racial fall. Alternatively, since, to the racist, the loss of racial purity and race-mixing is a sin against the Creator,[15] racist theology has to teach that, the superior race experiences a fall whenever it allows its blood to mix with the inferior race.[16]

The Bible does not teach such a doctrine. For if it were true, (1) the superior race would have no need for the atonement of Jesus Christ, since it does not accept its fallen condition, and (2) the inferior race would have no hope of redemption since it would need a second sacrifice of Jesus to atone for their second racial fall. Ultimately, the racist doctrine of the fall is an affront to the character of God.

**The Doctrine of the Great Controversy.** The Bible teaches that there exists a great controversy between Christ and His people on one hand, and Satan and his people on the other (Eph 6:10ff). In this cosmic conflict the issue centers upon the character of God, as is reflected in the sinless life of the incarnate Christ and expressed in the moral Ten-Commandment Law.[17]

The religion of racism also acknowledges that there is a cosmic conflict between two major forces. However, it challenges the biblical teaching by redefining the participants in the conflict along racial lines.

Thus, when racists talk about the great controversy in the supernatural realm, they recast God and His angels in the image of the superior race. And they perceive Satan and his evil angels as the essence of the inferior race. Racists concept of the great controversy is simply an amplification of a race war on earth.

And when racists bring this cosmic war or dualism into the natural realm, they create a "We versus Them" dichotomy among people. In the context of black/white racism, even non-human objects are assigned to their black and white spheres (e. g., black sheep, black market, black list), and personal problems between people of different races are recast along racial lines. There are even different colors for sin as, for example, white lies, blue-collar crimes, etc.

Racists accept as an *a priori* truth that there is an unbridgeable gulf between the races, and that there is a cosmic conflict between them in which each individual is expected to stand up for his or her kind.[18] In this kind of dualism, racial harmony, according to racist theology, is ensured when members of the different races know "their place" in society.

In other words, to avoid conflict the two worlds must be kept apart, separated or segregated (in housing, jobs, churches, or marriage). Racism believes that the different races must live their lives apart from each other as if the other does not exist.[19]

Thus, Christians who are racists can live in the same town or city, without ever visiting the home of another race, attending their church, or school. In the context of the race-based conferences in North America, racists may belong to the same Union, but hardly be aware of the existence of the other Conference. Out of sight means out of mind. And when the other race comes to the racist's church, the racist Christian will politely suggest: "there is another church over there where you will feel more comfortable." Furthermore, the racist minister make no efforts to evangelize other races in his area. Even when a member of the despised race seeks membership in his church, the minister will piously transfer the new member to a congregation next door that belongs to the despised race.

Writes an Adventist sociologist:

> It is a well-documented reality across a broad range of institutions in American society that most Whites leave when the percentage of Blacks exceeds 25 percent. Almost all of the integration that has taken place within the North American church has been in one direction: Black Adventists joining predominantly White congregations. How many Adventist churches, Black or White, would welcome a minister of a different race?[20]

Whenever we attempt to regulate the growing numbers of certain ethnic groups in our communities, churches, or institutions, and whenever we resort to race flight when other races join our church, we are simply putting in practice a key doctrine of the racist faith.

**Philosophy of History.** In the Bible's view, all of history unfolds under God's planning and direction. This is because it was God who brought creation into being to be the "arena of history"; He also created time to measure the "movement of history" and He formed the human being to be an "entity inhabiting history."[21] Thus, history always proceeds under God's divine sovereignty. Ellen G. White captures this God-centered (or theocentric) view of history in this way:

> In the annals of human history the growth of nations, the rise and fall of empires, appear as dependent on the will and prowess of man. The shaping of events seems, to a great degree, to be determined by his power, ambition, or caprice. But in the word of God the curtain is drawn aside, and we behold, behind, above, and through all the play and counterplay of human interests and power and passions, the agencies of the all-merciful One, silently, patiently working out the counsels of His own will.[22]

The religion of racism, however, overthrows this biblical view of history. In this religion, the superior race, not God, is the center of human history. And the forces which shape history are the polar opposites of races—the clash between the superior and inferior races.

The view in racism is similar to that in the secular religion of communism. But whereas, in communism, economic forces (or substructure) are believed to create the proletariat and bourgeois social classes, and whereas the clash between the two becomes the basis for the interpretation of the meaning of history, in the religion of racism, the shaping forces of history are determined by genetic (not economic) forces. Also, because in the racist religion it is only "one race [the superior race that] has carried progress throughout human history and can alone ensure future progress,"[23] meaningful history is that which is associated with the superior race. Unless the superior race is involved somehow in an event, there is no history.

Thus, for example, the racist not only ignores, discounts, or distorts the histories of other races, but also, will not want to listen or learn from other races. After all, the only history worth recording or paying attention to is the history of, or the history interpreted by, the superior race.[24]

While racism cannot be blamed for every failure to recognize the contributions and potentials of people of color, one may wonder if racial arrogance plays no part in the Christian Church's seeming unwillingness to give equal opportunity and recognition to Christians of all races in the theological, missiological and administrative activities of the church's life?

A recapture of the true biblical conception of God's leading in history (cf. Acts 11:17) can correct the pervasive spirit that is actuated by racism's morality of pride and contempt for the other race when it comes to the Church's life and work.

**Value of Human Life.** Christianity's ethic of race relations is predicated on the belief in the "*sanctity* of human life"—the belief that since human beings were created in the image of God, all human lives have *equal* value and worth, and should, therefore, be treated with respect and dignity. Thus, the commandment, "Thou shall not kill," applies to all human life, regardless of any external characteristics.

Racism, however, upholds the "*quality* of human life" doctrine. This belief maintains that since the personhood of human beings is supposedly determined by their biological or genetic characteristics, some human lives have only a *relative* value.

According to the quality-of-human-life ethic (also known as utilitarianism or situation ethics),[25] since some human beings are not true persons, where necessary (i.e. to enhance the quality of life of the superior persons), they may be exploited and even killed.

The institution of slavery in the United States is one classic example of racism's "quality-of-human-life" ethic. Thus, in 1857 the US Supreme Court ruled, in the *Dred Scott* case, that the Black race was less than human and that a slave could be treated as the personal property of the owner. Chief Justice Roger Taney (himself a slave owner) argued:

> They [Blacks] had for more than a century been regarded as beings of an inferior order, and altogether unfit to associate with the white race, either in social or political relations; and so far inferior, that they had no rights which the white man was bound to respect; and that the negro might justly and lawfully be reduced to slavery for his benefit. He was bought and sold, and treated as an ordinary article of merchandise and traffic, whenever a profit could be made by it.[26]

The quality-of-human-life ethic which the religion of racism embraces leads to a devaluation of human life. By dying on the cross for them, the God of Christianity paid a high price in order to elevate human beings. But the racist faith seeks to dehumanize them for profit.

**Doctrine of Redemption.** Biblical Christianity teaches that the redemption of the human race, secured once and for all by Jesus Christ through His substitutionary atonement on Calvary, will be ushered in at His second coming (John 14:1-3; 1 Thess 4:14ff.; 2 Pet 3) and be consummated in the earth made new (Rev 21). In other words, the redemption of the human race is a divine act graciously extended to all—Jews and Gentiles—who have accepted Jesus Christ as their Lord and Savior.

However, in the religion of racism, since the Fall means racial impoverishment, the mixing of the blood of the superior race with that of inferior, "the essence of redemption is racial renewal, the revivification of the superior race by techniques of purification."[27] In other words, racist theology teaches that human beings (the super-race) can effect their own redemption. This doctrine that has led to the subordination, oppression, deprivation and extermination of the alleged inferior races (Blacks, Jews, poor, mentally ill, deformed, weak, criminals, etc.). The belief flows out of racism's mechanistic doctrine of human nature.

Given its belief in biological or genetic determinism, the reasoning of racists regarding the future hope (eschatology) may go somewhat like this: Since changing the environment cannot change behavior, the superior race must take steps to protect itself and its superior genes from being diminished by members of the inferior race. When this kind of reasoning is adopted as a social policy, it leads to a delimitation, degradation, and dehumanization of some races.

In the legal racism of Nazi Germany and apartheid South Africa, for example, this doctrine led to the promulgation of laws that curtail the freedom of movement, or rights of property, or citizenship, or freedom of marriage, and in some extreme cases, collection, or "concentration" of the inferior races and, perhaps, the ultimate or final solution to ensure permanent protection of the superior race. For if some races are inherently superior and others inferior, the superior race must be bred and the inferior race must be eliminated.

Charles Darwin is often cited for laying the scientific foundation for this aspect of the racist faith. The second half of the title of Darwin's famous book, *The Origin of Species by Means of Natural Selection, or the Survival of Favored Races in the Struggle for Life*, was understood by some to justify the extermination of people of other races.[28] However, Friedrich Nietzsche was a more blatant advocate of "the survival of favored races in the struggle for life." Nietzsche is widely believed to have provided Hitler with a philosophical justification for his "final solution" to the problem of inferior races.[29]

The racist doctrine of redemption ultimately leads to the extermination of inferior races. It is this belief that Ruth Benedict has in mind when she defines racism's second dogma as a belief that "the hope of civilization depends upon eliminating some races and keeping others pure."[30]

In pursuing racism's future (eschatological) dream, a number of techniques have been used over the years. These range from race improvement techniques (such as psychological motivation or group affirmation of self, or identity seminars) to "scientific" programs of social engineering like positive and negative eugenics. The eminent English scientist, Francis Galton, a cousin of Charles Darwin is credited with proposing in 1883 a new science—eugenics (from the Greek, meaning "good in birth" or "noble in heredity")—which aimed at ensuring that the best of human stock survived. As explained by D. J. Kevles, in his book *In the Name of Eugenics*, this new science was intended to give "the more suitable race or strains of blood a better chance of prevailing speedily over the less suitable."[31]

Positive eugenics involves the multiplication of the superior race by careful selection and breeding of people possessing superior genes. This is one reason why racists do not encourage inter-racial marriage. Such marriages allegedly taint the pure blood of the racist.

Negative eugenics, on the other hand, may take several forms, including efforts that prevent procreation by inferior races (e.g., by using contraceptives, sterilization, etc.), and those involving ethnic or racial cleansing or the elimination of the unwanted inferior race (whether it is by warfare, lynching, eugenic-abortions, euthanasia, or even nuclear experimentation).

## Conclusion

The forgoing discussion has outlined the belief system of the secular religion called racism. On the fundamental question of how to know truth, a study philosophers call epistemology, racists believe you have to be part of their group in order to fully understand the truth about reality. In this regard, racism is no different from gay and feminist ideologies, both of which also maintain that a person must be part of the in-group (i.e., be born a homosexual or a woman) in order to gain an accurate knowledge about a situation.

Racism's religious faith denies the biblical doctrine of creation by questioning the character of God in creating all races and declaring them all as good. Not only does it undermine the nature *of* creation, but also its teaching of the supremacy of a race inverts the order *in* creation by maintaining that some races of human beings belong to the natural order and are, thus, not a part of the human family. In questioning God's creation order and intent, racism shares the basic framework of feminism's egalitarian ideology which repudiates male-female role distinctions (the biblical doctrine of headship) as a consequence of the Fall, rather than a part of God's original creation. Whereas racism errs, saying God created inequality of race at creation, feminism errs when, in the name of equality, it decries God's creational order regarding gender role-distinctions in the home and in the church.

Racism's doctrine of the great controversy is the basis of its practice of racial segregation and all race based facilities and institutions. Racism's philosophy of history makes the superior race the center of history, and gives credibility to the practice of ignoring, discounting, or distorting the history and contributions of people of other races. Racism's *quality* of human life ethic allows racist to treat other human beings not as true persons, but as things to be exploited for profit. And racism's doctrine of redemption provides the theological foundation for the delimitation, degradation, dehumanization, and ultimate destruction of people deemed inferior.

It should now be clear that racism, in whatever form it may appear, is indeed antithetical to biblical religion. If this is the case, then Bible-believing Christians—individuals who have been saved by grace and are seeking to live under the Lordship of Jesus Christ—cannot accept this secular religion. To do so is to deny the biblical faith.

---

**Endnotes**

[1]One notable exception is George D. Kelsey, *Racism and the Christian Understanding of Man* (New York: Scribners, 1965). To my knowledge, this work, to which I am indebted for insights expressed in this chapter, is probably the most detailed analysis of racism as a faith system.

[2]For a helpful discussion of the nature, characteristics, and types of religion, see Elizabeth K. Nottingham, *Religion and Society* (New York: Random House, 1954), 1-11. Our analysis, in this section, of racism as a religion builds upon this work by Nottingham.

[3]The following are adapted from the comparison between Christianity and Communism, provided by Richard J. Gehman, *African Traditional Religion in Biblical Perspective* (Kijabe, Kenya: Kesho Publications, 1989), 38.

[4]The Frenchman, Count Joseph Arthur de Gobineau, is recognized as the "Father of Modern Racism" and one of the first contributors to the science of racism (see Bruno Leone, ed., *Racism: Opposing Viewpoints*, 207; Michael D. Biddiss, *Father of Racist Ideology: The Social and Political Thought of Count Gobineau* [New York: Weybright and Talley, 1970]). Gobineau used the word *Aryan*, a word that had been used by linguistic scholars

for a number of related languages, including German and Latin) to denote a supreme and original white race. David A. Rausch, *A Legacy of Hatred: Why Christians Must Not Forget the Holocaust*, 2nd ed. (Grand Rapids, MI: Baker, 1990), 34-35, summarizes Gobineau's views on race: "Gobineau claimed that race was the determining factor in the rise and fall of civilizations, postulating a hierarchy of humanity ranging from the superior white race to the inferior black race. Racial mixing had brought decline to the Latin and Semitic peoples, whereas Aryan Germans—the western Germanic tribes—held the key to a successful human destiny. These powerful people, he said, could be brought down only by the degenerative effect of race mixing" (cf. Biddiss, 112-121). Building on the work of Gobineau, Adolf Hitler articulated in his *Mein Kampf*, "a book that became the bible of the Nazi movement in Germany," why the Aryan race was superior to all others (see *Racism: Opposing Viewpoints*, 211).

[5]Patriotic citizens of various nations handle their flags with reverential awe. For example, reading through the U.S. Flag Code, adopted in 1923 and which prescribes the following rules for proper handling of the flag, one gets the impression that the flag is a religious object of worship : (1) Always display the flag with the blue union field up; never display the flag upside down, except as a distress signal. (2) Always hold the flag carefully; never let it touch anything beneath it: the ground, the floor, water or merchandise. (3) Always carry the flag aloft and free; never carry it flat or horizontally. (4) Always keep the flag clean and safe; never let it become torn, soiled or damaged. (5) Always dispose of a flag properly; it should be destroyed by burning it in a dignified manner. (6) Always treat the flag with respect; never embroider it on household items or pieces of clothing. See "Our Flag: How to Honor and Display It," available through the National Flag Foundation, Flag Plaza, Dept. A., Pittsburgh, PA 15219-3630. Or review it on the web site: www.AmericanFlags.org.

[6]The naturalistic world view is built on the assumption that nothing exists outside the material mechanical natural order. This world view was "born in the eighteenth century, it came of age in the nineteenth and grew to maturity in the twentieth" (see James W. Sire, *The Universe Next Door* [Downers Grove, IL: Intervarsity, 1988], 82). According to Ronald Nash, the naturalistic world view offers "the major competition" to the Christian world view ( Ronald H. Nash, *Worldviews in Conflict* [Grand Rapids, MI: Zondervan, 1992], 116). For a discussion of how a world view shapes a person's lifestyle, see Samuel Koranteng-Pipim, "Contemporary Culture and Christian Lifestyle: A Clash of Worldviews," *Journal of the Adventist Theological Society* 4 (Spring 1993): 129-150.

[7]Ruth Benedict, *Race: Science and Politics* (New York: Viking Press, 1959), 98.

[8]For a discussion of some of the texts used to justify racism, see Cain Hope Felder, "Race, Racism and the biblical Narratives," in *Stony the Road We Trod*, ed. Cain Hope Felder, (Minneapolis, MN: Fortress Press, 1991), 127-145; T. B. Maston, *The Bible and Race*, 105-117; Douglas Bax, "The Bible and Apartheid [Part] 2," in *Apartheid Is a Heresy*, 112-143.

[9]Talbert O. Shaw, "Racism and Adventist Theology," *Spectrum* 3:4 (Autumn 1971): 33.

[10]Ellen G. White, *The Acts of Apostles* (Mountain View, CA: Pacific Press, 1911), 238.

[11]T. F. Torrance, *Calvin's Doctrine of Man* (London: Lutherworth Press, 1949), 24.

[12]"From the standpoint of classical Christian thought, of course, racial prejudice is not

one of a catalogue of sins, but is a facet or expression of the single sin of pride, the rejection of the Infinite Sovereign Source of life and the attempt to set up as final some substitute sovereignty derived from the finite. Insofar as fallen man tends to make of himself or some collective projection of himself the center of love and value. Racial pride within and discriminatory practices are one ready way among many to 'exchange the truth of God for a lie,' and to worship the creature rather than the Creator." See Waldo Beach, "A Theological Analysis of Race Relations," in *Faith and Ethics*, 211.

[13]James I. Packer, *Concise Theology* (Wheaton, IL: Tyndale House, 1993), 85.

[14]SDA Fundamental Belief 7; for the full statement and a discussion of Adventists understanding of the fall, see *Seventh-day Adventists Believe . . . : A Biblical Exposition of 27 Fundamental Doctrines* (Washington D.C.: Ministerial Association of the General Conference of Seventh-day Adventists, 1988), 78-96.

[15]Hitler, *Mein Kampf*, 392-393.

[16]Hitler maintains that whereas everything in the world can be improved as long as the blood remains preserved in its purity, "Alone the loss of the purity of blood destroys the inner happiness forever; it eternally lowers man, and never again can its consequences be removed from body and mind" (Hitler, *Mein Kampf*, 452). Lothrop Stoddard concurs: "Racial impoverishment is the plague of civilization"; it is a "hideous disease" that has reduced "the proudest societies to charred and squalid ruin" (Stoddard, *The Revolt against Civilization* [New York: C. Scribner's Sons, 1922], 88).

[17]See *Seventh-day Adventists Believe . . .* , 98-105, for a summary discussion of "the great controversy" doctrine. For a more detailed and theological discussion of the theme, see the five volume Conflict of the Ages series by Ellen G. White [*Patriarchs and Prophets, Prophets and Kings, Desire of Ages, Acts of the Apostles, and the Great Controversy*] (Mountain View, CA: Pacific Press, 1890-1917). The implication of "the great controversy" doctrine for ethics can be found in my "Contemporary Culture and Christian Lifestyle," 143-147, see footnote #41.

[18]Lewis C. Copeland, "The Negro as a Contrast Conception," in Edgar T. Thompson, ed., *Race Relations and the Race Problem* (New York: Greenwood Press, 1968), 168.

[19]*Racial* segregation must be distinguished from various forms of *voluntary* segregation or separation, that are functionally necessary to accomplish a task. For example, there may be nothing wrong when churches are organized for groups that cannot understand a particular dominant language. "[*Racial*] Segregation is born in hatred, fear, pride, and contempt. It knows nothing of love and does not aim at the general well-being; it is inspired by the spirit of pride and hostility, generated by the racist faith. Segregation is anticommunity. It is the structured will to deprive and reduce the life of the other. The appointed 'place' of the other is *below*, and the functions of the other are the structured servilities of society" (Kelsey, 98).

[20]David Williams, "The Right Thing To Do," *Adventist Review,* February 20, 1997, 26.

[21]Gerhard Maier, *Biblical Hermeneutics,* trans. Robert W. Yarbrough (Wheaton, IL: Crossway, 1994), 23.

[22]Ellen G. White, *Education* (Mountain View, CA: Pacific Press, 1903), 173.

[23]Benedict, *Race: Science and Politics,* 98; thus, Joseph Gobineau, the "Father of Modern Racism," argues that history "shows us that all civilizations derive from the white race, that none can exist without its help, and that a society is great and brilliant

only so far as it preserves the blood of the noble group that created it, provided that this group itself belongs to the most illustrious branch of our species" (see Bruno Leone, *Racism: Opposing Views*, 13, 210).

[24]For an example of Eurocentric and Afrocentric reinterpretations of history, see Robert Hughes, *Culture of Complaint: The Fraying of America* (New York: Oxford University Press, 1993), 102-147.

[25]Joseph Fletcher is a leading proponent of this quality of life ethic. See his *Humanhood: Essays in Biomedical Ethics* (Buffalo, NY: Prometheus, 1979), 12-18, where he provides fifteen positive and five negative criteria for measuring the quality of one's life and whether a person achieved humanhood; elsewhere, Fletcher reduces the criteria to "four indicators" (see his "Four Indicators of Humanhood—The Enquiry Matures," *The Hastings Center Report 4*, no. 6 (December 1974): 4-7.

[26]*Dred Scott v. Sandford*, 60 U.S. 393 at 404. A detailed discussion of the *Dred Scott* decision is found in Curt Young, *The Least of These* (Chicago, IL: Moody Press, 1984), 1-20; see also Richard Fredericks, "Who Deserves to Live?: Toward an Ethic of Compassion," *Signs of the Times*, April 1990, 3-5.

[27]Kelsey, 162.

[28]See, for example, Jacques Barzun, *Race: A Study in Superstition* (New York: Harper and Row, 1965), 47-48.

[29]Refer to Friedrich Nietzsche, *The Antichrist* (New York: Alfred Knopf, 1931), 41-60.

[30]Benedict, *Race: Science and Politics*, 98.

[31]D. J. Kevles, *In the Name of Eugenics* (New York: Knopf, 1985), ix,

# 21

# WHY IS RACISM WRONG?

When Christians who claim to be saved by grace choose to live by race, they are essentially embracing a form of legalism. They depend on their race, rather than on our Lord Jesus Christ, to save them. This is no different from the legalism adopted by believers in the Galatian Church. The apostle Paul raised this issue when he demanded to know why the Galatian believers, having begun in the Spirit, were seeking to live by the works of the (flesh) law (Galatians 3:2, 3).

According to Paul, such an effort on the part of believers is tantamount to "seeking to be justified by the law"—instead of by grace (Gal 5:4). He referred to their action as a perversion of and departure from the gospel (Gal 1:6, 7) and from Christ (5:4). He argued that those "bewitched" by this "folly" were in bondage and under a curse. Paul's goal in the epistle to the Galatians was not only to show the incompatibility of being saved by grace and at the same time living by the works of the law, but also to emphasize the fact that there is an ethical dimension to the gospel of grace.

We should not miss the analogy. Christians respond, all too often, to issues of racism only when the sociopolitical realities force them to do so. Even then, instead of living by the moral imperatives of the gospel, those who claim to be saved by grace tend to depend and live by the (secular) law—affirmative action, threats of economic sanctions, protests, etc.—as the sole basis for their ethical conduct.

This chapter will build on the previous chapter's discussion of racism as a religion. We shall attempt to show that racism violates God's Moral Law, contradicts the teaching and practice of Jesus Christ, hinders Christ's Gospel commission, and raises barriers to unity among believers.

**Racism Violates the Ten Commandments**

God has given to us His Moral Law, the Ten Commandments, to guide us on decisions of right and wrong (1 John 3:4) This Law is a transcript of God's perfect character as exemplified in the life and teaching of our Lord Jesus Christ. Given the fact that the teachings of racism's religion compete against the teachings of the Bible, it should come as no surprise that racism breaches each single one of the Ten Commandments:[1]

(1) Racism nullifies the first commandment, because it substitutes race for God as the organizing center of life.

(2) Racism overturns the second commandment, because it turns the face of a particular race into a graven image, then bows down and worships "the likeness" of what is "in the earth beneath."

(3) Racism profanes the third commandment's prohibition against taking God's name in vain when the Christian who is a racist piously cries "Lord, Lord," but does not do the will of God by showing the love of God—which is value blind, creed blind, color-blind—to his neighbor (cf. Matt 7:21-23).

(4) Racism desecrates the fourth commandment in that on the Sabbath, instead of bringing Christians together because of their common faith, it keeps them apart despite the common faith.

(5) Racism disrespects the fifth commandment to "honor thy father and thy mother," because it defines kinship in terms of blood rather than faith (cf. Matt 12:48-50).

(6) Racism destroys the sixth commandment not only because the racist literally kills the despised race, but also because the derogatory words of the racist "can be just as murderous as the sword or bomb in the hands of a maniac" (cf. Matt 5:21-22).

(7) Racism annuls the seventh commandment, because among other things, it equates adultery with *adulteration* of blood.

(8) Racism breaks the eighth commandment, in that it robs the inferior race of equal access to opportunities and respect and dignity due them as human beings;

(9) Racism abrogates the ninth commandment, in that it bears

false witness about both races by ascribing the undeserved advantages of the superior race to extraneous considerations (such as his industry, superior intelligence, moral rectitude, etc.), while the denial of basic rights to the despised race is justified on the grounds that he is lazy, unintelligent, or immoral.[2]

(10) Racism encroaches upon the tenth commandment, by making one race covet what truly belongs to the despised race.

Even if the practice of racism undermined only one of the Ten Commandments, racism would still be guilty of breaking all. "For whosoever shall keep the whole law and yet offend in one point, he is guilty of all" (James 2:10). And as Jesus Himself said, "Till heaven and earth pass, one jot or one tittle shall in no wise pass from the law, till all be fulfilled. Whosoever therefore shall break one of these least commandments, and shall teach men so, he shall be called the least in the kingdom of heaven: but whosoever shall do and teach them, the same shall be called great in the kingdom of heaven" (Matt 5:18-19).

**Racism Contradicts the Teachings and Practice of Jesus**

Jesus' earthly life and teaching also refuted the ethics of racism. The story of the Syrophoenician woman is a classic example of how Jesus viewed the morality of racial prejudice and bigotry. In the form of an acted parable, Jesus portrayed to His followers the unchristian manner in which they (the Jewish people) had often treated people of other ethnic and racial backgrounds. He thereby sought to teach them the compassionate manner in which they ought to deal with the despised race.

In this dramatized account (Matt 15:21-28; Mark 7:24-30), Jesus actually acted out the way Jewish people tended to act towards non-Jews. Let's observe a few things.

First, there was a desperate need (the woman's child needed help). Yet, those who were in a position to help chose to be apathetic to the need and therefore ignored the woman ("Jesus did not answer a word,"Matt 15: 23).

Second, when His closest associates could no longer pretend the need was not there, they pressured Jesus to refuse the needed help. The reason was that it was inconvenient ("she keeps crying after us," the disciples said; v. 23). Here is illustrated how pressure is often applied so that we conform to ambient expectations, and show an unwillingness to go against popular opinion and practice.

Third, there was a shift of the responsibility to others. Notice in verse 24 that when Jesus finally felt compelled to do something about it, He indicated that the specific need of the woman could only be met by someone else. "I was sent only to the lost sheep of Israel," Christ said. The implication was that, He could only offer help to the superior "in-race."

Fourth, He justified His reason for denying the help by first labeling the woman as a dog and then rationalizing that it was not appropriate to give what is due to humans to a subhuman (dog; v. 26).

In this acted parable, Jesus not only confronted the national and religious pride that had developed as a result of Israel's status as a favored people, but He also condemned the resulting racial and religious prejudice and bigotry—the contempt and heartless treatment of other races, as well as the polarization of groups into Greeks and Barbarians, Jews and Samaritans, and Jews and Gentiles. Christ dramatized how prejudice leads to the devaluing of others, breeding "in-group" favoritism, and sanctioning discrimination against the "out-group."

Speaking about the "wider purpose" of Christ's dealing with the Syrophoenician woman, Ellen White suggests that, by His life and teaching (cf. Matt 15:21-28; Luke 15:1, 2; John 4), Christ sought to instruct His "slow to learn" followers that not only was His love "not to be circumscribed to race or nation," but He demonstrated that any form of caste—"distinction of age, or rank, or nationality, or religious privilege"—"is hateful to God" (*The Desire of Ages,* 402, 403).

Beyond passing a negative judgment on racism, Jesus "laid the foundation" for a completely different religion "by which Jew and Gentile, black and white, free and bond, are linked together in one common brotherhood, recognized as equal in the sight of God" (*Testimonies for the Church,* 7:225)."

> No distinction on account of nationality, race, or caste is recognized by God. He is the Maker of all mankind. All men are of one family by creation, and all are one through redemption. Christ came to demolish every wall of partition, to throw open every compartment of the temple, that every soul may have free access to God. His love is so broad, so deep, so full, that it penetrates everywhere" (*Christ's Object Lessons,* 386).

### Racism Hinders the Gospel Commission

Racism obstructs Christ's Gospel commission. When He commissioned His followers to be His witnesses "both in Jerusalem, and in all Judea and Samaria, and even to the remotest part of the earth" (Acts 1:8), Jesus embraced all races as objects of salvation.

Christ deliberately included the phrase "and Samaria"[3] because of all the racial conflicts in His day. The Jewish-Samaritan problem was probably "the most acute racial, national, and religious conflict of His [Christ's] day." By thus commissioning them, "Jesus intended to challenge the strongest prejudice of His followers of that day."[4]

The racial animosity between Jews and Samaritans is comparable, to no small extent "in its depth and viciousness" to the racial conflict between Blacks and whites in the United States. Let's point to some parallels.[5]

(1) In both instances, racial division is manifested in a "We-You" relationship. Thus, the Jews proclaimed in John 8:33, "we are descendants of Abraham," and charged Jesus (and hence, anyone who did not agree with them), "you are a Samaritan" (John 8:33, 48, RSV). In this "we-you" relationship, the Jews saw themselves as the favored race, and the Samaritans as the unfavored race (an incipient superior/inferior race dichotomy).

(2) Like the black-white racism in our day, the cause of this racial prejudice had some historical basis (cultural, religious, political, economic—2 Kngs 17:24; Ezra 4, Neh 13:28).

(3) Because of the racial prejudice, "Jews have no dealings with Samaritans" (John 4:9, RSV). In this kind of racial segregation, Jews had a difficult time associating with, offering and accepting food and drink from Samaritans, and even rendering helping hands to wounded persons of the opposite race—as the story of the good Samaritan suggests (cf. Luke 10:25-37; 17:11-18).

(4) Just as we demonize other races, for the Jews, Samaritans were the embodiment of evil; thus, the religious leaders told Jesus: "You are a Samaritan and have a demon" (John 8:48, RSV). Even the disciples of Christ were not totally free from this racial prejudice. On one occasion James and John asked Jesus to call fire from heaven to consume the Samaritans.

(5) But the racial prejudice of Jews against Samaritans was not entirely one-sided. The Samaritans also were prejudiced against the Jews. This is reflected in the statement of the Samaritan woman at the well, when she

asked Christ: "How is it that you, a Jew, ask a drink of me, a woman of Samaria" (John 4:9, RSV).

This reverse racism on the part of the Samaritans was equally as sinful and deadly as that perpetrated by those on the other side. It led to the creation of a myth of spiritual superiority in which, for example, Samaritans considered their form of worship to be superior to all others (John 4:20), a view that may have contributed to their initial rejection of Jesus (Luke 9:52, 53).

It is a matter of passing interest that the Samaritans' superior form of worship style (which was one of their arguments for worshiping on the mountain) played no role in the conversion of people in one Samaritan village. They later said to the woman who met Jesus at the well: "Now we believe, not because of thy saying: for we have heard him [Christ] ourselves, and know that this is indeed the Christ and the Savior" (John 4:42).

Racism hinders the Gospel commission as long as we hold on to our Samarias, or areas of prejudice. Christ's message of "and Samaria" (Acts 1:8) suggests that there are no national or racial lines in Christ's Commission. We must leave our race based mountains (communities, churches and Conferences) and cross over the border to Samaria. As long as we keep referring to our unique worship styles as a reason for our racial churches and Conferences, we obstruct the Gospel commission to "go into all the world" (Matt 28:18-20). What really matters is knowing Christ and worshiping "the Father in spirit and in truth" (v. 23).

Heeding Christ's "and Samaria" commission means that we must "move beyond that which is expedient to that which is morally right. Racially oriented evangelism can produce racially insensitive and even racially prejudiced congregations."[6] But more importantly, it is disobedience to the One who has asked us to preach the everlasting gospel "unto them that dwell on the earth, and to every nation, and kindred, and tongue, and people . . . and worship him that made heaven, and earth, and the sea, and the fountains of waters" (Rev 14:6-7).

**Racism Raises Barriers to Unity**

Racism's doctrine of race-based separateness raises a hindrance to the unity Christ prayed for. We must understand that John 17 records Christ's most sublime prayer for the church. It captures His last words of instruction to his apostles before His crucifixion. Within less than twenty-four hours, He would be killed. Thus, in this prayer Christ reveals His innermost thought.

Without doubt, His chief concern was for unity. At least five times He prayed for His followers that "they may be one, as we are" (v. 11), "that they all be one" (v. 21a), "that they also may be one in us" (v. 21b), "that they may be one, even as we are one" (v. 22), and "that they may be made perfect in one" (v.23).

But the unity of the church for which Christ prayed was not primarily that we may be one with each other. It was not simply the integration or fellowship of believers from different ethnic groups. As Evangelical scholar John Stott has shown, the unity for which Christ prayed is first, a unity with the apostle's teaching. This is evident in verse 20 where He alludes to two groups of believers. The RSV designates them as "these" (i.e., the apostles) and "those" (i.e., all subsequent believers). "It seems beyond question that the 'all' of verse 21, whose unity Christ desires, are a combination of 'these' and 'those'."[7]

In other words, the church unity Christ wants to see in His church is one that is in harmony with the teachings of Christ's inspired apostles. Like the apostolic church, believers in God's end-time church must "devote them to the apostles' teaching and fellowship" (Acts 2:42). But as we have shown in the preceding chapter, the teaching of racism is contrary to the Bible. To the extent that this is the case, racism is a barrier to Christ's prayer for unity. Any ideology—gay theology, feminist egalitarian theology, racism, higher criticism—that is not in harmony with God's teaching is a hindrance to Christ's prayer.

But in addition to the unity with the apostles, Christ also prayed "that they also may be one in us" (John 17:.21b). This is a unity with the Father and the Son. It ensures that at all times the church lives in harmony with the leading of the life-giving Spirit whom the Father and Christ will send (John 14:15, 26;15:26; 16:7). Unity with the Father and Son means we shall accept the correction of the Spirit and His guidance into all truth (16:8-13). This includes the Spirit's leading through God's end-time gift of prophecy (Rev 12:17; 19:10).

Only as Christ followers are "in us" (i.e., with the Father and Son) can they truly "be one" among themselves (v. 21a). In other words, the horizontal unity (among Christ's followers) must be grounded in a vertical unity (oneness with Christ). We seek unity on this basis so that "the world may believe that thou hast sent me" (v. 21). Jesus declares: "I in them, and thou in me, that they may be made perfect in one; and that the world may know that thou hast sent me, and hast loved them, as thou hast loved me" (v. 23).

In other words, *a visible unity* results when Christ followers are in harmony with the apostles and with the Father and Son. This unity is readily evident to the world. It is not limited to a doctrinal or "invisible" unity. This visible unity convinces the world of the truthfulness of the Christian message. It demonstrates that the grace of Christ can triumph over the divisions of race. Conversely, racism's attempt to separate people according to their ethnic groups nullifies Christ's desire to see a visible unity in the church.

Writes Ellen White: "There is no person, no nation, that is perfect in every habit and thought. One must learn of another. Therefore God wants the different nationalities to mingle together, to be one in judgment, one in purpose. Then the union that there is in Christ will be exemplified (*SDA Bible Commentary*, 2:1029).

The visible unity that God expects to see in His church applies also to the structures of our organizations—our Conferences, Unions, and Divisions. In fact, in 1905, Ellen G. White wrote against proposals to organize conferences on the basis of nationality. She quoted John 17:17-21, stating that the segregation of Conferences along lines of nationality was out of harmony with Christ's prayer for unity. She wrote:

> Some of our ministers have written to me, asking if the work among the Germans and Scandinavians should not be carried forward under separate organizations. This matter has been presented to me several times. When I was in College View, the Lord gave me a straight testimony to bear, and since that time the matter has been presented to me again. . . . According to the light given me of God, separate organizations, instead of bringing about unity, will create discord. If our brethren will seek the Lord together in humility of mind, those who now think it necessary to organize separate German and Scandinavian conferences will see that the Lord desires them to work together as brethren. . . . If we are to carry on the work most successfully, the talents to be found among the English and Americans should be united with the talents of those of every other nationality. And each nationality should

> labor earnestly for every other nationality. There is but one Lord, one faith. *Our effort should be to answer Christ's prayer for His disciples, that they should be one* (*Testimonies for the Church*, 9:195-196; emphasis mine).

Racism is incompatible with the desire of Christ to see not just doctrinal unity, but also visible unity in all expressions of the church's life. Christianity wants believers to "work together as brethren," but racism wants to separate them. Christianity teaches that "There is no person, no nation, that is perfect in every habit and thought. One must learn of another. Therefore God wants the different nationalities to mingle together, to be one in judgment, one in purpose. Then the union that there is in Christ will be exemplified (*SDA Bible Commentary*, 2:1029). But racism's morality of pride and contempt for other races teaches that only the superior race is wise enough, understanding enough, capable enough, and experienced enough to work for its race.

**Conclusion**

In the previous chapter we showed that the *beliefs* of racism are incompatible with those of biblical Christianity. In this chapter we have attempted to show that racism's *practice* is at odds with Christianity. Racism is wrong because it violates God's moral law, contradicts the teaching and practice of Jesus Christ, hinders Christ's Gospel commission, and raises barriers to the doctrinal and visible unity among believers.

We understate our judgment on racism when we simply state that "racism is sinful."[8] One Christian author underscores the seriousness of racial sin when he argues that it is a "heresy."[9] The Jewish scholar, Abraham J. Heschel, goes even farther in his evaluation. He insists that racism is "worse than idolatry," it is "satanism," an "unmitigated evil," "a treacherous denial of the existence of God" and "blasphemy."[10]

The 1985 General Conference session in New Orleans, Louisiana, was correct in its denunciation of racism. With reference to human societies, racism is, indeed, "one of the odious evils of our day." As far as morality is concerned, racism is "a sin." And as judged by the Christian faith, racism is "a heresy and in essence a form of idolatry."[11]

One prominent Seventh-day Adventist church leader in North America has recently echoed the above sentiments:

> In spiritual and biblical terms, racism is a perverse sin that cuts to the very core of the gospel message. Racism is demonic. Racism negates the reason for which Christ died—the reconciling work of the cross. Racism is at the core of sin. It is a lack of trust in God and a denial of His transforming grace. The devil has used racism as a primary tool to divide not only nations but the Christian church as well. Racism denies the mission and purpose the church, which is to bring together, in Christ, those who have been divided from one another, to remove the middle wall of partition—Jew and Gentile—a division based on race.[12]

Given the heinousness of racism, it is quite puzzling, if not unpardonable, that very little is being done to eradicate its visible expression in our church. For example, instead of dismantling the racially separate conferences in the Adventist church in North America, some are still justifying these structures of racism. The next two chapters will candidly respond to the arguments often employed in their defense, showing why the church ought to do the right thing on this question of black and white conferences in the North American Division.

---

**Endnotes**

[1]Everett Tilson, "Segregation and the Ten Commandments," in Alfred T. Davies, *The Pulpit Speaks on Race* (Nashville, TN: Abingdon, 1965), 96-103.

[2]For example, if the Black person lives in a slum, he "is charged not with poverty, but laziness. If he works in a kitchen the reason is not discrimination, but limitation. If he fails as an engineer the reason is not lack of education, but a shortage of intelligence. If he goes to jail the reason is not environment, but heredity" (ibid., 102-103).

[3]With respect to the despised Samaritans, when Jesus first sent out the twelve, He specifically forbade them to preach to the Gentiles—particularly the Samaritans (Matt 10:5)—apparently because He knew that His followers were not adequately prepared at this time "to preach the gospel, or to do good works, either among Samaritans or Gentiles. Their hearts were too narrow, their prejudices too strong: there was too much of the [unconverted] Jew, too little of the Christian, in their character." (See A. B. Bruce, *The Training of the Twelve* [New York: Doubleday, Doran & Co., Inc., 1929], 101). But after His resurrection and shortly before His ascension, Jesus made it clear that the barriers of race must be overcome as they preached to all the world, including Samaria.

[4]Maston, *The Bible and Race*, 58, 62.

[5]Maston, *The Bible and Race*, 58; 53-67.

[6]Williams, "The Right Thing To Do," 25.

[7]John R.W. Stott, *Christ the Liberator* (Downers Grove, IL.: InterVarsity, 1946), 82.

[8]*Seventh-day Adventist Minister's Manual*, 53.

[9]Will D. Campbell, *Race and the Renewal of the Church* (Philadelphia, PA: Westminster Press, 1962), 13.

[10]Abraham J. Heschel, "The Religious Basis of Equality of Opportunity—The Segregation of God," in Matthew Ahmann, ed., *Race: Challenge to Religion* (Chicago: Henry Regnery Co., 1963), 56.

[11]"GC President Issues Statements on Racism, Peace, Home and Family, and Drugs," *Adventist Review*, June 30, 1985, 2-3.

[12]Harold L. Lee, *Church Leadership in a Multicultural World: Directions for Cultural Harmony in the Adventist Church* (Lincoln, Nebraska: Center for Creative Ministry, 2000), p. 14.

# 22

# A PROPHETIC VOICE ON CHURCH RACE RELATIONS

In the United States, the Seventh-day Adventist (SDA) church currently runs two racially separate administrative structures—one for the Black, and the other for the White. The Black conferences are also known as Regional conferences because of their distinctive geographical arrangement. Even though each Black (Regional) conference covers not merely one portion of the union area but all the Black churches in the whole region of the union, membership is open to all people.[1]

The original intention for the creation of separate Black conferences in 1944 was to correct the problem of the exclusion of Black Adventists from full participation in the life of the church. As one church leader has correctly pointed out, and as we shall show in the next chapter, "the emergence of the Black church was the product of exclusion and experience. Black Christians of all denominations have always desired to be included and integrated with their White brothers and sisters in the church. But they were not always admitted, welcomed, or treated as equals. There were shameful times when they were physically thrown out of White churches." Indeed, "the Black Church and Regional (Black) conferences" in the SDA church "were born from the womb of exclusion, inequality, and experience."[2]

*The SDA Encyclopedia* offers three major reasons why separate Black conferences were organized: (1) greater efficiency in reaching black people with the gospel, (2) creation of more opportunities for leadership and other participation by gifted and trained Blacks, (3) more adequate representation of Blacks in elected offices and on boards and committees outside the Black Regional conferences.[3] But it concedes that this arrangement is "not ideal."[4]

**An Embarrassment to the Church.** The continued existence of these racially distinctive structures of church governance has brought embarrassment and disrepute to the credibility of the SDA church, having created the image of the denomination as two churches—one Black and one White. It is true that no Christian denomination in the United States is innocent of racism. But for the Seventh-day Adventist church to claim to be God's end-time remnant church and yet refuse to dismantle the visible expressions of racism is a contradiction of the gospel.[5]

Many Bible-believing SDAs worldwide also believe that these black and white conferences in North America go against the teachings of Ellen G. White (1827-1915), a founding member of the denomination and one recognized to be the recipient of what SDAs have accepted as the true prophetic gift described in the Bible. During her lifetime, when various Christian denominations in America were split over the thorny issues of slavery and Black and White racism, her stirring messages kept the Seventh-day Adventist church united. She led the SDA church to confront some of the major events in the area of race relations in United States—slavery, the civil war (1861-1865), the Emancipation proclamation (1862), and the Reconstruction. As the church struggled with the issues of slavery, racial prejudice and discrimination, segregation, and its evangelistic and humanitarian responsibility in the South, she provided a prophetic voice.[6]

**Common Myths Defending Racially Separate Conferences.** In spite of the fact that today's Black (Regional) conferences "were born from the womb of [racial] exclusion, inequality and experience," despite the fact that they began as "non-ideal" arrangements, and even though their existence contradicts the message of the Bible and that of Mrs. White, some still defend the continued need of these racially separate church structures.

To address whether we still need separate Black and White conferences, this chapter and the next will look at some of the main arguments often advanced in their defense. The two chapters will challenge the following popular myths about racially segregated conferences:

(1) "The Church Has Always Been Black and White,"
(2) "The Church Has Never Been Interested in Blacks, and Never Will,"
(3) "Ellen G. White Called for Racially Separate Congregations,"
(4) "Racially Separate Conferences Preserve Fellowship, Unity, and Harmony."
(5) "Blacks Demanded Racially Separate Conferences,"
(6) "Separate Conferences Are Still Needed in the Church Today,"
(7) "The Time Has Not Yet Come to Dismantle the Racially Separate Conference,"
(8) "Blacks and Whites Are Different, and Must Be Reached in Different Ways."

The intention of these two chapters is to show that the time has come for our church to dismantle the visible structures of racism that currently operate in the North American Division. Among other things, I will allow the writings of Mrs. White to respond to the above arguments. Because Mrs. White traveled very widely—to England, France, Germany, Italy, Denmark, Norway, Sweden, and Australia—her perspectives on the Black and White relations in America also offer directions to Adventists today on how they should deal with racism in its various manifestations—tribalism, anti-semitism, anti-Arabism, etc.[7]

**An Untouchable Issue.** Readers should understand that the subject to be addressed in this chapter and the next is a forbidden issue in North America. Like the ideologies of homosexuality and women's ordination, anyone who dares to challenge the myths on racially separate conferences is likely to incur the unmitigated wrath of advocates—both Black and White. In the words of Ellen White,

> I know that which I now speak will bring me into conflict. This I do not covet, for the conflict has seemed to be continuous of late years; but I do not mean to live a coward or die a coward, leaving my work undone. I must follow in my Master's

footsteps" (*The Southern Work,* 10).

It is not without significance that Mrs. White. made this statement in the context of race relations in America. She was not silent; neither must we.

**"The Church Has Always Been Black and White"**

Those who argue for the continued existence of separate Black and White structures have often argued that the Seventh-day Adventist church, like many other Christian denominations in the United States, has from its very beginning existed as two churches—one black and one white. According to this view, this arrangement is the best way for the church to maintain racial harmony in a racially volatile American culture.

The argument that "the church has always been Black and White" is an oversimplification of Seventh-day Adventist history. Though the immediate context of Black conferences was in 1944, a background to the present racially segregated conferences can be traced back to the deplorable conditions created by American slavery, Emancipation of Black (or Negro) slaves, the ensuing Civil-War, and the worsening racial relationships created by Jim Crow segregation laws in the South during the 1870s and 1890s,

During its early years, there were no Black conferences or churches in the SDA church as we know them today. As we will later show, the creation in 1944 of Black (Regional) conferences by Seventh-day Adventists was a biblically compromising attempt to deal with slavery's legacy of racism *without splitting the church.* Many other Christian denominations in the United States had earlier divided into two racially separate denominations over the issue. While a few Christians opposed the practice of slavery on moral and biblical grounds, a majority defended it, arguing that it was an economic or political issue. The ambivalence of Christian denominations on the question of slavery led to splits in the various Christian churches. For example, in 1844 the Methodist church was divided between Black and White denominations. A year later it divided the Baptists. In 1861 three other denominations were torn apart: the Lutherans, Episcopalians, and Newside Presbyterians.

Though these denominations provided members to the emerging Seventh-day Adventist church, our church was spared from the racial split that plagued the other denominations. Three factors account for this.

**Abolitionist Stance of Pioneers.** Several of our leading Adventist pioneers had at an earlier time identified with the Abolitionist movement, a minority movement in the USA opposing slavery. Among these were Joseph Bates, the former sea-captain who did much to convince the early Adventists of the Sabbath truth; John Preston Kellogg, the father of Dr. John Harvey Kellogg (the famous surgeon, inventor of surgical instruments, and resident physician at the Battle Creek Sanitarium), William K. Kellogg (the cornflakes manufacturer); and John Byington, pioneer minister and the first president of the General Conference of SDAs. Some of the early Adventists were also closely associated with Sojourner Truth, the itinerant anti-slave lecturer, and Frederick Douglas, a distinguished Abolitionist.[8]

**Strong Words from Ellen G. White.** Ellen G. White's strong opposition to slavery predisposed the attitudes of early Adventists on Black and White race relations. Mrs. White spoke out against slavery at a time when many Christian writers were defending the practice. Arguing on the basis of Scripture, she maintained that Christ "laid the foundation for a religion by which Jew and Gentile, black and white, free and bond, are linked together in one common brotherhood, [and are] recognized as equal in the sight of God" (*Testimonies for the Church,* 7:225).

Explaining why Whites should not despise and ostracize Blacks, she wrote: "The religion of the Bible recognizes no cast or color. It ignores rank, wealth, worldly honor. God estimates men as men. With Him, character decides their worth. And we are to recognize the Spirit of Christ in whomsoever it is revealed. No one need be ashamed to speak with an honest black man in any place or to shake him by the hand. He who is living in the atmosphere in which Christ lives will be taught of God and will learn to put His estimate on men" (*Testimonies for the Church,* 9:223).

Mrs. White also argued: "The same price was paid for the salvation of the colored man as for that of the white man, and the slights put upon the colored people by many who claim to be redeemed by the blood of the Lamb, and who therefore acknowledge themselves debtors to Christ, misrepresent Jesus, and reveal that selfishness, tradition, and prejudice pollute the soul. They are not sanctified through the truth. Those who slight a brother because of his color are slighting Christ" (*Southern Work,* 13).

During the late 1700s and early 1800s, a number of laws were enacted in the United States to maintain the system of slavery. For example, the Fugitive Slave Act (1850) required "all good citizens" to return runaway slaves to their masters. Those who failed to do so risked paying a heavy penalty. In an effort to circumvent this law, some courageous individuals employed the Underground Railroad, a resistance effort that was dangerous and fraught with misunderstanding. During this critical period, when laws were made to keep Black slaves in perpetual servitude to their White masters, Ellen G. White took a very strong position in favor of the ostracized Black race. She urged civil disobedience on theological grounds:

"When the laws of men conflict with the word and law of God, we are to obey the latter, whatever the consequences may be. The law of our land requiring us to deliver a slave to his master, we are not to obey; and we must abide the consequences of violating this law. The slave is not the property of any man. God is his rightful master, and man has no right to take God's workmanship into his hands, and claim him as his own." (*Testimonies for the Church,* 1:201-202). Mrs. White's position was not just a civil disobedience, but a moral disobedience—consistent with the biblical teaching[9]

Explaining why the slaves needed to escape, she wrote: "I was shown how our leading men have treated the poor slaves who have come to them for protection. Angels have recorded it. Instead of breaking their yoke and letting the oppressed go free, these men have made the yoke more galling for them than when in the service of their tyrannical masters. Love of liberty leads the poor slaves to leave their masters and risk their lives to obtain liberty. They would never venture to leave their masters and expose themselves to the difficulties and horrors attending their recapture if they had not as strong a love for liberty as any of us. The escaped slaves have endured untold hardships and dangers to obtain their freedom, and as their last hope, with the love of liberty burning in their breasts, they apply to our Government for protection; but their confidence has been treated with the utmost contempt. Many of them have been cruelly treated because they committed so great a crime as to dare to make an effort to obtain their freedom." (*Testimonies for the Church,* 1:257).

In a stirring rebuke to Christians who apparently supported the Fugitive Slave Act of 1850, the law that demanded the return of slaves to their masters, Mrs. White responded: "Great men, professing to have human hearts, have seen the slaves almost naked and starving, and have abused them, and sent them back to their cruel masters and hopeless bondage, to suffer inhuman cruelty for daring to seek their liberty. Some of this wretched class they thrust into unwholesome dungeons, to live or die, they cared not which. They have deprived them of the liberty and free air which heaven has never denied them, and then left them to suffer for food and clothing. In view of all this, a national fast is proclaimed! Oh, what an insult to Jehovah! The Lord saith by the mouth of Isaiah: 'Yet they seek Me daily, and delight to know My ways, as a nation that did righteousness, and forsook not the ordinance of their God'" (ibid, 257).

In a 1863 statement entitled "Slavery and the War," Ellen G. White declared that God Himself was bringing judgment against America for "the high crime of slavery." She explained that the reason for the protracted Civil War in America was twofold: "He [God] will punish the South for the sin of slavery, and the North for so long suffering its overreaching and overbearing influence" (*Testimonies for the Church*, 1:264).

According to Ellen White, slavery of Blacks was in the sight of God "a sin of the darkest dye." She, therefore, demanded that any Adventist who publicly defended the practice should be disfellowshipped from the church. "Some have been so indiscreet as to talk out their pro-slavery principles—principles which are not heaven-born, but proceed from the dominion of Satan. These restless spirits talk and act in a manner to bring a reproach upon the cause of God." She wrote to one such individual: "I was shown some things in regard to you. I saw that you were deceived in regard to yourself. You have given occasion for the enemies of our faith to blaspheme, and to reproach Sabbathkeepers. By your indiscreet course, you have closed the ears of some who would have listened to the truth. I saw that we should be as wise as serpents and as harmless as doves. You have manifested neither the wisdom of the serpent nor the harmlessness of the dove. . . . Your views of slavery cannot harmonize with the sacred, important truths for this time.

She continued, "You must yield your views or the truth. Both cannot be cherished in the same heart, for they are at war with each other. . . . You have cast your influence on the wrong side, with those whose course of life is to sow thorns and plant misery for others. I saw you casting your influence with a degraded company, a Godforsaken company; and angels of God fled from you in disgust. I saw that you were utterly deceived. Had you followed the light which God has given you, had you heeded the instructions of your brethren, had you listened to their advice, you would have saved yourself and saved the precious cause of truth. But notwithstanding all the light given, you have given publicity to your sentiments. Unless you undo what you have done, *it will be the duty of God's people to publicly withdraw their sympathy and fellowship from you, in order to save the impression which must go out in regard to us as a people. We must let it be known that we have no such ones in our fellowship, that we will not walk with them in church capacity*" (*Testimonies for the Church,* 1:355-359, emphasis mine).[10]

In summary, Ellen G. White maintained that, (1) all races are equal and deserve just treatment; (2) slavery was a sin; it was for this reason God visited judgment on America during the Civil War between the North and the South; (3) SDAs should not support any form of slavery—subtle or blatant; those who did so should be disfellowshiped; (4) SDAs and all Christians should assist slaves and former slaves "to improve their condition."

Given the abolitionist stance of influential Adventist figures, and the strong words of Ellen G. White against slavery, it was unthinkable for the early Adventist church to be a divided church—one for Whites and another for Black. Notes one Adventist historian: "Because of William Miller's Negro following, one is not surprised that later, when Seventh-day Adventist churches were formally organized, throughout New England congregations that were largely white included Americans of African descent."[11]

Thus, the argument that the Adventist church has always been black and white is without merit.

**Relatively Small Black Presence.** A final reason why the SDA church was not split over the racial issue was because there was initially only a relatively small presence of Blacks in the Adventist church. They could not have formed congregations of their own, let alone a conference. Blacks who were part of the Advent (Millerite) movement worshiped with White believers. The Seventh-day Adventist church was formally organized in 1863. It was only eight years later (1871) that some work for Blacks in the South was reported.[12] It took repeated appeals and admonitions from Ellen G. White in the 1890s before the work for Blacks moved ahead with momentum.[13]

### "The Church Has Never Been Interested in Blacks, and Never Will"

Advocates of racially exclusive conferences sometimes argue that the church has not always been interested in the well-being and evangelism of Blacks. They fear that dismantling Black (Regional) conferences will seriously undermine the Black work.

This argument is partly true and partly false. It can be demonstrated that Whites have not always been eager to advance work among Black people. But there is no logical correlation of this historical fact with the fear of dismantling today's Black conferences. The argument would be valid if it can be shown that today's church in North America is still not interested in outreach to Blacks. And even when that is proven be the case, the solution would not necessarily require racially separate church structures.

**Neglect of the Black Work.** Without question, a compelling case can be made to show that between the 1870s (when some work was reported among Blacks in the South) and 1890s (when Ellen White repeatedly appealed to the church to labor among Blacks), White Adventists, by and large, acquiesced to their ambient culture. They accepted the racially segregated status quo in society, showing little interest in the deplorable plight of Blacks and manifesting disdain for Blacks.

Ellen White spoke to this sad situation. Beginning in the early 1890s she made repeated appeals to the church, urging its evangelistic forces to enter the great harvest field of the South (where a large majority of Blacks were located). In 1891 she presented her first comprehensive appeal to the thirty church leaders at the twenty-ninth session of the General Conference in Battle Creek, Michigan. It was titled "Our Duty to Colored People." It was by far the most courageous and far-reaching statement of Mrs. White. She anticipated some opposition. Thus, she wrote:

"I know that which I now speak will bring me into conflict. This I do not covet, for the conflict has seemed to be continuous of late years; but I do not mean to live a coward or die a coward, leaving my work undone. I must follow in my Master's footsteps" (*The Southern Work,* 10).

She continued: "It has become fashionable to look down upon the poor, and upon the colored race in particular. But Jesus, the Master, was poor, and He sympathizes with the poor, the discarded, the oppressed, and declares that every insult shown to them is as if shown to Himself. I am more and more surprised as I see those who claim to be children of God possessing so little of the sympathy, tenderness, and love which actuated Christ. Would that every church, North and South, were imbued with the spirit of our Lord's teaching" (*The Southern Work,* 10-11).

**Major Thrust in the Black Work.** Ellen G. White's 1891 appeal to church leaders outlined principles to develop work among Black people. Copies of the message were distributed to key leaders, ministers in the South, and lay persons. It was also circulated in manuscript form and later printed in a leaflet. Two years later, this appeal stirred the missionary zeal of her son James Edson White, leading him to launch evangelistic and educational work among the neglected people of the South. In 1894, he constructed a 75-foot steamboat, christened *The Morning Star,* and sailed it down the Mississippi River. The $3,700 boat provided residence, chapel, school room, a library, photographic room with a darkroom, printshop for publishing educational and agricultural work among blacks. Thus, began his evangelistic work at Vicksburg, Mississippi, in January 1895.

Despite Edson White's tireless labor, there was still a continued lack of interest in the Black work. One reason for this could have been the economic and political unrest between the 1870's and 1890's. Partly for fear, and partly from comfort, White Adventists in the North were not easily disposed to labor for Blacks in the South. During this period, Ellen White continued to urge more Adventists to go into the vineyards of the South. She gave reasons why they should go, counsels on how they should conduct themselves there, and encouragement to those already laboring there. Her appeals have been preserved in the small booklet *The Southern Work*, in *Testimonies for the Church* volumes seven (pages 220-245), and in *Testimonies for the Church* volume eight (pages 34, 59-61, 91, 137, 150, 205). Some of the titles of her articles in *The Southern Work* will give some idea of the burden of Mrs. White.[14]

On March 20, 1891, she appealed to church leaders: "Sin rests upon us as a church because we have not made greater effort for the salvation of souls among the colored people. It will always be a difficult matter to deal with the prejudices of the white people in the South and do missionary work for the colored race. But the way this matter has been treated by some is an offense to God. We need not expect that all will be accomplished in the South that God would do until in our missionary efforts we place this question on the ground of principle, and let those who accept the truth be educated to be Bible Christians, working according to Christ's order" (*The Southern Work,* 15).

On April 2, 1895, she wrote: "I have a most earnest interest in the work to be done among the colored people. This is a branch of work that has been strangely neglected. The reason that this large class of human beings, who have souls to save or to lose, have been so long neglected, is the prejudice that the white people have felt and manifested against mingling with them in religious worship. They have been despised, shunned, and treated with abhorrence, as though crime were upon them, when they were helpless and in need, when men should have labored most earnestly for their salvation. They have been treated without pity. The priests and the Levites have looked upon their wretchedness, and have passed by on the other side" (ibid., 19)

Again, she wrote on November 26, 1895: "Why should not Seventh-day Adventists become true laborers together with God in seeking to save the souls of the colored race? Instead of a few, why should not many go forth to labor in this long-neglected field? Where are the families who will become missionaries and who will engage in labor in this field? Where are the men who have means and experience so that they can go forth to these people and work for them just where they are? There are men who can educate them in agricultural lines, who can teach the colored people to sow seed and plant orchards. There are others who can teach them to read, and can give them an object lesson from their own life and example. Show them what you yourself can do to gain a livelihood, and it will be an education to them. Are we not called upon to do this very work? Are there not many who need to learn to love God supremely and their fellow men as themselves? In the Southern field are many thousands of people who have souls to save or to lose. Are there not many among those who claim to believe the truth who will go forth into this field to do the work for which Christ gave up His ease, His riches, and His life?" (ibid., 27).

**A Key Question.** Without doubt, White Adventists for the most part neglected to labor among Blacks in the 1890's. The question before us now is whether dismantling Black (Regional) conferences will lead to the same neglect. That case is yet to be made. It is, however, a historical fact and a matter of encouragement that, stirred by Ellen White, the church in her day came to an understanding of its duty and began a work among Black people that was to grow and prosper. Why can't the same message stir us even after we dismantle today's Black conferences—the visible expression of America's post-slavery racism?

**"Ellen G. White Called for Racially Separate Congregations"**

Another argument often employed in defense of the current Black and White conference system is that in 1895 and 1896, Ellen G. White called for the separation of the two races as the most practical way to advance the work among the respective groups of people. Advocates—both Black and White—of the current *status quo* argue that racially separated churches necessarily require racially separated conferences.

**Statements Often Misquoted.** Those who hold the above view often misquote and misinterpret the following statements from *Testimonies*, vol. 9:

> "In regard to white and colored people worshiping in the same building, this cannot be followed as a general custom with profit to either party—especially in the South. The best thing will be to provide the colored people who accept the truth, with places of worship of their own, in which they can carry on their services by themselves" (*Testimonies for the Church,* 9:206).

> "Let colored workers labor for their own people, assisted by white workers as occasion demands. They will often need counsel and advice. Let the colored believers have their place of worship and the white believers their place of worship. Let each company be zealous to do genuine missionary work for its own people and for the colored people wherever and whenever they can" (ibid., 210).

> "But for several reasons white men must be chosen as leaders. . . . The mingling of whites and blacks in social equality was by no means to be encouraged (ibid, 202, 206).

In addition to the above 1895 statements from *Testimonies,* vol. 9, the following 1896 counsel recorded in *The Southern Work* is also often quoted:

> "Common association with the blacks is not a wise course to pursue. To lodge with them in their homes may stir up feelings in the minds of the whites which will imperil the lives of the workers. . . . The breaking down of distinctions between the white and the colored races unfits the blacks to work for

their own class, and exerts a wrong influence upon the whites (*The Southern Work,* 95, 96).

The above justification for racially separate churches (and hence conferences) takes the statements of Mrs. White out of context. Advocates fail to recognize that the above counsels were made at a very difficult time in American history of race relations, a period in which White Adventists "who attempted to work for the black race had to suffer persecution, and many were martyrs to the cause" (ibid., 43). Those familiar with the writings of Mrs. White know that given her biblical understanding of the inherent worth of all races, she would not yield to racism in the matter of separate worship services.

Before looking at the often-quoted 1895 statement, let me call attention to one pertinent statement by Mrs. White to refute the assertion that she believed in racially segregated congregations. In 1891, she wrote:

> "You have no license from God to exclude the colored people from your places of worship. Treat them as Christ's property, which they are, just as much as yourselves. They should hold membership in the church with the white brethren. Every effort should be made to wipe out the terrible wrong which has been done them" (*The Southern Work,* 15).

Since in 1891 Mrs. White discouraged any attempts at excluding Blacks from worshiping with Whites, why would she later (1895 and 1896) argue for separate work for Blacks and Whites? A brief historical context will show that she was addressing a specific situation in which the life and work of missionaries to the South were being threatened. The oft-misquoted statements were ad hoc and not a timeless policy. They were judicious counsels on how the church at that time was to handle the life threatening racial condition, not a mandate for racially separate congregations or conferences.

**A Historical Background.** As we pointed out earlier, during its beginnings the SDA church did not seriously have to deal with the problem of racial prejudice and segregation. However, when Adventist missionaries went to the South in the 1890s, they discovered a social system based on the separation of the races. This system was also in place in many of the

Christian denominations, from which the Adventist missionaries obtained a bulk of their new members.[15]

Our Adventist missionaries to the South were also caught in the middle of a racial war raging in the country. Abraham Lincoln signed the Emancipation proclamation on September 22, 1862, freeing all people held as slaves in areas of the Confederacy (the South), effective January 1, 1863. Three legal enactments gave friends of the abolition movement a further cause to celebrate: (1) the Thirteenth Amendment to the US Constitution (1865) ended slavery and involuntary servitude; (2) the Fourteenth (1868) recognized the rights of Negroes to citizenship; and (3) the Fifteenth (1870) gave Negroes the right to vote.

But in the South, there was a counter-reaction to the freedom of Blacks. The Ku Klux Klan emerged and inspired violent raids and acts of terrorism against Blacks and White supporters and sympathizers. There were widespread civil disorders as new laws were enacted that further restricted freedmen. Lynching of Black people increased at an alarming rate. The racial segregation flourished greatly with the promulgation of Jim Crow laws. These laws first banned interracial marriages (1875). They were followed by the construction of segregated schools (in 1885) and by the 1890's, new Jim Crow laws spread rapidly to trains, streetcars, employment, and hospitals.[16]

So, on one hand, we had pro-slavery segregation laws and violence in the South. On the other hand, we had anti-slavery agitations against them by people who believed in the "social equality" of Blacks and Whites. This volatile racial climate created unfavorable conditions to advance the work among Blacks. Though to a lesser extent than in the South, this racial war was also going on in the North.[17]

Adventist missionaries in the South were most vulnerable to attacks from slaveholders in the South. This is because "the entire South's economy strongly depended on the barbaric system of bondage, delicately balanced as it was—always tenuous, ever subject to insurrection by its victims. Slaveholders seemed little disposed to risk indoctrination of their work force by outsiders, especially by invaders from the North who might question the propriety of one man's holding another in a lifetime of unrecompensed servitude. Hard work for slaves was looked upon as a prime necessity, and anyone who advocated a rest day for them, a Sabbath as set forth in the Ten Commandments, or any free time other than Sunday, would do so at the peril of his life."[18]

Perhaps we can use two incidents that occurred in the late 1800s to illustrate what Ellen White was trying to avoid four years earlier in *Testimonies* volume nine. On December 18, 1898, a week before Christmas, Edson White (the son of Mrs. White and the builder of *The Morning Star* steamboat) received a letter from J. A. Crisler, a friendly physician in Yazoo City, Mississippi. At that time Edson was at Vicksburg, Mississippi, while F. R. Rogers, his assistant in the mission work in the South, was operating the school for Blacks in Yazoo City, Mississippi. The physician's letter alerted Edson of a plot to attack the Whites who were helping the Blacks. Dr. Crisler's letter said:

> Mr. Rogers was ordered to leave here by some kind of a committee, who claim to have been informed by some colored people, that the Negroes were going to rise and slaughter the whites on Christmas eve, or shortly after. These informers (colored) state that these uprising Negroes are being wrought up by white people, and they (the committee), have gone no further into the investigation, but take these informers' words as being correct, and have ordered all whites who are in any way connected with the colored race here to leave. . . . They, of course, do not represent the good people of this section. . . . Please do not connect our name in this matter to anyone as it would destroy our usefulness to you in helping adjust this great and uncalled-for calamity. I will quietly do whatever I can to peaceably settle things.[19]

The next morning, Edson received another letter. This time from F. R. Rogers himself, whose work among the Blacks had earned him a reputation as a "Nigger-lover."[20] The letter of Rogers read:

> Satan is loosed here. We are in trouble. Today at 1:30 p.m. two men rode up to the chapel where we are holding school and called me out and asked my name and told me 'This business must stop. We went to the river last night to *sink* the boat *Morning Star*, but could not find it. It will never land here again, SO BEWARE.' . . . Well, Bro. White, we are resting in the Lord and have left the case to Him. However, I applied to the Mayor for advice as to leaving

> the organ and other things in the chapel, as burning was threatened. The Mayor said all was safe and he would see me protected.[21]

Commenting on the above two events Edson White wrote: "On receiving these communications we all felt that great caution and much heavenly wisdom was required to enable us to take the proper course in this matter. The testimonies [counsels from the Mrs. White] instruct us that great caution must be exercised so that these evilly disposed persons shall not be aroused and the work closed up as a result." [22]

James Edson White understood that their lives and their work were in danger because of the racial prejudice and animosity in the South. Five months later, in May of 1899, new trouble arose, this time from a white mob. On May 25, 1899, Edson wrote a letter to his mother, reporting the incident that had taken place:

> Two weeks ago tonight, a mob of about 25 white men came to our church at Calmer at about midnight. They brought out brother Stevenson, our worker, and then looted the church, burning books, maps, charts, etc. They hunted for brother Casey, our leading colored brother of that place, but he had escaped in time so they did not reach him. They then went to the house of brother Alvin, called him out, and whipped him with a cowhide. I think they would have killed him if it had not been for a friendly white man who ordered them to stop whipping after they had struck a few blows. They did not pay any attention to him at first, but he drew his revolver and said that the next man who struck a blow would hear from him, and then they stopped. During this time they shot at brother Alvin's wife and struck her in the leg, but did not hurt her seriously. They took brother Stevenson to the nearest railway station, put him on the cars and sent him out of the country. They posted a notice on our church, forbidding me to return, and forbidding the steamer, *The Morning Star*, to land between Yazoo City and Vicksburg. The whole difficulty arose from our efforts to aid the colored people. We had given them clothing where in need, and food to those who were hungry and taught them some better ideas about farming, introducing different seeds such as peanuts,

> beans, etc. that bring a high price, . . . and these the whites would not stand[23]

Edson's May 25, 1899 letter from Mississippi had a profound impact on his mother. A few days after receiving the letter she wrote on June 5, 1899 to A.F. Ballenger (a one-time Adventist minister and secretary of the National Religious Liberty Association) on the subject of race. "It is the prejudice of the white against the black race that makes this field hard, very hard. The whites who have oppressed the colored people still have the same spirit. They did not lose it, although they were conquered in war. They are determined to make it appear that the blacks were better off in slavery than since they were set free. Any provocation from the blacks is met with the greatest cruelty. The field is one that needs to be worked with the greatest discretion." Mrs. White continued:

> The white people will stir up the blacks by telling them all kinds of stories; and the blacks, who can lie even when it is for their interest to speak the truth, will stir up the whites with falsehoods, and the whites who want an occasion will seize upon any pretext for taking revenge, even upon those of their own color who are presenting the truth. This is the danger. *As far as possible, everything that will stir up the race prejudice of the white people should be avoided. There is danger of closing the door so that our white laborers will not be able to work in some places in the South*" (*The Southern Work,* 83, 84; emphasis mine).

The words in italics are identical to those quoted in *Testimonies* volume 9, p. 214, suggesting that it is this kind of situation Mrs. White was trying to avoid when she wrote that there should be separate worship services and separate lines of labor for blacks and whites, and that blacks should not agitate for "social equality."[24] It is the same reason that lies behind her strong counsel against inter-racial marriage.[25]

When she urged caution in the South, saying that future missionary labor among Blacks "would have to be carried on along lines different from those followed *in some sections* of the country *in former times*" (*Testimonies for the Church,* Vol. 9, p. 206), she herself indicated that her counsel must take *place* and *time* in consideration. It is not a universal or timeless admonition.[26]

Therefore, it is incorrect to argue, as some do, that "Mrs. White bowed to the white racism she had earlier tried to resist" or that her counsels inadvertently "helped those within the movement who wanted to keep blacks 'in their place' and who wanted to justify discrimination against them."[27] It is more accurate to say that her calls for "separate churches [were] a concession to necessity."[28]

In fact, those two statements often cited as evidence that today we need racially separate congregations and ministries are contained in a full section within *Testimonies for the Church* ("Among the Colored People," pages 199-226). Ellen White's whole point in that section was that if the customs and prejudices existing in certain areas could not be ignored, those laboring there must exercise great prudence. Failure to do so could jeopardize the work and even the laborers and those being labored for.

The reason why Mrs. White called for the change of method was the "strengthening opposition" from outside the church, the "danger of closing the door" to the work (*Testimonies,* 9:214); "we shall find our way blocked completely" (ibid.); "do nothing that will unnecessarily arouse opposition" (ibid., 208). She counseled that because of the changed situation, Blacks should have their own places of worship as "the course of wisdom," "where demanded by custom or where greater efficiency is to be gained" (ibid.). A careful reader will also observe that the course that she outlined was one that was to be followed to the best advantage "*until the Lord shows us a better way*" (ibid., 207).

**Ellen G. White's Statements in their Full Context.** It is, therefore, incorrect to argue for the continued existence of separate Black and White congregations or conferences on the basis of statements from *Testimonies* volume nine, statements which were clearly addressing a unique problem threatening the life and work of our missionaries in the South. Bearing in mind the historical and contextual background presented above, we may now read the *Testimonies,* vol. 9, quotations in their full context:

> In regard to white and colored people worshiping in the same building, *this cannot be followed as a general custom* with profit to either party—*especially in the South.* The best thing will be to provide the colored people who accept the truth, with places of worship of their own, in which they can carry on their services by themselves. *This is particularly necessary in the South* in order

that the work for the white people may be carried on without serious hindrance. Let the colored believers be provided with neat, tasteful houses of worship. Let them be shown that *this is done not to exclude them from worshiping with white people,* because they are black, but in order that the progress of the truth may be advanced. Let them understand that this plan is to be followed *until the Lord shows us a better way.* The colored members of ability and experience should be encouraged to lead the services of their own people; and their voices are to be heard in the representative assemblies. The colored ministers should make every effort possible to help their own people to understand the truth for this time. As time advances, and race prejudices increase, it will become almost impossible, in many places, for white workers to labor for the colored people. Sometimes the white people who are not in sympathy with our work will unite with colored people to oppose it, claiming that our teaching is an effort to break up churches and bring in trouble over the Sabbath question. White ministers and colored ministers will make false statements, arousing in the minds of the people such a feeling of antagonism that they will be ready to destroy and to kill. The powers of hell are working with all their ingenuity to prevent the proclamation of the last message of mercy among the colored people. Satan is working to make it most difficult for the gospel minister and teacher to ignore the prejudice that exists between the white and the colored people (*Testimonies for the Church,* 9:206-208; emphasis mine).

While men are trying to settle the question of the color line, time rolls on, and souls go down into the grave, unwarned and unsaved. Let this condition of things continue no longer. Let men and women go to work, and let them labor as the Spirit of God shall impress their minds. We need the talent of the colored believers, every jot of it, in this work. Let colored workers labor for their own people, assisted by white workers as occasion demands. They will often need counsel and advice. Let the colored believers have their place of worship and the white believers their place of worship. Let each company be zealous to do genuine missionary work for its own people and for the colored people wherever and whenever they can. . . . *But we must not unnecessarily arouse prejudice that would close the way against the proclamation of the third angel's message to the white people* (ibid., 210; emphasis mine).

*The time has not come for us to work as if there were no prejudice.* Christ said: 'Be ye therefore wise as serpents, and harmless as doves.' Matthew 10:16. If you see that by doing certain things which you have a perfect right to do, you hinder the advancement of God's work, refrain from doing those things. Do nothing that will close the minds of others against the truth. There is a world to save, and we shall gain nothing by cutting loose from those we are trying to help. All things may be lawful, but all things are not expedient.

*The wise course is the best.* As laborers together with God, we are to work in the way that will enable us to accomplish the most for Him. Let none go to extremes. We need wisdom from above; for we have a difficult problem to solve. If rash moves are made now, great mischief will be done. The matter is to be presented in such a way that the truly converted colored people will cling to the truth for Christ's sake, refusing to renounce one principle of sound Bible doctrine because they may think that the very best course is not being pursued toward the Negro race.

We must sit as learners at the feet of Christ, that He may teach us the will of God and that we may know how to work for the white people and the colored people in the Southern field. We are to do as the Spirit of the Lord shall dictate, and agitate the subject of the color line as little as possible. We must use every energy to present the closing gospel message to all classes in the South. As we are led and controlled by the Spirit of God we shall find that this question will adjust itself in the minds of our people" (ibid., 215; emphasis mine).

In giving the above counsels, Mrs. White made it clear that her counsel "cannot be followed as a general custom." To suggest that she encouraged separate churches as a rule is to grossly misunderstand her writings. She also circumscribed the context of her counsels—namely the volatile racial situation in the United States, especially in the South. Her concern was "in order that the work for the White people may be carried on without serious hindrance." In other words, her concern was for the advancement of the work, not for the color of the skin.

**Additional Evidence.** Another indication that the above statements cannot be used as a justification for racially exclusive churches and conferences can be found in Edson White's understanding of his mother's counsel. On October 10, 1899, four months after Edson had sent his letter to his mother, he wrote to a woman in Washington, D.C., who was planning to work for Blacks over there. In this letter, Edson, interpreted the *Testimonies* as he understood them to apply to integrating schools:

> Now in regard to the testimonies respecting colored schools unmixed with whites. *I understand that this refers to the South only where mixed schools will not be tolerated. God forbid that we should build up color lines where they do not now exist.* You say, 'I have been asked by several whether that testimony [from Mrs. White] would apply here and whether they should separate them.' I would not undertake anything of the kind myself. *I should feel that I would sin in so doing.*
>
> I think there is a rule that we may safely follow in this color line business. *We must regard it only as it affects the outside element in such a way as to close up our work and injure its usefulness.* If you disregard [White probably meant to use "regard"] the sons and daughters of Christ you cannot make divisions where God regards us all blood relation to the Lord, God Almighty and brethren and sisters of our Lord and Savior Jesus Christ. For us to build up anything of the kind will be a s bad as the 'Middle Wall of Partition' built up by the ancient Jews.
>
> God has made [of] one blood all nations of the earth and He so regards them. If we are true children of God we will regard them in the same way. We are not to regard the prejudice of men in matters of this kind only as we are compelled to do so in

> order that we may be allowed to work for them where a different course would close the field to our work and make it difficult and impossible to reach the people at all. I do not think I have any further advice to give upon this point.[29]

Finally, Mrs. White herself explains to us how we should understand her counsels in *Testimonies* volume nine. Speaking to Black students at Oakwood College, Hunstville, Alabama, on June 21, 1904, she said:

> We need, O so much, colored workers to labor for their own people, in places where it would not be safe for white people to labor. White workers can labor in places where the prejudice is not so strong. This is why we have established our printing office in Nashville. . . . You can labor where we can not, in places where the existing prejudice forbids us to labor. Christ left Jerusalem in order to save His life. It is our duty to take care of our lives for Christ's sake. We are not to place ourselves, unbidden, in danger, because He wants us to live to teach and help others. God wants the colored students before me today to be His helping hand in reaching souls in many places where white workers cannot labor (*Manuscript* 60, 1904 ["The Work of the Huntsville School"]).

It must be pointed out that Oakwood College (until 1943 known as Oakwood Industrial School) was established in 1896 in response to the appeals of Ellen G. White to develop a training center in the South for Black leaders.

The inescapable conclusion from our investigation of the context of Mrs. White's statement in *Testimonies* volume nine is that no one can legitimately use her words as a justification for today's separate Black and White churches (and hence conferences) in the United States. Ellen White was addressing a specific situation during which the lives and work of Adventist missionaries were being threatened by strong racial prejudice and hatred. It is true that racism still exists in America. But the situation today is far more different from what it used to be in Ellen White's day. Even in those difficult days, she said her counsel was valid "until the Lord shows us a better way."

### "Racially Separate Conferences Preserve Fellowship, Unity, and Harmony"

One popular myth regarding the creation and existence of the present racial structures in the North American church is that the path of separate Black and White conferences is "a road to fellowship," the only realistic hope of "preserving unity in the Seventh-day Adventist church," and the divine way for the different races "to get on together."[30] Can this argument be sustained today?

It is paradoxical to explain how "separate" conferences preserve "fellowship," "unity" and "getting on together." In the context of our discussion, how is it possible for the word "separate" (which means being apart, at a distance, cleavage, division) lead to "fellowship" "unity" and "getting together"—expressions that imply "brotherhood," "accord," "company," "oneness," "solidarity," etc.?

More importantly, given our discussion in the previous chapter about Christ's prayer for unity, and Ellen White's desire for the Lord to show us "a better way," can we still hold on to the racially segregated structures of church governance as though they are the ideal means to redeem us from our racial quagmire?

**An Equivocal Answer.** Seventh-day Adventists don't have to second-guess an answer. Almost a century ago, Ellen White was presented with a similar question. Her unequivocal answer shows that racially separate organizations do not foster unity, but rather discord. She gave her answer when she was asked about the desirability of creating separate German and Scandinavian conferences in America. It is significant that her response is found in a chapter titled "The Spirit of Unity." On September 1, 1905, she wrote from Loma Linda, California:

> Dear Brethren: Some of our ministers have written to me, asking if the work among the Germans and Scandinavians should not be carried forward under separate organizations. This matter has been presented to me several times. When I was in College View, the Lord gave me a straight testimony to bear, and since that time the matter has been presented to me again. . . .
>
> According to the light given me of God, *separate organizations, instead of bringing about unity, will create discord. If our*

*brethren will seek the Lord together in humility of mind, those who now think it necessary to organize separate German and Scandinavian conferences will see that the Lord desires them to work together as brethren.*

"Were those who seek to disintegrate the work of God, to carry out their purpose, some would magnify themselves to do a work that should not be done. *Such an arrangement would greatly retard the cause of God.* If we are to carry on the work most successfully, the talents to be found among the English and Americans should be united with the talents of those of every other nationality. And each nationality should labor earnestly for every other nationality. There is but one Lord, one faith. *Our effort should be to answer Christ's prayer for His disciples, that they should be one*" (*Testimonies for the Church,* 1:195-196; emphasis mine).

Now, if the path of separate conferences is "a road to fellowship," the only realistic hope of "preserving unity in the Seventh-day Adventist church.," and the divine way for the different races "to get on together," and if a race is any group of people distinguishable by easily noticed features (such as color of the skin, eye, hair, or shape of the face or body, or age, gender, etc.), then would we be justified in calling for Hispanic conferences? Korean conferences? African conferences? Haitian conferences? Polish conferences? If Black and White conferences are justifiable, why is it not legitimate to have women's conferences? youth and teenage conferences? etc.

And why stop at racially exclusive conferences? Why not demand separate Unions?—and even, Divisions and General Conference (i.e., an organization separate from the SDA)?

I may be exaggerating in the above rhetorical questions. But my point is to highlight the utterly unconvincing nature of arguments that racially separate conferences preserve fellowship, unity, and togetherness in the North American church.

**Visible Unity, A Divine Mandate.** No, the Bible calls for visible unity. "A unity that will convince the world must be visible and readily evident. It cannot be limited to doctrinal unity or some mystical 'invisible' unity. The world must see a unity in practice that demonstrates that the gospel of Christ is strong enough to destroy the sectarianism, selfishness, and ethnocentrism that is natural to human nature."[31]

"Where this oneness exists," says Ellen White, "it is evidence that the image of God is being restored in humanity" (*The Desire of Ages,* 678). In other words, the absence of a visible unity in the church is evidence that we are not converted. But where there is true conversion, we are able to transcend the artificial barriers sin has erected. Conversion makes us "one in Christ"—regardless of our color, nationality, or station in life. Writes Mrs. White:

> When the sinner is converted he receives the Holy Spirit, that makes him a child of God, and fits him for the society of the redeemed and the angelic host. He is made a joint heir with Christ. Whoever of the human family give themselves to Christ, whoever hear the truth and obey it, become children of one family. The ignorant and the wise, the rich and the poor, the heathen and the slave, white or black—Jesus paid the purchase money for their souls. If they believe on Him, His cleansing blood is applied to them. The black man's name is written in the book of life beside the white man's. All are one in Christ. Birth, station, nationality, or color cannot elevate or degrade men. The character makes the man.
>
> If a red man, a Chinaman, or an African gives his heart to God, in obedience and faith, Jesus loves him none the less for his color. He calls him his well-beloved brother. The day is coming when the kings and the lordly men of the earth would be glad to exchange places with the humblest African who has laid hold on the hope of the gospel. To all who are overcomers through the blood of the Lamb, the invitation will be given, 'Come, ye blessed of my Father, inherit the kingdom prepared for you from the foundation of the world.' Arranged on the right and left of the throne of God are the long columns of the heavenly host, who touch the golden harps, and the songs of welcome and of praise to God and the Lamb ring through the heavenly courts. "He that hath an ear, let him hear what the Spirit saith unto the churches; To him that overcometh will I give to eat of the tree of life, which is in the midst of the

paradise of God" (*The Southern Work,* 12-13).

---

**Endnotes**

[1]There are presently nine Black (Regional) conferences in the North American Division, having largely Black constituency and leadership. However, the Pacific and North Pacific unions currently have no Regional conferences. Instead, they have union and conference Regional Departments that serve in an advisory capacity for the Black constituency in their respective areas. In Canada, there are churches that are predominantly Black, churches that are predominantly White, and churches that are fully integrated—but no separate conferences. In Bermuda, most of the churches have a majority of Black members and the conference has a Black president (cf. *SDA Encyclopedia* [1976], 1191).

[2]Helvius L. Thompson, "Do We Still Need Regional (Black) Conferences?" in Delbert W. Baker, ed., *Telling the Story: An Anthology on the Development of the Black SDA Work* (Loma Linda, Calif.: Loma Linda University Printing Services, 1996), 2/53.

[3]The *SDA Encyclopedia* notes that the Regional conferences were formed "in the hope that the new organizations might, with concentration on work within a specific ethnic group, achieve greater results in a shorter space of time than would be achieved under the previously existing organizations (in some cases under a departmental or mission arrangement). The plan has been responsible for an evangelistic penetration into the Negro [Black] community that had not been possible under the organizations that formerly administered the work among the nation's Negro membership. The Regional conferences also have created more opportunities for leadership and other participation by gifted and trained Negro young people of the church whose selection in the same or similar capacities had not worked out in the years prior to the formation of the Regional conferences. Another practical result has been that colored members of the SDA Church have been more readily and more naturally represented in elected offices and on boards and committees outside the Regional conferences than appears to have been true formerly" (*Seventh-day Adventist Encyclopedia* [Hagerstown, Md.: Review and Herald, 1976], 1192)

[4]The first edition (1966) of the *SDA Encyclopedia,* 1059-1060, prefaces the above success story of Regional conferences (see previous note), stating that "church leaders admit it is not ideal." The "not ideal" preface is, however, omitted in the revised (1976) edition. It appears that, within 10 years of existence, what started out as a non ideal arrangement had become ideal. We shall later show that indeed, today's leadership of the North American Division has no desire to dismantle the Black/White structure.

[5]I say "refuse" because even after the much publicized October 27-30, 1999 "Summit on Race," a parenthetical paragraph in the document, *Suggested Activities Plan and Timetable for North American Division Race Relations Follow-up,* makes it clear that its strategic plan to achieve "inclusiveness and racial harmony" does not include the dismantling of the race based conference structure in the NAD. See the *Suggested Activities Plan and Timetable for North American Division Race Relations Follow-up*, 3, 4. The Document contains the recommendations from the 1999 Race Summit, and was prepared by the Office of Human Relations and presented to the President of the North American Division. Later in this chapter, I will take a closer look at this Document.

[6]"Ellen White can rightfully be called the initiator of the Black work. No person had a greater impact on the inclusion and status of Black people in the Adventist church;

it is impossible to talk about Black Adventist history without constantly referring to her contributions. All significant workers in the early Black work, either directly or indirectly, pointed to either Ellen White or her writings as the source of their inspiration and guidance. There would have been little hope for the Black work had Ellen White not championed the cause" (Delbert W. Baker, *Adventist Review,* "In Search of Roots: Adventist African-Americans," Part 1 ["Exploring the History"], February 4, 1993, 14.

[7]For insights and primary sources on this subject, I am indebted to Ronald D. Graybill, *E. G. White and Church Race Relations* (Washington D.C.: Review and Herald, 1970) and Delbert W. Baker, "The Dynamics of Communication and African-American Progress in the Seventh-day Adventist Organization: A Historical Descriptive Analysis" (Ph.D. Dissertation, Howard University, 1993); idem, "Black Seventh-day Adventists and the Influence of Ellen G. White," in Calvin B. Rock, ed., *Black Seventh-day Adventists Face the Twenty-first Century* (Hagerstown, Md.: Review and Herald, 1996), 21-27; idem, "Ellen White: A Pioneer in Race Relations," in Delbert W. Baker, ed., *Make Us One: Celebration Spiritual Unity in the Midst of Cultural Diversity* (Boise, Id.: Pacific Press, 1995), 83-103; idem, *The Unknown Prophet* (Washington, D.C.: Review and Herald, 1987).

[8]Joseph Bates (1792-1872) helped found the Abolitionist movement in his home town. John Preston Kellogg (1807-1881) harbored fleeing slaves on his Michigan farm. John Byington (1798-1887) had maintained a station of the Underground Railroad at his home in Buck's Bridge, NY, illegally transporting slaves from the South to Canada. Sojourner Truth (c. 1797-1883), one of the Black heroes of abolition, was closely associated with the SDA work in Battle Creek. This itinerant lecturer against slavery enjoyed the friendship of John Byington, Dr. J. H. Kellogg, and other prominent SDAs. Not only did she regularly attend the Battle Creek Tabernacle church and camp meetings, but many students of the Battle Creek college visited her home near Battle Creek regularly. In fact, one of her books was printed by the Adventist publishing house. Frederick Douglas's was attracted to the faith; though he never joined the church his daughter became an Adventist. The fact that leading Adventist figures had previously been Abolitionists undoubtedly influenced the attitude of the early SDA church on the question of the relationship between Blacks and Whites. For a sympathetic discussion, see F. D. Nichol, *The Midnight Cry* (Washington, D.C.: Review and Herald, 1944), 54, 175-178, 301; Roy Branson, "Ellen G. White: Racist or Champion of Equality?" *Review,* April 9, 1970, 3; Ronald D. Graybill, "The Abolistionist-Millerite Connection," in Ronald L. Numbers and Jonathan M. Butler, eds., *The Disappointment: Millerism and Millenarianism in the Nineteenth Century* (Bloomington, Ind.: Indiana University Press, 1987), 139-152; Louis B. Reynolds, *We Have Tomorrow: The Story of American Seventh-day Adventists With an African Heritage* (Hagerstown, Md.: Review and Herald, 1984), 22-27. For an alternate assessment, see Malcolm Bull and Keith Lockhart, *Seeking A Sanctuary: Seventh-day Adventism and the American Dream* (San Francisco: Harper and Row, 1989), 194-197.

[9]See my *True to Principle: Radical Discipleship in God's End-Time Church* (Ann Arbor, Mich.: Berean Books, 2000), 25-34.

[10]Ellen White also chided White Adventists who apparently found unattractive the task of working among "degraded" and "repulsive" Blacks. She wrote: "God cares no less for the souls of the African race that might be won to serve Him than He cared for Israel. He requires far more of His people than they have given Him in missionary work among the

people of the South of all classes, and especially among the colored race. Are we not under even greater obligation to labor for the colored people than for those who have been more highly favored? Who is it that held these people in servitude? Who kept them in ignorance, and pursued a course to debase and brutalize them, forcing them to disregard the law of marriage, breaking up the family relation, tearing wife from husband, and husband from wife? If the race is degraded, if they are repulsive in habits and manners, who made them so? Is there not much due to them from the white people? After so great a wrong has been done them, should not an earnest effort be made to lift them up? The truth must be carried to them. They have souls to save as well as we" (*Southern Work,* 14-15).

[11]Louis Reynolds, *We Have Tomorrow,* 22.

[12]*SDA Encyclopedia,* 1192.

[13]At the time of Mrs. White's 1891 appeal, "there were not more than 20 colored Seventh-day Adventists south of the Mason-Dixon Line . . . at a time when we had a world membership of about 30,000" (Arthur L. White, "Survey of the E. G. White Writings Concerning the Racial Question." A paper presented to the Human Relations Committee, September 13, 1961, available at the E. G. White Research Center as Document DF 43-e). Helvius Thompson also mentions that "by 1890, there were about 50 Black Adventists in the south" (Thompson, "Do We Still Need Regional (Black) Conferences?" 2/50).

[14]"Our Duty to the Colored People," "Work Among the Colored People," "An Appeal for the Southern Field," "An Example in History," "The Bible the Colored People's Hope," "Spirit and Life for the Colored People," "'Am I My Brother's Keeper?'," "Lift Up Your Eyes and Look on the Field," "Volunteers Wanted for the Southern Field," "Proper Methods of Work in the Southern Field," "The Field Becoming Difficult," "A Neglected Work." Most of these articles were published by the same titles in *Review and Herald,* April 2, 1895; Nov. 26, 1895; Dec. 3, 1895; Dec. 10, 1895; Dec. 17, 1895; Dec. 24, 1895; Jan. 14, 1896; Jan. 21, 1896; Jan. 28, 1896; Feb. 4, 1896.

[15]It seems that a majority of Christians in the South simply acquiesced to the status quo in American society. Prior to the slave Emancipation and Civil-War days in America, there were no separate Black churches or denominations as we know them today. In the South, Black slave church members belonged to their masters' congregations. Though the churches were interracial, at meetings and church gatherings the Negroes were separated—often relegated to the back seats. For a brief discussion of the reaction of the early SDA missionaries to the South, see *SDA Encyclopedia,* 1192-1193.

[16]It is a matter of record in American history that "in the 1890's, in a period of economic and political unrest, segregation increased sharply, and many legal restrictions date from that time." See *Seventh-day Adventist Encyclopedia,* revised edition (Washington, D.C.: Review and Herald, 1976), 1193.

[17]A case in point was the situation in the Washington, DC., area churches, where some were unwisely urging the association of Blacks and Whites on the grounds that they were equal in society. Ellen White acknowledged that, indeed, Blacks and Whites were equal: "Both white and colored people have the same Creator, and are saved by the redeeming grace of the same Saviour. Christ gave His life for all. He says to all, 'Ye are bought with a price.' God has marked out no color line, and men should move very guardedly, lest we offend God. The Lord has not made two heavens, one for white people and one for colored people. There is but one heaven for the saved." (*Manuscript Releases,* vol. 4, 33). But while

acknowledging the equality of Blacks and Whites in society, Ellen G. White warned that the unwise agitations and hasty actions by some churches could flare up the already volatile racial feelings in society and, consequently, thereby jeopardize the missionary work among both races. It was for this reason that she encouraged separate lines of work for Blacks and Whites. Mrs. White wrote: "There is a work to be done for both the white and the colored people in Washington, and in the neighboring States. Many obstacles will arise to retard this work. Inconsiderate or premature movements would bring no real satisfaction, and would make it far more difficult to carry forward any line of work for the colored people. The work in behalf of this people has been sadly neglected, and the powers of darkness are prepared to work with intensity of effort against those who take up this work. From the light given me, I know that every injudicious movement made in or about Washington, or in other parts of the Southern field, to encourage the sentiment that the white and the colored people are to associate together in social equality, will mean more in retarding our work than any human mind can comprehend." She continued: "There is too much at stake for human judgment to be followed in this matter. If the Conference should say that no difference is to be recognized and no separation is to be made in church relationship between the white people and the colored people, our work with both races would be greatly hindered. If it should be recommended and generally practiced in all our Washington churches, that white and black believers assemble in the same house of worship, and be seated promiscuously in the building, many evils would be the result. Many would say that this should not be, and must not be" (ibid., 32). Ellen White did not consider laboring along separate racial lines as jeopardizing her strong stand against racism. "Those white people who appreciate the ministry of Christ in their behalf, cannot cherish prejudice against their colored brethren" (ibid., 33).

[18]Louis B. Reynolds, *We Have Tomorrow: The Story of American Seventh-day Adventists With an African Heritage* (Hagerstown, Md.: Review and Herald, 1984), 42.

[19]J. A. Crisler, Letter to James Edson White, quoted in letter from James Edson White to "Friend and Fellow-Worker," December 18, 1898.

[20]Some twelve years after the incidents in the late 1890s, A. W. Spalding visited Yazoo City to interview the workers there for his book. It was reported that Rogers was often "accompanied by a string of boys holding his coat-tails, chorusing, "Nigger-lover! Nigger-lover." Spalding also mentioned how on one occasion, Rogers was knocked down, pelted with brickbats, had his hat shot off, and was chased to his home by a bloodthirsty mob. See Arthur W. Spalding, Letter to William C. White, September 26, 1912; cf. his letter to W. C. White, October 6, 1912.

[21]F. R. Rogers to James Edson White, quoted in a letter from James Edson White "Friend and Fellow-Worker," December 18, 1898.

[22]Ibid. In his reply to Rogers the same day, Edson White wrote: "Of course we are willing to trust all these matters to the Lord, and yet He requires us to be very cautious; and the Testimonies [counsels from Mrs. White] point out to us the necessity of such extreme care that prejudice shall not be aroused among this class of people down here, for, if it is, it will shut us off from the work entirely." J. E. White, Letter to F. R. Rogers, December 1898.

[23]See also Ron Graybill, *E. G. White and Church Race Relations* (Washington, D.C.: Review and Herald, 1970), 56-57; idem, *Mission to Black America* (Mountain View, Calif.: Pacific Press, 1971), 130-131; cf. Reynolds, *We Have Tomorrow*, 102-104;

Charles E. Dudley, Sr., *"Thou Who Hath Brought Us . . ."* (Brighton, NY: Teach Services Inc., 1997), 179.

[24]Wrote Mrs. White:"We are to avoid entering into contention over the problem of the color line. If this question is much agitated, difficulties will arise that will consume much precious time to adjust. We cannot lay down a definite line to be followed in dealing with this subject. In different places and under varying circumstances, the subject will need to be handled differently. In the South, where race prejudice is so strong, we could do nothing in presenting the truth were we to deal with the color line question as we can deal with it in some places in the North. The white workers in the South will have to move in a way that will enable them to gain access to the white people. . . . Let colored laborers do what they can to keep abreast, working earnestly for their own people. I thank God that among the colored believers there are men of talent who can work efficiently for their own people, presenting the truth in clear lines. There are many colored people of precious talent who will be converted to the truth if our colored ministers are wise in devising ways of training teachers for the schools and other laborers for the field. *The colored people should not urge that they be placed on an equality with white people.* The relation of the two races has been a matter hard to deal with, and I fear that it will ever remain a most perplexing problem. So far as possible, everything that would stir up the race prejudice of the white people should be avoided. There is danger of closing the door so that our white laborers will not be able to work in some places in the South" (*Testimonies for the Church,* 9:213-214).

[25]In 1896, Mrs. White wrote: "There is an objection to the marriage of the white race with the black. All should consider that they have no right to entail upon their offspring that which will place them at a disadvantage; they have no right to give them as a birthright a condition which would subject them to a life of humiliation. The children of these mixed marriages have a feeling of bitterness toward the parents who have given them this lifelong inheritance. For this reason, if there were no other, there should be no intermarriage between the white and the colored races" (*Selected Messages,* 2:343-344; cf. 481-488). Again she wrote in 1912: "In reply to inquiries regarding the advisability of intermarriage between Christian young people of the white and black races, I will say that in my earlier experience this question was brought before me, and the light given me of the Lord was that this step should not be taken; *for it is sure to create controversy and confusion.* I have always had the same counsel to give. No encouragement to marriages of this character should be given among our people. Let the colored brother enter into marriage with a colored sister who is worthy, one who loves God, and keeps His commandments. Let the white sister who contemplates uniting in marriage with the colored brother refuse to take this step, for the Lord is not leading in this direction. *Time is too precious to be lost in controversy that will arise over this matter. Let no questions of this kind be permitted to call our ministers from their work. The taking of such a step will create confusion and hindrance. It will not be for the advancement of the work or for the glory of God"* (Letter 36, 1912; emphasis mine).

[26]For an insightful discussion of the relationship between the incidents in Yazoo City, Edson's letter to Mrs. White, Sis. White's letter to Ballenger, and her statement in *Testimonies for the Church,* volume nine, see Ronald Graybill's *E. G. White and Church Race Relations,* 57-68.

[27]Bull and Lockhart, *Seeking A Sanctuary,* 195-196, 201. They are, however, correct in suggesting that "what began as an evangelistic expedient eventually became the denomination's preferred method of dealing with the races, especially as the black

membership grew" (ibid., 197).

[28]*SDA Encyclopedia,* 1193.

[29]J. E. White, Letter to M. A. Cornwell, October 10, 1899; emphasis mine. It is true that Edson White cannot be regarded as an inspired interpreter of his mother's counsels any more than anyone else. But as Graybill correctly noted, Edson "worked more closely with her on this subjet of race relations than any other person and was certainly closer to the situation than anyone else. It is significant, then, to notice that he interprets her testimonies concerning separate schools as given in order that the work for Negroes might not be closed by white prejudice, and says that the prejudice is only to be regarded when a different course would make it difficult and impossible to reach the people at all" (Graybill, *E. G. White and Church Race Relations,* 65-66).

[30]A chapter describing the creation of Black (Regional) conferences is titled: "Separate Conferences: A Road to Fellowship" (see Louis B. Reynolds, *We Have Tomorrow: The Story of American Seventh-day Adventists with An African Heritage* [Hagerstown, Md.: Review and Herald, 1984), 292. Another work mentions that the reason why some influential Blacks urged the then GC president [J. L. McElhany] to organize "separate conferences for Black members [was] in the hope of preserving unity in the Seventh day Adventist church" (see W. W. Fordham, *Righteous Rebel: The Unforgettable Legacy of a Fearless Advocate for Change* [Hagerstown, Md.: Review and Herald, 1990], 76; cf. Reynolds, *We Have Tomorrow,* 294). A prominent leader of the General Conference (one time president of the Michigan Conference), is also quoted in *Righteous Rebel* as saying, "Racial segregation originated in the Bible as the divine way for nations to get on together" (ibid., 75).

[31]David R. Williams, "The Right Thing to Do," *Adventist Review,* February 20, 1997, 25.

# 23

# TWO CHURCHES—ONE BLACK AND ONE WHITE?

Can the good news of God's amazing grace address the baneful shortcomings of our mazing (confusing) race? Every Christian denomination has had to deal with this thorny question as it has confronted racism in its manifold expressions. Whether we are talking about tribalism in Africa, ethnic cleansings and neo-Nazism in Europe, Black and White racism in North America, etc., the challenge is the same. What should be the Christian's response to racial prejudice and discrimination?

Our Seventh-day Adventist church is today grappling with what to do with its racially separate conference system in North America. Should we continue to maintain this structure? Or should we tear down the walls? This chapter continues our discussion from the previous chapter, looking at four more myths regarding the validity of separate Black and White conferences. We shall look at how these racially segregated conferences came into being, and what we ought to do about them.

### "Blacks Demanded Racially Separate Conferences"

Those who are unwilling to dismantle the existing racial structures in the church sometimes argue that the current arrangement was demanded by Blacks. The unspoken assertion implied in this argument is that either Blacks are responsible for the structural racism that exists or, at the very least, they prefer to maintain the current Regional (Black) conference system.

This popular myth is a naive oversimplification of what actually prompted the Regional conferences. It also erroneously assumes that whatever a group of people prefer is necessarily right.

A little over a decade ago, two non-Adventist scholars offered an unflattering critique of the Seventh-day Adventist church. They noted that "although the relationship between whites and blacks in the church was never one of master-servant, it was certainly one of master-pupil." In their assessment, "the Adventist black, who, although perhaps loved by his white brothers, has never been totally convinced that they want him to sit with them." It is against this background that these scholars identify the formation of Black (Regional) conferences in 1944 as "the most important institutional development" in the SDA church.[1]

The above comment may be a little exaggerated. But there is some validity in their claims regarding Black-White church relations in the United States—at least in the years following Ellen G. White's death in 1915. During this period, many loyal Adventists suffered racial discrimination simply because they were Black. A number of prominent Black Adventist ministers and layperson also gave up their affiliation with the Adventist church because of its treatment of Blacks.[2]

One Adventist scholar writes: "White Adventist congregations and administrative leadership positions were rarely accessible to Blacks prior to the 1940s. The first Black person to work at the General Conference was the director of the Negro Department. Neither he nor Black visitors to the General Conference were permitted to eat in the Review and Herald cafeteria (the eating place for the General Conference workers at the time). Segregation was the norm for the first half of the 1900s. Across the United States the denomination's schools and institutions did not yet have an equitable admissions policy."[3]

**The Creation of Black (Regional) Conferences.** Although serious discussions had been going on since 1889 for the creation of separate Black conferences,[4] the spark that ignited the flame for immediate action to organize Regional conferences was an unfortunate racial incident at our Washington Adventist hospital in 1943.[5]

In October 1943, Bro. Byard took his wife, Lucy, to the Washington Adventist Sanitarium and Hospital in Takoma Park, Maryland for medical treatment. Both Bro. Byard and his wife were Black, but of a very light complexion. They were also longtime Adventists from Brooklyn, New York.

Because she was gravely ill, Lucy Byard was brought by an ambulance and was admitted without hesitation. But before treatment was begun, her admission slip was reviewed. When her racial identity was discovered, she was told a mistake had been made. Without examination or treatment, she was wheeled from her hospital room into a corridor as the hospital staff called around to other hospitals to transfer the patient. She was transferred by automobile—not even granted the use of an ambulance—across State line to the Freeman's Hospital, where she later died of pneumonia. According to rumor, she contracted this pneumonia while waiting in the hallway of the hospital wearing only a hospital gown. This incident, along with similar cases of racial discrimination stirred the Black constituency immeasurably.

They demanded that the General conference act to ensure that such discriminatory and inhumane treatment of blacks would not occur again. The Black members were not only concerned about admittance to hospitals, but the whole questions of quotas in schools, lack of employment in church institutions, and a general absence of solicitude for them in the church were subjects of their protest. They employed the press and pulpit to whip up sentiment in their favor.

To quiet the brethren, Elder W. G. Turner, an Australian and President of the North American Division, went to the Ephesus church in Washington, D.C. (now the DuPont Park church), the next Sabbath, October 16, 1943. He chose as his text 1 Peter 4:12: "Beloved, think it not strange concerning the fiery trial which is to try you as though some strange thing happened unto you." He had hardly sat down after completing his message when brother James O. Montgomery (father of Alma Blackmon, for many years the director of Oakwood College's choir) stepped to the front of the congregation and delivered his speech.

Montgomery, who was sitting near the front of the church, placed his violin in the seat he occupied near the organ, stepped up front and declared: "Think it not strange? Yes, I think it is very strange that there is an Adventist college (Washington Missionary, now Columbia Union) nearby to which I cannot send my children. Yes, I think it is strange! A denominational cafeteria [at the Review and Herald] in which I cannot be served, and now this incident. I think it mighty strange." Among other things, he said in his speech: "I am not prepared to hear you say 'servants obey your masters,' meaning the General Conference is our master."[6]

After the service, a group gathered around him and promptly formed a committee.[7] That Saturday night, October 16, 1943, this group of lay people met in the back room of Joseph Dodson's bookstore and hastily organized the National Association for the Advancement of Worldwide Work Among Colored Seventh-day Adventists. Joseph Dodson was elected as chairman and Alma J. Scott as vice-chairman. To accomplish their objective of arousing Black members throughout the country, they made telephone calls and, after a quick printing of stationery, dispatched scores of letters. John H. Wagner, secretary of the Colored Department in the Columbia Union, acted as advisor. The meeting closed officially after the president of the General Conference, Elder J. Lamar McElhany, agreed to meet the committee at the General Conference office building the next day, Sunday, October 17, 1943. Because of Elder McElhany's promise to report all the proceedings to the General Conference Committee and because of the very pointed discussion, a longer one was held on Sunday October 31, 1943.

It should be pointed out that the idea of forming a separate Black conference was *not* the stated goal of the group. It was the complete integration of Blacks into the church. This lay group was simply demanding the end of discriminatory practices in the church.[8] In response, the General Conference president voted to call in all of the Black Departmental men and pastors of the leading Black churches from all over America in order to discuss the race problem at a special meeting during Spring Council, April 8-19, 1944. The agenda called for the *integration* of White conferences. But during the meeting, the idea of Black conferences evolved as a new type of organization for the Black worker.

Not all—Black or White—favored the creation of a racially separate conference. Some were fearful that "the decision for the organization of Black conferences might lead ultimately to a complete separation from the Adventist church. Furthermore, some of our Black brethren were suspicious that some of the leaders had ulterior motives."[9]

There were also differences of opinion as to the proper solution to the racial impasse. "Some advocated the status quo approach, which would essentially leave conditions as they were—hoping that the situation would evolve into a more acceptable state. Others wanted full and complete integration, regardless of the mind-set of the White Adventist membership. Then there was the group that believed that the regional conference arrangement would resolve the tensions without compromising the essential unity of the body. Still others advocated more radical solutions."[10]

So as a strategic move to overcome the diversity of opinions among Whites and Blacks, it was decided that the GC president, Elder McElhanny, was to make the request for the separate Black conference. The rationale was that "Black leaders who oppose the idea of a separate administrative organization will readily accept the proposal if it comes from the General Conference president . . . . It will receive support from the White leadership as well."[11]

Indeed, the fears of some of the Black brethren opposed to the idea were put to rest by the unequivocal support voiced by the church's top White leaders. For example, the GC president argued: "To me it is wonderful to see that the colored have large churches efficiently led and directed by colored men. We have some colored churches with more members than we have in some conferences. I think our colored men do a very good job. This gives me confidence in their being leaders. To say that a man could be a pastor of a thousand membership [church] if they were divided into conferences seems to me to be inconsistent in reasoning."[12]

A former president of the General Conference, Elder William A. Spicer, also spoke in favor of separate Black conferences: "Brethren, in Europe we have German conferences, French conferences, Swedish and Polish conferences; why not Black conferences?" Elder J. J. Nethery, president of the Lake Union Conference, and later a vice president of the General Conference, also supported the idea with a powerful speech. He said: "There are Black leaders who are qualified to become administrators."[13] Most important, by having separate conferences they would "be able to save more souls in their territory."[14]

In the end, on April 10, 1944, after a heated debate, the question was presented to the floor to vote: "Shall Regional conferences be organized?" The vote to accept and implement the proposal was unanimous:

> In union conferences, when the Colored constituency is considered to be sufficiently large enough, and when the income and territory warrant, separate conferences for the Colored membership shall be organized. Such conferences are to be administered by Colored officials and Colored committees.[15]

Thus, begun the "non-ideal" practice of separate Black (Regional) conferences.[16] What started as an unfortunate racial incident, propelled into a demand for racial *integration*, but ended up in a racial *separation*.

Though many of the Black lay people called for integration, many of the black ministers, aided by the white leadership, wanted black conferences due to the inequalities that were occurring. For them, separation with power was better than the status quo at that time.

One Black writer emphasizes: "The National Association for the Advancement of World-Wide Work Among Colored Seventh-day Adventists did not ask for Negro conferences either in their original presentation or in their agenda. They asked for complete integration." He continues by quoting the words of Joseph T. Dodson, chairman of the above lay group that was organized after the tragic incidence of Lucy Byard, "They gave us our conferences instead of integration. We didn't have a choice. In the end it was better to have segregation with power, than segregation without power."[17]

**Segregation with Power.** Contrary to the protests by some, the Black (Regional) conference in North America can be viewed as "segregation with power."[18] The argument that won the day was not a biblical or theological one, but a pragmatic or political (some will say racist) argument. For, if, indeed, the Blacks were doing "a very good job," if it gives confidence "in their being leaders," and if some Black leaders were "qualified to become administrators," why couldn't they be integrated into the existing (White) conference structure?

If there was any theology at all in the arguments for Black (Regional) conferences, it is a theology of separation, not reconciliation and unity. This theology of separation is no different from the argument used by an earlier group of Black Adventists who had separated themselves from the organized Seventh-day Adventist church. In 1921, the General Assembly of Free Seventh-day Adventists was organized in Savannah, Georgia. The group explains why they broke away from the SDA church:

> It is a fact that many Black workers could not tolerate the injustices shown them because of their color. They gave up their positions in the work, with their church membership, too humiliated to accept 'crumbs' any longer. We stand upon the principle advocated by our father Abraham when he saw that other methods of peaceable coexistence [with Lot] failed. For the sake of peace and unity of spirit, we saw that

> a separation was necessary. . . . Black leaders suggested a course of action, separation, hoping to eliminate friction arising from prejudice in many areas of the United States. The impasse seemed irremovable except by a vital change, a separate Negro organization.[19]

So, we may ask: Did Blacks demand the creation of racially separate conferences? The answer is No. It can only be answered Yes if we qualify it by saying, "Blacks demanded the creation of racially separate conferences as a response to White racism."

In the words of a Black church administrator, the "proposal to formulate segregated units of organization," and thus the idea of racially segregated conferences, was "foisted upon them [Blacks] by White leadership" He explains further: "It is fair to say that the Black Adventist leadership early on agitated for total and complete integration. Failing to achieve that goal prior to the 1940s because of the near monolithic resistance of White leaders and the general membership, many African-American SDAs accepted a partial separatist status as a means of working successfully for the Lord among their people. . . . It is important to emphasize that the formation of Black conferences was proposed by the White leadership as a response to Black SDAs' request for integration."[20]

**Separate Conferences, A Concession to Racism.** We must, therefore, see the current black and white conference arrangement in North America as an unfortunate concession to racism. Though today we often try to reinterpret the existence of the separate conferences as due to a cultural difference between the two races, the sad truth is that White leaders at that time were not willing to share "power" with their qualified Black leaders. And the Black leaders were forced to seek separation as a way of exercising the power that had for a long time been denied them. Both Black leadership and White leadership wanted segregation with power. In other words, because Whites preferred "racism that is *in power*", Blacks opted for "racism that is *out of power.*"[21]

In the long run, anyone—Black or White— who continues to justify the existing racially inspired conference structures and who undertakes to defend it by constructing a dubious theology of racially separate churches has without knowing it embraced the racist's ideology of power (see chapter 19 of this book). Since racial prejudice, pride, hatred, and ill-treatment lie at the root of our black and white conferences, rather than pretending that our differences are simply cultural, we must recognize that we have a spiritual problem, and must humbly seek God's forgiveness as we work towards reconciliation and healing. The concern is not who is right, but what is right.

Two non-Adventist scholars have perceptively observed: "There have always been two poles in the history of the Negro in the United States. One is the push for integration and equal rights. The other, the desire for separation and withdrawal from white society. Integration is perhaps the initial goal, but if competition [between Blacks and Whites] becomes too fierce and the white majority proves too intransigent, blacks are likely to see separation as the best way forward. Segregation is then seen as the answer to discrimination. Certainly, in the Adventist case, blacks proposed regional conferences after they felt integration was an unobtainable goal."[22]

But racial segregation or separation is never a true answer to the sin of racism. The biblical answer is repentance and conversion, demonstrated by visible acts of reconciliation and unity. Thus, when Black leaders still defend the "propriety of the continuation of Regional organizations," it is only because they have effectively abandoned themselves to the mistaken notion that racial segregation is an effective "bridge leading to racial understanding and brotherhood."[23] And as we will later show, when the North American Division's 1999 Race Summit suggests that "inclusiveness and racial harmony" do not extend to the dismantling of the Black (Regional) conferences, our church leadership (mostly White) has essentially capitulated to the "segregation with power" arrangement foisted upon the church for half a century.[24] Both groups are betraying the gospel imperative for reconciliation and unity.

The black and white conference arrangement currently operating in North America is a non-ideal situation brought about by a church leadership which was unwilling to confront racism in the 1940s. The question before us is: Do we still need separate Black (and hence, white) conferences? Do we still need the separate but equal church structure? Should the policy of segregation with power continue in the Remnant church? *These questions are not about who is right, but what is right.* The questions simply challenge us to offer biblically legitimate reasons for continuing to maintain these visible manifestations of racism. Should we prefer a theology of separation to that of unity?

**"Separate Conferences Are Still Needed in the Church Today"**

Those who consider Black and White conferences as viable and valuable in the church today laud the progress and growth of the Black churches since 1944 as evidence that the current racially separate arrangement is still needed. But this argument fails to recognize that disobedience to God's instructions deprive us of His full blessings and, thus, greatly retard His cause.

There is no doubt that separate conferences have provided Blacks opportunities for evangelistic outreach, given them new opportunities for training and experience in ministry, leadership, service, and participation in church governance, and have afforded them eligibility for elected offices, and ex-officio representation on boards, councils and committees.[25] But are these pragmatic reasons compelling enough to justify the continued existence of the racially inspired church structures? Does the end justify the means? Should the "non-ideal" be viewed as ideal?

**What Could Have Been?** True, Black conferences and churches have experienced more impressive growth than had occurred before. It's also a fact that Black leaders have demonstrated administrative acumen that has matched, and in some cases surpassed, that considered to be the norm in the general church. But is it possible that the growth rates would have been even greater if we had been following God's will on race relations? If we (the church) decided to choose leaders solely on the basis of criteria in Scripture (e.g., 1 Tim 3; Titus 1, etc.), and not on skin pigmentation, is it possible that there would be far greater opportunities for minorities in leadership positions?

It is also true that church growth experts confirm that racially and culturally distinct churches make for more efficient evangelism. But one Adventist sociologist has poignantly responded: "Is it ever right to sacrifice the truth of the gospel for the expediency of efficient evangelism? If we win persons by distorting and compromising the gospel, what have we won them to? Christians must move beyond that which is expedient to that which is morally right. Racially oriented evangelism can produce racially insensitive and even racially prejudiced congregations."[26]

Some also justify the black and white arrangement on the grounds that Whites feel uncomfortable worshiping with Blacks and vice-versa. They point to "race flights" that have occurred in White congregations as Whites moved away because there were either too many Black members or too many

Black church officers. But do we really believe that we help the situation by catering to the prejudices of certain segments of our society? Are we more interested in quantity than in quality? Do the number of people in the church books really make up the kingdom of God? Are we not worsening the racial problem by creating artificial barriers which lessen black and white encounters within our church?

Black and White conferences necessarily require black and white churches and institutions to support the conferences. The only way to bring people together is to ensure that we remove the structural barriers that necessarily keep them apart. The point is that we cannot expect racial harmony at the grassroots level if the leaders are not prepared to work together at the conference levels. Racism is not an option for the Christian church, regardless of the perceived advantage it brings to both races.

**The Church in Antioch.** The apostolic church demonstrates that if we surrender to the Bible's teaching and the Holy Spirit's guidance, it is possible to have integrated churches, spirit-filled leadership, and church growth. For instance, we read in Acts 13:1:

"Now there were in the church that was at Antioch certain prophets and teachers; as Barnabas, and Simeon that was called Niger, and Lucius of Cyrene, and Manaen, which had been brought up with Herod the tetrarch, and Saul. As they ministered to the Lord, and fasted, the Holy Ghost said, Separate me Barnabas and Saul for the work whereunto I have called them. And when they had fasted and prayed, and laid their hands on them, they sent them away."

The church in Antioch was a multiracial, multi-class, and cross-cultural church. The Lord had called into the fellowship and into leadership positions people from several nations and different social backgrounds. The names include those of Jews, Africans, and Roman aristocrats. There was no fight about ethnic identity, styles of worship, or leadership quotas. The church at Antioch was simply a fellowship from the then known world committed to reaching the world with the gospel. One Bible commentary summarizes:

> The Lord knew what He was doing! Note the magnificent mixture: Barnabas ["a Levite from Cyprus"; Acts 4:36], who had the rich background of the infant church in Jerusalem from Pentecost or shortly thereafter; Simeon, also called Niger, a

> Latin name showing two strong cultures in one person; Lucius of Cyrene, also a Latin name, clearly identified as coming from North Africa; Manaen, who had been raised (*súntrophos*) in the court of Herod the tetrarch (that is the court of Herod Antipas, father of Agrippa); and Saul, the converted Pharisee. It was a world fellowship to start a world movement. Even Mark, brought from Jerusalem, would add his own contribution later.[27]

There were no race flights in the church at Antioch, for neither Jew nor Gentile fled from the church when believers from the other ethnic group joined. There were no strategizing sessions behind closed doors to keep minorities from leadership positions. And there was no caucausing to map out how to put minorities in positions of leadership. Neither group opted for some non-ideal segregation with power. And they did not defend their theology of separation with pragmatic reasons or some questionable doctrine of "unity in diversity."

Jewish scholars in Antioch never thought of their Gentile counterparts as incapable of serious theological and ethical reflection. And the Gentiles never thought of Jews as incapable of preaching. In their institutions, no single ethnic or racial group was considered to have a monopoly on the treasury department, theology department, church ministry department, music department, or church human relations office (if one existed). At their church business meetings, Annual Council meetings, and General Conference sessions, there were no parliamentary maneuvers to legislate questionable theological views. And there was no effort on either side to circumvent or rebel against their biblically grounded GC session decision. On the contrary, the believers in this apostolic church proved that the gospel has power to transform human hearts and create racial reconciliation and harmony.

It is obvious that these early believers did not employ a quota system to elect or appoint their leaders. For the Lord Himself helped the church in Antioch to choose the right kinds of leaders. But He did so while the believers were worshiping together and fasting together. No wonder Antioch was the city in which believers were first called Christians (Acts 11:26). And no wonder that as they preached the Lord Jesus, "the hand of the Lord was with them: and a great number believed, and turned unto the Lord" (11:20).

**What about the American Church?** The Seventh-day Adventist church is also a world fellowship with a global mission to every nation, kindred, multitude and tongue. The United States should be a microcosm of the world church. For many years, this great nation has sent missionaries to foreign fields to spread the word that all men are brothers and that we have one Father. The success of overseas missions strongly suggests that the gospel message can cross boundaries of race, nationality, and culture. Why can't the same gospel message cut across the color line in the United States?

Many people overseas are now asking those of us in America: "If you have a superior God, religion, and message, then why hasn't He changed the hearts of Blacks and Whites on this question of racism? Why do you still operate a racially segregated church structure? Can't you forgive one another? On issue after issue, you have conducted yourselves as if you arc more mature or principled than the rest of the church. Thus, you have worked hard to dismantle the racial structures in the church in South Africa. When are you going to confront your own pride, prejudice, ignorance, and superstitions on Black and White racism?"

What will be our response? To simply say we are not perfect is a cop-out. For whatever the Lord bids us to do, He also enables us to accomplish it. Racism, in its myriads of expressions, goes contrary to the Lord's will. It is out of our Lord's mercy and longsuffering that our present segregated conferences have seen growth. God has blessed us in spite of our disobedience. But His mercy will not wait for too long. This is the time to dismantle the walls of black and white conferences. If we are not willing to be led by the Bible, we should at least learn from our society, which has taken major strides integrating the work place, schools, sports, and entertainment.

### "The Time Has Not Yet Come to Dismantle the Racially Separate Conference"

Those who still defend the existence of the Black and White conferences see the need to bring the church's practice in line with its biblical teaching. Yet they often argue that the time has not yet arrived to dismantle the racial structures in the church. They contend that the work for Blacks and Whites will not be very successful without the separate organizations. They sometimes misquote Mrs. White's *Testimonies* volume nine statement ("The time has not come for us to work as if there were no [racial] prejudices"; *Testimonies for the Church,* Vol. 9, p. 215) to support their contention that the current arrangement is the best way to reach the different ethnic groups.

In making the above claim, advocates fail to realize that the separate but equal conference system that was put in place in 1944 is a repudiation of the biblical teaching of reconciliation and unity, and an endorsement of the segregationist standard of racism, as the norm for Christian race relations.[28] They also overlook the fact that until Jesus comes, racism will always remain a human problem, and that Christ calls upon His church to transcend this particular sin as evidence of His power to change lives.

**Revisiting A Discredited [Kilgore] Policy.** Given Mrs. White's prophetic voice on the issue of race relations (as discussed in the previous chapter), she would not endorse the non-ideal practice if she were alive today. In fact, the argument that the work among Blacks and Whites will not be very successful without the separate church organizations is a racist argument that Mrs. White challenged in the 1890s when she was responding to what has come to be known as the Kilgore policy. Her commentary on this policy will be useful in our evaluation of the continued legitimacy of the existing Black (Regional) conferences.

In 1889, Charles M. Kinny, the first black minister to be ordained in the Seventh-day Adventist church was confronted by efforts to segregate him and his members at camp meeting. The embarrassing event took place when that year Kinny was ordained by Robert M. Kilgore "to the work of the ministry *among his own people*."[29] Kilgore was the leader of the SDA work in the South.[30]

According to Kilgore's report in the *Review and Herald*, that camp meeting at Nashville, Tennessee was not well attended as had been expected. There were several reasons for the poor turnout. But the main reason was this: "Another reason offered was the race question (the mingling of the colored brethren and sisters with those on the ground), the prejudices of the people keeping many away."[31] Later at a workers' meeting at the camp grounds Kilgore suggested that "Colored members [should] be separated from the rest of the audience at the camp meeting."

But Kinny, the Black minister, argued that segregation of Blacks at camp meetings was against "the unity of the third angel's message." Besides, "the recommendation would be one of great embarrassment and humiliation, not only to myself, but to [all] Colored members and future converts."

Despite the thorough discussion, this leader of the Adventist work in the South, Elder Kilgore, maintained his position: "The camp meeting is literally a failure because the White people object to the presence of Colored people at the camp meeting."[32]

It was at this point that Kinny proposed the idea of a separate black conference. For him, a "total separation" was preferable to "a separate meeting for the Colored people to be held in connection with the general meetings, or a clear-cut distinction by having them occupy the back seats." He then suggested his solution: "To solve this problem, there should be the organization of a Colored conference. Until there are enough Colored members to form a conference, let the Colored churches, companies and individuals pay their tithe and make other contributions to the regular state office. And when Colored conferences are formed, they should bear the same relation to the General Conference that White Conferences do."[33]

Unable to resolve that issue at the Nashville, Tennessee, camp ground, Kilgore brought the issue to the General Conference Committee in 1890, and led out in a resolution to establish a policy of segregated churches: "The work in the South for the White population will not be successful until there is a policy of segregation between the races." [34]

The Kilgore policy of 1890 was significant in that it was the first time a General Conference had voted to endorse racially segregated work. Attempts to do so at previous General Conferences had failed because the policy was deemed to be out of harmony with Scripture. However, in 1890 this Kilgore policy was established on the grounds of expediency, not sound theology.[35]

As the *SDA Encyclopedia* points out, this "policy of separation, at first adopted for the sake of advancing the gospel, eventually came to be so taken for granted that probably a majority of SDA members in areas where segregation was the custom believed it to be a fundamental teaching of the church."[36] This so-called Kilgore policy is the same justification being advanced by advocates of the present Black and White conferences.

Was this policy right? Did Ellen White endorse it? And would she endorse similar arrangements today? We already know what Ellen G. White's position was on the creation of separate conferences. In 1905, she rejected the idea when a proposal was made for separate German and Scandinavian conferences (*Testimonies for the Church,* 1:195-195). But what was her reaction to the Kilgore policy of racially separating the races presumably to advance the work among both Black and White?

Mrs. White addressed this very question in an 1891 appeal titled "Our Duty to the Colored People." In it, she referred to the 1889 meeting and indicated that the matter had been presented to her a year before "as if written with a pen of fire." Her reasons for opposing the Kilgore policy may be applicable to our present Black (Regional) conferences. She wrote:

> *To The Church:* At the General Conference of 1889, resolutions were presented in regard to the color line. Such action is not called for. Let not men take the place of God, but stand aside in awe, and let God work upon human hearts, both white and black, in His own way. He will adjust all these perplexing questions. We need not prescribe a definite plan of working. Leave an opportunity for God to do something. We should be careful not to strengthen prejudices that ought to have died just as soon as Christ redeemed the soul from the bondage of sin.
>
> Sin rests upon us as a church because we have not made greater effort for the salvation of souls among the colored people. It will always be a difficult matter to deal with the prejudices of the white people in the South and do missionary work for the colored race. But the way this matter has been treated by some is an offense to God. We need not expect that all will be accomplished in the South that God would do until in our missionary efforts we place this question on the ground of principle, and let those who accept the truth be educated to be Bible Christians, working according to Christ's order. You have no license from God to exclude the colored people from your places of worship. Treat them as Christ's property, which they are, just as much as yourselves. They should hold membership in the church with the white brethren. Every effort should be made to wipe out the terrible wrong which has been done them. At the same time we must not carry things to extremes and run into fanaticism on this question. Some would think it right to throw down every partition wall and intermarry with the

colored people, but this is not the right thing to teach or to practice (*The Southern Work,* 15).

On the basis of the above statement, we conclude that Ellen White would reject the current racially separate conferences in the United States: Her reasons for repudiating the "separate but equal" conference arrangement would be as follows: (1) "It is uncalled for"; (2) It is due to "a heart problem—both white and black"; (3) It will "strengthen prejudices that ought to have died" a long time ago; (4) "Sin rests upon us," for the way we may have handled the matter may be "an offense to God"; (5) Our missionary efforts to the different races must be "on the ground of principle"; (6) Church members must be "educated to be Bible Christians, working according to Christ's order"; (7) Blacks must hold "membership in the church with the white"; (8) Whites must make efforts "to wipe out the terrible wrong which has been done"; (9) Even when doing the right thing, "We must not carry things to the extremes"; (10) "Throwing down every partition wall"—including inter-racial marriage[37]—may not always be wise.

**Now Is the Time.** The above counsel was given at a time when the racial problem in the United States was far more serious than today's. If the Kilgore policy was "uncalled for" at that time, and if "sin rests upon us" for adopting that policy, what better reason do we have for refusing to break down the walls of separate conferences? If the time has not come to dismantle these separate church structures, when will be the best time to do so?

Let's remember that *now* is always the best time to do right. For obedience deferred is always disobedience. Now is, therefore, the time to dismantle our racially separate conferences in the North American Division.

### "Blacks and Whites Are Different, and Must Be Reached in Different Ways"

Advocates of the separate Black and White conferences often argue that Blacks are different from Whites. Therefore, we need different ways to reach each group Different worship and evangelistic styles are often cited as reasons why we need the separate churches and conferences.

But this argument also fails to recognize that Blacks and Whites are fundamentally the same. They are both sinners, have the same need of a Savior, and can only be reached by the same gospel. Moreover, the only worship styles the Bible recognizes are not Black and White styles of worship, but true and false worship styles. Every style of worship in the church should be subjected to biblical scrutiny. Culture should not be the norm. In the Jew-Samaritan situation we discussed in an earlier chapter, we showed that Jesus was not interested in any culture's worship style. He insisted that "all who worship the Father must worship Him in spirit and in truth" (John 4).

Finally, to argue for racially separate conferences in the United States on grounds that Blacks and Whites must be reached "in a certain way" also overlooks Ellen White's categorical rejection of this argument. She addressed a similar situation on September 24, 1885, when she addressed the third session of the European Union Council in Basel, Switzerland.

Because of the clash between different nationalities of Europe, she expressed her fears:

> I was almost afraid to come to this country because I heard so many say that the different nationalities of Europe were peculiar and had to be reached in a certain way. But the wisdom of God is promised to those who feel their need and who ask for it. *God can bring the people where they will receive the truth. Let the Lord take possession of the mind and mold it as the clay is molded in the hands of the potter, and these differences will not exist. Look to Jesus, brethren; copy His manners and spirit, and you will have no trouble in reaching these different classes.* We have not six patterns to follow, nor five; we have only one, and that is Christ Jesus. If the Italian brethren, the French brethren, and the German brethren try to be like Him, they will plant their feet upon the same foundation of truth; the same spirit that dwells in one will dwell in the other—Christ in them, the hope of glory. I warn you, brethren and sisters, not to build up a wall of partition between different nationalities. On the contrary, seek to break it down wherever it exists. We should endeavor to bring all into the harmony that there is in Jesus, laboring for the one object, the salvation of our fellow men (*Testimonies for the Church,* 9:181; emphasis mine).

To encourage the different nationalities of Adventists to work together, avoiding the ethnic conflicts within society, she presented a series of messages on unity. Her topics included "Love and Forbearance Among the Brethren," "Unity Among Laborers," and "Unity Among Different Nationalities." She urged:

> Some who have entered these missionary fields have said: 'You do not understand the French people; you do not understand the Germans. They have to be met in just such a way.' But I inquire: Does not God understand them? Is it not He who gives His servants a message for the people? He knows just what they need; and if the message comes directly from Him through His servants to the people, it will accomplish the work whereunto it is sent; it will make all one in Christ. Though some are decidedly French, others decidedly German, and others decidedly American, they will be just as decidedly Christlike. . . . God wants the different nationalities to mingle together, to be one in judgment, one in purpose. Then the union that there is in Christ will be exemplified (*Testimonies for the Church,* 9:180-183).

Ellen White's final warning to the leaders in Europe is applicable to our situation today. Shall we tear down the walls of racially separated conferences in America? We need to heed the prophetic voice:

> I warn you, brethren, and sisters not to build up a wall of partition between different nationalities. On the contrary, seek to break it down whenever it exists . . . We are to demonstrate to the world that men of every nationality are one in Christ Jesus. Then let us remove every barrier and come into unity in the service of the Master (ibid, 183-196).

**The 1999 Race Summit: Form or Substance?**

Recently, the North American Division (NAD) of Seventh-day Adventists organized a Race Summit at the Church's Headquarters in Silver Spring, Maryland, from October 27-30, 1999. "Rather than merely talk about critical racial issues," the organizers of the meeting sought to "concentrate on the important question of how to bring about positive change in race relations, recommend bold initiatives for dismantling racism, and create an on-going mechanism to continually motivate, expand, and monitor the progress of those initiatives." More than 300 administrators and institutional heads were summoned to the summit. About fifty "renowned thought leaders" were invited to speak.[38]

But despite their best intention, it seems that the NAD was not prepared to do the "unglamorous" thing of breaking down the visible expression of racism in the church. Following the much publicized 1999 Summit on Race, the NAD Office of Human Relations prepared a document detailing a set of "bold new initiatives" so that the church's "public and internal image will be one of inclusiveness and racial harmony." The detailed initiatives, and the corresponding timetables for each recommendation, are contained in an 8-page document titled *Suggested Activities Plan and Timetable for North American Division Race Relations Follow-up.*[39]

Consistent with its stated goal "to create a church body that transcends the social barriers of race, culture, class, ethnicity, gender, disabilities, etc., by reflecting the love and oneness of *a new humanity in Christ*,"[40] the Document offers several laudable suggestions. Among other things, the Document (1) calls for the appointment of a committee to "design and implement" the recommendations of delegates of the 1999 Summit on Race; (2) urges the leadership of NAD to approve October 24-27, 2001 as the dates for a second "Summit on Race"; (3) suggests to the NAD leadership to "build on the moral imperative of Jesus that will lead to a true diversity that incorporates culture, race, gender, and disability"; (4) calls upon the Office of Strategic Planning working with NAD to "create a vision for the future of our church based on values so its public and internal image will be one of inclusiveness and racial harmony"; and (5) urges various entities of the Division "to create a strategic plan to achieve that vision [of inclusiveness and racial harmony]."

**An Intriguing Parenthesis.** Bear in mind that participants at the 1999 Race Summit were "to recommend bold initiatives for dismantling racism."[41] Thus, each of the broad recommendations above contains detailed or specific activities, with their corresponding timetables. But there is an intriguing parenthesis in the Document's discussion of how to restructure the NAD's "ecclesiastical [church organizational] structure"[42]

That baffling parenthesis suggests that "inclusiveness and racial harmony" does not extend to the dismantling of the non-ideal Black

(Regional) conferences that were occasioned by White racism. This fact is captured in the most intriguing paragraph of the strategic plan regarding "ecclesiastical structure." For, immediately after it had urged the NAD leadership to conduct "leadership dialogues that will focus on how best to restructure to remove the image of the denomination as two churches—one black and one white," the Document adds these parenthetical words:

> "(Restructuring must not be seen as an attempt to eliminate black conferences and leaders but as an activity that will eliminate conference overlapping and that will result in the possibility of increased conference leadership opportunities for qualified blacks and other people of color.)"[43]

Let's reflect on the terse statement above. Our church in North America wants a restructuring in the ecclesiastical structure that would "remove the image of the denomination as two churches—one black and one white." And yet, it is unwilling to "eliminate black conferences and leaders." Why should this be so?

It seems to me that there is only one way to remove the image of the North American church as two churches: dismantle the Black (Regional) conferences *that were initially created as a concession to White racism. For, once we decide to eliminate Black conferences, the church would at the same time be forced to deal with the future of exclusively White conferences.* In other words, the elimination of Black conferences necessarily demand the elimination of White conferences.

The forbidden question then is this: Are we afraid to touch the issue of "Black conferences and leaders" because *Blacks leaders* are afraid to lose their power (hence the assurance of "the possibility of increased conference leadership opportunities for qualified blacks and other people of color")[44]? Or is it rather the *White leaders* who are afraid of losing their power (as a result of "the possibility of increased conference leadership opportunities for qualified blacks and other people of color")?

Or must we interpret the parenthetical statement as a calculated attempt to conceal the fears of *both* White and Black leaders in North America? As I see it, Blacks generally think that Whites are racists. And Whites generally think that Blacks hate them. Blacks see Whites as unwilling to relinquish power. Whites think Blacks want quotas to reward their perceived incompetence. Both groups agitate their congregations and constituencies into believing that it is the other race that has racial problems. And both refuse to see the issue as a spiritual one that calls for confession and reconciliation. Are these not the real issues behind the unwillingness of the NAD to break down the racial walls? And are these not evidence that we all need to be converted lest we perish together?

Candid answers to the above questions will reveal whether the 1999 Race Summit really sought "to do more than merely talk about our critical racial issues." The responses will also make clear to what extent the participants at the summit really sought to "concentrate on the unglamorous but very important question of how to bring about positive change in our race relations."[45]

I must repeat again. The issue I'm focusing on is not about who is right, but rather, what is right.

The North American Division is correct in noting that "it is through leadership that the outcomes of the Summit will reach communities throughout the Church—particularly [at] the congregational level, which is the place where we really do church!"[46] This is because conference leaders set the racial tone for pastors and members at the congregational levels. In other words, racially exclusive conferences encourage the creation of racially exclusive churches, camp meetings, schools, and workers.

Now, if the conference leaders—Black and White—remain segregated, as the "bold initiatives"of NAD's *Suggested Activities Plan* indicate, how can we expect church members and pastors at the local levels to work toward racial reconciliation and harmony?

How can we fulfill the stated goal of the Race Summit Follow-Up (namely, "to create a church body that transcends the social barriers of race, culture, class, ethnicity, gender, disabilities, etc., by reflecting the love and oneness of *a new humanity in Christ*"),[47] when we are unwilling to eliminate the racially segregated conferences created by the racism of a previous generation? Does not our action bolster "the image of the denomination as two churches—one black and one white?" Can we honestly and legitimately speak about "inclusiveness and racial harmony" when our leadership at the Conference administrative levels chooses to live apart? Wouldn't segregation at the conference level ultimately lead to demands for racially segregated Unions?[48]

**Bold Initiatives or Photo Op?** Unless we are willing to eliminate Black (Regional) conferences (which also necessitates the dismantling of exclusively White conferences), then the elaborate plans for a second summit in October 2001 will be legitimately construed as another photo-op designed to convince no one but us that our refusal to eliminate the racially separate structures do not stem from our lust for power. Let me be more specific.

The *Suggested Activities Plan* Document contains many laudable suggestions for a second summit. But what is the use of hosting "continental prayer breakfasts" and "diversity banquets" for racial healing if we cannot regularly sit at the Lord's communion table (because we choose to worship in racially exclusive churches)?

What is the use of planning many "burying the hatchet handle services" to "rid participating individuals of all racial prejudices and hindrances to racial reconciliation as a result of being pointed once again to the cross of Jesus Christ" if we are unwilling to talk candidly about why we still need racially separate conferences?

And what value is there in conducting "diversity celebration services" if we are unprepared to remove the organizational structure that discourages us from worshiping together weekly? Occasional diversity services is not the same as worshiping together. Jesus did not commute between heaven and earth to conduct some regular diversity celebration services; He came and dwelt among us.

I want to emphasize again that I am not opposed to the "bold new initiatives" calculated to heal our racial wounds and restore racial harmony. Even though I question some of the cosmetic proposals, I see some merits in some of the suggested activities. My point is simply that unless we are willing to dismantle our racially separate conferences in the United States, the series of NAD proposals will be perceived as nothing more than a photo op—the adoption of meaningless forms without any substance. Here is a summary of those "bold initiatives":

—highlighting many "successful events . . . with awards ceremonies"

—contracting and paying many "diversity professionals" to conduct "leadership training sessions"

—inviting GC Presidents to "generate enthusiasm" to encourage initiative in other divisions

—purchasing from vendors additional materials "for growth in race relations"

—denouncing racism as "sin, [and] an evil that must be addressed"
—issuing many "public commitments" to all entities of the Division challenging them on how to deal with differences
—instituting many "series of sermons on racism" for the "education of the faith community"
—developing many "organizing principles" as foundations for "anti-racist approaches using scripture, sacred writings, shared values, human service, human dignity"
—developing or revising "Vision, Values, and Mission Statements" that are not driven by economic or political forces "but by the egalitarian factors of the gospel"[49]
—creating "strategic plans" to achieve the vision of inclusiveness and racial harmony in *"ecclesiastical structure,"* a restructuring "to remove the image of the denomination as two churches—one black and one white"
—promoting and adopting the term "*inclusion* as a new paradigm for the Division," and making use of it in our programs, policies, personnel appointments, and practices
—developing mechanisms to "conduct policy and practice audits that will eliminate policies and practices which, directly or indirectly, disadvantage people of color and women"
—creating additional "strategic plans" to achieve the vision of inclusiveness and racial harmony in *congregations,* and developing approaches "to increase sensitivity to each other's history, culture, personal experience, dreams for the future, and the intentional cooperation and exchange of members of diverse congregations"[50]
—creating many more "strategic plans" for racial inclusivity and harmony in *"education,"* utilizing all the media of the Church, "reaching all levels of the church, and presenting practical pathways"
—developing youth programs to address racism and classism "as essential mechanisms to eliminate racism in the life of the individual and the Church structure"[51]
—working at "minimizing racism in schools by carefully examining the total educational program"—its curricula, instructional methods, assessment practices, etc.

Yes, we may do all the above laudable things, and even more, "so that the Holy Spirit may have full say in the community of faith, preparing us on earth for the fellowship of heaven where all forms of diversity will be affirmed and celebrated forever." But unless we are willing to take the first step of eliminating the racially inspired conferences, none of the above "bold initiatives for dismantling racism" will be effective.

Moreover, do church leaders have the right to demand from local church pastors and members what they themselves are not prepared to do? The rubber meets the road when we decide to take away the color code from our church structure in North America.

We must be prepared to eliminate black conferences *in such a manner as would allow for increased conference leadership opportunities for all qualified Adventists not just for Blacks.* Qualified Adventists are not necessarily those who have previously patronized and benefitted from the racial structures, nor those with impressive degrees or political acumen. Rather, all leaders for the structures of our church organization must meet the biblical requirements of 1 Timothy 3:1-7, 2 Timothy 4:1-5, and Titus 1:5-9. In other words, all Adventists aspiring for leadership roles must, in the words of Martin Luther King, Jr., not be judged by the color of their skin but by the content of their character.

**Beyond the Prudence of Racial Prejudices.** The current black and white conference arrangement in North America is a concession to racism. It is based on pragmatic expediency, not sound theology. This system, and the separate houses of worship it encourages, must not continue till Jesus comes. The first step in any bold initiative for dismantling racism in the church must be the elimination of black conferences in North America, a step which necessarily calls into question the existence of separate White conferences.

If we are not willing to dismantle the racial structures *now*, we must truthfully ask ourselves why not. Is it because *we* are afraid to admit our own racism and unwilling to do something about the sin? And if we are not prepared to vote the elimination of black and white conferences at the next Summit on Race, we must seriously question the purpose and morality of again spending hundreds of thousands of dollars for an event that will be more talk than substance.

In the words of Ellen G. White, "I call upon every church in our land to look well to your own souls. . . . Whatever may be your prejudices, your wonderful prudence, do not lose sight of this fact, that unless you put on Christ, and His Spirit dwells in you, you are slaves of sin and of Satan" (*Southern Work,* 13).

Is it not time for us to pursue a better way? This may be our finest hour to do something about the wall of racism.

---

**Endnotes**

[1]Malcolm Bull & Keith Lockhart, *Seeking A Sanctuary: Seventh-day Adventism and the American Dream* (San Francisco: Harper and Row, 1989), 202, 206, 197. For a documentation of how blacks were treated in the church, see ibid, 197-206. At the time of publishing their work, Malcolm Bull was a junior research fellow at Wolfson College, Oxford, and Keith Lockhart was a journalist who wrote for the London *Independent* and the London *Guardian*. A more sympathetic critique of the church's policies and practices on race relations can be found in W. W. Fordham's *Righteous Rebel*: *The Unforgetable Legacy of a Fearless Advocate for Change* (Hagerstown, MD: Review and Herald, 1990); cf. Louis B. Reynold's *We Have Tomorrow: The Story of American Seventh-day Adventists with An African Heritage* (Hagerstown MD: Review and Herald, 1984). W. W. Fordham is a retired church leader, who lived through and played major roles in the church's Black-White struggles; he was the first president of the Southwest Regional conference, and later served at the General Conference as Director of the Regional Department; Louis B. Reynolds had served the church as editor of *Message* magazine, as scriptwriter for Breath of Life telecast, and as field secretary of the General Conference of SDA.

[2]During the period between 1915-1950, the church accepted the social patterns of racial segregation and discrimination in our schools, hospitals, etc. Blacks had given tithes and offerings to support these institutions; yet they were excluded from them. Church leaders felt that Blacks were incapable of leading and governing in any respect. See J. Messar T. Dybdahl, "The Utopia Park Affair and the Rise of Northern Black Adventists," *Adventist Heritage* (January 1974), 36-41. Robert H. Carter, the late Lake Union president , recalled that in 1941, during a Literature Evangelism Institute held at the Southern Publishing Association, black colporteurs were asked to enter the building where the meetings were being held from the rear. They were to use separate restrooms, drinking fountains and dine at a separate time from whites. During this same period of time, black ministers were paid approximately one third that of his [*sic*] white counter-part. While black ministers were expected to minister to three to four churches, they were discouraged from purchasing automobiles. In the late 1940s the dining room at the Review and Herald Publishing Association was segregated. Elder G. E. Peters was the only black staff member of the General Conference and as Secretary of the Negro Department occupied an office located in the basement of the office." Refer to Alan Curtis Perez, "Factors in the Development of Regional Conferences and Black Union Movement," Unpublished term paper (Andrews University, 1978), 10; available at the Andrews University E. G. White Research Center in Document File #DF42.

[3]Delbert Baker, "Regional Conferences: 50 Years of Progress," *Adventist Review,*

November 1995, 12. See also, W. W. Fordham's *Righteous Rebel,* 60-77.

[4]See Appendices 6 and 7 in Fordham's *Righteous Rebel,* 131-141.

[5]The historical account that follows is a condensation from Louis Reynold's *We Have Tomorrow,* 292-322; Louis Fordham's *Righteous Rebel,* 66-83; Jacob Justiss, *Angels in Ebony,* 43-51.

[6]Jacob Justiss, *Angels in Ebony,* 43, 44.

[7]The committee included some prominent Black Adventists in the Washington, DC, area. Among them were: Joseph T. Dodson, Chairman, who had operated his own funeral service; Alma James Scott, the Vice-Chairman, was the founder of the first social Settlement House for Negroes in the entire world; Eva B. Dykes was the first Black woman in the US to receive a Ph.D; and Valerie Justiss, Secretary, who would be the second Black SDA to receive a Ph.D.; and Arna Bontemps, a noted Black author of the Harlem Renaissance.

[8]In April 1944, the group printed an 8-page pamphlet entitled "Shall the Four Freedoms Function Among Seventh-day Adventists"? The document stated that "the present policy of the white Adventists in responsible positions will not stand the acid test of the Judgment." It cited examples showing that "colored people are not admitted generally to our institutions as patients, students and nurses," "no academies like the Shenandoah Academy are available in the East for our colored youth," "academies that might accept colored students are not easily accessible," "there is no standard satisfactory creditable academy for our colored youth," "injustice was the policy of Emmanuel Missionary College [now Andrews University]," "the 'quota' Policy of our institutions of higher learning with its limitations of equal opportunities for our colored youth to obtain a Christian education is indefensible," there are no negroes so far as we know on staffs of Adventist institutions," "there is a policy of evasion and futile appeasement relative to our work," "negroes do not have adequate representation on committees at all levels—local, union, and general conferences," "the policy in the field of employment is unfair, partial and un-Christlike," and "the policy in spiritual matters is too one-sided and narrow." See "Shall the Four Freedoms Function Among Seventh-day Adventists"? in Delbert W. Baker, ed., *Telling the Story: An Anthology on the Development of the Black SDA Work* (Loma Linda, Calif.: Loma Linda University Printing Services, 1996), 2/10-2/16.

[9]Fordham, *Righteous Rebel,* 78.

[10]Baker, "Regional Conferences: 50 Years of Progress," 12.

[11]Fordham, *Righteous Rebel,* 78.

[12]Minutes of the first meeting of black delegates at a special meeting of General Conference Committee, held at Stevens Hotel, Chicago, April 8-19, 1944.

[13]Fordham, *Righteous Rebel,* 79; Reynolds, *We Have Tomorrow,* 295.

[14]General Conference Spring Council premeeting (April 8-9, 1944) and the Spring Council minutes of the General Conference of SDA (April 10, 1944).

[15]*Actions of the Spring Meeting of the General Conference Committee,* April 10-16, 1944, 15, 16; cf. *SDA Encyclopedia,,* 1195. Lake Region lead the way with a constituency meeting in Chicago, IL (1944); Northeastern Conference followed with a meeting in New York City (1944); Allegheny Conference had its in Pine Forge, Pennsylvania (1945); South Atlantic in Atlanta Georgia (1945); South Central Conference in Birmingham, Alabama (1945); Southwest Region Conference in Dallas, Texas (1946), with W. W. Fordham as president; Central States Conference in Kansas City, Missouri (1947). But there was

a notable exception: "Plans were modified in the Pacific Union because local black leaders felt regional conferences would not be acceptable to the membership in the Far West. The Pacific Union was thus the only union with large congregations that did not organize a separate administration for its minority membership" (Reynolds, *We Have Tomorrow,* 295).

[16]*SDA Encyclopedia* (1966 edition), 1059.

[17]See Jacob Justiss, *Angels in Ebony,* 61.

[18]Some Adventists take offence at the suggestion that the current separate church structures evidence racial segregation. For example, Helvius L. Thompson writes: "Some misguided Adventists, Black and White, have called Regional conferences 'church-structured segregation.' However, they fail to realize that there is a big difference between segregation and separation. Segregation is forced separation and degrading isolation. But voluntary separation is the freedom to choose or decide where you want to go and who you want to be with. Black conferences are no more segregation that your choice of which church you attend and hold membership in" (Helvius L. Thompson, "Do We Still Need Regional [Black] Conferences?" in *Telling the Story,* 2/53). But J. T. Dodson, one of the founders and chairman of the National Association for the Advancement of World-Wide Work Among Colored Seventh-day Adventists puts Thompson's protest into a better perspective: "They gave us our conferences instead of integration. We didn't have a choice. In the end it was better to have segregation with power, than segregation without power" (see Jacob Justiss, *Angels in Ebony,* 61).

[19]The General Assembly of Free Seventh-day Adventists was led by a former Adventist preacher. Like other Black denominations that broke off from their White brethren on account of racism, John Manns also left the church and set up his own denomination because he felt that the lack of acceptance of Black leaders was a breach in the "brotherhood of believers." The above theological rationale for establishing a new denomination is set forth in a pamphlet he put out. See W.W. Fordham, *Righteous Rebel,* 70.

[20]He concludes: "In the main, African-American Adventist have always desired to follow what they consider to be the model of the Bible when it related to race relations among Christians. However, lacking full and complete inclusion, Black SDA leadership has made the best of the situation. They settled for 'self-determination' and have opted to take full advantage of the separation that was foisted upon them by White leadership" (Ricardo B. Graham, "Black Seventh-day Adventists and Racial Reconciliation," in Calvin B. Rock, ed., *Black Seventh-day Adventists Face the Twenty-first Century* [Hagerstown, Md.: Review and Herald, 1996], 136-136).

[21]As explained in an earlier chapter, "racism in power" (or imperialistic/aggressive racism) is full-blooded, in that "it can walk on its feet and strike with its feet because its spirit permeates the institutions of power"—political, economic, educational, ecclesiastical and other cultural institutions. On the other hand, "racism that is *out of power"* (i.e., counter/reverse racism) is a racism that "lacks feet to walk on and fists with which to strike. The spirit is present; the hope is compelling; but the will to power cannot find the institutions of power through which it can express itself"( Kelsey, *Racism and the Christian Understanding of Man,* 10-11).

[22]Bull and Lockhart, *Seeking A Sanctuary,* 202-203.

[23]For example, in their response to "questions about the propriety of the continuation of Regional organizations," the leadership of the Black conferences argued their case in

the following resolutions: "WHEREAS, It is the opinion of this council that the Regional conferences and the Regional Department are not only relevant for the times, but were used of God especially for these days, and WHEREAS, The years have proven the wisdom of Regional organizations as attested by the phenomenal growth of the constituency and the unprecedented financial support which has come to the church through the channels of Regional organizations, and WHEREAS, These Regional organizations have served effectively as a bridge leading to racial understanding and brotherhood, *We recommend,* That a positive statement be prepared reaffirming our support and belief in our present form of organization, and that this statement appear in the *Review and Herald,* the union papers and the INFORMANT, thus making crystal clear to the church that the responsible leadership of the approximately 70,000 Regional constituents meeting at the Quadrennial Advisory Council of the General Conference of Seventh-day Adventists in Miami, Florida, is not divided, but is united in reaffirming the loyal support of our present constituted form of organization, namely the Regional Department and Regional conferences." See "Actions of the Regional Advisory Committee in Miami, April 7-9, 1969," reproduced as Appendix B in Louis Reynold's *We Have Tomorrow* (1984), 365-366; cf. Helvius L. Thompson, "Do We Still Need Regional (Black) Conferences [in 1995]?" in Delbert W. Baker, ed., *Telling the Story,* 2/49-2/56.

[24]See, *Suggested Activities Plan and Timetable for North American Division Race Relations Follow-up,* 4-5. The document, a series of recommendations from the 1999 "Race Summit," was prepared by the Office of Human Relations and presented to the President of the North American Division. Among other things, it urged the NAD leadership to conduct "leadership dialogues that will focus on how best to restructure to remove the image of the denomination as two churches—one black and one white." But the Document immediately adds these parenthetical words: "(Restructuring must not be seen as an attempt to eliminate black conferences and leaders but as an activity that will eliminate conference overlapping and that will result in the possibility of increased conference leadership opportunities for qualified blacks and other people of color.)" (ibid).

[25]See the *SDA Encyclopedia,* 1192; Delbert W. Baker, "Regional Conferences: 50 Years of Progress," *Adventist Review,* November 1995, 11; cf. Helvius L. Thompson, "Do We Still Need Regional (Black) Conferences [in 1995]?" in Delbert W. Baker, ed., *Telling the Story,* 2/49-2/56; Louis Reynold's *We Have Tomorrow* (1984), 365-366;

[26]David R. Williams, "The Right Thing to Do," *Adventist Review,* February 20, 1997, 25.

[27]Lloyd J. Ogilvie, "Acts," in *The Communicator's Commentary* (Waco, Texas: Word Books, 1983), 207.

[28]"In some ways, the events of 1944 [when Black conferences were created] put into practice the Supreme Court decision of 1896, which saw the two races, at least in theory, as 'separate but equal.' Given the racial climate in the nation as a whole, it might be thought that the development of black Adventist conferences was inevitable. But this is not necessarily true. The Jehovah's Witnesses, however, showed a markedly greater capacity for racial integration than did the Adventists. The Mormons, on the other hand, unashamedly held to a doctrine of white supremacy, barring blacks from the priesthood and avoiding contact with them. It was Adventism that most closely followed national trends in that it accepted blacks into its community but adopted segregationist policies" (Bull and Lockhart, *Seeking A Sanctuary,* 198).

[29]Robert M. Kilgore, in *Review and Herald,* Oct. 29, 1889, 683. This kind of ministerial ordination to one region of the church, is equivalent to the "division based" women's ordination request at Utrecht in 1995. Or, even the rebellious ordination services for "women pastors" in certain influential churches in North America.

[30]In 1889, the General Conference divided the United States and Canada into six districts. District number 2 included all the Southern States east of the Mississippi (the only exception was Virginia and Maryland). Elder R.M. Kilgore, an Iowan and former officer in the Civil War, was chosen Superintendent of this district in 1890. At the General Conference in April 1901, the nine states of this field were organized into the Southern Union.

[31]Ibid.

[32]It is likely that Kilgore's segregational policy may have been influenced by his earlier experience in Texas. A noted Adventist historian notes that "Kilgore's eight years of labor in Texas [1877-1885] were not without difficulties; several times he was threatened with lynching, and on one occasion his tent was burned down. Public opposition may have led to the curtailing of the church's unofficial educational work for blacks. As an ex-Union officer, Kilgore was sensitive to the charge that Adventists were 'Yankees' come 'to preach nigger equality'; a charge he denied. Opposition from prejudiced whites may also have contributed to the early demise of a school for freedmen begun in 1877 by Mrs. H. M. Van Slyke in Ray County, Missouri" (R. W. Schwarz, *Light Bearers to the Remnant* [Mountain View, Calif.: Pacific Press, 1979], 233-234).

[33]W. W. Fordham, *Righteous Rebel,* 67. Kinny reasoned: "Where the two races cannot meet together without [trouble] in the church, it is better to separate. That missions be established among them [the Colored race], thus raising up separate churches. . . . That in view of the outside [world's] feeling on the race feeling, and the hindrances it makes in accomplishing the work desired among the Whites, the attendance of the Colored brethren at the general meetings should not be encouraged, yet not positively forbidden. . . . I would say in this connection that in my judgment a separate meeting for the Colored people to be held in connection with the general meetings, or a clear-cut distinction by having them occupy the back seats, etc., would not meet with as much favor from my people as a total separation. . . . That when Colored conferences are formed they bear the same relation to the General Conference as the White conferences" (see "Statement by C. M. Kinny, Nashville, Tennessee, SDA Camp Ground," October 2, 1889, reproduced as Appendix 6, in Fordham's *Righteous Rebel,* 131-133); cf. Reynolds, *We Have Tommorrow,* 296-297.

[34]Fordham, *Righteous Rebel,,* 67; Reynolds, *We Have Tomorrow,* 297; *SDA Encyclopedia,* 1194.

[35]One church historian has accurately pointed out that during the General Conferences of 1877 and 1885, "the question of whether or not to bow to Southern prejudices by establishing separate work and separate churches for blacks was debated. Most speakers believed that to do so would be a denial of true Christianity since God was no respecter of persons. In 1890, however, R. M. Kilgore, the Adventist leader with the most experience relative to the South, argued for separate churches. D. M. Canright had urged this policy as early as 1876 during a brief period of labor in Texas. Eventually their recommendation prevailed, but the policy was never defended on grounds other than those of expediency" (Schwarz, *Light Bearers to the Remnant,* 234).

[36]*SDA Encyclopedia,* 1194. "The practice of separate Negro congregations has not been

uniformly followed. In many parts of the country there are no separate churches, and even in areas where the Regional conferences operate, not all colored members are in the Regional churches. In some places the colored congregations were established by members who chose to withdraw from white congregations in order to have their own groups and work better for Negro evangelism; in other places, 'where demanded by custom,' the separation was the result of local necessity" (ibid).

[37]Ellen White's judicious counsel above—as also reflected in her "Counsel Regarding Intermarriage" (*Selected Messages,* 2:343-344)—goes beyond the *color* line to include any kind of incompatibility (be it of religion, age, social status, ethnicity, etc.) that is likely to adversely affect the couple and the children who are involved in the marriage relationship. Mrs. White points out some of the problems and pressures experienced by couples and children of interracial marriages. These factors add to the stresses commonly experienced in marriage.

[38]The "renowned thought leaders" included: Dr. Samuel Betances, futurist, author, motivational speaker, and senior consultant for Chicago based Souder, Betances, and Associates, Inc.; Dr. Tony Campolo, professor of Sociology at Eastern College in St. Davids, PA, author of 26 books, and producer of "Hashing It Out," a weekly television show on the Odyssey Network; Dr. Edwin Nichols, a Washington, D.C.-based psychologist, motivational speaker, and director of Nichols and Associates, Inc.; Dr. Betty Lentz Siegel, nationally recognized lecturer and president of Kennesaw State University in GA; and Dr. Cain Hope Felder, professor of New Testament in the School of Divinity at Howard University in Washington, D.C. See, Celeste Ryan, "Adventist Church Hosts Race Relations Summit," *Adventist News Network* [ANN], October 19, 1999; cf. *Modeling the Ministry of Christ: Making It Happen!* (the Summit on Race Relations Program Booklet).

[39]*Suggested Activities Plan and Timetable for North American Division Race Relations Follow-up,* 1, 4. The document was prepared by the Office of Human Relations and presented to the President of the North American Division.

[40]*Suggested Activities Plan and Timetable for North American Division Race Relations Follow-up,* 1 (emphasis in original).

[41]Rosa T. Banks, "Making It Happen," in an invitation brochure prepared for potential attendees to the October 27-30, 1999 "Race Summit." See also the "Terms of Reference" in the same brochure.

[42]The Document offers detailed strategic plans to achieve the church's vision of "inclusiveness and racial harmony" in (1) the "ecclesiastical [church organizational] structure," (2) local congregations, and (3) education of various levels of the Church, including the youth department and the institutions of learning. Since this chapter is dealing with the racially segregated church structure in North America, the first item (recommendations dealing with "ecclesiastical structure") is of particular interest to us (*Suggested Activities Plan,* 4-5).

[43]*Suggested Activities Plan and Timetable for North American Division Race Relations Follow-up,* 4-5. The document was prepared by the Office of Human Relations and presented to the President of the North American Division.

[44]The fourth suggestion under the strategic plan for "ecclesiastical structure" aims at "developing a mechanism for encouraging administrators of the North American Division to conduct policy and practice audits that will eliminate policies and practices

which, directly or indirectly, disadvantage people of color and women." See *Suggested Activities Plan,* 5.

[45]Rosa T. Banks, "Making It Happen," in an invitation brochure prepared for potential attendees to the October 27-30, 1999 "Race Summit."

[46]Ibid.

[47]*Suggested Activities Plan and Timetable for North American Division Race Relations Follow-up,* 1.

[48]Some Black leaders argued in the past for the creation of Black unions, the next level of government in the SDA polity. For example, rightly recognizing the current Black-White conference arrangement as one of racial power, E. E. Cleveland supports Black unions because it is "imperative that black men have someone at Union Conference level to speak for them" (see E. E. Cleveland, "Regional Union Conferences," *Spectrum* 2:2 [1970]: 44). Calvin Rock also argues for Black unions on the grounds of the genuine cultural differences that exist between Blacks and Whites (Calvin Rock, "Cultural Pluralism and Black Unions," *Spectrum* 9:3 [1978]: 4-12). Observe that the church has repeatedly rejected the proposals for Black Unions; see Benjamin Reeves, "The Call for Black Unions," *Spectrum* 9:3 (1978): 2-3; cf. Jonathan Butler, "Race Relations in the Church," 4, *Insight,* February 20, 1979, 13-14.

[49]In the next chapter I will offer a different perspective on the "egalitarian factors of the gospel."

[50]My point is simply this: The best way to "to increase sensitivity to each others' history, culture, personal experience, and dreams for the future" is to encourage people to work together. Also the "intentional cooperation" mentioned in the NAD document can take place only when the different races are working, studying, and worshiping together. When this happens, there would be no need for an "exchange of members of diverse congregations."

[51]This suggested plan calls upon youth to help in combating racism in the life of the individual "and the Church structure." But are leaders running the church structures willing to do their part—namely, dismantle the racial structures of church organization?

# 24

# IS THERE A BETTER WAY?

Of all the Christian churches today, Seventh-day Adventists are the best equipped to deal with the challenge of racism. If we believe, as Ellen White did, that one day—in our day—the walls of racial prejudice and bigotry "will tumble down of themselves, as did the walls of Jericho, when Christians obey the Word of God, which enjoins on them supreme love to their Maker and impartial love to their neighbors" (*Christian Service,* 217), then Bible-believing Adventists who are eagerly awaiting the Lord's return have a unique opportunity to address racism in both society and the church. Three reasons can be given for this assertion.

**Our Unique Identity.** First, the Seventh-day Adventist church's self-understanding as *the remnant Church*—the true Israel of God—recognizes the fact that membership in the New Israel does not depend on natural birth but on the spiritual birth of conversion (Jn 3:3-21); not on ethnic blood but on the redeeming blood of Christ (Heb 9:14, 15; Rev 5:9). The only kind of race the Bible recognizes is not a superior race, but a holy race (1 Pet 2:9); and the only kind of segregation or *apartheid* (an Afrikaans word that means separation) acceptable in the biblical religion is separation from sin. The Bible requires us to display the beauty of racial harmony.

**Our Unique Mission.** Second, the Seventh-day Adventist church understands its reason for existence to be found in its unique *global mission* in the world. Members of this church have been called to praise Jesus Christ, the One who "has redeemed us to God by [His] blood out of every kindred, and tongue, and people, and nation" (Rev 5:9) and to proclaim His everlasting gospel unto "every nation, and kindred, and tongue, and people" (Rev 14:6). This mission demands that we transcend all the barriers of race that currently exist in our midst.

**Our Unique Name.** Third, the *unique name* by which the church is identified—Seventh-day Adventist—calls for an unparalleled display of racial harmony. The "Seventh-day" component of the name announces our theology of the Sabbath, a doctrine pointing to God as the Creator (and hence, re-Creator or Redeemer) and Father of all human races. The Sabbath is designed to remind believers, at least every week, of the inherent worth of every person and the need to treat each one—irrespective of gender, ethnic origin, religion or class—with respect and dignity (Exod 20:8-11).[1] Indeed, their doctrine of creation is "the antidote to idolatry," is the "foundation of true worship," is "the basis for true worth," and is "the basis for true fellowship."[2]

The "Adventist" component of the name recognizes that in the church awaiting Christ's return and in the earth made new will be people from "every nation, tribe, people, and language." That such a community should actually exist in a world torn by ethnic and racial divisions and hatred will be a wonder and a marvel to the world. The church could be "a kind of preliminary model, on a small and imperfect scale, of what the final state of mankind is to be in God's design."[3]

The above three defining characteristics of the church—its identity as a remnant, its global mission, and its unique name—compel the church to exhibit to the world a kind of racial harmony that has, perhaps, not existed since the early church. Describing how the early church conceived itself in the world, one second century writer noted:

> Christians are not to be distinguished from other men by country, language, or customs. They have no cities of their own, they use no peculiar dialect, and they practice no extraordinary way of life. Residing in cities of the Greek world and beyond it, as is the lot of each, they follow the local customs in clothing,

> diet, and general manner of life, but at the same time they exhibit the constitution of their own commonwealth as something quite paradoxical. They reside in their homelands—but as aliens. Every foreign land is home to them, every homeland a place of exile. . . .[4]

### Towards Racial Harmony

As Ellen White states, "The same agencies that barred men away from Christ eighteen hundred years ago are at work today." The spirit of pride and prejudice "which built up the partition wall between Jew and Gentile is still active."[5] If the racial problem is not to "ever remain a most perplexing problem" for the Adventist Church,[6] then the time is ripe for the church to seek biblical insights to address the problem of racism in the church.[7]

We must speak candidly to this forbidden subject. The suggestions that follow will be drawn from Acts 10, the Jew and Gentile encounter of Peter and Cornelius.

**1. Acknowledge Our Racial Prejudices.** Expounding upon the meaning of the holocaust for Christians today, David A. Rausch has stated: "The most dangerous attitude we can have is to think that we have no prejudice. The next danger is to believe that it cannot make us cold and indifferent—that it does not harm our society and that it takes no toll on our spiritual life."[8]

To begin the process of racial healing and harmony we must be humble enough to acknowledge the fact that we too, like the people in the world, have often harbored racial attitudes and engaged in racially discriminatory acts. This should not be too hard for us to accept since the Bible records that even in the apostolic church, among the pillars of the Christian faith, racial and ethnic prejudice thrived.

Thus, when Peter declared in the house of Cornelius, "Of a truth I perceive that God is no respecter of persons: But in every nation he that feareth him and worketh righteousness is accepted with him" (Acts 10:34), he was speaking for many of the early Jewish Christians. That Peter was not alone in "perceiving" that God is no respecter of persons is indicated by the fact that those who had come with Peter from Joppa "were amazed" at seeing the Gentiles in Cornelius home receive the outpouring of the Holy Spirit (Acts 10:45). Apparently, they thought that Gentiles were not worthy of such a gift. Even more, we are told in Acts 11 that when the brethren in Jerusalem heard the news, they were very upset. Therefore, Peter's statement of Acts 10:34 is a clear indication that the early Jewish Christians failed to fully grasp the fact that no form of ethnic or racial prejudice is justifiable under the gospel.

One rather surprising thing about the apostle's declaration is that it took some ten years after Pentecost for Peter—an apostle of Christ and a prominent leader in the Apostolic church, a Spirit filled Pentecost evangelist whose preaching on one day yielded some 3,000 souls—"to perceive" that God is no respecter of persons, and that his favor is not along racial or ethnic lines. Like the other believers, Peter had a theoretical knowledge of the truth of the gospel, yet he did not fully understand that it had some practical, ethical implications for his own life.

The truth of God being no respecter of persons, and His insistence that His followers be impartial, are recorded in several places in the Old Testament Scriptures (Deut 10:18, Job 34:19, 2 Chron 19:7). Peter and the others may have known this Bible truth, and their association with Jesus provided a living demonstration of this truth to them. Sadly, Peter and the others did not "perceive" that racism or ethnic prejudice is not acceptable to God.

Apparently, the disciples had bought so much into the established societal norms ("For we know that it is an unlawful thing for me who is Jew to. . ." [Acts 10:28; 11:1, 2]) that if they had their own way, they would certainly have maintained segregated churches on Sabbaths, they would have preferred to run segregated schools in the same towns and cities, and wherever possible, would have had segregated dining hall facilities (Gal 2:11ff). But for the Spirit of God, the privileged group in the early church (Jews) would have wanted to control the leadership and resources of the Church (Acts 6), paying little attention to the needs of the deprived members and making little effort to train leaders among the unfavored group.

We can be thankful that God gave clear instruction on this matter to Peter, instruction preserved in His Word.

Could the Scriptures be suggesting that even Bible-believing Seventh-day Adventists—God-fearing church members, well-meaning missionaries, successful evangelists, capable church administrators, articulate professors of religion or theology, prolific writers and editors, etc.—can exhibit racial or ethnic prejudice, without fully realizing it?

**2. Confess the Sins of Racism.** Peter's statement, "Of truth I perceive that God is no respecter of persons . . ." may also be understood as a public act of confession. He may have understood that injustice cannot be easily forgotten, but it can be freely forgiven upon confession. Therefore, if we desire racial harmony, we must confess our sins for whatever part we may have played, deliberately or unknowingly, in perpetuating racism.

We must confess our sin:

- for remaining silent when there was opportunity for us to act nobly and courageously in treating people of all races as equal;

- for shirking our responsibility to show concern for the poor, weak and oppressed, instead of blaming them for the racial injustices they suffer;

- for the racial slurs, epithets and jokes, and the innocent caricatures and stereotypes we have used for other races *when we were behind closed doors;*

- for our paternalistic "love" for the despised race—as long as we kept them "in their place";

- for the will-to-power that is often exhibited by covert political maneuvers at church council deliberations, elections, and appointments;

- for encouraging race-flight in the churches when other races begin to worship with us;

- for equating Christianity with Western civilization, and Seventh-day Adventism with ideologies of certain political systems or parties;[9]

- for placing prejudicial stumbling blocks in the path of our children, and letting them mimic our racial attitudes and actions.

But those of us who have been historic *victims* of racial prejudice and bigotry must also share moral responsibility for racism. We must confess our sins for being as much a part of the racial problem as the perpetrator.

We also must confess our sins:[10]

• for mirroring the prejudice we ourselves have experienced and retaliating with prejudice, bitterness and anger;

• for being suspicious of the intentions behind all genuine gestures of goodwill from persons belonging to the favored race and for rebuffing them as hypocritical;

• for accusing and blaming the children of the favored race for the wrongs committed by their parents;

• for the times when we, like Uncle Toms, have hypocritically eulogized the perpetrators of racism;

• for the occasions when, for personal gain, power, or anger, we have argued for the existence and perpetuation of racially exclusive churches, schools and institutions;

• for casting every conflict between us and others as a racial problem, and for blaming the results of our lack of responsibility upon other races.

• for our failure to empathize with victims of reverse discrimination, and for gloating in our hearts when we say to them, "Now you know how we have always felt."

For if we all confess our racial sins, He is faithful and just to forgive us and to cleanse us from all unrighteousness (1 Jn 1:9).

**3. Seek Biblical Solutions.** In the home of Cornelius, Peter called attention to what "God hath shewed me" about other races (Acts 10:28); similarly, all the Gentiles present sought to "hear all things that are commanded . . . of God" (v. 33). In other words, they asked for divine guidance. This means that since the inspired Scriptures express the mind and will of God (2 Tim 3:16-17), we must always seek *biblical* solutions to the problems that confront us. Three points have special bearing on our discussion of racial or tribal conflicts:

First, we must clearly understand that the root cause of racism is not merely economic or political exploitation, but *human pride.* If the problem of racism is a heart problem, then, the cure for it is not "education, culture, the exercise of the will, [or] human effort," all of which "may produce an outward correctness of behavior, but they cannot change the heart." There is a need to have a born-again experience. "There must be a power working from within, a new life from above, before men can be changed from sin to holiness. That power is Christ. His grace alone can quicken the lifeless faculties of the soul and attract it to God, to holiness" (*Steps to Christ,* 18).

Henry Ward Beecher put it well: "The moment a man's heart touches the heart of Christ in living faith, he becomes, whether he knows it or not, the brother of every other, in heaven or on earth, who has come into the same relationship with Christ. Whoever is united to Christ is brother or sister to everybody else that is united to Him."[11]

Second, in the pursuit of racial harmony, we must be clear about our objective. For example, we must pursue the path of *reconciliation,* not a forced *integration.* For while integration—a political pursuit that makes it illegal for one to discriminate against the other on the basis of his race—may be helpful in reducing the effects of racism, a lasting solution is only possible through the transforming power of Christ (2 Cor 5:16-21). The gospel imperative for reconciliation is much stronger than the legal urge for racial integration (Matt 5:24; 2 Cor 5:18-20).[12]

Third, we must not confuse the Christian's pursuit of *unity* among the various races, with the secular agitation for *equality*[13]—a political declaration that is enshrined in the constitution or laws of nations, and which can be redefined or revoked by legislators, when they so wish (e.g., the *Dred Scott* decision during the era of slavery, and the *Roe v. Wade* ruling with respect to the abortion issue). The Bible calls upon believers to pursue unity at all times (Jn 17:20-23), but as for equality, we must distinguish clearly between ontological equality and functional equality.

Ontological equality suggests that human beings *are* equal—in their standing before God, in all having been created in His image, in all needing salvation through Christ, in all having been called to the same destiny (Gen

1:26, 27; Gal 3:28; 1 Pet 3:7). The Christian recognizes that this equality results solely from God's action and purposes and not from any intrinsic qualities that human beings possess by themselves. It is a gift of God to every member of the human race, regardless of ethnicity, status or gender. This is what Paul had in mind when he wrote in Galatians 3:28 that "in Christ Jesus" there is "neither Jew nor Greek, neither slave or free, neither male nor female."

But as we showed in our discussion of the Galatians 3:28 text in chapter 10 ("The Feminist Campaign for Full Equality"), the Bible's teaching on ontological equality does not do away with functional role distinctions. Thus, ontological equality must not be confused with *functional* equality, the view that there is equality of ability, skill, gifts, office, or position. The Bible does *not* teach functional equality, since the Holy Spirit gives to each "severally as He wills" (see 1 Cor 12; Rom 12:3-8).

The *unity* to which Christians are called affirms ontological equality, not functional equality. Such unity seeks to employ our functional differences in a complementary manner for the advancement of God's kingdom. This understanding will correct some of the excesses of the various racial or gender equal rights movements.

**4. Develop Interracial Relationships.** Since racism is kept alive by ignorance of other races—the absence of genuine intimate knowledge of others, and an unwillingness to engage in genuine interaction—racial harmony can be restored and strengthened as we make the effort to move beyond our segregated homes, neighborhoods, schools, churches, conferences, etc., and relate meaningfully with people of other races. Such an attitude does not renounce the natural affinity we feel for those with similar culture, but it endeavors to expand our horizons through our coming to know, understand, and appreciate people of different backgrounds.

The process that led to Peter's perceiving that God is no respecter of persons began with *prayer* on the part of both Peter and Cornelius. Then, contrary to the restrictions imposed by social customs and traditions (Acts 10:28), Peter risked his life, career, and position in order to establish a *relationship* between himself, a representative of God from the favored race, and Cornelius, a member of the despised race. Whether the underlying division was ethnic or religious is immaterial; the gulf was wide, but God bridged it decisively. Peter allowed the messengers from Cornelius "to be his guests" (Acts 10:23 NIV), and Cornelius, apparently, permitted Peter and his fellow Jews to stay with him "for a few days" (Acts 10:48; cf. 11:3).

As a result of the encounter, Peter rejected the two extreme views people tend to adopt towards one another: 1) treating the superior race as divine and hence, "falling down at his feet and worshiping him" (see vv. 25-26), and 2) treating the inferior race as subhuman, as "common or unclean" (v. 28). "Peter refused both to be treated by Cornelius as if he were a *god,* and to treat Cornelius as if he were a *dog.*"[14]

Can we imagine what would happen if the different races in our church, in every part of the world, would interact with one another, visiting, praying, and sharing their homes, meals, and resources? When we truly get to know people of other races as real human beings, we shall:

- begin to identify our next door neighbors as Sue and John and not as "my white neighbors"; we shall recognize the physician as Dr. Kofi, not as a "fine black doctor";

- not only allow them to speak, but make efforts to *hear* them in our church publications and at our church council meetings;[15]

- put an end to the cultural snobbery that leads us to think and act as if we exhibit a far greater sense of ethical sensitivity—on issues of justice, fairness, equality, etc.—than do other races in the church;

- hire them in our churches and institutions, not in order to fulfill some racial quotas, but because they are the best qualified and most gifted personnel available;

- work toward developing models that show the spiritual and social significance of cohesive worship and ministry, and a missionary enterprise that allows workers to move "from everywhere to everywhere";

- celebrate their histories not as monuments to tokenism, but because their experiences have kinship with our own;

- carefully evaluate our attitude toward them if, despite our strong and wise counsel to the contrary, they enter into interracial or intertribal marriages with those of our race; for then, it will be easier for us to accept the members of the other race not only as our brothers and sisters in Christ, but also as our brothers and sisters-*in-law*.[16]

**5. Take a Stand Against Racial Injustice.** Restoring and strengthening racial harmony requires that we take a stand against any form of racial injustice, wherever and whenever it appears—and not only when the problem concerns our own tribe, race, or group. It compels us to be ethically sensitive to social issues affecting all human beings (war, abortion, capital punishment, euthanasia, gender and age discrimination, poverty, unemployment, ecology, etc). In this effort, those who have historically been perpetrators and beneficiaries of legal and institutional racism must take the lead.

The New Testament suggests that those in privileged positions and who benefited from their favored status—i.e., those who were slow to recognize that "God is no respecter of persons"—were foremost in speaking out in God's name against partiality, whether based on ethnic origin, religious background, or other distinctions. For example, Peter (1 Pet 1:17), Paul (Rom 2:11; Gal 2:6), and James (2:1) all proclaimed this doctrine without fear. John, the disciple, who once wished Jesus to call fire from heaven to consume the Samaritans, was the one who went on a loving mission to the Samaritans (Acts 8:14-25).

This may explain Ellen White's rhetorical question: "Is there not much due to them [the colored race] from the white people? After so great a wrong has been done them, should not an earnest effort be made to lift them up?"[17] This is the true spirit of Christianity, which teaches the believer "not to think of himself more highly than he ought to think" (Rom 12:3), "but in humility count others better than yourselves" (Phil 2:3, RSV).

Taking a stand for justice means that:

- some of us will have to go the extra mile by equipping, in whatever way possible, some members of the underprivileged race in the harness of their talents and gift as missionaries, administrators, theologians, etc.;[18]

• when there are opportunities for employment or advancement, etc., we shall not ignore or overlook some races;

• we shall not judge the intelligence, capability, or spiritual maturity of other races by how articulate they are in their use of particular languages;

• since English has been adopted as the lingua franca of the church, and yet a majority of the church does not speak it, in some instances, such as at major business sessions, the world wide church will have to make an alternate provision to enable the majority to voice their opinions (in say, Spanish, Swahili or Russian) on issues that affect the general direction of the church;

• in a world-wide church such as our own, no region of the world field will be encouraged to blackmail, defy, or circumvent the consensus of the church on theological issues;

• we shall quit masquerading our contempt for some races by acting as if the church in some parts of the world is more progressive or principled, enlightened or mature than the rest of the church;

• we shall emulate the example of Adventists in post-apartheid South Africa in overcoming the scandal of racially segregated conferences that currently exist in North America;

• whenever the church is called upon to compute its success, we will insist that the computation should not be in terms of numbers, dollars, or degrees, but in terms of faithfulness to historic Christian truths and in terms of costly discipleship.[19]

From the encounter of Peter and Cornelius in Caesarea (Acts 10), we may conclude that whenever we make genuine efforts at racial harmony, there will not only be an outpouring of the Holy Spirit, but there will also be conversions and baptisms (Acts 10:44-48; 11:15-18). Are we eager for the same?

### Conclusion

Human history records the tragic consequences of the disgrace of race. Racism has created in its victims a sense of inferiority, defeatism, resentment, and a determination to get even. It has despised, beaten, wounded, robbed, bruised, and left unconscious people of other races, while those who are in a position to show compassion and bind up the wounds of the victims of racism, like the priest and Levite in Christ's parable, have often passed by on the other side. Worse still, racism has murdered many innocent people just because of the shape of their noses, the color of their skin, eyes, or hair, or some other external feature—including age, weight, gender, or disability.

Can anyone still doubt the fact that the tenets of the secular religion called racism are so incompatible with the Christian faith that anyone who claims to be saved by grace, cannot live by race? Can it still be disputed that if a Christian is found to be a racist, his profession is a syncretistic faith, and hence a departure from the everlasting gospel?

The good news, however, is that Bible-believing Christians do not have to worship at any of the shrines of racism. In the person of Jesus Christ we have the God of all races. The children's Sabbath School song summarizes this:

> Jesus loves the little Children,
> All the children of the world.
> Red and yellow, black and white,
> They are precious in His sight.
> Jesus loves the little children of the world.[20]

These words state a very profound truth of biblical Christianity: the principle of love is the foundation of the supernatural religion that Christ Himself has founded[21]—love for God, and love for our neighbors—irrespective of their race. Even more, Christ Himself can effect the necessary transformation in our lives to follow in His steps.

Racism has disgraced the grace of race. It has left our world wounded, bleeding, and dying. Part of our mission in proclaiming the everlasting gospel to "every nation, and kindred, and tongue, and people" is to demonstrate visibly the triumph of grace over race. This triumph does not eliminate the differences among groups of people but transcends them through respect, acceptance, and Christlike love. Through the Savior's enabling power, we can show the world that, indeed, the remnant church is a beautiful model of what humanity's final state will be in God's design. Our strongest motivation to display the beauty of the grace of race is found in the teaching and personal example of our Lord Jesus Christ.

"Our remembrance of the love of Jesus, a love that directed Him to declare that even *enemies* are to be loved, should strengthen the Christian on this journey. If we are to love our enemies, should we not also love our fellow neighbor of a different race, ethnic origin, or religious faith?"[22]

Ellen G. White is emphatic: "When the Holy Spirit is poured out, there will be a triumph of humanity over prejudice in seeking the salvation of the souls of human beings. God will control minds. Human hearts will love as Christ loved. And the color line will be regarded by many very differently from the way in which it is now regarded."[23]

Indeed, Seventh-day Adventists maintain that:

> The church is one body with many members, called from every nation, kindred, tongue, and people. In Christ we are a new creation; distinctions of race, culture, learning, and nationality, and differences between high and low, rich and poor, male and female, must not be divisive among us. We are all equal in Christ, who by one Spirit has bonded us into one fellowship with Him and with one another; we are to serve and be served without partiality or reservation. Through the revelation of Jesus Christ in the Scriptures we share the same faith and hope, and reach out in one witness to all. This unity has its source in the oneness of the triune God, who has adopted us as His children (*Fundamental Beliefs of Seventh-day Adventists,* #13).

Can we imagine the powerful impact our Christianity will have, if we live out the ethical implications of this belief?

With prophetic insight, Ellen White looked beyond her day to ours and proclaimed, "When the Holy Spirit is poured out, there will be a triumph of humanity over prejudice in seeking the salvation of the souls of human beings. God will control minds. Human hearts will love as Christ loved. And the color line will be regarded by many very differently from the way in which it is now regarded" (*Testimonies for the Church,* 9:209).

She was most emphatic: "Walls of separation have been built up between the whites and the blacks. These walls of prejudice will tumble down of themselves as did the walls of Jericho, when Christians obey the Word of God, which enjoins on them supreme love to their Maker and impartial love to their neighbors. *For Christ's sake, let us do something now"* (*The Southern Work,* 43, emphasis mine).

Shall we respond to this *ethical* challenge of the three angels' messages? Are we eager for the Holy Spirit to knock down our walls of tribal and racial prejudices? Are we willing to allow God's impartial love to triumph over our pride, our hurt, and our hate? Are we prepared to let His amazing grace triumph over the disgrace of our mazing race? *"For Christ's sake, let us do something now"!*

---

**Endnotes**

[1]Refer to my "'Remember' the Sabbath Day," *Adventists Affirm* 8/3 (Year-End 1994), 5-14.

[2]*Seventh-day Adventists Believe . . . ,* 73-74.

[3]C. H. Dodd, *Christ and the New Humanity,* Facet Books Social Ethics Series 6 (Philadelphia, PA: Fortress, 1965), p. 2.

[4]*Epistle to Diognetus,* 5-6, quoted by C. H. Dodd, *Christ and the New Humanity,* Facet Books Social Ethics Series 6 (Philadelphia, PA: Fortress, 1965), 3-4.

[5]Ellen G. White, *Desire of Ages,* 403.

[6]Cf., Ellen G. White, *Testimonies for the Church,* 9:214.

[7]There is a sense in which we all are prisoners of our time and the cultures of our age. Consequently we do not always see some aspects of our respective cultures, however hard we try, until we are made to stand outside of it, and measure it by the standards that are not part of it. In order to address the contemporary problem of racism in the Church, it may be necessary to look at the subject as it manifested itself during the NT times. From the vantage point of the past, we may be able to assess our present situation, and thereby avoid the inescapable mind-set in which we have been set. Testing our contemporary presuppositions by the NT Church can help us avoid some mistakes on the subject of race relations (cf. Packer, "The Comfort of Conservatism," in *Power Religion,* ed. Michael Scot Horton, (Chicago: Moody Press, 1992), 291, where, in his discussion of the benefits of the Christian Tradition, he speaks about the sense of realism Christians gain when they learn from the experiences of the past).

[8]David A. Rausch, *Legacy of Hatred,* 1.

[9]Roger L. Dudley and Edwin I. Hernandez suggest that American Seventh-day Adventism tends to identify with the Republican Party. See Roger L. Dudley and Edwin I. Hernandez, *Citizens of Two Worlds: Religion and Politics among American Seventh-day Adventists* (Berrien Springs, MI: Andrews University Press, 1992), 149-211.

[10]George Kelsey, "Racial Patterns and the Churches," 74-76.

[11]W. L. Emmerson, *The Bible Speaks,* 2 vols. (Warburton, Victoria, Australia: Signs Publishing Co., 1949), 2:439, attributes the above statement to Henry Ward Beecher.

[12]Spencer Perkins, "Integration Versus Reconciliation," *Christianity Today,* October 4, 1993, 23.

[13]Equality is a concept introduced by scientists in their effort to define the basic relationship between some separate items. What is not generally recognized, however, is that the concept of equality is not scientific; it is neither provable nor disprovable. It is valid only when one *assumes* it. In other words, the idea of equality must be accepted by faith. As applied to human beings, individuals and groups are said to be equal solely because they are so declared. The Christian must therefore be clear in his or her mind regarding who it is that grants that equality and on what basis it is granted.

[14]John Stott, *The Spirit, the Church, and the World* (Downers Grove, Ill.: InterVarsity, 1990), 189 (emphasis mine).

[15]Ellen White: "Their [Blacks'] voices are to be heard in the representative assemblies" (*Testimonies for the Church,* 9:207).

[16]Adventists contemplating interracial marriage need to be cautioned by Ellen White's judicious "Counsel Regarding Intermarriage" (*Selected Messages,* 2:343-344), which points out some of the problems and pressures experienced by couples and children of interracial marriages. These factors add to the stresses commonly experienced in marriage. In most parts of the world, such factors make interracial marriages inadvisable at best and impossible to recommend. My concern here, however, probes the racial attitude that frowns on interracial/intertribal marriage or adoption for the *wrong* reasons, such as assuming that (1) some races are inherently inferior, or (2) intermarriage results in "blood mixing" or "mongrelization," or that (3) it is a case of spiritual "unequal yoking together." Such assumptions lead to the faulty conclusion that it is wrong or sinful for converted, Bible-believing Adventists of different tribes or races to be married. Too often this conclusion results in their rejection and isolation. Is it possible that some of our opposition to interracial marriages has more to do with our own racial biases than with Ellen White's judicious counsel—a counsel that goes beyond the *color* line to include any kind of incompatibility (be it of religion, age, social status, ethnicity, etc.) that is likely to adversely affect the couple and the children who are involved in the marriage relationship? This question calls for honest searching of heart.

[17]*Southern Work,* 11-12; "Every effort should be made to wipe out the terrible wrong which has been done them [colored race]" (ibid., 13); "The American nation owes a debt of love to the colored race, and God has ordained that they should make restitution for the wrong they have done them in the past. Those who have taken no active part in enforcing slavery upon the colored people are not relieved from the responsibility of making special efforts to remove, as far as possible, the sure result of their enslavement" (ibid., 74); "The Lord demands restitution from the churches in America . . . The Lord calls upon you to restore to his people the advantages which they have so long been deprived" (ibid., 144).

[18]Ellen White urged: "Special efforts should be made to increase the force of colored workers" (*Testimonies for the Church,* 9:207). "Among the negro race, there are many who have talent and ability" and "Many wise, Christian men will be called to work" (ibid., 202).

[19]Ellen White: "Many of the colored race are rich in faith and trust. God sees among them precious jewels that will one day shine out brightly. . ." (*Testimonies for the Church,* 7:229).

[20]It is very remarkable that this biblical truth is taught to our children at a very early age. The fact that this truth is put in a song, and repeated every week, suggests that adults expect their children to remember this cardinal teaching of Christianity, as they grow and live in a world torn by ethnic and racial hatred. It is therefore, a matter of surprise that by the time the children become adults and take their places in the pews and pulpits of the Church, and at the desks in classrooms and administrative offices of the Church's institutions, this truth is either misunderstood or largely forgotten, ignored, discredited, or even rejected. And with this attitude towards the theology undergirding the truth of God's love for the "Red and yellow, black and white," the church is left in a position in which it is totally incapable of confronting ethnic and racial prejudice and bigotry within and without the Church. Abdicating this responsibility, the Church then waits upon an ungodly society to demonstrate and prescribe ways by which racism should be addressed.

[21]The religion that was established by the life and message of the Incarnate Christ is one in which there is no caste, "a religion by which Jew and Gentile, black and white, free and bond, are linked in a common brotherhood, equal before God." See Ellen G. White, *Testimonies for the Church*, 7:225 (cf. idem, *Ministry of Healing*, 25-26).

[22]David A. Rausch, *Legacy of Hatred*, 15.

[23]White, *Testimonies for the Church*, 9:209; "Walls of separation have been built up between the whites and the blacks. These walls of prejudice will tumble down of themselves as did the walls of Jericho, when Christians obey the Word of God, which enjoins on them supreme love to their Maker and impartial love to their neighbors. For Christ's sake, let us do something now" (*Southern Work*, 54).

# 25

# "NO HUTU, NO TUTSI!"—A Testimony

*Must We Be Silent?* was inspired by the uncompromising faith I recently witnessed among our believers in the Central African countries of Rwanda and Congo. The report you are about to read was written by the Africa Indian-Ocean Division administrator who accompanied me on the trip to those countries. It reveals how and why some of our African believers transcended the barriers of race—even in life threatening situations.

**Christian Lifestyle in action**[1]

*"He that loveth father or mother more than me is not worthy of me; and he that loveth son or daughter more than me is not worthy of me. And he that taketh not his cross, and followeth after me is not worthy of me. He that findeth his life shall lose it: and he that loseth his life for my sake shall find it" (Matthew 10:37-39).*

One of the saddest realities of Christianity is that there are many Christians but few disciples. There are many intellectually convinced believers but few converted. Many have the knowledge about God but do not know Him experientially. Their religion does not touch the reality of life but remains only at a theoretical level.

But there are some notable exceptions. There are actually some

Christians today who truly believe that "We are called to be a godly people who think, feel, and act in harmony with the principles of heaven" (*Fundamental Beliefs of Seventh-day Adventists*, #21). In their general manner of life, they demonstrate that they not here to stay, but to get ready. And because they have already been crucified with Christ, they are not intimidated by the fear of poverty, reproach, separation from friends, suffering, or even death.

These individuals (i.e, those who are seeking to put Christian lifestyle into action) can be found in different parts of the world. Their lives challenge us to be true disciples of Christ. Recently, I spent one of the most enriching and rewarding trips of my ministry in the company of such believers in the Central African countries of Rwanda and the Democratic Republic of Congo (formerly Zaire). Let me share with you a few of their stories.

**1. Don't Deny Me From . . .**

Have you been so hurt that you find it difficult to forgive. If so, I'd like you to reflect on the experience of one woman in Rwanda.

As a result of the tribal genocide in Rwanda there are many widows and orphans. The Seventh-day Adventist church was not spared from this tragic experience. More than 15,000 of our members were killed. But our mighty God turned this tragedy into a wonderful opportunity to witness for Him.

An Adventist widow was told that the man who had killed her loved ones had been captured and was in a prison not far from where she lived. Upon hearing this, she went to the prison guards and requested to see the man. When asked why she wanted to see him, she told the guards that the man murdered her relatives but she wanted to take care of him according to the teaching of Christ. They couldn't believe their ears. Thinking she cherished a revengeful or sinister motive, they declined her request. But she persisted. In disbelief, the guards asked, "How can you do such a thing?"

Our dear sister explained that she was a Seventh-day Adventist Christian and had decided to follow what the Bible teaches no matter what. "It is written," our dear sister quoted, "'Love your enemies, bless them that curse you, do good to them that hate you, and pray for them which despitefully use you, and persecute you; that ye may be the children of your father which is in heaven . . . ' and 'Dearly beloved, avenge not yourselves, but rather give place unto wrath: for it is written, Vengeance is mine; I will repay, saith the Lord. Therefore, if thine enemy hunger, feed him; if he thirsts, give him drink . . . Be not overcome of evil, but overcome evil with good'" ( Matt. 5:44,45; Rom. 12:19-21).

After quoting the Scriptures, she pleaded with the prison guards: "Please, don't deny me from practicing my Christian duties: to love my enemy, feed him and give water to him."

Moved by her words, the guards granted her the permission to take care of the one who killed her loved ones. On a regular basis, she visited the man in the prison, fed him, gave him water to drink, and provided for his daily needs..

Here is Christian lifestyle in action. If you ask whether this kind of lifestyle is it worth it, our dear sister will most likely refer you to the following words in Matthew 25:34-40:

> Then shall the king say to them on his right hand, Come, ye blessed of my Father, inherit the kingdom prepared for you from the foundation of the world: For I was hungry, and ye gave me meat: I was thirsty, and ye gave me drink: I was a stranger, and ye took me in: Naked, and ye clothed me: I was sick, and ye visited me: I was in prison, and ye came unto me. Then shall the righteous answer him, saying, Lord, when saw we thee hungry, and fed thee? Or thirsty, and gave thee drink? When saw we thee a stranger and took thee in? Or naked, and clothed thee? Or when saw we thee sick, or in prison, and came unto thee? And the King shall answer and say unto them, Verily I say unto you, Inasmuch as ye have done it unto one of the least of these my brethren, ye have done it unto me.

Why should we forgive those who have hurt us so badly? Jesus answers with the parable of two debtors, and concludes:

> "O thou wicked servant, I forgave thee all that debt, because thou desireth me: Shouldest not thou also have had compassion on thy fellow servant, even as I had pity on thee? . . . So likewise shall my heavenly Father do also unto you, if ye from your hearts forgive not every one his brother their trespasses" (Matt 18:32-33, 35). And any time we say in the Lord's prayer, ". . . forgive us our debts, as we forgive our debtors," let us

also remember the words of Christ: "For if ye forgive men their trespasses, your heavenly Father will also forgive you: But if ye forgive not men their trespasses, neither will your Father forgive your trespasses (Matt 6:14-15).

**2. No Hutu, No Tutsi!**

One of the tragedies plaguing the African continent is the endless circle of civil wars and violence. Sometimes these are fueled, if not inspired, by tribal hatred. Tribalism is the belief that one ethnic group, distinguished by certain easily noticed characteristics, is inherently superior to all others. Taken to its logical conclusions, this belief allows the supposedly superior ethnic group to dehumanize, oppress, and even kill the inferior group.

But Africa does not hold a patent right to tribalism. The spirit of tribalism is alive wherever we despise, separate, exploit, and wound people just because of the shape of their noses, the color of their skin, eyes, or hair, or some other external feature—including age, weight, gender, disability, language , or even economic or social status. What exists in Africa as tribalism exists also in other parts of the world as black and white racism, anti-Semitism, anti-Arabism, male-female chauvinism, classism, etc.

Can the Christian lifestyle transcend these different manifestations of tribalism? Some of our believers in Africa think so. Consider this incident that took place during the 100-day genocide in Rwanda.

One evening, a Seventh-day Adventist choir was in church practicing when armed militia men suddenly walked in. They stopped the practice and separated the singers into their Hutu and Tutsi ethnic groups. Then they ordered the Hutus to kill their fellow Tutsis or lose their own lives as well. But the Hutu choir members said that in the church there is no Hutu and Tutsi, all are brothers and sisters. The killers put a lot of pressure on them, threatening them with deadly weapons , but those members kept on saying that they could not kill their brothers and their sisters. When no amount of pressure could cause them to do otherwise, all choir members, except very few who could escape, were ruthlessly massacred.

After the genocide, a new choir was reconstituted. The Emmaus Choir (Luke 24) emerged from the ashes of their martyred members. Today, this new choir is singing about the soon coming of Jesus to resurrect their fellow believers who died believing that in Christ, there is neither Hutu nor Tutsi.

This also, is Christian lifestyle in action. Is it worth it? Jesus said, "If any man come to me and hate not his father, and mother and wife, and children, and brethren, and sisters, *yea, and his own life also,* he cannot be my disciple." "He that findeth his life shall lose it: *and he that loseth his life for my sake shall find it*" (Luke 14:26; cf. Matthew 10:39). "This is my commandment, That ye love one another, as I loved you. Greater love hath no man than this, that a man lay down his life for his friend" (John 15:12-13).

Can we imagine the powerful impact our Christianity will have, if we live out the implications of this teaching by Christ? Writes Ellen G. White: "If Christians were to act in concert, moving forward as one, under the direction of one Power, for the accomplishment of one purpose, they would move the world" (*Christians Service,* 75).

### 3. Ready to Live and to Die

Sometimes believers are called upon to bear some unbearable loads. These heavy burdens may involve some painful losses, illness, betrayal, or even death. Like Paul's enigmatic "thorn in the flesh," relief seems to defy their persistent prayers. This is the case with some of our believers in the Democratic Republic of Congo, formerly Zaire.

This region is currently occupied by two rebel forces, both of which are fighting the ruling government based in the Congolese capital of Kinshasha. The occasion of my most recent trip to this area was to conduct two ministerial council meetings for our pastors and wives who are living in the two war zones of this region (due to the war, the East Congo Union has been divided into two sectors, each headed by a Coordinator). I was joined by Dr. Samuel Koranteng-Pipim, Director Public Campus Ministries, Michigan Conference.

After spending few days in Rwanda, we flew on a small aircraft to Gisenyi, a northern border city in Rwanda. The first indication that we were entering a war zone was the presence of several heavily armed soldiers and military aircrafts at the airport. The Coordinator of the Northern Congo Sector was at hand to meet us and drive us across the border into Goma, a Congolese city of about one and half million inhabitants. This is the city to which many Rwandees fled during the genocide. Hundreds of thousands of people lost their lives in this city through the violence of war, famine, and cholera.

This was not the first time I have been in Congo. In fact, I was serving in that country when I was called to my new assignment at the Africa-Indian

Ocean Division headquarters in Cote d'Ivoire. My recent trip, however, was my first visit since the civil war erupted in Congo. Knowing how the city of Goma used to look, I was particularly saddened by the war's devastation: dilapidated buildings; widows patiently sitting in a public square awaiting job assignments in exchange for food, soldiers at every turn, the presence of the international organizations like Red Cross, UN personnel, etc. The war's ruin of property and lives verifies the saying that "war does not decide who is right but who is left."

We spent the night in Goma, and the following day we flew 350 km northward in a 25 small seater aircraft from Goma to Butembo (a city of one million people). Ten church pastors, led by the local field President, were at the airport to meet us. I cannot describe the joy in their faces in seeing us. They were not sure we could make it. From there, we drove the distance of 40 Km in one hour to Lukanga, where we have the Adventist University-Wallace and a Mission headquarters. This location was the site of our first assigned Ministerial Council meeting.

As we drove the one hour journey from the Butembo airport to Lukanga, the local field President shared with us the plight of the believers living everyday with evidence of war surrounding them. He explained that they live as though each day was their last day to be alive. They could die (and several had already died) at the hands of soldiers, armed robbers, militiamen,etc. They could be imprisoned for no valid reason. Many pastors and church members had lost their homes. For their own "safety" they live in the bush/jungles. In order to attend meetings, some wake up at 4:00 am and have to walk 3-5 hours to be at Sabbath School at 9:00 am, then walk back to their jungles.

When asked about the nature of theological questions church members ask in the face of these endless wars, deaths, loss, etc., the field President replied, "Our members are not asking why all of these are happening. They already know the answer. They know that we are living in the last days, perilous days. And as long as we live in this world, we shall continue experiencing these tragedies. This is why our people are actively preparing themselves and others for the second coming." In his opinion, the main reason why those of us in the free world are engaged in frivolous theological discussions is because we have nothing else to do. We are too comfortable in this world, oblivious of the fact that it is headed for destruction.

But our believers in East Congo have counted the cost and are willing to bear their cross. They have made a commitment to take seriously Christ's words: *"And Whosoever doth not bear his cross, and come after me, cannot be my disciple"* (Luke 14:27). Though the burden is heavy, they hear Christ saying to them, "My grace is sufficient for thee: for my strength is made perfect in weakness" (2 Cor 12:9). "In the world ye shall have tribulation: but be of good cheer; I have overcome the world" (John 16:33).

### 4. Faithful No Matter What

There are times when God also calls upon us to leave the comforts and securities of our jobs, pay checks, homes, or retirement benefits. In their selfless ministry, they also display Christian lifestyle in action. This fact was also confirmed to us in East Congo, after we returned to Goma (from Lukanga). We came back to conduct a meeting with another group of pastors and their wives.

One Sabbath, we spoke to some 5000 church members as they sat and stood quietly in the hot sun—since there was no place available that could hold the large number of people. The leaders told us that many districts in that part of the country were empty. The members have been displaced or they had to flee to the forest because a lot of killings are still going on. They have to hide there otherwise the killers may come and exterminate them. But it is extremely difficult to live in the jungle. Because of the war there is not enough food to live on in the forests.

But the most moving part of this story is that the pastors who have been the district pastors of those members, even though they are not obliged to do so, decided to follow the members in the forest to minister to them, to feed the flock. They said they cannot abandon the sheep. With salary or without salary, they made up their minds that they would be faithful to their calling, no matter what. Because there is no food there, a pastor ventured to go out and look for food for his family; the killers saw him, he was assassinated. And that was two months ago.

Since the members of their districts are scattered in the forests, those faithful ministers go looking for them. They visit them by the jungle streams, in the caves, and under trees and conduct meetings for them. Without cars or bicycles, they continue to minister in spite of all of the obstacles.

When the pastors and their wives heard of the ministerial councils, they really wanted to attend. They were eager to be spiritually charged. They longed to be with their fellow ministers. They desired to attend the meetings to learn how to be better ministers for God. But they also knew that it was not easy to sneak out of the forest without being noticed by the killers. Yet, risking their lives, eighteen of them walked through the jungle for three days. They came one by one. The Lord helped them to make it even though they could not start with us.

Some of them arrived at the last meeting, which was a communion service. The ordinance of foot washing takes on a whole new meaning when you are called upon to wash the dirty feet of a fellow pastor whose shoes and socks are completely worn out The profound nature of their prayers and the kinds of things they pray for will rebuke us for the kinds of prayer requests that often escape our lips. Their enthusiastic hymn singing and hearty "amens" will not only wake us up from our ice-cold lethargy, formalism, and lukewarmness at our worship services, but also put to shame those of us who are allowing so-called praise music and applauses in some of our churches today.

The pastors and wives of our churches in East Congo seek to be totally committed to Christ. Even in the face of extreme poverty, homelessness, famine, sickness, and death, they are seeking to do God's will and God's work. This life of total commitment is Christian lifestyle in action. It takes Christ's words seriously: *"So likewise, whosoever he be of you that forsaketh not all that he hath, he cannot be my disciple"* (Luke 14:33).

Such a lifestyle of radical discipleship arises as a grateful response to God's magnificent salvation through Christ. Church members and pastors whose lives have been spared in the civil war are asking "What can I give back to the Lord for saving me?" In response, they are giving their time, means and talents for the advancement of the God's cause in spite of the difficulties.

This life of total commitment is that which is expected of those who have been truly called by their Master. And without doubt, these pastors have heard the charge from God through Paul : "But you be watchful in all things, endure afflictions, do the work of an evangelist, fulfill your ministry" (2 Tim 4:5).

But should ministers sacrifice the comforts of this life for that of affliction and hardship? Shouldn't they be concerned about their homes, cars, paycheck, even their lives? When asked these questions, our pastors in East Congo would most assuredly reply with the words of the apostle Paul: "But none of these things move me; nor do I count my life dear to myself, so that I may finish my race with joy, and the ministry which I received from the Lord Jesus, to testify to the gospel of the grace of God" ( Acts 20:24 ).

Paul finished his race. These dear believers in Africa will finish theirs also. And what the Apostle of old said about himself is applicable to them: "I have fought the good fight, I have finished the race, I have kept the faith. Finally, there is laid for me the crown of righteousness, which the Lord, the righteous Judge, will give to me on that Day, and not to me only but also to all who have loved His appearing." ( 2 Tim 4 :7,8). Real crowns are reserved for our faithful workers in Congo. They believe that when Jesus Christ, "the Chief Shepherd," appears they "will receive the crown of glory that does not fade away" ( 1Pet. 5:4).

## The Price and the Prize

The experiences I have just shared are just samples of what is happening in the Africa Indian Ocean Division. Many parts of our Division are disturbed by wars and troubles. But we praise God, the Holy Spirit is using men and women to do everything to glorify His name. They are ready to sacrifice everything including life itself.

Time is short. Let us also ask God to help us be uncompromisingly loyal to Him. Let no one deny us from practicing our Christian duties. Let there be no Hutus nor Tutsis (or any other form of tribalism) in the church. Let us be ready to live and to die on account of our allegiance to Him. Let us be faithful, no matter what. This is the essence of Christian lifestyle in action.

Though eternal life is free, it is not cheap. It cost our Savior His life. Today, He bids us to follow in His steps. The *prize* of eternal life is worth the *price* of the Christian lifestyle.

---

**Endnotes**

[1]This article by Paul Ratsara, secretary of the Africa-Indian Ocean Division, was originally published in *Adventists Affirm* 14/1 (Spring 2000): 40-46. *Adventists Affirm* is currently published three times a year, each issue focusing on a contemporary problem facing the church. For a one-year subscription, send your check for $9.00 (US) or $12.00 (overseas) too: Adventists Affirm, P.O. Box 36 Berrien Springs, Michigan 49103, USA.

Phone/Fax (616) 471-2300.

**Web site: www.adventistsaffirm.org**

E-mail: info@adventistsaffirm.org

**Australia:** PO Box 658, Cannington, W.A. 6987; e-mail: aaffirm@space.net.au

Why are our scholars divided into conservative and liberal camps? What is the nature of the cold war over the Bible? Why are some of our thought leaders revising certain of our Bible based beliefs and practices? What are the key issues regarding biblical inspiration and interpretation?

Section IV

# The Babble Over the Bible
## (The Ideology of Liberal Higher Criticism)

# 26

# A Brief Background

*"Scripture is the foundation of the Church: the Church is the guardian of Scripture. When the Church is in strong health, the light of Scripture shines bright* [sic]*; when the Church is sick, Scripture is corroded by neglect; . . . and as a rule the way in which Scripture is being treated is in exact correspondence with the condition of the Church."*

**—John Albert Bengel**

At a recent Michigan Conference camp meeting, a speaker shared with us the following story by an unknown author:

One Sunday, the minister was giving a sermon on baptism and in the course of his sermon he was illustrating the fact that baptism should take place by sprinkling and not by immersion [the method prescribed in the Scriptures]. He pointed out some instances in the Bible. He said that when John the Baptist baptized Jesus *in* the River Jordan, it didn't mean "in"; it meant "close to, round about, or nearby." And again when it says in the Bible that Phillip baptized the eunuch *in* the river, it didn't mean "in"—it meant "close to, round about, or nearby."

After the service, a man came up to the minister and told him it was a great sermon, one of the best he had ever heard, and that it had cleared up a great many mysteries he had encountered in the Bible. "For instance," he said, "the story about Jonah getting swallowed by the whale has always bothered me. Now I know that Jonah wasn't really in the whale, but close to, round about, or nearby, swimming in the water. Then there is the story about the three young Hebrew boys who were thrown into the furious furnace, but were not burned. Now I see that they were not really in the fire, just close to, round about, or nearby, just keeping warm. But the hardest of all the stories for me to believe has always been the story of Daniel getting thrown into the lions' den. But now I see that he wasn't really in the lions' den, but close to, round about, or nearby, like at the zoo. The revealing of these mysteries has been a real comfort to me because I am a wicked man. Now I am gratified to know that I won't be in Hell, but close to, round about, or nearby. And next Sunday, I won't have to be in church, just close to, round about, or nearby. Thanks. You have really put my mind at ease."

We may laugh at this story. But we need to remember that, in the realm of the church's life and mission, there is also a subtle effort by entrenched liberalism within the church to overthrow biblical teaching and practice by undermining the Bible's full inspiration, trustworthiness, and sole-authority. Let me explain.

**Assault on the Bible.** Throughout centuries the Bible has come under vicious attack from critics outside the church. In some instances, the Bible was ridiculed, banned, and even burned. Yet the Bible not only has survived, but Christians have also received the Word as the inspired, reliable, and authoritative revelation of God's will.

Today, however, an assault on the Bible is coming from people claiming to be Christians and occupying positions of responsibility in the church. A careful look at the contemporary theological scene will reveal that much of today's theological activity is directed towards discrediting the Bible or creating doubts over its trustworthiness and absolute reliability. Many theologians in the classrooms, many preachers in the pulpits, and many leaders in administrative positions are subtly creating doubts in the minds of their hearers by suggesting that the Bible can no longer be fully trusted on almost any issue.

**Nature of the Doubts.** Contrary to the claims of the Bible, these dissenting theological voices allege that fulfilled prophecies of the Bible were actually written after the events took place. The Bible's history, they say, is not historical, its science is not scientific, its stories are myths, its facts are fables, its heroes were immoral, and its ethics are not practical today.

All these they present as new views of the Bible that will bring about a greater "appreciation" of the "beauty" of the Bible! To make this perspective palatable to unsuspecting believers, these critics have come up with different theories to explain the *nature* of the Bible (inspiration) and the appropriate *method* for its interpretation.

These two subjects—inspiration and interpretation—have a bearing on whether the Bible is fully trustworthy, absolutely dependable, and completely reliable in all that it deals with. These questions of biblical inspiration and interpretation have contributed to doubting the Word.

**Theological Divisions.** In my earlier book *Receiving the Word,* I explained how this crisis over the Word has caused division in various denominations. For lack of standard terminology, I described the three major positions in contemporary theology as: (i) the Liberal (Radical) position, (ii) the Conservative (Bible-believing) position, and (iii) the Moderate (Progressive/Accomodationist/neo-liberal) position.[1]

Because the theological labels—liberal, conservative, and moderate—also describe political views, and because today the usage of these terms often varies from its use in the past, my own preference would have been the following terms: *Bible-rejectors, Bible-believers,* and *Bible-doubters.* However, I have chosen to maintain the above theological labels because, rightly or wrongly, they are the best known. To avoid confusing the three warring factions in the Christian church's ongoing quarrel over the Word, I will now (a) briefly describe each of the theological divisions and (b) explain why they are engaged in this family feud.

These three factions are divided over their use of the method of higher criticism (or the historical-critical method), an approach growing out of the Enlightenment assumption (or basic presupposition) that denies miracles or supernatural intervention in history. [2] Radical liberals employ the method with its naturalistic (anti-supernaturalistic) presupposition; moderates/accommodationists believe they can use the method without its underlying assumptions; and conservatives find the method unacceptable since it cannot be separated from its basic presuppositions.

**Liberals: Bible Rejectors.** Theological liberals deny the full trustworthiness of the Bible. Seeking to accommodate Bible truth to modern culture or science, they deny the validity of miracles and the supernatural, and they adopt the methods of higher criticism as the way to restore the truthfulness of the Bible. In terms of numbers, the liberals are relatively few, but they hold prominent positions in various theological institutions and sometimes in the churches.

Their impact stems largely from the articles, books and commentaries on the Bible that they have published. These works are treated as the standard criteria for scholarship, and those who do not accord with them are treated as academic misfits. Because their publications tend to be reference works, when new believers or untrained students are exposed to them their faith in the Bible and its teachings is shaken.

**Conservatives: Bible Believers.** Theological conservatives, as their name implies, seek to conserve or preserve the traditional view of Scripture against the newer views. This does not mean that they accept tradition uncritically or that they refuse to be open to new ideas. Rather, they aim to preserve the view of Scripture set forth in the inspired Word which has been the consensus of Christendom from its very beginning until modern times. Bible-believing conservatives accept the full reliability and trustworthiness of the Bible in matters of salvation as well as on any other subject the Bible touches upon. Conservative scholars also reject even a moderate use of the higher critical methodologies.

As a conservative denomination, Seventh-day Adventists historically have affirmed their faith in the inspiration, unity, authenticity, and authority of the Bible as the Word of God in its totality. The very first of their Fundamental Beliefs reads: "The Holy Scriptures, Old and New Testaments, are the written Word of God, given by divine inspiration through holy men of God who spoke and wrote as they were moved by the Holy Spirit. In this Word, God has committed to man the knowledge necessary for salvation. The Holy Scriptures are the infallible revelation of His will. They are the standard of character, the test of experience, the authoritative revealer of doctrines, and the trustworthy record of God's acts in history." The conservative implications of this fundamental belief are reflected in the 1986 "Methods of Bible Study Report" voted by church leaders in Rio de Janeiro, Brazil, and published in the *Adventist Review*, January 22, 1987, pages 18-20 (and reproduced as appendix C in *Receiving the Word*).

Generally, a large majority of church members tend to be conservative Bible-believing Christians. Recognizing the power of Christ in their own lives, they submit to the authority of their Savior and His written Word. In their search to know Christ and His Word better, these Christian believers sometimes find themselves confused and shaken by the discordant notes of liberals and moderates in the church.

**Moderates or Accommodationists: Bible-Doubters.** Theological moderates give the appearance of being conservatives, and yet they hold onto a liberal agenda. Because they accommodate conservative beliefs to liberal thought, moderates can very well be described as accommodationists. Unlike liberals, moderates accept *some* or even *all* of the Bible's miracles and supernatural events, but they maintain that the Bible is not fully reliable in everything it says since it contains some minor "mistakes," "discrepancies," "inconsistencies," "inaccuracies," or even "errors."

By errors they do not simply refer to the ones that apparently crept into the text during the process of copying the manuscripts (e.g., occasional discrepancies due to the copyists' glosses, slips, misspellings, etc.) and which can be ascertained and corrected by comparing the various available manuscripts.[3] When moderate liberals speak of errors or discrepancies, they are referring to mistakes that are purported to have originated with the Bible writers themselves. These alleged errors include statements in the Bible that deal with chronology, numbers, genealogy, history, geography, and science, which the scholars insist are inaccurate.

Moderates, however, argue that these "inaccuracies" are few and largely trivial factual mistakes. They also add that in the areas of religion and ethics, and especially in the central teachings regarding God, Christ, and salvation, the Bible is most dependable. Those in this group generally believe that it is possible to make a moderate use of the higher critical methodologies.

Although the moderates do not come out as strongly as the radical liberals, yet in subtle ways they present modified and popular versions of liberalism to unsuspecting believers. Moderates tend to occupy high positions in the church where their neo-liberal influence is felt in the classrooms, in the pulpits, and in administrative decision-making. Therefore, when many church members speak of "liberals," they are actually referring to these accommodationists in their churches.

In short, (1) radical liberals accept the method of higher criticism with its basic presuppositions denying miracles; (2) moderate liberals (accommodationists) believe that modified versions of the method can be used apart from its basic presupposition; and (3) conservatives hold that the method is unacceptable because it cannot be isolated from its basic presupposition.

**Issue Dividing Factions.** All the three factions—theological liberals, moderates/accommodationists, and conservatives—claim to take the Bible very seriously. Their quarrel over the Word started when some confronted seemingly unresolvable difficulties in Scripture. While the three groups all claimed that in the face of difficulties they would allow the Bible to speak for itself, it became apparent that letting the Bible "speak for itself" meant different things to liberals and moderates on the one hand and to Bible-believing conservatives on the other.

Unlike conservatives who take very seriously the claims of the Bible to be truthful, liberals and accommodationists who come across difficulties in the Bible do three things. (1) They declare these problems as inaccuracies, contractions, or errors. (2) Then, to account for these alleged errors or contradictions in the Bible, they redefine the meaning of inspiration or the nature of the Bible to allow for the possibility of mistakes or inaccuracies in the Bible. (3) They adopt different versions of the higher critical methodology as appropriate in resolving the scriptural difficulties.

**Adventism's Challenge.** In *Receiving the Word*, I also argued that the on-going theological debates in our own Seventh-day Adventist church, result largely from the cracks created in our theological foundation as some scholars have attempted to marry Adventism's high view of Scripture with the moderate use of liberalism's historical-critical method. I brought readers up-to-date, by documenting how entrenched liberalism within the church is attempting to undermine our biblical faith and lifestyle.

*Receiving the Word* generated considerable interest, discussion, and heart-searching in the Adventist church. [4] On the whole, the overwhelming majority of Bible-believing Adventists worldwide–scholars, leaders, members, and students–embraced the book as reflective of the church's long-standing position. Predictably, however, scholars who are sympathetic to the use of higher criticism loudly denounced the book for generating the energyfor the Adventist church's alleged drift towards fundamentalism. [5]

Also, because the book attempted to uplift the trustworthiness of Scripture by demonstrating that many of its alleged errors, mistakes, or contradictions are either distortions due to the transmission process of its original text, or our failure to understand its true meaning, [6] some of the book's critics mistakenly suggested that *Receiving the Word* teaches "inerrancy and verbalism," popular expressions used to suggest a mechanical or verbal dictation view of Scripture. [7]

As will become evident in the next chapters, these criticisms of the book came from individuals who have either embraced aspects of liberal higher criticism or who have seriously misunderstood the key theological and hermeneutical issues involved in matters dealing with the inspiration and interpretation of the Bible.

**Key Issues.** The critical issue we must address in the Adventist debate over the Word is whether or not we can legitimately use any version of contemporary higher criticism (the historical-critical method), since the method ultimately denies the full inspiration, reliability, unity, and normative authority of Scripture. The specific issues raised by the above question are as follows:

(a) Are there degrees of inspiration in the Bible, so that some parts of the Bible are more inspired than others?
(b) Are there inaccuracies, mistakes, or errors in Scripture, so that some of the Bible's accounts (e.g., on history and science) are not fully trustworthy?
(c) Does one part of the Bible contradict another, so that there are conflicting theologies in the Bible?
(d) Does an insistence on *sola scriptura* (the Bible and the Bible only) allow Bible students to reinterpret Scripture by external norms like contemporary culture, psychology, philosophy, or science?

In other words, does the Bible merely contain "a great deal of accuracy" in its historical and scientific details? Or should the inspired Book be trusted as fully reliable in the areas and issues it teaches and touches upon?

**Forbidden Issue.** What is really behind the mistaken claim that those who uphold the longstanding Adventist view on the Bible's inspiration, trustworthiness, and sole authority are fundamentalists and verbal inspirationists?

As we address this forbidden question we shall understand why some of our scholars oppose key concepts in our Fundamental Belief #1. We shall also identify the crucial questions one must ask to ascertain whether a person is using the methodology of liberal higher criticism.

---

**Endnotes**

[1]As I explained in *Receiving the Word,* 58-59, although the terms, "liberal," "conservative," and "moderate," are now employed in theological discussions, one crucial point should be emphasized in the use of these labels, namely: the terminology is also used, if not borrowed from, the world of politics. Because of the political undertones undergirding the use of these words and because it is very easy to mistakenly assume that the terms liberal, conservative, and moderate mean the same things in both politics and theology, it would have been preferable to avoid these labels altogether. Besides, these terms sometimes have completely opposite meanings from their usage in the past.

For example, there was a time when a Christian could proudly carry the label of a liberal and boast of being warm-hearted or generous, open-minded, or free from narrow-minded thinking, prejudice or arbitrary authority. But as we shall show in the succeeding pages, today, when a Christian is described as a liberal, it connotes one who has betrayed the truths of the biblical religion, which if cherished can make a person truly generous, open-minded and free.

Similarly, in the past the term conservative had negative undertones. In those days a conservative Christian described a person who blindly fastened himself to prevalent views; was cautious toward or suspicious of change or innovation and had a tendency to avoid open-minded discussions for fear of being won over to the other side. In fact, most of Ellen G. White's usage of this term carried this negative meaning. Notice the context in which she employed the word: "But as real spiritual life declines, it has ever been the tendency to cease to advance in the knowledge of truth. Men rest satisfied with the light already received from God's word, and discourage any further investigation of the Scriptures. They become conservative, and seek to avoid discussion" (*Counsels to Writers and Editors*, 38; cf. *Testimonies to the Church*, 5:706, 370; *The Signs of the Times,* December 10, 1894)

Ellen G. White's uncomplimentary use of the term conservative in other places of her works could aptly describe today's theological liberals. She, for instance, classed the conservatives in her day among the "worldly" and "superficial" class; those whose influence retard the progress of God's work by putting "worldly conformity" first and God's cause second, or whose sympathies are with the enemies of God's truth; those who instead of being true to biblical convictions would rather shape the scriptural message "to please the minds of the unconsecrated"; those who betray the cause of truth by compromises and concessions; those who choose to be "self-centered," instead of "living the unselfish life of Christ"; and those who defer to the "traditions received from educated men, and from the writings of great men of the past," instead of seeking guidance from the "holy principles revealed in the word of God." (See *Christian Service*, 158; cf. *Testimonies to the Church*, 3:312; 5:463; *Testimonies to the Church*, 5:263; cf. *Christian Leadership*, 73; *Advent Review and Sabbath Herald*, May 21, 1914; *Selected Messages*, 3:397; cf. *The*

*Signs of the Times*, January 3, 1884; *Testimonies for the Church*, 3:165; *Advent Review and Sabbath Herald*, May 30, 1899; *Advent Review and Sabbath Herald*, February 7, 1893; cf. *Medical Ministry*, 99).

[2]Contemporary higher criticism or the historical-critical method is based on three key assumptions: (1) the principle of correlation, which says that every historical event must be explained solely by natural causes; (2) the principle of analogy, which holds that past events must be explained on the basis of present occurrences; and (3) the principle of criticism, which maintains that skepticism is the key to establishing truth. The German theologian and historian Ernst Troeltsch (1865-1923) holds the distinction of formulating the three cardinal principles of the historical-critical method. For his contribution, see Robert Morgan, Introduction to *Ernst Troeltsch: Writings on Theology and Religion*, trans. And ed. Robert Morgan and Michael Pye (Atlanta, Ga.: John Knox, 1977). For a summary discussion of "Nineteenth-Centuy Protestant Liberalism," see my "The Role of the Holy Spirit in Biblical Interpretation: A Study in the Writings of James I. Packer," (Ph.D. Dissertation, Andrews University, 1998), 86-93.

[3]A detailed discussion of these transmission errors is found in chapter 8 of *Receiving the Word*, 225-236.

[4]For conflicting reviews of the book, see George W. Reid (pro) and George R. Knight (con) in *Ministry*, December 1997, 30-31. Reid is director of the General Conference's Biblical Research Institute, and Knight is a professor of Church History at the SDA Theological Seminary.

[5]See Charles Scriven, "Embracing the Spirit," *Spectrum* 26 (September 1997): 28-37; Norman H Young, "'Moderate Liberalism' Threatens Adventism," *Spectrum* 26 (May 1997): 49-50.

[6]See *Receiving the Word*, 279-304.

[7]George R. Knight, "Review of *Receiving the Word*," in *Ministry*, December 1997, 30; cf. his, "The Case of the Overlooked Postscript: A Footnote on Inspiration," *Ministry* August 1997. Cf. Timothy E. Crosby, "The Bible: Inspiration and Authority," *Ministry*, May 1998, 18-20; Robert M. Johnston, "The Case for a Balanced Hermeneutic," *Ministry*, March 1999, 10-12.

# 27

# THE BUG IN ADVENTIST HERMENEUTICS

There is a bug in Seventh-day Adventist hermeneutic, a deadly virus attacking the church's approach to Scriptures. This bug threatens the church's message and mission. The good news is that, as a result of the heated discussions on homosexuality, women's ordination, divorce and remarriage, and contemporary worship styles, ordinary church members are becoming aware of this problem. The bad news is that some of the experts and leaders of the church who are supposed to fix the problem are pretending that the problem is not real.

This chapter identifies the hermeneutical bug, arguing that the on-going crisis within contemporary Adventism arises from the attempts by some to employ modified aspects of liberalism's higher criticism. The chapter also summarizes how this cold-war over the Bible has been waged in our church during the past decade.

### The Cold War in the Church: 1990-2000

For almost 30 years now, a cold war has been waged in the Seventh-day Adventist church over the nature of the Bible's inspiration, trustworthiness, and interpretation. This crisis over the Bible has divided our church scholars into liberal and conservative factions. The liberals believe that, in the study of the Scriptures, Adventists can legitimately employ the method of higher criticism without its anti-supernaturalistic assumptions.

The conservatives disagree, arguing that the method cannot be isolated from its basic assumptions, and that the use of the method ultimately leads to a rejection of basic biblical teachings.

In the 1980s, following years of internal debate over the Bible, the Seventh-day Adventist church expressed its official position in two carefully worded documents, both of which express a high view of Scripture. The first is our Fundamental Belief #1 (1980):

> The Holy Scriptures, Old and New Testaments, are the written Word of God, given by divine inspiration through holy men of God who spoke and wrote as they were moved by the Holy Spirit. In this Word, God has committed to man the knowledge necessary for salvation. The Holy Scriptures are the infallible revelation of His will. They are the standard of character, the test of experience, the authoritative revealer of doctrines, and the trustworthy record of God's acts in history.

The second church document sets forth the hermeneutical presuppositions, principles, and methods that are to govern its members' approach to Scripture. Approved at the 1986 Annual Council of church leaders, held in Rio de Janeiro the Methods of Bible Study" document (or the Rio Document," as it is popularly referred to) is addressed to all members of the Seventh-day Adventist Church with the purpose of providing guidelines on how to study the Bible, both the trained biblical scholar and others." Among other things, the church rejects even a modified use" of the historical-critical method as inconsistent with the teachings of Scripture itself.[1]

These two works—Fundamental Belief #1 and "Methods of Bible Study"—became the basis of the exposition found in the book *Seventh-day Adventists Believe . . . A Biblical Exposition of 27 Fundamental Doctrines* (1988).[2]

But in spite of the overwhelming support of the church's position by members around the world, certain segments of Adventist scholarship have never fully accepted the church's view. They continue to argue that (1) some parts of the Bible are more inspired than others, (2) there are inconsistencies, discrepancies, contradictions, or inaccuracies in Scripture, (3) the Bible contains "factual mistakes" or "factual errors"and, therefore, it is not always accurate in its historical and scientific details, and that (4) some teachings of the Bible are culturally conditioned," that is, they suffer from the cultural limitations, prejudice, and ignorance of the Bible writers.

These assertions grow out of liberalism's higher criticism (the so-called historical-critical method). Because they undermine the authority of the Bible and threaten the church's message and mission, Bible-believing Adventists throughout their history have always rejected these positions.[3] However, during the past decade moderate liberals have attempted to domesticate these aberrant views in the church by employing some of our leading denominational publishing houses and publications.

**The Debate in the Early 1990s.** As a result of the attempt to challenge the church's established position, the 1990s witnessed a renewed debate within our ranks over what the church's understanding ought to be on the Scriptures. The debate was intensified by the publication of the controversial *Inspiration: Hard Questions, Honest Answers* (1991).[4] Apart from its use of the historical-critical method, *Inspiration* was controversial because the method led the book's author to question some longstanding Seventh-day Adventist teachings.

For example, among other things, the author of *Inspiration* (a) makes a dichotomy between saving acts and factual statements, so that in scriptural accounts some things are "essential" and others are "debatable"; (b) rejects the Bible's claim that the original sanctuary in the wilderness was constructed as a copy of the heavenly (Ex 25:40), suggesting that the idea was borrowed from surrounding Canaanites; (c) claims that when the book of Hebrews referred to the "heavenly" sanctuary, the reference should be understood in terms of Platonic dualism; (d) accepts the miracle of the Exodus but maintains that the exact "number of people involved in the Exodus is not that crucial"; (e) acknowledges a miraculous flood in Noah's day but holds that the biblical flood was "less than [a] universal event"; (f) believes in biblical history and yet argues that information on numbers, genealogies, and dates may have been "distorted."[5]

Despite the book's troubling conclusions, *Inspiration* was endorsed by certain thought leaders and has been widely promoted in some quarters of the church.[6] This book has also become the hermeneutical compass for church scholars who have uncritically embraced the assumptions of moderate liberalism or who want to marry the church's high view of Scripture with the methodology of higher criticism.

However, church scholars who understood the full theological and hermeneutical implications of the book raised some serious concerns.[7] The most detailed response to *Inspiration* was provided by eight well-known scholars in their book *Issues in Revelation and Inspiration* (1992).[8] In the assessment of these church scholars, the earlier book *Inspiration* evidenced an uncritical reliance on liberalism's historical-critical method[9] and a serious lack of understanding of the crucial theological issues involved in the doctrine of Scripture.[10]

In any case, these two works—*Inspiration* and *Issues in Revelation and Inspiration*—were influential in bringing the scholarly debate on the Bible from the scholarly arena into the churchly domain. During the first half of the 1990s, opinions in the church divided along the views expressed in those works.

**Developments in the Late 1990s.** The second half of the 1990s witnessed an escalation in the cold war over the Bible. As noted by a perceptive church historian and theologian, during this period two works came to represent "the two main conflicting poles around which gravitate[d] the contemporary discussions on inspiration."[11] They were *Receiving the Word* (1996)[12] and *Reading Ellen White* (1997).[13]

The impetus for this round of debate was the book *Receiving the Word* (1996). In addition to challenging the method of moderate liberalism, this work also documented how the use of contemporary higher criticism (the historical-critical method) was undermining key Seventh-day Adventist beliefs and practices.

Reactions to *Receiving the Word* were predictable, tending to follow those manifested towards *Inspiration* and *Issues in Revelation and Inspiration.* Generally, scholars who embrace the church's official positions were very supportive of the book.[14] But others with a different hermeneutical temperament denounced the book.[15]

As noted in the previous chapter, because *Receiving the Word* attempted to uplift the trustworthiness of Scripture by demonstrating that many of the Bible's alleged errors, mistakes, or contradictions are the result of our failure to understand its true meaning,[16] some of the book's critics mistakenly suggested that *Receiving the Word* teaches fundamentalism's "inerrancy and verbalism," popular expressions often used to suggest a mechanical or verbal dictation view of Scripture.[17]

Though lacking any factual basis, the critics of *Receiving the Word* employed the terms "fundamentalism and "verbal inspiration" as rhetorical decoys to divert attention from the attempts by certain church scholars to deny the Bible's full inspiration, complete reliability in history and science, and internal consistency.[18]

One such scholar, who had earlier endorsed the controversial book *Inspiration*, set forth his own view in his book *Reading Ellen White* (1997).[19] There is much to be appreciated in this author's book. A careful reading of this work, however, shows that while purporting to describe Ellen White's understanding of the Scripture's inspiration, the author injected his own views into what he claims was Mrs. White's position on the Bible. Unfortunately, not everyone who reads *Reading Ellen White* will readily discern where Sister White's views on the Bible leave off and the book's author's begin.

For instance, when the author of *Reading Ellen White* argued that "inspiration is not infallible, inerrant, or verbal," he set up a straw man, a false dilemma, by implying that one must choose between two mistaken notions on the Bible: (1) the erroneous belief that the Bible was the product of a verbal word for word dictation (which he rejects), and (2) a defective view of inspiration which allows for historical and scientific mistakes in the Bible (which he proposes).

The author of *Reading Ellen White* was correct in asserting that the historic Adventist position, including that of Ellen G. White, has always been to reject verbal inspiration, *understood to mean a mechanical dictation inspiration,* in which the Bible writers functioned as passive secretaries to transcribe what the Holy Spirit dictated to them.[20] As long as we use the term verbal inspiration and explain to our audience that by it we are referring to mechanical (dictation) inspiration, there is no problem with such a usage. And we can affirm that Adventists, including Ellen G. White, *do not* believe in verbal inspiration.[21]

But while the author of *Reading Ellen White* correctly rejected "verbal inspiration" (understood as mechanical dictation), he proceeded to argue (erroneously) that since God did not dictate Scriptures to the Bible writers, the words of the inspired writers cannot always convey God's message in a trustworthy manner. For him, the Bible is not fully trustworthy in the realms of science and history; it merely contains "a great deal of accuracy."[22]

In other words, he went beyond discrediting mechanical-dictation theory of inspiration when he suggested that there are factual mistakes in inspired writings, and that those writings are infallible only "as a guide to salvation"—not necessarily infallible in the areas of history or science.[23]

In making this assertion, the author of *Reading Ellen White* was simply re-echoing his earlier attempt in 1993 to make Ellen White a party to his own "moderate stance on inspiration" which he also terms a "common-sense flexibility on inspiration." Without any shred of support from Ellen White and contrary to what she unambiguously asserted in several places in her works, this scholar popularized the revisionist reinterpretation of Ellen White's position. He wrote: "The Bible, she held, was infallible in the realm of salvation, but it was not infallible or inerrant in the radical sense of being beyond any possibility of factual difficulties or errors."[24]

But is it true that Sister White believed in the possibility of factual errors in Scripture, as claimed by the author of *Reading Ellen White*?[25] A careful study of Ellen White's writings will show that while she acknowledged the possibility of *copyist* and *translational* errors, she did not teach that there were factual mistakes (e.g., errors in history and science) traceable to the Bible writers themselves. Mrs. White wrote:

> Some look to us gravely and say, 'Don't you think there might have been some mistake *in the copyist or in the translators [of the Bible]?'* This is all probable, and the mind that is so narrow that it will hesitate and stumble over this possibility or probability would be just as ready to stumble over the mysteries of the Inspired Word, because their feeble minds cannot see through the purposes of God. Yes, they would just as easily stumble over plain facts that the common mind will accept, and discern the Divine, and to which God's utterance is plain and beautiful, full of marrow and fatness. *All the mistakes will not cause trouble to one soul, or cause any feet to stumble,* that would not manufacture difficulties from the plainest revealed truth (*Selected Messages,* 1:16, emphasis supplied).

Ellen G. White's recognition of copyist and translator errors in the Scriptures should not be misconstrued to mean the existence in the Bible of factual errors in history, science, geography, etc. To make this kind of claim is to woefully misunderstand, if not completely misrepresent, Mrs. White's position on the trustworthiness of Scripture.

Also, Mrs. White's rejection of a "mechanical/dictation" theory of inspiration should not be interpreted to mean that Scripture is not trustworthy in some of its historical or scientific assertions. She acknowledged that in the giving of the Bible to human beings, God did not communicate in a "grand superhuman language." Instead He enabled the Bible writers to use "imperfect" human language to communicate divine truths. Yet, she never suggested that the truthfulness of Scripture was compromised when the writers embodied "infinite ideas" in "finite vehicles of thought."[26]

Contrary to the claims in *Reading Ellen White,* Sister White never drove a wedge between biblical statements of salvation (deemed to be infallible) and other statements (believed to be riddled with "possible factual difficulties or errors"). She held that God's Word was "infallible," and should be accepted "as it reads" (*Review and Herald,* February 11, 1896; cf. *The Great Controversy,* vii; cf. 68, 102) and as "the only sufficient, infallible rule" (ibid., 173; cf. 89, 177, 238).

For Ellen White, Scripture shares in the infallibility of God. "God and heaven alone are infallible" (*Selected Messages,* 1:37; cf. *Testimonies to Ministers,* 30, 105). "Man is fallible, but God's Word is infallible" (*Selected Messages,* 1:416). She repeatedly argued for the trustworthiness of Scripture in all that it teaches and touches upon—whether in the realm of salvation or in the sphere of history, science, etc. She left no doubt that the Bible is "an unerring counselor and infallible guide," the "perfect guide under all circumstances of life"; "an unerring guide," "the one unerring guide," "the unerring standard," "an unerring light," "that unerring test," and "the unerring counsel of God."[27]

Against those who questioned the historical reliability of Scripture, she asserted that because the Holy Spirit "guided the pens of the sacred historians" (*Gospel Workers,* 286), biblical history is truthful, authentic, and reliable (*Fundamentals of Christian Education,* 84-85; *Testimonies for the Church,* 4:9-10). The accounts in the Bible are "unsullied by human pride or prejudice" (*Education,* 173); *Patriarchs and Prophets,* 596; *Testimonies for the Church,* 5:25). "The unerring pen of inspiration" traces biblical history with "exact fidelity" (ibid., 4:370). The Bible is equally trustworthy even in its statements having to do with scientific issues—e.g., questions about origins and geology (*Education,* 128-130).

Summarizing his findings from an extensive study of Ellen's White's writings, one careful Adventist professor of church history and historical theology wrote: "Although Ellen White recognized the existence of *transmission errors* and *difficulties* in Scripture, I have been unable to find any instance in which she mentioned specific factual errors in Scripture. As silent as the writers of the New Testament had been in pointing out factual errors in the Old Testament, so was Ellen White in regard to the total canon."[28]

### What Difference Does It Make?

Whenever scholars teach the existence of factual errors in Scripture, they are compelled to explain the source of these mistakes and how to identify them. One explanation liberals often offer is that these alleged factual errors (in history, science, etc.) result from the Bible writers' limited knowledge and/or cultural prejudice and not from God Himself. Others suggest that God accommodated Himself to popular opinions, even opinions that are in error. Consequently, these scholars find it necessary in their study of Scripture to isolate the human aspects of Scripture (deemed riddled with factual mistakes) from the divine aspect (considered infallible).

Our discussion in subsequent paragraphs will show that this "pick and choose" approach to the Bible ultimately leads one to repudiate established biblical teachings, including a six-day creation and a worldwide flood in Noah's day.

**1. Dissection of God's Word.** The pick and choose approach to the Bible, separating the human from the divine, is best illustrated in an article by an Adventist scholar who, like the author of *Reading Ellen White,* also advanced the questionable view that there were factual errors in Scripture. This scholar is a vice-president at one of the church's leading publishing houses and was also the editor of the 1991 controversial book *Inspiration.* In a *Ministry* magazine article, he suggested that we can isolate the divine from the human in Scripture.[29] He argued:

> So contrary to what some suggest, it is not heretical to deal with merely the human aspect of the Bible in isolation from its divine side, or vice versa. That's not heresy but simple necessity. The heresy occurs when we deny the unity, wholeness, and complementarity principle in relation to inspiration.[30]

Notice, however, that Ellen White challenged this tendency of moderate liberalism to separate the human and divine elements in Scripture and confer uninspired status upon some portions of the written Word. She wrote:

> The union of the divine and the human, manifest in Christ, exists also in the Bible. . . . And this fact, so far from being an argument against the Bible, should strengthen faith in it as the word of God. Those who pronounce upon the inspiration of the Scriptures, accepting some portions as divine while they reject other parts as human, overlook the fact that Christ, the divine, partook of our human nature, that He might reach humanity. In the work of God for man's redemption, divinity and humanity are combined (*Testimonies for the Church,* 5:747; cf. *The Great Controversy,* vi).

Despite this statement, another professor has suggested in a *Ministry* article that because God's messages were delivered through human instrumentalities, thus bearing the impress of human expression, in Scripture, "It is necessary to sort out what is human expression and divine message, even though all are inspired." For him Scriptures are reliable and trustworthy, only in the sense that they guide the hearer or reader "in the direction God wants him or her to go." However, he explained, the "attendant details with which the message is infleshed, but which are not an essential part of it, may have their origin in the culture or personality of the human messenger."[31]

In the carefully worded statement above, our scholar is suggesting that because the Bible is a record of God's communication to people who lived in a particular historico-cultural setting, part of Scripture's message (the "non-essential" part) is culturally conditioned. To discern the "direction" God wants today's interpreter to go, we must "sort out" which sections of God's Word are human (non-essential) and which are divine (essential).

It is instructive that while this professor of New Testament explicitly endorses the use of the historical-critical method in his *Ministry* article, Ellen White warned against higher criticism's attempts at sorting out from Scripture what is essential from the non-essential. Because the entire Scripture is inspired, Mrs. White warned:

> Do not let any living man come to you and begin to dissect God's Word, telling what is revelation, what is inspiration and what is not, without a rebuke. . . . We call on you to take your Bible, but do not put a sacrilegious hand upon it, and say, 'That

> is not inspired,' simply because somebody else has said so. Not a jot or tittle is ever to be taken from that Word. Hands off, brethren! Do not touch the ark. . . . When men begin to meddle with God's Word, I want to tell them to take their hands off, for they do not know what they are doing (E. G. White comments, *Seventh-day Adventist Bible Commentary,* 7:919-920).

Again she wrote:

> The warnings of the word of God regarding the perils surrounding the Christian church belong to us today. As in the days of the apostles men tried by tradition and philosophy to destroy faith in the Scriptures, so today, by the pleasing sentiments of higher criticism, evolution, spiritualism, theosophy, and pantheism, the enemy of righteousness is seeking to lead souls into forbidden paths. To many the Bible is a lamp without oil, because they have turned their minds into channels of speculative belief that bring misunderstanding and confusion. The work of higher criticism, in dissecting, conjecturing, reconstructing, is destroying faith in the Bible as a divine revelation. It is robing God's word of power to control, uplift, and inspire human lives (*The Acts of the Apostles,* 474).

**2. Reinterpretation of Traditional Bible Teachings.** Indeed, as we have seen in the previous sections of *Must We Be Silent?* the rejection of the Bible's teaching on homosexuality and role distinctions between male and female stems from liberalism's argument that we can pick and choose from Scripture or separate the essential truth from the allegedly culturally conditioned parts. By cultural conditioning liberal authors mean that the Bible mirrors the prejudices or limitations of its writers' culture and times.

This is the reason why some of the authors in the pro-ordination book *The Welcome Table* maintained that the apostle Paul erred in his interpretation of Genesis 1-3 when he grounded his teaching of role distinctions between male and female in Creation and the Fall. Reasoning along feminist and higher-critical lines, they claimed that the apostle Paul's statements were merely expressions of uninspired personal opinions—opinions that reflect his culture and hence do not apply to us. To these authors, Paul was "a man of his own time." He occasionally glimpsed the ideal that Jesus established during His time on earth; yet he never fully arrived at "the gospel ideal" of "full equality" or complete role interchangeability in both the home and the church.[32]

In certain denominations proponents of the cultural conditioning argument dismiss the Bible's condemnation of pre-marital and extra-marital sex, claiming that in contrast with our enlightened age, the Bible writers lived in a "pre-scientific" era with no antibiotics for venereal diseases, and no condoms and contraceptives to prevent pregnancies. The Bible writers' views, these liberal scholars contend, were consistent with the conditions of their times. But, they continue, if the Bible writers had lived in our day, they would have viewed pre- or extra-marital sex differently.

In my earlier work, I showed how some of our church scholars are employing similar arguments to reject the Bible's teaching against the wearing of jewelry, eating of unclean meats, drinking of alcohol, divorce and remarriage, etc. They maintain that these Christian lifestyle practices are culturally-conditioned to the pre-scientific Bible times or, perhaps, to the nineteenth-century Victorian age of Ellen White.[33]

The cultural-conditioning argument implies that in some cases the Bible writers wrote from ignorance or a distorted view of reality. In effect, today's historical-critical interpreters believe that they can decide which parts of the Bible are inspired and valid and which are not—the latter being the alleged culturally-conditioned sections of the Bible, not fully binding on all people in all ages. But they fail to show by what criteria they are able to sort out those parts tainted by the inspired writers' so-called cultural prejudices or ignorance.

**Rejection of Six-Day Creation and Worldwide Flood.** Some of our scholars are arguing that the Bible is culturally-conditioned because the Bible's teachings conflict with certain assumptions they hold on key issues of science. Thus, one former editor of the Review and Herald Publishing Association, who more recently served as an editor of the liberal publication *Adventist Today,* has carried liberalism's cultural condition argument to its logical conclusions by repudiating the Bible's teaching on creation and the flood in Noah's day. He argued for his new view in the liberal book *Creation Reconsidered* (2000).

Working on the assumption that "in matters of science, the Bible writers were on a level with their contemporaries," this thought leader suggested that on these issues our understanding should be informed by the more reliable data from modern science. He concluded that "at an unspecified time in the remote past, the Creator transmuted a finite portion of his infinite power into the primordial substance of the universe—perhaps in an event such as the Big Bang."[34]

This position essentially negates God's special direct creation, His creation from nothing (technically referred to as *creatio ex nihilo*), and undercuts the creation basis of the seventh-day Sabbath.

The reason for his repudiation of a literal six-day creation is his view that we must make a distinction between the "inspired message" of the Bible and the "uninspired message on record in the Bible," which he views as "culturally conditioned" or "historically conditioned." He wrote: "Historical conditioning permeates the entire Bible. It is not incidental, nor is it exceptional and unusual; it is the invariable rule."[35]

Like the author of *Inspiration,* the above scholar also concludes that the Genesis Flood did not extend beyond the known "lands bordering the Mediterranean Sea." In his opinion, "only by reading our modern worldview of 'all the earth' [Gen 7:3] back into the Hebrew text can the idea of a world-wide flood be established."[36]

Observe that this new view represents a major departure from the traditional Adventist understanding of the universal flood, as described in the *Seventh-day Adventist Bible Commentary,* of which this scholar himself was an associate editor. The commentary reads: "This description [of Gen 7] renders utterly foolish and impossible the view set forth by some that the Flood was a local affair in the Mesopotamian valley."[37]

Significantly, the above thought leader for years had argued for the use of higher criticism, discrediting the traditional Adventist approach as "prooftext subjectivity." This same scholar criticized the church's Rio document (as "Methods of Bible Study" is also called) as representing a "myopic position, . . . altogether unacceptable."[38]

This scholar's adoption of higher criticism may also explain why he claims that a significant number of scholars and church administrators, including himself, seek to revise our traditional Sanctuary doctrine (Article 23 of our Fundamental Beliefs).[39] Perceptive readers of his chapter in the pro-ordination book, *The Welcome Table* (1995), will notice that his analysis of Daniel 9:25 also repudiates the Adventist belief that the 2300 day prophecy of Daniel 8:14 ended in 1844.[40]

### Re-Affirming the Adventist Position

In the face of a growing awareness of historical-critical challenges bearing fruit in the church, it is not surprising that during the second half of the 1990s the church took steps to reaffirm its long established position on the nature, authority, and interpretation of Scripture. The then president of the General Conference set the tone in his 1995 *Adventist Review* article:

> Our unequivocal, historic emphasis upon the divine inspiration and trustworthiness of Scripture has strengthened our church. It has helped us resist the error of treating some parts of Scripture as God's Word, while ignoring or rejecting other parts. If we accept it as God's Word, we must accept it all, whether or not we like what it says. To us the Scriptures should be the ultimate revelation of God's will for our lives.[41]

Indeed, a careful study of official church actions during the latter half of the 1990's confirms that the positions of the Seventh-day Adventist church on the nature, authority, and interpretation of Scriptures have not changed since they were last formulated in the 1980's. For example, having designated 1998 as the "Year of the Bible," the world church chose as its theme "Experience the Power of His Word" for that year's annual Week of Prayer readings.[42] Similarly, the sermon theme for the 1998 Spirit of Prophecy Day (or as it is sometimes called, Heritage Sabbath) was entitled "God's Word Elevated."[43] The materials put forth by the church in the above world wide events affirm its longstanding position on the Bible.

Also, in response to the liberal challenge, a June 1998 International Bible Conference was convened in Jerusalem to urge Adventist scholars and leaders around the world to reaffirm their commitment to the authority of Scripture. The Jerusalem Bible Conference was sponsored by the Biblical Research Institute of the General Conference of Seventh-day Adventists, the Adventist Theological Society, the Institute of Archaeology at Andrews University Theological Seminary, and other Adventist entities. Noteworthy is the fact that the plenary speakers at the Jerusalem Bible Conference were all conservative thought leaders.

The worldwide church made another significant effort to curtail liberal scholars' attempt to erode confidence in God's Word. The Adult Sabbath School Lessons for the first quarter of 1999 and its companion book titled *Show and Tell* centered on "revelation and inspiration." Both works affirmed the longstanding Adventist position on the full inspiration, infallibility, and trustworthiness of Scriptures.[44] The principal author was one of the editors of the Adventist Theological Society book *Issues in Revelation and Inspiration* (1992).

Though other scholars wrote to affirm the longstanding Adventist position,[45] the clearest presentation of the church's position on the Bible is reflected in the recently released *Handbook of Seventh-day Adventist Theology* (2000), volume 12 of the commentary series.[46] This work was commissioned by the delegates "from all parts of the world" assembled at the 1988 Annual Council meeting in Nairobi, Kenya. The volume was "to strengthen unity among a body of believers diffused through more than 220 countries and in widely diverse cultural settings. . . . [and] to review carefully the biblical teachings undergirding the dynamic Adventist movement."[47]

The *Handbook of Seventh-day Theology* article on "Revelation and Inspiration" asserts that "the Scriptures are fully human and fully divine. Any idea that some parts of the Bible are merely human while other parts are divinely inspired contradicts the way the biblical writers present the matter." In an apparent response to liberalism's cultural-conditioning argument, the volume affirms "the complete veracity of Scripture," arguing that "the historical narratives of the Bible are to be accepted as reliable and true":

> Many today claim that there are numerous errors, contradictions, historical inaccuracies, anachronisms, and other flaws in the Scriptures. Worse still, it is alleged, the Bible contains deliberate distortions of historical events (e.g., the Exodus), narratives colored by national pride and prejudice (e.g., the story of Esther), and pseudonymous authorship (e.g., that the book of Daniel was not written by a sixth-century prophet). Such claims and allegations constitute a serious indictment against the truthfulness of Holy Scriptures.[48]

Similarly, the article on "Biblical Interpretation" in the *Handbook of Seventh-day Adventist Theology* affirms the "inseparable union of the Divine and Human." While recognizing "some minor transcriptional errors in Scripture," it affirms the reliability of the Bible's history and rejects the liberal attempt to question "the accuracy or veracity of numerous historical details in the biblical record."[49]

**Conclusion**

This chapter has highlighted how the cold war over the Bible has played out in the church during the past decade. In their attempt to marry Adventism's high view of Scripture with aspects of the historical-critical method (higher criticism), some of our scholars are teaching that (1) parts of the Bible are culturally conditioned, since God sometimes accommodated Himself to the personal or cultural opinions of the Bible writers, even opinions that were in error, (2) there are factual mistakes (e.g., scientific or historical) in the Bible, and that (3) we can sort out the statements on God's acts of salvation (deemed to be infallible) from the nonessential statements (believed to be riddled with possible factual inaccuracies).

Because of the sophistication of these liberal arguments, and in view of the manner in which some of our publications and publishing houses have been employed to domesticate the liberal views, it is important to summarize the theological concerns raised by the subtle attempts to inject assumptions of higher criticism into traditional Adventist and Ellen White positions.

**1. The Question of Divine Accommodation.** Does God accommodate Himself to popular opinion, even opinions that are in error? Does God in Scripture ever make an incidental affirmation of a so-called fact that was untrue? Some scholars think so. They would argue that even though God or Jesus was aware of the truth of certain minor historical, scientific, or geographical facts, (a) for the sake of the people at that time whose knowledge of those truths was limited, and (b) for the sake of effectively communicating His ethical and theological teachings to them, He deliberately accommodated His message to the needs of the people—sometimes by adopting mistaken views prevalent in those days.

This view is not only contrary to Scripture's own testimony, it raises many theological questions:[50]

1. If this view of divine accommodation is right, that is to say, if God intentionally affirmed incidental falsehoods in order to present greater truths, then God is guilty of telling "white lies." But the Bible teaches that it is "impossible for God to lie" (Heb 6:18); God "cannot lie" (Titus 1:2); "thy word is truth" (John 17:17; cf. 10:35).

2. If such a view of accommodation is correct, it raises moral problems for Christians since they are called to imitate the character of God (Lev 11:44; Eph 5:1).

3. If this position on accommodation is right, it denies the Bible writers' unanimous affirmation in the absolute truthfulness of *every* statement in Scripture—not some, or most (Ps 12:6; 18:30; 119:96; Prov 30:5; Matt 22:44-45; Luke 24:25; John 10:35; Acts 3:18; 24:14; Rom 15:4; 2 Tim 3:16-17; etc.).

4. If such a view of divine accommodation is valid, it is contrary to Jesus' claim that "He who sent me is true, and I declare to the world what I have heard from Him" (John 8:26, 38).

5. Finally, adopting this view of divine accommodation is contrary to the practice of Jesus, who refused to accommodate Himself to the mistaken views current in his day. His statements, "You have heard that it was said of old . . . . But I say unto you" (Matt 5; cf. John 8:24, 44), illustrate this fact. For this reason, Jesus took contrary positions on divorce, oath-taking, and traditions regarding food (Matt 19:9; 23:16-22; 15:11-20). If Jesus, the Incarnate Word, deliberately accommodated Himself to mistaken views of His day, He was a liar and therefore a sinner. But the Bible says that He "did no sin, neither was guile found in his mouth" (1 Pet 2:22).

**2. The Problem of Mistakes or Errors.** By mistakes or errors, we are *not* referring to those that may have crept into the text as a result of transmission (e.g. occasional or apparent discrepancies due to copyist glosses, slips, misspellings, additions, etc.) which can be corrected by comparing the various manuscripts.[51]

The question at hand has to do with mistakes or errors alleged to have originated with the Bible writers themselves at the time they wrote their accounts. For example, was Moses mistaken when he wrote of a literal six-day creation, a literal Adam and Eve, a literal universal flood, a miraculous Exodus consisting of over 600,000 males, etc.? Was Matthew deceived or mistaken about the virgin birth or about the crucifixion and the bodily resurrection of Jesus? Was Paul misguided when he condemned homosexuality because he lacked knowledge of an alleged genetical basis for homosexuality? These are the kinds of so-called mistakes or errors we have in mind.

Are the details (however minor) in the Bible accurate and trustworthy, or are they mere theological statements, void of any factual certainty? How do we define what constitutes an error in Scripture? Does an interpreter possess superior wisdom and spiritual insight enough to determine the mistakes, contradictions, or errors of the Bible? What if the person's judgment is wrong? What if that individual condemns as mistaken what is correct and endorses as correct what is erroneous?

Bible-believing Christians accept the biblical command: "Trust in the Lord with all thine heart; and lean not unto thine own understanding. In all thy ways acknowledge him, and he shall direct thy paths" (Prov 3:5, 6). Therefore, when Bible-believers perceive difficulties in Scripture, rather than judging the Bible to be contradictory, they question their own assumptions. As they study prayerfully, they ask God to shed more light on the difficult passages. God has done so in the past.

For example, through the painstaking studies of the Adventist scholar Edwin Thiele, the world came to recognize that there are no contradictions in the chronology of the Hebrew Kings; through the discovery of scientists, He proved that rabbits (Lev. 11) chew the cud; through archaeologists He showed the trustworthiness of historical details of the Old Testament.[52]

The decision to suspend judgment as they wrestle with difficult biblical texts is one of the reasons why Bible-believing scholars study the Bible so thoroughly. It would be easier for them simply to declare unresolved difficulties as errors, thereby avoiding the challenge of seeking biblical solutions.

**3. Saving Acts vs. Factual Statements.** As we have shown, some of our scholars suggest that we can accept the Exodus miracle but that the *exact number* of people involved in the Exodus is not that crucial; they claim that there was a miraculous flood in Noah's day but that it was less than a *universal* event. In effect, these scholars suggest that in Scripture some things are "essential" and others are "debatable." Their model for biblical inspiration allows for human imperfections in what they call the lesser matters of Scriptures.[53]

Can we make a distinction between theological statements of God's saving acts and their accompanying historical descriptions? Is there a dichotomy between true doctrine and true science? For example, can we separate the theology of creation (the who of creation) from the scientific issues (the how and the how long of creation)? Can we separate the miracles of the exodus from the actual number of people who left Egypt and the biblical dating of that event? On what basis do we accept one and not the other?

Bible writers make no such distinction between saving acts and the historicity of the details. Some 400-500 years after the events of Moses' day later Old Testament writers reaffirm their historicity (see for example, Ps 105; 106; Isa. 28:21; 1 Kings 16:34).

The New Testament writers, more than a thousand years after the events, trusted even the smallest details of the Old Testament narratives. They wrote about detailed aspects in the Old Testament accounts of Abraham, Rebecca, and the history of Israel (Acts 13:17-23; Rom 4:10, 19; 9:10-12; 1 Cor. 10:1-11). They gave a detailed description of the Old Testament sanctuary (Heb 9:1-5, 19-21), the manner of creation (Heb 11:3), the particulars of the lives of Abel, Enoch, Noah, Abraham, Moses, Rahab and others (Heb 11; 7:2; James 2:25), Esau (Heb 12:16-17), the saving of eight persons during universal flood (1 Pet 3:20; 2 Pet 2:5; 3:5, 6), and the talking of Balaam's donkey (2 Pet 2:16), etc.

Moreover, Jesus, our example, accepted the full trustworthiness of the Old Testament accounts, making no distinction between history and theology. For example, He believed in the historicity of Adam and Eve, Cain and Abel, Noah's universal flood, and Jonah's story (Matt 19:4, 5; 23:35; 24:38, 39; 12:40).

On the basis of the Scriptures, Bible-believing scholars make no dichotomy between so-called essential and debatable aspects of Old Testament saving acts. They do not claim to be more Christlike than Christ, or more apostolic than the apostles, in their use of Scripture. Like their Savior, they accept every historical detail—chronology, numbers, events and people—as a matter of faith and practice. Such scholars are not verbal inspirationists nor fundamentalists, as alleged by their critics. They are simply Bible-believing Adventists!

---

**Endnotes**

[1]At the 1986 Annual Council meeting in Rio de Janeiro, Brazil, church leaders representing all the world fields of the Seventh-day Adventist church approved the report of the General Conference's "Methods of Bible Study Committee as representative of the church's hermeneutical position. This document was published in the *Adventist Review*, January 22, 1977, pages 18-20, and reproduced as Appendix C in my *Receiving the Word*, 355-362. Generally, loyal Adventists embrace the 1986 "Methods of Bible Study" document as reflective of the principles of interpretation that have been accepted historically by Adventists. For a discussion of how Adventist scholars have reacted to the "Methods of Bible Study" document, see my *Receiving the Word*, 75-99.

[2]*Seventh-day Adventists Believe . . . A Biblical Exposition of 27 Fundamental Doctrines*

(Washington, DC: Ministerial Association of the General Conference of Seventh-day Adventists, 1988), 4-15. Produced by some 194 Seventh-day Adventist thought leaders around the world, this "carefully researched" volume is to be received "as representative of . . . [what] Seventh-day Adventists around the globe cherish and proclaim," and as furnishing "reliable information on the beliefs of our [SDA] church" (ibid., vii, iv, v).

[3]The most detailed discussion of Seventh-day Adventist views on the nature and authority of the Bible can be found in Alberto R. Timm's "A History of Seventh-day Adventist Views on Biblical and Prophetic Inspiration (1844-2000)," *Journal of the Adventist Theological Society* 10/1-2 (1999): 486-542. For a brief history of Adventist hermeneutics, see C. Mervyn Maxwell, "A Brief History of Adventist Hermeneutics," *Journal of the Adventist Theological Society* 4/2 (1993): 209-226; Don F. Neufeld, "Biblical Interpretation in the Advent Movement," in *Symposium on Biblical Hermeneutics*, ed. Gordon Hyde (Washington, DC: Biblical Research Institute, 1974), 109-125; George Reid, "Another Look At Adventist Hermeneutics," *Journal of the Adventist Theological Society* 2/1 (1991): 69-76; cf. Samuel Koranteng-Pipim, *Receiving the Word: How New Approaches to the Bible Impact Our Biblical Faith and Lifestyle* (Berrien Springs, Mich.: Berean Books, 1996), 75-99.

[4]Alden Thompson, *Inspiration: Hard Questions, Honest Answers* (Hagerstown, MD: Review and Herald, 1991). Thompson is a professor of biblical studies at an Adventist college in the United States.

[5]Thompson, *Inspiration*, 248, 202, 222, 247, 248, 229, 214-236.

[6]Besides George R. Knight, J. David Neuman, and Ralph Neall, whose endorsements appear on the back jacket of Alden Thompson's *Inspiration,* other scholars who recommended the book include Gosnell L. O. R. Yorke (in his review of the book in *Ministry*, December 1991, 28) and Gerhard van Wyk (in his "A Practical Theological Perspective on Adventist Theology and Contextualisation," *Journal of Adventist Thought in Africa* 1/1 [November 1995]:132-149). Evidence of the book's continued appeal in certain quarters of Adventism is indicated by the fact that in 1998 *Inspiration* was translated into German.

[7]See, for example, Norman R. Gulley's review in *Ministry,* December 1991, 28-30; cf. Peter van Bemmelen's review in *College and University Dialogue* 3/3 (1991): 27-28; Fernando Canale's review in *Andrews University Seminary Studies* 29 (Autumn 1991): 278-279; Robert K. McIver, "The Historical-Critical Method: The Adventist Debate," *Ministry,* March 1996, 15.

[8]Frank Holbrook and Leo van Dolson, eds., *Issues in Revelation and Inspiration*, Adventist Theological Society Occasional Papers vol. 1 (Berrien Springs, MI: Adventist Theological Society, 1992). The book contains articles by Raoul Dederen (two), Samuel Koranteng-Pipim, Norman R. Gulley, Richard A. Davidson, Gerhard F. Hasel, Randall W. Younker, Frank M. Hasel, and Miroslav Kis. Summing up the consensus of the above writers in their rejection of *Inspiration's* conclusions, the editors of the Adventist Theological Society book point out in their Preface that *Inspiration* evidences "the fruits of the historical-critical method," a method that the 1986 Annual Council rejected as "unacceptable" for Adventists (Holbrook and Dolson, "Preface," *Issues in Revelation and Inspiration,* 7). *Issues in Revelation and Inspiration* has recently been translated into German, *Offenbarung und Inspiration* (2000) by the Adventist Theological Society, Haydnstr. 10, D-35075 Gladenback.

[9]Cf. Richard M. Davidson, "Revelation/Inspiration in the Old Testament: A Critique of Alden Thompson's 'Incarnational' Model," in *Issues in Revelation and Inspiration,*

105-135; Gerhard F. Hasel, "Reflections on Alden Thompson's 'Law Pyramid within a Casebook/Codebook Dichotomy," in ibid., 137-171; Randall W. Younker, "A Few Thoughts on Alden Thompson's Chapter: Numbers, Genealogies, Dates," in ibid., 173-199.

[10]See especially Raoul Dederen's two articles in *Issues in Revelation and Inspiration*: "The Revelation-Inspiration Phenomenon according to the Bible Writers," and "On Inspiration and Biblical Authority," 9-29, and 91-103; cf. Frank M. Hasel, "Reflections on the Authority and Trustworthiness of Scripture, in ibid., 201-220; Samuel Koranteng-Pipim, "An Analysis and Evaluation of Alden Thompson's Casebook/Codebook Approach to the Bible," in ibid., 31-67.

[11]Alberto Timm, "A History of Seventh-day Adventist Views on Biblical and Prophetic Inspiration (1844-2000)," *Journal of the Adventist Theological Society* 10/1&2 (Spring-Autumn, 1999): 535.

[12]Samuel Koranteng-Pipim, *Receiving the Word: How New Approaches to the Bible Impact Our Biblical Faith and Lifestyle* (Berrien Springs, Mich.: Berean Books) 1996.

[13]George R. Knight, *Reading Ellen White: How to Understand and Apply Her Writings* (Hagerstown, Md.: Review and Herald, 1997).

[14]Besides the favorable review of the book by the Director of the Biblical Research Institute of the General Conference, George W. Reid, in *Ministry,* December 1997, 30-31, *Receiving the Word* was also endorsed by the following prominent thought leaders of the church: Norman R. Gulley, Paul Gordon, Raoul Dederen, Clifford Goldstein, Alberto R. Timm, William H. Shea, Keith Burton, C. Raymond Holmes, Artur A. Stele, and Randall W. Younker.

[15]George R. Knight, "Review of *Receiving the Word,*" in *Ministry,* December 1997, 30; cf. his, "The Case of the Overlooked Postscript: A Footnote on Inspiration," *Ministry* August 1997. See also Charles Scriven, "Embracing the Spirit," *Spectrum* 26 (September 1997): 28-37; Norman H. Young, "'Moderate Liberalism' Threatens Adventism," *Spectrum* 26 (May 1997): 49-50; cf. Timothy E. Crosby, "The Bible: Inspiration and Authority," *Ministry,* May 1998, 18-20; Robert M. Johnston, "The Case for a Balanced Hermeneutic," *Ministry,* March 1999, 10-12.

[16]See *Receiving the Word,* 279-304.

[17]See, especially, Charles Scriven, "Embracing the Spirit," *Spectrum* 26 (September 1997): 28-37; George R. Knight, "Review of *Receiving the Word,*" in *Ministry,* December 1997, 30; cf. his "The Case of the Overlooked Postscript: A Footnote on Inspiration," *Ministry,* August 1997; Norman H. Young, "'Moderate Liberalism' Threatens Adventism," *Spectrum* 26 (May 1997): 49-50.

[18]Notice that in the doctrine of Scripture the expression "verbal inspiration" is a technical theological phrase that means different things to different people. Used negatively, it means "verbal *mechanical* or *dictation* inspiration." Positively, it refers to a "verbal *plenary* inspiration," a view which maintains that even though the Holy Spirit did not dictate the words of Scripture (as, for instance, a man would dictate to a stenographer), He nonetheless guided the Bible writers in their choice of words. While rejecting mechanical/dictation inspiration, to preserve the truth that the Holy Spirit guided the Bible writers in the choice of their words, I employed the clumsy phrase "verbal propositional inspiration" in my book *Receiving the Word.* On one hand, when inspiration is described as "propositional," it suggests (contrary to neo-orthodox views) that God actually communicated information to the recipients of divine revelation. On the other hand, when I describe inspiration as

"verbal" I argue that despite the inadequacies of human language, because of the Spirit's guidance, the thoughts, ideas, and words of the Bible writers accurately convey God's message revealed to them (see 368). Apparently misunderstanding my phrase "verbal (propositional) inspiration," and most likely believing that the Bible contains some historical and scientific inaccuracies, George Knight has mistakenly claimed that *Receiving the Word* teaches mechanical (dictation) inspiration (see, his review in *Ministry*, December 1997,:30; cf. his "The Case of the Overlooked Postscript," 9-11). Note, however, that in the two places I employed the expression "verbal (propositional) inspiration," I was always careful to add that this expression should not be confused with mechanical (dictation) inspiration, a mistaken theory which claims that the Holy Spirit dictated each single world of Scripture (see *Receiving the Word*, 51, 265), and a view in which the Bible writers are perceived as passive junior secretaries who merely transcribed what the Holy Spirit dictated to them (ibid., 366-367).

[19]George R. Knight, *Reading Ellen White: How to Understand and Apply Her Writings* (Hagerstown, Md.: Review and Herald, 1997).

[20]For more on this, see Alberto Timm, "A History of Seventh-day Adventist Views on Biblical and Prophetic Inspiration (1844-2000)," 493-499.

[21]While it appears that Ellen G. White herself never used the expression "verbal inspiration" in her writings, her son W. C. White employed that phrase in its popular usage as a reference to the mistaken theory of mechanical (dictation) inspiration, a theory that would also not allow an inspired writer to make revisions in his/her original manuscripts. W. C. White argued accurately that none of the leading Seventh-day Adventist pioneers, including Ellen G. White, ever subscribed to verbal inspiration (understood here to mean mechanical [dictation] inspiration). Notice how W. C. White and Arthur L. White explained the meaning of verbal inspiration and why the pioneers rightly rejected such a view:

"Mother has never laid claim to verbal inspiration, and I do not find that my father, or Elder Bates, Andrews, Smith, or Waggoner, put forth this claim. *If there were verbal inspiration in writing her manuscripts, why should there be on her part the work of addition or adaptation?* It is a fact that Mother often takes one of her manuscripts, and goes over it thoughtfully, *making additions that develop the thought still further*" (W. C. White Letter, July 24, 1911; cf. *Selected Messages*, 3:437; 454; emphasis mine). Writing to S. N. Haskell in 1911, W. C. White again pointed out that: "There is danger of our injuring Mother's work by claiming for it more than she claims for it, more than Father ever claimed for it, more than Elders Andrews, [J. H.] Waggoner, or [U.] Smith ever claimed for it. I cannot see consistency in our putting forth a claim of verbal inspiration when Mother does not make any such claim (W. C. White to S. N. Haskell, October 31, 1912).

Arthur L. White concurs: "To make any changes at all in the text of a book written under the inspiration of the Spirit of God, especially a book as widely circulated and studiously read as *The Great Controversy*, was recognized by Ellen White and the staff at Elmshaven as something that would raise questions in the minds of Seventh-day Adventists. There were many who, jealous for Ellen White and the Spirit of Prophecy, held, for all practical purposes, to a theory of verbal inspiration in the work of God's prophets. An action disavowing this stance was taken by the General Conference in session in 1883. But by 1911 this was either unknown or forgotten by Adventists generally" (*Ellen G. White Volume 6: The Later Elmshaven Years, 1905-1915*, 322; cf. 337). "Many of the questions had their foundation in faulty concepts of inspiration. The prophet was thought of as a mechanical agent, speaking or writing each word dictated by the Holy Spirit. This 'verbal inspiration' concept at times led to the expectation of more from Ellen White than was justified—more than was demanded of the prophets and apostles of old" (ibid., 91; cf. 365-366).

It is clear from the above statements that the historic Adventist position has been to reject verbal inspiration, *understood to mean a mechanical dictation inspiration,* a mistaken theory that would also prevent an inspired writer from revising or expanding upon his/her earlier manuscripts. Thus, in the revised edition of the *Seventh-day Adventist Encyclopedia* (1976), the entry under the "Inspiration of Scripture" states that "SDA's do not believe in verbal inspiration according to the usual meaning of the term, but in what may properly be called thought inspiration." See, Don F. Neufeld, ed., *Seventh-day Adventist Encyclopedia*, vol. 10 of commentary series, revised edition (Hagerstown, Md.: Review and Herald, 1976), 648.

[22]George R. Knight, *Reading Ellen White*, 116, 111, 110; cf. his *Anticipating the Advent: A Brief History of Seventh-day Adventists* (Boise, Id: Pacific Press, 1993), 106-107.

[23]George R. Knight, *Reading Ellen White: How to Understand and Apply Her Writings* (Hagerstown, Md.: Review and Herald, 1997), 105, 110, 111, 113-118.

[24]George R. Knight, *Anticipating the Advent: A Brief History of Seventh-day Adventists* (Boise, Idaho: Pacific Press, 1993), 106-107. He wrote: "The loss of Ellen White's and Adventism's moderate stance on inspiration during the 1920s set the church up for decades of difficulties in interpreting the Bible and the writings of Ellen White. The resulting problems have led to extremism, misunderstandings, and bickering in Adventist ranks that exist, unfortunately, until the present" (ibid., 107). Knight's nuanced endorsement of Alden Thompson's book is found on the jacket cover of the latter's *Inspiration.* For helpful correction to the above reinterpretation of Ellen White's and Adventism's position, see James H. Burry, "An Investigation to Determine Ellen White's Concepts of Revelation, Inspiration, 'The Spirit of Prophecy,' and Her Claims About the Origin, Production and Authority of Her Writings," M.A. Thesis, Andrews University, 1991. Cf. P. Gerard Damsteegt, "The Inspiration of Scripture in the Writings of Ellen G. White," *Journal of the Adventist Theological Society* 5/1 (Spring 1994): 155-179; Peter van Bemmelen, "The Mystery of Inspiration: An Historical Study About the Development of the Doctrine of Inspiration in the Seventh-day Adventist Church, With Special Emphasis on the Decade 1884-1893," unpublished manuscript (1971), available at the James White Library, Andrews University.

[25]George R. Knight, *Reading Ellen White,* 116, 111, 110; cf. his *Anticipating the Advent: A Brief History of Seventh-day Adventists* (Boise, Id.: Pacific Press, 1993), 106-107.

[26]Ellen White wrote that rather than speaking in grand superhuman language, "The Lord speaks to human beings in imperfect speech, in order that the degenerate senses, the dull, earthly perception, of earthly beings may comprehend His words. Thus is shown God's condescension. He meets fallen human beings where they are. . . . Instead of the expressions of the Bible being exaggerated, as many people suppose, the strong expressions break down before the magnificence of the thought, though the penmen selected the most expressive language" (*Selected Messages,* 1:22). Again, "The Bible is not given to us in grand superhuman language. Jesus, in order to reach man where he is, took humanity. The Bible must be given in the language of men. Everything that is human is imperfect.

Different meanings are expressed by the same word; there is not one word for each distinct idea" (ibid., 1:20). Thus, in their attempt to communicate infinite ideas in finite human language, the inspired writers sometimes employed figures of speech, like parables, hyperbole, simile, metaphor, and symbolism. But even this figurative language conveys clear, literal truth.

[27]*Fundamentals of Christian Education,* 100; *The Acts of the Apostles,* 506; *Testimonies for the Church,* 5:389; *The Ministry of Healing,* 462; *Testimonies for the Church,* 5:247; ibid., 4:441.

[28]Alberto Timm, "A History of Seventh-day Adventist Views on Biblical and Prophetic Inspiration (1844-2000)," *Journal of the Adventist Theological Society* 10/1-2 (1999): 497. Timm is also the director of the Ellen G. White Research Center in Brazil.

[29]Richard W. Coffen, "A Fresh Look at the Dynamics of Inspiration," two-part series in *Ministry,* December 1999, 9-14, 29; February 2000, 20-23. Coffen, vice-president of editorial services at the Review and Herald Publishing Association, was the editor of Alden Thompson's *Inspiration: Hard Questions, Honest Answers.* According to church historian Alberto Timm, Coffen "showed himself very close to Thompson's theory of inspiration" (see Alberto Timm, "A History of Seventh-day Adventist Views on Biblical and Prophetic Inspiration [1844-2000]").

[30]Richard Coffen, "A Fresh Look at the Dynamics of Inspiration—Part 2," *Ministry,* February 2000, 22.

[31]Robert M. Johnston, "The Case for a Balanced Hermeneutic," *Ministry,* March 1999, 11.

[32]Jeane Haerich, "Genesis Revisited," in *The Welcome Table: Setting A Place for Ordained Women,* eds. Patricia A. Habada and Rebecca Frost Brillhart (Langley Park, Md.: TEAMPress, 1995), 99-101; David R. Larson, "Man and Woman as Equal Partners: The Biblical Mandate for Inclusive Ordination," ibid., 131, 132; Raymond F. Cottrell, "A Guide to Reliable Interpretation," in ibid., 87; Fritz Guy, "The Disappearance of Paradise," in ibid., 142-143. Although the book's introduction and back-cover recommendations state that *The Welcome Table* comprises "carefully thought-through expositions by some of our most competent writers" and "is a definitive collection of essays for our time from respected church leaders," others have observed that, regarding the key hermeneutical issues of women's ordination, this volume is more noteworthy for its breadth than for its depth. For example, Keith A. Burton, an Adventist New Testament scholar, has exposed the historical-critical assumptions underlying some of the essays in *The Welcome Table.* He concludes his insightful critique of this pro-ordination book: "The table around which we are warmly invited to sit is one that already accommodates those who have attacked the relevance of biblical authority; those who wish to pretend that the gnostic image of the primeval and eschatological androgyne is the one toward which Adventists should be moving; those whose interest is in the acquisition of corporate power rather than the evangelization of a dying world; and finally, those who confuse the undiscriminating limitation of the familial and ecclesiastical roles that have been defined by the same Spirit." See Burton, "The Welcome Table: A Critical Evaluation" (unpublished manuscript, 1995), available at the Adventist Heritage Center, James White Library, Andrews University. In my earlier work *Receiving the Word* ( 119-129), I spotlighted a few of the troubling aspects of *The Welcome Table's* arguments for women's ordination.

[33]For more on this see my *Receiving the Word,* 115-142, 155-180.

[34]Raymond F. Cottrell, "Inspiration and Authority of the Bible in Relation to Phenomena of the Natural World," in James L. Hayward, ed., *Creation Reconsidered: Scientific, Biblical, and Theological Perspectives* (Roseville, Calif.: Association of Adventist Forums, 2000), 199, 219. Cottrell's article was originally presented at a 1985 Conference on Geology and Biblical Record sponsored by the Association of Adventist Forums (the liberal Adventist organization that publishes *Spectrum* magazine).

[35]Ibid., 195-196, 199, 200, 205, 218.

[36]Raymond F. Cottrell, "Extent of the Genesis Flood," in Hayward, ed., *Creation Reconsidered,* 275.

[37]*Seventh-day Adventist Bible Commentary,* vol. 1, 257. For a detailed response to the liberal reinterpretation of the creation and flood accounts of the Bible, see John T. Baldwin, ed., *Creation, Catastrophe, and Calvary : Why a Global Flood is Vital to the Doctrine of Atonement* (Hagerstown, Md.: Review and Herald, 2000); cf. Marco T. Terreros, "What Is an Adventist? Someone Who Upholds Creation," *Journal of the Adventist Theological Society* 7/2 (Autumn 1996): 142-167.

[38]Raymond F. Cottrell, "Blame it on Rio: The Annual Council Statement on Methods of Bible Study," *Adventist Currents,* March 1987, 33. Since at least 1977 Cottrell has employed the euphemism "historical method," to describe his historical-critical method. For more on this, see my *Receiving the Word,* 94, 95 notes 9, 11, 15.

[39]Raymond F. Cottrell, "1844 Revisionists Not New: President Indicts the Church's Scholars," *Adventist Today,* January-February, 1995, 16. The front cover of the defunct *Adventist Currents* (October 1983) places Cottrell's picture alongside "some of the Seventh-day Adventist leaders who either doubted or discarded the traditional teaching of the sanctuary: O. R. L. Crosier, D. M. Canright, E. J. Waggoner, A. F. Ballenger, J. H. Kellogg, A. T. Jones, L. R. Conradi, W. W. Prescott, Raymond Cottrell, Desmond Ford" ( 3). Careful readers can discern Cottrell's "revised" views on the sanctuary doctrine by reading his assessment of Ford's position in the same issue of *Adventist Currents* in which his picture appears on the cover page. See Raymond F. Cottrell, "'Variant Views' Digested," *Adventist Currents,* October 1983, 4-9, 34.

[40]See Raymond F. Cottrell, "A Guide to Reliable Interpretation," *The Welcome Table,* 74-75.

[41]Robert S. Folkenberg, "Standing on Solid Ground—The Bible," *Adventist Review,* August 3, 1995, 22.

[42]See *Adventist Review,* October 29, 1998.

[43]The Heritage Sabbath, October 17, 1998, document *God's Word Elevated* was written by Allan G. Lindsay, who currently serves as director of the Ellen G. White SDA Research Center and senior lecturer in Adventist church history at Avondale College in Australia. He also narrated the "Keepers of the Flame" video series on denominational history.

[44]Leo R. van Dolson, *Show and Tell: How God Reveals Truth to Us* (Nampa, ID: Pacific Press, 1998).

[45]See for example, Gerhard Pfandl, "The Authority and Interpretation of Scripture," *Record* (South Pacific Division), April 26, 1997 [supplement, 1-16]; Ekkerhadt Mueller, "The Revelation, Inspiration, and Authority of Scripture," *Ministry,* April 2000, 21-22, 24-25; Roy Gane, "An Approach to the Historical-Critical Method," *Ministry,* March 1999,

5-7, 9; Merling Alomia, "Some Basic Hermeneutic Principles Established by Christ," *Journal of the Adventist Theological Society* 10/1-2 (Spring-Autumn 1999): 475-485; P. Gerard Damsteegt, "New Light in the Last Days," *Adventists Affirm* 10/1 (Spring 1996): 5-13; C. Mervyn Maxwell, "Take the Bible As It Is," *Adventists Affirm* 10/1 (Spring 1996):26-35; George W. Reid, "Another Look at Adventist Methods of Bible Interpretation," *Adventists Affirm* 10/1 (Spring 1996): 50-56; Miroslav Kis, "Biblical Interpretation and Moral Authority," *Journal of the Adventist Theological Society* 6/2 (Autumn 1995):52-62.

[46]Raoul Dederen, ed., *Handbook of Seventh-day Adventist Theology*, vol. 12 of commentary series (Hagerstown, Md.: Review and Herald, 2000). Observe that "although each article [in the *Handbook*] is signed, it was agreed from the start that all contributions would be subject to review and suggestions from the Biblical Research Institute Committee (BRICOM), a group of 40 persons predominantly scholars but including a few administrators. With its international composition BRICOM was called to function as an efficient sounding board. . . . This book is not simply a collection of parts written separately by individual contributors. In fact, no part of it is the work of a single author. As the text proceeded through editing and consultation, all parts of the book and the book as a whole profited from this cooperative approach. The whole working team, i.e., authors and BRICOM members—many of whom were authors—could claim to be genuinely international . . . They wrote this work for a worldwide readership" (see Raoul Dederen's "Preface" in *Handbook of Seventh-day Adventist Theology*, x-xi).

[47]George W. Reid, "Foreword," in *Handbook of Seventh-day Adventist Theology*, ix.

[48]Peter M. van Bemmelen, "Revelation and Inspiration," in *Handbook of Seventh-day Adventist Theology*, 40, 43, 45.

[49]Richard M. Davidson, "Biblical Interpretation," in *Handbook of Seventh-day Adventist Theology*, 62, 73, 72.

[50]Those who desire to speak knowledgeably about this issue will benefit greatly from Peter van Bemmelen's article on "Revelation and Inspiration," in the *Handbook of Seventh-day Adventist Theology*, 22-57; cf. his "Divine Accommodation in Revelation and Scripture," *Journal of the Adventist Theological Society* 9/1-2 (Spring-Autumn 1998): 221-229.

[51]I have given examples of these in *Receiving the Word*, 227-236.

[52]Edwin Thiele, *A Chronology of the Hebrew Kings* (Grand Rapids, Mich.: Zondervan, 1977). Regarding the questions raised about rabbits chewing the cud, studies comparing cows and rabbits have concluded that "it is difficult to deny that rabbits are ruminants" (Jules Carles, "The Rabbit's Secret," *CNRS Research* 5 [1977]:37). For a brief summary and bibliography of scientific studies on the issue, see Leonard R. Brand, "Do Rabbits Chew the Cud?" *Origins* 4/2 (1977):102-104; cf. *Fauna and Flora of the Bible* (London: United Bible Societies, 1972), 39. For how archaeological discoveries have confirmed the Bible, see, for example, Siegfried H. Horn, *The Spade Confirms the Book* (Washington, D.C.: Review and Herald, 1980).

[53]See for instance, Alden Thompson, *Inspiration*, 202, 222, 229, 248, 249; Raymond F. Cottrell, "Inspiration and Authority of the Bible in Relation to Phenomena of the Natural World," and "Extent of the Genesis Flood," in Hayward, ed., *Creation Reconsidered*, 199, 219, 275; Jeane Haerich, "Genesis Revisited," in *The Welcome Table: Setting A Place for Ordained Women*, eds. Patricia A. Habada and Rebecca Frost Brillhart (Langley Park, Md.: TEAMPress, 1995), 99-101; cf. George Knight, *Reading Ellen White*, 116, 111, 110; cf. his *Anticipating the Advent*, 106-107.

# 28

# EMBRACING WHAT SPIRIT?

Although the theological term *fundamentalist* is quite elastic, it is usually employed as a caricature of, if not put-down for, Bible-believing Christians who reject the higher criticism of theological liberalism. Their "progressive" counterparts often perceive such Christians as anti-intellectual, pre-scientific, third world, or intolerant (according to the canons of pluralism, the belief that contradictory theological views must be allowed to flourish in the church).[1]

In the context of recent Seventh-day Adventists' debates over the Bible, scholars who are attempting to revise the church's beliefs and practices often invoke the term fundamentalist against their counterparts who seek to uphold the longstanding Adventist position on the Bible.[2] One such effort is contained in a document titled, *Embracing the Spirit* and circulated as an "Open Letter to the Leaders of Adventism."[3]

The author of *Embracing the Spirit,* until recently a Seventh-day Adventist college administrator, argues thus:[4]

(1) he applauds the efforts of North American thought leaders who are "refining and renewing" Adventist belief, and who are offering "substantive critique and revision" of the church's theology,

(2) he denounces those persons who are standing in the way of this "renewal," "revision," and "adventure of truth," charging them with aiding the Seventh-day Adventist church in a "drift" towards religious fundamentalism,

and with "nullifying the work of the Holy Spirit,"

(3) he states that "the energy" for the church's alleged movement towards fundamentalism has been partly generated by *Receiving the Word*, a work that explains why some within our ranks are challenging cardinal Adventist doctrines (e.g., the substitutionary atonement of Christ, a literal six-day creation, the infallible authority of Scripture, etc.) and embracing lifestyle practices that are incompatible with the tenets of Adventism (e.g., moderate use of alcohol, the eating of unclean foods, endorsement of homosexuality, the use of jewelry, etc.), and

(4) he prescribes "the embrace of the Holy Spirit" as the antidote to the presumed drift of Adventism towards fundamentalism, claiming that through the Spirit's guidance believers would be given insights into new truths, sometimes "hard to bear" and "unforseen by the disciples [of Christ]."

*Embracing the Spirit* deserves some attention for the following reasons: (1) it may well represent the views of those seeking to "refine and renew" Adventist theology; (2) it is designed to be taken seriously by the leaders of Adventism; and (3) its contents have a bearing on, and illustrate, the concerns addressed in this present volume and my earlier work, *Receiving the Word*.[5]

This chapter argues that before "embracing any Spirit" we must first "try the spirits" (1 John 4:1), determining whether the "embraced Spirit" is the Spirit of Him who inspired the written Word to be the norm of Christian belief and practice. The chapter also challenges the claim that the Adventist church is moving in the direction of religious fundamentalism. Finally, it identifies some crucial issues that should be addressed by those who subscribe to the views expressed by the author of *Embracing the Spirit*.[6]

## The Spirit of the Pioneers

**The Birth of A Movement.** More than a century ago, in 1844, a group of young people embarked upon a genuine adventure of truth—truth grounded in God's inspired Word. They were no ordinary young people, for they were *converted* and *biblically knowledgeable* young people who were willing to learn and to do God's will no matter the cost.

Among them was James White, who began preaching at 23, and Ellen White, who started telling her visions publicly at 17. J. N. Andrews held evangelistic meetings at age 21, and by age 24 he had published 35 articles. Uriah Smith became editor of the *Review* at age 23, having already written a

35,000-word poem called "The Warning Voice of Time and Prophecy" that the *Review* published in installments the year before.

These Adventist pioneers humbly received God's Word as fully inspired, trustworthy, internally consistent, and the sole authoritative norm for belief and practice. Following the example of the Protestant Reformers, they took the Bible in its plain, literal sense, without adopting a literalistic interpretation.[7]

While searching the Scriptures, they also spent considerable time in prayer, asking the Holy Spirit to guide them into truths already revealed in His Word. With the Bible in their hands, and the love of Christ in their hearts, our young pioneers did not hesitate to challenge the unbiblical thinking of theological liberalism, and its method of higher criticism, that were pervasive in their day.[8]

Identifying themselves as the end-time Remnant prophesied in Scripture, they called themselves Seventh-day Adventists, fully aware that they were a divinely constituted people, commissioned to declare the everlasting gospel "to every nation, and kindred, and tongue, and people" (Rev 14:6). The unique system of beliefs which our Adventist pioneers consequently developed is summarized by the following distinctive S's:

(1) Scripture's sole and infallible authority, (2) the Substitutionary atonement of Christ, (3) Salvation by grace alone through faith in Jesus Christ, (4) the Sanctuary message, presenting Christ as our Sacrifice and heavenly High Priest (5) the imminent, literal Second Coming of Christ, (6) the seventh-day Sabbath of the fourth commandment, (7) the unconscious State of the dead and the teaching of a future resurrection (8) the Spirit of Prophecy as an identifying mark of God's end-time remnant church, (9) Stewardship of body, time, talents, and possessions, and (10) Standards regarding food, drink, dress, entertainment, relationships, etc.

Inasmuch as these doctrines are rooted in the inspired Word of God, our pioneers lived and proclaimed these distinctive truths with a sense of urgency. The result is that today, millions of people around the world have embraced the Adventist pioneers' unique identity, message and mission. One can point to the inspiring mission reports and growth of the church, even in the industrialized areas of Australia, Europe and North America, as evidence that the spirit of the pioneers is alive and well.

**Startling Development.** But alongside this revival and rapid growth come disturbing indications that some Seventh-day Adventists in certain parts of the world are facing an identity crisis. The church's most distinctive theological doctrines are being challenged—from within. Uncertainty prevails over the church's unique identity and mission, and its worldwide organizational unity is being defied.

As a result of this identity crisis many students in our institutions are confused. There exists a generation of church members, preachers, Bible teachers, leaders, writers, and publishers who are unsure of some of our historic beliefs. And in the areas where the situation prevails, vibrant church growth and church life have been adversely affected.

This startling development is well-known.[9] Yet not everyone sees this sophisticated internal challenge to our Adventist belief and practice as a threat. The advocates of theological change see themselves as offering bold and visionary guidance to the Seventh-day Adventist church by "refining" or renewing our beliefs and practices. In their estimation, their adventure of truth is veering the church off the course of fundamentalism, an overused theological slur often invoked against anyone refusing to embrace the spirit of the age.

The document, *Embracing the Spirit*, is a classic example of such a use of the "fundamentalist" epithet. Since this document has been circulated as an "Open Letter to Leaders of Adventism," we shall now briefly review its contents.

### Review of *Embracing the Spirit*

Although the document, *Embracing the Spirit: An Open Letter to Leaders of Adventism*, reads like the private opinion of its author, it was written and signed in its author's capacity as college president, and mailed out with the approval stamp of the college's development office.[10] Inasmuch as this "Open Letter" seeks to be treated as the official position of the college and the constituency represented by its development office, the document deserves a brief analysis and evaluation.

**Summary of Document.** *Embracing the Spirit* expresses concern over what its author describes as Adventism's "drift toward hostility to truth," "antagonism to the adventure of truth," "stifling [of] the church's quest for deeper understanding,"[11] and fearful accusation against "every prospect of substantive critique and revision of Adventism's speech about God."[12]

While our scholar applauds the efforts of North American thought leaders who are "offering energetic and visionary guidance to Seventh-day

Adventist conferences and congregations" by "refining and renewing [SDA] belief,"[13] he denounces those persons who are standing in the way of this "renewal of understanding," arguing that their alleged "drift toward hostility to the adventure of truth . . . moves the church ever closer to religious fundamentalism."[14]

In so many words he repeats his opinion that "the church's current drift . . . toward anathematizing the adventure of truth and nullifying the work of the Spirit"[15] is evidence that "the church is drifting in the fundamentalist direction."[16] By fundamentalism, he indicates three tendencies: (1) a tendency toward a flat, mechanical reading of the Bible, (2) a tendency toward rigidity and arrogance with regard to customary understanding, and (3) a tendency toward reactive, inward looking separatism.[17]

*Embracing the Spirit* intimates that Adventism's alleged drift towards fundamentalism is a grave situation that "admits of one protection only: the embrace of the Holy Spirit."[18] For our author, "embracing the Spirit" means that while the church has "the right and obligation to *require them* ["those charged with intellectual leadership" in our colleges and universities] to be faithful and effective in that leadership," we must also expect them "to nudge us toward the insights, sometimes hard to bear, that Jesus said would come."[19]

When our scholar writes about "insights, sometimes hard to bear," he explains that through the Spirit's guiding presence Christians would be led "in ways unforseen by the disciples [of Christ]." He asserts: "The unmistakable implication is that new insight, insight yet to enter Christian minds, would sometimes entail a difficult departure from the customary. It would be insight the disciples themselves were not ready, at that moment, to bear."[20] According to our Adventist scholar, such an openness to the Spirit will rule out "the narrow, unimaginative thinking that develops from the three tendencies of fundamentalism."[21]

Interestingly, our author suggests that *Receiving the Word*, my earlier work challenging liberal reinterpretations of traditional Adventist beliefs and practices, is partly responsible for generating "the energy" or a "rallying point for those who (effectively, if not deliberately) are stifling the adventure of truth within Adventism."[22] One can understand our scholar's exasperation over the book's "larger-than-expected readership,"[23] given the fact that *Receiving the Word* has been warmly embraced by very large numbers of Bible-believing Adventists around the world—church members, pastors, students, scholars, and leaders.

Though the author of *Embracing the Spirit* is careful to state that those he disagrees with—styled, "persons with the outlook and attitude expressed in Koranteng-Pipim's writings"[24]—are not "*pure* fundamentalists," he asserts: "Still, to the degree that the church is drifting in the fundamentalist direction, he [the author of *Receiving the Word*] is abetting the drift, and so are those who endorse his writing."[25]

Perceptive readers of the above comment will readily observe that our scholar is opposed, primarily, to the theological direction of the Adventist church, which he characterizes as fundamentalist. His criticism of *Receiving the Word*, and hence of those persons who share the outlook expressed in this work, stems from the fact that the book is encouraging readers to keep moving in the direction of the church's beliefs, not in the adventurous paths being suggested by the self-styled "energetic visionaries."

Those who fail to recognize this overriding concern of the writer of *Embracing the Spirit* may be missing the primary thrust of his "Open Letter to the Leaders of Adventism." Our author has a complaint against the theological direction of the Seventh-day Adventist Church. This is why he purposes with all his "heart and mind" to "oppose the effort of a few in our circle to align the rudder of the church with the direction of the drift."[26] He is distressed by the writings of the author of *Receiving the Word* mainly because the latter "illustrates and reinforces the church's current drift."[27]

**A Brief Evaluation.** Our scholar must be commended for his stated commitment to a "full-hearted openness to the adventure of truth"[28]—even if he is silent on what that truth is or on whether each of the fundamental beliefs of Seventh-day Adventism is to be bracketed within that truth.

He is also to be lauded for emphasizing an "embrace of the Spirit"—though he fails to clearly specify whether the Spirit he speaks about is the Spirit of Him who inspired the written Word to be the norm of all beliefs and practices (2 Tim 3:15-17; 2 Pet 1:19-21), or whether it is another Spirit which is none other than the spirit of our age. Such a clarification would also have been in order especially since there are presently some within our ranks who are jumping on the wings of the "Third Wave of the Holy Spirit" (i.e., the contemporary charismatic movement), in their flight from the biblical truths and practices upheld by Seventh-day Adventists.

He must also be complimented for recognizing that "the Bible story *ascends* toward Jesus, who is the *final* 'Word' of God, and the *final* authority for thought and life"[29]—despite the fact that he fails to note that we cannot recognize the true Jesus Christ apart from the written Word (John 5:39). Such an emphasis would have been in order so as to distance our scholar's views from Barthianism or neo-orthodoxy, a mistaken theological view that jettisons the authority of the Bible for some undefined or nebulous concept called "the final authority of Jesus Christ."

The author of *Embracing the Spirit* also deserves our admiration for asserting the right of the church to "hire teachers and researchers who, in their various ways, assist in promoting and refining that [the church's distinctive] vision"—even if he fails to state what recourse is available to the church when our institutional thought leaders teach, preach, or publish works that deny or fail to be "partisan to the mission implicit in the church's calling as the Remnant."[30]

Again, our scholar must be applauded for accurately describing the "listlessness," "stunted faith," and the "alarming tedium (and non-participation) associated with many Sabbath Schools of North America and other strongholds of Adventism"[31]—even though he misdiagnoses the cause as fundamentalism, and follows it up with a wrong prescription, namely, an "embrace of the Spirit," including a "substantive critique and revision of Adventism's speech about God."[32] He also fails to give evidence that his prescription will produce genuine church growth, faithfulness to God's written Word, and vitality in "the church's older strongholds [which are] suffering from flat or declining enthusiasm and faithfulness."[33]

Finally, the author of *Embracing the Spirit* deserves our appreciation for calling attention to the "destructive tendencies of fundamentalism"—though he fails to justify his claims to have discovered fundamentalism in *Receiving the Word*.

**Areas of Concern.** But with all due respect, I beg to differ with our scholar's assessment of developments within contemporary Adventism, with his debatable analysis and evaluation of a work that defends the church's beliefs and practices, and with his puzzling silence on crucial issues on biblical authority and biblical truth.

There may be a place for denouncing a book for abetting the Seventh-day Adventist church's alleged fundamentalist drift. But negative criticisms that fail to demonstrate objectively that the position upheld in *Receiving the Word* is unbiblical or out of harmony with traditional Adventist belief does not deserve serious attention nor serve the cause of truth—however loudly one invokes the emotional catch phrase of fundamentalism.

Therefore, instead of focusing on the straw man erected by the author of *Embracing the Spirit,* I will simply state the facts and identify some unanswered questions in our scholars work. In this way, I hope to correct our scholar's diagnosis of, and prescription for, the church's theological condition.

**The Facts.** The book *Receiving the Word* argues that some within our ranks have been infected by the virus of contemporary higher criticism (the historical-critical method). The symptoms of this infection can be seen by all who care about the health of the body of Christ: it has created theological uncertainty among our people and paralyzed the growth and vitality of the church in the areas where the product of higher criticism has been embraced. Since this new approach to Scripture denies the full inspiration, trustworthiness, internal harmony, and sole authority of the Bible, *Receiving the Word* challenges the method as unbiblical and incompatible with Seventh-day Adventist beliefs.[34]

But while opposed to contemporary higher criticism, *Receiving the Word* does not seek to promote the three tendencies of our scholar's dreaded fundamentalism. Contrary to the subtle insinuations in *Embracing the Spirit,* Bible-believing scholars—whether in the first world or third world—do not shy away from intellectual pursuits nor seek to create "congregations of poorly educated members who win converts, it is true, but have great difficulty passing their vision to succeeding generations and make little if any transformative difference in their surrounding cultures."[35]

Besides, chapters 9 and 10 of *Receiving the Word* dismiss any intimation that we argue for a mechanical or literalistic reading of the Bible. Moreover, our call for upholding the ideals of God's end time "Remnant" does not encourage the kind of "inward-looking separatism" alluded to by our scholar.[36]

*Embracing the Spirit* would have gained some credibility if its author had pointed out that those who are promoting "inward-looking separatism" are: (1) the persons who fail to motivate "Spirit-filled" church members to be active in the outreach, evangelistic, and soul-winning mission of the Remnant church ; (2) those who have embraced a spirit that says, "I'll defy or go my own way without regard to what the community of believers has to say on theological and ecclesiastical issues"; (3) the individuals who have accepted the so-called "principle," "progressive," or "dynamic" approach to biblical interpretation and, consequently, relativize biblical truth—all in the name of being led by the Spirit.

The Bible-believing Adventism that is advocated in *Receiving the Word* and embraced by an overwhelming majority of Seventh-day Adventists around the world is not afraid to investigate, advance in, or clarify biblical truth. But its quest for biblical truth, the whole truth, and nothing but the truth, compels it to challenge the kind of unbiblical thinking that for some has become the hallmark of scholarly enlightenment and spiritual insight.

The Adventism encouraged in *Receiving the Word* is a vibrant Christian movement that rejoices that Jesus Christ died for our sins in fulfillment of Bible prophecy and has called us to walk in His steps through a faithful, obedient commitment to Him. This kind of Adventism does not pander to the spirit of our age while believing or congratulating itself that it is transforming its ambient culture or renewing the beliefs of the church.

Our college administrator is a scholar who claims to write "neither lightly nor recklessly."[37] Hence his *Embracing the Spirit* should not be dismissed for being more noteworthy for its breadth than for its depth. He indicates that he has "considered the subject matter" and written his thoughts "with all the care" that he can muster.[38] Thus, he should be admired for the brilliant way he attempted to invoke the fundamentalist epithet as a decoy for diverting attention from the key issues raised in my earlier book.[39] Still, in all fairness, it must be stated that his *Embracing the Spirit* can win the sympathy of only those who have already bought into the critical heterodoxy challenged in *Receiving the Word*.

**Some Unanswered Questions.** One cannot help but notice that, in *Embracing the Spirit*, there is a deafening silence regarding major questions of biblical truth. A few examples will illustrate our observation.

Our college administrator's "Open Letter to Leaders of Adventism" speaks of "adventure to truth." But he is vague on whether that adventure has a destination—i.e., a body of beliefs that may be accepted as the truth. One is left wondering if the emphasis on "adventure of truth" is not an euphemism for parrying with the truth.

He encourages the "refining," "renewing," and "substantive critique and revision" of Adventist theology. However, he does not specify which of our Fundamental Beliefs needs this kind of modification. Is possible that the call for a change in Adventist theology is actually a clamor for the abandonment of some of our biblically established doctrines and practices?

The author of *Embracing the Spirit* sees the Adventist church drifting in the direction of fundamentalism. Yet he fails to notice that his observation of the church comes from the vantage point of one who is riding a fast train of change called the "adventure of truth." Could it be that those riding this speeding train are rather the ones who are drifting away from Adventism towards an unknown destination?

He speaks about "embracing the Spirit." Yet he is mute over whether that Spirit will ever contradict the Spirit who inspired the written Word to be the test of all spirits. One is left in a quandary over whether the call to "embrace the Spirit" is not a proposal for a paradigm shift so that the "People of the Book" will now see themselves as "the People of the Spirit"—as if the Holy Spirit ever quarrels with His inspired Book.[40]

Bible-believing Seventh-day Adventists have always insisted: "The Spirit was not given—nor can it ever be bestowed—to supersede the Bible; for the Scriptures explicitly state that the word of God is the standard by which all teaching and experience must be tested" (*The Great Controversy,* vii). "To the law and to the testimony: if they speak not according to this word, it is because there is no light in them" (Isa 8:20; cf. Gal 1:8, 9).

Finally, our scholar and college administrator acknowledges the church's "right and obligation" to require our thought leaders to be totally committed to the message and mission of the church.[41] Yet when the advocates of theological change are called upon to give account of their stewardship, he characterizes it as an eagerness to "track down and penalize every effort at constructive innovation."[42] Should we not expect those who take upon themselves the responsibility of a "substantive critique and revision of Adventism's speech about God"[43] to (a) show why the church's beliefs and practices are unscriptural, and (b) offer solid *biblical* basis for their new insights or adventure of truth?

Since the author of *Embracing the Spirit* is silent on the above questions, it may now be necessary for us to call attention to some specific aspects of our Adventist faith that are currently being challenged by the advocates of theological change. Perhaps our author and all others who share his attempt at "refining and renewing" Adventist belief will, in the spirit of truth, offer candid answers to the questions that follow.

## In the Spirit of Truth

Since the author of *Embracing the Spirit* failed to mention that key aspects of our faith are being challenged by some who seek "substantive critique and revision" of Adventist theology, I will do so in the next few paragraphs. Calling attention to these contentious areas of our theological disagreements will enable and encourage church members and leaders in their efforts to uphold sound teaching (1 Tim 6:20; 2 Tim 1:13) and counteracting false teaching and false teachers (1 Tim 1:3; 4:1, 6; Titus 1:9-11).

**Adventist Faith and Practice.** As we noticed in the previous discussion, our author correctly recognizes the church's "right and obligation *to require*"[44] its thought leaders to commit themselves to the message and mission of the church. Church institutions have a confessional responsibility to demand this, and church employees have a moral obligation to honor it—unless it can be shown that the church's biblical teachings are not biblically defensible.

For this reason, the leaders of Adventism to whom *Embracing the Spirit* is addressed should demand from the document's esteemed author, as well as those persons who presumably mandated him to send out his official document, to honestly declare if they still believe in the following time-honored Seventh-day Adventist affirmations—teachings that are being challenged in certain quarters of the Adventist church:

(1) the substitutionary atonement of Christ—i.e., His death in our place pays the penalty for sin, provides forgiveness, and creates saving faith;[45]

(2) the deity, virgin birth, miracles, *bodily* resurrection and the *literal* second coming of Jesus Christ;

(3) the Bible as the Word of God—a fully inspired, internally consistent, infallible revelation of propositional truth. The Bible is its own interpreter, provides the foundation and context for scholarship and the totality of life, and is the unerring standard for doctrine;

(4) Ellen G. White, as an inspired writer, possesses more than pastoral authority so that her writings are an invaluable tool for illuminating Scripture and confirming church doctrines;

(5) the literal reading and meaning of Genesis 1-11 as an objective, factual account of earth's origin and early history; that the world was created in six literal, consecutive, *contiguous* 24-hour days;[46] that the entire earth was subsequently devastated by a literal world-wide flood, and that since creation

week the age of our world is "about 6000 years." (This point is especially crucial since *Embracing the Spirit* seems to have problems with what its author refers to as "the arithmetic of the creation story"[47]);

(6) a literal sanctuary in heaven, the pre-advent judgment beginning in 1844, and an eschatology that identifies the Seventh-day Adventist church as the remnant of Bible prophecy called to proclaim the three angels' messages which prepare the world for Christ's second coming; and

(7) faithfulness to the Seventh-day Adventist church's lifestyle practices, including the rejection of homosexuality, polygamy, wearing of jewelry, eating of unclean foods, moderate use of alcohol, women's ordination, divorce and remarriage, and worldly entertainment and amusements.

This last point is particularly critical in light of the apprehension expressed in *Embracing the Spirit* over certain distinctives that distinguish God's people from others. When our author writes that "All too often, these markers—sometimes highly contestable, often merely external—have little to do with the mind of Christ and the soul of discipleship,"[48] does he include the Adventist lifestyle practices identified in #7 above, and is he suggesting that some of these are "highly contestable"?

**Method of Biblical Interpretation.** Besides the above theological affirmations, the "Leaders of Adventism" must also call upon the author of *Embracing the Spirit* and his fellow energetic visionaries to address the underlying hermeneutical questions that has occasioned much of the reinterpretations of our biblical beliefs and practices.

Specifically, these advocates of theological change (the self-styled "refiners" or "renewers" of our beliefs) must be asked if they believe in the use of the time-honored Adventist method of biblical interpretation (the plain reading of Scripture), the necessity of relying on the Holy Spirit in this effort, and a rejection of the use of any form of contemporary higher criticism (i.e., the historical-critical method of Bible study).

To encourage the champions of *Embracing the Spirit* to address the forbidden issues of hermeneutics, I will in the next chapter offer a brief summary of the most crucial questions of the current Seventh-day Adventist debate.

I trust that the author who speaks so eloquently and admirably of "adventure of truth" and of "embracing the Spirit," together with the "visionaries" of theological change, will, *in the Spirit of truth*, offer candid answers to the above questions and those which follow. For as Martin Luther said:

If I profess with the loudest voice and clearest exposition every position of the truth of God except precisely that little point which the world and the devil are at that moment attacking, I am not confessing Christ, however boldly I may be professing Christ. Where the battle rages, there the loyalty of the soldier is proved; and to be steady on all the battle field besides, is mere flight and disgrace if he flinches at that point.[49]

**Endnotes**

[1]James Barr's suggestion that the word *fundamentalism* connotes "narrowness, bigotry, obscurantism, and sectarianism" highlights this point (Barr, Fundamentalism [Philadelphia, Penn.: Westminster, 1977], 2). For a discussion of Protestant fundamentalism, see C. T. McIntire, "Fundamentalism," in Walter A. Elwell, ed., *Evangelical Dictionary of Theology* (Grand Rapids, Mich.: Baker, 1984), 433-436; G. M. Marsden, "Fundamentalism," in Sinclair B. Ferguson, David F. Wright, and J. I. Packer, eds., *New Dictionary of Theology* (Downers Grove, Ill.: InterVarsity, 1988), 266-268.

[2]In a lecture given in Wycliffe Hall at Oxford University, British scholar Gordon J. Wenham aptly described the situation: "I suspect that if either you [a student] or your lecturers discover during your study that you are a Sabellian montanist or semipelagian gnostic [these were christological heresies in the early church], it will not cause over-much excitement. Such deviants are common place today and in this pluralistic society are usually accepted without much fuss. However should you be diagnosed as a fundamentalist your fate may be very different. In the modern theology faculty fundamentalism is the great heresy. It is regarded as nearly as dangerous as the HIV virus and is treated with similar fervour but with rather less tact and sympathy." See, Gordon J. Wenham, "The Place of Biblical Criticism in Theological Study," *Themelios* 14/3 (1989):84. Bible-believing Christians should not be intimidated by any pejorative labels—labels that are calculated to induce Christians to accept some "progressive" ideas (theological codeword for deviations from Scripture).

[3]Charles Scriven, *Embracing the Spirit: An Open Letter to the Leaders of Adventism* (Columbia Union College, Takoma Park, MD, August 1997).

[4]Until very recently, Dr. Charles Scriven was the president of Columbia Union College, a Seventh-day Adventist institution in Takoma Park, Maryland.

[5]The entire content of Scriven's *Embracing the Spirit: An Open Letter to Leaders of Adventism* document was subsequently published in the liberal Adventist journal *Spectrum*, September 1997, 28-37. The editor, however, explained to me that because of space constraints only a portion of my response could be published alongside Scriven's (see my "In the Spirit of Truth: Pipim Responds," *Spectrum* 26 [September 1997], 38-44).

[6]My complete response to *Embracing the Spirit* was originally published as *In the Spirit of Truth* [A Review of an Open Letter Titled *Embracing the Spirit*, in the Light of Key Issues on Biblical Inspiration and Interpretation] (Berrien Springs, Mich.: Berean Books, 1997).

[7]An excellent review of the historic Adventist approach to Scripture can be found in

C. Mervyn Maxwell's "A Brief History of Adventist Hermeneutics," *Journal of the Adventist Theological Society* 4/2 (1993):209-226; "'Take the Bible as It Is,'" *Adventists Affirm* 10/1 (Spring 1996):26-35; cf. George W. Reid, "Another Look at Adventist Methods of Bible Interpretation," *Adventists Affirm* 10/1 (Spring 1996):50-56. A recent restatement of the historic Adventist hermeneutics is found in the carefully worded "Methods of Bible Study" document approved at the 1986 Annual Council meeting in Rio de Janeiro, Brazil. The entire document is published in the *Adventist Review* (January 22, 1987), pages 18-20, and reproduced in Appendix C of my recent book *Receiving the Word: How New Approaches to the Bible Impact Our Biblical Faith and Lifestyle* (Berrien Springs, MI: Berean Books, 1996), 355-362.

[8]A detailed discussion of the Seventh-day Adventist pioneers' attitude toward higher criticism can be found in Peter van Bemmelen's paper, "Seventh-day Adventists and Higher Criticism in the Nineteenth Century," Andrews University, 1977, available at the Ellen G. White Research Center of the James White Library, Andrews University, in Document File 391-h.; cf. idem, "The Mystery of Inspiration: An Historical Study About the Development of the Doctrine of Inspiration in the Seventh-day Adventist Church, With Special Emphasis on the Decade 1884-1893," unpublished manuscript (1971), available at the James White Library, Andrews University.

[9]For example, the then president of the General Conference stated this concern in 1995: "In many of the more developed and sophisticated areas of the world, I sense that an increasingly secular value system is negatively impacting many of our members. I sense a growing uncertainty about why we exist as a church and what our mission is." See Robert S. Folkenberg, "When Culture Doesn't Count," *Ministry,* December 1995, 7. A brief documentation, detailing the underlying causes, of this identity crisis may be found in chapters 4 to 6 of my *Receiving the Word*, 75-206.

[10]Charles Scriven, *Embracing the Spirit: An Open Letter to the Leaders of Adventism* (Columbia Union College, Takoma Park, MD, August 1997). Until recently, Dr. Charles Scriven was the president of Columbia Union College, a Seventh-day Adventist institution in Takoma Park, Maryland.

[11]Scriven, *Embracing the Spirit,* (3:3, 4). Note that figures in parentheses show the page numbers and the full paragraphs in which the quotations are found in his original document. Thus, (3:3, 4) refers to page 3, paragraphs 3 and 4.

[12]Ibid., (12:2).

[13]Ibid., (3:4; 4:3).

[14]Ibid., (5:1).

[15]Ibid., (4:1).

[16]Ibid., (6:3).

[17]Ibid., (5:2-8:2).

[18]Ibid., (5:1); cf. (6:1); (8:3-10:2).

[19]Ibid., (12:3-13:3).

[20]Ibid., (10:1). As examples of the new insights that entail a "difficult departure from the customary," our author continues: "Down the centuries, minds indeed would change in ways unforeseen by the disciples: Christians would come to favor complete abolition of slavery; they would defend liberty over despotism; they would further weigh, and further support, equal rights and opportunity for women" (ibid., 10:1). In making this assertion, our Adventist scholar seems to be unaware of the fact that the Bible has never supported

the practices of slavery, despotism, and denial of women's equal rights, and that many of the people who championed the cause of the abolition of slavery, defense of liberty over despotism, and the support of equal rights and opportunity for women, did so on the basis of *truth already revealed in Scripture.* Readers will benefit from the following works: John Stott, *Issues Facing Christians Today* (Basingstoke, Hants: Marshall Morgan & Scott, 1984), 2-28, 45-61; Theodore D. Weld, *The Bible Against Slavery: Or, An Inquiry into the Genius of the Mosaic System, and the Teachings of the Old Testament on the Subject of Human Rights* (Pittsburgh: United Presbyterian Board of Publication, 1864); cf. Dale B. Martin, *Slavery As Salvation: The Metaphor of Slavery in Pauline Christianity* (New Haven: Yale University Press, 1990); Guenther Haas, "Patriarchy as An Evil that God Tolerated: Analysis and Implications for the Authority of Scripture," *Journal of the Evangelical Theological Society,* September 1995, 321-326; George W. Knight III, *The Role Relationship of Men and Women: New Testament Teaching* (Chicago, IL: Moody Press, 1985), 7-15.

[21]Scriven, *Embracing the Spirit,* (14:2).

[22]Ibid., (4:1-2); cf. 8:2.

[23]Ibid, (4:1).

[24]Ibid, (4:2).

[25]Ibid., (6:3).

[26]Ibid., (3:3).

[27]Ibid., (4:1).

[28]Ibid., (16:2).

[29]Ibid., (7:0).

[30]Ibid., (12:3-13:1).

[31]Ibid., (11:3).

[32]Ibid., (12:2).

[33]Ibid., (5:2).

[34]An excellent exposition of the Seventh-day Adventist position on the inspiration, trustworthiness, unity and authority of Scripture is found in *Seventh-day Adventists Believe . . . A Biblical Exposition of 27 Fundamental Doctrines* (Washington, DC: Ministerial Association of the General Conference of Seventh-day Adventists, 1988), 5-15. This work, produced by 194 thought leaders around the world, is to be received "as representative of . . . [what] Seventh-day Adventists around the globe cherish and proclaim," and as furnishing "reliable information on the beliefs of our [SDA] church" (ibid., iv, v). For the general Seventh-day Adventist understanding of biblical interpretation, see "Methods of Bible Study," *Adventist Review* (January 22, 1987), 18-20, reproduced as Appendix C in *Receiving the Word,* 355-362. "Methods of Bible Study" rejects as "unacceptable to Adventists" "even a modified use" of the historical-critical method.

[35]Scriven, *Embracing the Spirit,* (5:3).

[36]Ibid., (6:4-8:2).

[37]Ibid., (3:3).

[38]Ibid., (2:1).

[39]These key issues have been summarized in the next chapter of this present work (*Must We Be Silent?)* as a set of ten questions on inspiration and interpretation.

[40]Readers interested in a detailed treatment of the Holy Spirit's role in Bible interpretation may want to consult my "The Role of the Holy Spirit in Biblical Interpretation: A Study in the Writings of James I. Packer" (Ph.D. dissertation, Andrews

University, 1998). This 410-page work explores how the relationship between the Spirit and the inspired Word has been understood by major theological figures and movements since the sixteenth century Reformation and culminating in the works of one of contemporary Evangelicalism's most widely respected theologians.

[41]Scriven, *Embracing the Spirit*, (12:3-13:1).

[42]Ibid., (7:1).

[43]Ibid., (12:2).

[44]Ibid, (12:3-13:1).

[45]In 1994, one of Scriven's published works generated considerable discussion in Adventist circles when it challenged the penal substitutionary atonement of Christ, the biblical teaching that Jesus Christ died in our stead, taking upon Himself the penalty of death that we deserved. See his "God's Justice, Yes; Penal Substitution, No," *Spectrum*, October 1993, 31-38; see also his follow-up letter, "Scriven Says Penal Substitutionary Atonement is Still Unbiblical," *Spectrum,* July 1994, 63-64. For a brief analysis and critique of these works, see Samuel Koranteng-Pipim, "A Critique of Dr. Charles Scriven's 'God's Justice Yes: Penal Substitution, No'," unpublished manuscript, December 1994, available at the Adventist Heritage Center, James White Library, Andrews University.

[46]The word "contiguous" is used to emphasize the fact that the six days of creation are not merely consecutive (in the sense of following in a successive order), but also that there are no gaps between the consecutive days. Thus, the days of creation touch one another, so that the second day begins just at the point when the first day ended.

[47]Scriven, *Embracing the Spirit*, (7:0).

[48]Ibid., (8:1).

[49]I am indebted to the Internet website *http://www.gospelcom.net/cquod/cquodlist.htm* for the above quote. Each day this Christian web site provides a noteworthy quotation for reflection. The above statement was posted on the site on May 1, 1997. I have yet to track down successfully the exact source reference in Luther's writings.

# 29

# KEY QUESTIONS ON THE BIBLE'S INSPIRATION

Sometimes proponents of contemporary higher criticism resort to straw man arguments to articulate their views, or they employ impressive scholarly jargon to camouflage their babble over the Bible. They carefully ignore the substantive theological issues raised by their use of the liberal methodology. The result is that very few are able to see through the smokescreen of the ideology of higher criticism.

The purpose of this chapter is to focus on the key questions being raised by those opposing the church's official positions. Clarifying the issues and identifying the relevant theological concerns in the Adventist debate over the Bible will enable readers to determine whether or not a person is employing the assumptions of higher criticism.

### Clarifying the Issues

During the last decade scholars representing the two major sides in the Seventh-day Adventist cold war over the Bible published conflicting articles and books on the Bible.[1] As significant as these works may be, it is a mistake to treat any of them as the reference point for any serious discussion of the church's understanding of the Bible's inspiration, authority, and interpretation.[2]

The Adventist church has explicitly expressed and clearly articulated its position on the Bible's inspiration and interpretation. Therefore, those who discuss the hermeneutical crisis within the Adventist church should be encouraged to reckon with the official views before pointing to unauthorized opinions.[3]

**1. Two Facts.** Two facts are often ignored in present discussions. First, the Seventh-day Adventists Church upholds the Bible as God's inspired, trustworthy, and solely authoritative Word. This high view of Scripture is expressed in the first article of the church's Fundamental Beliefs. Among other things, the first article of faith affirms that: (1) Scripture is of divine origin though written by human hands, (2) Scripture is an "infallible" revelation of God's will, (3) Scripture is the sole-authoritative norm for religious doctrine, and (4) Scripture's record of God's acts in history is "trustworthy."[4]

Second, the Seventh-day Adventist Church has a hermeneutic. The church's position, setting forth the hermeneutical presuppositions, principles, and methods that are to govern its members' approach to Scripture, was approved at the 1986 Annual Council of church leaders. The "Methods of Bible Study" document (or the "Rio Document," as it is popularly referred to) is "addressed to all members of the Seventh-day Adventist Church with the purpose of providing guidelines on how to study the Bible, both the trained biblical scholar and others." Among other things, the church rejects "even a modified use" of the historical-critical method as inconsistent with the teachings of Scripture itself.[5]

Indeed, a careful study of official church publications during the past decade confirm that the positions of the Seventh-day Adventist church on the nature, authority, and interpretation of Scriptures have not changed, since they were last formulated in the 1980s. For example, the Adult Sabbath School Lessons for the first quarter of 1999 and its companion book titled *Show and Tell,* as well as the articles on "Revelation and Inspiration" and "Biblical Interpretation" in the recently released *Handbook of Seventh-day Adventist Theology* (2000), volume 12 of the commentary series, confirm the long-standing Adventist position on the full inspiration, infallibility, and trustworthiness of Scriptures.[6]

**2. Why the Controversy.** As mentioned earlier, the current hermeneutical controversy in the church arises from the fact that some scholars within our ranks do not want to accept the established views of the church in their entirety.[7] Some take issue with aspects of Fundamental Belief#1, raising questions about the nature of the inspiration of the human and divine aspects of Scripture, and also about the nature of the Bible's authority, infallibility and trustworthiness.

Others are opposed to the hermeneutical position reflected in the 1986 "Methods of Bible Study" document, objecting to the church's categorical rejection of the historical-critical method.[8] Still, others would not want to accept the authoritative guidance of Ellen G. White on theological and hermeneutical issues.[9]

Even though the above concerns underlie Adventism's ongoing civil-war over the modified use of the historical-critical method, much of the recent discussions have carefully avoided to mention these facts. Some prefer not to engage in the discussion, maintaining that debates over the Bible are unimportant trivial domestic squabbles among quarrelsome Adventists.

Other scholars are more negative in their assessment of these debates, claiming that they are attempts towards a theological witch hunt. To such, recent discussions over the Bible's inspiration and interpretation are lamentable symptoms of "extreme fundamentalism" in the church, a theological neurosis believed to have been brought about by divisive individuals seeking to make mountains from mole hills. Those who share this view believe that consensus in Adventist interpretation can be reached merely by moving beyond these annoying discussions about the Bible and "embracing the Spirit."[10]

The failure to grasp the importance of the issues at stake in the debate have led some scholars to suggest that the term "historical-critical method" be abandoned altogether, ostensibly because it is so loaded and often misunderstood. They seem to assume that if the expression is not employed, the method will cease to be identified as historical-critical. Others have also simply dropped the word "critical" in the phrase "historical-critical method," referring to their scholarly approach as the historical method or a historical analysis. Still, others prefer to disguise the method by repackaging it as principle approach, progressive approach, casebook approach, commonsense approach, contextual approach, matured approach, developmental approach, sensible approach.[11]

These proposals are seriously misleading, in that they fail to discuss the real differences between the advocates and opponents of the historical-critical method.

## The Differences Between the Two Approaches

It is possible that many who engage in discussions over the Bible are not fully aware of what the real issues are. As a first step in clarifying the questions associated with the use of contemporary higher criticism, I will briefly set forth the differences between the liberal methodology and the long-standing Adventist approach to the Bible.

**1. Methodological Assumptions.** The difference between Adventists who seek a modified use of the historical-critical method and those who reject it does not lie in the fact that one method is *scholarly* and the other not. Both groups of scholars seek an understanding of Scripture that takes into account the historical and literary contexts of the Bible. The difference lies in the assumptions which undergird the respective methods.

Unlike the official Adventist approach, advocates of the higher-critical methods assume that: (a) the Bible is not fully inspired (i.e., some parts of the Bible are more inspired than others); (b) the Bible is not fully trustworthy (because of alleged mistakes in some of the Bible's historical and scientific assertions); (c) the Bible is not absolutely authoritative in all that it teaches or touches upon (portions allegedly shaped by the personal or cultural prejudices of the writers and their times are uninspired and not binding on us); and (d) there are internal discrepancies, contradictions, or inconsistencies in Scripture; this diversity in Scripture (i.e., pluralism or conflicting theologies in the Bible) is believed to be caused by the Bible's many human writers. Are these assumptions valid?

**2. Historical Inquiry.** The Adventists opposing the modified use of the historical-critical method do not object because they do not want to study the *historical* or cultural backgrounds of the Bible. They welcome the inquiry of those who accept what Scripture says as trustworthy and who desire simply to learn its meaning. What they reject is the intrusion of unbiblical assumptions drawn from secular thought, culture, or subjective experience as the basis to judge the credibility of the biblical record and to conjecture and reconstruct what may or may not have actually happened.

The historical interpretation of the historical-critical method, if adopted, will breed a new papalism of scholars, since ordinary laypeople who are not trained as historians will be expected to depend on the experts for understanding the real historical backgrounds of the contents of the Christian faith. Besides, such a historical approach fails to show a way out should the historical experts disagree.

How much easier it would be to follow the example of Jesus in simply taking the Bible as historically reliable. He believed in the historical trustworthiness of the account about Adam and Eve, Satan, Cain and Abel, Noah's universal flood, and Jonah's story (Matt 19:4, 5; 23:35; 24:38, 39; 12:40; etc.). Should we not?[12]

**3. Critical Reasoning.** The difference between the traditional or official Adventist approach to Scripture and the historical-critical approach is not that the latter is *critical* while the former is not; both are critical, depending upon how one defines the term.

If by *critical* interpretation we mean the answering of questions about the date, place, sources, background, literary character, credentials, and purposes of each biblical book or composition, then Adventists upholding the church's position will have no difficulty in describing their own approach as critical. If, however, the term implies *charging the Bible with untrustworthiness or fraudulence of any kind* (which is what proponents of the historical-critical method intimate), then they are opposed to it.

Adventists who are tempted to adopt the reasoning of the historical-critical method face a major dilemma. How do they exalt the Bible as the judge of human errors and at the same time keep the human interpreter as the arbiter of Scripture's errors? How can they commend the Bible as a true witness yet charge it with falsehood? Is this not theological double-talk? It seems to me that those seeking to use modified versions of the higher-critical methodologies are riding two convictional horses—religious certainty about the Bible's power, and an intellectual uncertainty about its full truth.

**4. Scientific Objectivity.** The difference between the official Adventist approach and the historical-critical method is not that the latter is *scientific* or *objective* while the former is not. Such an assessment can only be made after understanding the meanings of the terms.

If by scientific or objective is meant that one is neutral in one's assumptions, then it must be pointed out that there has never been, and indeed, can never be, complete scientific objectivity or neutrality in the study of the Bible. For the moment anyone begins to interpret the biblical data, presuppositions set in. Therefore, the claim to divorce the study of Scripture from presuppositions (whether biblical or non-biblical), in the hope of achieving a scientific objectivity is not only impossible, but also an illusion.

An interpretation can only be said to be genuinely scientific, in the proper sense if, and only if, it is wholly determined by the object of study—which in this case is Scripture itself, the self-revelation of God. Since the historical-critical method is shaped by some *a priori* philosophical presuppositions that are brought from outside to Scripture, it cannot legitimately be described as a scientific method. Only the church's official position can correctly make that claim, for it seeks to interpret Scripture solely on the basis of correct inferences from Scripture.

**5. Doubts and Skepticism, the Result.** In rejecting even a modified use of the historical-critical method, Seventh-day Adventists opposed to the method are guarding against the repudiation of biblical teaching and lifestyle that inevitably results once the method is adopted.

This point is best illustrated from the published works of some of our scholars who have embraced modified versions of the method. As we have shown elsewhere, these scholars are not only questioning the trustworthiness of some scriptural accounts, but they are also raising doubts over basic Adventist teachings like a literal six-day creation, a worldwide flood, the Ten Commandments, the substitutionary atonement of Christ, the sanctuary, clean and unclean meat, homosexuality, etc.[13]

It is evident from the above example that once we start questioning or passing judgment upon the Word of God, it does not take long before we begin to criticize or reject its message. This skepticism may explain why the Adventist pioneers were opposed to the use of higher criticism.[14] It may also explain Ellen G. White's unfavorable view about the method, tracing it to Satan himself. She writes:

> Satan had the highest education that could be obtained. This education he received under the greatest of all teachers. When men talk of higher criticism, when they pass their judgment upon the word of God, call their attention to the fact that they have forgotten who was the first and wisest critic. He has had thousands of years of practical experience. He it is who teaches the so-called higher critics of the world today. God will punish all those who, as higher critics, exalt themselves, and criticize God's Holy word (*Review and Herald*, March 16, 1897).

The knowledge that "God will punish all those who, as higher critics, exalt themselves, and criticize God's Holy word," should caution us against the temptation of using even a modified version of the historical-critical method.

### Ten Crucial Questions on the Bible

To help focus the debate over the appropriateness of the historical method in Seventh-day Adventist scholarship, I will now briefly summarize the crucial issues that underlie the present hermeneutical debates in the church, pointing out some possible areas of agreement and disagreement.

**1. Divinity and Humanity of Scriptures:** There is a unanimous recognition of the fact that the Bible is *both* divine *and* human. Like Jesus at his incarnation, the Bible is a mysterious union.

***Issue #1:*** *Can Adventist interpreters separate the human from the divine? If so, by what criteria?*

Notice that Ellen White challenged the tendency of some to separate the human and divine elements in Scripture, conferring uninspired status upon some portions of the written Word.[15] Indeed, Bible-believing Adventists recognize the impossibility of separating what is divine from what is human in Scripture. They also recognize that attempting to do so denies the basic *unity* of Scripture.

Against this liberal view, Adventists assert that the Bible is ultimately the product of one Divine mind, the Holy Spirit; hence, a theological unity runs through the Bible from Genesis to Revelation. This unity means that we may compare Scripture with Scripture to arrive at correct doctrine. It makes the later inspired writers the best interpreters of earlier inspired writers.

**2. The Use of Human Sources:** Both sides of the hermeneutical quarrel affirm that, in addition to direct divine revelation through visions, dreams, and theophanies, the inspired writers also used human sources in composing their material.[16]

***Issue #2:*** *Does the use of human sources render some parts of Scripture as uninspired? In other words, are visions or dreams (the "I saw" and "I heard" parts of Scripture) more inspired than the biographical sections that are not based on direct divine revelation? Did the New Testament writers correctly use the Old Testament sources they cited?*

Bible-believing Adventists have always recognized that because the Holy Spirit guided the Bible writers in their selection and use of historical and literary sources, all Scripture is inspired and manifest a remarkable unity in content. Therefore, Ellen White warned: "Do not let any living man come to you and begin to dissect God's Word, telling what is revelation, what is inspiration and what is not, without a rebuke" (E. G. White, *Seventh-day Adventist Bible Commentary,* 7:919-920). Contrary to the claims of liberal (source) critics, the Spirit's superintendence of the Bible writers is the grounds for comparing Scripture with Scripture to arrive at a biblical doctrine.[17]

**3. The Use of Imperfect Human Language:** Seventh-day Adventist scholars acknowledge that God did not dictate each word of Scripture to the Bible writers. Instead of a mechanical (dictation) mode of inspiration, the Holy Spirit condescended to the level of the Bible writers, guiding them even as they employed their own imperfect human language to communicate divine truth.[18]

***Issue #3:*** *Does the use of imperfect human language to communicate divine truth mean that the words the Bible writers employed are not important? Does the fact that "infinite ideas cannot be perfectly embodied in finite vehicles of thought"*[19] *imply that the truthfulness of Scripture's message is thereby compromised?*

Bible-believing Adventists maintain: "The very fact that God selects fallen beings to convey the revelation of Himself to other fallen beings, in human language, with all its foibles and imperfections, is by itself an unfathomable act of condescension. While we do recognize divine accommodation in the Scriptures, we must guard against pressing the concept of accommodation so far as to deny or distort the true meaning of Scripture."[20]

**4. Cultural Elements in Scripture:** As a perfect Communicator to human beings, God has spoken in the language of His listeners, using the cultural expressions, idioms, thought forms, etc. of the listening audience living at a particular time in history. Thus Scripture, being *historically constituted*, contains certain cultural elements, some of which are relative to the Bible times.[21]

***Issue #4:*** *Does God's communication to people in a particular historico-cultural setting imply that Scripture is culturally conditioned—that is, does the* *message of Scripture suffer from the limitations, prejudice, or ignorance of the Bible writers?*[22] *If so, by what criteria can interpreters isolate the culturally conditioned content from its trans-cultural message?*

Adventists reject liberalism's "cultural conditioning" argument which relativizes and arbitrarily picks and chooses from the message of the Scriptures. Instead, they insist: "Although it was given to those who lived in an ancient Near Eastern/Mediterranean context, the Bible transcends its cultural backgrounds to serve as God's word for all cultural, racial, and situational contexts in all ages" ("Methods of Bible Study" Report). They also recognize that "although the biblical instruction is relevant to all cultures and time, it was given to a particular culture and time. [Therefore,] Time and place must be taken into account in application." As a general principle, Bible-believing Adventists "assume the transcultural and transtemporal relevancy of biblical instruction unless Scripture itself gives criteria limiting this relevancy."[23]

**5. Diversity in Scripture:** It is generally recognized by Adventist scholars that each Bible writer had a particular theological purpose in mind in composing and presenting the relevant materials. Thus, there are diversities, different styles, and different emphases in Scripture.

***Issue #5:*** *In composing their respective accounts, did the Bible writers embellish, change, or distort the facts? That is, were the inspired writers sometimes untruthful in what they wrote (however minor or unimportant their alleged embellishment, changes, or distortions may have been)? Are things said by the different Bible writers in different ways at different times, and with different wordings and emphasis, necessarily inconsistent? Or should we view the different emphases as different aspects of the same truth, with a perfect harmony through all?*

Bible-believing Adventists affirm: "A superficial reading of the Scriptures will yield a superficial understanding of it. Read in such a way, the Bible may appear to be a jumble of stories, sermons, and history. Yet, those open to the illumination of the Spirit of God, those willing to search for the hidden truths with patience and much prayer, discover that the Bible evidences an underlying unity in what it teaches about the principles of salvation" (*Seventh-day Adventists Believe . . .*, 14; cf. *The Great Controversy*, vi[24]).

Contrary to the claims of our contemporary higher critics, Ellen White wrote: "As presented through different individuals, the truth is brought out in its varied aspects. One writer is more strongly impressed with one phase of the subject; he grasps those points that harmonize with his experience or with his power of perception and appreciation; another seizes upon a different phase; and each, under the guidance of the Holy Spirit, presents what is most forcibly impressed upon his own mind—*a different aspect of the truth in each, but a perfect harmony through all.* And the truths thus revealed unite to form a perfect whole, adapted to meet the wants of men in all the circumstances and experiences of life" (*The Great Controversy,* vi).

**6. Parallel Biblical Accounts:** Adventist Students of the Bible have always recognized that sometimes when Bible writers report even the same events, their accounts tend to vary in specific details and in some cases, some do not mention certain details (e.g., 2 Sam 24 and 1 Chron 21; 2 Kings 18-20 and 2 Chron 32; Mark 5:2 and Luke 8:27; Matt 21:33-44, Mark 12:1-11 and Luke 20:9-18, etc.).[25]

***Issue #6:*** *Should different parallel accounts be viewed as complementary or contradictory? Beyond a mere spiritual unity, are the parallel accounts actually consistent with the facts the writers reported?*

For Bible-believing Adventists, rather than looking for alleged contradictions in the parallel accounts (e.g., the different ways the Gospel writers presented their accounts), we must look for underlying harmony. They agree with Ellen White: "The Creator of all ideas may impress different minds with the same thought, but each may express it in a different way, *yet without contradiction.* The fact that this difference exists should not perplex or confuse us. It is seldom that two persons will view and express truth in the very same way. Each dwells on particular points which his constitution and education have fitted him to appreciate. The sunlight falling upon the different objects gives those objects a different hue" (*Selected Messages,* 1:22, emphasis supplied; cf. *The Great Controversy,* v, vi).[26]

**7. Mistakes, Inaccuracies, and Errors in Scripture:** Adventist scholars are agreed that there are transmission errors in Scripture—errors that apparently crept into the text during the process of copying the manuscripts (e.g., occasional discrepancies due to copyist glosses, slips, misspellings, etc.) and which can be ascertained and corrected by comparing the various available manuscripts.

***Issue #7:*** *Apart from copyist and translator errors, can we find* *factual errors in the Bible, such as errors in the historical and scientific details in the Bible?*

While acknowledging with Ellen White that "there might have been some mistake in the copyist or in the translators,"[27] Bible-believing Adventists reject liberalism's claim that there are factual mistakes(e.g., errors in history and science) which are traceable to the Bible writers themselves.[28] "It is clear that while the ancient manuscripts vary, the essential truths have been preserved. While it is quite possible that copyists and translators of the Bible made minor mistakes, evidence from Bible archeology reveals that many alleged errors were really misunderstandings of the part of scholars. Some of these problems arose because people were reading Biblical history and customs through Western eyes. We must admit that humans only know in part—their insight into divine operations remains fragmentary." Because perceived discrepancies in the Scriptures are often "products of our inaccurate perceptions rather than actual mistakes," Bible-believing Adventists are cautious in declaring the things they cannot understand as errors (*Seventh-day Adventists Believe*, 11).

**8. Biblical Infallibility:** The Seventh-day Adventist Fundamental Beliefs #1 states in part: "The Holy Scriptures are the *infallible revelation* of His will. They are the standard of character, the test of experience, the authoritative revealer of doctrines, and *the trustworthy record of God's acts in history*". Ellen G. White also repeatedly refers to the Bible as an "infallible" guide for faith and practice.[29]

***Issue #8:*** *Should Seventh-day Adventists continue to uphold and defend the assertions in their Fundamental Belief #1 and the writings of Ellen G. White that the Bible is infallible?*[30] *If so, what is the nature and extent of this infallibility? Is it limited only to issues of salvation but does not extend to non-salvific issues that the Bible touches upon (e.g., science, history, ethical lifestyle, etc.)? Specifically, should instantaneous creation out of nothing(" creatio ex nihilio") be excluded from the "matters of faith"? Should a literal 24-hour six-day creation be outside the matters of faith? Should a literal world-wide flood in Noah's day be separated from the matters of faith? etc. In short, can we extricate matters of faith from their accompanied facts of history, science, geography, etc.?*

Against the claims of higher critical scholars, Bible-believing Adventists affirm the full trustworthiness or reliability of Scripture in all that it touches and touches upon. In the words of the just released (2000) *Handbook of*

*Seventh-day Adventist Theology* (vol. 12 of the SDA Commentary series), "Scripture is true in everything it says": "The implications of the complete veracity of Scripture are clear. Not only do its authors tell the truth in what they say about God and salvation but also in regard to other matters. The historical narratives of the Bible are to be accepted as reliable and true. Among these authentic accounts of real events are the creation of the world and the first human beings in six days, the fall of Adam and Eve, the universal flood, the lives of the patriarchs, the history of Israel, the Gospel narratives, and the story of the Spirit-led origin and development of the apostolic church."[31]

**9. Thought Inspiration and Verbal Inspiration:** How should Adventists describe their view of inspiration without being misunderstood? The expressions "thought inspiration" and "verbal inspiration" are now so loaded that they mean different things to different people. Because liberal scholars have hijacked these terms and injected them with new meanings, a brief discussion is in order.

In the revised edition of the *Seventh-day Adventist Encyclopedia* (1976), the entry under the "Inspiration of Scripture" states that "SDA's do not believe in verbal inspiration according to the usual meaning of the term, but in what may properly be called thought inspiration."[32] The usual meaning of "verbal inspiration" referred to is "verbal dictation" or the mechanical view of inspiration, which sees the Bible writers as some passive junior secretaries who merely transcribed what the Holy Spirit dictated to them.[33]

Also, Adventists have historically employed the phrase "thought inspiration" to emphasize that the Spirit did not dictate the words of the Bible to its human writers. Instead, when God inspired the Bible writers, their personalities were not effaced nor their style set aside. They still retained their individual human traits, even their forms and styles of literary expression, as the Holy Spirit infallibly guided them in their communication of divine truth using their own vocabularies. Though the Bible writers were "God's penmen, not His pen" (*Selected Messages,* 1:21), their messages can be trusted "not as the word of men but as what it really is, the word of God" (1 Thess 2:13).[34]

However, in recent times some within our ranks have employed the phrase "thought inspiration" to mean that because God did not dictate the messages that are recorded in Scripture, therefore in revelation God did not impart any messages to the Bible writers. (This is neo-orthodoxy or

Barthianism disguised as thought inspiration!)[35]

Observe that neo-orthodox theologians (or Barthians, following the Swiss theologian Karl Barth) are liberal scholars who hold that the Bible is *not* the word of God but can *become* the word of God at the moment the Bible speaks to a person in a significant personal encounter. In a subtle denial of the Bible's inspiration, these theologians suggest that until the Bible becomes the Word of God, it is merely the word of humans, or at best a human document that *contains* the Word of God. In the words of a former assistant professor of New Testament at Andrews University, we cannot equate the Bible with the Word of God. For, "the words of the book [Bible] are the words of the prophets which only tangentially reflect the Word of God. Nothing on earth is the ultimate expression of God. To make the Bible such is bibliolatry, just another form of idolatry." For him, "the Bible as a book can and must be studied as any other book."[36]

In effect, liberal scholars have hijacked the term thought inspiration to propagate their neo-orthodox view. At the same time that some within our ranks are re-interpreting thought inspiration along Barthian lines, some are also employing the term verbal inspiration to suggest that the Bible is not always trustworthy in its historical or scientific assertions. The tendency within such quarters of Adventist scholarship is to utilize the expression verbal inspiration to caricature the views of Bible-believing Adventists who are still upholding the church's position on the full inspiration and trustworthiness of Scripture.

For example, among those who have understood verbal inspiration in the popular sense of the word, some have proceeded to argue (erroneously) that since God did not dictate Scriptures to the Bible writers, the human words of the inspired writers cannot always convey God's message in a trustworthy manner (cf. issues #3, 7, and 8 above). To such, the Bible is not fully trustworthy in the realms of science and history; it merely contains "a great deal of accuracy."[37]

Because of the non-uniform and confusing manner in which contemporary Adventists use the terms "thought inspiration" and "verbal inspiration," it is important to demand from those who use these expressions a clear explanation of what they mean. In *Receiving the Word*, I have employed the clumsy phrase "verbal propositional inspiration." On one hand, when inspiration is described as "propositional," it suggests (contrary to neo-orthodox views) that God actually communicated information to the recipients of divine revelation. On the other hand, when I describe inspiration as "verbal," I argue that despite the inadequacies of human language, because of the Spirit's guidance, the thoughts, ideas, and words of the Bible writers accurately convey God's message revealed to them.[38]

***Issue #9:*** *Given the fact that the terms "thought inspiration," and "verbal inspiration" are quite elastic, is the above definition of "verbal propositional inspiration" an adequate description of the SDA position, or should we employ a different expression to avoid being misunderstood as subscribing to either a neo-orthodox view of inspiration or a mechanical (dictation) view of inspiration?*

Adventists would need to come up with an adequate expression to capture their high view of inspiration and trustworthiness of Scripture.[39] Such an expression must take into consideration the facts that in the inspiration of the Scriptures (1) "God inspired men—not words"; (2) "the Bible, then, is divine truth expressed in human language"; (3) "the Bible is the written Word of God"; (4) "the Bible does not teach partial inspiration or degrees of inspiration"; (5) the guidance of the Holy Spirit "guarantees the Bible's trustworthiness"; and (6) "many alleged errors" or "perceived discrepancies" are "really misunderstandings on the part of scholars" or are often the "products of our inaccurate perceptions rather than actual mistakes" (*Seventh-day Adventists Believe . . .*, 8, 10, 11).

**10. Hermeneutical Implications of *Sola Scriptura*:** As a Protestant denomination, Seventh-day Adventists historically have embraced the idea that "the Bible and the Bible only" is our rule of faith and practice. This *sola scriptura* principle raises a number of crucial questions: For example:

***Issue #10a: Biblical Assertions or Phenomena.*** *In developing a doctrine of Scripture, should the so-called phenomena (apparent mistakes and discrepancies) of Scripture hold priority over clear, explicit, biblical assertions? (This issue concerns the inductive and deductive approaches.)*[40]

***Issue #10b: The Use of Extra-Biblical Data.*** *Should an insistence on sola scriptura require interpreters to interpret Scripture solely on the basis of the Bible, and not by any extra-biblical data—whether ancient (e.g., data from ancient Near-Eastern cultures, Jewish, Greco-Roman, and traditions of the church Fathers), or modern (archaeology, science, psychology, public opinion, etc.)? In other words, should Scripture be its own interpreter?*[41]

***Issue #10c: The Place of Ellen G. White.*** *Given the fact that the Bible itself teaches us to listen to God's true prophets, and given the fact that Seventh-day Adventists recognize Ellen G. White as a recipient of the true gift* *of prophecy, what should be the relationship between her writings and the Bible? Should her inspired counsels and insights on biblical truth be given more weight than the theological/exegetical insights of any uninspired authority or expert, whether church leader or scholar?*[42]

***Issue #10d: New Light from the Spirit.*** *Can the Holy Spirit lead believers today into new truths or new light that contradict truths already established in His inspired Word?*[43]

***Issue #10e: The Question of Science and History.*** *Which authority should be accorded the highest authority when the interpretations and conclusions of modern science and secular history conflict with that of Scripture?*[44]

The above questions constitute the hermeneutical implications of our historic stance on the Protestant affirmation of the Bible and the Bible only (*sola scriptura*). In addressing these questions, Bible-believing Adventists are guided by Fundamental Belief #1, which reads in part: "The Holy Scriptures are the infallible revelation of His will. They are *the standard of character, the test of experience, the authoritative revealer of doctrines,* and the trustworthy record of God's acts in history."

Indeed, "the Word of God is the great detector of error; to it we believe everything must be brought. The Bible must be our standard for every doctrine and practice. We must study it reverentially. We are to receive no one's opinion without comparing it with the Scriptures. Here is divine authority which is supreme in matters of faith. It is the Word of the living God that is to decide all controversies" (*The Ellen G. White 1888 Materials,* 44, 45).

Bible-believing Adventists respond to the above questions in the following words of Ellen G. White: "God will have a people upon the earth to maintain the Bible, and the Bible only, as the standard of all doctrines and the basis of all reforms. The *opinions of learned men, the deductions of science, the creeds or decisions of ecclesiastical councils,* as numerous and discordant as are the churches which they represent, *the voice of the majority—not one nor all of these* should be regarded as evidence for or against any point of religious faith. *Before accepting any doctrine or precept, we should demand a plain 'Thus said the Lord' in its support*" (*The Great Controversy,* 595, emphasis mine).

### Conclusion

In the heated debate over the legitimacy of employing aspects of contemporary higher criticism to interpret the Bible, much of the discussion have tended to be more noteworthy for their breadth than for their depth. Very often false issues have been raised and straw man arguments have been presented to mask what is really at stake in the battle over the Bible. The purpose of this chapter was to clear away the smokescreen so as to identify the real issues in the debate.

While other important questions can also be raised, in my opinion, the issues outlined in this chapter constitute the key hermeneutical questions in the current Seventh-day Adventist conflict over the Bible. If Adventist biblical scholars are "to reach consensus on principles of interpretation,"[45] they would have to candidly answer the following questions: Is the Bible fully inspired, internally consistent, and the sole-governing authority for faith and lifestyle? Does inspired Scripture present a fully trustworthy/reliable account in all of its assertions, or does it merely contain "a great deal of accuracy" in its historical and scientific details? These questions define the nature of the bug in Adventist hermeneutic.

The responses we give to the specific questions identified in this chapter will determine whether or not we subscribe to the historical-critical method. More importantly our candid responses will ultimately determine what our attitudes toward God's Word will be: trust or doubt, confidence or skepticism, submission or criticism. The implications and consequences of our responses have been captured by Ellen G. White:

> Man can be exalted only by laying hold of the merits of a crucified and risen Savior. The finest intellect, the most exalted position, will not secure heaven. Satan had the highest education that could be obtained. This education he received under the greatest of all teachers. When men talk of higher criticism, when they pass their judgment upon the word of God, call their attention to the fact that they have forgotten who was the first and wisest critic. He has had thousands of years of practical experience. He it is who teaches the so-called higher critics of the world today. *God will punish all those who, as higher critics, exalt themselves, and criticize God's Holy word* (*Review and Herald,* March 16, 1897).

As we grapple with the above hermeneutical issues, may we be led to humbly *receive the Word.* For, by receiving the Word of the Lord, we are also receiving the Lord of the Word. This is the ultimate corrective to the hermeneutical bug in contemporary Adventist approaches to the Bible.

---

**Endnotes**

[1]In addition to several articles, four significant books emerged during the past ten years. In the early 1990's the two major works were Alden Thompson, *Inspiration: Hard Questions, Honest Answers* (Hagerstown, MD: Review and Herald, 1991), and a response by Frank Holbrook and Leo van Dolson, eds., *Issues in Revelation and Inspiration*, Adventist Theological Society Occasional Papers vol. 1 (Berrien Springs, MI: Adventist Theological Society, 1992). In the later half of the 1990's the two conflicting views were articulated in the books by Samuel Koranteng-Pipim, *Receiving the Word: How New Approaches to the Bible Impact Our Biblical Faith and Lifestyle* (Berrien Springs, Mich.: Berean Books, 1996) and George R. Knight, *Reading Ellen White: How to Understand and Apply Her Writings* (Hagerstown, Md.: Review and Herald, 1997). For more on this, refer to our discussion in chapter 27 of this present volume.

[2]Besides the superficial nature of the discussions, the focus on *Inspiration* and *Receiving the Word* at the expense of the church's longstanding position is one of the major flaws in some recent articles. See, for example, Timothy E. Crosby, "The Bible: Inspiration and Authority," *Ministry* (May 1998): 18-20; Robert M. Johnston, "The Case for a Balanced Hermeneutic," *Ministry* (March 1999): 10-12.

[3]This point is particularly pertinent in light of a misleading editorial comment in the April 1999 issue of *Ministry*, a journal published for Seventh-day Adventist ministers. Instead of pointing to the church's official position, the editors recommend articles in their March 1999 issue as "more representative of our Church's position on biblical hermeneutics." An examination of their recommended articles, reveals, however, that at least one of them explicitly advocates the modified use of the historical-critical method, an approach that is rejected by the church. See editorial comment to P. Gerard Damsteegt's article, "Scripture Faces Current Issues," *Ministry* (April 1999): 23.

[4]Fundamental Belief #1 states: "The Holy Scriptures, Old and New Testaments, are the written Word of God, given by divine inspiration through holy men of God who spoke and wrote as they were moved by the Holy Spirit. In this Word, God has committed to man the knowledge necessary for salvation. The Holy Scriptures are the infallible revelation of His will. They are the standard of character, the test of experience, the authoritative revealer of doctrines, and the trustworthy record of God's acts in history."

[5]At the 1986 Annual Council meeting in Rio de Janeiro, Brazil, church leaders representing all the world fields of the Seventh-day Adventist church approved the report of the General Conference's "Methods of Bible Study Committee as representative of the church's hermeneutical position. This document was published in the *Adventist Review*, January 22, 1977, pages 18-20, and reproduced as Appendix C in my *Receiving the Word*, 355-362. Generally, loyal Adventists embrace the 1986 "Methods of Bible Study" document as reflective of the principles of interpretation that have been historically accepted by Adventists. For a discussion of how Adventist scholars have reacted to the "Methods of Bible Study" document, see my *Receiving the Word*, 75-99.

[6]The principal author of the first quarter 1999 Adult Sabbath School Lessons was

Leo R. van Dolson; his companion book to the quarterly is titled, *Show and Tell: How God Reveals Truth to Us* (Nampa, ID: Pacific Press, 1998). See also the articles by Peter M. van Bemmelen, "Revelation and Inspiration" and Richard M. Davidson, "Biblical Interpretation,"in Raoul Dederen, ed., *Handbook of Seventh-day Adventist Theology*, vol. 12 of commentary series (Hagerstown, Md.: Review and Herald, 2000), 22-57 and 58-104, respectively. Observe that "although each article [in the *Handbook*] is signed, it was agreed from the start that all contributions would be subject to review and suggestions from the Biblical Research Institute Committee (BRICOM), a group of 40 persons predominantly scholars but including a few administrators. With its international composition BRICOM was called to function as an efficient sounding board. . . . This book is not simply a collection of parts written separately by individual contributors. In fact, no part of it is the work of a single author. As the text proceeded through editing and consultation, all parts of the book and the book as a whole profited from this cooperative approach. The whole working team, i.e., authors and BRICOM members—many of whom were authors—could claim to be genuinely international . . . They wrote this work for a worldwide readership" (see Raoul Dederen's "Preface" in *Handbook*, x-xi).

[7]For more on this, see my *Receiving the Word*, especially chps. 4-6, 75-206. In response to this challenge, a June 1998 "International Bible Conference" was convened in Jerusalem to urge Adventist scholars and leaders around the world to reaffirm their commitment to the authority of Scripture. The Jerusalem Bible Conference was sponsored by the Biblical Research Institute of the General Conference of SDAs, the Adventist Theological Society, the Institute of Archaeology at Andrews University Theological Seminary, and other SDA entities. The opening address was given by the President of the General Conference of SDAs.

[8]Because of the "Methods of Bible Study" document's categorical rejection of even a moderate use of the historical-critical method, some advocates of the method have also fought against it using the argument that it was an "approved," and not a "voted," document. In response, it should be noted that the intent of the world church regarding the the 1986 document's place in Adventist practice is not only indicated by its publication in *Adventist Review* (1987), but also in the reference to it in the 1988 book *Seventh-day Adventists Believe*, where it is cited among works furnishing "the general Seventh-day Adventist understanding of biblical interpretation" (see page 15, note 5). The introductory comment about this book is equally applicable to the "Methods of Bible Study" document: "While this volume is not an officially voted statement—only a General Conference in world session could provide that—it may be viewed as representative of 'the truth . . . in Jesus' (Eph. 4:21) that Seventh-day Adventists around the globe cherish and proclaim" (*Seventh-day Adventists Believe*, iv).

[9]Just as every Christian denomination respects the interpretative insights of leading figures in their respective traditions, the Seventh-day Adventist church takes seriously the works of Ellen G. White. In fact, given their belief that Ellen G. White received the true prophetic gift, Adventists value her theological insights more highly than any uninspired authority or expert: "As the Lord's messenger, her writings are a continuing and authoritative source of truth which provide for the church comfort, guidance, instruction, and correction. They also make clear that the Bible is the standard by which all teaching and experience must be tested" (SDA Fundamental Belief # 17). Thus, any credible discussion of Adventist hermeneutic must not fail to pay heed to Ellen White's written statements.

[10]See, for example, Charles Scriven's *Embracing the Spirit: An Open Letter to the Leaders of Adventism* (Columbia Union College, Takoma Park, MD, 1997). For a response, see my *In the Spirit of Truth: A Review of An Open Letter Titled "Embracing the Spirit"* (Berrien Springs, MI: Berean Books, 1997).

[11]For more on this, see *Receiving the Word,* 79-92, 167-175.

[12]Ellen G. White also affirmed the full trustworthiness of the Bible's historical accounts. The Holy Spirit "guided the pens of the sacred historians" in such a manner that "the Bible is the most instructive and comprehensive history that has ever been given to the world. . . . Here we have a truthful history of the human race, one that is unmarred by human prejudice or human pride" (*Gospel Workers,* 286; *Fundamentals of Christian Education,* 84-85; cf. *Education,* 173). There are no distortions in the biographies and history of God's favored people for, in the words of Ellen White, "this history the unerring pen of inspiration must trace with exact fidelity" (*Testimonies for the Church,* 4:370). Whereas uninspired historians are unable to record history without bias, the inspired writers "did not testify to falsehoods to prevent the pages of sacred history being clouded by the record of human frailties and faults. The scribes of God wrote as they were dictated by the Holy Spirit, having no control of the work themselves. They penned the literal truth, and stern, forbidding facts are revealed for reasons that our finite minds cannot fully comprehend" (ibid., 9).

[13]Besides the examples cited in chapter 22 of *Must We Be Silent?,* one may also refer to *Receiving the Word,* 105-111, 144-148, 156-163, 169-175, 181-194.

[14]A detailed discussion of the Seventh-day Adventist pioneers' attitude toward higher criticism can be found in Peter van Bemmelen's paper, "Seventh-day Adventists and Higher Criticism in the Nineteenth Century," Andrews University, 1977, available at the Ellen G. White Research Center of the James White Library, Andrews University, in Document File 391-h.; cf. idem, "The Mystery of Inspiration: An Historical Study About the Development of the Doctrine of Inspiration in the Seventh-day Adventist Church, With Special Emphasis on the Decade 1884-1893," unpublished manuscript (1971), available at the James White Library, Andrews University.

[15]Mrs. White wrote: "The union of the divine and the human, manifest in Christ, exists also in the Bible. . . . And this fact, so far from being an argument against the Bible, should strengthen faith in it as the word of God. Those who pronounce upon the inspiration of the Scriptures, accepting some portions as divine while they reject other parts as human, overlook the fact that Christ, the divine, partook of our human nature, that He might reach humanity. In the work of God for man's redemption, divinity and humanity are combined" (*Testimonies for the Church,* 5:747; cf. *The Great Controversy,* vi).

[16]See my *Receiving the Word,* 48-49.

[17]Observe the following distinction between liberalism's literary (source) criticism and Adventism's literary analysis. Higher criticism's *literary (source) criticism* is the attempt "to hypothetically reconstruct and understand the process of literary development leading to the present form of the text, based on the assumption that Scriptures are the product of the life setting of the community that produced them (often in opposition to specific scriptural statements regarding the origin and nature of the sources." But in the Adventist approach, *literary analysis* is simply the "examination of the literary characteristics of the biblical materials in their canonical form, accepting as a unity those parts of Scriptures that are presented as such, and accepting at face value the specific scriptural statements regarding the

origins and nature of the biblical materials" (Richard M. Davidson, "Biblical Interpretation," in *Handbook of Seventh-day Adventist Theology,* 95).

[18]Rather than speaking in grand superhuman language, "The Lord speaks to human beings in imperfect speech, in order that the degenerate senses, the dull, earthly perception, of earthly beings may comprehend His words. Thus is shown God's condescension. He meets fallen human beings where they are. . . . Instead of the expressions of the Bible being exaggerated, as many people suppose, the strong expressions break down before the magnificence of the thought, though the penmen selected the most expressive language" (*Selected Messages,* 1:22). Again, "The Bible is not given to us in grand superhuman language. Jesus, in order to reach man where he is, took humanity. The Bible must be given in the language of men. Everything that is human is imperfect. Different meanings are expressed by the same word; there is not one word for each distinct idea" (ibid., 1:20). Thus, in their attempt to communicate infinite ideas in finite human language, the inspired writers sometimes employed figures of speech, like parables, hyperbole, simile, metaphor, and symbolism. But even this figurative language conveys clear, literal truth.

[19]White, *Selected Messages,* 1:22.

[20]Peter van Bemmelen, "Revelation and Inspiration," in *Handbook of Seventh-day Adventist Theology,* 33.

[21]For more on this, see Angel Manuel Rodriguez, "Culture's Role in Writing Scripture," *Adventist Review,* October 12, 2000, 30.

[22]Robert M. Johnston, for example, seems to hold this view when he writes that because God's messages were delivered through human instrumentalities, thus bearing the impress of human expression in Scripture, "It is necessary to sort out what is human expression and divine message, even though all are inspired." For him Scriptures are reliable and trustworthy only in the sense that they guide the hearer or reader "in the direction God wants him or her to go." However, he explains, the "attendant details with which the message is infleshed, but which are not an essential part of it, may have their origin in the culture or personality of the human messenger" (Johnston, "The Case for a Balanced Hermeneutic," *Ministry* (March 1999):11).

[23]Richard M. Davidson, "Biblical Interpretation," in *Handbook of Seventh-day Adventist Theology,* 85, 86.

[24]Writes Ellen White: "Written in different ages, by men who differed widely in rank and occupation, and in mental and spiritual endowments, the books of the Bible present a wide contrast in style, as well as a diversity in the nature of the subjects unfolded. Different forms of expression are employed by different writers; often *the same truth* is more strikingly presented by one than by another. And as several writers present a subject under varied aspects and relations, *there may appear, to the superficial, careless, or prejudiced reader, to be discrepancy or contradiction, where the thoughtful, reverent student, with clearer insight, discerns the underlying harmony*" (*The Great Controversy,* vi. emphasis mine).

[25]Ellen White wrote: "In our Bible, we might ask, Why need Matthew, Mark, Luke, and John in the Gospels, why need the Acts of the Apostles, and the variety of writers in the Epistles, go over the same thing? The Lord gave His word in just the way He wanted it to come. He gave it through different writers, each having his own individuality, though going over the same history. Their testimonies are brought together in one Book, and are like the testimonies in a social meeting [testimony service]. They do not represent things in just the same style. Each has an experience of his own, and this diversity

broadens and deepens the knowledge that is brought out to meet the necessities of varied minds. The thoughts expressed have not a set uniformity, as if cast in an iron mold, making the very hearing monotonous. In such uniformity there would be a loss of grace" (*Selected Messages,* 1:21-22).

[26]For a detailed discussion of how to deal with "Seeming Discrepancies in Parallel Biblical Accounts," see Richard M. Davidson, "Biblical Interpretation," in *Handbook of Seventh-day Adventist Theology,* 72-74; cf. section O of "Methods of Bible Study."

[27]Ellen G. White's recognition of copyist and translator errors has often been misquoted to mean the existence of factual errors (e.g., errors in history, science, geography, etc.) traceable to the Bible writers themselves. This is her statement: "Some look to us gravely and say, 'Don't you think there might have been some mistake *in the copyist or in the translators?'* This is all probable, and the mind that is so narrow that it will hesitate and stumble over this possibility or probability would be just as ready to stumble over the mysteries of the Inspired Word, because their feeble minds cannot see through the purposes of God. Yes, they would just as easily stumble over plain facts that the common mind will accept, and discern the Divine, and to which God's utterance is plain and beautiful, full of marrow and fatness. *All the mistakes will not cause trouble to one soul, or cause any feet to stumble,* that would not manufacture difficulties from the plainest revealed truth" (*Selected Messages,* 1:16, emphasis supplied).

[28]For examples of some of the alleged discrepancies or mistakes in Scripture, and a response to some of them, see *Receiving the Word,* 241-247, 279-302.

[29]Regarding scriptural infallibility, Ellen White states that the Holy Scriptures "are to be accepted as an authoritative, infallible revelation of His [God's] will" (*The Great Controversy,* vii; cf. 68, 102); they are "the only infallible authority in religion" (ibid., 238; see also 89, 177), and "the only sufficient, infallible rule" (ibid., 173). For Ellen White, Scripture shares in the infallibility of God. "God and heaven alone are infallible" (*Selected Messages,* 1:37; cf. *Testimonies to Ministers,* 30, 105). "Man is fallible, but God's Word is infallible" (*Selected Messages,* 1:416). She left no doubt that the Bible is "an unerring counselor and infallible guide" and the "perfect guide under all circumstances of life" (*Fundamentals of Christian Education,* 100); "an unerring guide," "the one unerring guide," "the unerring standard," "an unerring light," "that unerring test," and "the unerring counsel of God" (*Acts of the Apostles,* 506; *Testimonies,* 5:389; *Ministry of Healing,* 462; *Testimonies,* 5:247, 192; *Testimonies,* 4:441).

[30]The words "infallible/infallibility" derive from the Latin *infallibilitas,* suggesting the quality of neither deceiving nor misleading. Thus, to declare Scripture as infallible means "to assert the Bible's divine origin, truthfulness, and trustworthiness, never denying, disregarding, or arbitrarily relativizing anything that the Bible writers teach" (*Receiving the Word,* 366).

[31]Peter van Bemmelen, "Revelation and Inspiration," in *Handbook of Seventh-day Adventist Theology,* 43.

[32]"Inspiration of Scripture," in Don F. Neufeld, ed., *Seventh-day Adventist Encyclopedia,* vol. 10 of commentary series, revised edition (Hagerstown, Md.: Review and Herald, 1976), 648.

[33]While it appears that Ellen G. White herself never used the expression "verbal inspiration" in her writings, her son W. C. White employed that phrase in its popular usage as a reference to the mistaken theory of mechanical (dictation) inspiration, a theory that

would also not allow an inspired writer to make revisions in his/her original manuscripts. W. C. White argues accurately that none of the leading Seventh-day Adventist pioneers, including Ellen G. White, ever subscribed to verbal inspiration (understood here to mean mechanical [dictation] inspiration). Notice how W. C. White and Arthur L. White explained the meaning of verbal inspiration and why the pioneers rightly rejected such a view (understood to mean mechanical dictation inspiration):

"Mother has never laid claim to verbal inspiration, and I do not find that my father, or Elder Bates, Andrews, Smith, or Waggoner, put forth this claim. *If there were verbal inspiration in writing her manuscripts, why should there be on her part the work of addition or adaptation?* It is a fact that Mother often takes one of her manuscripts, and goes over it thoughtfully, *making additions that develop the thought still further*" (W. C. White Letter, July 24, 1911; cf. 3 *Selected Messages*, 437; 454; emphasis mine). Writing to S. N. Haskell in 1911, W. C. White again pointed out that: "There is danger of our injuring Mother's work by claiming for it more than she claims for it, more than Father ever claimed for it, more than Elders Andrews, [J. H.] Waggoner, or Smith ever claimed for it. I cannot see consistency in our putting forth a claim of verbal inspiration when Mother does not make any such claim" (W. C. White to S. N. Haskell, October 31, 1912).

Arthur L. White concurs: "To make any changes at all in the text of a book written under the inspiration of the Spirit of God, especially a book as widely circulated and studiously read as *The Great Controversy*, was recognized by Ellen White and the staff at Elmshaven as something that would raise questions in the minds of Seventh-day Adventists. There were many who, jealous for Ellen White and the Spirit of Prophecy, held, for all practical purposes, to a theory of verbal inspiration in the work of God's prophets. An action disavowing this stance was taken by the General Conference in session in 1883. But by 1911 this was either unknown or forgotten by Adventists generally" (*Ellen G. White Volume 6: The Later Elmshaven Years, 1905-1915*, 322; cf. 337). "Many of the questions had their foundation in faulty concepts of inspiration. The prophet was thought of as a mechanical agent, speaking or writing each word dictated by the Holy Spirit. This 'verbal inspiration' concept at times led to the expectation of more from Ellen White than was justified—more than was demanded of the prophets and apostles of old" (ibid., 91; cf. 365-366).

It is clear from the above statements that the historic Adventist position has been to reject verbal inspiration, *understood to mean a mechanical dictation inspiration,* a mistaken theory that would also prevent an inspired writer from revising or expanding upon his/her earlier manuscripts.

[34]Ellen White continues: "It is not the words of the Bible that are inspired, but the men that were inspired. Inspiration acts not on the man's words or his expressions but on the man himself, who, under the influence of the Holy Ghost, is imbued with thoughts. But the words receive the impress of the individual mind. The divine mind diffused. The divine mind and will is combined with the human mid and will; thus the utterances of the man are the word of God" (*Selected Messages,* 1:21).

[35]Neo-orthodoxy, it must be remembered, "perceives revelation as a subjective personal divine-human encounter rather than as an objective communication of propositional truth. The Bible is, therefore, reduced to a mere human testimony of that encounter." See Alberto R. Timm, "A History of Seventh-day Adventist Views on Biblical and Prophetic Inspiration (1844-2000)," *Journal of the Adventist Theological Society* 10/1-2 (1999): 514. In

a well-documented study, Timm, a scholar in Adventist studies, noted that the Association of Adventist Forums and its *Spectrum* magazine became the main forum for those who assumed a "revisionist-critical stand" on the church's understanding of the inspiration of Bible writers and Ellen White. "Several articles advocating encounter revelation and the use of the historical-critical method came out in *Spectrum,* setting the agenda for many discussions on inspiration during the period under consideration (1970-1994)" (ibid.). He backed this by citing all the articles published in this magazine that had historical-critical assumptions. An extended bibliography of such historical-critical works is found in footnotes that almost fill pages 517-519, notes 204-217.

[36]Harold Weiss, "Revelation and the Bible: Beyond Verbal Inspiration," *Spectrum* 7/3 (1975):53, 49-50. For a response to the neo-orthodox or "encounter" view of the Bible, see Raoul Dederen, "Revelation, Inspiration and Hermeneutics," in Gordon M. Hyde, ed., *A Symposium on Biblical Hermeneutics* ([Washington, DC]: Biblical Research Committee of the General Conference of Seventh-day Adventists, 1974), 1-15.

[37]See, for example, the following works by George R. Knight: *Reading Ellen White: How to Understand and Apply Her Writings* (Hagerstown, Md: Review and Herald, 1997), 105-118; "The Case of the Overlooked Postscript: A Footnote on Inspiration," *Ministry* (August 1997):9-11; *Anticipating the Advent: A Brief History of Seventh-day Adventists* (Boise, Id: Pacific Press, 1993), 106-107. While Knight seems to define verbal inspiration as mechanical dictation (a view that he correctly rejects), he suggests that inspiration does not guarantee a fully trustworthy biblical account in all of Scripture's historical and scientific details (a subtle error we challenge in *Receiving the Word*). In his opinion, the Bible is only trustworthy "as guide to salvation," not fully trustworthy in the realms of history and science. When he writes that the Bible contains "a great deal of accuracy" in its historical and scientific detail, he is suggesting that there are "factual errors" in the inspired Book (Knight, *Reading Ellen White,* 116, 111, 110; idem, *Anticipating the Advent,* 106-107).

[38]See *Receiving the Word,* 368. Apparently misunderstanding my phrase "verbal (propositional) inspiration," one reviewer of my *Receiving the Word* has claimed that I believe in mechanical (dictation) inspiration (see, George Knight's review in *Ministry* [December 1997]:30; cf. his "The Case of the Overlooked Postscript," *Ministry,* August 1997, 9-11). It should, however, be pointed out that in the two places I employed the expression "verbal (propositional) inspiration," I was always careful to add that this expression should not be confused with mechanical (dictation) inspiration, a mistaken theory which claims that the Holy Spirit dictated each single word of Scripture (see *Receiving the Word*, 51, 265), and a view in which the Bible writers are perceived as passive junior secretaries who merely transcribed what the Holy Spirit dictated to them (ibid., 366-367). Because I am not fully aware of the theological dynamics in the non-English speaking regions of the Adventist world, I have not utilized the clumsy phrase "verbal (propositional) inspiration" in translations of *Receiving the Word* into other languages.

[39]Roger Coon, for instance, has suggested the expression "plenary (thought) inspiration," to distance himself from both verbal inspiration (i.e., mechanical dictation) and encounter inspiration (i.e., neoorthodoxy or Barthianism). See Roger W. Coon, "Inspiration/Revelation: What It Is and How It Works—Part I," *Journal of Adventist Education* 44 (October-November 1981): 24-30. He, however, allows for "inconsequential errors of minor, insignificant detail" in Scripture. Among these are Matthew's alleged error in quoting Jeremiah instead of Zechariah (Matt 27:9, 10; cf. Zech 11:12, 13;

Jer 19:1-13), and the different wordings of the inscription on the cross of Christ. See Roger W. Coon, "Inspiration/Revelation: What It Is and How It Works—Part II," *Journal of Adventist Education* 44 (December 1981-January 1982): 18-19, 24-26. For my own response to these alleged "inconsequential errors of minor, insignificant detail," see *Receiving the Word,* 295-296, 298-300.

[40]Those who desire to speak knowledgeably about this issue will benefit greatly from the excellent discussion in Peter M. van Bemmelen's *Issues in Biblical Inspiration: Sanday and Warfield* (Berrien Springs, Mich.: Andrews University Press, 1988), 313-327. See also Paul Feinberg, "The Meaning of Inerrancy," in *Inerrancy,* ed. Norman Geisler (Grand Rapids, MI: Zondervan, 1980), 267-304.

[41]Ellen White repeatedly emphasized, "Make the Bible its own expositor, bringing together all that is said concerning a given subject at different times and under varied circumstances" (*Child Guidance,* 511). "I saw that the Word of God, as a whole, is a perfect chain, one portion linking into and explaining another" (*Early Writings,* 221). We must submit to "the Bible as the word of God, the only sufficient, infallible rule," which "must be its own interpreter" (*The Great Controversy,* 173). "Scripture interprets scripture, one passage being the key to other passages" (*Evangelism,* 581). "The Bible is its own expositor. Scripture is to be compared with scripture" (*Education,* 190).

[42]While upholding *sola scriptura* and thus referring to her works as the lesser light, Ellen White herself described her two-fold function in the church as follows: "God has, in that Word [the Bible], promised to give visions in the *'last days';* not for a new rule of faith, but for the comfort of His people, *and to correct those who err from the Bible truth*" (*Early Writings,* 78; emphasis mine). The light God gave her, she explains, "has been given to *correct specious error and to specify what is truth*" (*Selected Messages,* 3:32; emphasis mine). Notice that the writings of Ellen White are not to establish a new rule of faith apart from the Bible. Rather, they have been given the church to "comfort" God's people (when they are in the right path), to "correct" them (when they err from the truth) and to "specify" what is truth (when they are not sure). With so many confusing, conflicting voices involved in biblical interpretation, can anyone doubt the importance and urgency of the Spirit of Prophecy in the hermeneutical enterprise?

[43]For Ellen White, the answer is very simple: "The Spirit was not given—nor can it ever be bestowed—to supersede the Bible; for the Scriptures explicitly state that the word of God is the standard by which all teaching and experience must be tested" (*The Great Controversy,* vii). Again, "The old truths are essential; new truth is not independent of the old, but an unfolding of it. It is only as the old truths are understood that we can comprehend the new" (*Christ's Object Lessons,* 127-128). Ellen White discredits the claims of the revisionist proponents of "present truth" or "progressive revelation." Anticipating the modern reinterpretations and applications of Scripture which contradict Scripture, she wrote: "When the power of God testifies as to what is truth, that truth is to stand forever as the truth. No after suppositions contrary to the light God has given are to be entertained. Men will arise with interpretations of Scripture which are to them truth, but which are not truth. The truth for this time God has given us as a foundation for our faith. One will arise, and still another, with new light, which contradicts the light that God has given under the demonstration of His Holy Spirit. . . . We are not to receive the words of those who come with a message that contradicts the special points of our faith" (*Selected Messages,* 1:161).

[44]Ellen G. White affirmed the full trustworthiness of the Bible's historical and scientific accounts. First, the Holy Spirit "guided the pens of the sacred historians" in such a manner that "the Bible is the most instructive and comprehensive history that has ever been given to the world. . . . Here we have a truthful history of the human race, one that is unmarred by human prejudice or human pride" (*Gospel Workers,* 286; *Fundamentals of Christian Education,* 84-85; cf. *Education,* 173). There are no distortions in the biographies and history of God's favored people for, in the words of Ellen White, "this history the unerring pen of inspiration must trace with exact fidelity" (*Testimonies for the Church,* 4:370). Whereas uninspired historians are unable to record history without bias, the inspired writers "did not testify to falsehoods to prevent the pages of sacred history being clouded by the record of human frailties and faults. The scribes of God wrote as they were dictated by the Holy Spirit, having no control of the work themselves. They penned the literal truth, and stern, forbidding facts are revealed for reasons that our finite minds cannot fully comprehend" (ibid., 9).

Second, the Bible's science is also authentic. "Its sacred pages contain the only authentic account of the creation. . . . There is harmony between nature and Christianity; for both have the same Author. The book of nature and the book of revelation indicate the working of the same divine mind" (*Fundamentals of Christian Education,* 84-85). "Inferences erroneously drawn from facts observed in nature have, however, led to supposed conflict between science and revelation; and in the effort to restore harmony, interpretations of Scripture have been adopted that undermine and destroy the force of the Word of God." Ellen White rejected naturalistic evolution and the long ages of geology. "Geology has been thought to contradict the literal interpretation of the Mosaic record of the creation. Millions of years, it is claimed, were required for the evolution of the earth from chaos; and in order to accommodate the Bible to this supposed revelation of science, the days of creation are assumed to have been vast, indefinite periods, covering thousands or even millions of years. Such a conclusion is wholly uncalled for. The Bible record is in harmony with itself and with the teaching of nature" (*Education,* 128-129).

[45]William G. Johnsson, "Nine Foundations for An Adventist Hermeneutic," *Ministry* (March 1999): 13.

# 30

# "SUFFERING MANY THINGS" —A SERMON

In response to liberalism's sophisticated challenge to our beliefs and practices, the world church sponsored the First International Jerusalem Bible Conference, June 8-14, 1998. The goal of this convocation in Israel was to urge our Bible teachers and thought leaders around the world "to remain faithful to God's holy Word and the teachings of the Seventh-day Adventist Church." I was invited to be one of the plenary speakers at the conference, apparently because of the impact of my book *Receiving the Word*.[1]

My original objective was to describe candidly the theological situation in the church, showing the baneful impact of contemporary higher criticism on the church's life and witness and suggesting a response to it. I chose my title ("Suffering Many Things") from Mark 5:25-26, with the intent of drawing an analogy between the condition of the woman with an issue of blood and that of today's Seventh-day Adventist church. However, upon arriving in Jerusalem I felt impressed to speak to the hearts of the church's thought leaders, not just to their minds. But not wanting to deviate from the printed title, I preached a sermon from the same chapter of Mark 5, focusing this time on Jairus instead of the woman with the issue of blood.

Perceptive readers of the following plenary address will recognize that the introductory comments preceding the sermon, "The Story Within the

Story," captured the essence of what I had originally set out to do.[2]

**Introduction**

1998 is "The Year of the Bible." And at the request of the Biblical Research Institute of the General Conference of Seventh-day Adventists (SDA), the Adventist Theological Society, the Institute of Archaeology at Andrews University, and other SDA institutions, we have gathered here in Jerusalem from different parts of the world for two major reasons:

> (1) To reaffirm our whole-hearted commitment to the authority of Scripture, and
>
> (2) To renew our pledge to uphold the message and mission of the Seventh-day Adventist church.

Although we refer to this meeting as the "First International Jerusalem Bible Conference," perhaps it is worth remembering that exactly twelve years ago, in another part of the world, there was a similar convocation of the church's foremost administrators and scholars.

The year was 1986. The venue was Rio de Janeiro, Brazil. The purpose was to set forth the hermeneutical implications of our Fundamental Beliefs #1, by specifying the assumptions and principles of Bible study that are consistent with the teachings of Scripture itself. That Annual Council meeting has bequeathed to the church a historic document known as the "Rio Document" or the "Methods of Bible Study Report," a document that has since been embraced by an overwhelming majority of Seventh-day Adventist Bible students around the world.[3]

Ever since I was asked to be one of the plenary speakers at this 1998 Jerusalem Conference, I have asked myself two questions: Given the fact that the world church, as well as the organizers and sponsors of this International Conference whole-heartedly uphold the authority of Scripture and the principles of biblical interpretation outlined in the Rio Document,

> (1) Why has the General Conference of the SDA church designated 1998 as "The Year of the Bible," a year to emphasize and experience the power of the Word"?

> (2) And why have the various SDA entities sponsoring this meeting invited our church's scholars and leaders from around the world to attend another Bible Conference dedicated to upholding God's Word?

In seeking answers to the above questions, I reflected on the theological situation in the SDA church, especially during the past twelve years (1986-1998). After pondering over the direct correlation that exists between the health of the church and its attitude to God's Word,[4] I came to the conclusion that, perhaps, I should use this occasion to briefly, but candidly, describe the present theological situation in the church, and then suggest what we need to do.

### Why "Suffering Many Things"?

Permit me to explain why I chose the title *"Suffering Many Things"* as a launching pad for my plenary address. Perceptive Bible students may probably recognize that this title is taken from Mark 5:25-26 (KJV):

> "And a certain woman, which had an issue of blood twelve years, and had *suffered many things* of many physicians, and had spent all that she had, and was nothing bettered, but rather grew worse" (emphasis mine).

My intention is to draw an analogy between the condition of the woman with an issue of blood and that of today's Seventh-day Adventist church. It seems to me that our church is also slowly bleeding to death because the authority of Scripture, the church's life-blood, has been infected by the deadly virus of contemporary higher criticism.

On this analogy, the twelve years of the woman's suffering correspond to the period between the 1986 Annual Council meeting in Rio de Janeiro, Brazil, and this Jerusalem Conference of 1998.

The "many physicians" at whose hands the woman had "suffered many things" may refer to the theological specialists and professional elite who shape the theological thinking of the church. Such "physicians" include the doctors in New and Old Testament theology, systematic theology, church history, Christian ministry, missions, etc. The "many physicians" also include experts in education, administration, psychology, anthropology, sociology, science, business, etc.

At no time has the church boasted itself of so many academic and professional doctorates. In this auditorium alone we may be able to count at least one hundred "doctors" in one field or another. And yet, at no time has the church "suffered many things" at the hands of so "many physicians." Thus:

—Our *teaching of the Bible* has suffered at the hands of "many physicians," whose exegesis have created uncertainty about virtually every single Bible passage.

—Our *distinctive doctrines* (literal six-day creation and the seventh-day Sabbath, sanctuary, Spirit of Prophecy, second coming, the substitutionary atonement of Christ, etc) have also suffered at the hands of "many physicians," whose subtle reinterpretations make of none effect our unique identity, message, and mission.

—Furthermore, our *distinctive lifestyle practices* have suffered at the hands of many physicians, who are suggesting that we should abandon certain historic Adventist practices (e.g., Sabbath observance, distinction between clean and unclean, bodily adornment, etc.) or embrace new ones (e.g. homosexuality, moderate use of alcohol, divorce and remarriage, etc.)

—Still, our *worship and preaching* have suffered at the hands of many physicians. As our preaching has become hazy and our worship insipid, we have staggered from one gimmick to another, nibbling at every fad in the shopping malls of today's megachurches and charismatic fellowships so as to "meet the felt needs" of our congregations.

—Again, our *mission and evangelism* have suffered at the hands of many physicians, who are suggesting that we shift the focus of our soul-winning efforts to the "unchurched" instead of to the unsaved (whether churched or unchurched).

—And our *publishing houses, publications,* and *book centers* have also suffered many things at the hands of many physicians, who are producing and distributing materials that are not Bible-centered in content and unifying in effect.

But it may be asked: What has been the *cost* to our church, and what has been the *outcome* of the painful surgeries endured by the church during the twelve years that she had "suffered many things" at the hands of our "many physicians"?[5]

The Bible describes it best when it states that, having "suffered many things of many physicians," and having "spent all that she had," the woman "was nothing bettered, but rather grew worse."

I will leave you to speculate on how this applies to the contemporary Seventh-day Adventist church. But one thing is certain: The woman needed a healing touch, not from "many physicians" but from the Master Physician. The anemic condition of the church can be cured only if we receive, reaffirm, and remain faithful to Christ's inspired Word. This is the reason why we have gathered in Jerusalem this week.

**Message From GC President**

Perhaps it is fitting, at this time, to call your attention to Elder Folkenberg's welcoming letter to participants to this conference. This letter from our GC president (printed on page 2 of the brochure for the Jerusalem Conference) describes what we need to do. It reads:

> Dear Fellow Bible Student,
>
> Welcome to the First International Jerusalem Bible Conference. Your church has encouraged you to come to this event to enrich your love of the Bible and, thus, enrich the church.
>
> As the president of your church, I must tell you, the Seventh-day Adventist Church needs you. It needs you to *remain faithful to God's holy Word and the teachings of the Seventh-day Adventist Church.* At no time in the history of this world has the Bible been more needed than in this day and at no time has the Bible been more under attack, than at this time. Rightly studied, God's Word always brings revival.
>
> May this Conference renew and invigorate your faith. Please do

not leave this Jerusalem Bible Conference without recommitting yourself to meet me, your fellow teachers, and your students in the New Jerusalem.

God bless you during this week! (italics mine)

Note that, according to the president of our church, if we are to experience a true revival in God's end time church, we must *remain faithful* to God's holy Word and the teachings of the Seventh-day Adventist Church.

**A Call to Faithfulness**

This evening, I will attempt to move beyond a mere theoretical adherence to the principles of interpretation outlined in the 1986 Rio Document. Consequently, I will not dwell upon the theological condition of the church and how it has "suffered many things" at the hands of its "many physicians" during the past twelve years. Instead, the message will call upon each one of us to *remain faithful*, even if we have to "suffer many things" on account of our commitment to Jesus Christ and His Word.

We shall still be studying Mark 5. But rather than focusing on the condition of the woman with an issue of blood, we shall concentrate on the faith of Jairus. By the close of the sermon, we shall discover that we cannot separate the experience of Jairus from that of the woman. Thus, a more fitting title to my message tonight would be "The Story Within the Story."

As a prelude to the message, I've requested one of the Quartets in our Ghanaian SDA church in Tel Aviv to sing for us a special song. The song, titled *Hwan Ne Wo Yehowah* [translated, "Who Is Like Unto Thee, Jehovah?"], is in the Ashanti language of Ghana. It presents to us Jesus Christ as the Creator and Redeemer. Because Christ Himself suffered and died for us, the song urges us to remain faithful to Him, even if we also have to suffer many things for Him.

[*At this point, there was a song from the Ghanaian Quartet, followed by prayer*]

**The Story within the Story**

**Experience of Ellen Dipenaar.** You may have read about the experience of Ellen Dipenaar, a dedicated Christian who lived in South

Africa several years ago. Almost unannounced this fine Christian lady came down with leprosy and was sent into quarantine. While receiving treatment at the leprosarium, her only son died of polio, her husband succumbed to cancer, and her sister died in a car accident. As if these were not enough, she soon discovered that strange growths on her legs were actually gangrene, a condition that demanded and led to the amputation of both legs. Saddest of all, when Ellen's doctor prescribed some eye drops to take care of problems in her eyes, the nurse who administered the medication made a serious mistake: Instead of eye drops, she dropped in Ellen's eyes acid—a mistake that led to her becoming blind!

**Crucial Questions.** *Why is it that when one makes a commitment to be faithful to Christ, sometimes one's situation goes from bad to worse?*

This afternoon, as we toured Yad Veshem, the Holocaust Museum in Jerusalem, I couldn't help but think of many Seventh-day Adventists around the world, who today are also suffering many things on account of their faith.

I think of some Adventists who are in prison or who have lost their jobs because they would not compromise their biblical convictions about Sabbath work, lying, or fighting in their tribes' or nations' wars.

I also think of Adventist refugees who are literally starving to death in troubled regions of the world because they will not eat unclean foods, sometimes the only available provision to keep themselves alive.

I think also of the plight of Adventists who have been disowned by their families, divorced by their spouses, and killed by their neighbors because of their religious convictions.

As I think of such cases, I ask myself: *Where is God when His children suffer many things? And what should Christians do when, after taking a stand for God, sometimes things go from bad to worse?*

An answer to these perplexing questions may be partly found in Mark 5. This chapter in the gospel of Mark may well be described as a chapter of sorrows.

### Mark 5: A Chapter of Sorrows

Mark 5 begins with the painful account of a man living in a tomb, possessed by evil spirits. As you read further, we see another man emerge from his house brokenhearted, because his only daughter is seriously ill. A little further in the chapter, we are told of a woman who, for twelve years, had been slowly bleeding to death. And by the time the chapter closes, we are taken into a home where a young girl lies dead.

Thus, Mark 5 is a chapter of sorrows. It describes the accounts of individuals who are suffering many things—demon possession, sudden/acute illness, chronic, incurable illness, poverty, ridicule/scorn, and death.

Today we shall focus on verses 21 to 43. Turn to this section of your Bibles as we briefly look at how the account of the woman with an issue of blood is intricately woven together with Jairus's experience.

**Structure of Mark 5:21-43.** The Bible passage under consideration divides into three distinct parts:

Part I (verses 21-24) begins on a note of urgency. In these verses we read of an emergency in the house of Jairus, a ruler of the synagogue. He comes to Jesus, pleading that He should go to his home and heal his dying daughter (cf. Lk 8:42-"only" daughter). Jesus responds immediately. As He moves towards the home of Jairus, a large crowd goes with Him.

Part II (verses 25-34) opens abruptly. Almost unannounced there is a shift from the emergency situation of Jairus to an anonymous woman with an issue of blood. Her arrival on the scene causes a delay or interruption in the journey to the home of Jairus. For twelve years this woman had unsuccessfully tried everything. Finally, she decides to go to Jesus by pressing through the crowd and touching the hem of Christ's garment. Just then, Jesus asks what seems to the disciples to be a rather ridiculous question: "Who touched my clothes?" At Christ's persistence, the woman confessed what had happened and Jesus encourages her to go home in peace.

In Part III (verses 35-43) the narrative shifts back again to Jairus. Here we read that messengers from Jairus's house arrive with the bad news of the child's death. Jesus ignores the news, urges Jairus to have faith, and goes to his home with Peter, James and John. In spite of the scorn and ridicule by professional mourners, Jesus raises the dead child back to life and charges the parents not to publicize the miracle.

We see, therefore, that the Mark 5:21-43 passage consists of three segments. It initially focuses on Jairus, then shifts to the woman, and finally moves back again to Jairus. The passage under consideration sandwiches one story (the woman's) within another story (Jairus's).

Because the passage begins and concludes with Jairus, we can say that Jairus is the principal focus of the entire passage. However, the key to understanding the Jairus story lies in the story of the woman with an issue of blood. This story within the story may offer to us some valuable lessons on what we must do when, after taking a stand for Jesus, our situations go from bad to worse.

### A Closer Look at "The Story Within the Story"

A casual reading of Mark 5:21-43 will reveal some general parallels/similarities in the two stories of Jairus and the woman: Both had desperate needs; both went to Jesus for help; and both were helped by Jesus.

However, the closer we study the accounts of Jairus and the Woman, the more contrasts we will discover:

***1. Names.*** Whereas Jairus is identified by name, in the case of the woman her name is not given; she is simply identified as "a certain woman" (v. 25). Thus, we have prominent/well-known person and an anonymous/unknown individual.

***2. Condition.*** The woman's condition may be described as chronic (she was battling with an incurable illness for twelve years). On the other hand, Jairus daughter's situation was acute (a sudden terminal illness that would soon lead to her death).

***3. Time/Duration.*** The woman had suffered in her condition for twelve years. This period of time captures the age of Jairus daughter (we are told that "she was of the age of twelve years," v. 42). In other words, the year in which the child was born was the exact year in which the woman started getting sick Thus, while Jairus's daughter experienced 12 years of vitality and health, the woman, on the other hand suffered twelve years of continuous death. Jairus experienced twelve years of progressive joy and hope, the woman suffered twelve years of deterioration and despair.

***4. Religious Status.*** We understand that Jairus was a ruler of the synagogue. But the woman, because of her issue of blood, would be an outcast of the synagogue. For according to Lev 15:25-33; Num 4, the woman's condition made her unclean, and her contact with others made them also unclean.

***5. Social/Economic status.*** The woman was economically handicapped, having spent all that she had on many physicians. But Jairus was a man of means, one with servants and social respectability.

***6. Options.*** For the woman, Jesus was the *last* resort. She had unsuccessfully tried other remedies and options. But apparently, for Jairus, Jesus was His *first* choice; he went straight to Jesus when his child took ill.

***7. Advocate.*** The woman had no one to plead her case with Jesus, so she had to go herself. Jairus served as a mouthpiece to plead the case for his daughter.

***8. Manner of Coming.*** The woman went to Jesus secretly/anonymously. But Jairus went to Jesus publicly or openly.

***9. Direction of Approach.*** The woman approached Jesus from behind (v. 27), falling later at His feet at the end of her encounter with Him. On the other hand, Jairus came to Jesus face to face, falling at Jesus's feet at the beginning of his encounter.

***10. Result of Delay.*** Because of Jesus's delay in going to Jairus home, the woman was healed. But, because of the delay, Jairus's daughter dies.

***11. Word from Jesus.*** Jesus speaks to the woman only after *good* news of her healing. But He speaks to Jairus only after *bad* news of his child's death.

***12. Testimonies.*** Though the woman came to Jesus secretly, her healing was made public. On the other hand, though Jairus came publicly to Jesus, the healing of his child was to be kept a secret (v. 43).

The above contrasts in the two stories will help us understand why the story of the woman is sandwiched within that of Jairus. Later on, we shall return to consider the significance of the differences. Right now we shall focus on Jairus, inasmuch as the passage begins and concludes with him.

## The Trial of Jairus's Faith

Jairus exercised great faith when he came publicly to Jesus. His act of coming publicly to Jesus was an unpopular decision that could cost him his job as a ruler of the synagogue. He could have come to Jesus secretly like the woman or like Nicodemus, another ruler of the synagogue (John 3). But Jairus took a stand for the Man of Galilee. He recognized that the Man who associated with sinners and tax collectors was non other than the Messiah.

Jairus had come to a point in his life where nothing, not even his social standing, job or wealth, mattered any more to him. His child was dying. Only a Savior could save her. Every other earthly consideration paled into insignificance. Thus, he made a costly decision for Christ. He did right because it was right and left consequences with God. And God always honors those who take a stand with Him, regardless of foreboding circumstances.

Christ rewarded his faith by immediately setting out to Jairus's house. But since every true faith requires public testing, Jairus's faith was also tried. Notice how Jesus allowed Jairus's faith to be tested.

**1. Delay by the crowd.** Jesus was on a life and death errand—an emergency situation in Jairus's home, an emergency that did not need a crowd to impede his movement. Jesus could have driven away the throng that surrounded him (v. 21). But He deliberately chose not to do so. Later on, when the child dies, Christ would send away the crowd (cf. v. 37). But now, when we expect Him to do something about the crowd which is jostling and obstructing His movement, Christ does not do anything about it.

Can you imagine the driver of an ambulance, caught in a trafficjam and yet refusing to sound his sirens? And can you imagine how Jairus may have felt when the crowd caused the delay in the movement of Jesus to his home? *Why does the Lord often delay when we trust Him with our urgent cases?*

**2. Silence and interruption.** Jairus experienced another trial. Do you notice that besides not speaking to the crowd to give way, Jesus also did not speak a word of encouragement to Jairus, assuring him that all would be well? Instead, Jesus allows his movement to be interrupted by the woman (v.25-34).

*Why does the Lord often allow our cherished plans to be interrupted? Why did the Lord speak to others, but not to Jairus? Why does He sometimes seem to care about others but, often appears to be indifferent to our plight?*

And worse still, why did Jesus *stop* and ask a seemingly pointless question "Who touched my clothes" (v. 30)?

To His disciples this was not logical since Jesus had been jostled and touched by a host of individuals (v.31). The fact, however, remains that what Jesus says may not always be logical to our rational minds. It is illogical to insist that we should never lie, steal, kill, or break any of God's Ten Commandments to save life. The Christian does not always operate on human logic but by faith in God and His Word. We are urged to "Trust in the Lord with all thine heart, and lean not on your own understanding. In all your ways acknowledge Him and He shall direct your path" (Prov 3:5, 6).

But these questions still remain: *Why is it that when we put our trust in the Lord, He sometimes allows our plans to be interrupted? Why does the Lord seem silent to us when, at the same time, He appears to pay attention to others? Why does He call on others while He appears to pass us by?*

To Jairus, the delay by the crowd, the interruption by the woman, and Christ's silence and stopping were a real trial of his faith. I can imagine Jairus saying to himself: "Master, if we continue delaying, my child will die! Our immediate mission is to assist a dying girl. Why are you concerned about the insignificant question about who touched your clothes? Further delay will be catastrophic."

But Jesus still delays.

**3. Further Delay by the Woman.** Jesus looks in direction of the woman and speaks to her (v. 32, 34). But not a word to Jairus. Can you imagine what was going through Jairus's mind? I can hear him saying to himself: "Lord, this woman's situation is chronic but not an emergency as mine!"

In verse 33 we read that, "in fear and trembling," the woman falls at Christ's feet and tells all. She was afraid because: (a) she had broken the rules of the Torah (God's law) regarding ritual uncleanness. By touching Jesus, she feared that she had made Him ritually unclean (Num 5:1-4; cf. Lev 15:25ff.). (b) Even more she would be acknowledging her uncleanness in the presence of a leader of her local synagogue. Besides the courage such a step would involve, Jesus was asking her to also do something humiliating: To talk about her problem in front of men. It is one thing for a woman to discuss this kind of problem with her fellow women in small groups or at home; it is another to declare the uncleanness before a large crowd, including the disciples of Christ and the ruler of the synagogue.

Meanwhile, as the woman tells "all the truth" (v. 33). Jairus waits impatiently. Can you imagine what telling *all* the truth entailed? I can hear the woman saying to Jesus:

> Master, when my problem started, I thought it was my normal monthly period. But it prolonged beyond the regular time. Therefore, I consulted with my family doctor, who also referred me to some brilliant Jewish specialists in a leading Tel Aviv hospital. When the specialists were unable to do anything about the situation, I was encouraged to try some alternative or non-traditional (read as New Age) medicine—acupuncture, hypnotism, yogi, biofeedback, homeopathy, massage therapy, therapeutic touch, etc. These were no help either. Then, I heard that I should go and swim in the Dead Sea. I tried it, but it didn't work. Some friends of mine also urged me to try some African and Indian herbs. These helped a little bit. But I soon realized the situation was getting worse. Then I was told by some TV evangelist that by touching the TV screen the demons causing my ailment would be cast out. Master, I even sent a thank offering ("seed of faith money") to the Televangelist. But it did not help. I also tried. . . . etc. My health insurance has been cancelled; I have exhausted my entire pension and social security funds; I am currently on welfare and food stamps; besides, I am. . . ."

The Bible simply says that the woman "came and fell down before him, and told him all the truth" (v. 33). While she tells "all the truth," Jairus is seemingly ignored by Christ. Jesus patiently listens and gives encouragement to the woman: "Daughter, your faith (not your superstitious touch of my garment) has saved you; go in peace." But not a word to Jairus.

**4. From Bad to Worse.** Just then messengers from Jairus's home arrive with bad news: "Thy daughter is dead" (v. 35). I can overhear Satan whispering into Jairus' ears: "I told you so! I knew that with all these delays, this is what it would come up to. Your daughter is dead!"

The account here is almost similar to the incident involving Lazarus. Jesus deliberately delays when news reached Him of Lazarus's illness. He allows time for him to die, be buried, to decompose, before he goes there. Anyway, news reaches Jairus, "thy daughter is dead."

Have you ever heard those words?

"Your loved one is dead!"

"Your job is ended!"

"Your career is over!"

"Your future is hopeless!"

"Your marriage is over!"

"Your cancer is terminal!"

Often, these cruel words come when you've just committed or rededicated your life to Christ. The verdict is announced when you're trying to do what is right, such as getting out of an immoral relationship or returning a faithful tithe.

*Why is it that when you are trying to do the right thing, it is then that things go from bad to worse?* You do your best to honor God's Sabbath only to lose your job; you try to do God's will and your husband threatens divorce; you try to tell the truth under dire circumstances, and you are fired from your job.

Have you ever experienced that? Have you ever been told: "Yours is a hopeless case. Don't waste Christ's time"? Jairus experienced this when he was told: "Your daughter is dead. Do not trouble the Master."

**5. More Trials.** But Christ's words and actions after the bad news may even have tested the faith of Jairus even more. Observe that when the situation became hopeless, Jesus then spoke some strange words to Jairus: "Be not afraid . . . only believe [i.e keep on believing." (v. 36).

To us, this may sound hopeful. But think of how it might have sounded to Jairus to be told, "Be not afraid . . ." "Afraid?" What was there to fear now? The worst has occurred. And "believe?" What was there to believe? The girl is dead!

A friend of mine has said that whenever God says, "Don't be afraid," it is time to start worrying, because God is about to ask you to do the impossible (think of Abraham, Moses, Gideon, Jeremiah, Mary, etc.)

But note that whenever Jesus says, "Be not afraid," that *command is also a promise.* Someone has estimated that there are some 365 "Fear

Nots" in the Bible—at least one for each day's need. Therefore, when you're told, "You are finished," Jesus says "Fear not. It's not the end." When you're told, "I'm sorry, that's the end," Jesus says "Fear not. It is the beginning; it is to be continued."

The real question for us to answer is: Do you trust God enough to believe in His word? Do you believe that He knows what is best for you? Do you believe He has power to save—even in difficult situations?

Those words of Jesus, "Be not afraid . . . only believe [literally, keep on believing"] (v. 36), were calculated to encourage Jairus so that he would not give up. For just then Jesus does another strange thing.

In verse 37, we are told that Jesus drives away the crowd save Peter, James and John. Why does he now send away the crowd? Why did He choose to do so now that all is lost? Why didn't Christ send away the crowd earlier, when there was hope for the child to be healed?

Perhaps Jesus was teaching Jairus that God's ways are not our ways. His timing is always the best. All we have to do at all times is to trust Him.

**6. Trials at Home.** The trial of Jairus was not over when he got nearer home (v. 38-40). He was greeted with the weeping of mourners, confirming that, indeed, the child was dead. What would Jesus do now that the situation had gone from bad to worse?

Speaking to Jairus, whose faith was then wavering, Jesus declares that the child was not dead but only sleeping. You see, though death is the most hopeless condition in this life, Jesus calls it sleep. And if death is simply sleep, then there is hope for the most hopeless situation. That's why we are to be "faithful unto death" (Rev 2:10). And this is why we must not attempt to save our jobs, positions, or even our lives at all cost.

But Jairus's faith was to be tried one last time. To the words of Jesus that the child was not dead but asleep, the mourners stop their weeping and laugh Him to scorn. Their ridicule was not so much directed to Christ as it was to Jairus. The funeral professionals seemed to say: "What does this man think? Doesn't he know the difference between death and sleep? And, you Jairus, is this the kind of person you are willing to stake your career and child's life on?"

Have you ever experienced ridicule, derision, or scorn, on account of your faith? Have you experienced ridicule from the experts/specialists, family, friends, church members—people who should know better? And have you ever wondered why the wicked often mock the righteous? Jairus went through that experience. He may have asked: *Why does the Lord delay in times of emergency? Why does He keep silent when His children need to hear from Him? Why does He allow other people to interrupt the plans of His children? Why does the Lord allow things to go from bad to worse? And why does He permit enemies to subject His children to scorn and ridicule?*

**Reward of Faith**

I want to believe that in all these trials, Jesus is always very near. If we remain faithful He would honor our faith—even as He did for Jairus. For in verse 41, we are told that the One who once stood at Lazarus tomb and said "come forth" now goes to Jairus daughter's room, takes the child by the hand and commands: "TALITHA CUMI."

Observe that by the phrase, "Talithah Cumi," Jesus did not speak in some unintelligible ecstatic utterance. He spoke in a known human language—Aramaic—not some charismatic gibberish masquerading as the biblical "speaking in tongues." For the sake of those who may not understand this human tongue, the gospel writer Mark translates it: "Damsel [or Little girl], I say unto thee arise" (v. 41).

Jesus statement is emphatic in the Greek. He seemed to say: "Little girl, *it is I who says unto thee*, arise"

> —Some may say that you are dead, but "I say unto thee, arise."
> —Others may say that your case is hopeless, but "I am the resurrection and life. I say unto you arise."
> —Some may tell you your future is ended, but "I am the alpha and omega. I say unto you arise."
> —Others may think that I am delaying and silent, but "I am He that died and am alive. I say unto you arise."
> —Some may think there is no way out, but "I am the way, the truth and the life. I say unto you arise."
> —Others may think that no power on earth can save your situation, but "All power is given unto me . . . I say unto you arise."

The same Jesus who could bring life out of death can transform our hopeless situations today. Our responsibility is to remain faithful, no matter what.

Perhaps we may be asking what Jesus was seeking to teach Jairus by the delay, silence, bad news, scorn, etc.? Let me call attention to four possible reasons:

**1. Divine Timing.** One reason is to teach Jairus and us something about the mystery of Divine timing: despite what may appear as a delay or interruption in our plans and expectations. To the child of God, God's timing is never late.

Never talk about delay, unless you know of God's arrival time. Let me illustrate: Sometime ago, my flight was scheduled to arrive at the Dulles International Airport in Washington, DC at 11:09 a.m. The one picking me up from the airport was waiting. But due to mechanical difficulties with the aircraft, I got there at 3:00 p.m.! In this instance, the friend who was waiting for me can legitimately speak of a delay. But we cannot speak about a delay when discussing the second coming of Christ. This is because Jesus has not given us His arrival time. In the same way, we cannot speak about delay in God's plan for our lives—unless we fully know what He is seeking to do in our individual lives. Since God's time never knows a delay, we must always trust Him, no matter how long it may seem to us.

> To all who are reaching out to feel the guiding hand of God, the moment of greatest discouragement is the time when divine help is nearest (The *Desire of Ages*, 528).

> Jesus sees the end from the beginning. In every difficulty He has His way prepared to bring relief. Our heavenly Father has a thousand ways to provide for us, of which we know nothing. Those who accept the one principle of making the service and honor of God supreme, will find perplexities vanish and a plain path before their feet (*The Desire of Ages*, 330).

> When in faith we take hold of His strength, he will change, wonderfully change, the most hopeless, discouraging outlook. He will do this for the glory of His name (*Prophets and Kings*, 260).

**2. Nature of True Faith.** Jesus was also teaching Jairus and us that true faith steps forward regardless of humiliation, intimidation, scorn, or even loss. It is the nature of true faith to take a stand—even in the face of obstacles. One cannot secretly hold to faith. Faith requires public testing—it calls for a public stand regardless of consequences.

The woman with an issue of blood took a courageous and humiliating step of faith when she stepped forward publicly to talk about her uncleanness. Jairus took a courageous step of faith when he decided to come to Jesus publicly—even amidst derision and the risk of his job as ruler of the synagogue.

We must also dare to take a stand for Christ and His truth, no matter what. If teachers can't take a stand for unpopular theological truth, how would our students do so? If pastors and church leaders are unwilling to take unpopular stands, why would they expect their members and churches to do so? And if parents are unprepared to honor the Lord, how can their children be expected to make decisions of faith for the Lord?

The days in which we live call for men and women who would dare to stand for truth, regardless of consequences. Ellen G. White wrote:

> In deciding upon any course of action we are not to ask whether we can see that harm will result from it, but whether it is in keeping with the will of God (*Patriarchs and Prophets*, 634).

> True Christian principle will not stop to weigh consequences. It does not ask, What will people think of me if I do this? or, How will it affect my worldly prospects if I do that? (*The Sanctified Life*, 39).

> Christ's ambassadors have nothing to do with consequences. They must perform their duty, and leave results with God (*The Great Controversy*, 609-610).

> It is better to die than to sin; better to want [be in need] than to defraud; better to hunger than to lie (*Testimonies for the Church*, 4:495).

3. **Reward for Faithfulness.** Jesus was also teaching Jairus and us that divine blessing will always attend those who are faithful to the Lord. He will never fail anyone who puts his/her trust in Him.

> Those who take Christ at His word, and surrender their souls to His keeping, their lives to His ordering, will find peace and quietude. Nothing of the world can make them sad when Jesus makes them glad by His presence (*Desire of Ages*, 331).

> Those who surrender their lives to His guidance and His service will never be placed in a position for which He has not made provision. Whatever our situation, if we are doers of His word, we have a Guide to direct our way; whatever our perplexity, we have a sure Counselor; whatever our sorrow, bereavement, or loneliness, we have a sympathizing Friend (*The Ministry of Healing*, 248-249).

**4. Not Alone in Suffering.** Perhaps the most important reason why Jesus allowed the faith of Jairus to be tried was to instruct him through the experience of the woman. Though Jarius's ordeal was bitter, he was not alone in his pain. There was another person also suffering (a woman, for twelve long years). Sometimes our trials are designed to help us appreciate others. Pains make us more sympathetic disappointments make us more humble; and hardships keep us dependent on God.

Jesus was teaching Jairus from the experience of the woman. *It is here that the contrasting characteristics we identified earlier, between the woman and Jairus, become most helpful.* If Jesus was able to help the woman's hopeless case, what about Jairus?

> —If Jesus could help the woman's chronic disease (twelve years of slow death), what about Jairus daughter's recent illness after twelve years of full life?
> —If Jesus could help a woman without a name, what about a person with a name (Jairus)?
> —If Jesus could help an outcast of the synagogue, what about a ruler of the synagogue?
> —If Jesus could help a woman who came secretly, what about Jairus, who came publicly/openly?

—If Jesus could help a woman who had no intercessor/advocate, what about Jairus's child whose father was her advocate?
—If Jesus could help a woman who came from behind and superstitiously touched His garment, what about Jairus who exercised faith by coming face to face to Christ, kneeling and pleading?
—If Jesus could help a woman who came to Him as a last resort, what about Jairus who apparently made Jesus his first choice?
—If the one who made a silent request can give public testimony, what about Jairus, one who made a request in public?

Jesus did not needlessly delay, keep silent, or utter ridiculous or strange words. Christ permitted the woman's path to cross Jairus's so He could instruct Jairus on faith. This is, perhaps, the most important message contained in the story within the story: If Jesus did it for the woman, how much more would He not do for Jairus?

**Some Lessons for Us Today**

What lessons then can we draw from the Story Within the Story? First, all of us have some pain. Yours may be similar to Jarius's. Perhaps it is a loved one (child, husband, wife, parents, sister, relative, friend, etc.) who is in some serious difficulty. Or it may be that your situation is similar to the woman. You are the one actually bleeding to death. Perhaps it is your health, finances, or family situation that is slowly but hopelessly bleeding.

Whatever our situation, we must go to Jesus with our burdens. We may choose to go to Him like the woman—secretly in the closets of our homes, or silently/anonymously in church (as Hannah, the mother of Samuel did, 1 Samuel 1:9-17). Or we may choose to go to Jesus like Jairus did—openly in church/prayer meeting, during the time for prayer request.

Another lesson we learn is that we must not fear taking a stand for Jesus. The times in which we live call for men and women who dare to risk all for Jesus sake. If we do not stand up for something, we shall fall for anything. Fear of censure from our critics and fear of losing our jobs should not prevent us from doing the right thing. Neither should we wait until retirement before declaring where we stand on issues. Both the woman and Jairus took risks; and so must we.

> Often the follower of Christ is brought where he cannot serve God and carry forward his worldly enterprises. Perhaps it appears that obedience to some plain requirement of God will cut off his means of support. Satan would make him believe that he must sacrifice his conscientious convictions. But the only thing in our world upon which we can rely is the word of God . . . Matt. 6:33. Even in this life it is not for our good to depart from the will of our Father in heaven. When we learn the power of His word, we shall not follow the suggestions of Satan in order to obtain food or to save our lives. Our only questions will be, What is God's command? and what is His promise? Knowing these, we shall obey the one, and trust the other (*Desire of Ages*, 121).

Finally, when we take a stand for the Lord and He seems to delay, and our prospects grow darker and darker, we are still to trust Him. Each of us should say with Job: "Though he slays me, yet will I trust in him" (Job 13:15). With the three Hebrew children, we must be able to say that, "Our God whom we serve is able to deliver us from the burning fiery furnace, and he will deliver us out of thine hand, O king. *But if not, be it known unto thee, O king, that we will not serve thy gods, nor worship the golden image which thou hast set up*" (Dan 3:17-18; emphasis mine).

> As in the days of Shadrach, Meshach, and Abednego, so in the closing period of earth's history the Lord will work mightily in behalf of those who stand steadfastly for the right. He who walked with the Hebrew worthies in the fiery furnace will be with His followers wherever they are. His abiding presence will comfort and sustain. In the midst of the time of trouble—trouble such as has not been since there was a nation—His chosen ones will stand unmoved (*Prophets and Kings*, 513).

> The season of distress before God's people will call for a faith that will not falter. His children must make it manifest that He is the only object of their worship, and that no consideration, not even that of life itself, can induce them to make the least concession to false worship. To the loyal heart, the commands of sinful, finite men will sink into insignificance

beside the word of the eternal God. Truth will be obeyed though the result be imprisonment or exile or death (*Prophets and Kings* 512-513).

**Appeal**

Perhaps you are seated here tonite, and it appears that the Lord is delaying in answering your prayers.

—You have asked for light, but all you experience is darkness.
—You have asked for health, but you are experiencing more sickness.
—You've asked the Lord for companionship in life, but you are still experiencing loneliness.
—You have asked Him for success, but you see only failure.
—You asked Him for deliverance, yet you know only of distress.
—You asked him to clear your name, but no one seems to vindicate you.
—And you've asked for life, but death is what you get.

The story within the story tells us that when we take a stand for Jesus and things go from bad to worse, we are still to trust Him. Trust Him still even if He delays, and even if our plans are interrupted.

When you are told that because of your faith, your daughter is dead, tell them she is only asleep; she will rise again.

When you are told your future is finished, tell them that your future is in God's hands, and that He has better plans for your life. What may seem like the end may very well be the beginning of real life.

When you are told that your prospects are bleak, tell them that as long as Jesus lives there is hope.

And when you are ridiculed, and told "don't trouble the Master," its a waste of time, there's no hope, tell them that no one who goes to Jesus is ever a trouble to Him.

There is hope for everyone of us who makes a decision of faith to serve the Lord and do His will. Therefore, in all our afflictions, sorrows, pains, let us go to Jesus, and in the words of that familiar hymn plead: "Pass me not Oh gentle Savior; Hear my humble cry. While on others Thou art calling do not pass me by."

Your situation may be desperate. You may have experienced sorrow after sorrow, trouble after trouble. You may have lost your health, wealth, job, friend, or family. You may have been misunderstood/persecuted. Whatever your situation, let's remember that it was this same situation that Jesus dealt with when He met Jairus and the woman. Someone has said: "Every sorrow is a summons to us to go Jesus."

So when Jesus appears to delay, when He seems silent, or when things go from bad to worse, we must still keep trusting Him. Everything will be all right in the long run.

> The Elder Brother of our race is by the eternal throne. He looks upon every soul who is turning his face toward Him as the Savior. He knows by experience what are the weaknesses of humanity, what are our wants, and where lies the strength of our temptations; for He was in all points tempted like as we are, yet without sin. He is watching over you, trembling child of God. Are you tempted? He will deliver. Are you weak? He will strengthen. Are you ignorant? He will enlighten. Are you wounded? He will heal. The Lord 'telleth the number of the stars;' and yet 'He healeth the broken in heart, and bindeth up their wounds.' Ps. 147:4, 3. 'Come unto Me,' is His invitation. Whatever your anxieties and trials, spread out your case before the Lord. Your spirit will be braced for endurance. The way will be opened for you to disentangle yourself from embarrassment and difficulty. The weaker and more helpless you know yourself to be, the stronger will you become in His strength. The heavier your burdens, the more blessed the rest in casting them upon the Burden Bearer (*The Desire of Ages*, 329).

May the Lord help us to *remain faithful*, even if we have to suffer many things. This is my prayer for each one of us gathered here at this First International Jerusalem Bible Conference.

---

**Endnotes**

[1]The following thought leaders were invited to be the plenary speakers at the 1998 Jerusalem Bible Conference: Robert S. Folkenberg (President, General Conference), George Reid (Director, Biblical Research Institute of the General Conference), Mark Finley (Speaker and Director, "It Is Written" Telecast), Alberto Timm (Director of the Ellen

G. White & SDA Research Center, Brazil), Samuel Koranteng-Pipim (author of *Receiving the Word*), Angel Rodriguez (Associate Director, Biblical Research Institute of the GC), Randall W. Younker (Director, Institute of Archaeology, SDA Theological Seminary, Andrews University), Walter L. Pearson, Jr. (Speaker and Director, Breath of Life Telecast), Norman R. Gulley (Professor, Southern Adventist University), Ed Zinke (Silver Spring, MD; Former Associate Director of Biblical Research Institute of the GC), and Dwight K. Nelson (Senior Pastor, Pioneer Memorial Church, Andrews University).

[2]Though I have already published my sermon at the Jerusalem Bible Conference in the *Journal of the Adventist Theological Society,* I did not include the introductory comments. See my "Suffering Many Things," *Journal of the Adventist Theological Society* 9/1&2 (Spring-Autumn 1998):128-148. This chapter of *Must We Be Silent?* carries my unabridged address at the Conference.

[3]At the 1986 Annual Council meeting in Rio de Janeiro, Brazil, church leaders representing all the world fields approved the report of the General Conference's "Methods of Bible Study Committee (GCC-A)." This carefully worded document was published in the *Adventist Review* (January 22, 1987), pages 18-20. Generally, all Bible-believing conservatives embrace this report as reflective of the principles of interpretation that have been historically accepted by Seventh-day Adventists. The "Rio Document" is reproduced as appendix C in my *Receiving the Word* (Berrien Springs, MI: Berean Books, 1996). For a discussion of how Adventist scholars have related to this document, see Chapter 4 of *Receiving the Word*, 75-99.

[4]As explained by John Albert Bengel, some two centuries ago (in 1742), "Scripture is the foundation of the Church: the Church is the guardian of Scripture. When the Church is in strong health, the light of Scripture shines bright [sic]; when the Church is sick, Scripture is corroded by neglect; . . . and as a rule the way in which Scripture is being treated is in exact correspondence with the condition of the Church" (John Albert Bengel, *Gnomon of the New Testament*, ed. Andrew R. Fausset, 5 vols. [Edinburgh: T & T Clark, 1857-1858], 1:7).

[5]For more on this see the General Conference document, "The Use of Scripture in the Life of the SDA Church," a discussion paper at the 1995 General Conference Session, Utrecht, Netherlands. It is reproduced as Appendix B in my *Receiving the Word*, 349-354.

*What are the threats to our church unity? What's wrong with using worldly gimmicks to proclaim the gospel? What happens when a GC session votes a biblically questionable practice into the* Church Manual*? What about situations where the Spirit-guided decision of the church body seem to clash with the Spirit's leading of a person's life and with the person's conscience? Must we be concerned about innovations in contemporary worship styles?*

Section V

# The Vocal Few and the Local Pew

## (The Ideology of Congregationalism)

# 31

# A Brief Background

*"When to unite and when to divide, that is the question, and a right answer requires the wisdom of a Solomon. . . . To divide what should be divided and unite what should be united is the part of wisdom. Union of dissimilar elements is never good even where it is possible. Nor is the arbitrary division of elements that are alike; and this is as certainly true of things moral and religious as of things political or scientific."*

**A.W. Tozer**

The liberal agenda is dividing our church and threatening our worldwide unity. Yet those pushing this agenda often accuse anyone opposing it as being divisive. Liberals are fond of trumpeting "unity in diversity." Yet theirs is a counterfeit unity. For the unity they preach is nothing more than theological pluralism, the peaceful coexistence of truth and error.

In this final section of *Must We Be Silent?* I am going to call attention to the ideology of congregational discord, explaining how certain liberal ideas and practices are creating confusion in local churches, splitting others, and threatening our worldwide unity. More specifically, in subsequent chapters, I will share my thoughts on:

(1) the gospel gimmicks being introduced in some of our churches, including gospel rock, gospel clowns, gospel cafés, gospel magicians, etc.
(2) the questionable divorce and remarriage decision that was voted into the *Church Manual* at the 2000 Toronto General Conference session,
(3) the rebellious ordinations that have taken place in some North American churches, and

(4) the innovative worship styles being pushed in certain quarters of our church.

But before I take up these issues, it is important that I briefly explain why we must not be silent on these and other divisive practices that are being imposed upon the local pew by the vocal few. The discussion in this chapter challenges the superficial and erroneous doctrine of "unity in diversity." I will explain what true biblical unity entails, contrasting it with the counterfeit unity being advocated in certain quarters of our church.

**Unity: A Divine Imperative**

Ever since there was rebellion in heaven there has been division. And alongside this division have been conflicts, wars, and bloodshed. Recent events in the Middle East, Balkans, Africa, and other places testify to the urgent need for unity and harmony in the world.

The religion of the Bible is about restoring unity—unity between God and man, unity between husband and wife, unity between members of the church, and unity among members of the human family.

The last prayer request of our Lord Jesus Christ before His death was for unity among his followers. He prayed:

> "I do not ask in behalf of these alone, but for those also who believe in Me through their word; that they may all be one; even as Thou, Father, art in Me, and I in Thee, that they also may be one in Us; that the world may believe that Thou didst send Me. And the glory which thou hast given Me I have given them; that they may be one, just as We are one; I in them, and Thou in Me, that they may be perfected in unity, that the world may know that Thou didst send Me, and didst love them, even as Thou didst love Me" (John 17:20-23).

As we explained in our discussion in chapter 21, the unity that Christ prayed for in this John 17 passage is a unity grounded in the Word of God and forged by the Holy Spirit Concerning this prayer, Ellen G. White wrote:

> "The Lord calls for men of genuine faith and sound minds, men who recognize the distinction between the true and the false. Each one should be on his guard, studying and practicing

> the lessons given in the seventeenth chapter of John, and preserving a living faith in the truth for this time" (*Testimonies for the Church,* 8:239).

**The Basis of Our Unity.** As a global movement, comprising people from "every nation, and kindred, and tongue, and people" (Rev 14:6), the Seventh-day Adventist church seeks to manifest this unity to an unbelieving world. Without the church's worldwide unity, this prophetic movement would disintegrate into a pattern of local options, weakness, and confusion. Moreover, our strength and credibility as a church depends, to a large extent, on our organized unity. For how else can we convince the world that we have a message that heals wounds of division if we ourselves choose to go in different directions?

Throughout our history, three major factors have greatly contributed to our worldwide unity:

> (1) *Our distinctive doctrine and lifestyle.* Despite obvious cultural differences, Adventists everywhere in the world have held the same doctrines and embraced the same lifestyle. As a group, they have manifested a distinctive personality of faith. The near unanimity in belief and lifestyle practices has been possible because of our adherence to the teachings of God's Word.
>
> (2) *Our sense of mission.* Accepting Christ's commission (Matt 28:18-20), we have always understood our reason for existence to be the clear and persuasive proclamation of God's Word within the context of the end-time (Rev 14:6-12). The sending forth of hundreds of missionaries around the world every year and the movement of our workers "from everywhere to everywhere" have been constant reminders to all that ours is a worldwide church and the mission of the church can only be accomplished by a united body of people from all nations of the world.
>
> (3) *Our unique church polity (the form of organizational structure in the church).* Despite its limitations, the Adventist church's unique church structure—uniting local churches, conferences, and unions at the divisions of the General Conference—has not only maintained the stability of the church, but has also

> ensured doctrinal unity and purity, and has facilitated the equitable distribution of the resources of the church for the accomplishment of its mission.[1]

These factors, together with the Lord's blessings, may explain why the Seventh-day Adventist church is enjoying an unprecedented growth around the world today.

**Threats to Our Church Unity.** There are, however, disturbing indications that our unity as a people is being threatened. For example, as apathy and the spirit of Laodiceanism have crept into the church, there are tensions in some places about our distinctive doctrinal beliefs and practices. Also, as worldly gimmicks and entertainment are gaining inroads into our preaching and worship styles, we are slowly losing our sense of mission. Still, in other places, ideologies as well as conflicts like tribalism, racism, nationalism, and classism (economic, social, or educational), and liberalism are testing the strength of our organizational unity.

As a result of these and other factors, we are witnessing the increased activities of dissident or offshoot movements. Inspired by both the "independent right" and the "liberal left," these movements are disrupting the unity within local congregations. As the offshoots of the left and right continue sowing seeds of discord, there is also a real danger of congregationalism (autonomous breakaway independent congregations) within the church's polity or form of organization. When the spirit of defiance or rebellion goes unchecked, and when they are cherished and encouraged at the conference, union, and division levels, there is the additional risk of fracturing our worldwide unity.

This chapter takes a look at some of the recent developments in the church that are threatening the unity of our church. It will focus on the offshoot streaks of the liberal left.

**Offshoots of the "Liberal Left" and "Independent Right"** In my earlier work, *Receiving the Word,* I explained that the Seventh-day Adventist church is caught in the middle of a crossfire of attacks from the "liberal left" and the "independent right."

The liberals, often educated and influential, operate within the church structure; the independents, appearing spiritual and orthodox, operate from without by establishing organizations and structures of their own.

Both groups are critical of the church because they believe that today's Adventism is not what it should be. So both attempt to "rehabilitate" the church.

In order to make Adventism "relevant" for this generation, the liberals seek to "liberate" the church from its alleged fundamentalist doctrines and nineteenth-century lifestyle. In their attempt to bring a "revival" to the church, the independents desire to "reform" the church from its ways of "apostasy." The liberals reinterpret Adventism's historic doctrines; the independents oppose any tampering with the Adventist pillars.

Regarding lifestyle or conduct, the liberals emphasize love, acceptance, and inclusiveness. The independents stress law, perfectionism, and uniqueness.

When the liberals on the left speak about the Adventist church, they often seem to see only the independents on the right; and when the independents discuss the church, one could almost believe that all members of the church are liberals.

The independent right is often perceived as siphoning off tithe from the church; the liberal left, which includes many church workers, is paid with tithe money while it often appears to be challenging, if not undermining, the beliefs and practices of the church.

The independent right destroys church unity by encouraging faithful members to separate from the church. The liberal left destroys the church's unity by remaining in the church and introducing its counterfeit unity doctrine, a doctrine that allows truth and error to coexist.

The activities of both groups are often encouraged by the silence and indifference of mainstream Adventism.

Although in recent times an effort has been made to inform church members (not always accurately) about the activities of the independent right,[2] little has been done to alert unwary Adventists to the influence of the entrenched liberal left. Ellen G. White stated that "we have far more to fear from within than from without" (*Selected Messages,* 1:122). If this applies to our current situation, then the mainstream Seventh-day Adventist church, caught in the crossfire, should be more concerned about the liberals within than about the independents without.

Inasmuch as liberalism's spurious doctrine of unity is creating confusion and division in local congregations and threatening the worldwide unity of our church, the remainder of this chapter will contrast this doctrine with the biblical one.[3]

## Liberalism's Counterfeit Unity

Satan has a counterfeit for every truth in the Bible (miracles, angels, love, faith, Sabbath, etc.). He even counterfeits our Savior Himself (Mat 24:24). So it should not surprise us that, in his plan to deceive, Satan also offers a counterfeit unity as well. The counterfeit unity being promoted by theological liberalism adopts a two-fold strategy. First, liberalism teaches that God and all good men are for unity, while the devil and all bad people are for division. Second, it confuses true unity with the absence of conflict or the tolerance of error. Let's briefly take a look at these.

**Unity, Not Always Good.** Those who followed the 2000 United States presidential election campaign may be familiar with the political slogan, "I am a uniter, not divider." Unfortunately, many interpret this slogan to mean unity is always good and division is always bad. Christians who have bought into this concept unknowingly extrapolate this campaign slogan into a belief that God is for unity and Satan is for division. They blindly support or promote any views or practices that are carried out in the name of unity.

Such people will not raise a voice against false ideologies like homosexuality, women's ordination, liberal higher criticism, questionable worship styles, divorce and remarriage, etc. because it is "divisive" to do so. And isn't division always bad?

But is this belief correct? Is unity always good and division always bad? Let's not forget that Satan's goal is always to deceive. If good people were all for union and bad folks are all for division, or vice versa, would it not make it very easy for people to detect error? If it could be shown that God always unites and the devil always divides would it not be easy to find our way around in this confused and confusing world?

Against this mistaken notion of unity, we must make three brief comments:

*1. God Is Sometimes a Divider.* The first divider was God who at the creation divided the light from the darkness. This division set the direction for all God's dealings in the natural and spiritual realms. Light and darkness are incompatible. If we try to have both in the same place at once, we attempt the impossible and end by having neither the one nor the other, but dimness rather, and obscurity.

*2. Satan Is Sometimes a Uniter.* Ever since Satan tempted our first parents to partake of the tree of knowledge of good and evil, he has always sought to unite that which God Himself had divided. Thus, we read in the Scriptures about how the "sons of God" married the "daughters of men" (Gen 6: 1ff.). We also read how the priests of Judah "put no difference between the holy and profane, neither have they shewed difference between the unclean and the clean" (Eze 22:26).

*3. Unity Not Always Good, Division Not Always Bad.* Uniting things that should never be united in the first place is never good even where it is possible. Similarly, the arbitrary division of things that should be united is never right. This fact is not only true in the realm of nature and politics, but especially so in moral and religious realms. To divide what should be divided and unite what should be united require a clear knowledge of God's Word and the Holy Spirit's gift of discernment.

Much blood has been shed in tribal wars in Africa because attempts were made during the colonial era not only to divide peoples of the same tribes/nations, but also to forcibly unite tribes and nations that historically never got along. In the same way, there will be confusion in the church if we attempt to unite truth and error, light and darkness. Unity achieved this way is not unity at all; it is compromise. It is sin. And it can be fatal to one's salvation.

Let us be careful that in our quest for unity, we don't attempt to harmonize right and wrong. Writes the apostle Paul: "What fellowship hath righteousness with unrighteousness? And what communion hath light with darkness" (2 Cor 6:14)? Ellen White was emphatic: "Light and darkness cannot harmonize. Between truth and error there is an irrepressible conflict. To uphold and defend the one is to attack and overthrow the other" (*The Great Controversy*, p. 126).

**Unity, Not the Same As Absence of Conflict.** To counterfeit the biblical teaching of unity, Satan seeks to confuse it with peaceful coexistence of truth and error. Those who have embraced this mistaken view think that unity is putting aside theological differences and pretending they don't exist or don't matter. Thus, in some of our churches, there are different Sabbath School classes to allow for different theologies. Pluralism in beliefs and the desire to get along with everyone is confused with true unity.

Proponents and supporters of this counterfeit unity sometimes employ Christ's parables of the wheat and tares, and of the sheep and goats to teach that the church has no business in separating the true from the false. To such, anyone who challenges conflicting or erroneous theologies in the church is "divisive" or "intolerant."

Two brief comments are in order:

*1. Coexistence is not the same as unity.* It is true that in the church today, the wheat grows with the tares, the sheep and the goats coexist, and the farms of the just and the unjust lie side by side in the landscape. It is also true that the hour is coming when Christ Himself will divide the sheep from the goats and separate the tares from the wheat. But while a fruit of unity is harmony, co-existence is not the same as unity.

The question is not about coexistence, but of union and fellowship. The fact that the wheat grows in the same field with the tares does not mean the two should cross-pollinate. The fact that the sheep graze near the goats does not mean that the two should seek to interbreed. The unjust and the just enjoy the same rain and sunshine, but shall they forget their deep moral differences and intermarry? The prophet Amos asked: "Can two walk together except they be agreed" (Amos 3:3)?

*2. Absence of conflict is not the same as unity.* Counterfeit unity is popular because it argues that the absence of conflict is evidence of true unity. But this is not necessarily true. Sometimes, striving to uphold true unity, the unity founded on Christ's Word, inevitably results in conflict and persecution (2 Tim 3:12). We must not purchase unity at the expense of biblical fidelity. Loyalty to God and faithfulness to His truth are jewels more precious than gold or diamond. For these jewels men and women have suffered the loss of property, imprisonment and even death.

In the last days of the world's history, an attempt will be made to enforce this counterfeit unity. Different religions and churches will be united on falsehood, and demand all to follow the path of disobedience. But God's true followers will not embrace this type of unity. They will choose to separate themselves from the path of disobedience (Rev 13 & 14). As someone observed, when confused sheep start over a cliff the individual sheep can save himself only by separating from the flock. For perfect unity at such a time can only mean total destruction .

**The Bible's Teaching about Unity**

The Bible rejects pluralism of belief and practice. It rejects the notion that conflicting or contradictory theological views are legitimate and must be allowed to cohabit in the church. In contrast to today's counterfeit unity, the Bible teaches that members of God's church should uphold a unity of faith and practice.

**Unity of Faith.** Doctrinal unity is the teaching that (1) all God's people should uphold a common faith, and that (2) any new teachings or interpretations purporting to come from God must be in harmony with previous truth communicated to God's true prophets. In the Old Testament, the unity of doctrine was best captured by the prophet Isaiah when he challenged Israel: "To the law and to the testimony; if they speak not according to this word, the light is not in them" (Isa 8:20).

The apostles in the New Testament upheld this teaching when they constantly sought to establish their understanding of Christ's redemptive work by appealing to the Old Testament. The early believers also recognized that the unity which our Lord prayed for (in John 17) is one which is founded on "a common faith" (Titus 1:4; 2 Peter 1:1), "the faith which was once delivered unto the saints" (Jude 3, KJV). In the New Testament church, this spirit of unity was conveyed in a number of ways.

Believers in the early church understood that they did not exist as independent congregations, each choosing to go their own separate ways, believing their own different doctrines, and caring only for their own local interests. Rather, they saw themselves as a God's special commonwealth, comprising Christians in every region of the Roman world.

Sometimes the spirit of unity was done through greetings from church to church (Rom. 16:16; 1 Cor. 16:19; Phil. 4:22). The conveyance of greetings reminded local churches that they belonged to a global network of churches. This spirit of unity was also reflected in the letters of recommendation sent from one church to another or from well-known leaders, commending God-given teachers to other churches (Acts 18:24-28; 2 Cor. 3:1; Rom. 16:1, 2; Col. 4:10).

When, on one occasion, the Corinthians cherished a spirit of independence, the apostle Paul wrote that he had sent Timothy to remind them of "my ways in Christ, as I teach everywhere in every church" (1 Cor. 4:17). He also reprimanded them for their independent attitude: "Did the word of God originate with you? Or are you the only people it has reached?" (1 Cor. 14:36, NIV).

In order to preserve the "unity of the faith" (Eph 4:13), the apostles urged believers to uphold sound teaching (1Tim 6:20; 2 Tim 1:13) and counteract false teaching and false teachers (1 Tim 1:3; 4:1, 6; Titus 1:9-11).

They occasionally exposed the false teachings of certain individuals (1 Tim 1:20; 2 Tim 2:17; 4:19; cf. Phil 4:2-3). Even John, the apostle of love, and Jude, the brother of our Lord Jesus Christ, also found it necessary to call attention to those who were departing from the teachings of the apostles (3 John 9-10; Jude). The Christians in Berea were commended for constantly subjecting the teachings of the apostle Paul to the scrutiny of Scripture (Acts 17:11).

It is, therefore, evident that the New Testament believers embraced a unity of doctrine. If they lived in our day, they would reject any proposals for theological pluralism. The apostle Paul was emphatic when he said, "though we, or an angel from heaven, preach any other gospel unto you than that which we have preached unto you, let him be accursed" (Gal 1:8).

The above understanding of unity is the theological basis for the church's requirement that all Seventh-day Adventists—including our pastors, church leaders, teachers in our institutions, publishers and editors of our church publications—must adhere to all our 27 Fundamental Beliefs. Wherever the biblical teachings summarized in our Fundamental Beliefs are questioned or challenged, the result is always pluralism in beliefs and congregationalism or offshootism in church polity.

**Unity of Practice.** The New Testament also teaches that unity of doctrine should not remain at the intellectual level. It also extends to practice as well as in cooperative actions. This is indicated in a number of ways.

For example, the apostle Paul repeatedly pointed the churches to what was going on in other parts of the Roman empire. He reminded the believers of the common gospel that brought them together (Col. 1:6, 23; 1 Tim. 3:16). In the same way, Corinthian believers were to see themselves united "with all who in every place call upon the name of our Lord, Jesus Christ," who is both "their Lord and ours" (1 Cor. 1:2).

The apostles taught that what happened in other congregations or parts of the world must have their full interest (cf. 2 Cor. 9:2-5; Col. 4:16). They exhorted the believers to participate in all that was being done elsewhere and to accept the guidelines that were offered for all the churches (1 Cor. 16:1-4; 11:16). "This is the rule I lay down in all the churches," writes Paul to the Corinthians (1 Cor. 7:17, NIV), adding that "God is not a God of confusion, but of peace" (1 Cor. 14:33).

Basing themselves on the above theological understanding, Seventh-day Adventists have sought to uphold their worldwide unity through a number ways: reading the same mission stories and reports, giving mission offerings to finance specific projects, and respecting the *Church Manual* and other church policies that have been agreed upon to govern the operation of the church at its different levels. Churches that ignore these practices tend to lack a global vision, tend to be inward looking, and tend to be suspicious or disrespectful of our unique system of church governance.[4] The result is always the same: rebellion and a gravitation towards offshootism of either the independent right or the liberal left.

**Conclusion**

Because unity is a biblical teaching, and because unity among believers is the most powerful witness we can give about Christ, it is not surprising that Satan also has manufactured his own version of unity to confuse and deceive God's people. It attempts to unite that which God has divided, and divide that which God has united. This counterfeit unity poses the greatest threat to the church. For it undermines our doctrinal beliefs and lifestyle practices, our sense of mission, and our unique form of church organization.

Bible-believing Adventists must not remain silent when error is being taught and practiced, and when truth is being undermined. Doing nothing when God's cause is being threatened is equivalent to the "sin of Meroz" (Judges 5:23).

With this thought in mind, I will proceed in the next chapters to share my thoughts on:

> (1) the gospel gimmicks—gospel rock, gospel clowns, gospel cafés, gospel magicians, etc.—being introduced in some of our churches,
> (2) the questionable divorce and remarriage decision voted into the *Church Manual* at the 2000 Toronto General Conference session,
> (3) the rebellious ordinations that have taken place in some North American churches, and
> (4) some of the innovative worship styles being pushed in certain quarters of our church.

**Endnotes**

[1]Contrary to what is held by some, the SDA polity is not just the result of the pragmatic concerns of our pioneers. Instead, it has a very strong theological undergirding. Our pioneers felt the urgency of their time and message; they believed that organizational unity was necessary for both doctrinal unity and the accomplishment of the church's mission. It was this conviction that influenced the subsequent concrete form of our present church government. The success of our church bears eloquent testimony to the importance of such a authoritative (not authoritarian), centralized church structure. For more on this, see Andrew Mustard, "James White and the Development of Seventh-day Adventist Organization, 1844-1881" (Ph.D. Dissertation, Andrews University, 1987).

[2]See, for example, the North American Division's *Issues: The Seventh-day Adventist Church and Certain Private Ministries* (Silver Spring, Md.: North American Division, 1993). This work takes issues with the activities of private organizations such as Hope International, Hartland Institute, Prophecy Countdown, Inc., and Steps to Life. For a response to the above work, see Hope International's *Issues Clarified: A Clarification of Issues: The Seventh-day Adventist Church and Certain Private Ministries* (Eatonville, Wash.: Hope International, 1993); cf. Hartland Institute's *Report and Appeal of Hartland Institute to Seventh-day Adventist Leadership and Worldwide Membership* (Rapidan, Va.: Hartland Institute, 1993). Although some independent self-supporting ministries are often lumped with the independent right, readers should understand that there are many legitimate independent ministries whose goals and methods complement the work of the mainstream church. Recently the Biblical Research Institute also published its "Report on Hope International and Associated Groups" and "Primacy of the Gospel Committe

Report" (see, "Report on Hope International and Associated Groups," *Adventist Review,* August 2000, 34-37; cf. "Decision on Hope International and Associated Groups by a General Conference-Apointed Committee," *Ministry* August 2000, 28-31; these reports are available on the BRI website: *http://www.biblicalresearch.gc.adventist.org/independentminis.htm*). For Hope International's response, see "An Open Letter from Hope International" (August 2000), available on the website: *http://www.hopeint.org/NewHome/Issues/Response.htm#Letter.* For the response from the Hartland Institute, see "Appeal and Report in Response to the Biblical Research Institute Report about Hope International, Hartland Institute and Remnant Ministries" (August 2000), available at the website: *http://www.hartland.edu/appeal_and_report.htm*; cf. Kevin Paulson's "The Crying Stones: A Reply to the Recent Articles in the *Adventist Review* and *Ministry* on Hope International and Associated Ministries'" (August 14, 2000; revised edition September 7, 2000; available on the Great Controversy.Org website: *http://www.greatcontroversy.org/documents/papers/pau-cryi.html*)

[3]For my discussion on counterfeit unity, I am greatly indebted to sermons preached by Richard O'Ffill and Matthew A. Bediako. Some of O'Ffill's sermons are available on audio cassette and obtainable through the American Cassette Ministry (1-800-233-4450; www.americancassette.org); the sermons may also be accessed via his website: *http://www.revivalsermons.org.* My treatment of the biblical teaching on church unity is informed by Raoul Dederen, "The Church: Authority and Unity," Supplement to *Ministry,* May 1995. This excellent paper, originally presented to the Commission on World Church Organization at Cohutta Springs, Georgia, in 1994, presents a biblical basis for church authority—its source, nature, and expression. This work deserves a far wider dissemination and a more serious attention than it has been given. The

entire document, together with another one of his ("Unity and Tensions within the Adventist Church") is available on the GC's Biblical Research Committee website: *http://www.biblicalresearch.gc.adventist.org/documents/churchauthority.htm*

[4]In recent times, there is a mood in certain quarters of the church that seems to be antagonistic to centralized authority or almost any kind of ecclesiastical authority. The reasons often cited for this challenge include the following: (a) the present hierarchical structure of the church has led to authoritarian tendencies by those in leadership roles; (b) power is very far removed from the people—stiffling accountability and greater lay participation in decision making. It must be conceded that challenge to the church's authority is not unique to the Adventist church alone. Authority in almost every area of life is in crisis. Some of the challenges to the church's authority are well justified—especially in situations where leaders have dispositions towards infallibility and dictatorship. Such human inclinations must be confronted wherever they appear in the church. But it must be emphasized that while the attitudes of those running the system may leave much to be desired, there is no compelling reason to jettison our theologically grounded church polity for a congregational model.

It seems to me, however, that the most serious threat to ecclesiastical authority is that which is induced by the spirit of liberalism. Thus, in certain quarters of the church, there are voices against the present church structure. Some are pushing for a certain kind democratization in which even the doctrines of the church must be subject to referendum or vote. Others are seeking growth and efficiency on a model of corporate business. In scholarly circles, some are opposed to our centralized church organization because they feel it stands in their way of academic freedom or dissent. Such scholars consider it an infringement on their liberty to have their conduct and teaching submitted to any kind of ecclesiastical authority or discipline.

There are also a few who are yet to realize that the SDA church is not a Western church, but a worldwide church. They feel frustrated by the growing numbers of believers from the so-called Third World. These individuals—scholars, leaders, and lay people—give the impression that Christianity has its seat in America, Australia, or Europe from which all missionaries and theological wisdom should emanate. They act like parents who have struggled and sacrificed to rear children but are quite unready for their adolescence and the emergence of distinctive personalities. The attitude of this latter group is evident in the manner in which they have conducted themselves with respect to issues that have come up at General Conference sessions. Losing sight of the worldwide nature of the church, they even wish that the church was congregational in its polity, with each region of the church doing its own thing. They seem to be saying: "We don't care if Africa chooses to baptize polygamists, neither should it care if we ordained women." Those holding these views hardly remember that in a worldwide church a baptized polygamist (with his many wives) can transfer their membership to Europe or Australia, and that an ordained woman minister can be sent "from everywhere to everywhere."

# 32

# GOSPEL GIMMICKS:

*"My people have committed two sins: They have forsaken me, the spring of living water, and have dug their own cisterns, broken cisterns that cannot hold water. . . . Now why go to Egypt to drink water from the Shihor? And why go to Assyria to drink water from the River?"* (Jer 2:13, 18, NIV).

Throughout Bible times, and ever since, the clear and persuasive proclamation of God's Word has been the most effective medium to communicate God's truth. The apostle Paul refers to the method as the *foolishness of preaching* (1 Cor 1:21).

Today, however, we seem to be moving away from simple Bible-based preaching to some rather ridiculous and sometimes bizarre gimmicks from the secular world. We may convince ourselves that there is nothing wrong with these gimmicks. But perceptive unbelievers, observing the way we are blindly mimicking worldly methods, may justifiably dismiss our message as the *preaching of foolishness.* Let me explain.

**Gospel Magician?** Recently I received an urgent e-mail from a Seventh-day Adventist graduate student at a public university in the United States. He urged me to share my views with him on "a troubling issue" that had arisen in one of the local churches of his conference. The issue relates to the plan by that local church to invite a "gospel magician" to be guest speaker for a week of prayer. The student expressed his concerns this way:

"I fear that in engaging in practices of magical tricks (that are also done by many secular magicians) we are blurring the line between what is good and what is not. Even though I do not necessarily believe that those engaged in sleight of hand are using any supernatural powers, I fear that the use of illusion to pass across some gospel truth is missing the point and only putting temptation before our children.

"The brethren in the church I referred to do not believe that this is a matter of black and white. They believe that those of us who are opposing this practice in the church (for children's story) and in the church school (for both entertainment and now week of prayer) are 'ultra conservatives' and that we are looking for evil where there is none. I do not know if there is a very clear distinction between black and white in this case. For now (I am still hoping to do further study on this matter), I see it as 'black' because of the potential for evil and because it blurs he line between the good and the bad (these brethren even argue that the Bible is really not opposed to 'magic.') I feel that if the line we are dealing with is gray then we, as a church, need to keep away from it. We should shun all 'appearance' of evil.

"I do not know therefore whether the church has a position on this. I have been challenged to show from the Spirit of prophecy or Bible where this practice is condemned. I have been reminded that the local conference has sponsored some of the church members to seminars and conferences for gospel magicians. I have also been reminded that there were Adventist gospel magicians (or gospel illusionists) performing during the Toronto GC Session. I am groping in the large sea of information and arguments out there to even get some principles I can apply in this matter. I have asked that this particular local church appoint brethren to study the matter and to get a forum to discuss it. I tried the same in the school board, but the overwhelming number of members of this school board 'did not see' anything wrong with the practice. I am preparing to face the church board but cannot go with simple arguments without a biblical reason. Any ideas?"

Few would have thought that a Seventh-day Adventist congregation would one day even consider employing a so-called "gospel magician" to communicate spiritual truth at a church meeting. Yet this is one more evidence of a growing trend to introduce into the church some biblically-questionable styles of worship and evangelism. The surprising thing about this development is that an overwhelming number of members don't see anything wrong with it.

We have had gospel rock and praise dancing in worship services, gospel puppets, gospel clowns, gospel cafés/discos and gospel theatrics/dramas for our outreach to youth, young adults, and the "unchurched." Now, it seems, we must have gospel magicians for our church services and weeks of prayer. By resorting to these "gospel gimmicks," are we in danger of turning away from the *foolishness of preaching* to the *preaching of foolishness*?

In this article I will argue that in so far as gospel gimmicks accommodate the biblical religion to the tastes of unrenewed hearts, such contemporary methods evidence our welcoming of worldliness into the church. Even more, a reliance upon such worldly methods of communicating the gospel is misguided and contrary to the biblical teachings of the Seventh-day Adventist church.

**Worldliness in the Church**

The former Soviet leader Nikita Khruschev reportedly told the following story to teach the need for vigilance.

At a time when there was a wave of petty theft in the USSR, the story goes, the Soviet authorities put guards at many of the state-owned factories. At one of the timber works in Leningrad the guard knew the workers well. The first evening, Pyotr Petrovich came out with a wheelbarrow and, on the wheelbarrow, a great bulky sack with a suspicious-looking object inside.

Guard: "Come on, Petrovich. What have you got there?"

Petrovich: "Just sawdust and shavings."

Guard: "Come on, I wasn't born yesterday. Tip it out."

Petrovitch did, and out came nothing but sawdust and shavings. So he was allowed to put it all back again and go home. The same thing happened every night all week, and the guard was getting extremely frustrated. Finally his curiosity overcame his frustration.

Guard: "Petrovich, I know you. Tell me what you're smuggling out of here, and I'll let you go."

Petrovich: "Wheelbarrows."

While we may laugh at this story, we may also need to remember that in he arena of contemporary worship and outreach methods the laugh is on us as Bible-believing Adventist Christians. We have set up patrols to check for worldliness around us by developing our own schools, seminaries, radio and TV stations, publishing houses, book centers, etc. But the devil has wheeled worldliness and paganism right past our eyes into some of these institutions of our church. And many don't see it, let alone see anything wrong with it.

What is more, we are actually importing and actively promoting these questionable methods of worship and evangelism from both the secular world and from other religions and churches. In some instances Adventists have gone outside to study these methods at non-Adventist theological seminaries or have attended the training seminars on worship, soul-winning and leadership at Willow Creek and other inter-denominational, ecumenical, and charismatic organizations and churches. Yet we fail to recognize that when we fundamentally change our method of proclaiming spiritual truth, we change the message itself. And when we change the message of God, we change the God of the message.

Because these gimmicks compromise the credibility of our message, Adventists have been counseled against copying methods found in other churches.

**Our Temptation.** Throughout our history, there has always been a temptation for our ministers to pattern our practices after other churches. Ellen G. White warned against this in her day: "A new order of things has come into the ministry. There is a desire to pattern after other churches" (*Signs of the Times,* Dec. 27, 1899). She expressed her concerns about the influence of other churches on our ministers: "Some ministers are adopting the customs of other churches, copying their habits and manner of labor" (ibid., May 25, 1882).

Warning of the dangers inherent in responding to other churches' invitations to learn from them and employ their methods of labor, Mrs. White wrote: "They may desire us to unite with them and accept their plans, and may make propositions in regard to our course of action which may give the enemy an advantage over us" (*General Conference Bulletin,* April 13, 1891).

In embracing Mrs. White's counsel, Seventh-day Adventists are not suggesting that they alone have the truth. The Word of God is clear that every human being in God's world has at least a little light (Jn 1:9; Jas 4:17) and that God has revealed Himself in nature, history, human experience, and in many other ways (Ps 19; Rom 1 & 2; Heb 1:1, 2). Consequently, Adventists hold that some divine truth can be found in the secular world (whether atheistic or materialistic), in pagan and non-Christian religions, as well as in all Christian denominations—Catholic, Orthodox, Protestant, and Pentecostal. God is truth and the ultimate source of all truth. Wherever truth is found, we must embrace it.

**Present Truth.** Adventists, however, insist that whatever light can be found in other churches, they have also and much more besides. Believing that God has raised up their church as His end-time repository of truth, Adventists hold that they have the *present truth,* the *everlasting gospel* for these last days.

The issue, then, is not whether other faiths or churches have some truth. Instead, the question is whether our ministers ought to look to other churches for new light. Given our self-understanding as God's end-time depository of truth, is it necessary for us to go to churches that are still living in spiritual darkness to discover new light or additional truth from them? If those churches represent "Babylon," and if it is true that "Babylon is fallen," how can we call upon our brothers and sisters in "Babylon" to "Come out of her, My people" (Rev 18:4), when we ourselves are now returning to "Babylon" to receive instruction from her?

**Broken Cisterns.** Centuries ago, the prophet Jeremiah spoke out against this tendency on the part of God's people to mimic the gimmicks found in other faiths: "My people have committed two sins: They have forsaken me, the spring of living water, and have dug their own cisterns, broken cisterns that cannot hold water. . . . Now why go to Egypt to drink water from the Shihor? And why go to Assyria to drink water from the River?" (Jer 2:13, 18 NIV).

Ellen White explained why we must not drink from the broken cisterns: "We are in danger of making blunders in our missionary effort, in danger of failing to realize how essential is the work of the Holy Spirit upon the heart. A new order of things has come into the ministry. There is a desire to pattern after other churches, and simplicity and humility are almost unknown. Young ministers who desire to be original introduce new ideas and new plans for labor. They open revival meetings and call large numbers into the church. But when the excitement is over, where are the converted ones? Repentance for sin is not felt. The sinner is entreated to believe in Christ and accept Him, without any regard for his past life of sin and rebellion, and the heart is not broken. There is no contrition of soul. The professedly converted ones have not fallen upon the Rock Christ Jesus" (*Signs of the Times,* Dec. 27, 1889).

Earlier in our history, following the disappointment, Mrs. White warned our members not to seek "new light" even from denominations that had their roots in the Advent movement but had not accepted advancing truth: "The different parties of professed Advent believers have each a little truth, but God has given all these truths to His children who are being prepared for the day of God. He has also given them truths that none of these parties know, neither will they understand. Things which are sealed up to them, the Lord has opened to those who will see and are ready to understand. *If God has any new light to communicate, He will let His chosen and beloved understand it, without their going to have their minds enlightened by hearing those who are in darkness and error"* (*Early Writings,* p. 124, emphasis mine).

She continued: "I was shown the necessity of those who believe that we are having the last message of mercy, being separate from those who are daily imbibing new errors. I saw that neither young nor old should attend their meetings; for it is wrong to thus encourage them while they teach error that is a deadly poison to the soul and teach for doctrines the commandments of men. The influence of such gatherings is not good. If God has delivered us from such darkness and error, we should stand fast in the liberty wherewith He has set us free and rejoice in the truth. *God is displeased with us when we go to listen to error, without being obliged to go"* (ibid., pp. 124, 125, my emphasis).

In spite of these warnings, a growing number of our members and leaders "don't see anything wrong" with today's gospel gimmicks. We are adopting and actively promoting these worldly entertainment methods for our own worship and evangelistic services. Regrettably, those who raise concerns are mislabeled "ultra-conservatives." Why is this so?

### Why We "Don't See Anything Wrong"

Granted, many within our ranks who are resorting to the various types of gospel gimmicks—gospel rock, gospel clowns, gospel cafés, gospel magicians, etc.—sincerely desire to see spiritual renewal in the church and want to attract new souls to Christ. Many who advocate such things are persuaded that God will use these modified forms of entertainment from other churches to win and retain young people in our own church. Without judging their motives and sincerity, I'd like to suggest a few other reasons why some of us don't see anything wrong with these contemporary innovations.

**1. Desperation.** There are those of us whose witness and example as parents and teachers have been unconvincing to our young people.

The youth have observed that while we rightly affirm "the Bible and the Bible only," many of us do not have a living experience with the Bible's divine Author. Baptism seems more a graduation ceremony than the start of a new life in Christ. Our identity as God's "remnant" church makes us complacent instead of inspiring us to fulfill our divine mission to the world. We assert repeatedly that "we have the truth," but very often the truth does not have us. Our preaching, teaching and evangelism may cram the mind with information without bringing about the deep soul searching and humility of heart that results in transforming the character. Our ethical positions on social issues reflect pragmatic concerns rather than fidelity to Scripture. And instead of our worship being reverently vibrant, it tends to be either dull and sterile or emotional and superficial.

Having observed the above inconsistencies and hypocrisies, many of our young people are restless to sever all links with what they perceive as hypocritical faith. Their parents and teachers, in sheer desperation to hold them in the fold, encourage every worldly fad, even if it means importing "gospel rock," "gospel clowns," or "gospel magicians" into the church.

Although some of us who fit this description may sense that these new forms of worship and outreach are incompatible with biblical Christianity, we find ourselves unable to oppose the methods because, in fact, we share the same worldly values and do practically nothing for the Lord. On the other hand, our children and students want to be active in the church. But the only way they know how is through different forms of worldly idolatry.

**2. Weak Church Leaders.** Unfortunately, some of us pastors and church leaders are sometimes to blame for the introduction of gospel gimmicks into church. We appear to put popularity, job security, position, and the illusion of outward success above our duty to the Chief Shepherd. We seem to fear that if we were to take a stand against these forms of worldliness in our churches, we would create enemies and threaten our support among our constituencies.

In some instances, we have done less than we might have to lead our congregations in the direction of revival and meaningful evangelism. We seldom preach Bible-based messages. With hazy preaching and teachings paralyzed by uncertainty, our churches are dying. Consequently, when something *wrong* comes along in the name of evangelism and worship innovation, we have already forfeited our moral right to challenge it. We find it easier to jump on the bandwagon of what is *new* instead of courageously holding on to what is *true.*

**3. Denial of Faith.** Another reason why we may not see anything wrong with gospel gimmicks is that some of us have embraced liberal higher criticism. Consequently we do not really believe in the efficacy of God's Word to draw souls to Christ and keep them in the faith. We also do not believe that ours is the end-time church of Bible prophecy to which other faiths should come for truth. To those of us with this view, our church is not the remnant, but only "part of the remnant." Although we may accept some aspects of our faith, such as the Sabbath and our health principles, in the honesty of our hearts we do not see the uniqueness of our message, the distinctiveness of our identity, the end-time dimension of our hope, and the urgency of our mission.

Ethical integrity suggests that if we have lost the faith and certainties of our pioneers and cannot regain them, we should resign from our denominational employment. But not all of us have the courage to do so. (Some announce their views only after retirement). So, in our desire to shed the "cult" and "sectarian" labels that have often been used to characterize Seventh-day Adventists, we actively import gospel gimmicks from both the secular world and other religions and churches.

**4. Lack of Conversion.** There is another reason why some of us who advocate gospel gimmicks don't see anything wrong with them. Perhaps, unknown even to ourselves, we have never been fully converted. Our tastes and affections are still in the world. We are honest when we say that we see nothing wrong with these biblically-questionable innovations. This is because spiritual things are spiritually discerned.

Thus when the sanctuaries which were dedicated to the worship of a holy God are transformed into auditoriums to worship the god of entertainment, we do not see anything wrong. We may congratulate ourselves for finally coming up with "a contemporary church program that meets the needs of our generation." We don't realize that the God of this world has blinded us (see 2 Cor 4:4). Without a true conversion, there is no hope of changing our minds against the use of worldly methods in worship or evangelism.

**Worldly Entertainment to Communicate Gospel?**

It is often suggested that before we can reach the world with the gospel, we have to employ the world's methods to proclaim Christ's truth. But this reasoning is indefensible for at least two important reasons: (1) Worldly methods trivialize the message; (2) Worldly methods are contrary to biblical teaching.

**1. Trivializing the Message.** Even if we are actually proclaiming the everlasting gospel, we trivialize and cheapen the importance of the message when we adopt the world's entertainment methods to communicate the truth. Entertainment is entertainment and is generally not taken seriously by the public as a vehicle to proclaim important messages. If we adopt entertainment elements such as rock music, drama, clowns, puppets, and magicians, our message will fail to make any real moral demand upon the hearers.

If it is true that rock music (disguised as praise music and praise dancing) is the most effective medium to reach young people today, why is it that math teachers and chemistry professors don't set their classes to heavy-beat and hip-swinging music? Why don't politicians employ clowns and illusionists to present their political messages?

Common sense tells us that these entertainment media are not the most credible methods to communicate serious messages. A doctor, meeting an apprehensive patient, does not dress like a clown in order to tell his patient that she has cancer. If a doctor who wants to be taken seriously does not resort to this kind of frivolity, isn't it folly to announce God's message of warning and judgment to a dying world by resorting to entertainment?

Jesus did not use the gimmicks of entertainment to proclaim his Sermon on the Mount. On the day of Pentecost, Peter did not set up a drum set or ask Mary to lead out in praise dancing to announce the resurrection of Jesus and His enthronement in heaven. And Paul did not persuade people on Mars Hill using gospel magicians.

We are self-deceived if we believe that drums, disco lights, costumes, illusions, and loud noises are capable of representing the infinite holiness and mercy of God to a lost generation. Those of us who resort to these worldly gimmicks can only do so because we serve a different god from the One the apostles worshiped.

The apostle Paul makes it clear that the pre-eminent method of proclaiming spiritual truth is by the spoken word. "It pleased God by the foolishness of preaching to save them that believe. . . . Because the foolishness of God is wiser than men; and the weakness of God is stronger than men" (1 Cor 1:21, 25).

**2. Contrary to Scripture.** It is a mistake for us to think that the world will embrace our message when we use worldly methods. The New Testament tells us that when Christ came to the world, "the world knew him not" (Jn 1:10), for He was "not of this world" (Jn 8:23). What makes us believe that we can succeed where Christ failed?

Jesus Himself mentioned that Christians "are not of the world, even as I am not of it" (Jn 17:16; cf. vv. 9, 14). He stated emphatically that the works of this world are evil (Jn 7:7). He said that true believers are not of the world and prayed that they should be kept from its evil ways (Jn 17:14, 15). Because the Spirit of God stands against the spirit of the world (1 Cor 2:12), the gospel should not be presented in such a way as to be coupled with the standards of the world. "Be not conformed to this world: but be ye transformed . . . that ye may prove what is that good, and acceptable, and perfect, will of God" (Rom 12:2).

The apostles also taught that "friendship with the world is hatred toward God" (Jas 4:4) and that the world "pollutes" the believer (cf. 1:27). Therefore, Christians are urged: "Love not the world, neither the things that are in the world. If any man love the world, the love of the Father is not in him. For all that is in the world, the lust of the flesh, and the lust of the eyes, and the pride of life, is not of the Father, but is of the world" (1 Jn 2:15-16).

We depart from biblical teaching when we think that today's so-called gospel rock, gospel clowns, gospel magicians, and other forms of gospel entertainment can legitimately be employed to communicate spiritual truth. The Scriptures teach that the world is on its own, "without hope and without God" (Eph 2:12). Therefore, instead of borrowing worldly methods to reach the world, Christians are sent forth like the apostle Paul, "to open their eyes, and to turn them from darkness to light, and from the power of Satan unto God" (Acts 26:18).

### Bait-and-Hook Evangelism?

It is often suggested that because most people—especially young people—don't want to listen to the gospel, we have to "bait" them with gospel entertainment and gimmicks. Once we attract them by these contemporary methods, then we can "hook" them with the true message. The proof text to justify the use of worldly methods to reach people is Paul's statement:

"And unto the Jews I became as a Jew, that I might gain the Jews. . . . To them that are without law, as without law . . . that I might gain them that are without law. To the weak became I as weak, that I might gain the weak: I am made all things to all men, that I might by all means save some" (1 Cor 9:20-22). Thus, some argue, we must employ whatever people like to hear in order to get a hearing for the gospel.

But the context of the passage reveals that Paul was talking about *preaching* (see v. 16ff.), not the use of worldly methods of evangelism. The apostle stated that in his preaching and witnessing he always tailored his message to suit the level of understanding of his hearers. In other words, he always spoke *appropriately.* Therefore 1 Corinthians 9 does not teach that Paul employed or encouraged the "bait and hook" method for evangelism. On the contrary, he persuaded the people from the Word of God using preaching as his method.

Moreover, God's end-time church has been divinely entrusted with the everlasting gospel. This stewardship is a great privilege. But it is also a solemn responsibility. For "it is required in stewards, that a man be found faithful" (1 Cor 4:2). The faithfulness to which the church has been called compels us to preserve the integrity of the message by preserving the method we employ to communicate it.

The apostle Paul therefore urges us not to try to "catch" people with the entertainment "bait" so we can "hook" them with the gospel. He writes: "For our exhortation was not of deceit, nor of uncleanness, nor in guile. But as we were allowed of God to be put in trust with the gospel, even so we speak; not as pleasing men, but God, which trieth our hearts. For neither at any time used we flattering words, as ye know, nor a cloak of covetousness; God is witness" (1 Thess 2:3-5).

Note the following two facts from this passage. First, the Greek word translated "deceit" (*plané*) means error. The ultimate issue on any subject should always be truth. "The Gospel is either true or it is not. Paul stakes his entire life on the truth of the Gospel. There's a tendency in our day to judge values by the wrong standard. 'Does it work?' is often asked more than 'Is it true?' The test of the validity of the Gospel is truth. The danger in preaching to attract an audience is obvious. It is too readily disguised to provide solutions that work rather than truth that is to be confronted. The acid test for every sermon or Bible class must be: *Is it true?* If Christ is presented [merely] as a means by which we can be successful, happy, or whatever, we are betraying the Gospel of God. We are guilty of deceit and error even though we may be successful in drawing followers."[1]

Second, the Greek word *dolos,* translated "guile" in 1 Thessalonians 2:3, means "trick" or "bait" (or "craft," "subtilty," or "decoy"). There is no place for trickery or manipulation in evangelism. Thus the NIV translates the passage as: "For the appeal we make does not spring from error or impure motives, nor *are we trying to trick you"* (my emphasis).

We must not employ "deceit" in the proclamation of the gospel. Our message must determine the method. Paul tells us in 1 Corinthians 1 that when the Jews wanted to see miracles and the Greeks wanted to hear worldly wisdom, he refused to bow to their tastes and desires because God had commanded him to preach the gospel. Effective preaching is always the preferred biblical method to proclaim the gospel.

### Encouraging Youth Involvement

We sometimes hear that the use of these contemporary methods of entertainment is the only way to involve young people in church life. Advocates argue that because young people have many wonderful talents and abilities, the church must give them "a piece of the pie"—just as was done for our youthful Adventist pioneers. They further claim that failing to allow them to employ their unique gifts in the worship and outreach activities of the church makes young people lose interest in the church.

This argument is not entirely accurate, nor is it biblical. It is true that many of our Adventist pioneers were young people. For example, James White began preaching at 23 and Ellen White was telling her visions publicly at 17. J. N. Andrews held evangelistic meetings at age 21, and by age 24 he had published 35 articles. Uriah Smith became editor of the *Review* at age 23, having already written a 35,000-word poem called "The Warning Voice of Time and Prophecy" that the *Review* published in installments the year before. What set these youthful pioneers apart from many of today's youth is that they were *converted* and *studious Bible students.* As such, they would not bring themselves to using worldly entertainment methods in the Lord's service.

Many of today's young people have special gifts and abilities. But giftedness in performing certain functions does not necessarily mean those abilities should be employed in spiritual worship or outreach. The fact that a person can play a set of drums, or dance, or even perform magical illusions and acrobatics does not mean we need gospel rock, gospel dancing, gospel magicians or gospel acrobats in church. If this were the case, we would have to insist that gospel footballers and gospel baseball pitchers should use their special gifts during worship services. Rather, we must seek to encourage young people who are truly converted to use their gifts in ways appropriate to the worship service of the Holy God, while not putting them in positions that expose them too early to the dangers of spiritual pride and arrogance (see 1 Tim 3:6).

**The Foolishness of Preaching, Not the Preaching of Foolishness**

The clear proclamation of God's Word has always been the most effective method of communicating God's truth. Because this method went contrary to the gospel gimmicks of his day, the apostle Paul referred to it as "the foolishness of preaching." Adventist evangelist Carlyle B. Haynes has aptly illustrated the difference between preaching centered on the Word of God and preaching using the worldly method.

**Gospel Gimmicks.** Speaking to young ministers several decades ago, Haynes wrote:

"I once attended a meeting conducted by a well-known Adventist evangelist who had achieved an outstanding reputation, and whom many younger ministers were consulting for suggestions to improve their work. Some were diligently copying this man's manner of presentation. I had been out of the country for five years in mission work. Reports came to me regarding this man, who was looked upon as a successful winner of souls. His methods, which were certainly innovations among us, were the subject of much discussion.

"I was eager to get a firsthand look at this man and his techniques. My appointments brought me to the city where he was conducting an evangelistic campaign, and I made plans to hear and observe him in action. Mingling with the large number of people streaming in to the meetings, I sat in the middle of the audience, where I could see and hear without difficulty.

"The tabernacle was well lighted and decorated. . . . On the rafters above the platform were hung many lights, and on each side of the platform two spotlights centered on the preacher.

"There was music, much music—instrumental, vocal, choral, solos, duets, quartets, and two little tots who sang an amusing ditty which brought a round of laughter and a handclap or two. Then came an impressive theme song, which many seemed to know and I had never heard. At its close the preacher entered in a sort of hush.

"He attracted everyone's attention, including mine. I was not quite prepared for this. He could not fail to catch attention. Everything had apparently been done with that in mind. He was dressed in spotless white, with white tie, white socks, white shoes. Even the Bible he carried was bound in white. A woman at my back exclaimed breathlessly to her companion, 'Isn't he a honey?' and I had to agree. He was indeed. From that first moment he was the focus of attraction. No one could hear, see, or think of anything else but that 'honey' of a preacher. His words were little noticed, yet no one moved his eyes from the speaker, and all heads swung around with him as he stood or moved about in the glare of the spotlights. . . .

"I didn't listen, but I certainly looked. I couldn't help looking. It was an impressive performance. What he said, I don't know; but I can remember yet what he did as he skillfully moved about the platform. . . .

"Returning to my hotel room, I tried to recall what he may have read from the Bible. I could not remember his opening that beautiful white Bible at all. While I am sure he must have done so, I did not notice it. The last thing I remember passing through my mind before I sank into slumber was, 'He certainly is a "honey." '

"Traveling about the country for some months after that, I ran into a considerable number of white suits and spotlights. They broke out like an epidemic everywhere. The imitation ran its course, as epidemics do, and then subsided—I hope.

"I mention the incident only because I desire to contrast it with another experience that occurred while I was a pastor in New York City. For a number of years I had heard reports about the ministry of a great British expositor, George Campbell Morgan, pastor of London's Westminster Chapel. He had been making annual trips to America for Bible conferences, but I had not heard him. I had, however, read all his books. . . ."

**Biblical Preaching.** Haynes continued his advice to ministers:

"Learning that Morgan was coming to New York City to conduct a two-week series of studies in the Fifth Avenue Presbyterian Church, I was delighted at the prospect of hearing this great preacher and arranged my schedule so that I could attend these nightly meetings without interruption. They were to start on a Monday night which I thought to be a poor night to begin.

"I arrived at the church a half hour before the meeting was to begin. Knowing the church accommodated 2,500 easily, I had no worry about finding a seat. But I was wrong; the seats were all taken. The ushers directed me into the gallery, and fortunately one seat was left there. With a sigh of relief I sat down, astonished beyond measure that 2,500 people would turn out like this on a Monday night.

"The pastor and Dr. Morgan came onto the rostrum quietly and sat down. The congregation sang an old hymn, and during the singing I looked closely at the famous preacher. Never had I seen a more unprepossessing man in the pulpit. He was tall, lanky, awkward, and I thought I might hear his bones rattle if there were not so much rustling by the audience. His clothing was plain, and there was nothing conspicuous about him.

"After the pastor's prayer and simple introduction, Dr. Morgan walked to the pulpit, opened the Bible—not a white one—and in a pleasing voice, but entirely without dramatic effect, read the Scripture passage and immediately began to explain it. I am glad that I examined him before he began speaking, for I never noticed him again during the whole hour. Instead, I was utterly absorbed and entranced at the meanings he was bringing out of the treasure-house of the Word of God. It was one of the most thrilling hours of my life. I had never experienced anything like it before. And it was repeated nightly for two weeks.

"Dr. Morgan had no graces of gesture, no spectacular delivery, and no eloquence in the usual sense. He used no charts, blackboard, pictures, screen, or gadgets of any kind. Nothing in his talk, movements, dress, or manner attracted attention to himself or diverted attention from the Bible. His tremendous power was in what he did with and by the Word of God.

"I was in another world in five minutes, not because of any elocution or oratorical ability. He talked quite casually and in a conversational tone, reading with deep reverence and impressive feeling the passage he was to explore. I forgot the people about me, forgot the church, forgot the speaker, forgot everything but the wonders of the world into which I had been led . . . .

"I went home dazed with wonder at the effectiveness of the Bible alone as the source of great preaching. . . .

"I want to impress upon you that such preaching is wholly within the reach of every one of you, the most powerful that any man can ever use. Throw away your accessories, discard your gadgets and pictures, discontinue your shows and playlets, stop relying on entertainment and theatrical displays, and get back again to the simple, plain, powerful exposition of the Word.

"When I returned home the night after Dr. Morgan's first study, the prayer that burst from my deeply moved heart was, 'O God, make me a preacher of Thy divine Word, and help me never to rely on anything else.'"[2]

May this be our prayer, too.

---

**Endnotes**

[1]Gary W. Demarest, *The Communicator's Commentary Series,* Volume 9, *1, 2 Thessalonians, 1, 2 Timothy, Titus* (Waco, Texas: Word Books, 1984), p. 54.

[2]Carlyle B. Haynes, *Carlyle B. Haynes Speaks to Young Ministers* (Nashville, Tenn.: Southern Publishing Association, 1968), pp. 31-36.

# 33

# When Error Is Legislated

I was a delegate to the 2000 Toronto General Conference Session. More than any other issue, this session will be remembered for its controversial vote on divorce and remarriage. To many, this issue has come to symbolize the domestication of liberal ideas in the church.

Over the course of two days (Tuesday, July 4 and Wednesday, July 5), delegates at the session vigorously debated a proposed document on marriage, divorce, and remarriage before referring it back to the *Church Manual* Committee for further study. The understanding was that the issue would be taken up again at the next GC session in St. Louis, Missouri, USA, in the year 2005. However, during the opening minutes of the last business session on Friday, July 7, with only a small fraction of delegates present to vote, supporters of the document employed a series of parliamentary procedures to rescind the earlier decision and then voted the document for inclusion in the *Church Manual*. This questionable decision is now contained in Chapter 15 of the newly revised *Church Manual*.

Why should Bible-believing church members and pastors be concerned about what happened in Toronto? And how should they relate to this questionable policy now enshrined in the *Church Manual*? This chapter captures my views on the issue.

Immediately after the controversial decision, I was interviewed by a number of Adventist news outlets—spanning a wide spectrum of theological leanings. The following interview was conducted by the news editor of *Adventist Today*, a liberal publication based in La Sierra, California. Because we tend to stand on opposite sides of theological issues, this interview can be read as a conservative-liberal exchange on the subject.

**"The Parliamentary Maneuver" As Coup d'Etat[1]**

Dr. Samuel Koranteng-Pipim, a native of Ghana, seemed to be in the middle of every potential conservative-liberal debate during the entire 57th GC conference session. His cries for "theological integrity!" reverberated through the SkyDome on more than one occasion. More than any other individual, it was Pipim that represented the loyal opposition to the recommended divorce and remarriage amendment that was passed in a surprise parliamentary maneuver on Friday morning, July 7, 2000.

Pipim, although now living and working in the United States, was a delegate of the African Indian Ocean Division [AID], as he has been for every general conference session going back to New Orleans in 1985. He is currently employed by the Michigan Conference, serving as the Director of Public Campus Ministries, whose office is presently located on the campus of the University of Michigan in Ann Arbor, Michigan.

Pipim's continuing status as AID delegate despite working in the United States is explained by the fact that he has continued to play an active role in the African Division church work. He regularly returns to teach theology and ethics to their students, conduct ministerial workshops, and speak at various camp meetings. Since 1995, he had represented the AID at the GC's Biblical Research Institute Committee (BRICOM).

AT [*Adventist Today*] spotted Sam Pipim late Friday afternoon on July 7 as he was strolling through the exhibit hall near the AT booth in his yellow Ghanaian garb. When approached by AT, he was delighted to talk and in good spirits. When he saw my AT name tag his face actually lit up in a friendly smile, saying he read AT regularly and respected the fact that AT was not afraid to debate and take a stand on controversial issues, though he usually disagreed with its viewpoint. Pipim exudes a charming, radiant mental energy and self assurance. The discussion we had there was brief but productive. It was agreed that we would continue our discussion via e-mail. The framework for this interview is based on that meeting, supplemented by the subsequent exchange of e-mails that followed from it.

AT: Dr. Pipim, your voice echoed several times in the Toronto SkyDome. Were there any specific issues that were of particular concern to you?

SKP: Every issue was important to me, but I was particularly interested in theological issues, since they concern the message and mission of the church. Moreover, just as the accountants and treasurers spoke forcefully on the auditing procedures in the church, you should expect a systematic theologian to show keen interest in doctrinal proposals suggested for inclusion in the *Church Manual*. The auditors were seeking to preserve the financial integrity of the church. I was arguing for the theological integrity of the church.

AT: You were obviously keenly interested in the matter that was passed this morning. Will you tell me what your thoughts are concerning what happened?

SKP: Certainly! First of all, I want to make it clear that the General Conference spoke this morning, and I therefore accept that decision and will respect it as such. But I'm confident that when the issue is sufficiently explored, it will be reconsidered at a future GC session. My concern is that as a church, we are slowly legitimizing a process which I describe as "legislate now, find biblical answers later." This happened with the questionable Annual Council decision on baptizing wives of polygamists (1941);[2] then came another questionable decision on ordaining women as elders (1975 and 1984). Each of these Annual Council decisions have caused deep polarization and confusion in Churches. Now divorce and remarriage (2000) has been added to the list of controversial decisions.

But this most recent decision in Toronto is worse than the previous ones. For whereas polygamy and women elders were Annual Council actions, the divorce and remarriage decision was made at General Conference session. As such, it is now going to be enshrined in the *Church Manual*! But as I said, the decision this morning is now the church's official position. I will respect it as such, though I reserve the right to question it's theological legitimacy. That must be emphasized, and everything else that I say must be taken in that context.

It is no secret that I am not happy about the means by which the Divorce and

Remarriage amendment was passed this morning. The thought that went through my mind as it was being passed, was that these developed country delegates must think that those of us from the so-called third world are awfully dumb. As you must have seen, those from the developing world are generally more conservative and tended to have more reservations concerning this amendment. Well, just because we speak with a different accent, [he does not mention color] does not mean that we cannot think or learn. Some of these delegates from the non-industrialized world who saw this unfolding are prominent government officials in their own countries. They cherish and seek to uphold the ideals of representative democracy in their home nations. They are very intelligent and godly. I am afraid they will learn the wrong lessons from this.

Remember that the conservatives have numbers on their side. If we wanted to play power politics, we could have forced our views on North America and the world church. But I don't believe in that. Issues involving principles or ideas should be decided on merit, not on politics or parliamentary tricks. That's why I preferred to leave it up to a commission to study the matter dispassionately rather than having things settled on the floor in the heat of debate, as much as I enjoy that process. If the conservatives had tried to use force to get our way, I would have gotten up to oppose it passionately. This should not be about winning. It should be about coming to the right decision.

AT: Does that mean you did not hear Garry Hodgkin get up yesterday afternoon and announce what he was going to do this morning?[3]

SKP: No, I did not. I'm not sure many of our people did. Otherwise they'd have been there in great numbers. You know that the divorce remarriage issue was a hot potato item. The chair persons were at times confused.[4]

Delegates offered conflicting suggestions on how to proceed. But it was clear to most of us that the matter had all been settled for this session, and would not come up again until St. Louis. So we were caught completely by surprise. Hardly anybody from our delegation was there. It was Friday, the last working day of the week. Many went to confirm their air tickets for their departure on Sunday. Remember that there were rumors of an Air Canada strike. Others went shopping and packing.

AT: But most of the N[orth] A[merican] D[ivision] delegates were also absent.

SKP: Yes, but proportionally, I think our delegations were less represented. There were only about 150 delegates present altogether. How can it be fair for them to overturn a decision that passed with most delegates present?

AT: Do you accept parliamentary procedure as valid rules under which to conduct church business?

SKP: Oh, yes. I want to emphasize that what they did, procedurally or legally, was O.K. When a church business meeting is called, if you are there, you are there; if not, it is still a valid meeting. Some are questioning whether the decision was valid, given the fact that a quorum was not there. I say that's a waste of time and disagree with those who wish to make that an issue now, though I think it true that if quorum had been challenged then, that challenge would have been upheld.

But it is possible for things to be legal, while still violating the spirit of fairness. The question before us is not whether the action was legal in a technical sense, but whether the individuals from the industrialized countries acted "rightly and fairly" in a more fundamental sense.

Those who are really pushing this new view of divorce and remarriage—most of them from these industrialized countries such as North America, Australia, and Europe; regions that constitute less than 10% of the world Adventist membership—came in and staged their theological coup d'etat by utilizing parliamentary procedures to rescind the previous action, cut off all debate and overturn a prior decision taken by an overwhelming majority of delegates.

I say it was a coup d'etat, because the proponents decided to do so when the overwhelming majority of delegates from Africa, Inter-America, South America, the Pacific Islands, etc, were not there. Only about 150 people [about 7 or 8% of GC delegates] were present. Do you understand the dynamics? 150 people from certain segments of the industrialized countries took advantage of the absence of a large segment of the delegates, and over-turned a prior decision by an overwhelming majority of delegates.

Some may dispute the 150 number, but I believe my criticism would still be valid, even if 50% of the delegates took the decision to overturn the previous actions[[5] read this endnote.]

Remember, Dennis, the issue was considered so important that they had to suspend nominating committee meetings so its members could be there to speak to this issue. That was Tuesday and Wednesday. And with an almost full house of 2000 delegates present, we voted that the entire document, bearing in mind our concerns, be referred to the *Church Manual* Committee.

I have spoken to many people, including people who disagree with me theologically; I'm talking about even liberals. And they all concede that the action was really wrong. It didn't show maturity, sensitivity, or a sense of fairness.

Now our people from the developing countries can be faulted for not being there. Perhaps they were too naive or trusting, oblivious to the many ideological undercurrents at GC sessions. Undoubtedly, they have themselves to blame for this theologically questionable position now enshrined in the *Church Manual.*

AT: Let's set aside the parliamentary issue for one moment and consider the merits of the amendment that got passed, against what it will replace. I know you object to certain elements in it, but as a package, what do you think of it?

SKP: As a whole, I think there is much to like. There is no doubt that it appears more redemptive than what it replaces. Among its strengths is that, instead of the old *Church Manual* which began with a statement on "divorce and remarriage", the amended document begins with a positive statement on marriage. That chapter in the *Church Manual* now is titled, "Marriage, Divorce and Remarriage." I think that is positive. We distort things when we begin discussing a negative, ("Divorce and Remarriage") without first putting it in the context of something that is very positive (Marriage).

Another positive aspect of the document was the attempt to make it a little more user-friendly.' For example, instead of talking about "disfellowshipping", it talks about "removal from membership"; it's a change in terminology. Also, instead of talking about "the guilty party" in a marriage situation, it uses the phrase "the spouse who has violated the marriage vow"—a phrase which means the same thing, but doesn't look so judgmental. These were positive changes that I think they brought together, and I am happy about that.

AT: Now tell me about the problems you see in it.

**Role Distinctions in Marriage**

SKP: Let's start with the issue of role differentiation in marriage. For the first time, this document sets forth a new view of marriage, which I would describe as an "egalitarian" form of marriage. Some call it a "partnership" form of marriage.

AT: But you are not saying that there is something wrong with the idea that both partners in a marriage relationship are in principle equal, are you?

SKP: Of course not. The equality of men and a women is not an issue, though liberals and feminists try to portray it that way. God created Adam and Eve as equals with neither superior to the other. They were created as equal but complementary spiritual beings with different roles for male and female to govern the home and the first church. Role distinctions do not imply inequality.

The document that was initially submitted to the delegates for consideration suggested that male-headship and female submission began at the Fall, instead of its inception at the creation. The subtle implication here is that male headship may have been done away with at the cross.

By taking away role distinctions at creation, the document set a theological foundation for not only women's ordination, but by logical extension, the condoning of homosexuality and homosexual marriages. After all, if the roles of men and women in their relationship with each other are completely negotiable in God's view, then why not a homosexual relationship?

Many people may not appreciate the full implications of recognizing role differentiation. To them, homosexuality and women's ordination issues were unrelated to the discussion on the floor. In fact, one associate editor of *Adventist Review* expressed "surprise" at my comment. He apparently believes the comment by one delegate that those of us questioning the theological fuzziness of the proposal were appealing to those with "a scare mentality."[6]

I may be wrong. But my guess is that many have not seriously thought through the theological implications of the issues involved in the theologically ambiguous proposal. In fact, I myself at one time was a supporter of women's ordination because I did not recognize the validity of Bible based role distinctions for men and women. But after much Bible study, I changed my mind, publishing my reasons in my book, *Searching the Scriptures* (1995). I have opposed it since then. For my most recent attempt, see my three chapters in *Prove All Things* (2000).

At Toronto, we succeeded in removing some of the most blatant statements endorsing this egalitarian view before we were prevented from making any further amendments to the document. But some of it is still there in some fuzzy and feminist language. For example, they refer to Paul's teaching on headship and submission (Ephesians 5:21-28) as though it is discussing male superiority and female inferiority.

### Abandonment by an Unbelieving Partner

It also introduced another grounds for divorce, namely, "abandonment by an unbelieving partner." Historically, Adventists have insisted that the only ground for divorce is adultery and/or fornication. But the document which the *Church Manual* Committee presented before us introduces a new ground; they call it "abandonment by an unbelieving partner." Then they inserted 1 Corinthians 7:10-15 as their proof text that it is another ground for divorce! Now this is extremely problematic in terms of its hermeneutics, logic, internal coherence, as well as its application.

### Hermeneutics

The *Church Manual* committee has injected a reference to 1 Corinthians 7:10-15 into their document, as if that text is talking about divorce. Does it really? By making that assertion, they have raised the issue of hermeneutics—how to interpret the Bible. Responsible scholars and commentators seem to be in agreement that the precise meaning of 1 Cor. 7:15 is not crystal clear. So why do we build a theological position on an obscure passage? We never got a chance to discuss it.

**Questionable Logic**

Having read the document all the way through, it is apparent that a logical contradiction has been created that has serious ethical and practical implications. On the "Grounds for Divorce," the document states "Scripture recognizes adultery and/or fornication (Matthew 5:32) as well as abandonment by an unbelieving partner (1 Corinthians 7:10-15) as biblical grounds for divorce."

Yet they continue to assert that only adultery and/or fornication by the other partner allows one to remarry. This asymmetry is not logical, and in my opinion betrays the artificial mental gymnastics that were used to create this new ground for divorce in the first place. How can the grounds for remarriage logically be different from the grounds for divorce? The fact that one is not free to remarry implies that one is not really divorced. Shouldn't divorce mean divorce? Give us a break!

If the Scriptures really allow these two grounds for divorce, why shouldn't an abandoned believer who allegedly has biblical grounds for divorce, not to be permitted to remarry? It is this kind of theological ambiguity, fuzziness, and inconsistency that some of us were pointing out. This kind of theological "double speak" is always a common prelude to liberalism's revisionist theologies.

AT: Following your logic, one might argue that this logical asymmetry also will create practical problems, because it will create a class of single people who are left in limbo to live like nuns and priests.

SKP: Absolutely. If living this life of celibacy is biblically mandated, there would be no problem. But that case has not yet been made by proponents. I find parallels here with the debate on homosexuality. Some argue that being a homosexual is not a sin. But they proceed to argue illogically that homosexuals cannot get married!

As far as I'm concerned, there are only two logically sound alternatives. If homosexuality is not a sin, we should allow homosexuals to marry, and hold offices in the church. But if it is a sin (which is my position), the church should not allow homosexual marriage.

In the same way, if the Bible grants divorce on the grounds of abandonment, we should allow such divorcees to remarry. Otherwise, we create second class divorcees in the church. In this respect, the illogical *Church Manual* proposal is neither "compassionate" nor "redemptive."

**Internal Coherence**

For those people who still believe that Ellen White is an inspired writer, the *Church Manual* proposal also raises some troubling questions. Mrs. White states very clearly that the only ground for divorce is unfaithfulness to the marriage vow, understood by the church to mean adultery, fornication, and various forms of sexual immorality or perversion, including homosexuality and child [sexual] abuse. Mrs. White wrote:

> In the sermon on the Mount [Matthew 5:32; 19:9] Jesus declared plainly that there could be no dissolution of the marriage tie, except for unfaithfulness to the marriage vow. (*Thoughts From the Mount of Blessing*, p. 63).

This statement was quoted in the *Church Manual.* As some of the speakers rightly argued, the "abandonment clause" raises a direct contradiction to this Ellen G. White statement already in the *Church Manual.* So all these questions were raised.

Besides, Ellen White has spoken on this very question of "abandonment of the unbelieving partner," divorce, remarriage (see, for example, *Adventist Home*, pp. 340-352). We cannot adopt the *Church Manual* proposal without a careful discussion of all these concerns vis-a-vis the writings of Ellen White.

**Application**

Practically speaking, allowing the abandonment provision for divorce into the manual is like allowing the proverbial camel's head under the tent. The rest of the camel is bound to follow.

What constitutes "abandonment"? Is it ten years? Is it two years? Is it five weeks? The document is silent, but the camel will keep pushing. That's just the beginning. The second phase of the camel's invasion will be to argue for what could be termed "emotional abandonment". For example, I may not physically abandon my wife, but I or my wife (depending on which one of us wants to divorce) can say, "you know, even though we live in the same house, he or she has emotionally abandoned me". Then there will be the push for recognition of what may be called "sexual abandonment", when one spouse's sexual needs are not met. This logical extension of the definition of abandonment will eventually create room for anyone, for whatever reason, to seek divorce.

AT: Well, not quite. It has to be abandonment by "an unbelieving partner".

SKP: That phrase is also a problem. Who or what constitutes an "unbelieving partner"? During the debate, they defined an unbelieving partner as "one who has not embraced the three angels' message". In other words, an unbelieving partner is a non-Adventist.

So, according to this new proposal, if a Seventh-day Adventist who is married to a Baptist, or Methodist or Presbyterian, and this non-SDA spouse ("unbelieving partner") abandons the other on say his/her birthday, anniversary, or for two weeks, months, years, etc., the Adventist has grounds to go to the church and say, "See, my Baptist or Methodist husband/wife has abandoned me. Therefore, I have a right to a divorce".

Does this double standard make good theological sense when applied to divorce? Our church will begin to be known as that church which encourages splitting of families, creating some missiological problems.

For example, it wouldn't be too helpful in Utah where the Church of Jesus Christ of Latter-day Saints, the Mormons, score a lot of points with their family emphasis. It would also create problems in Africa, where our people are winning many converts from other churches. Sometimes under very difficult circumstances (e. g. when a wife is being persecuted by the husband for joining the SDA church), all they want to hear from the pastor is a license to go ahead and divorce the spouse. Under this new questionable *Church Manual* proposal, a person in this kind of situation can divorce the unbelieving partner. In the opinion of several of the delegates who spoke against the proposal, this liberalized position is going to open a can of worms.

AT: Speaking of worms or camels, I suppose one could also argue that since a non-believer is defined in terms of a negation of "belief" rather than official membership, an argument could be made that one's officially SDA spouse is not really "a believer" if he or she is a liberal or evangelical SDA.

SKP: Yes, if the terms "liberal" or "evangelical" implies a negation of some Fundamental Beliefs of the SDA church. And I'm sure some will also argue in this way: "My spouse, though officially an Adventist, is actually an Unbeliever because he/she does not practice the SDA lifestyle. He/she worships his/her TV, sports, computer, clothing, etc.; hence has violated the second commandment!" My point is that, this "unbelieving partner" provision in the divorce and remarriage package raises the fundamental question of who or what constitutes a true SDA believer? Don't we have a right to debate the issue?

To summarize, the questionable vote on Friday regarding the marriage and divorce proposal was more than a "change of wording." I therefore reject the "spin" that has been put on the issue in some of our official Publications and news outlets.[7] The vote was a calculated attempt by proponents to liberalize the Church's long-standing position on divorce and remarriage. And I'd hope that some fair-minded Adventist journalists will hold them accountable. It is the right thing to do—regardless of one's theological leaning.

Believing that "it is better to debate an issue without settling it, than settling an issue without debating it," I have always welcomed candid and vigorous debates on theological issues. But to maneuver the parliamentary process to rescind a decision made by an overwhelming majority of delegates, to cut off debate, and to vote into the *Church Manual* a document that is riddled with theological fuzziness, and which is arguably defective in theology, holds the potential of splitting the church. Some conscientious pastors and church members can argue that they cannot accept the *Church Manual* as an authoritative document to govern the church since this provision is contrary to biblical and Ellen G. White teaching. A rejection of the authority of the *Church Manual* will be a sure recipe for congregationalism.

Unless such tactics as were employed in the Friday Morning coup d'etat are repudiated, this is going to have serious consequences in future sessions, and cause a mistrust to grow that will only deepen the divisions that already exist between the industrialized and developing countries, between liberals and conservatives. This is why I felt compelled this morning to use a "privileged motion" to register my protest.

I knew that nothing would come out of it, but I wanted the world and future generations of Adventists to know that there was at least one person at Toronto who refused to be party to that theologically questionable decision. And of course, one day, God will hold all of us accountable for what we did and refused to do on this issue.

AT: Dr. Pipim, it has been a pleasure speaking with you. I truly admire your passion and the purity of your logic, although we may differ in our presuppositions and the underlying logic we employ. Would you be willing to discuss the underlying foundational issues sometime in the near future?

SKP: I would love to discuss the foundational issues. Unless our logical foundation is biblically sound, then everything built upon it becomes questionable. Let's continue to dialogue. Perhaps I will succeed in making you a good, happy conservative. Then we can have another kind of *Adventist Today*!

[***Note:*** *Following the publication of this interview, several asked me questions about (a) lessons I learned from Toronto, (b) the validity of the vote by a few members of delegates, and (c) what attitude church members should take now. The following is a summary of my response.*]

**Lessons from Toronto**

1. Those who are called upon to attend General Conference sessions do not go there for sight seeing or for their personal agenda. They are there to conduct the business of the church. Therefore delegates have a responsibility to attend all the sessions. To do otherwise is to be negligent in one's obligations.

2. The questionable vote on divorce and remarriage took place on the very last day of the working session—when most people thought the issue had

been settled already. Delegates must always remember that until a business session is adjourned, anything can happen. Typically, some of the most important issues tend to be brought to the floor during the closing hours of business sessions—when many are tired or not present.

3. As far as possible, delegates should be given copies (or summaries) of the issues that will come up for discussion long before they arrive for the session. It takes extra motivation after long travel hours for a person to comb through hundreds of pages. Some of the materials tend to be written in terse language. This suggestion is especially crucial in matters dealing with *Church Manual* revisions.

4. It costs thousands of dollars to send a delegate to a ten-day session (airfare, hotel, food, etc.).To ensure that God's tithe money is well spent, only knowledgeable individuals who have a burden for the work should be asked to serve as delegates. GC sessions are not designed to reward individuals for faithful service or for being political allies of leaders.

**Is the Decision Valid?**

Several years ago, Mrs. Ellen G. White stated what our attitude ought to be with respect to GC session decisions: "But when, in a General Conference, the judgment of the brethren assembled from all parts of the field is exercised, private independence and private judgment must not be stubbornly maintained, but surrendered. Never should a laborer regard as a virtue the persistent maintenance of his position of independence, contrary to the decision of the general body" (*Testimonies for the Church,* 9:260).

However, Mrs. White also indicated that in order for a GC session decision to have its full force of authority, such decisions should not be surrendered to a "small group of men." She considered it an "error" to accord "the full measure of authority and influence" to the judgment by a small and/or unrepresentative group of delegates. Sister White wrote:

> "God has ordained that the representatives of His church from all parts of the earth, when assembled in a General Conference, shall have authority. The error that some are in danger of committing is in giving to the mind and judgment of one man, or of a small group of men, the full measure of authority and influence that God has vested in His church in the judgment and voice of the General Conference assembled to plan for

the prosperity and advancement of His work" (*Testimonies for the Church,* 9:261).

In the light of the above statements, one can legitimately argue that the biblically questionable vote taken at Toronto on divorce and remarriage cannot be accorded the "full measure of authority and influence that God has invested in His church." How can the decision by a small "small group of men" represent that of the "the judgment and voice of the General Conference assembled to plan for the prosperity and advancement of His work"? It seems to me that those who attempt to implement this unbiblical policy can only do so at the peril of the "prosperity and advancement" of God's work (*Testimonies for the Church,* 9:260-261).

Proponents can flatter themselves into believing that they now have a policy on divorce and remarriage that is "compassionate" and "redemptive." The truth, however, is that this questionable policy now enshrined in the *Church Manual* will not solve the divorce problem. It will rather worsen it. More importantly, the policy will compromise the message and witness of the Seventh-day Adventist church as a counter-voice in today's world.

**What Can We Do?**

*1. There is judicious procedure.* Let's remember that the SDA church has a judicious procedure to address this kind of situation. Churches can direct their grievances to the appropriate quarters of the church—from the conference level, through the Union and Division levels to the General Conference level—requesting that the issue be re-visited again. When this happens, and when the issue is sufficiently explored, I am confident that this questionable policy will be overturned at a future GC session.

*2. Teach the dangers of violating biblical teaching.* Church members, elders, pastors, and leaders should counsel all who are contemplating divorcing and remarrying under the present policy about the dangers of violating biblical teaching. Jesus is coming soon, this is not the time to lose heart. The Lord Himself understands their painful situations. If we determine to do God's will, He will give us strength to cheerfully bear the cross. In some cases, He Himself will find a way out that does not contravene His teaching.

*3. Be Always Vigilant.* The church must constantly be alert. We must guard against the ever present temptation to "legislate now, find biblical answers later." As we noted in the interview, this happened with the questionable Annual Council decision to baptize wives of polygamists (1941), and to ordain women as elders (1975 and 1984). Each of these Annual Council actions have caused deep polarization and confusion in our churches. Now, divorce and remarriage (2000) has been added to the list of controversial decisions. What will come next? Homosexuality? Drinking alcohol? Eating unclean foods? Rock music and dancing in the churches? Evolution? The enemy will not rest. He will plant his tares when many of us are asleep (Matt 13). We must remain faithful watchmen over Zion. We must demand an immediate freeze or moratorium in the implementation of the questionable policies that have been slipped into the church.

*4. Pray for our leaders.* We must pray daily for our church leaders. They face constant pressures from different quarters. It is not always easy to be courageous. Send them words of encouragement from time to time, and let them know that you are counting on them to hold high the banner.

*5. Be faithful no matter what.* Finally, determine that when all choose to go the path of rebellion against God's truth, by God's grace you'll remain faithful—regardless of cost. And as we shall argue in the next chapter, you must always embrace and support GC session decisions that are in harmony with our established biblical teachings.

---

**Endnotes**

[1]The interview that follows was published in *Adventist Today*, July-August, 2000. I am grateful to Dennis Hokoma, news editor of *Adventist Today* for granting me permission to reproduce the entire interview here. I have inserted endnotes in a few places to clarify the issue being addressed during the interview. For another interview from a conservative perspective, see the Great Controversy website: *www.greatcontroversy.org/documents/papers/pip-interview10july2000.html.* This latter interview covers a broad range of issues.

[2]For more on this, see the introductory chapter in Ronald A. G. du Preez, *Polygamy in the Bible* (Berrien Springs, MI: Adventist Theological Society Publications, 1993), 21-22.

[3]Eld. Garry Hodgkin, President of the South New Zealand Conference and a delegate of the South Pacific Division, was at the epicenter of the great divorce-remarriage controversy in Toronto. He was the architect of the parliamentary process that led to the dramatic reversal.

[4]In a subsequent e-mail exchange with Eld. Garry Hodgkin, he explained that: (1) He sought nothing but fairness in the proceedings. This is indicated by the fact that a day before his motion, he expressed a wish to move to rescind the prior action. Though some of us did not hear it, he apparently gave notice of when he would like to make such a motion; (2) He himself did not expect his motion to pass, given the strong opposition to

the document on the previous days; (3) He did not anticipate that all debates would be terminated after his motion passed; in fact he expressed his "surprise" and regret that it turned out that way; (4) He identified the "two sticking points" in the theological debate to be (a) the proposed document's "lack of an understanding of role differentiation," and (b) the proposal's assertion that "abandonment" (1 Cor 7:10-15) was a valid scriptural basis for divorce. On the above points, Hodgkin and I can agree. I also agree with him that the authority that resides within a delegation can be a rather unpredictable thing, yet it is something we have chosen to respect. We, however, disagree on the following: (i) Was the event on that Friday morning carefully orchestrated by certain delegates from the industrialized world or was it wholly spontaneous? (ii) How many people were actually present that morning when the vote was taken (was it 150 or some 500+)? (iii) What reason motivated those who engineered and those who opposed the dramatic reversal?

[5]Some have taken issue with my 150 figure estimate for those present at that Friday morning session. I base my figure on my own personal estimate. When I saw what was going on that Friday morning, I asked myself in surprise: "But how many people are actually here? And what right do they have to attempt overthrowing a decision by a majority of delegates?" This led me to do a quick approximation (it was not very difficult to estimate, considering the handful of people who were present in the places earmarked for delegates from developing countries). Apparently, I don't seem to stand alone in my rough estimate of 150. A friend of mine in the United States, who followed the GC session proceedings on the Internet audio feed, has also confirmed that number to me. After he read claims that there were 300, 500, or even 600 people present, my friend sent me this e-mail: "I plainly heard, on the Internet audio feed, a delegate during the Friday business session state the number 150 and I plainly heard the chairman [of the afternoon session] confirm that it had appeared that 150 had been present. If an audio recording of the Friday business meeting exists, that would concretely prove it." But regardless of the exact number estimated, very few, can question the fact that the total number of people present that morning was (i) a substantially smaller figure than those present on Tuesday and Wednesday, and that (ii) of the delegates present, an overwhelming majority of them were from the industrialized countries of North America, Europe, and Australia & New Zealand. Therefore, rather than quibble over the 150 estimate I gave, I want to reiterate the point I stated in my interview: "Some may dispute the 150 number, but I believe my criticism would still be valid, even if 50% of the delegates took the decision to overturn the previous action." Let's therefore not waste time on this peripheral issue. Though I believe the number was around 150, this is not my main concern. It could have been 200, 300, even 500. That will not change my basic point that a very small number of people from the industrialized regions of the world church overturned a decision that a larger body of delegates took.

[6]See Roy Adams, "Fireworks in the Dome," *Adventist Review*, July 5, 2000, 2-3.

[7]Apparently because of the theologically worrisome content of the document and the manner in which it was voted, some of our church publications have attempted to put a positive "spin" on what actually happened and its theological significance. For example, reporting on the "surprising turn of events" on the morning of July 7, the editors of the *Adventist Online News* (an electronic publication of the *Adventist Review*) reported in the GC 2000 Bulletin 10 that the divorce-remarriage document "was eventually approved by a large majority of the delegates" (see the editors' introductory comment to the article

"Divorce/Remarriage Paper Voted"). As we have shown, this statement is ambiguous, if not totally misleading. If it refers to a majority of *the few* delegates present during the theological coup d' etat, the statement is accurate. However, without any qualification, the statement can give a wrong impression that it was approved by "a large majority of the [2000 GC session] delegates." Also, even though the Toronto vote introduces a new grounds for divorce, namely, "abandonment by an unbelieving spouse," a staff writer for the *Adventist News Network* reported that this new policy "doesn't substantially alter the church's previous position on divorce and remarriage" (see "2000 - A Year in Review: World Session in Toronto," *ANN*, December 27, 2000). While some of our publications continue to put a positive "spin" on what happened at Toronto and its theological significance, perceptive individuals, including even the liberals of the church, those who are most in favor of the new policy, recognize that the Toronto decision could have some repercussions. For example, commenting on the "early morning blitzkrieg of swift parliamentary maneuvers" that led to the questionable vote, the news editor of *Adventist Today*, the liberal publication based in La Sierra, wrote: "Although the event was hailed by many liberals as a sweet victory, judging from the way it has been criticized by some conservatives, and on some web sites, the backlash may turn that victory bitter in their stomachs" (see Dennis Hokama, "Further Reflections on the Toronto Experience," July 25, 2000).

# 34

# *Rebellion in the Spirit's Name*

How should individual members conduct themselves when an overwhelming majority of their brothers and sisters take a position that they sincerely believe to be biblically wrong? Should they rebel? Should they circumvent or reinterpret the collective decision? Should they, perhaps, withhold their tithe—or even leave the church and establish independent congregations?

These questions have arisen recently over such divisive issues as the ordination of women as elders and pastors, over the introduction of "alternative" styles of worship—yes, and over baptizing practicing polygamists, endorsing unbiblical divorce and remarriage, embracing homosexuality as an acceptable lifestyle, and so on.

To avoid the confusion that often results when we misdiagnose our consciences as evidence of "the Holy Spirit's leading," we need to understand clearly how the Spirit leads individual members of the church within a corporate body of believers.

To focus our discussion, I will call attention to the "local ordinations" that took place in a few North American congregations following the 1995 General Conference session in Utrecht; however, the concerns addressed in this article have implications far beyond those post-Utrecht developments.

### Post-Utrecht Developments

At the 1995 General Conference session in Utrecht, the Seventh-day Adventist church worldwide overwhelmingly voted to reject the request of the North American Division (NAD) to permit divisions desiring to do so to ordain women for service as pastors within their own divisions. The vote against granting this permission was 1481 to 673.

Those who opposed women's ordination did so partly for theological and hermeneutical reasons. In addition, they rejected the division-based ordination proposal because it would have undermined the worldwide purpose of ministerial ordination in the Seventh-day Adventist church. They feared that letting this happen would open the door to rampant congregationalism.

In the Seventh-day Adventist church, a minister ordained in any part of the world can function anywhere in the world. The *Church Manual* (1990) says that the church recognizes "the equality of the ordination of the entire ministry"(p38).

The Minister's Manual (1992), published by the Ministerial Association of the General Conference, makes the matter even more explicit. It understands ordination to be a call "to serve as a minister of the *gospel in any part of the world*." Ordination is the investment of ministers with "full ecclesiastical authority to act *in behalf of the church anywhere in the world field* where they may be employed by the church." Again, "Workers who are ordained to the gospel ministry are set apart *to serve the world church* Ordination to the ministry is the setting apart of the employee to a sacred calling, *not for one local field alone but for the world church* and therefore needs to be done with wide counsel" (pp. 75-79, emphasis supplied).

Thus, adopting the NAD's request at Utrecht for single-division ordination would have introduced unequal or even second-rate kinds of ministerial ordination. We can be grateful that the General Comference in session rejected the individual-division ordination proposal.

**"Spiritual Disobedience" or "Rebellion"?** Despite the decisive 2 to 1 ratio of votes at the 1995 General Conference session (1481 to 673), a few influential NAD congregations decided to defy this democratic decision of the church by ordaining women pastors anyway. Believing their position to be biblical and thus in harmony with "the Spirit's leading," organizers of the post-Utrecht ordinations chose not to submit their "freedom of moral conscience" to the worldwide decision of the church.

Because they earnestly believed that the church was unwilling to uphold the principles of equality, justice, and fairness, they justified their spiritual disobedience as a "moral imperative" and hence as a kind of "civil disobedience."[1]

However, other well-meaning Adventists viewed their "disobedience" differently. For example, expressing his "disappointment," the recently retired North American Division president issued a statement in which he said, "Whatever my personal view on this topic or any other, I have an obligation to lend my full support to help this church in its desire for worldwide unity. I will not do otherwise . The leaders of your church believe wholeheartedly that God speaks through the church in business session, and for this reason we will continue to support the [Utrecht] July 5, 1995, action."[2]

The former General Conference President also spoke out clearly against the post-Utrecht ordinations. He maintained that each case of local ordination "was the result of a rebellious leader(not always the church pastor) who felt 'morally justified' in attempting to impose their view on the world church(just like Korah, Dathan, and Abiram)."[3] He continued by suggesting a course of action for loyal church members: "We have no option but to pray that the membership (most of which were 'uninformed or uninvolved') wake up and decide if their congregation is going to be a Seventh-day Adventist congregation, which in part means they will respect the authority of the ever-broadening constituencies."[4]

**Some Crucial Issues.** Whatever one may think of the "spiritual disobedience" or "rebellion" manifested by the NAD congregations who organized these local ordinations, the ordinations raise some crucial questions about how the Holy Spirit leads a body of people when its members are wrestling with theological or ethical concerns. They also raise questions about what we should do personally if we find ourselves disagreeing with a particular decision of the church. Unless we clearly understand what we ought to do in such a situation, we may find ourselves engaging in the kind of rebellious activities often associated with "offshoots," independent groups of either the fanatical right or the radical left.

The issue I want to discuss is not about the rightness or wrongness of women's ordination in each individual congregation or division. (I have already spoken to this issue in a previous section of *Must We Be Silent?*[5]). Instead, the problem I am addressing here is the undergirding spirit or attitude that says, "I will go my own way regardless of what other members of the church family think or decide."

I seek to challenge the claims of "the Holy Spirit's leading" and of "individual freedom of moral conscience" often advanced as a reason to disregard the democratic decisions of the worldwide church, to despise the counsels of the church's appointed leaders, and in some cases, to try to blackmail the church by withholding tithes or threatening uncomplimentary media exposure. In making this challenge, I shall examine how the Holy Spirit guides individuals, the church community, and the councils of the church.[6]

### The Spirit Guides Individual Believers

Often, we don't correctly understand God's Word because we are so married to the unbiblical ideologies pervasive in our ambient cultures. It takes a miracle from God to enable us surrender those pet ideas. To overcome or counteract the baneful effects of our respective cultures in our quest to understand God's Word, God has made provision for believers through the work of the Holy Spirit.

Through His work in conversion and sanctification, the Spirit renews our minds, bringing them daily into conformity to His. The Holy Spirit continues to guide individual believers of the church through His inspired Word and through the godly counsels of members of His church.

The problem arises when an individual's or group's "Spirit-guided" understanding of the Word conflicts with the "Spirit-guided" views of the entire body of believers. What should a person do in such a situation?

Without belittling the valuable contributions of technical biblical experts, we need to remember that it is possible for everyone correctly to study Scripture without a mass of technical theological expertise. One of the functions of the Holy Spirit is to lead laypersons, no less than theologians, into "all truth" (John 14:26; 16:13-14; 1 Cor 2:10-14; 1 John 2:27). The assurance that "the testimony of the Lord is sure, making wise the simple" (Ps. 19:7) is still valid. Scripture is still able to make even little children "wise unto salvation" (2 Tim 3:15). The Holy Spirit will lead everyone who approaches the Word of God with the humble, teachable, and God-fearing attitude of the child Samuel: "Speak, Lord; for thy servant heareth" (1 Sam 3:9-10).

But the Bible offers some timely principles on the value of humbly subjecting one's theological views or interpretations of Scripture to the correction of the entire body of believers. For example, we are told that "the way of the fool is right in his own eyes, but a wise man is he who listens to counsel" (Prov 12:159. "Through presumption comes nothing but strife, but with those who receive counsel is wisdom" (Prov 13:10). "Where there is no guidance, the people fall, but in abundance of counselors there is victory" (Prov 11:14).

Ellen G. White once wrote to a man who had been studying the prophecies and had found what he thought was new light. She advised him to submit his assumed new light "to brethren of experience," and "if they see no light in it, yield to their judgment; for 'in the multitude of counselors there is safety'" (*Testimonies for the Church,* 5:293; see pp. 291-295). If that instruction were followed today, it would save a great deal of confusion.

**What about the Conscience?** The Bible's discussion of "conscience" is enlightening. The Bible urges us to do our best to "maintain a clear conscience" before God (Acts 24:16). But the Bible also speaks about different kinds of consciences. It tells us that the conscience can be "good" (Acts 23:1; 1 Tim 1:19), "evil" (Heb 10:22; cf. 9:14), "seared" (1 Tim 4:1-4), "weak" (1Cor 8:9-12), or "defiled" (Titus 1:15). Since the human heart is very deceptive, it is important to be sure that one's conscience has been shaped by Scripture, not by unexamined secular culture or ecclesiastical tradition.

Our English word "conscience," it must be remembered comes from two Latin words—*con* (which means "with" or "together") and *scire* (meaning "to know"). Thus, etymologically, the word conscience suggests "to know with" or "to know together." The same meaning is found in the New Testament Greek word for conscience, *suneidesis,* meaning "to know with," "to see together," or "to agree with." Therefore, conscience is never an independent authority for knowledge. It is always a knowing in partnership with others. A true conscience is one which knows *with God*—i.e. one which is in agreement with God and His Word, as it is led by the Holy Spirit (Rom 9:1)

Ellen G. White says, "It is not enough for a man to think himself safe in following the dictates of his conscience . The question to be settled is, Is the conscience in harmony with the Word of God? If not, it cannot safely be followed, for it will deceive. The conscience must be enlightened by God. Time must be given to a study of the Scriptures and to prayer. Thus the mind will be stablished, strengthened, and settled" (*Our High Calling,* p. 143).

Our consciences must be captive to the Word of God. This raises the question: If a Christian conscience finds its instruction and guidance in Scripture, how does the Spirit guide the individual in his or her understanding of Scripture in relation to His leading of the corporate church?

We can restate the question in another way: What should we do when two or more individuals all claim the Spirit's guidance in their contradictory understanding of the Word? In other words, how can we avoid the temptation of invoking the name of the Spirit to justify our questionable reinterpretations of Scripture? How do we avoid the danger of making Scripture mean anything we desire (polygamy, women's ordination, divorce and remarriage, homosexuality, etc.), and then giving the Holy Spirit the credit? How do we prevent the tendency of invoking the Spirit to circumvent the Bible's explicit teachings (on say, monogamous, heterosexual marriages, male-female role-distinctions in both the home and the church, etc.) or inventing some new theories to justify our biblically questionable ideologies?

The answer lies in what Scripture calls a "partnership with all the saints." This principle calls upon the interpreter to submit his findings to the correction, confirmation, and edification of his fellow believers. Comparing one's interpretation with others within the worshiping community, submitting it to their scrutiny and correction, is one way to reduce the effects of one's blind spots

### The Spirit Guides the Entire Church Community

While the Spirit guides individual believers in their study of Scripture, Paul says that believers will come to a knowledge of God "with all the saints" (Eph 3:18), suggesting that God also gives spiritual understanding through the Christian community.

Responsible interpretation therefore demands that the Bible student compare his understanding with the discoveries of other believers, from the first century through the sixteenth-century Protestant Reformers, the eighteenth-century Puritans and Methodists, the nineteenth-century Adventist pioneers, and twentieth-century Bible-believing scholars

We are not the only ones the Holy Spirit has been teaching. Others, in earlier generations and in our own, have also been enlightened by the Spirit, and we stand to benefit from their discoveries and mistakes. By studying the Bible in partnership with other members of the church, the believer recognizes that God has entrusted different gifts to different members of the church to edify the entire body (1 Cor 12). For Seventh-day Adventists, this means that all interpretations of Scripture should be checked with the writings of Ellen G. White, a person believed to be the recipient of the true gift of prophecy.

Reluctance to study the Bible "with all the saints" leads to "Lone Rangerism" in interpreting Scripture—the attitude that says, "I'll go my own way without regard to what the community of believers thinks." Studying the Scriptures "with all the saints" serves as a check on our tendency to believe that we alone are guided by the Holy Spirit.

"God has not passed His people by and chosen one solitary man here and another there as the only ones worthy to be entrusted with His truth. He does not give one man new light contrary to the established faith of the body. In every reform men have arisen making this claim . Let none be self-confident, as though God had given them special light above their brethren. Christ is represented as dwelling in His people. Believers are represented as 'built upon the foundation of the apostles and prophets, Jesus Christ Himself being the chief Cornerstone' [Eph 2:20-22]" (*Testimonies for the Church*, 5:291).

Furthermore, the Spirit's design that believers study His word "with all the saints" delivers us from the tyranny of being tied to our own thoughts and to our naïve cultural conceits. It is as Christians study the Bible together and share the Word with one another, not as solitary individuals or as groups of individuals from particular regions of the world, that they are given understanding most fully.

### The Spirit Guides at a Church Council

Just as there is safety and certainty "in the multitude of counselors" (Prov 11:14; 15:22), so also in the collective decision of the worldwide church at a council meeting there is safety. The Spirit's guidance at the Jerusalem Council (Acts 15) may be instructive for Seventh-day Adventists who are tempted to defy, circumvent, reinterpret, or rebel against decisions arrived at in a General Conference session.

The Jerusalem Council has all the earmarks of our General Conference session. Following discussion and disputation in the church at Antioch over the role of circumcision in salvation (Acts 15:1-5), Paul and Barnabas, "and certain others" were urged to go up to Jerusalem, "to the apostles and the elders" about this matter (verse 2). They were "sent on their way by the church" at Antioch (verse 3), as its representatives. As they made their way through Phoenicia and Samaria, telling everyone about the conversion of the Gentiles, their story gave "great joy to all the brethren" (verse 3).

Undoubtedly, the early believers placed great value on solidarity among local churches. They were not content to live in mutual isolation. They shared their experiences and sought reactions from each other. Thus, when the "General Conference session" delegates arrived in Jerusalem, "they were welcomed by the church," along with the apostles and the elders (verse 4). Note the following about the Jerusalem Council:

(a) *Theological (Not Cultural) Issue.* The problem confronting the apostolic church was whether to require circumcision and the observance of other elements of the Mosaic laws. It was not regarded as merely a sociological issue, shaped by culture or geography, to be resolved pragmatically by compromises and concessions. It was a theological issue, having to do with salvation, the law, and the teachings of Scripture (Acts 15:15-17).

(b) *Worldwide (Not Local) Representation.* Because it was a theological issue it became a church-wide issue, and could not, therefore, be settled by each different region of the church according to its cultural "readiness" or sociological structures. Delegates included apostles, elders, missionaries, etc., suggesting that on a theological issue of worldwide importance, we need informed input from all who have a burden for the work—administrators, theologians, evangelists, laity, and so on.

(c) *Impartial (Not Biased) Discussion.* Before making a final decision, the Jerusalem delegates had a free and open discussion of the issue, with theological input from both Gentile and Jewish Christians (vv. 7-12). On unresolved theological issues, leadership and church publications should evidently not publish only one view.

(d) *Literal (Not "Principle") approach.* After Peter, Paul, and Barnabas called attention to God's work among Jews and Gentiles, James appealed to Scripture as the basis for the theological solution (vv. 15-21). The literal principle they employed in their interpretation of Scripture was simple: "The words of the prophets [must be] in agreement with this, as it is written" (v.15).

(e) *Spirit-Guided (Not Pragmatic) Decision.* After a thorough discussion, they made their decision "with one accord" (v. 25 KJV). Their decision also met the approval of the Holy Spirit ("It seemed good to the Holy Spirit and to us " [v.28 NIV]) evidently because it was in harmony with His expressed will as revealed and recorded in inspired Scripture.

"The Spirit was not given—nor can it ever be bestowed—to supersede the Bible; for the Scriptures explicitly state that the word of God is the standard by which all teaching and experience must be tested" (The Great Controversy, p. vii).

(f) *Binding (Not Optional) Obligation.* The theological decision made at that Jerusalem "General Conference session" was not optional, to be accepted or rejected according to the "unique needs" or "peculiar circumstances" of the different churches. The council's prohibitions were "necessary," not optional (v. 28). Though the letter was addressed to the Christians in Antioch, Syria and Cilicia (vv. 23-29), it was binding on all the other Christian churches.

The binding nature of the Jerusalem GC session decision is clearly stated in the very next chapter (Acts 16). Paul, accompanied by Silas, came to Derbe and Lystra in Lycaonia, clearly west of Cilicia. On their westbound journey to the region of Phrygya and Galacia (see verse 6) "as they went through the cities, they delivered to them the decrees *to keep*, which were determined by the apostles and elders at Jerusalem" (verse 4, KJV). It is clear that the council's conclusions were regarded as binding upon the churches—and not merely those of Antioch, Syria, and Cilicia (cf. Acts 21:25; Rev 2:14, 20).

There was no room for "spiritual disobedience" or "rebellion" by a few influential congregations. "When, in a General Conference, the judgment of the brethren assembled from all parts of the field is exercised, private independence and private judgment must not be stubbornly maintained, but surrendered. Never should a laborer regard as a virtue the persistent maintenance of his position of independence, contrary to the decision of the general body" (*Testimonies for the Church*, 9:260).

(g) *Blessing (Not Confusion) as the Outcome.* Because the various churches submitted to the council decision, the mission of the church was greatly helped, resulting in a growing church membership: "As they [Paul and Timothy] traveled from town to town, they delivered the decisions [Greek. *dogma*] reached by the apostles and elders in Jerusalem for the people to obey. So the churches were strengthened in the faith and grew daily in numbers" (Acts 16:4-5 NIV). The strategy for church growth was to quit fighting and circumventing a worldwide decision and start working!

This is how the Spirit leads a worldwide democratic church. This is the example recorded in Scripture for our emulation.

### What If the Collective Decision is Wrong?

The 2000 Toronto GC session's questionable vote on divorce and remarriage leads us to ask some crucial questions about collective decisions by a church body: What about instances in which a church board or a conference (or even a union conference, a division, an annual council, or the General Conference in session) makes a decision that is unbiblical? What if the collective decision is actually the decision of a small group of hand-picked committee members who are motivated by some ideological or political agenda? What should we do when it is obvious to us that the Spirit was not leading in the collective decision of the church?

Specifically, what should individual members of the church do if the church takes a waffling or compromising position on such issues as abortion, ordaining women as elders and pastor, unbiblical divorce and remarriage, baptizing practicing polygamists, homosexual lifestyle, "alternate" forms of worship, and so on? What should they do if they discover that, instead of basing a decision on Scripture, their chosen representatives have buckled under the pressure of pragmatic consideration, such as finances (tithe, taxes, etc.), political lobbying, or the desire to be popular with the world?

Should these considerations lead members to withhold tithes or even perhaps to leave the church altogether? Here are some suggestions:

**1. Stay with the Church.** Since we believe that the Seventh-day Adventist church is God's end-time remnant movement according to Bible prophecy, we must make a commitment *ahead of time* that nothing, not even the failure of our fellow church members, scholars, leaders, or councils will cause us to leave the church.

"Although there are evils existing in the church, and will be until the end of the world, the church in these last days is to be the light of the world that is polluted and demoralized by sin. The church, enfeebled and defective, needing to be reproved, warned, and counseled, is the only object upon earth upon which Christ bestows His supreme regard" (*Testimonies to Ministers*, p. 49; cf. *Selected Messages*, 2:396).

**2. Strive for Unity, Not Separation.** "Some have advanced the thought that, as we near the close of time, every child of God will act independently of any religious organization. But I have been instructed by the Lord that in this work there is no such thing as every man's being independent" (*Testimonies for the Church*, 9:258).

**3. Respect and Support Leadership.** David set an example for us when he said: "The Lord forbid that I should stretch forth mine hand against the Lord's anointed . For who can stretch forth his hand against the Lord's anointed, and be guiltless?" (1 Sam 26:11, 9).

We do not show a responsible Christian spirit when we claim that the church is God's remnant and profess to be its loyal members, if at the same time we proceed to defy, disrespect, blackmail, rebel against, or undermine the church's authority. To do so is misguided, if not hypocritical.

**4. Prayerfully Work for a Change.** Let us ask the Lord to grant us wisdom as to how to effect biblical changes through our witness (by voice, pen, or example). While praying for courage to stand for the truth, let us ask the Lord to help us to be humble and courteous. Let us pray earnestly that the Lord will cause His church to see the light we have seen. Much more can be accomplished on our knees than through all the political pressures, tithe embargoes, strategic sessions, questionable church policy revisions, or other manipulations that we may be capable of mustering.

But while praying for a change, we must allow ourselves to be instruments of change. Those of us who are able to write should write. Those who are able to speak should speak. Those who are able to vote should make their voices heard. But by all means, *we must not be silent.*

**5. Remember that God Is in Control.** Over the years, I have found these statements by Ellen G. White reassuring: "There is no need to doubt, to be fearful that the work will not succeed. *God is at the head of the work, and He will set everything in order.* If matters need adjusting at the head of the work, God will attend to that, and work to right every wrong. Let us have faith that God is going to carry the noble ship which bears the people of God safely into port" (*Review and Herald*, September 20, 1892; *Selected Messages*, 2:30; emphasis mine).

"If I did not believe that God's eye is over His people, I could not have the courage to write the same things over and over again . God has a people whom He is leading and instructing" (*Selected Messages*, 2:397).

**Conclusion.** These are exciting days for worldwide Adventism. But they are also turbulent days. Ellen G. White described it as a time of sealing and shaking. We should not be surprised if in the coming days and months we witness all kinds of dissensions, rebellions, and independent congregations. Justification offered for such divisions will take various forms, including "the Spirit's leading," "freedom of moral conscience," "equality," "justice," "fairness," "revival," "purity," etc. Our only safeguard will be the Scriptures alone. This is why we must continue searching the Scriptures to see whether the things we are seeing and hearing around us are really of God (Acts 17:11).

While our discussion has focused on the post-Utrecht "rebellion" in a few NAD congregations, it should serve to alert us to the "ultimate rebellion"—the gathering storm or "shaking"—that looms on the horizon. We must use the intervening time to hunt for the solid Rock, dig deep, and lay our foundation sure. Then, when the rains begin to fall, the floods to rise, and the winds to blow, our individual houses will stand firm (cf. Matt 7:25).

---

**Endnotes**

[1]For an insightful analysis and response to this argument, see C. Raymond Holmes, "Post-Utrecht: Conscience and the Ecclesiastical Crisis," *Adventists Affirm*, Spring 1996, pp. 44-49, 56.

[2]For the NAD's response to the "local ordinations" see "McClure Reaffirms Division's Position," *Adventist Review* (NAD edition), February 1996, p. 6.

[3]"Will You Help Answer Elder Folkenberg's Prayer?" *Adventists Affirm*, Spring 1996, p. 36.

[4]Ibid., p. 35

[5]Samuel Koranteng-Pipim, *Searching the Scriptures: Women's Ordination and the Call to Biblical Fidelity* (Berrien Springs, Mich.: Adventists Affirm, 1995). Available for $5.00 U.S., $7.00 foreign, through *Adventists Affirm*, Box 36, Berrien Springs, MI 49103.

[6]The following discussion is adapted from my *Searching the Scriptures*, pp. 40-44, and also from my *Receiving the Word* (Berrien Springs, Mich.: Berean Books, 1996), pp. 273-374.

# 35

# INVENTING STYLES OF WORSHIP

Much discussion is taking place over what forms of worship are appropriate. Some alternative styles being tested are a combination of incompatible elements from other faiths. As long ago as December 17, 1990, a feature article in *Newsweek* magazine spoke of the 1990's as "an age of mix'em, match'em salad-bar spirituality—Quakerpalians, charismatic Catholics, New Age Jews—where brand loyalty is a doctrine of the past and the customer is king."[1]

In contrast to the present trend toward cafeteria-style worship, the Bible recognizes only two kinds of worship, true worship and false worship. An attempt to marry true and false worship is known technically as syncretism, and biblically as "Babylon."

Because God's faithful followers have always resisted drifting towards syncretism, throughout history there have been clashes between true and false worship. The Bible teaches that in the end-time—our time—there would be a final conflict over worship.[2]

Satan's rebellion against God centered on worship, the desire to be like the Most High (Isa 14:12-14). The first death in human history, the death of Abel at the hands of his brother Cain, was the result of a clash between true and false worship (Gen 4). The contest between Elijah and the priests of Baal had to do with worship (1 Kings 18). Daniel and the three Hebrew men in Babylon were tested on the issue of worship (Dan

3 and 6). In the days of Esther and Mordecai, the issue was worship (Esther 3-8). One of the temptations of Christ in the wilderness was over worship. Is it any wonder that the last conflict in human history is also over worship (Rev 13; 14)?

This chapter focuses on worship styles, drawing some valuable lessons from Jeroboam's innovative approach. We begin by explaining why this issue is so important.

### An End-Time Crisis over Worship

Some of the most fearful prophecies ever addressed to mortals are found in the book of Revelation. There, we are told that at the end of time there would be two rival powers, each demanding our highest allegiance in worship.

On one side of the conflict is a power masterminded by Satan (Rev 12:9). Concerning this power, we are told: "And there was given to him [beast with lamb-like horns] to give breath to the image of the beast, that the image of the beast might even speak and cause as many as do not *worship* the image of the beast to be killed. And he causes all, the small and the great, and the rich and the poor, and the free men and the slaves, to be given a mark on their right hand, or on their foreword. And he provides that no one should be able to buy or to sell, except the one who has the mark, either the name of the beast or the number of his name" (Rev 13:15-17; NASB).

On the other hand, the Lord warns inhabitants of the earth through the third angel of Revelation 14: "If anyone *worships* the beast and his image, and receives a mark on his forehead or upon his hand, he also will drink of he wine of the wrath of God, which is mixed in full strength in the cup of His anger; and he will be tormented with fire and brimstone in the presence of the holy angels and in the presence of the Lamb. And the smoke of their torment goes up forever and ever; and they have no rest day and night, those who *worship* the beast and his image, and whoever receives the mark of his name" (Rev 14:9-11; NASB).

Here is found "the hour of trial that is going to come upon the whole world to test those who live on the earth" (Rev 3:10). This crisis over worship will manifest itself as a great conflict of loyalties.

**The Nature of the Crisis.** Without getting distracted by the identity of the "beast," "the image of beast," "mark of the beast," and the cryptic number 666, it is worth exploring the nature of the worship crisis.

1. *A Global Conflict.* The rival powers in the end-time crisis will expect every inhabitant of the world to follow their respective commands. The adversary of God and His people will demand the worship of the "beast" and its "image." On the other hand, God will warn against such a worship, commanding instead the worship of Him who "made heaven, and earth, and the sea, and he fountains of waters" (Rev 14:7)—a strong allusion to the claims in the fourth Commandment (Exo 20:8-11). Inasmuch as everyone will worship one power or the other, we can conclude that in the last days, everyone will be religious. But while everyone will profess a belief in God, not everyone will believe God—His Word, His claims, His promises, and His power.

2. *Worship: The Ultimate Test.* It is significant that the crisis in the last days will end where it all began—over the issue of worship. Worship is a fitting issue upon which one's faith is put to test. Worship reveals who or what is number one in a person's life. It discloses where a person's ultimate allegiance lies, and to whom one will offer the highest devotion and service. It probes into what a person will live and die for. Moreover, in worship the worshippers conform to the likeness of the objects they worship (Rom 1:24-25; 2 Cor 3:18). When all is said and done, our stand on contemporary worship styles may determine where we shall stand in the end-time conflict over worship.

3. *God's Law: The Key Focus.* Human institutions and governments may legitimately legislate and enforce the last six of the Ten Commandments—those touching upon the relationship among individuals (honor to parents, prohibition against killing, adultery, stealing, lying, covetousness). However, the crisis over worship pertains to our moral duty to God. Since the end-time crisis is over worship, it stands to reason that the issue will center on the first four commandments of the Decalogue—who to worship, why to worship, how to worship, and when to worship. It appears that the end-time ethical crisis over worship will raise major questions about religious liberty.

4. *No Neutrality.* Each person in the world, regardless of race, gender, or status, will have to choose who to obey in this crisis over worship. In other words, everyone will have a choice and will be called upon to use their freedom of choice to declare where they stand. No one can

legitimately excuse his wrong moral decisions and actions by blaming them on his environment, circumstances, or even genes. At that time "theological neutrality" will be finally exposed to be a myth embraced by those unwilling to take a stand for biblical truth.

5. *Costly Decision.* There are dire consequences for either of the choices one makes. There is a price to pay—economic or survival concerns, as well as life or death. Since the kings and powers of the earth will all be involved, we should expect to see attempts in legislative halls and courts of justice to legislate and enforce human laws in defiance of God's law. The fusion of religious and secular powers suggest that those who conscientiously disobey will be pronounced obstinate, stubborn, contemptuous or enemies of society or state, and may thus be subject to fines, imprisonment, and capital punishment. It will become evident, then, that questions over worship styles go far beyond one's personal, cultural, or generational preferences for a particular kind of worship style.

6. *Beliefs and Lifestyle.* After the warning us against the beast and his image, the prophecy declares, "Here is the patience of the saints: here are they that keep the commandments of God and the faith of Jesus" (Rev 14:12; cf. 12:17; 19:10). Since those who "keep God's commandments" are placed in contrast with those who worship the beast, his image, and receive his mark, it follows that the loving obedience of God's law, on the one hand, and its violation on the other, will make the distinction between the true worshipers of God and the beast. Also, the reference to the "testimony of Jesus" suggests a faithfulness in maintaining the authoritative standard of the Christian faith. Ultimately then, the final crisis in the end-time will demand that God's people uphold sound doctrine and practice.[3]

7. *Assurance of Victory.* The reference to God's people as "saints" suggests that through a living faith in Christ, they will be able live ethically holy lives amidst the most trying circumstances. They will ultimately triumph in the great conflict over worship (Rev 20:4; cf. 12:11), proving to the entire world that, indeed, ethical holiness is possible even in this sinful world.[4]

Yes, true worshipers will prevail in the last great conflict over worship. Having faithfully persevered in the "great tribulation," these victors will forever be with their Lord: "They shall hunger no more, neither thirst any more; neither shall the sun light on them, nor any heat. For the Lamb which is in the midst of the throne shall feed them, and shall lead them unto living fountains of waters: and God shall wipe away all tears from their eyes" (Rev 7:13-17; cf. 21:3-7).

While the prospect of a triumph of God and His people is a strong motivation for the saints to be "faithful unto death" (Rev 2:10), false worship has its own enticement. Otherwise, why would an overwhelming majority of people in the end-time prefer spurious worship over the genuine (cf. Rev 13:8, 12, 15)?

To better understand the attractiveness of some of today's contemporary worship styles, I have chosen to provide an "update" on "The People's Community Church." Some readers may already be familiar with worship in this "church" since the Bible itself discusses it in 1 Kings 12. It is an account of the innovative worship style instituted by the charismatic King Jeroboam (931-910 BC), the son of Nebat.

### "Jeroboam's Innovative People's Church"

As soon as Jeroboam, son of Nebat, heard that king Solomon was dead, he returned from his forced exile in Egypt and took up his residence in his native town of Zeredah, in the hill country of Ephraim.

Meanwhile, Israel's political crisis had taken a turn for the worse. The people were already upset by Solomon's oppressive taxes. With the death of Solomon, they were expecting the new king to be a little more caring. But Rehoboam, son of Solomon, apparently did not understand their felt needs. He indicated that he was unwilling to lighten the tax burdens. "My father made your yoke heavy," Rehoboam told the people. "I will make it even heavier. My father scourged you with whips; I will scourge you with scorpion" (1 Kings 12:14; NIV).

Rehoboam's insensitive answer was the straw that broke the camel's back. Most of the people revolted: "When all Israel saw that the king refused to listen to them, they answered the king: What share do we have in David, what part in Jesse's son? To your tents, O Israel! Look after your own house, O David!" (vs. 16).

Unwilling to recognize this rebellion, Rehoboam sent aged Adoram, the finance minister who had been over the tax system, to quell the disaffection. However, this attempt failed. Adoram was stoned to death by the people. Fearing for his life, Rehoboam flees to Jerusalem, where he became king only of Judah.

It is at this time that Jeroboam comes into the picture again. "When all the Israelites heard that Jeroboam had returned [from Egypt], they sent and called him to the assembly and made him king over all Israel. Only the tribe of Judah remailed loyal to the house of David" (vs. 20).

Jeroboam seemed to be the perfect choice as leader of the northern kingdom. He was experienced, having served and excelled in Solomon's administration as minister of labor. Besides, God Himself had divinely set him apart to be king over Israel (1 Kings 11:26-40). And now, by the people's popular choice, he was unanimously elected as leader.

What else could this charismatic leader have asked for? God Himself, through the prophet Ahijah, had at an earlier time guaranteed his success: "If you do whatever I command you and walk in my ways and do what is right in my eyes by keeping my statutes and commands, as David my servant did, I will be with you. I will build you a dynasty as enduring as the one I built for David and will give Israel to you" (1 Kings 11:38).

Regrettably, instead of recognizing his rise to power as a divine call to faithfulness, Jeroboam chose to secure his position and success by inventing new styles of worship which, though popular with the people, were founded on principles contrary to God's Word.

Not only was Jeroboam the people's popular choice, his name can be interpreted to mean "the people contend" or "one who pleads the people's cause." He was true a charismatic leader, one who got along well with "the people," who had "the people's" interest at heart, and one who, lamentably, invented style of worship to please "the people" instead of God. His church would be, in the truest sense, the best example of what I term a "People's Community Church."

Popular as it was, Jeroboam's people's church departed from God's ideal in at least seven respects: (1) its motivation for worship, (2) its blueprint for worship, (3) its object of worship, (4) its demands on its worshipers, (5) the center of its worship, (6) its ministers of worship, and (7) its time for worship.

**1. The Motivation for Worship.** True worship, we all know, is based on love and is always actuated by a true conception of God.[5] Jeroboam's false worship, however, was motivated by fear. He feared that the appeal of worship in Jerusalem would draw people away from him to Rehoboam, his political rival (1 Kings 12:26-27), resulting possibly in his own overthrow and assassination. He feared for his political career, if not for his life. And fear is an expression of lack of faith in God.

How often has a lack of faith caused us to go on "a way that seemeth right in our own eyes." We are told that "every failure on the part of God's children was due to a lack of faith" (*Patriarchs and Prophets*, p. 657). Think of the times you failed God—lying, cheating, stealing, engaging in immoral relationships, etc. Was it not the result of fear, that is, a lack of faith in God? And in the end-time, is it not the fear of not being able to "buy or sell" or the fear of death that would lead many to opt for the worship "the beast and his image"?

And how often have leaders, driven by a fear of losing members or the votes of their constituencies, compromised the faith by adopting unbiblical practices, even as Jeroboam did.

**2. Blueprint for Worship.** "*The king took counsel,*" we read, "and made two calves of gold" (1 Kings 12:28). Quite obviously, the king did not seek counsel from the Lord. Instead, he consulted his team of "experts" for strategies to revitalize worship.

If Jeroboam had lived in our day, his church growth specialists would have encouraged him to learn from the successful strategies of the mega-churches of today's Canaan and Egypt. His experts would have encouraged him to adopt age-specific, gender-inclusive, and culturally-sensitive innovative schemes to attract the "bored, burned, and by-passed." Certainly, the sociologists and public relations experts would have urged him to take surveys and opinion polls to find out what unconverted church members really want.

Perhaps Jeroboam did not consult Moses or the Spirit of Prophecy (available to him in the person of prophet Ahijah; 1 Kings 11:29ff.) because he felt that these sources of information belonged to the "Victorian" era of king David, and therefore, not relevant to his current challenging situation. At all events, as we noted a moment ago, after consulting his advisors, Jeroboam made two golden calves, and said to the people, "Behold your gods" (1 Kings 12:28).

**3. Changing the Object of Worship.** Jeroboam's interest in, and favorable disposition toward, calf-worship may have been developed during his exile in Egypt. Though he did not study at an Egyptian Theological Seminary, he no doubt would have come in contact with the Egyptians' worship of Amon-Re, the sun-god, and its impressive worship ceremonies that included the representation of an invisible deity by a visible bull.

The challenge for the Jeroboam was how to introduce into Israel an identical style of worship. If only he could successfully combine Jehovah worship with "positive" elements from Egyptian sun-worship . . . Only if he could find justification for a visible representation of the invisible God . . . Where could he learn the carefully nuanced theology that he so desperately needed?

Where? In the example of Aaron at Mount Sinai, of course (Exo 32). Aaron's worship style was characterized by the ancient version of today's powerful synthesizers, bass guitars, electric drums, contemporary Christian rock and rap, and holy dances (cf. Exo 32:6).[6]

Of course, in order for such a creative worship style to be warmly embraced by mainstream believers in Israel, Jeroboam would have to construct a carefully nuanced theology of worship. As before, Jeroboam discovered some "new light" from Aaron as in 1 Kings 12:28 he used the identical language of Aaron: "Behold thy gods, O Israel . . ."

Let's follow this ingenious theological exercise to make worship "relevant." Inasmuch as the word "gods" (*Elohim*) is singular in meaning, the phrase could have been translated, "Here *are* your *God*." The plural verb ("are") with a singular object ("God") may have been designed to express his new theology. Jeroboam may have reasoned: "Though you see two golden-calves, I am not introducing idolatry or polytheism in Israel. What you see is simply an artistic expression, a creative symbol, of our historic belief in the *one* true God of Israel—even as we had the cherubim and seraphim on the cover of the ark. It is the same truth we are trying to express for our visually-sensitive MTV generation."

But despite Jeroboam's rationalization, God still condemned the worship of images. Through His Word, God had warned: "Thou shalt not make unto thee any graven image . . . Thou shall not bow down thyself to them, nor serve them . . ." (Exo 20:4-5).

The second commandment is not primarily against the worship of false gods (this is the concern of the first commandment) as it is against the worship of the true God in a false way. This commandment, rightly understood, forbids all kinds of man-made images—whether metal, mortal, or mental.

It does not only condemn Jeroboam's metal image, it also denounces the worship of likeness of things in heaven (sun, moon, stars), and in earth (mortal human beings, animals, birds, insects, stones, rivers, metals), and in the sea (fishes, mammals crustaceans).

I need to direct an essential parenthetical comment to those of us living in the Western world, who are often tempted to believe that the second commandment is directed solely against animistic practices in some far-away jungles. We need to think again. One leading Evangelical scholar has wisely observed that "just as it [second commandment] forbids us to manufacture molten images of God, so it forbids us to dream up mental images of Him. Imagining God in our heads can be just as real a breach of the second commandment as imagining Him by the work of our hands."[7]

Too often, expressions like, "*My view of* God is . . ."; "I *like to think* of God as . . ."; "*I have experienced* God to be . . ."; "*My reality of* God is . . .," etc. are but gross distortions, if not subtle denials, of what the Bible itself teaches of God.

Our author continues: "It needs to be said with the greatest possible emphasis that those who hold themselves free to think of God *as they think* are breaking the second commandment. At best, they can only think of God in the image of man—as an ideal man, perhaps, or a super-man. But God is not any sort of man. We were made in His image, but we must not think of Him as existing in ours. To think of God in such terms is to be ignorant of Him, not to know Him. All speculative theology, which rests on philosophical reasoning rather than biblical revelation is at fault here. . . . To follow the imagination of one's heart in the realm of theology is the way to remain ignorant of God and to become an idol-worshipper—the idol in this case being a false mental image of God, 'made unto thee' by speculation and imagination."[8]

If this scholar's observations are correct, those of us who feel at liberty to fashion the biblical faith according to the metal or *mental* images of our day are but repeating the mistake of Jeroboam, and our theological innovations are bound to produce a cheap religion, as did Jeroboam's.

**4. Changing the Demands on its Worshipers.** When Jeroboam told Israel, "*it is too much for you* to go up to Jerusalem" (1 Kings 12:28), he was offering them a discount religion, a religion of convenience rather than obedience.

By taking away the seventh-day Sabbath, Sunday-keepers today may generally be said to be offering a 10% discount on the Ten Commandments. And what about those within our own ranks who offer Christian lifestyles at sale prices, encouraging a *moderate* use of alcohol, a *tasteful* use of ornamental jewelry, the *occasional* eating of unclean meats, endorsing homosexual lifestyle for people who claim to be *born gay,* and legislating divorce and remarriage for *incompatible* unions and for reasons of *abandonment*?

The seriousness of discount religion lies in the assumption that in order to be a truly "caring church," a church must accept people "just as they are" without any sort of do's and don'ts. The *Newsweek* article we read from earlier noted that "unlike earlier religious revivals, the aim this time (aside from born-again traditionalists of all faiths) is support not salvation, help rather than holiness, a circle of spiritual equals rather than an authoritative church or guide. A group affirmation of self is at the top of the agenda, *which is why some of the least demanding churches are now in greatest demand.*"[9]

In this kind of worship, the *Newsweek* article continues, "each individual is the ultimate source of authority." Or as it quotes from an advertising campaign capturing the ethos of a consumer-driven church: "Instead of me fitting a religion I found a religion to fit me." The article explains that in this kind of worship members "inspect congregations as if they were restaurants and leave if they find nothing to their taste." Participation does not derive from a sense of commitment but if it meets their felt-needs. "They don't convert—they choose."[10]

Even more insightful is this observation from the magazine: "Theologically, the prospects are even blander. In their efforts to accommodate, many clergy have simply airbrushed sin out of their language. Like politicians, they can only recognize mistakes which congregants are urged to 'put behind them.' Having substituted therapy for spiritual discernment, they appeal to a nurturing God who helps His (or Her) people cope. Heaven, by this creed, is never having to say no to yourself, and God is never having to say you're sorry."[11]

Such is the nature of a cheap, Jeroboam-like worship style that murmurs sweetly, "*It is too much for you* to go up to Jerusalem" (1 Kings 12:28).

**Changing the Center of Worship.** Jeroboam was well in advance of today's "bold" innovators of worship in yet another way. The designated center of worship was in Jerusalem, where Solomon's temple stood. But Jeroboam changed it to two locations when "he set the one in Bethel, and the other put he in Dan" (1 Kings 12:29).

These sites were chosen strategically. Bethel, on the southern border, was historically the site where the patriarchs worshiped (Gen 28:10-12; 31:13; 35:1-7; Hos 12:4). On the other hand, Dan, in the north, was a place of worship associated with a renegade Levite who lived in the days of the judges (Judges 18). Bethel would appeal to *unconverted* "traditionalists" who could feel that they were holding the "old time religion." Dan would attract the "progressives," *unconverted* professionals mature enough to "adventure in truth" by "refining and renewing" old beliefs and practices.

In this way, Jeroboam, our charismatic leader offered a choice for those who wanted "traditional" worship and those who enjoyed "contemporary," alternative worship. If the two worships could have been conducted on the same location, perhaps he would have had two different types of services for each of the two groups—perhaps the traditional worship would be the first service and the contemporary one would come afterwards. Of course, the architecture of the building would have had to incorporate elements of the old as well as the new (resembling a suburban shopping mall, a disco, or movie theater).

Jeroboam had a very practical reason for choosing his two locations: "Why should the people go all the way to Jerusalem to worship? We need a community church, a church we can truly claim as our own—free from the control of authoritarian hierarchy of Jerusalem." Moreover, since Bethel was just 10 miles north of Jerusalem on the highway, the site would tempt Israelites to stop there instead of traveling the rest of the way to Jerusalem. And Dan, being the northernmost city in Israel, would be a more accessible place for people who would otherwise have to walk all the way to Jerusalem.

Apparently, convenience in worship was more important to Jeroboam than obedience in worship. This is why his "People's Community Church" would be very alluring to Israel.

Notice, however, that although this compromise worship from a shrewd political leader may have been popular with "the people," the Bible describes it as the "sin of Jeroboam the son of Nebat, wherewith he made Israel to sin" (1 Kings 12:30; 16:26). Whenever political expediency takes priority over faithful obedience to the Lord, the result, as we shall soon discover, is fatal to the innovators of the new styles of worship and also to all of God's people.

**Changing the Ministers of Worship.** Another of Jeroboam's innovations was his redefinition of the practice of ministry, making it more nearly "inclusive." We read that "he made an house of high places, and *made priests of the lowest of the people, which were not of the sons of Levi*" (1 Kings 12:31

We are not surprised that Jeroboam faced some strong opposition from many of the dedicated *conservative* priests (2 Chron 11:13-17). But how did he respond? He systematically silenced the voice of the conservatives and, at the same time, trained and ordained a new generation of priests. "Why," he apparently asked, "should ordination continue to be reserved for only males from the tribe of Levi?"

Perhaps, he reasoned, as some do today in another context, that the "priesthood of all believers" means that everyone can be a minister. "Certainly, anyone with an appropriate training or the gift of the Spirit should be ordained *as elder/minister*," Jeroboam rationalized. The old tradition that priests could only be males from the tribe of Levi was "culturally conditioned," going back to the time of Moses, the rigid and irritable administrator who dared to withstand the bold, innovative Aaron. And had not Korah, Dathan, and Abiram, notable men in Israel's history who had boldly challenged Moses, argued that "all the congregation are holy" (Num 15:3)?

Jeroboam embraced the egalitarian ideology of his day which taught "full equality." As far as he was concerned, in his new golden-calf religion, "there is neither Israelite nor Canaanite, slave nor free, male nor female." In his opinion, such an "inclusive ministry" would empower people for mission, restore Israel's credibility among the Canaanite churches, and appeal to the sense of fairness of all "justice-inspired" believers. To do otherwise was to be held hostage by the "fundamentalist fringe" of Israel.

**7. Changing the Time of Worship.** One more change that Jeroboam introduced had to do with the time of worship. He dared to change the date of the great annual fall festival from the seventh-month, where God had placed it, to the eighth month (see 1 Kings 12:32). "It does not matter which day a person worships—the important thing is Christ," contemporary Jeroboams would say. "Why be fussy over a specific day?"

For Jeroboam, failure to recognize the real principle behind God's call for specific times of worship can easily lead to triumphalism, bigotry, and intolerance towards God's many "remnant" peoples. In the context of discussions about the seventh-day Sabbath, modern Jeroboams would argue that holding on to God's appointed day of worship leads to "ethnocentrism," "xenophobia," and "paranoia." These inflexible attitudes would undermine the spirit of ecumenism and also ultimately hinder the church's witness to a twenty-first century world.

**Conclusion.** It is interesting to observe how the author of the book of Kings evaluates this new style of worship. "So did he in Bethel, sacrificing unto the calves that *he had made*: and he placed in Bethel the priests of the high places which *he had made*. So he offered upon the altar which *he had made* in Bethel the fifteenth day of the eighth month, even in the month which *he had devised of his own heart* . . ." (1 Kings 12:32-33).

Jeroboam's was a man-made religion. By inventing an alternative worship style in order to advance his own career, Jeroboam prostituted God's true worship. His independent "people's community church" altered the shape of true worship, by changing the (1) the motivation for worship, (2) the blueprint for worship, (3) the object of worship, (4) the demands on worshipers, (5) the center of worship, (6) the ministers of worship, and (7) the time of worship. For this cause, both his family and the entire nation of Israel were eventually punished.

What did Jeroboam gain? What did his people gain in the long run? Answered God through the prophet Ahijah:

> "'Go, say to Jeroboam, 'Thus says the Lord God of Israel, 'Because I exalted you from among the people and made you leader over My people Israel, and tore the kingdom away from the house of David and gave it to you—yet you have not been like My servant David, who kept My commandments and who followed Me with all his heart, to do only that which was right in My sight; you also have done more evil than all who were before you, and have gone and made for yourself other gods and molten images to provoke Me to anger and have cast Me behind your back—therefore, behold, I am bringing calamity on the house of Jeroboam, and will cut off from Jeroboam every male person, both bond and free in Israel, and I will make a clean sweep of the house of Jeroboam, as one sweeps away dung until it is all gone. . . . For the Lord will strike Israel, as a reed is shaken in the water; and He will uproot Israel from this good land which He gave to their fathers,

> and will scatter them beyond the Euphrates River, because they have made their Asherim, provoking the Lord to anger" (1 Kings 14:7-10, 15)

There are other lessons for us: "When today's politicians join the church to get votes, when high achievers unite with a prestigious congregation for 'social reason,' when opportunists identify with a certain religious group because it is popular, are their actions any better than Jeroboam's? Not really. Not really. A religion of convenience, devised in one's own heart, is an abomination to God and is condemned by history as was the substitute faith of Jeroboam. He was branded forever as, 'Jeroboam the son of Nebat, who made Israel sin' (2 Kings 23:15)."[12]

Before embracing the gospel gimmicks and other innovations in use among the mega-churches of our modern Canaan, would we not do well to remind ourselves of the following counsel, as we reflect on the fact that the end-time worship crisis looms dead ahead?

"If God has any new light to communicate, He will let His chosen and beloved understand it, without their going to have their minds enlightened by hearing those who are in darkness and error. . . . God is displeased with us when we go to listen to error, without being obliged to go . . . and the light around us become contaminated with the darkness" (*Early Writings*, pp. 124-125).

---

**Endnotes**

[1]*Newsweek* (December 17, 1990):50.

[2]For detailed discussion of this age-long conflict between true and false worship, see Ellen G. White, *The Great Controversy.*

[3]The reference to the "commandments of God and the testimony of Jesus" (cf. Rev 20:4) suggests that God's end-time people will be "characterized by the restoration of the *historic* commandments of God and by the *historic* testimony of Jesus, that is, of the everlasting gospel." See Hans La Rondelle, *How to Understand the End-Time Prophecies of the Bible* (Sarasota, FL: First Impressions, 1997), 290. Notice that besides the apostle Paul who uses the phrase "testimony of Christ," "testimony of God," and "testimony of our Lord" (1 Cor 1:6; 2:1; 2 Tim 1:8), John the Revelator also uses the phrase in at least two major ways. In it's broader usage, the term "testimony of Jesus" (or "testimony of God") refers to the book of Revelation itself, as an objective and authoritative body of truth from Jesus Christ, given through the gift of prophecy, to His church (Rev 1:2; 19:10; 22:16). In its narrow usage, it emphasizes the body of truth that distinguishes true worshippers of God from the apostate. Thus, John was on the island of Patmos "for the word of God, and for the testimony of Jesus Christ" (Rev 1:2, 9). Countless martyrs

sacrificed their lives in the course of Christian history "for the word of God, and for the testimony they held" (Rev 6:9). During the end-time conflict with the antichrist, the remnant church will "keep the commandment of God, and have the testimony of Jesus" (Rev 12:17). Those who reigned with Christ during the millennium, had earlier refused to worship the beast and its image and had been killed "because of the testimony of Jesus and the word of God" (Rev 20:4; NASB). We may conclude from these passages that God's people, from the beginning till the end of the church age are characterized by the same authoritative standard of Christian faith. When, therefore, God's end-time people are described as keeping "the commandments of God" and having the "faith of Jesus," the latter expression should be understood in the manner described by William G. Johnsson: "They keep the faith of Jesus. The expression does not mean that the people of God have faith *in* Jesus (although they do), because the faith of Jesus is something they *keep*. 'The faith' probably refers to the Christian tradition, the body of teaching that center in Jesus. Jude 3 may provide a parallel: 'the faith which was once for all delivered to the saints.' When God's loyal followers keep the faith of Jesus they remain true to basic Christianity—they 'keep the faith'" (W. G. Johnsson, "'The Saints' End-Time Victory Over the Forces of Evil," in *Symposium on Revelation*, Book II, ed. Frank B. Holbrook [Hagerstown, MD: Review and Herald, 1992], 38, 39; cf. Gerhard Pfandl, "The Remnant Church and the Spirit of Prophecy" in *Symposium on Revelation*, Book II, chapter 10). For a helpful summary discussion, see Hans LaRondelle, *How to Understand the End-Time Prophecies of the Bible*, 130-131, 281-290.

[4]See my "Shining Like Stars: Ethical Holiness in Dark Times," *Adventists Affirm* 11/3 (Fall 1997):13-19.

[5]God is worthy of worship because of His: *(a) Eternal Existence*; He is worthy because He is the God "who was and who is and who is to come" (Rev 4:8); *(b) Creatorship*; He is worthy because He did "create all things, and because of Thy will they existed, and were created" (Rev 4:11; 14:7); *(c) Redemptive work*; He is worthy because He is the Lamb who was slain, and whose blood purchased "men from every tribe and tongue and people and nation" (Rev 5:9); *(d) Sovereignty as Lord and Judge*; He is worthy of worship because He alone determines the destiny of human kind and renders just and true judgment (Rev 11:16-18; 15:3-4); *5. Glorious triumph*; He is worthy of worship because "His judgments are true and righteous" and because "He has avenged the blood" of His people by being victorious over His enemies.

[6]It is, perhaps, more than a coincidence that Jeroboam's eldest sons bore identical names as Aaron's. The sons of Aaron were Nadab and Abihu (Exo 6:23; Num 3:2; 26:60); Jeroboam's were Nadab and Abijah (1 Kings 14:1, 20; 15:25). There are other parallels: (a) They were both responding to public opinion (Exo 32:1-6; 1 Kings 12:28); (b) They both made identical responses (Exo 32:4; 1 Kings 12:28); (c) Altars and feasts were part of the calf-worship (Exo 32:5: 1 Kings 12:32, 33; 2 Kings 23:15); (d) A non-Levitical priesthood was established (Exo 32:26-29; 1 Kings 12:31; 13:33); (e) The resulting sin adversely affected the entire nation (Ex 32:21, 30-34; Deut 9:18-21; 1 Kings 12:30; 13:34; 14:16; 15:26, 30, 34; 2 Kings 3:3; 10:29-31); (f) The golden calves were destroyed in a similar fashion (Exo 32:20; Deut 9:21; 2 Kings 23:15); (g) The punishment upon the people were also similar (Exo 32:35; 2 Chron 13:20). For more on the parallels between Aaron and Jeroboam, see article on "Jeroboam" in Walter Elwell, ed., *Encyclopedia of the Bible* (Grand Rapids, Mich.: Baker, 1988): 2:1121.

[7]James I. Packer, *Knowing God* (Downers Grove, IL: InterVarsity, 1973), 42.
[8]Packer, *Knowing God*, 42.
[9]*Newsweek* (December 17, 1990):56.
[10]Ibid., p. 56, 52.
[11]Ibid., 56.
[12]*Communicators Bible Commentary*, page, 164.

# 36

# *Epilogue: Why We Must Not Be Silent*

This chapter concludes my discussion of the ideological issues currently dividing our church—homosexuality, women's ordination, racism and racially separate conferences, liberal higher criticism, and congregationalism. Because these ideologies have been actively promoted by influential thought leaders, and because the church has been far too willing to embrace these fads of worldly opinion, I have spoken candidly and passionately on these issues. My hope is that the Seventh-day Adventist church will clearly see the theological dangers inherent in these ideologies and respond biblically and decisively.

Some will, no doubt, disagree with me on some points. I respect their right to do so and welcome their painstaking effort to refute the arguments in the book. As I mentioned in my introduction to *Must We Be Silent?* I will also appreciate the labors of those who offer compelling scriptural correctives to the positions I have advanced in this volume. But I will ignore all negative criticisms that fail to demonstrate objectively that the views presented in this volume are biblically incorrect or out of harmony with the long-standing Seventh-day Adventist beliefs and practices.

**Expectation from the Critics.** Judging from the reaction from certain quarters of the church to my earlier apologetic book, *Receiving the Word,* I anticipate that this book, too, will invoke the displeasure of advocates and supporters of the views I have challenged. In fact, prior to its publication, several individuals—scholars and leaders—who read sections of the book manuscript alerted me to this very possibility. One of them fired this e-mail to me after reading only the table of contents and my introduction:

> Dear Samuel:
>
> To be honest, I face the prospect of your new book with the sort of enthusiasm I usually reserve for when a doctor tells me, "You're going to need surgery." Or should I say with the enthusiasm of Johoiakim when his secretary said, "Hey, you have another letter here from Jeremiah!" Whether or not the book is needed, it's not going to be received with equanimity—by anyone.

Undoubtedly, believers in gay and feminist theologies will not receive the book kindly. The entrenched liberal establishment will also be irritated. Supporters of the racially separate church structure in North America—Blacks and Whites—will castigate the book. And promoters of pluralism, independence, gospel gimmicks, and new worship styles will take offense at this work.

Besides these predictable reactions, it is also conceivable that some of my conservative friends will not deal kindly with me for publishing the book. Lacking the courage of Elijah, and desperately seeking to please the liberal establishment, these "good Obadiahs" don't want to be branded "troublers of Israel" (cf. 1 Kings 18), lest they tarnish their conservative image as "centrist Adventists." In fact, the friend who had sent me the above e-mail forewarned me about this likelihood: "I think it should be pretty clear to you that the book is also not going to lead to more [conservative] speaking appointments . . . [and] you aren't likely to get an invitation to be a plenary speaker at the next Jerusalem Bible Conference."

My friend may have had in mind the potential consequences for my vigorous critique of the arguments for women's ordination and racially separate conferences—questionable arguments which some influential church administrators and conservative scholars are still using to prop up the secular ideologies. The concerns expressed in my friends e-mail faintly describe what I mentioned in the introduction to this book:

> I am aware that it is risky these days for anyone to question the biblical legitimacy of the ideologies that are invading our church. Scholars and leaders who courageously stand up against them are often vilified, if not persecuted. The issues have torn apart friendships and churches. In places where the ideologies have become entrenched, opposing views have not always been welcome, even if those views are still embraced by an overwhelming majority of the church through official action. And sometimes it is very difficult for loyal Adventists to be hired or retained, despite the fact that they may be the most qualified. The policy is usually unwritten, but those familiar with several situations can testify to the intolerant attitude toward those who uphold the longstanding biblical position on the ideological issues.

But must we be silent? Are the above consequences compelling reasons to justify our continued silence on homosexuality, women's ordination, racism and racially separate conferences, liberal higher criticism, and congregationalism? I don't think so.

**Why We Must *Not* Be Silent.** In my introduction to the book, I mentioned that in certain quarters of our own church, individuals who forthrightly express their views on the issues addressed in this volume are considered "divisive," "controversial," "intolerant," "fundamentalist," "immature," or even "third world." I also indicated that these uncomplimentary labels have exerted powerful psychological pressure on some church leaders and scholars to either endorse the unbiblical practices or, at a minimum, remain silent. Permit me to state some reasons why we must not be intimidated into silence.

> *1. We betray a sacred trust if we remain silent.* Writes the apostle Paul to Timothy: "I charge thee therefore before God, and the Lord Jesus Christ, who shall judge the quick and the dead at his appearing and his kingdom; Preach the word; be instant in season, our of season; reprove, rebuke, exhort with all longsuffering and doctrine. For the time will come when they will not endure sound doctrine; but after their own lusts shall they heap to themselves teachers, having itching ears; And

> they shall turn away their ears from the truth, and shall be turned unto fables. But watch though in all things, endure afflictions, do the work of an evangelist, make full proof of thy ministry" (2 Tim 4:1-5).

*2. We expose others to danger if we remain silent.* Anyone who has a charge over the spiritual well-being of others is a "watchman over Zion." This includes church administrators, professional theologians, editors of our church publications, local church pastors and elders, Sabbath school teachers, and parents in the home.

If these watchmen over Zion fail to sound the alarm, the people under their care will be exposed to dangers inherent in believing false doctrines. When this happens, the Lord will hold them accountable for anyone who needlessly loses his soul because of the negligence. The prophet Ezekiel warned:

> "But if the watchman sees the sword coming and does not blow the trumpet to warn the people and the sword comes and takes the life of one of them, that man will be taken away because of his sin, but I will hold the watch man accountable for his blood. Son of man, I have made you a watchman for the house of Israel; so hear the word I speak and give them warning from me" (Eze 33:6, 7; NIV).

One Adventist newspaper refers to ministers who refuse to sound the alarm as "silent watchmen [and] dumb dogs." It explains:

> A watch dog that won't bark when a prowler comes is of no value as a watch dog. God called the pastors of Judah blind watchmen, "dumb dogs" that cannot bark (Isa 56:10). He didn't accuse them of false doctrine but of being asleep at a time when they should have been warning the flock.
>
> Calvin said: "A dog barks when his master is attacked. I would be a coward if I saw God's truth attacked and yet remained silent without giving a sound."
>
> Christ's undershepherds have a duty to speak out, take sides,

> take a stand. Neutrality helps God's enemies not His cause. . . . "A Silent watchman is more dangerous than no watchman, because people feel a sense of security if they know a watchman is on the job 24 hours a day."
>
> Silence encourages the compromiser, not the contender for Truth.[1]

*3. We commit a criminal act if we remain silent.* When powerful secular ideologies undermine the biblical faith, indifference and inaction with respect to the cause of God is viewed by Him as a crime. This was the sin of Meroz, an Israelite town in Naphtali: "Curse ye Meroz, said the angel of the Lord, curse ye bitterly the inhabitants thereof; *because they came not to the help of the Lord, to the help of the Lord against the mighty"* (Judges 5:23).

Ellen White makes it more plain when she wrote: "If God abhors one sin above another, of which His people are guilty, it is doing nothing in case of an emergency. Indifference and neutrality in a religious crisis is regarded of God as a grievous crime and equal to the very worst type of hostility against God" (*Testimonies,* vol. 3, p. 281).

*4. The stones will cry out if we remain silent.* It is a privilege to be entrusted with God's end time saving message. But lets remember that God can get His message out—with or without our cooperation. In the words of Jesus Christ, "the stones would immediately cry out" if we refuse to speak out (Luke 19:40). In fact, the Lord can even raise up "babes and sucklings" to speak for Him (cf.Ps. 8:2).

Mordecai's statement to Esther is applicable in our context: "For *if you remain silent* at this time, relief and deliverance for the Jews will arise from another place, but you and your fathers family will perish. And who knows but that you have come to royal position for such a time as this?" (Esther 4:14; NIV).

*5. The Lord has been good to us, we cannot be silent.* A most compelling reason for not remaining silent is that the Lord has done so much for us. We show ingratitude to Him, if for fear of job, position, fame, or whatever reason, we choose to remain silent.

The four lepers who lived in the days of Elisha, and who witnessed a mighty deliverance from the Syrian hosts, said it best: "We are not doing right. This day is a day of good news; *if we are silent* and wait until the morning light, punishment will over take us; now therefore come, let us go and tell the king's household" (2 Kings 7:9; RSV).

Peter and John also could not keep silent—even though they were threatened, beaten, and imprisoned. When, on one occasion, the Sanhedrin called them in and "commanded them not to speak or teach at all in the name of Jesus" (Acts 4:19; KJV), Peter and John replied: "Whether it is right in the sight of God to listen to you rather than to God, you must judge; *for we cannot but speak* of what we have seen and heard" (Acts 4:20; RSV).

On another occasion, when the Jewish religious leaders brought them in and set them before the council, the high priest asked them: "Did not we straitly command you that ye should not teach in this name [Jesus Christ]? and, behold, ye have filled Jerusalem with your doctrine, and intend to bring this man's blood upon us. Then Peter and the other apostles answered and said, We out to obey God rather than men" ( Acts 5:27-29).

**Why *I* Cannot Be Silent.** There are many more reasons why a Christian must not be silent. I will offer one personal reason: It is the challenge of actually seeing and talking to believers who refuse to allow their witness to be silenced. I am speaking about the uncompromising faithfulness of our Adventist believers in Rwanda and Congo, the people to whom this book is dedicated.

In fact, the inspiration to write this book, the book's title *Must We Be Silent?* and the basic outline of the book's content all took place while I was visiting these Central African believers a few months ago. Perhaps you will appreciate my reason for not being silent if you read the following e-mail. Originally addressed to the young people involved in my current ministry to public university students on the campus of the University of Michigan, the e-mail captures the motivation for this present apologetic work. This *unedited* e-mail, dated April 6, 2000, is a brief report on my trip to Congo and Rwanda:

> Dear Friends:
>
> I am by this e-mail expressing my appreciation to all of you for your prayers during the time I was away. Of all the overseas trips

I have undertaken on behalf of the church, my recent assignment in Rwanda and Congo (March 26-April 4, 2000) has been the most challenging, and yet life-transforming. If I had known the full extent of the risks involved, perhaps I would have declined to go. But I'm glad I didn't know. As a result, I was able to witness first-hand, what it means to be a Christian in a war situation. Let me share some highlights of the trip.

**Background**

My ten-day trip to Central Africa was at the request of the Africa-Indian Ocean Division, one of the twelve divisions of the Seventh-day Adventist church world-wide. The trip, which would take me through the post-genocide country of Rwanda, was to terminate in the Democratic Republic of Congo (formerly known as Zaire). My assignment was to speak at two ministerial conferences in East Congo, a war-zone that is currently under two rebel leaders who are fighting against the Kinshasha-based Kabila government (the present leader who overthrew Mobutu Sese Seko). This would be the first time since the eruption of the civil-war that outsiders would go there to meet and speak to all the ministers and their wives.

I was joined by Pastor Paul Ratsara, the Division's Ministerial Director.[2] We had a good "feel" of the situation in Rwanda—the country was recovering from the genocide; church members were making efforts at reconciliation; accused war criminals (including an Adventist church leader) were being tried for genocide. But we were not quite sure of the situation in East Congo—would we be permitted into the "country" (read "rebel-held territories")? Would we be safe? Would the pastors and their wives be able to congregate at the designated locations? Would our mission be successful?

**Report on Rwanda**

My anxiety for the trip was fueled by the "resignation" of the president of Rwanda, a few days before my arrival in that country (African leaders [typically] don't voluntarily resign from their positions of authority). But to my surprise, the country's capital, Kigali, seemed relatively at peace. Rwanda has over 300,000 SDAs (official government records indicate that there are over a million people in the country who identify themselves as Adventists). Last year alone, Rwanda baptized 57,000. In Kigali, the capital city, there are over 20,000 Adventists.

During the 100-day genocide in Rwanda, over 15,000 church members and 100 pastors were killed. Those still alive lost several members of their families, children, and friends. For example, the current Union president lost 68 members of his family—including his wife, 6 children and 8 grand-children. It was a moving experience talking to several genocide-survivors. What is most remarkable is the forgiving spirit of those who had been victimized and hurt. Equally remarkable is their whole-hearted commitment to sharing the message. A few examples:

* The Women's Ministry Director of the Union is at the fore-front of women's evangelism. Last year alone, 5,000 people were baptized through evangelistic campaigns conducted by women. While eating in the home of this Women's Ministry leader, she explained to me that many of the women believe that the best way to say "thank you" to God for sparing their lives is to share the gospel. She herself escaped by standing neck-deep in a river for 24 hours (with grass camouflage on her head) as she witnessed the murder of 2 members of her family. Her husband, after hiding in a cealing for one month, could not walk, until he had to be taught again.

* Students are also active in evangelism. Pierre, a 5th-year medical student, informed me that in his university alone, there are over 600 Adventists. The Adventist students in this public university conduct evangelistic meetings and are presently planning to build a church building.

* Many conversions are also taking place in prisons. The Union president, who was at one time imprisoned for five and half

months, mentioned the presence of active and vibrant Adventist churches in the prisons. Some of the converts, who were involved in the genocide, have been won over because of the love and forgiveness of some church members. For example, one Adventist woman, who goes regularly to the prison to feed some of the prisoners who killed her relatives, could not be discouraged from doing so. She told the prison guards: "Don't deny me from practicing my Christian duty to love my enemies, feed them, and give water to them."

The church in Rwanda comprises many widows and orphans. Others are still traumatized by the genocide. Some have lost their memories Many have lost their homes, limbs, and other parts of their bodies. Others are still hurt and angry on account of what happened, and by the apparent inaction by the world and even by God. I spoke two times in Kigali—first to lay church-leaders (Sunday evening, October 26), and the following day to church members in the city. I emphasized the gospel imperative of reconciliation and the good news of the second-coming of Christ to right all wrongs and to make all things new.

The most moving experience for me was to hear Kigali's Emmaus [Resurrection] Choir sing. This group was reconstituted after most of the members of the previous church choir were killed. Why were they killed? One evening, while the choir was in the church practicing, armed militiamen walked in. They separated the singers into their Hutu and Tutsi ethnic groups, and ordered the Hutu Adventists to kill their fellow Tutsis or lose their own lives as well. When the former protested that in the church there is no Hutu and Tutsi, and when no amount of pressure could cause them to do otherwise, members of the choir were ruthlessly massacred . The Emaus choir (Luke 24) emerged from the ashes of the martyred choir members.

As the choir sang about the "blessed hope" of Christ's second coming and how that event is just on the horizon, the phrase "Advent Hope" (which we have adopted to describe the focus of our own public university student organizations) took on a whole meaning. I wish I could describe the mood in the church as the choir sang the song titled *Mwana W'umuntu* (I brought with me a cassette recording of the choir).

**Report on Congo**

It's Tuesday, March 28. From Kigali we flew on a small air-craft to Gisenyi, a northern border city in Rwanda. The first indication that we were entering a war-zone was the presence of several heavily-armed soldiers and military aircrafts at the Gisenyi airport. The Northern Congo Union president was at hand to meet us and drive us across the border into Goma, a Congolese city of one and half million. This is the city to which many Rwandese fled during the genocide. More than 700,000 people died in this city—through the violence of war, famine, or cholera.

The contrast between Rwanda and Congo was very apparent in this city: dilapidated buildings; widows patiently sitting in a public square awaiting job assignments in exchange for food; soldiers at every turn; the presence of international organizations like the Red Cross, UN personnel, etc. For our own safety, we were housed that night in a heavily guarded "hotel." We were "briefed" about the complex situation in Congo (perpetrators of the Rwanda genocide were active in the city, where they organize how to attack Rwanda; different war-factions in the Congolese civil-war; the presence of foreign mercenaries, etc.). All these required that we be very careful in what we say and do, lest our peaceful mission could be in jeopardy.

The following day (Wednesday, March 29), we flew 350 km. northward in a small 16-seater air-craft from Goma to Butembo (a city of 1 million people in a region under the control of another rebel leader). From there, we drove the distance of 40 km (25 miles) in one hour to Lukanga, where we have the Adventist University of Central Africa, the site of my first assigned ministerial conference. I don't have to inform you that we needed special authorization from one town to the other, and that every piece of luggage was heavily scrutinized. We were also carefully interrogated.

To give you an idea of how even innocent-looking items can give reasons for suspicion in a war-zone, let me illustrate: Consider how a foreigner holding a passport identifying himself as a "minister" (myself) and carrying a laptop computer can be easily perceived as a foreign government official ("minister") with sophisticated military intelligence equipment! To make matters worse, I was carrying in my computer bag John Mac Arthur's book titled "*How To Meet the Enemy: Arming Yourself for Spiritual Warfare*" and [my presentation] handouts titled "Uncompromising Loyalty: Radical Commitment in the End-time" (think about the implications of the words in each title). As if that was not enough, I also had with me a new Sabbath School quarterly titled "*The Certainty of the Second Coming*" and with a cover picture of what looks like a laser-guided explosion and the words "Object in Mirror is Closer than it Appears"! I leave you to use your creative imagination to decode what these religious "manuals" can mean in a war-situation.

Anyway, the Lord was on our side. Ten church pastors were at the airport to meet us. I cannot describe their joy in seeing us (they were not sure we could make it). As we drove the one hour journey from the airport to the Adventist University of Central Africa in Lukanga, the local field president shared with us the plight of believers living everyday with evidence of war surrounding them. He explained that they live as though each day was their last day alive; they could die (and several have already died) at the hands of soldiers, armed robbers, militiamen, etc. They could be imprisoned for no valid reason (and there are no "human rights" in jails). Many pastors and church members have lost their homes; they live in the bush/jungles. In order to attend meetings, some wake up at 4.00 a.m. and have to walk 3-5 hours to be at Sabbath school at 9:00 a.m, then walk back to their jungles. Pastors walk through these bushes/jungles looking for and ministering to their flock. According to the field president, these difficult experiences have proven to be the most spiritually healthy for the members, making them to live one day at time in anticipation of death or the second advent.

When I asked about the nature of theological questions that church members are asking in the face of these endless wars, deaths, loss, etc. the field president replied: "Our members are not asking 'why all these?' They already know the answer—namely, we are living in the last days, perilous days. And as long as we live in this world, we shall continue experiencing these tragedies. This is why our people are actively preparing themselves and others for the second coming." In his opinion, the main reason why those of us in the free-world are engaged in frivolous theological discussions is because we have nothing else to do. We are too comfortable in this world, oblivious of the fact that it is headed for destruction. In Congo, the church members whose lives have been spared in the civil war are asking: "What can I give back to the Lord for saving me?" In response, many are giving their time, means, talents for the advancement of God's cause.

I wish space could allow me to mention the sacrifice of our members and pastors in Congo. As I reflect on their total commitment to Christ even in the face of extreme poverty, famine, sickness, and death, I feel ashamed by the abundance that surrounds me. The profound nature of their prayers and the kinds of things they pray for are a rebuke to me for the kinds of prayer requests that often escape my lips. Perhaps we also need some major crisis to wake us up.

After spending two days in Lukanga, we returned to Goma on Friday (31 March) to meet with another group of pastors and their wives. On Sabbath, I spoke to some 5,000 members sitting and standing quietly in the hot sun—since there was no place that could hold the large number of people.

We concluded the ministerial conference in Goma with a communion service—perhaps the most sobering communion service I've participated in. The ordinance of foot-washing takes

> on a whole new meaning when you are called upon to wash the dirty feet of a fellow pastor whose shoes and socks are completely worn out. Some of these pastors walked through the jungle for three days to be at the meeting, arriving just in time for the closing communion service. The parting words of many of them was: "Thank you for coming to East Congo. Now we know we have not been forgotten."
>
> As I mentioned at the beginning of this brief highlight of my trip, if I had known the full extent of the risks involved, perhaps I would have declined to go to Congo. But I'm glad I didn't know. My life is richer because of the trip. In comparison to what our believers are going through, what I considered a "risk" pales into insignificance. I am more determined, by the grace of God, to give Him my best. For God's sake, and for the sake of the faithful believers in Rwanda and Congo, let us not compromise the faith. Let us also be faithful unto death. And let us work to hasten the coming of our Lord Jesus Christ—our blessed hope.
>
> —Samuel Koranteng-Pipim
> Director Public Campus Ministries, Michigan Conference

**A Most Compelling Reason for Not Remaining Silent.** The last paragraph aptly explains why I decided to write *Must We Be Silent*? Our biblical faith is being undermined by secular ideologies. Despite the anticipated harsh treatment from the book's critics, I could not remain silent.

It's true there are risks involved in challenging unbiblical views being pushed upon the church by some influential scholars and administrators. But, in comparison to what our believers in Central Africa are going through, what I consider a "risk" pales into insignificance. As I stated in the e-mail, "For God's sake, and for the sake of the faithful believers in Rwanda and Congo, let us not compromise the faith. Let us also be faithful unto death."

I sent a copy of the above e-mail to the President of the Africa-Indian Ocean Division. One week later (on April 13, 2000) he sent me the following reply:

Dear Dr. Koranteng-Pipim,

Greetings . . .
Many thanks for sharing glimpses of your last Missionary Journey to Rwanda and East Congo. Just as you said repeatedly that if you had known the risks (and they are many), you would have declined, I just want to tell you that some of us wished you declined for the same reason. But we voted the call in faith that the Lord may lead you to respond to the glory of His name. Thanks to God that you made the trip and the devil has been put to shame, while God has taken the glory!

The "Great Lakes Region", as Rwanda, the Congo and Burundi are known, is one of the two riskiest spots in our Division. Liberia and Sierra Leone constitute the second riskiest. Note the use of the superlative. Because other places are risky but not as these two spots. In spite of all these risks which are not only imagined but real, soul-winning continues unabated. By the end of last year [1999] we had added over 569,000 to our church membership so far in this quinquennium, which is over 69,000 above our quinquennial goal. That is why some times we think God loves our Division more than any other Division. This is because we constantly live with God's miracles and the reality of the Great Controversy—physical and spiritual.

May the Lord continue to bless your noble ministry . . .

Marana tha,

President, Africa-Indian Ocean Division[3]

**We Also Must Not Be Silent.** Based on the uncompromising loyalty of our believers in Rwanda and Congo, I want to conclude *Must We Be Silent?* by challenging you, the reader, not to be silent on the ideological issues currently dividing our church.

With so many of these believers willing to die rather than sin, we also must not be silent on the sin of homosexuality parading under the banner of born a gay theology.

With so many of their godly women demonstrating that it is possible to be actively involved in the soul-winning ministry without ordination, we also must not be silent on the unbiblical campaign for women's ordination.

With so many of these church members willing to die because in Christ "there is no Hutu or Tutsi," we also must not be silent on the ideology of racism and racially separate conferences.

With so many of their pastors and teachers faithfully proclaiming the Word, even at the risk of their lives, we also must not be silent on the ideology of liberal higher criticism which seeks to nullify the power of the Word.

And with so many of their students and young people actively doing the work of evangelism, we also must not be silent on the ideology of congregationalism which is splitting our churches by introducing pluralism, instigating a rebellious spirit in certain parts of our worldwide church, and which is introducing ridiculous, and sometimes bizarre, gospel gimmicks and worship styles in the name of reaching young people.

I challenge you, dear reader, not to be silent. In the language of Ellen G. White, "My message to you is: No longer consent to listen without protest to the perversion of truth. . . . God calls upon men and women to take their stand under the blood-stained banner of Prince Emmanuel. I have been instructed to warn our people; for many are in danger of receiving theories and sophistries that undermine the foundation pillars of the faith" (*Selected Messages,* 1:196-197).

As you resolve not to be silent, may you find the words of the familiar song on page 304 of our *Seventh-day Adventist Hymnal* to be a constant source of encouragement, even in the face of opposition and persecution:

Faith of our fathers! Living still
In spite of dungeon fire, and sword,
O how our hearts beat high with joy
Whene'er we hear that glorious word.
Faith of our fathers! Holy faith!
We will be true to thee till death.

Our fathers, chained in prisons dark,
Were still in heart and conscience free;
How sweet would be their children's fate,

If they, like them, could die for thee!
Faith of our fathers! Holy faith!
We will be true to thee till death.

Faith of our fathers! We will love
Both friend and foe in all our strife,
And preach thee, too, as love knows how,
By kindly words and virtuous life.
Faith of our fathers! Holy faith!
We will be true to thee till death.

---

**Endnotes**

[1]See, "For Preachers," *Hour of Prophecy,* December 2000, p. 4. The *Hour of Prophecy* is the official publication of the Hour of Prophecy Radio Broadcast, a supporting organization in the Seventh-day Adventist church. For more information contact:
address: Hour of Prophecy, P.O. Box 1417, Ft. Worth, TX 76101
telephone: (817) 641-9897
e-mail: hourofprophecy@juno.com
webpage: *www.tagnet.org/hop.*

[2]Eld. Ratsara was elected as the Division's secretary at the 2000 Toronto GC session. For his account of our shared experience in Rwanda and Congo, read his article, "No Hutu, No Tutsi!" found in chapter 25 of this present volume.

[3]The e-mail was sent by Luka T. Daniel, President Africa-Indian Ocean Division